Occupational Health and Safety

Psychological and Behavioral Aspects of Risk Series

Series Editors: Professor Cary L. Cooper and Professor Ronald J. Burke

Risk management is an ongoing concern for modern organizations in terms of their finance, their people, their assets, their projects and their reputation. The majority of the processes and systems adopted are very financially oriented or fundamentally mechanistic; often better suited to codifying and recording risk, rather than understanding and working with it. Risk is fundamentally a human construct; how we perceive and manage it is dictated by our attitude, behavior and the environment or culture within which we work. Organizations that seek to mitigate, manage, transfer or exploit risk need to understand the psychological factors that dictate the response and behaviors of their employees, their high-flyers, their customers and their stakeholders.

This series, edited by two of the most influential writers and researchers on organizational behavior and human psychology explores the psychological and behavioral aspects of risk; the factors that:

- define our attitudes and response to risk;
- are important in understanding and managing "risk managers"; and
- dictate risky behavior in individuals at all levels.

Titles Currently in the Series Include:

New Directions in Organizational Psychology and Behavioral Medicine
Edited by Alexander-Stamatios Antoniou and Cary Cooper

Risky Business
Psychological, Physical and Financial Costs of High Risk Behavior in Organizations
Edited by Ronald J. Burke and Cary L. Cooper

Safety Culture
Assessing and Changing the Behaviour of Organisations
John Bernard Taylor

Corporate Reputation
Managing Opportunities and Threats
Edited by Ronald J. Burke, Graeme Martin and Cary L. Cooper

Occupational Health and Safety

Edited by

RONALD J. BURKE,
SHARON CLARKE
and
CARY L. COOPER

GOWER

Gower Applied Business Research
Our programme provides leaders, practitioners, scholars and researchers with thought provoking, cutting edge books that combine conceptual insights, interdisciplinary rigour and practical relevance in key areas of business and management.

Published by
Gower Publishing Limited
Wey Court East
Union Road
Farnham
Surrey, GU9 7PT
England

Gower Publishing Company
Suite 420
101 Cherry Street
Burlington,
VT 05401-4405
USA

www.gowerpublishing.com

British Library Cataloguing in Publication Data
Occupational health and safety. — (Psychological and behavioural aspects of risk)
1. Industrial safety. 2. Industrial accidents. 3. Work environment—Psychological aspects.
4. Hazardous occupations. 5. Employee health promotion. 6. Risk assessment.
I. Series II. Clarke, Sharon, 1968– III. Burke, Ronald J. IV. Cooper, Cary L.
658.3'8-dc22

Library of Congress Cataloging-in-Publication Data
Occupational health and safety / edited by Sharon Clarke, Ronald J. Burke, and Cary L. Cooper.
p. cm.— Psychological and behavioural aspects of risk)
Includes index.
ISBN 978-0-566-08983-1 (hardback : alk. paper) 1. Industrial hygiene. 2. Industrial safety.
I. Clarke, Sharon, 1968– II. Burke, Ronald J. III. Cooper, Cary L.
RC967.O265 2010
616.9'803—dc22

2010043529

ISBN 9780566089831 (hbk)
ISBN 9781409432074 (ebk)

Printed and bound in Great Britain by the
MPG Books Group, UK

Contents

PART IV OCCUPATIONAL FACTORS

PART V INNOVATIVE ORGANIZATIONAL APPROACHES

List of Figures

List of Tables

List of Contributors

Ronald J. Burke is Professor of Organizational Behavior, Schulich School of Business, York University, Toronto, Canada. He is the editor or co-editor of 31 books and has published over 500 journal articles. He was the founding Editor of the *Canadian Journal of Administrative Sciences* and has served on the editorial boards of over 20 journals. His current research interests include work and health, crime and corruption in organizations, occupational health and safety, corporate reputation, and women in management. He has participated in numerous management development courses and consulted with both private and public sector organizations on human resource management issues.

Sharon Clarke, PhD, is Reader in Organizational Psychology at Manchester Business School, University of Manchester. She has research interests in safety culture, safety climate, leadership, and workplace accidents. Her work has been published in *Journal of Occupational and Organisational Psychology, Journal of Organizational Behaviour, Journal of Occupational Health Psychology, Applied Psychology: An International Review*, and other leading journals. She is Associate Editor for the *Journal of Occupational and Organizational Psychology*. Recent research grants have focused on the impact of safety interventions on safety climate; this work was awarded first place in 'Best Practice in Interventions Competition' 2008 by National Institute for Occupational Safety and Health (NIOSH).

Cary L. Cooper is Distinguished Professor of Organizational Psychology and Health at Lancaster University. He is the author of over 100 books (on occupational stress, women at work, and industrial and organizational psychology), has written over 400 scholarly articles, and is a frequent contributor to national newspapers, TV, and radio. Professor Cooper is a Fellow of the British Academy of Management and also of the Academy of Management (having also won the 1998 Distinguished Service Award). In 2001 he was awarded a CBE in the Queen's Birthday Honours List for his contribution to organizational health. He was the lead scientist to the UK Government Office for Science on their Foresight programme on Mental Capital and Well Being (2007–2008) and was appointed a member of the expert group on establishing guidance for the National Institute for Health and Clinical Excellence on "promoting mental wellbeing through productive and healthy working conditions" in 2009. Professor Cooper is Chair of the UK's Academy of Social Sciences.

Thomas A. Arcury, PhD, is Professor and Vice Chair for Research in Family and Community Medicine. He is also Director of the Center for Worker Health and Director of the Program on Community Engagement and Implementation of the Translational Sciences Institute of Wake Forest University School of Medicine, North Carolina. Dr Arcury directs a comprehensive and prolific program of research focused on all aspects of immigrant farm worker health. His research is supported by grants from the National Institutes of Health, the Centers for Disease Control, and the Environmental Protection Agency. Dr Arcury is co-recipient of the National Institute for Occupational Safety and Health R2P award, and has authored over 200 peer-reviewed articles.

Elyce Anne Biddle is a Senior Research Economist at the National Institute for Occupational Safety and Health. She holds a Master's degree in Resource Economics and a doctorate in Occupational Safety and Health (West Virginia University, West Virginia). Her work, presented throughout the world, focuses on economic cost modeling and health outcome measurements for occupational injuries and fatalities. She co-chaired the Social and Economic Consequences of Workplace Illness and Injury team charged to set the US National Occupational Research Agenda. In addition to numerous other awards, the International Association of Industrial Accident Boards and Commissions presented her the Samuel Gomper's Award for her outstanding efforts in improving the working conditions of the masses.

Brita Bjørkelo is a licensed Clinical Psychologist and has written a PhD thesis on "Whistleblowing at work: Antecedents and consequences". She has also contributed to papers and book chapters about bullying, workaholism, and sexual harassment. Dr Bjørkelo is a member of the research group "Digital Learning Communities" and works in teacher education at the Department of Education, University of Bergen, Norway. She is involved in research projects on Ethics, Social Media and Teacher Education.

Catherine Briand, PhD, is an Occupational Therapist, an Assistant Professor at the University of Montréal (School of Rehabilitation) and a Reseacher at the Fernand-Seguin Research Center, Hôpital Louis-H. Lafontaine (research in mental health). She holds a PhD in Biomedical Sciences (Psychiatry) and achieved a post-doctorate in the field of work integration of people with mental illness (FRSQ and REPAR grants). Her research expertise is the design and evaluation of rehabilitation programs for people with mental health problems particularly among people with severe mental disorders. In recent years, Professor Briand has developed expertise in evaluation research and knowledge translation. She contributes in several projects to analyze the factors that facilitate or impede the implementation of evidence best practices.

Vilma G. Carande-Kulis, PhD, is an Economist at the Office of the Associated Director for Science, Center for Disease Control and Prevention (CDC). Dr Carande-Kulis has an undergraduate degree in Agronomical Engineering from Argentina and MSc and PhD degrees from Colorado State University, Colorado. Her graduate program was supported by a Fulbright Scholarship. As Lead Economist for the Guide to Community Preventive Services, Dr Carande-Kulis developed the methods to conduct systematic reviews of economic evaluations. Her work has been presented in Italy, the Netherlands, the UK, and Germany. Dr Carande-Kulis has also been the Chief of the CDC Prevention Effectiveness Branch. She pioneered the concept of public health economics which has been presented in Spain and adopted by several US institutions. She has been a consultant for the World Health Organization and has more than six departmental and agency awards. Her work has been nominated three times to the CDC Science Charles C Shepard Award.

Nearkasen Chau is Research Director of the French National Institute for Health and Medical Research (Inserm, Unit 669) and Paris-Sud/Paris Descartes Universities. He was born in 1948 in Cambodia and holds a PhD in mathematics from the Henri Poincaré, Nancy 1 University, France. His main research areas are public health and epidemiology. Recent studies have assessed the role of occupational, health-behavioral, and other individual risk factors in injury, disability, mental health, respiratory health, substance use, and mortality, in general and specific populations. The studies have also evaluated the social inequalities and mediated role of these factors. Dr Chau has contributed to over 300 publications and conferences and is a member of the Lorhandicap Research Group.

Eva Cifre is Associate Professor of Work Psychology at the University Jaume I, Castellón, Spain. She has been a member of the WONT Research Team since 1995. She received her PhD Extraordinary Award in 2000. Her research interests are mainly focused on the effects of technology at work (including telework), psychosocial health promotion at work (including psychosocial well-being and flow at work) and work/home interaction strategies (a topic for which she received a national award in 2004). Dr Cifre provides consultancy on work risk-prevention and is a member of professional and scientific associations such as the Spanish Association of Psychologists, the European Association of Work Psychology (EAWOP) and the International Association of Applied Pyschology (IAAP).

Marc Corbière, PhD, is an Associate Professor at the University of Sherbrooke, School of Rehabilitation and a researcher (FRSQ Junior II) at the Centre for Action in Work Disability and Rehabilitation (CAPRIT). Specializing in counselling psychology, work psychology, and social psychiatry, Professor Corbière examines the factors that help people with mental disorders obtain and maintain employment. His research evaluates individual determinants (for example, self-esteem, work history, work motivation) and programmatic determinants (for example, rapid job search, competences in employment specialists) associated with the work integration of people with mental illness. For example, he is analyzing the implementation of supported employment programs, recognized as evidence-based practice, in three Canadian provinces.

Marie-José Durand, PhD, is an Occupational Therapist, Full Professor with the School of Rehabilitation of the Université de Sherbrooke, and Director of the Centre for Action in Work Disability Prevention and Rehabilitation (CAPRIT). She is also the Director of the master program in rehabilitation practices offered at the Université de Sherbrooke. She holds a senior FRSQ Investigator Award and a research Chair in work rehabilitation (J. Armand Bombardier—Pratt & Whitney Canada). Her research projects aim at the development and assessment of work rehabilitation tools and programs.

A. Ian Glendon, PhD, is Associate Professor at the School of Psychology, Griffith University, Gold Coast, Australia. He has previously held full-time or visiting positions at universities in Beijing, Birmingham, Brisbane, Edinburgh, Hong Kong, and Manchester. His research interests include transportation psychology, driver stress/behavior, safety/risk management, and safety culture/climate. He has contributed to over 100 publications including five books. He has consulted for over 60 clients on safety auditing, safety culture/climate analysis, injury/incident analysis, task analysis, and human error/reliability analysis. He is a registered Psychologist in Australia, a Chartered Fellow of the Institution of Occupational Safety and Health, a Chartered Occupational Psychologist (UK), and Past President (2006–2010) of the International Association of Applied Psychology's Traffic and Transportation Psychology Division. He is on the editorial board of four international journals, including *Transportation Research Part F: Traffic Psychology and Behaviour*, and *Safety Science*. (http://www.griffith.edu.au/health/school-psychology/staff/associate-professor-ian-glendon)

Lonnie Golden, PhD, is Professor of Economics and Labor Studies and Employment Relations, Penn State University, Abington. His research focuses on working hours, work scheduling, well-being consequences, Fair Labor Standards Act (FLSA) overtime law, overwork, daily time use, work-life balance and students' work hours. He is co-editor of *Working Time: International Trends, Theory and Policy* and of *Nonstandard Work: The Nature and Challenge of Changing Employment Arrangements*. His research has appeared in journals such as *Industrial Relations, Monthly Labor Review, Journal of Business Ethics, Cambridge Journal of Economics, Journal of Family and Economic Issues, Journal of Socio-Economics and American Journal of Economics and Sociology.* He is an affiliate of the Economic Policy Institute and Sloan Work and Family Research Network. He is on the editorial board of the *Review of Social Economics* and *Journal of Socio-Economics*.

Maja Graso has a Master's degree from the Washington State University, Vancouver and is currently a doctoral candidate in Experimental Psychology in the area of Industrial/Organizational Pyschology. Her research focuses on job insecurity, workplace safety, and organizational justice.

Joseph G. Grzywacz, PhD, is Associate Professor of Family and Community Medicine, and Associate Director for Research, Center for Worker Health, Wake Forest University School of Medicine. Dr Grzywacz, an interdisciplinary family scientist, studies the interface of everyday work and family life, and its implications for adult and child health. Supported by grants from the National Institute of Health, Dr Grzywacz's research is published in premier interdisciplinary and discipline-specific journals such as the *Journal of Applied Psychology*, *Journal of Marriage and Family*, *Journal of Health and Social Behavior*, *Journal of Occupational and Environmental Medicine*, and *Behavioral Medicine*.

Evelyn Kedl is a research professional at the Canada Research Chair on Occupational Integration and the Psychosocial Environment of Work at Université Laval. She has training in industrial relations and is a member of the Association of Human Resource Professionals. She also has expertise in mediation, labour conflict resolution, workplace psychological harassment, and is a member of the Canadian Institute for Conflict Resolution. She has also worked for many years in the field of occupational health and safety in a bipartite organization relating to the construction sector.

Kathleen M. Kowalski-Trakofler, PhD, is a Research Psychologist at the Office of Mine Safety and Health Research (OMSHR) with the US National Institute for Occupational Safety and Health (NIOSH), Center for Disease Control and Prevention (CDC). She received her PhD in Psychology from the University of Pittsburgh, her MS in Counseling and BS in Education from the University of Wisconsin-Madison. Over the past 18 years in mining, her research interests have focused on human behavior as related to mine safety, with a present focus on escape and rescue in mine emergencies. Dr Kowalski Trakofler serves on the editorial board of a number of international journals, is a member of the American Psychological Association, and a licensed counselor with a small private psychotherapy practice.

David Lester has doctoral degrees from Cambridge University (UK) in social and political science and Brandeis University (USA) in psychology. He is Distinguished Professor of Psychology at the Richard Stockton College of New Jersey. He has been President of the International Association for Suicide Prevention, and he has published extensively on suicide, murder and other issues in thanatology. His recent books include *Katie's Diary: Unlocking the Mystery of a Suicide* (2004), *Suicide and the Holocaust* (2005), *Is there Life after Death?* (2005) and *Understanding Suicide: Closing the Exits Revisited* (2009).

Susana Llorens, PhD, is Associate Professor in Work Psychology at the Universitat Jaume I, Castellón, Spain. She was awarded the PhD Extraordinary Grant in Social Sciences and was the first European to graduate with a PhD in Work Psychology from this university. Beside publications on the implications of technological innovation and training process, burnout and engagement, self-efficacy, and healthy and resilient organizations, she is also immersed in an organizational consultancy as a member of the WONT research team. She has membership of European Association of Work and Organizational Psychology (EAWOP) and and Society for Occupational Health Psychology (SOHP) and is on the editorial committee of the Spanish Journal *Psicología del Trabajo y de las Organizaciones*.

Laura Lorente, PhD, is a Research Assistant in Work and Organizational Psychology for the WONT research team. Her research interests are mainly focused on efficacy beliefs, work engagement, and healthy organizations. She has had work on these subject areas published nationally and internationally. She is also member of the Society for Occupational Health Psychology (SOHP).

Linda Jansen McWilliams is a Supervisory Statistician in the National Institute for Occupational Safety and Health's Mining Program. She received a BSc degree in Microbiology and a BSc degree in Psychology from the University of Pittsburgh, and an MSc degree in Research Methodology from the University of Pittsburgh. Ms McWilliams oversees and guides the surveillance and statistics team, and also provides statistical and research design consultation, and reviews of research manuscripts. She is the Principal Investigator for several mining surveillance projects, including a probability-based sample survey of US mining operations and mine employees.

Peter F. Martelli is a PhD candidate in the organizational theory track of the Health Services and Policy Analysis program at the University of California, Berkeley. His professional interests are in evidence-based management, expertise, social networks, and risk. He is also a Doctoral Research Fellow of Berkeley's Center for Catastrophic Risk Management, and has worked on high reliability research in patient safety, wildland fire and emergency response, and civil and industrial infrastructure. Before returning to university, Mr Martelli was a Research Coordinator at the American College of Physicians, where he helped establish and manage the ACPNet practice-based research network.

Isabel M. Martínez is Associate Professor in Work and Organizational Psychology at University Jaume I Castellón, Spain where she is also a member of the WONT research team. Her research interests are focused on the work stress, burnout, and well-being of people at work and cooperative work groups, especially in group support systems. Her research is currently directed toward the positive aspects of work (such as engagement and flow) and health organizations. She is member of European Association of Work and Organizational Psychology (EAWOP), International Association of Applied Psychology (IAAP), and Society for Occupational Health Psychology (SOHP).

Stig Berge Matthiesen, PhD, is Professor of Work and Organizational Psychology at the University of Bergen, Norway. His PhD was in the area of Workplace bullying. His current research interests covers areas such as ethical leadership, whistleblowing, organizational conflicts, in addition to workplace bullying. Professor Matthiesen is also interested in topics such as work stress, burnout, workaholism, and job engagement, and has experience as a researcher in crisis and grief psychology. Professor Matthiesen is a member of the Bergen Bullying Research Group.

Kathryn Mearns, PhD, is Senior Lecturer at the School of Psychology, University of Aberdeen and co-director of the Industrial Psychology Research Centre. Her research interests encompass human factors in industrial safety, safety culture and climate, safety leadership, trust, risk perception, and psychological aspects of workplace well-being. Dr Mearns is Editor-in-Chief for *Safety Science* and a member of the American Psychological Association (APA) and the Society for Risk Analysis (SRA). She has worked on a range of projects in high-hazard/high-reliability industries including the offshore industry, shipping, air traffic control, and power generation.

Steve Newell is a Director of ORC Health, Safety & Environment Networks for Mercer ORC Networks, a membership-based consulting business that services large multinational corporations on safety, health, and environmental matters. He contributes to several different Mercer ORC networks, including the Executive Business Issues Forum, the main Occupational Safety and Health Group, the OSH Lawyers Group, and the Global Safety and Health Forum. Steve joined ORC in January 1998. Prior to ORC, he was on the Executive Staff of the federal Occupational Safety and Health Administration (OSHA), as the Director of the OSHA Office of Statistics with responsibility for targeting OSHA inspections and measuring agency performance. Before joining OSHA he headed the ongoing safety and health statistical programs for the Bureau of Labor Statistics (BLS). Steve obtained his B.S. degree in economics from the University of Maryland and his J.D. degree from the Columbus School of Law, Catholic University. He is a past member of the District of Columbia and Maryland State Bars.

Mariève Pelletier is a research professional at the Canada Research Chair on Occupational Integration and the Psychosocial Environment of Work at Université Laval. She is also a doctoral student in Orientation Sciences and the recipient of an SSHRC Canada Joseph-Armand-Bombardier Graduate Scholarship. She holds a post-graduate Diploma in Occupational Health and Safety Management and Prevention and has training in psychology and industrial relations. She has worked for several years as a research professional in projects related to interventions in mental health at work and the return to work.

Tahira M. Probst, PhD, is a Professor of Psychology at Washington State University, Vancouver. Her research interests include economic stress, organizational safety climate, and accident under-reporting. She has published over 60 articles and chapters on these and related topics with her research appearing in outlets such as the *Journal of Occupational Health Psychology, Applied Psychology: An International Review*, the *Journal of Occupational and Organizational Psychology*, and the *Journal of Applied Psychology*. She has served as a consultant to the National Academies Institute of Medicine to assess workplace health promotion programs at NASA. In addition, she has collaborated with the International Labor Organization to evaluate the effectiveness of workplace interventions designed to prevent and mitigate psychosocial risk factors in the workplace. Dr Probst currently serves as an Associate Editor of *Stress & Health* and sits on the editorial boards of three additional journals.

Sara A. Quandt, PhD, is Professor of Epidemiology and Prevention in the Division of Public Health Sciences, and Associate Director for Education and Translation, Center for Worker Health, Wake Forest University School of Medicine. Dr Quandt directs a substantial research program funded by the National Institute of Health and the Center for Disease Control and Prevention (CDC) that is focused on immigrant and minority health, and on rural aging. Dr Quandt is a co-recipient of the National Institute for Occupational Safety and Health R2P award, and has published over 200 peer-reviewed articles in journals such as *Lancet, Environmental Health Perspectives*, and the *Journal of Immigrant and Minority Health*.

Dori B. Reissman, PhD, holds the rank of Captain in the US Public Health Service and and is Senior Medical Advisor for the National Institute for Occupational Safety and Health (NIOSH), a part of the US Centers for Disease Control and Prevention (CDC). She has been working on strategies to integrate health, safety, and resiliency into incident management for emergency responders and to address organizational dynamics for workers in hazardous occupations. Professional contributions include emergency response service, expert consultation, applied behavioral research, and policy guidance. Dr Reissman initiated efforts to address community resiliency and responder resiliency as public health protection strategies at the Center for Disease Control and Prevention (CDC).

Karlene H. Roberts, PhD, is Professor at the Walter A. Haas School of Business, University of California at Berkeley. She earned her bachelor's degree in Psychology from Stanford University and her PhD in Industrial Psychology from the University of California at Berkeley. She also received the docteur honoris causa from the Universite Paul Cezanne (Aix Marseilles III). Professor Roberts has done research on job attitudes, cross-national management, and organizational communication. She has also contributed to the research methodology literature. Since 1984 she has been investigating the design and management of organizations and systems of organizations in which error can result in catastrophic consequences. She has studied both organizations that fail and those that succeed in a variety of industries, including the military, commercial marine transportation, healthcare, banking, and community emergency services.

Marisa Salanova is Professor of Social Psychology at the University Jaume I, Castellón, Spain. She specializes in Work and Organizational Psychology and is Director of the WONT (Work and Organization Network) Research Team at that University (http://www.wont.uji.es). She has contributed to over 200 national and international publications on about the subjects of work-related stress, HR development, and the latest movement of the Positive Psychology. Her recent research interest is focused on "healthy and resilient organizations" from a multilevel approach. She has published in high-impact journals, such as *Journal of Applied Psychology, Applied Psychology: An International Review, Anxiety, Stress & Coping, Journal of Cross-Cultural Psychology, and Computers in Human Behavior*, and is on the editorial board of *Applied Psychology: An International Review, Journal of Occupational Health Psychology*, and *European Journal of Work and Organizational Psychology*, among others.

Reepa Shroff is a Consultant with ORC Worldwide and manages the Occupational Safety and Health Network Group for ORC. She joined ORC in 2007 bringing a special background in incident investigation, regulatory compliance as well as experience in Environmental Health and Safety. Previously, she served as a Chemical Incident Investigator for the United States Chemical Safety and Hazard Investigation Board (CSB). While with CSB, she participated in numerous investigations involving explosions, equipment failures, human errors, chemical reactions, and other hazards at fixed industrial facilities. Notable investigations that Ms Shroff participated in include the BP America Refinery Explosion in Texas City, Texas and the Combustible Dust Hazard Investigation. She has experience as a Storm Water Quality Inspector for the Gwinnett County Storm Water Management Division within the Department of Public Utilities where she inspected industrial facilities for compliance with storm water ordinances. She is completing her MSc degree in Engineering Management with a concentration in Environment and Energy at The George Washington University. She holds a BSc degree in Environmental Science with a concentration in Environmental Economics and Management from the University of Georgia.

Louise St-Arnaud, PhD, is a Professor and holds the Canada Research Chair on Occupational Integration and the Psychosocial Environment of Work at the Faculty of Education, Université Laval in Québec City. She is also a member of CRIÉVAT (Center for Research and Interventions in Education and Worklife). She is a psychologist and holds a Doctorate in Biomedical Science from the Faculty of Medicine, Université de Montréal, as well as a Master's in Public Health and a DEA in Occupational Health. Her research interests relate to the study of occupational integration and job retention processes. She has also been pursuing research in the fields of the psychodynamics of work and mental health in the workplace for many years.

Charles Vaught, PhD is a Certified Mine Safety Professional. He received his PhD degree in Industrial Sociology from the University of Kentucky, Lexington. Prior to this, he worked as a rank-and-file underground coal miner and was a member of the United Mine Workers of America. His primary research interest is the behavior of groups engaged in emergency response activities. Dr Vaught is a member of the American Sociological Association and the United States Mine Rescue Association. He is also an associate member of the National Mine Rescue Association and the United Mine Workers of America. He holds a 501 Trainer Certification from the Occupational Safety and Health Administration, and has been approved as an Instructor by the US Mine Safety and Health Administration.

Barbara Wiens-Tuers is an Associate Professor of Economics at Penn State Altoona, Pennsylvania, with affiliate status in the Labor Studies and Employment Relations program at University Park. Most recently, she has published articles in the *Labor Studies Journal, Labor Family News,* and *Journal of Socio-Economics.* She has also published articles in the *Journal of Economic Issues, Review of Social Economy,* the *American Journal of Economics and Sociology,* and a chapter in a labor text.

Dee Woodhull is Director of Safety, Health, and Environmental Networks at ORC Worldwide in Washington, DC. Ms Woodhull is certified in both occupational safety and industrial hygiene, and holds a MSc degree in environmental health. She brings 32 years of experience in the environment, health and safety arena, including assignments in both corporate and operating-level positions in several Fortune 100 companies and experience as an OSHA Field Compliance Officer. Prior to joining ORC, Ms Woodhull was Corporate Manager, Safety, Industrial Hygiene, and Workers Compensation for United Technologies Corporation in Hartford, CT, currently a $58.7 billion global company.

Acknowledgements

I have always learned a lot from every volume that I have edited and this one was no exception. I have been interested in the effects of work experiences on individual psychological and physical well-being for some time: this collection enlarged the focus of my thinking. Although I have sometimes included accident-related measures in my work they were peripheral to my central interests. Working on this collection made me realize that broadening one's view on health and well-being to include workplace injuries and illnesses gave the research a much broader perspective. Millions of workers around the globe experience injury, illness, and death every year. Workplace injuries, illnesses, and deaths not only affect individuals but also their families and communities. While injury and illness rates have dropped slightly in some countries, they remain stable or have increased in others. In addition, there is considerable individual and organizational under-reporting of injuries and illness so the magnitude of the challenge is vast. We have considerable understanding of the causes of workplace injuries and illnesses and making use of this knowledge was one objective of this collection.

This venture was a group effort. I acknowledge the commitment of my co-editors to this collection. Sharon Clarke has been studying occupational safety and health for some time, making significant contributions to both research and practice. I continue to be a big fan of her work. I have worked with Cary Cooper for several years on various projects and continue to value his energy and openness.

My contributions were supported in part by York University.

I thank our international authors for their contributions.

Susan, Sharon, Rachel, Jeff, and Jay—my family—continue to keep me young.

And, last but not least, Jonathan Norman and the gang at Gower provided outstanding support along the way. Their efforts and professionalism were first rate.

Ronald J. Burke
Toronto, Canada

PART I

Occupational Health and Safety—Key Issues

CHAPTER **1**

Building a Safe and Healthy Workplace

RONALD J. BURKE

This collection, consistent with our emphasis on the psychological, behavioral, and social aspects of risk in organizations (Burke and Cooper, 2010), focuses on understanding the causes of accidents, injuries, and illness in the workplace and increasing employee occupational safety, health, and well-being. In the first part of this chapter, central concepts, themes, research findings, and practical recommendations are reviewed. The second part of the chapter summarizes the contributions that follow.

Consider these facts and incidents:

- Between 1962 and 2002 there were 13,337 work-related highway deaths in the US. In 2002, there were 808 truck driver deaths; 62 percent of highway accidents. Semi-trailer trucks were involved in the greatest number of work-related driver deaths. Older drivers accounted for more deaths than did younger drivers. The cost of a single work-related truck driver fatality in a highway incident was an average of $821,049 with a median cost of $928,322. Costs to US society from truck driver incidents range from $316 million in 1992 to $506 million in 2000. Driver fatigue was a major factor in driver incidents, accounting for 31 percent of driver deaths. Forty seven percent of drivers in New York State reported falling asleep at the wheel at least once during their career. To combat driver fatigue, drivers are limited in the number of hours they can drive each day or each week. Unfortunately, 73 percent reported violating these limits, 56 percent of drivers worked more hours than they recorded, 25 percent of drivers worked 75 hours, and 10 percent worked more than 90 hours.[1]
- About 1,000 deaths and 240,000 accidents each year in the US are the result of individuals being on cell-phones while driving their vehicles A recent US study (January 2010) found that cell-phone use was cited in 28 percent of road crashes. Even drivers using hands-free phones exhibit reduced skill and attention while on electronic devices (texting).[2]
- Almost 1.3 million people are killed and between 20 and 50 million are injured each year on the world's roads according to a study by the World Health Organization (WHO). Road deaths are the leading cause of death in people aged 25 to 44. Countries differ widely in number of reported road deaths with the Netherlands, Sweden, and

1 Source: www.bts.gov/publications/transpsortation_statistics_annual_report/2000/chapter3/index/html.

2 Source: www.nhtsa.gov.

Britain being low and the Eastern Mediterranean and African region being high. About half the deaths occur in motor vehicles with half involving pedestrians, bicyclists, and motorcyclists. The WHO estimates that road deaths will reach 2.4 million per year by 2030.[3]

- Within a two to three week period in late March/early April 2009 there were at least three helicopter crashes involving fatalities. Eight people were killed after a helicopter crashed in the North Sea as it returned from an oil-rig offshore. The second helicopter crash also occurred in the North Sea, making it the third crash in six weeks involving oil-rig helicopters. In Canada, 17 people died on March 12 when another oil-rig helicopter fell into the Atlantic. Analysis of this fatal crash by the Transportation Safety Board of Canada indicated that the Sikorsky helicopter gearbox failed ten minutes into a test designed to show that it could run half an hour without oil, a failure rate judged to be 267 times worse than the standard. Some accidents and workplace fatalities result from faulty equipment. The lone survivor and the families of 17 people who died in a helicopter crash of Newfoundland in March 2009 recently settled their lawsuit against the aircraft's manufacturer (January 2010). There were obvious safety concerns with the Sikorsky helicopter.[4]
- A sight-seeing helicopter carrying Italian tourists and a small plane crashed over the Hudson River in mid-2009 resulting in 11 deaths. Two air traffic controllers were punished; one was on the phone at the time of the crash and the second was absent from the office.[5]
- A fatal commuter train crash in September 2008 in Los Angeles led to the company involved passing a ban on the use of cell-phones and related electronic devices by engineers operating trains. The engineer of a train involved in this crash had been text messaging shortly before the crash that killed 25 and injured 130 people. This ban was in place but apparently was often ignored.[6]
- Two transit trains crashed in Washington DC in June 2009 killing nine and injuring over 50 people. Investigators were focusing on the train's computer systems that failed to stop an oncoming train though there was evidence that the operator (killed in the crash) tried to slow the train down. Investigators were also examining cell-phone records from the operator to see if she was distracted before the crash. The operator had been in her job only four months prior to the crash.[7]
- A ferry sank in the northern Philippines (December 26, 2009) making it the second sea disaster in three days. Three were killed and 22 people missing. On December 24, a ferry sank after colliding with a fishing boat near Manila Bay with 24 people still missing. Previous ferry accidents have been the result of ferries being over-loaded and going out in too rough waters.[8]
- A gas explosion in a coal mine in Northern China (February 2009) left at least 74 miners dead and 114 hospitalized. A mine explosion in China in December 2007

---

3 Source: http://whqlibdoc.who.int/publications/2009/9789241563840_eng.pdf.

4 Source: http://dcnonl.com/article/id37044.

5 Source: www.reuters.com/article/idUSTRE5771L520090808.

6 Source: www.latimes.com/news/local/la-me-traincrash14-2008sep14,0,3460884.story.

7 Source: www.washingonpost.com/wpdyn/content/article/2009/06/22/AR2009062202508/html.

8 Source: www.reuters.com/article/rdUSTRE5BQ03K20091227.

killed 105 miners when gas exploded in an unventilated tunnel. China's mining industry has been described as the deadliest in the world (Wright, 2004).

- Another gas explosion in a state-run Chinese mine on November 21, 2009 killed at least 104 people. The chief engineer and two mine directors were fired after the disaster. A later story blamed overcrowding in this coal mine disaster as management attempted to increase output; making it very difficult to evacuate workers promptly. China closed about 1,000 dangerous small mines in 2008 reducing the number of fatalities. Yet hundreds still die in accidents each year in China.[9]
- One miner was killed and another injured on November 28, 2009 in Saskatchewan when a raw ore storage bin in Mosaic's Esterhazy mine collapsed on them.[10]
- DeMont (2009) writes about the Westray mine disaster in New Glasgow, Nova Scotia in May 1992 in which 26 miners died. He sees these men as victims of corporate arrogance, greed, bad mining practices, and bad luck.
- Many individuals have attempted suicide or committed suicide by throwing themselves under trains in Toronto's subway system. The Toronto Transit Commission (TTC) has kept the numbers of attempted or successful suicides confidential. Just recently these have been made public. From 1998 to 2007 there were 100 unsuccessful attempts and 150 successful attempts. Both unsuccessful and successful suicides are sometimes viewed by other passengers and/or subway operators. Both subway operators and subway bystanders who have seen suicides indicate that they recollect these incidents for a long time. Subway drivers are kept away from the incident until other help arrives. Toronto police, firefighters, emergency personnel, the coroner's office, and TTC supervisors and management are sent to the scene after a suicide incident. Subway drivers are typically traumatized, in shock, and may experience long-term depression and psychology trauma. One subway operator said that he once had three suicides over a four-month period. The TTC works with a Toronto hospital and health center to provide a support structure of train operators who suffer post-traumatic stress disorder (PTSD), at a rate found to be four times higher than for Toronto's police officers. The TTC also has a program aimed at helping people in distress who may be thinking about suicide. This program trains operators, supervisors, and special officers to see potential warning signs that someone may be thinking about taking their own life.[11]
- Death awareness—there are some jobs in which the incumbents face concerns about their own death (for example, soldiers, miners, police officers, and power plant operators) because they work in dangerous jobs. Other employees work in jobs that expose them to the death of others (for example, doctors, nurses, paramedics, funeral directors, grief counselors, and rescue workers). Employees in several jobs suffer accidents and illness that can remind others of death (for example, truck drivers and construction workers). The Haitian earthquake (January 2010) has exposed not only trained rescue workers and soldiers to seeing and recovering dead bodies but also many Haitian men, women, and children. Grant and Wade-Benzoni (2009) suggest that making employees aware of death may bring about changes in their behavior. They propose a four-stage model of death awareness at work that includes situational

9 Source: www.wsws.org/articles/2009/nov2009/mine-n23.shtml.

10 Source: http://Coalmountain.wordpress.com/2009/11/29/potash-worker-killed-by-bin-collapse/.

11 Source: www.thestar.com/News/GTA/article/295876.

triggers (mortality triggers such as mortality exposure), death awareness (anxiety, reflection), individual and work context contingencies (coping behaviors, individual work orientation, job design factors) and work behaviors (for example, stress-related withdrawal behaviors such as absenteeism, tardiness, and turnover, and cooperative behaviors such as helping others and change to a service job). Their model serves as a useful starting point for future research. Managers might foster discussions about mortality-related events in the hope of encouraging more generative responses to them. Managers in organizations where safety and physical dangers are high (mining, construction) might encourage death reflection to increase adherence to safety practices. Some employees may become motivated to also support and assist the safety of others as a result.

- More Canadian soldiers committed suicide in 2008 than in 2007 (15 versus 11) (Burke, 2010). The military does not track suicides among reservists who are filling in increasing numbers of positions. The US army confirmed 128 suicides in 2008 (Burke, 2010). The US army confirmed record levels of suicides in 2009, with at least 140 among active duty soldiers and 71 suspected suicides by service members no longer on active duty.
- The job of a soldier has been described as "killing people and breaking things." On May 11, 2009, a career soldier serving his third tour of duty killed five people in Iraq (Burke, 2010). He was having financial difficulties back home and had a conflict with his commanding officer who took away his gun and ordered him to receive psychological counseling. He had a confrontation with clinic staff and returned with a gun killing the five. Fourteen soldiers in a Colorado unit were accused in May 2009 of nearly a dozen slayings since returning home from Iraq. Half these soldiers reported seeing war crimes including the killing of civilians during their tours (Burke, 2010).
- A fire at a Mexico City daycare center in 2009 killed 41 children, most under the age of two. There were 142 children in the daycare center, most taking their afternoon nap when the fire began. There were only two doors, one of which was locked, and the windows were located very high on the walls. The daycare center was located in an industrial area near facilities having flammable materials.[12]
- A fire, apparently caused by pyrotechnics, killed 146 at a Russian nightclub in Perm on December 4, 2009. Enforcement of fire safety standards in Russia are very lax with blazes in apartment buildings and drug treatment facilities occurring over the past few years. Russia records about 18,000 fire deaths per year, the highest rate among develop (western) countries. Apparently managers of this Russian nightclub were fined twice previously for breaking fire safety regulations. Four people were taken into custody. Nightclub fires have killed thousands of people worldwide (for example, in the US and Indonesia).[13]
- The death of two Chinese workers at a large oil-sands project in Northern Alberta, Canada in 2007 resulted in the laying of 53 charges against Canadian Natural Resources Ltd and two other companies. A giant holding tank collapsed killing the two workers.[14] The maximum penalty for a first offense under Alberta's Health and Safety Act is $500,000 for each charge.

12 Source: http://online.wsj.com/article/SB125999892775378299/html.

13 Source: http://online.wsj.com/article/SB125999892775378299/html.

14 Source: www.dcnonl.com/article/id20792.

- More than 4,000 children between the ages of four and 19 were injured in one year in the Ottawa, Ontario area, based on data collected in hospital emergency rooms (severe hand injuries, eye injuries, broken bones, bruises, sprains). These were school-related injuries that required medical attention (MacKay, Osmond and MacPherson, 2009).
- Unions at the Centre for Addiction and Mental Health (CAMH) in Toronto made complaints in December 2008 about their staff members being attacked. During the week of November 12, patients injured three nurses: one suffered a broken shoulder and the second a broken jaw. Twenty-three violent incidents occurred in a six-week period beginning in October.[15]
- Domestic violence is now being seen as both a personal and business issue. Domestic violence is reported to cost US business $6 billion a year in absenteeism, turnover, health care costs, and lowered productivity.[16]
- Athletes in several sports (boxing, football, and hockey) suffer concussions in their playing days. Athletes suffering concussions are more likely to show mental decline as they age (for example, memory loss, slower reaction times, and mild cognitive impairment when can be a risk factor for Alzheimer's disease).The National Football League (NFL) in the US released the results of research indicating a link between concussions and Alzheimer's disease in October 2009. A survey of 160 NFL players conducted by the Associated Press in early November 2009 indicated that 30 admitted hiding concussion symptoms. Players saw this as an inevitable part of their jobs. The NFL data indicates 120 to 130 concussions occur during their regular playing season.[17]
- "I was going to write a book about my career in hockey but I couldn't remember it.": Comments made by Ron Duguay, forward for the New York Rangers and the last player to play without the now required helmet. Hockey is Canada's national game. There has been an increase in hockey violence and racial slurs among children, often as young as 13, who play the game. This increase is partly the result of aggressive coaches and efforts to imitate adult players of the National Hockey League. Young players on the losing teams were more likely to initiate these acts. Hockey referees also indicated an increasing fear for their own safety.[18]
- There are also country differences in workplace injuries and deaths. Italy has recorded a high number of these, particularly among immigrants. Immigrants often get injured or die on their first days on the job. In Italy, an average of 1,376 employees die each year in workplace accidents; and there were 5,252 workplace deaths between 2003 and 2006. The International Labor Office reported that Italy had a fatality rate of 6.9 per 100,000 workers, second highest of the European Union (EU) member states included in the study, about one-quarter of the workplace deaths in the EU.[19]
- More than 25 chemicals used in the workplace are known to cause cancer and another 100 are likely causes of cancer. Studies suggest that 2 to 8 percent of cancer-related deaths may be linked to carcinogens experienced at work. Occupational-

15 Source: www.thestar.com./comment/article/562137.

16 Source: www.allbusiness.com/crime-law/criminal-offenses-crimes-against/14876492-1.html.

17 Source: www.suite101.com/content/nfl-waking-up-to-danger-of-brain-injuries-a170123.

18 Source: www.globalpost.com/notebook/canada/090204/canada-debates-its-tradition-hockey-violence.

19 Source: www.hse.gov.uk/statistics/european/background.htm.

related cancers include lung, bladder, and skin cancers, leukemia, and mesothelioma. Common carcinogens include radon, benzene, coal, tar, and asbestos. Coal dust has long been known to contribute to black lung disease among miners.[20]

- Canada is one of the world's largest producers of asbestos. Although asbestos is now shunned in many parts of the developed world, there is a huge asbestos market in the developing world. India, followed by Indonesia and Thailand, are the biggest importers of asbestos. Thus, a dangerous product remains in demand.
- Miners in Sept-Iles, Quebec are pressing the Quebec Government to study the effects of working in uranium mines (December 2009).[21] There are now more than 80 uranium exploration sites in Quebec, up from less than five a few years ago given the current high financial value of uranium today in health care. Local physicians and concerned citizens want an inquiry; miners and their union leaders want uranium mining to proceed.
- The National Cancer Institute (NCI) added formaldehyde to the list of cancer-causing agents in May 2009,[22] based on long-term studies of workers at formaldehyde-producing or formaldehyde-using plants. Workers exposed to higher levels of formaldehyde were more likely to incur certain types of cancers of the blood and lymph systems than workers exposed to lower levels. The health of funeral directors has also been found to be affected by this chemical.[23]
- People working in cattle, swine, and poultry barns were also found to have a higher prevalence of respiratory symptoms and decreased lung function compared to control individuals (Mazan et al., 2009). They attributed this to organic dust exposures and horse dander allergies.
- It has long been known the radioactive material from the Chernobyl disaster was associated with increased health problems. A recent study (Almond, Edlund and Palme, 2009) of children in Sweden reported that higher levels of prenatal exposure to the Chernobyl fallout was associated with reduced cognitive functioning.
- Finally, recent evidence has demonstrated an association of workplace bisphenol A (BPA) and male sexual performance difficulties including difficulties in maintaining erections and ejaculating in studies of Chinese males working in factories that either manufactured BPA (ingesting dust containing BPA) or used BPA in their products (epoxy products, lining of bottles).[24]
- The Congo has experienced war, child soldiers, genocide, rape, and the destruction of property over the past two decades. And financing wars isn't cheap. Blood diamonds provided a source of case earlier and now it seems that blood gold is serving this purpose.[25]
- Gold mining is carried out by men using mainly their hands and primitive panning supplies. Miners mix mercury with "mud" containing gold, the mercury binding the

---

20 Source: www.cdc.gov/niosh/topics/cancer/.

21 Source: www.theglobeandmail.com/report-on-business/industry-news/energy-and-resources/protesters-seek-debate-on-uranium-mining/article1393708/.

22 Source: www.cancer.gov/cancertopics/factsheet/Risk/formaldehyde.

23 Source: www.cancer.gov/cancertopics/factsheet/Risk/formaldehyde.

24 Source: www.theglobeandmail.com/life/health/workplace-bpa-tied-to-male-sex-problems/article1360318/.

25 Source: www.diamondfacts.org/conflict/index.html.

gold together. Then they burn off the mercury. The toxic fumes from the mercury causes neurological damage that is likely to show up only years later.[26]

- It is estimated that poverty has forced over 225,000 children in Haiti's cities into slavery as unpaid household servants.[27] Most of these children, particularly young girls, experience sexual, psychological, and physical abuse. Most were sent by their parents who could not afford to take care of them.
- Mattel and its Fisher-Price subsidiary paid a US$7.3 million penalty for importing and knowingly selling toys with excessive levels of lead. The company recalled almost 2 million toys in 2007 (Teagarden, 2009). Lead poisoning can cause neurological damage and delayed mental and physical development in young children (Teagarden, 2009).
- More recently, Maclaren, the makers of strollers for children, had to recall tens of thousands of its product as they led to dozens of fingertip amputations among children.[28] Some companies unfortunately make products that are later found out to be dangerous to consumers. Families in North America are suing a manufacturer of baby cribs that have killed infants who got caught on a drop-side.
- A national sample of 2,048 US worker (Ettner and Grzywacz, 2001) showed that those who had higher levels of perceived constraints and neuroticism, who worked nights or overtime, or who reported serious ongoing stress at work or higher job pressure, reported negative effects on their physical and mental health as result of their jobs. More extraverted workers, the self-employed, those who worked part time, or reported greater decision latitude or use of skills on their jobs, reported that their jobs had a positive effect on their physical and mental health (Ettner and Grzywacz, 2001).
- Robert Stewart shot eight people in a North Carolina nursing home in March 2009. His recently estranged wife worked as a nursing assistant at the home. This was the twentieth shooting spree in the US in less than a month.[29]
- In November 2009, Jason Rodriguez, a disgruntled ex-employee, returned to his former workplace killing one person and wounding five others. He shouted "They left me to rot" as he was taken into custody. It was the second such shooting in the past two days in the US.[30]
- On December 31, 2009, a gunman in Finland killed his former girlfriend and four employees at a supermarket where the girl worked, then committed suicide. The girlfriend had a restraining order against the man. Several shoppers witnessed the shootings. Finland has had several such shootings and has a preponderance of guns among the population.[31]
- Wendy Craig, a Professor of Psychology at Queens University, Kingston, Ontario, Canada undertook a study of bullying in schools in cooperation with the WHO. In 2009, they collected data from more than 200,000 students aged 11, 13, and 15 from 40 countries. Bullying was defined as the "use of power and aggression to cause distress or control another," and distinguished between verbal, physical, sexual, or racial. My country, Canada, ranked 36th, just ahead of Israel, the US, and Lithuania.

26 Source: http:// news.bbc.co.uk/1/hi/health/271598.stm.

27 Source: http://www.theworld.org.//2010/02/01/haitis-child-slaves/.

28 Source: news.bbc.co.uk/1/hi/8351424.stm.

29 Source: www.mahalo.com/robert-stewart.

30 Source: www.reuters.com/article/idUSTRE5A54FB20091106.

31 Source: www.nola.com/crime/index.ssf/2009/12/gunman_kills_five_then_himself.html.

Craig reported that 14 percent of 11-year-old Canadian boys alleged being physically bulled and 30 percent reported verbal abuse. In addition, it has been shown that bullying among children also affects bystanders. Only about 10 percent of bystanders intervene to help the victim while the others feel threatened and anxious.[32]

- On October 21, 2009, a Northwest Airlines jet from San Diego to Minneapolis with 144 passengers on board over-flew Minneapolis by over 100 miles and did not respond to calls from air traffic controllers and other airplanes for over an hour. Early explanations have the two pilots sleeping or arguing. They later admitted that they were on their PCs during this time, an admission likely to have them both fired. Being out of contact for whatever reason is cause for termination. Both pilots have since had their pilot's licenses revoked.[33]
- In 2009, an Air Canada pilot, scheduled to serve in a back-up role on a nine-hour flight from London, UK to Calgary, was not allowed to board the airplane after a security agent at London's Heathrow airport smelled alcohol on his breath. Air Canada pilots cannot consume alcohol for 12 hours before a flight. A United Airlines pilot was found to be too drunk to fly from London to Chicago (November 9, 2009) and his employment was terminated.[34]
- Canadian pilots are asking for changes in regulations that would reduce the risk of pilot fatigue. In fact, airline pilots around the world have fought for such changes over the past two years. Canada has had several accidents in which pilot fatigue was implicated as a cause. For example, on August 12, 1999, Regionnair Beechcraft 1900 crashed in poor visibility near Sept-Iles, Quebec. The captain was killed. Both pilots were over their time limit. The first officer, flung at the time of the crash, did not have a day of uninterrupted sleep for a month.[35] On August 22, 1997, an improperly loaded Piper Aztec crashed on takeoff killing two passengers. The pilot had slept only three hours on each of the two previous nights.[36]
- A passenger plane with a recent history of technical problems crashed into the airport VIP lounge in Kigali, Rwanda, killing one passenger (November 2009). The plane had indicated technical problems a few days before this crash.[37] Equipment malfunctions also contribute to accidents, injuries, and fatalities.
- A bus driver in Vancouver was featured on a video posted on YouTube (October 20, 2009) doing a Sudoku puzzle while driving. Apparently there are no explicit policies indicating what drivers can and cannot do while driving, other than following the law and using common sense.[38]
- Nearly one-fifth of Canada's nurses admit to making occasional or frequent errors in giving medication to patients. Nurses working overtime, or where staffing and resources were inadequate, were more likely to report that a patient had received the wrong medication or dosage. These findings came from a 2005 study of 19,000

32 Source: www.canadiancrc.com?Bullying_in_Canada_study_2009. aspx.

33 Source: www.heraldtribune.com/article/20091022/BREAKING1910229952.

34 Source: www.reuters.com/article/idSTRE5AQ4X220091110.

35 Source: www.planecrashinforcom/1999/1999.htm.

36 Source: www.tsb.gc.ca/eng/publications/reflexions/aviation/2003/numero-issue_26/aviation-numero-issue-26-sec1.asp.

37 Source: www.airsafenews.com/2009/11/rwandair-jet-crashes-into-vip-terminal.html.

38 Source: www.cbc.ca/canada/british-columbia/story/2009/10/21/bc-sukoku-bus-driver-vancouver-surrey.html.

nurses.[39] Factors associated with medication errors included working overtime, work overload, staffing shortages, unsupportive colleagues, and poor relations with doctors.

- Workers perceiving higher levels of job insecurity exhibited decreased safety motivation and compliance, which in turn were related to higher levels of workplace injuries and accidents (Probst, 2002; Probst and Brubaker, 2001).
- Anyone visiting London has likely seen the ceremonial guards, known as Beefeaters, at the historic Tower of London. The first female Beefeater was recently appointed. She has since successfully claimed workplace harassment and bullying by male Beefeaters which resulted in two of them being fired (November 25, 2009).[40]
- The EU is now setting limits on the level of noise permitted both at work and outside of work after concluding that prolonged exposure to loud noise could cause permanent hearing damage.[41]
- Tainted food products (listeria in meat in Canada, tainted peanut butter in the US, tainted peppers in the US) have resulted in dozens of deaths and hundreds of illnesses.
- Menu Foods Income Fund, the owner of a company that sold pet food tainted with melamine in 2008, paid $24 million to satisfy North American lawsuits of people whose pets had died.[42]
- The Workers Safety and Insurance Board (WSIB) in Ontario reported about 100 job-related deaths and more than 80,000 "lost-time" workplace injuries in 2007.[43]
- There is occasional tension between government agencies mandated to help injured workers and the workers themselves. Workers sometimes feel they deserve more support than they receive. A disgruntled injured worker armed with a rifle held nine people hostage for ten hours in the Edmonton offices of the Workers Compensation Board (WCB) on Wednesday, October 21, 2009, before giving himself up. The gunman, a client of the WCB, felt his knee was injured during an examination by a doctor at the WCB and, though the doctor thought he was fit to return to work, the man disagreed.[44] There have been previous incidents of worker frustration moving into anger. In 1991, a worker committed suicide with a gun in the Calgary WCB parking lot.[45] In 1993, a gun-toting worker took several hostages at the Calgary office before surrendering.[46] And in 2007, an injured and depressed worker whose compensation claim had been rejected deliberately drove his truck into the WCB office in Winnipeg.[47] WCB offices across Canada have been criticized by disgruntled workers.
- There are some organizations in which errors can have catastrophic consequences for employees and the wider community. These disasters have included the Chernobyl nuclear power plant, the pesticide plant of Union Carbide in Bhopal, India in 1986,

39 Source: www.statcan.gc.ca/daily-quotidien/080514/dq080514b-eng.htm.

40 Source: www.guardian.co.uk/money/2009/nov/02/tower-london-beefeaters-harassment-inquiry.

41 Source: www.mycontactcentre.com/wp-content/uploads/2010/11/noise_at_work_VistaPlus_White_Paper.pdf.

42 Source: www.lawyersandsettlements.com/articles/menu-foods/pet-food-crisis-00717.html.

43 Source: www.insurance-canada.ca/consinfobusiness/infonews/2007/WSIB-workplace-injuries-fatalities-712.php.

44 Source: www.edmontonsun.com/news/edmonton/2009/10/21/11475841.html.

45 .Source: www.edmontonsun.com.

46 Source: www.edmontonsun.com/news/edmonton/2009/10/22/11495146.html.

47 Source: www.edmontonsun.com.

the grounding of the Exxon Valdez with the resulting oil spill in 1989, the explosion and sinking of the Russian submarine, the Kursk in 2000, the Petrobas oil-rig collapse in 2001, and the fire at a British Petroleum refinery in Texas City, Texas in 2005. In the latter case, the fire was attributed to cost-cutting measures, not enough training being provided, and a culture that made it acceptable to cut corners. We are beginning to understand what makes these "high reliability organizations" more likely to be error free (Roberts, Desai and Kuo, 2008).
- A propane blast in Toronto killed two people and led to the evacuation of 12,000 in the summer of 2008. One year after this event, concerns were still being raised about the inspection of propane facilities in other locations in and around Toronto.[48]
- 96 people have died in Canada as of October 27, 2009 from the H1N1 virus.[49] Severe illness and death are part of this pandemic. Organizations are taking precautions within their facilities (for example, encouraging hand washing, asking employees to stay home if sick). Some organizations (for example, Dupont Canada) are having their doctors give vaccine shots in their facilities. Schools have reported an increase in student absences.
- Family-to-work conflict was found to be associated with decreased compliance with safety rule and less willingness to participate in discretionary safety meetings in a sample of 243 health care workers (Cullen and Hammer, 2007).

Incidence and Costs of Workplace Injuries, Illnesses, and Deaths

These examples suggest that a consideration of workplace injuries, illnesses, and deaths and their prevention is both timely and relevant for individual workers, their families, employing organizations, communities in which these organizations are located, and society at large.

The International Labor Organization (ILO) estimated 2.2 million people die every year from accidents at work or occupational diseases and these numbers may be increasing. In addition, the ILO estimates that there are 270 million non-fatal accidents each year, causing injury worldwide.[50] Workplace accidents and errors have a cost of hundreds of billions of dollars each year. There are also wide country differences (for example, China has higher rates on some types of accidents and in some sectors), and wide occupational differences (for example, construction and transportation have higher rates) in incidence of accidents and errors.[51]

Organizations incur both direct and indirect costs from workplace accidents and injuries: direct costs include payments to injured workers and costs of their treatment, and costs of health and accident insurance; indirect costs include lost productivity and overtime charges. The health care system gets stretched, given increased usage and efforts by governments to constrain costs, and the injured worker and their families endure considerable financial and emotional suffering.

48 Source: www.thestar.com/generic/article/476267.

49 Source: http://www.conferenceboard.ca/HCP/Details/health/mortality-respiratory-system.aspx.

50 Source: www.ilo.org/global/topics/safety-and-health-at-work/lang-en.index.htm.

51 Source: www.ilo.org/global/topics/safety-and-health-at-work/lang-en.index.htm.

Executives in the German steel maker Thyssen Krupp's Italian unit faced charges ranging from murder to manslaughter following a fire at their steel plant in December 2007 that killed seven people. Survivors said that the fire extinguishers were empty and that safety standards in general were lax in the Turin factory. If convicted, the CEO, charged with murder, could face 21 years in prison. Organizations are increasingly being held legally responsible for not addressing known risks to health and safety (Susser, 2006).

A hospital in Windsor, Ontario, Hotel-Dieu Grace, reached a settlement in a lawsuit brought by the family of a slain hospital nurse who was killed by a doctor, a former boyfriend. The doctor had a long history of disruptive and sometimes aggressive and violent behavior toward hospital staff. The doctor had his hospital privileges reinstated after he was suspended and ordered to seek counseling after a suicide attempt. The hospital has instituted a number of initiatives to prevent such an event occurring again.[52]

Organizations are now taking a more proactive approach to accidents, safety, and health by engaging in risk assessment and risk management. The accumulating evidence shows that investing in occupational safety and health results in improved financial and social responsibility performance—increasing employee safety, health, and well-being pays. And although there has been a reduction in workplace accidents in some countries, further improvements seem to have stalled.

Organizational Liability

Organizations are being increasingly held liable for contributing to unsafe or unhealthy workplaces, failing to address known workplace hazards, and failing to inform employees of these hazards (Susser, 2006). Virginia Tech University experienced the worst campus shooting spree in US history on April 16, 2007, which left 33 dead including the shooter. Investigations of this incident found the University employees and administrators made some "mistakes" during this event. The University has reached financial settlements with most of the relatives of the victims.

What is Occupational Injury and Illness?

These include the obvious occupational injuries and illness such as sprains, cuts, loss of a limb, and illness due to coal dust (generally due to physical demands and chemical job hazards) as well as broader concepts of occupational illness such as carpal tunnel syndrome, back pain, noise-induced hearing loss, cardiovascular diseases, cancers, and chronic respiratory diseases. This collection deliberately takes a broad view on employee safety and health, consistent with recent writing that views work and working as major social determinants of individual and family health and well-being (Dembe, 1996; 2005). In addition, we will consider worker and organizational behaviors and actions that impact on the health and safety of users and consumers of their products, the safety of the products and services that are provided, citizens in communities in which these

52 Source: http://workplaceviolencenews.com/2010/01/05/settlement-reached-in-case-of-slain-windsor-nurse/.

organizations are located, and wider external threats to the health and safety of employees (for example, the H1N1 virus and SARS).

Under-Reporting of Workplace Accidents and Illnesses

While the number of worldwide workplace injuries, illnesses, and deaths are staggering, there is considerable evidence that these reported rates are under-estimates of the actual numbers of injuries and illnesses. Under-reporting occurs both at the individual level and the organizational level (Leigh, Marcin and Miller, 2004; Probst, Brubaker and Barsotti, 2008). Under-reporting occurs for several reasons: the injury or illness is minor, the reporting procedures are onerous, the organization "discourages" the reporting of injuries or illnesses, and the criteria for defining accidents, injuries, or illnesses are confusing. The actual number of injuries and illnesses may in fact be double that reported by data-gathering and monitoring bodies (Hämäläinen, Takala and Saarela, 2006)

Organizations in Canada get rewarded by under-reporting the numbers of injuries and their severity and rushing injured workers back to work. Workers are pressured or bribed not to report major injuries. Some companies pay the injured to do "odd jobs," others report injuries as less serious than they are. These organizational actions reduce their insurance premiums.

Impact of Workplace Injuries and Illness on Families and Children

The impact and costs of workplace injuries and illnesses have typically considered only the worker. Dembe (2005) rightly broadens our consideration of occupational injuries and illnesses to include families and children. Occupational health events have economic, employment, and legal implications. These affect workers' lives, their families and children, and their communities. Workplace injuries and illnesses affect those injured or ill in terms of physical impairment, functional limitations, lost wages, and limiting the worker's ability to do their job. But workplace injuries and illnesses can also affect the workers family and children.

Dembe (2005) identifies five impacts on those who become injured or ill from work experiences. These are:

1. medical care and recovery—hospitalization, surgery, medication use, need for home care;
2. psychological and behavior responses—depression, anger, stress, isolation and loneliness, use of drugs, use of alcohol;
3. functional responses—limitations to daily activities, household tasks, community activities;
4. vocational responses—reduced hours, less productive in employment, job changes; and
5. economic responses—lower income, more expenses, asset losses, increased debt, worker compensation claims.

These then affect the workers' family and children in terms of their own physical and mental health, their social relationships, their domestic and household relationships, and their economic circumstances.

There are likely hidden organizational costs when employees have to worry about and take care of a family member who has been injured at work, as well as caring for family members who may have mental illnesses. About one-quarter of US adults aged 18 and older suffer from a diagnosed mental disorder in any given year (Dembe, 2005). Organizations need to be sensitive to and support their employees who are caring for another. Employees should feel free to ask for help that is needed in supporting another family member, managers should model supportive behaviors, and the organizational culture should reflect these values.

Human Error in Medicine

Individuals who become sick or injured almost always to go a hospital for care and treatment. But hospitals themselves and the health care system, because of human error, sometimes can make sick or injured people worse, or even cause deaths. Human error occurs in all aspects of human activity so it is not surprising that human error occurs in hospitals as well, but the errors and deaths they cause have been kept under wraps and most people see hospitals, and the health care system more generally, as a safe environment. Bogner (1994; 2010) put the issue of medical error on the radar. While adverse health care outcomes are often the result of errors by care providers, other factors are involved as well. Errors result from the use of medical equipment, poor or fatigued decision making, surgical mistakes, stress, and cognitive overload. Human error in medicine could have disastrous consequences (Peters and Peters, 2007).

The Committee on Quality of Health Care in America (2000) estimated that about 98,000 people die annually from medical errors in hospitals, more than die from motor vehicle accidents, breast cancer, or AIDS. More people die from medication errors than from workplace injuries. Their view, that to err is human, emphasized the role of the health care system in medical errors. Unfortunately liability issues discourage the reporting of errors and thus limits one's ability to learn from them. Wachter (2010), an expert on hospital safety, gave the health care system a grade of B-, up from the grade of C+ he gave the same system in 2004 (Wachter, 2004). Thus, while progress has been made over the ten years, there is still plenty of room for improvements.

What is Safety Performance?

Safety performance includes two related but different concepts (Christian et al., 2009). One concept refers to a way of measuring safety outcomes, a tangible metric, for example, number of workplace injuries or deaths per year. The second concept refers to a metric for safety-related behaviors, for example, wearing protective equipment. Safety performance behaviors can be better predicted than can safety outcomes. Safety outcomes (workplace injuries, deaths) are relatively rare events and yield skewed distributions.

Burke et al. (2002) defined safety performance as "actions or behaviors that individuals exhibit in almost all jobs to promote the health and safety of workers, clients, the public, and the environment" (p. 432). They note four factors in safety performance: using personal protective equipment, engaging in work practice to reduce risk, communicating hazards and accidents, and exercising employee rights and responsibilities. Neal, Griffin and Hart (2000) make a distinction between safety "compliance" and safety "participation," the first referring to required or mandated safety behaviors and the second to voluntary safety behaviors.

Christian and his colleagues (2009) develop an integrative model of workplace safety having five major panels of variables (p. 1105). Two distal panels of variables (for example, situation-related and person-related factors) lead to proximal person factors (for example, safety motivation, safety knowledge) which in turn lead to safety performance (for example, safety compliance, safety participation) which in turn lead to safety outcomes (for example, accidents, injuries). Distal situation-related factors include managerial commitment, human resource management (HRM) policies, safety systems, supervisor support, informal group processes, degree of job risk, and work pressures. Distal person-related factors include personality (for example, risk taking, neuroticism) and job attitudes (for example, safety attitudes, broader job attitudes). Safety compliance includes following procedures, using protective equipment, and practicing risk reduction. Safety participation includes communication and voice, helping stewardship, whistleblowing, civic virtue, and facilitating safety-related dialogue.

They review and integrate available health and safety research studies into their model and analyze findings across studies using meta-analytic techniques. They found support across these studies for the following relationships (p. 1123). First, safety climate had significant relationships with both safety knowledge and safety motivation. Second, one aspect of personality (conscientiousness) had a significant relationship with safety motivation. Third, safety motivation had a significant relationship with levels of safety knowledge. Fourth, both safety knowledge and safety motivation had a significant relationship with safety performance (behaviors). Finally, safety performance had a significant relationship with accidents and injuries.

Causes of Unsafe Workplace Behaviors

What causes unsafe workplace behaviors, accidents, and errors in the workplace? The accumulating research data point to individual factors (for example, personality factors—a macho attitude among oil-rig workers, and fatigue—25 percent of driving accidents and 19 percent of workplace accidents are fatigue-related), organizational factors (for example, a production emphasis on off-shore oil platforms), and technological factors (for example, computer usage and carpal tunnel syndrome/repetitive strain injury).[53]

Factors that have been associated with increasing risk of accidents include individual, group, and organizational characteristics (Hoffman, Jacobs and Landy, 1996; Clarke, 2010). Hoffman, Jacobs and Landy (1996) review individual factors or human error (cognitive errors, slips, fatigue, alcohol consumption, safety motivation, and attitudes), micro-organizational factors (safety objectives, safety commitment, role of senior executives, collecting complete safety data) and macro-organizational factors (organizational structure, personnel specialization, technology, centralized decision making).

53 Source: www.car.accidents.com/car-accidents-ca.

Accidents result from negligent worker behaviors and/or faulty company practices. Young workers are particularly vulnerable to workplace accidents; young workers may be over-confident or fail to follow instructions. Since human error is typically involved in a high number of accidents, initial attention had focused on the individual. More recently, attention has shifted to the interaction of the individual with their social, technical, and organizational work environment.

Individual Factors

Early studies focused on accident-prone individuals of accident repeaters (Davids and Mahoney, 1957) but it has proven difficult to identify consistent characteristics of accident-prone individuals. One potential common factor appears to be a propensity to take risks, associated with sensation seeking. Other individual factors found to be linked with accidents were neuroticism (Clarke and Robertson, 2005; Lajunen, 2001), affectivity (Cellar et al., 2001; Iverson and Erwin, 1997), and conscientiousness (Fallon et al., 2000).

Sleep Deprivation and Fatigue

Barnes and Wagner (2009), using data on workplace injuries among miners from 1983–2006, found that changes to daylight savings time, that resulted in a loss of one hour, was associated with increased injury rates on the Monday following the time change. Changes in time that added one hour were not related to accidents on the following Monday. Their work indicated that workers slept 40 minutes less in the former case, suggesting that sleep loss influenced workplace injuries, by increasing them.

Barnes and Hollenbeck (2009) reviewed literature on sleep deprivation and team functioning and concluded that sleep deprivation had a negative effect on team decision-making accuracy and problem solving. Their conclusions fit the results of sleep deprivation research and human functioning more broadly, showing negative effects.

Many major disasters at work (for example, Chernobyl, Three Mile Island, Exxon Valdez, and the Space Shuttle Challenger accident) occurred at night or early morning. Sleep deprivation has been suggested as a cause of 7.8 percent of all the US Air Force's Class A mishaps (Barnes and Hollenbeck, 2009).

Individuals who suffered from insomnia took sick days twice as often as those not suffering from insomnia. Over a six-month period, insomnia cost organizations an average of 4.4 days of wages for each untreated sufferer, plus direct costs due to lower productivity and mistakes made because of lack of sleep (The Center of Medicine in the Public Interest).[54] In addition, about one-third of American adults have high blood pressure or hypertension, a condition that accounts for seven million deaths worldwide per year.[55] Knutson and his colleagues (2009) report that individuals sleeping fewer hours were significantly more likely to have higher systolic and diastolic blood pressures. Each hour of sleep reduction was associated with a 37 percent increase in the probability of developing high blood pressure.

---

54 Source: www.cmpi.org/uploads/File/Insomnia-paper-5.15.09_final.pdf

55 Source: www.cmpi.org/uploads/File/Insomnia-paper-5.15.09_final.pdf.

Vila (1996), a former police officer turned college professor, makes a number of connections between police officer fatigue and the performance, health, and safety of patrol officers. Police officers are required or choose to work overtime, and Vila contends that police administration can do a much better job controlling these hours.

These findings are important since it appears that more adults are now sleep deprived (that is, sleeping less) than previously, particularly in North America (Czeisler, 2006).

Alcohol and Drugs

A young man, driving while drunk, sliced a Honda minivan in half killing three people in Toronto on October 17, 2009. He was driving 200 km (120 miles) per hour in a 60 (36 miles) km zone. The 21-year-old driver had been charged in 2007 with failing to provide a breathalyzer sample but for unexplained reasons this charge was withdrawn.[56] Drunk driving is a significant cause of car accidents, injuries, and deaths.

Not Following the Rules

Colgan Air blamed the pilot for a plane crash that killed 50 people near Buffalo, New York in early 2009 for inattention and failure to follow safety rules.

Organizational and Social Risk Factors

Glendon (2008a; 2008b) notes increasing interest in the concepts of safety culture and safety climate. Most articles on these topics, not surprisingly, were published in safety-related journals, followed by psychology and health care journals. Researchers and writers in the US, UK, and Scandinavia are major contributors to this body of work. Manufacturing health care, transport, and petrochemicals are the most commonly studied industrial sectors.

A poor "safety culture" has been shown to be a risk factor in safety behaviors and accidents. Safety cultures reflect senior management's commitment to safe workplace practices. Neal and Griffin (2006) define safety culture as "individual perceptions of policies, procedures and practices relating to safety in the workplace" (pp. 946–947). This includes the priority that the organization gives to safety in relation to other factors. An important issue here is the relationship between safety and productivity (Antonsen, 2009). Safety climate has been show to influence safety behavior and workplace accidents (Burke et al., 2002; Clarke, 2006b; Cooper and Phillips, 2004; DeJoy et al., 2004; Glendon, 2006; Johnson, 2007; Neal and Griffin, 2006, Neal, Griffin and Hart, 2000; Zohar, 2000; 2002a; 2002b). The concept of safety climate reflects both individual-level and organizational factors. Safety climate, in turn, is influenced by management decisions and actions, leadership style, manager-worker relationship quality, work group processes, and work processes.

56 Source: www.alcoholalert.com/drunk-driving-statistics.html.

On December 24, 2009, a scaffold holding five workers doing balcony repair work on the thirteenth floor of a high-rise outside Toronto broke, sending four to their death, with a fifth unlikely to recover from his injuries. Their swing stage platform broke in the middle causing them to fall: it was later determined that the workers were not wearing safety harnesses. Observers commented that use of this large platform allowed workers to work on two balconies at the same time, a more efficient approach, but that longer platforms are more vulnerable to breaking. This site was visited by government inspectors about two months earlier who stopped work on the site because of concerns about the safety of the scaffolding. Work was allowed to resume about a week before the accident after a visit by a safety inspector.

Hoffman and Marks (2006), in a large sample of US hospitals, found that safety climate predicted medication errors, nurse back injuries, urinary tract infections, patient satisfaction, patient assessments of nurse responsiveness, and nurse satisfaction. Interestingly, the effects of safety climate with various outcomes was stronger for more complex patient conditions.

Organizations also differ in the safety and health performance. Some organizations are viewed as industry leaders (for example, Dupont), and these have often offered their learning, wisdom, and practices to other organizations to help them improve their performance in these areas. Key elements in these programs include employee selection and training, fostering employee understanding, participation, and engagement in safety and health matters, developing a health and safety culture at group/work unit and organizational levels, communicating and reinforcing safe workplace practices, learning from accidents and errors, and bench-marking one's organization against the industry leaders. Borofsky and Smith (1993) and Fullerton and Stokes (2007) illustrate how a pre-employment screening inventory reduced accidents. Eklof (2002) and Eklof and Turner (2005) use the analysis of accidents and incidents to increase safety behavior of fishermen designing an intervention that increased their perception and control of occupational injury risks.

Work Demands

Forty years or more of research has provided considerable support for the adverse effects of particular work demands, termed "work stressors" by some, on worker psychological and physical health (see Barling, Kelloway and Frone, 2005; Schabracq, Winnubst and Cooper, 2003, for reviews). These work demands have included hours worked, overtime work, types of shift work, and work intensity (Burke and Cooper, 2008; Dembe, 2009; Dembe, Erickson and Delbos, 2008; Dembe et al., 2005; 2006; 2007; Green 2008). There is also evidence that employees holding high-quality jobs are both more satisfied and display safer work behaviors (Barling, Kelloway and Iverson, 2003) In addition, there is emerging evidence that workaholic and work addiction also has negative effects on individual health and well-being (Burke, 2006; Schaufeli, Taris and Bakker, 2008).

A recent study of health care workers in Canada found that nearly three in five workers were suffering from overload that contributed to increased absenteeism, lower productivity, and greater staff turnover. Overload was caused by the complexity of the work, the urgency of the work, and difficulties in saying "no" rather than by sheer number of hours worked. Hours worked played a role in that some nurses choose or are required to work overtime and some work two shifts back-to-back. About one-quarter of the nursing respondents indicated they planned to leave their nursing jobs.[57]

Nearly one-third of European workers see workplace stress as one of the most common threats in their work environment according to a recent study (September 2009) conducted by the European Union.[58] The UK economy alone loses 13.7 million working days yearly due to workplace stress, costing the economy US$50 billion a year due to lost productivity.[59] At least 25 employees at France Telecom committed suicide in 2009 as a result of corporate restructuring according to their unions.[60]

Statistics Canada reported that assaults against peace offices in Canada (police officers, correctional officers, bailiffs, justices of the peace, bylaw officers) had increased by almost 29 percent over the past decade.[61] A guard was killed in a courthouse shooting in Las Vegas (January 2010). Threats against US judges and federal prosecutors rose almost 12 percent in 2008. Judges, court officials, and prosecutors reported 1,278 threats in 2008.[62]

Workplace incivility is an increasing problem associated with increased negative emotions, frustration, and annoyance by the victims (Cortina and Magley, 2009). The biggest complaint individuals have about their workplace is their boss. Bosses also emerge as the main focus of bullying in the workplace (Roscigno, Lopez and Hodson, 2009). The following joke captures this finding: "What is the difference between the Pope and your boss? The Pope only expects you to kiss his ring."

There is also a potential health risk in having little to do. Ironically, male workers in unchallenging jobs in which they engage in passive work are more likely to be "couch potatoes" at home, a lifestyle associated with poorer health (Gimeno et al., 2009). Such individuals engaged in less leisure-time physical activity. This effect was not found for female workers however. In addition, being unemployed is likely to also be associated with poorer physical health (more smoking, more drinking, less physical activity).

Managers and Workers See it Differently

Organizational research has typically found that managers tend to have a more positive view of workplace practices and outcomes in their organizations than workers do. This is often the case for health and safety issues. Spielholz et al. (2008), in a study of truck drivers, found that managers were more positive about their safety climate than their employees were.

57 Source: www.theglobeandmail.com/life/health/health-care-staff-close-to-burnout-study-finds/article1436101/.

58 Source: www.eurofound.europa.eu/ewco/studies/tn1004059s/tn1004059s_9.htm.

59 Source: www.nytimes.com/2010/04/10/business/global/10ftel.html.

60 Source: http://www.cbsnews.com/stories/2009/11/20/eveningnews/main5726974.shtml.

61 Source: http://ywcacanada.ca/data/research_docs/00000039.pdf.

62 Source: www.nytimes.com/2010/01/05/us/05vegas.html.

Presenteeism

Presenteeism refers to employees coming to work, being present at work, even though they are sick or unhealthy. A US survey of 12,000 employees, conducted online by Monster.com, found that 70 percent feared losing their jobs or falling behind in their work, and this made them come into work when sick.[63] In a Swedish study, Bergstrom et al. (2009) found that those coming in sick were more likely to take off more sick time later. Individuals coming in sick on more than five occasions in the base year (2000) reported more than 30 sick days in 2002 and 2003. He also reported that 39 percent came in because of a heavy workload, 37 percent feared losing their jobs, 10 percent worked at home while sick, and 19 percent undertook rest to get better.

The Globalization of Business

Over the past decade, organizations have become increasingly global and international. This movement was driven by the search for new markets, efforts to capitalize on economies of scale, and lower labor costs in developing countries. This often resulted in the building of new factories and the introduction of new technologies. As a consequence of this, workplace accidents, injuries, illnesses, and deaths have increased in developing countries (Hämäläinen, 2009; Hämäläinen, Saarela and Takala, 2009). Baram (2009) believes that developing countries are vulnerable to exploitation since they lack the safeguards, expertise, and public pressures that prevent harm to their workers. He concludes that previous efforts to address workplace hazards in developing countries (for example, soft and hard laws, codes of conduct, and voluntary self-regulation) have failed. Reports of the use of child labor, workers living and working in sweat-shop conditions, abusive supervision, long work hours, low rates of pay, and unsafe work practices have been on the rise. Baram suggests a new approach that defines a standard of care that provides equivalent treatment of worker health and safety across all nations and establishing contractual relationships between multinational companies and host countries as a way of implementing and achieving equivalent treatment.

Olsen and Lindee (2009) also note that the transfer of technology can increase the risk of new failures, misuse, accidents, and unhealthy workplaces. Using longitudinal data from the Norwegian petroleum industry, they found that the first phase in a technology transfer process created high technological risks, sometimes requiring years for the risk levels to become normalized.

Unsafe Products

In November 2009 there were two product recalls prompted by injury to children in one case and death of children in the other. In the first instance, strollers were recalled after a dozen or more young children had the tips of fingers amputated; in the second case, over 2 million infant cribs were recalled after at least four infants died after being caught in a drop-side. On December 16, 2009, health and safety agencies in the US and Canada

63 Source: www.monster.ca.

recalled more than 50 million Roman-style and pull-up blinds sold by such major retail chains as Well-Mart, J.C. Penney, and Pottery Barn. At least five child deaths and 16 serious injuries were associated with these blinds since 2006 and 200 infant and child deaths since 2000.

Do Countries Differ in Safety Performance?

This is a difficult question to answer since countries also likely differ in accident reporting. Mearns and Yule (2009) examined the role of national culture in determining safety performance in the global oil and gas industry. They report that more proximal factors such as management commitment to safety and the effectiveness of safety measures had more impact on workforce safety behaviors and subsequent accident rates than did basic national values. It is likely that whatever differences exist in accident rates across various countries may better reflect country legislation and differences in worker education and skill levels.

Integrating What We Currently Know

A few scholars (for example, Christian et al., 2009; Clarke, 2006a; Griffin and Neal, 2000; Neal and Griffin, 2006) have developed frameworks or models attempting to integrate antecedents. processes, and health and safety outcomes. Brown, Willis and Prussia (2000) developed and tested a sociotechnical model for predicting safe employee behavior in the steel industry. These efforts have identified areas in which research findings have been relatively consistent, suggested high-priority areas for future research, and highlighted potential applications and interventions to improve safety behaviors and safety outcomes.

Physician—Heal Thyself

It is somewhat ironic that the men and women committed to helping others with their health and well-being so often fail to take care of themselves. Wallace, Lemaire and Ghali (2009) review the literature examining the link between physician workplace stress and their health. Physicians experience considerable stress at work. But physicians apparently are not very good at taking care of themselves. They note that about 18 percent of physicians are depressed, but only 25 percent of these seek help. Many physicians themselves do not have family doctors. It is unlikely that unwell physicians can have a positive effect on the health care system. Unwell physicians are more likely to make errors and have poorer treatment outcomes.

Initiatives for Improving Occupational Health and Safety

We will now review some of the efforts being undertaken by individuals and employing organizations to improve occupational safety and health.

Clarke (2010) identifies four types of interventions to improve workplace safety and health based on (1) whether they are reactive or preventative, and (2) whether the target is individuals or the group/organization.

- Individual and reactive—rule enforcement, behavior-based safety programs.
- Organizational and reactive—safety audits, ergonomic changes.
- Individual and preventative—health and safety training aimed at problem solving and hazard awareness.
- Organizational and preventative—employee participation in the identification of workplace risks and their solution, changes in supervisory behaviors, safety training for supervisors, improving management and worker commitment to health and safety.

Being Prepared

Organizations need to be prepared for life-threatening emergencies at work. The sudden death of NBC's Tim Russert (age 50) of a heart attack at his workplace indicated how life-threatening health emergencies (for example, strokes, heart attacks, choking, aneurisms) can take place at work. This is particularly important as the population ages; it is expected that more people will experience these at work in future.

The Heart and Stroke Foundation of Canada noted that Canadians suffer 50,000 stokes each year and 14,000 die; Canadians also suffer 70,000 heart attacks each year with 10,000 dying. Only a small percentage of these happen at work (less than 5 percent)—most happening at home or in public places—but this figure is also expected to grow.[64]

NBC did not have a defibrillator on site leading some to wonder whether Russert might have been saved if there had been access to one.

People see offices as low-risk environments. Yet planning for such life-threatening emergencies makes sense. Companies need to undertake the following:

- have equipment available (for example, defibrillators, first aid kits, oxygen supplies) and trained employees;
- hold staff meetings to discuss how to handle emergency situations. Who is trained? Where is the equipment? Who would call an ambulance?
- organize "lunch and learn" sessions that address major concerns; and
- encourage wellness (fitness, stress reduction).

Federal and provincial laws in Canada require companies to have a given number of trained employees able to provide first aid. Many companies have occupational health and safety committees, depending on the company size and type of industry.

How Organizations Manage Accident Risk

Organizations manage accident risk by:

---

64 Source: www-03.ibm.com/press/us/en/pressrelease/26268.wss.

- creating a positive safety culture;
- focusing on system failures, not blaming individuals when accidents occur;
- developing flexible organizational structures;
- emphasizing organizational learning to better understand and anticipate potential hazards in the workplace; and
- proactively focusing on health and safety.

Food Safety

Fewer than 20 percent of American consumers trust food companies to produce food that is safe and healthy, according to an IBM survey. They found that 83 percent could name a food product that had been recalled in the past two years (46 percent named peanut butter, 15 percent spinach). Companies also faced a hard time rebounding after a food safety scare. Thus, 49 percent of those surveyed indicated that they would be less likely to buy a once-recalled product even after the source of the contamination had been found and addressed. Unfortunately it also takes several months or more to trace the source of some contaminated products.

Raising Safety Issues and Concerns

Mullen (2005) found, in a sample of 178 workers, that top management openness and norms favoring raising issues predicted an individual's perceived probability of success and perceived image risk; perceived probability of success, in turn, predicted employee willingness to raise safety issues and concerns. The whistleblower literature is relevant here.

Use of Checklists

Pilots have been using checklists for years to make flying safe. A recent study showed that the use of checklists among surgical staff before, during, and after operations, reduced complications and deaths from surgery by more than one-third. Checklists have the added advantage of being inexpensive and straightforward. The Province of Ontario introduced a 26-item checklist for physicians which took effect in January 2009. This checklist became mandatory for all surgeries in the province and hospitals became required to report compliance with its use. The checklist must be completed before the anesthesis, the first incision, and before the patient leaves the operating room.

Sax et al. (2009) have shown that the use of aviation-based team training in hospitals produced sustainable behavioral change among nurses, doctors, and ancillary personnel. Perceptions of safety culture increased and staff felt more empowered to self-report errors.

Reducing Road Deaths and Injuries

The WHO recommends the following measures to reduce deaths and injuries from traffic accidents:

- better built and safer cars;
- reducing country speed limits;
- monitoring blood alcohol levels to reduce drunk driving;
- making the use of helmets mandatory for cyclists, motorcyclists, and their passengers;
- making seat belt use mandatory;
- making seat belts mandatory for children;
- building bicycle lanes; and
- building more sidewalks.

Avoiding Hazardous Design Flaws

Although Chinese manufacturing organizations have come under fair criticism for their role in toy recalls, most errors are the result of design flaws made by the companies that create and develop these products (Bapuji and Beamish, 2008) and these mistakes are preventable. Organizations need to do a better job of learning what these flaws are and how to prevent them. Bapuji and Beamish studied about 600 US toy recalls from 1988 through 2007 and interviewed design engineers, manufacturing managers, and consumer protection advocates. They identified several steps in avoiding design flaws. These involved establishing a learning culture in which employees feel safe to report their concerns so mistakes are not ignored, engaging in reactive learning when a flaw is discovered so that an examination and improvement in the systems and process that resulted in the flaw can be corrected, studying competitors' recalls, regulator comments, and medical journals, listening to design and test engineers for their concerns, and testing products for safety issues, and soliciting feedback from customers.

The Requirement of Booster Seats for Children

Children were 20 percent less likely to die in car accidents if the crash occurred in a jurisdiction that had a law requiring booster seats for children. The study examined 14,571 children, aged four to eight, who were involved in head-on automobile crashes involving at least one death in the US between 1995 and 2008.[65]

Helping the Injured/Ill Worker and Their Families

Dembe (2005) offers the following strategies for reducing the negative effects of workplace injuries or illnesses:

65 Source: http://www.aap.org/healthtopics/carseatsafety.cfm.

- counseling for the injured worker and their family members about possible coping responses and ideas for addressing the stresses created by the worker's injury or illness;
- improving communication between employer, medical provides, the injured/ill worker, and their family;
- information to family members on how to support the injured worker at home;
- counseling or medical treatments to address psychological symptoms in the injured worker (for example, depression, isolation) and, if relevant, for other family members;
- psychological and medical treatment to manage the injured workers pain and disability;
- help to injured workers and their families in applying for social benefits to address financial and physical losses;
- using worker's compensation insurance to pay for counseling and other services for family members of injured/ill workers.

No Lifting Policies

Nurses report a high incidence of back injury resulting from the heavy physical loads involved in lifting and transporting patients (for example, Engkvist, 2004). Studies carried out in single institutions (Collins et al., 2004) or across an entire health care system (Martin et al., 2009) have shown that the implementation of a no lifting policy reduced both injuries and back injury compensation claims.

Drug and Alcohol Testing

The TTC, responsible for buses, the subways and connecting commuter trains, is considering the use of an on-the-job drug and alcohol testing program. A private bus company, Canada Coach, uses both random and pre-employment tests on drivers and others in its 800 employee workforce.

Participatory Ergonomic Interventions

Participatory Ergonomic Interventions (PEIs) involve the use of ergonomics teams representing both management and workers, who attempt to reduce workplace risk exposure through redesign of work processes, tools, and equipment. Reviews of five PEIs using some economic data (Tompa, Culyer and Dolinsch, 2008) reported cost benefits to their organizations.

Tompa, Dolinsch and Laing (2009) undertook an economic evaluation of a PEI process in an auto manufacturing plant. They first describe the PEI process following the University of Waterloo Ergonomics Process and Program Blueprint (Wells et al., 2001). It involves the formation of a steering committee and a worksite ergonomics change team (ECT). The ECT included management and workers, a union representative, individuals from all three shifts, HR representatives, a mechanical engineer, and other managers from the Health, Safety, and Environment Department. The ECT received training in anatomy, principles of ergonomics, physical and psychosocial risk factors, and tools for undertaking ergonomic observations and analyses. The ECT identified and prioritized projects based on previous injury rates, pain reports, and worker suggestions and complaints. The research team worked with and helped the ECT. Ten physical change projects were undertaken during the 11-month intervention period. The results were positive. Disability injury claims and number of denied worker compensation claims were reduced and financial benefits were evident.

Safety-Specific Transformational Leadership

Barling, Loughlin and Kelloway (2002), in two separate investigations, found that safety-specific transformation leadership predicted occupational injuries through perceived safety climate, safety consciousness, and safety-related events. Transformational leadership has been shown to influence important worker attitudes and outcomes (Avolio, 1999). In addition, leadership more generally has been shown to be associated with safety practices (Clarke and Ward, 2006; Clarke and Flitcroft, 2008; Hoffman, Jacobs and Landy, 1996; Shannon, Mayr and Haines, 1997; Zohar, 2002a). These writings suggest that training supervisors and managers in safety-specific transformational leadership had value.

Zohar (2002b) found that training supervisors to monitor and reward subordinate's safety performance and engage in safety discussions with them was accompanied by significant and stable changes in minor injury rates, earplug use, and safety climate scores.

Safety Climate

A construction worker was killed in Toronto on December 15, 2009 when a concrete slab fell on him at a job site. He was cutting a concrete slab on a bridge when the concrete slab and the cutting machine fell on him. The cause of the accident is still under investigation.

The construction industry ranks as one of the most hazardous industries in terms of injury compensation payments and mortality. For example, Im et al. (2009) reported that there were 10,276 fatal occupational injury victims in Korea over eight years (1997–2004). McDonald et al. (2009) studied a large university construction project site. Lost time injury rates were considerably lower in this project than those reported for the industry as a whole. Interviews, focus groups, observations, and objective records supported the conclusions that both the consideration of safety in the awarding of contracts and safety climate (for example, top-down management commitment to safety, clear communication of these priorities, and worker commitment to safety) played major roles in keeping injuries low.

Safety Artifacts

Luria and Rafaeli (2008) studied the effects of "safety artifacts," safety signs that were clearly evident in the workplace, and safety climate. Employees in three factories interpreted the safety signs with both safety compliance and commitment to safety. These interpretations were significantly correlated with perceptions of a stronger safety climate. They conclude that perceptions and interpretations of safety signs can support assessments of a stronger safety culture and potentially lead to greater understanding of safety and improvements in the level of factory safety.

The Marlin Company describes their work with Allied Waste's Grand Rapids, Michigan-based 100-employee unit. Waste management is a dangerous business. Allied Waste began its safety program to communicate safety statistics to employees using a low-tech method of posting safety numbers on a white board outside the driver service area where employees begin their work day. This made employees aware of the need for safety but did not produce the dramatic reduction in accidents that Allied Waste wanted. The Marlin Company then created an electronic communication station that was able to make safety information engaging and timely. This resulted in a drop in accidents.[66]

Quick et al. (2008) and Stephenson et al. (2005) increased the use of hearing protection equipment among miners by sending them positive or neutral postcards and exposing them to posters promoting such behaviors.

Improved Safety as a By-Product of Organizational Effectiveness Initiatives

van Ginneken and Hale (2009), using a case study of decision making in a steelworks maintenance department, reported that efforts to improve the overall morale, functioning, and effectiveness of the department when a new senior manager arrived also resulted in improvements in occupational safety. Change efforts involved changing the culture of the department from one of suspicion, blame, and poor work to one of a sense of purpose, of pride in achievement, and cooperation between workers and management. In addition, efforts to improve safety performance can also be a spearhead for wider organizational changes.

Safety Observations

Research has shown that conducting observations of another's safety performance increases the safety performance of the observer (Sasson and Austin, 2005). Alvero, Rost and Austin (2008) found that conducting safety observations of the postural safety performance of individuals undertaking assembly tasks resulted in improvements in postural safety of the observers after their observations, and these improvements did not affect individual productivity.

66 Source: www.themarlincompany.com/site/page.ca.

Training in Safe Workplace Behaviors

There is considerable support for the use of training to change employee job behaviors in an attempt to reduce occupational injuries, illnesses, and deaths (Krause, Seymour and Sloat, 1999). Burke and his colleagues (Burke et al., 2008; Burke, Holman and Birdi, 2006) apply learning theory in efforts to develop effective safety and health training. Goal setting and feedback have been successfully incorporated into training and behavior change programs (Cooper et al., 1994; Fellner and Sulzer-Azaroff, 1984).

There are a number of organizations that provide a range of short courses for firms in various industries. For example, Grey Owl Aviation Consultants offer courses in safety management systems for employees and managers, and in human factors for aviation technicians. Grey Owl also has a number of printed materials that address various aspects of aviation safety (for example, management's role in error prevention, accountability, goal setting, communication, and distraction.). The Marlin Company also assists clients with health and safety concerns though the use of high-tech displays.[67]

Information Sharing

The new technology has made it possible for individuals interested in and responsible for occupational health and safety to collect and disseminate information rapidly. For example, in the health care sector with its focus on patient safety, the Patient Safety Monitor offers online access to briefings on patient safety, safety cultures, diagnostic errors, and patient safety. RL Solutions has developed software solutions for safer health care that have been adopted by health care organizations.[68]

Hospitals in the US and in Ontario, Canada have developed health and safety courses that address a variety of subjects (for example, communicable diseases, disability management, healthy work environments, and patient safety), made consulting services available to hospitals on health and safety issues (for example, Ontario Health Association), disseminated information on emergency preparedness and pandemic planning (the Ontario Health Association offering an emergency preparedness toolkit), and information on dealing with chemical, biological, radiological, and nuclear events.

Government Regulations

All industrialized countries have developed government-level agencies responsible for monitoring workplace injury, illness, and death rates and developing policies and programs to reduce their incidence. These include the National Institute for Occupational Safety and Health (NIOSH) in the US and the Workers Insurance and Safety Board (WISB) in Ontario, Canada, among others. These agencies monitor workplace injuries, illnesses, and deaths, distribute information on workplace practices supporting safer workplaces, and sponsor research.

67 Source: www.themarlincompany.con/site/page.ca.

68 Source: www.rlsolutions.com/risk-management/patient-safety.html.

Accidents, in the US at least, have fallen modestly over the past decade, one of the factors in this being increasing government regulations.[69] Coal mining is another hazardous occupation, and the evidence indicates that coal mining safety in the US (and in the UK as well) has increased as reflected in reductions in the mortality rate of miners (see Chapter 9). Shi (2009) examined the potential impact of government regulations on the safety of miners in a province in China from 1995 to 2006. China's coal mining industry has been labeled the most dangerous industry in the world (Wright, 2004). Government safety regulations were expected to initially reduce the most serious accidents and later to improve overall mining safety performance. Shi reports that government regulations regarding improved mine safety did reduce the frequency of disastrous accidents but did not reduce the mortality rate, one indication of overall safety performance. Shi offers some additional policy recommendations for government regulation including more mine inspections and more state regulation. It also takes time for government regulations to work, estimated to be five years at least (Chapman et al., 2008; Shi, 2009).

In the US, NIOSH launched its national Prevention through Design (PtD) initiative as a comprehensive national strategy for preventing and controlling occupational injuries, illness, and fatalities (Schulte et al., 2008). This effort attempts to "design out" hazards and hazardous exposures from the workplace. The program advocates a demand for safer designs that will protect workers; these involve tools used, the ways workers sit and stand, physical mental and psychological demands, and physical and social ways individuals interact with their work environment. Four areas of action will be targeted: practice, policy, research, and education, over a seven-year period. For PtD efforts to be implemented, organizational and union leaders need to be on side.

Bullying is one of the fastest-growing complaints of workplace violence according to the ILO.[70] Some countries, and two Canadian provinces, have passed workplace bullying laws.

Ontario passed its first seat belt laws in 1976. In 1988, 4,154 people died in car collisions, by 2008 that number had dropped to 2,800. In 1993, 84 percent of drivers used seat belts; when the punishment for not using them was increased in 1994, this figure increased to 91 percent and by 2004 was 92 percent.

Prevention through Design and Reducing Healing Loss in the Mining Industry

Noise-induced hearing loss (NIHL) is one of the ten leading work-related diseases and injuries in the US (Kovalchik et al., 2009). NIHL is a permanent illness with no recovery possible. Fifty percent of miners will experience hearing loss by age 50 compared to only 9 percent of the general population. Kovalchik et al. (2008) used the PtD strategy to "design out" noise hazards in underground coal mining. The intervention involved the design of a noise control for a conveyor on a continuous mining machine.

69 Source: www.osha.gov.

70 Source: www.ilo.org/publ.

A Time-Consuming Process

Chapman et al. (2008) evaluated a four-year intervention to reduce musculoskeletal hazards among berry growers. Their efforts began with the dissemination of information with the hope that this would lead to the adoption of new practices. They found that while managers indicated greater awareness of "better" and safer practices, adoption of these newer practices remained unchanged. The authors conclude that the adoption of their safer practices may take more time.

Reducing Workplace Violence

Wassell (2009) summarizes literature on workplace violence interventions in both health care and retail, the two most common workplace sources of violence. Health care workers have typically been given training in how to better cope with violent patients and how to avoid injury. Interventions in retail typically focus on preventing robbery and violence to retail workers and involve increased lighting to improve visibility, the use of cameras in retail locations, having two employees present, and a low cash handling policy (McPhaul et al. 2008).

Brenda Healey, aged 27, was killed by her supervisor, Stephen Daniel, in March 2008. Both worked for the same bus company. Daniel used a pretense to get Healey to come to a house where he killed her and then committed suicide. Daniel had attacked a woman with a knife in April 1999 and served jail time for aggravated assault. Healey's parents are asking the government to make it mandatory to inform individuals at work of any staff members in their unit with a history or violence. The Healey's said that if they knew of Daniel's violent history they would have discouraged their daughter from working with him.[71]

Safety for Funeral Directors

Funeral directors face risks as they undertake their job responsibilities. The National Funeral Directors Association created a document for their members that lays out the types of hazards (for example, manual handling, slips, trips and falls, and infection control) and ways of managing these risks.[72] They offer some suggestions for handling formaldehyde, recently found to increase certain types of cancers. These include choosing embalming fluids with low levels of formaldehyde, buying small containers rather than large drums, installing ventilation systems in embalming rooms, cleaning up any spillages promptly, wearing full protective clothing, and regular monitoring of employees exposures using personal dose meters.

71 Source: www.newsdurhamregion.com/article/95112.

72 Source: www.nfda.com.

Protective Equipment

British actress Natasha Richardson died from a blood clot following a fall while skiing at Mont-Tremblant in Quebec in late 2008. The company that operates the resort announced that helmets would be a requirement for all children and youths in skiing and snowboarding programs at their resorts. This requirement does not extend to adults however.[73]

Banning the Use of Hand-held Electronic Devices While Driving

"Honk if you love Jesus. Text while driving if you'd like to meet him."

Seen on a bumper sticker.

A study conducted by Drews et al. (2009) found that texting while driving was riskier than talking on a cell-phone or with another passenger. Text-messaging drivers were six times more likely to get into an accident than drivers who do not text.

Ontario, the province in which I live, banned the use of all hand-held electronic devices for car drivers starting October 26, 2009.

Monitoring Airline Pilot Fatigue

Scientific methods have been developed to monitor pilot fatigue and manage its risk. The Fatigue Risk Management System (FRMS) uses computers to analyze a pilot's work history, the timing of work, and rest period that identifies potential fatigue concerns. Pilots in some cases wear wrist watches that monitor their fatigue and sleep patterns and in others are attached to a portable electroencephalogram (EEG) device. Some airlines are now using FRMSs.

Preventing H1N1 Flu

Organizations should have some interest and responsibility in protecting the health and safety of their employees even when the threats lie outside the organization (Harvard Business Review, 2006). Organizations rely on healthy employees to achieve their objectives.

Tens of thousands of people worldwide have died from the H1N1 flu virus, several hundred thousands have become sick, tens of millions of work hours worldwide have been lost to the flu virus, and millions of people have had to work overtime to perform the jobs of their absent colleagues. It is an organization's self-interest to protect their employees from such illnesses, and many have responded.

The Public Health Agency of Canada recommends these simple steps to reduce the likelihood of employees contracting the H1N1 virus:

---

73 Source: www.telegraph.co.uk/news/newstopics/celebritynews/5013887/Natasha-Richardson-Obituary.html.

1. Get an annual flu shot and ensure your family members get one to.
2. Wash your hands frequently.
3. Cover up when you cough or sneeze.
4. Keep shared surfaces (for example, doorknobs, light switches, telephones, and keyboards) clean.
5. If you get sick, stay home.

Contents of This Collection

The contributors to this volume come from various countries, reflecting both the worldwide importance of workplace injury and illness and the unique interest and knowledge in particular areas (for example, the UK and Norway in off-shore oil-rig installations, the US and China regarding mining and construction), as well as company representatives describing their best practices.

Part I, Occupational Health and Safety—Key Issues, contains three chapters. Ronald Burke sets the stage for the chapters that follow by reviewing some important concepts, issues, and research findings related to occupational safety and health. He first provides vignettes from the print media to illustrate the variety of workplace accidents, injuries, and illnesses, and what these examples show as potential "causes" of them, and both the direct and indirect costs of them. He offers a broad definition of safety and health consistent with the view that work and working are major contributors to individual and family health and well-being. Unfortunately, workplace accidents and injuries are both widespread and under-reported. Accidents and illness affect individuals and their families. He then defines safety performance and outlines its elements. Individual and organizational factors associated with workplace accidents, injuries, and illnesses are reviewed. He concludes with a description of a wide range of initiatives for improving occupational health and safety; some are simple (for example, the use of checklists for both air plane pilots and physicians) others being complex (for example, participatory ergonomic studies and remedial actions) and still others being legislative (for example, prohibition of hand-held texting devices while driving). He also includes unsafe products that harm consumers and outlines the role of individuals and employers in combating pandemics in his consideration of health and safe workplaces.

Why make the business case for occupational safety and health (also known as OSH) initiatives? Organizations need to see value from their OSH efforts given competition for scarce resources. Elyce Biddle, Vilma Carande-Kulis, Dee Woodhull, Steve Newell, and Reepa Shroff lay out a basis for determining the value of OSH efforts and provide practical approaches to estimating the value of OSH initiatives. They first consider different definitions of value employing a definition that is understood and accepted within the business community, typically in economic, accounting, and general business terms—ultimately, the impact and effect OSH efforts have on the organization. They then consider ways that value is measured, key to a useful business case. They address the use of both quantitative and qualitative data. They review tools used to measure value of occupational safety and health. Considerable progress has been made here over the past 20 years. The Value Proposition approach is described in some detail. Various accounting standards are used to calculate financial metrics. Use of such business cases, while still relatively new in occupational safety and health, have demonstrated the worksite health promotion and disease prevention programs save health care costs and generate positive returns for employers while protecting employees. In addition, preparation of a business case is informative to OSH managers in understanding the costs and benefits of various intervention options.

Tahira Probst and Maja Graso deal with the reporting and investigating of accidents. Although the numbers of workplace accidents, injuries, illnesses, and deaths may appear to be high, there is concern that these figures may seriously underestimate the actual numbers of non-fatal occupational injuries. This gap occurs when organizations do not report employee injuries and illnesses to appropriate bodies (organizational-level under-reporting) or when employees fail to report injuries and illnesses at work (individual-level under-reporting). They first review commonly used practices/processes organizations and countries use to report, investigate, and track employee injuries and illnesses. Then they define accident under-reporting and review research on individual and organizational correlates of under-reporting. The empirical evidence indicates significant individual-level and organization-level under-reporting of accidents and injuries. They conclude with suggestions for increasing injury and illness reporting including rewards, benefits of reporting, education, recognizing signs of under-reporting, developing action plans to address under-reporting, better methods/tools for accident reporting, and making reporting easier to do.

Part II, Individual Factors, includes two chapters. The concept of "accident proneness" may be back in style. Sharon Clarke examines the history of accident proneness research and psychological factors associated with accident proneness, and offers suggestions for organizational policies and practices in reducing workplace accidents. An increasing number of studies using sophisticated designs and analysis techniques support the concept of accident-proneness are not distributed randomly. Clarke then reviews individual difference factors associated with accidents. These include cognitive abilities (for example, inattention, information processing), personality (for example, neuroticism, conscientiousness), and core self-evaluations (for example, self-efficacy, locus of control). The experience of stress at work and at home also affects accidents. Clarke believes that individual factors, both stable and transient, need consideration to more fully understand workplace accidents and injuries. She concludes with several practical implications for organizations. These include: providing more support to inexperienced workers, widespread safety training, helping workers build personal resources and stress management skills, training workers to be more proactive, increasing worker's perceptions of control, and using training to improve levels of self-efficacy.

Nearkasen Chau examines injury proneness. Occupational injuries are affected by working conditions and the ability of workers to deal with them. Chau first considers working conditions. These include environmental hazards, technical malfunctions, poor organization, high physical workloads, a fast work pace, awkward positions, adverse weather, and noise, cold, and heat. He then reviews the role of lifestyle and personal characteristics. These include an unhealthy lifestyle (smoking, alcohol, and drug use), fatigue, sleep disorders, and old age. The risk of these personal factors was also found to vary across occupations and age groups. He concludes his chapter by addressing the causes of injuries. These include improving working conditions (work environment, work organization, tools and materials used); improving training to increase job knowledge and occupational hazard assessment, matching worker skills to job requirements, improving employee physical fitness and physical health, and helping injured workers rehabilitate and ultimately return to work.

Part III, Work Environment Factors, contains three chapters. Lonnie Golden and Barbara Wiens-Tuers examine the association between overtime work, schedule inflexibility, and worker's physical well-being. One source of inflexibility is the inability to refuse extra work hours, the other is the inability to change starting and quitting times of work on a daily basis. About 25 percent of workers have to work extra-hours, and 50 percent of workers do not control their start or stop times at work, and about 15 percent face both of these inflexibilities. They analyzed data using three indicators of pain, as well as considering the effects of work stress and daily fatigue. The effects of overtime work were exacerbated when overtime work was mandatory and work schedules were inflexible. In general, overtime work was associated with chronic pain and cumulative injury more than acute injuries from work, and with both higher levels of work stress and daily fatigue. The mandatory nature of overtime was more important than working overtime itself. They suggest greater flexibility, a little cost option, as one way to improve worker physical health.

Stig Matthiesen and Brita Bjørkelo review the emerging research on workplace bullying. Bullying results from the interplay of individual, social, and organizational factors. Bullying results in job dissatisfaction, diminished psychological health, higher levels of absenteeism and turnover, and workplace violence as well as lawsuits against employers for disregarding such negative aggressive acts. Workplace bullying reduces individual and organizational effectiveness, besides raising ethical issues. Bullying ranges from the mild to the severe. Some bullying is unconscious while others are deliberate. Although exact figures on the prevalence of bullying are debated, about 10 percent of employees are likely victims. Women may be victims of bullying more than men. Bullying tends to be long lasting. The authors describe different types of bullies and different types of bullying and offer suggestions on how individuals and organizations might address bullying. It starts with policies that spell out what bullying is, why it will not be tolerated, how it will be investigated, and consequences for perpetrators. Investigations of reported or suspected bullying need to be prompt, thorough, skilled, impartial, and confidential. Organizations also need to be proactive rather than reactive in addressing bullying. In concluding, Matthiesen and Bjørkelo describe possible intervention programs to reduce the prevalence of workplace bullying.

David Lester addresses violence in the workplace. Workplace violence takes many forms, ranging from harassment to murder, and from many sources including present and former co-workers, customers, patients, and intimate partners. Observers of workplace violence can also experience psychological distress. Some occupations or workplaces are also prone to violence including soldiers, police officers, nurses, psychiatric and home care staff. Lester provides an in-depth review of mobbing or bullying (non-lethal violence) and murder in the workplace. A profile of the typical workplace killer is summarized. Work stressors are a common "cause" of murder in the workplace, being terminated, bullied, and job dissatisfaction being frequent contributors. Lester concludes with thoughts on how to prevent mass murder. These include: design of the work environment, pre-employment screening of workers, psychological testing, terminating employees with sensitivity, supervisor training in anger management and in detecting "problem" workers, helping battered women, and critical incident stress counseling following a violent incident.

Part IV examines Occupational Factors in five work settings. Kathleen Kowalski-Trakofler, Charles Vaught, Linda Jansen McWilliams, and Dori Reissman examine OSH issues in mining from a psychological perspective. They pay particular attention to coal mining. The past two decades have emphasized psychological aspects of occupational safety and health, complementing the earlier work on the physical mine environment. Most underground mines are coal mines; injury rates underground are higher than the rates for surface mines. They offer a rich description of coal mining at the outset to provide a context for their writing. Government legislation has addressed many of the causes of OSH events over several decades. They use a three-tier model for intervening to improve mine safety: engineering controls (for example, mine support roof technology), administrative controls (for example, safety programs), and behavioral controls (for example, training workers to wear protective equipment). They review recent research on miner behavior in mine escapes, hazard recognition, communication, expectations training, and mandated refuge chambers. Much of the recent intervention work has emphasized training. Their review is a "good news" story. Mine injuries and deaths have dropped dramatically over the past 100 years.

Finding, extracting, and processing oil is hazardous. Over the past several decades, offshore safety has improved however. Kathryn Mearns first reviews disasters that have occurred in the offshore oil and gas industry in the UK, identifying causal factors associated with them (for example, technological factors, inadequate safety regimes, and poorly maintained equipment). She then considers the research evidence linking safety culture, safety climate, and safety outcomes. Perceptions of management and supervisor commitment to safety emerged as the best predictors of safety performance (for example, accidents, injuries, safety compliance). Safety culture was found to have several dimensions and oil and gas installations have been shown to differ on them. Auditing activities of safety culture and practices were associated with favorable health and safety outcomes. Some researchers have found an association of work stress and accident involvement while others have not, suggest an area of future consideration. The role of top management and senior executives in creating and supporting a positive safety culture was central.

Ian Glendon considers safety in four modes of transport—air, sea, rail, and road. All forms of transport involve some risk. He begins by illustrating uses of these four modes of transport, relative costs and benefits, and perceived risk, risk exposure, and sphere of risk. Transport risk can be managed simultaneously across several levels (for example, individual, team organization, country national, and international). He then summarizes traditional strategies of managing transport hazards and risk (for example, regulation, enforcement, education, and training along with more recent strategies (for example, safety culture, mindfulness, human factors, and resiliency engineering). Risk factors in transport stem from workload, fatigue, stress, system complexity, terrorism, and rapid environmental change. He indicates how key hazards/high risks for each of the modes of transport are typically addressed. Ironically, knowledge and resources to address hazards and risks in transport are greater in the developed world, yet most of the incidents occur in the developing world.

Joseph Grzywacz, Sara Quandt, and Thomas Arcury examine the health risks of pesticides among Latino farmworkers. It is estimated that 10,000 to 20,000 physician-diagnosed cases of acute pesticide exposure occur in the US annually among nearly 2 million farmworkers (see Chapter 12). High-dose exposures can have serious health consequences; low-dose exposures have less severe consequences but the long-term effects of chronic low-dose exposure are still unknown. Illnesses have been associated with low-dose exposures (for example, asthma, diabetes, and premature abortion). In addition, pesticides are brought home affecting family members. Grzywacz and his colleagues describe the farmworker population, review what is known about pesticide exposure among farmworkers, consider the role of job stressors in pesticide exposure, and conclude with a research agenda. Job stressors include crowded living conditions, heat, rain, and associated lost wages, and separation from family. Their work reported an association of job stressors with pesticide exposure. Work intensity and low job control were particularly important here. Stressors may encourage behaviors that put farmworkers at greater risk of exposure to pesticides or may "prevent" farmworkers from protecting themselves from pesticide exposure. They suggest some useful "modifiers" of the job stressor-pesticide exposure relationship. These include pesticide training, taking showers at the end of the day, increasing farmworker control, better farmworker housing, and an improved safety climate.

Marisa Salanova, Eva Cifre, Susana Llorens, Isabel Martínez, and Laura Lorente focus on safety, climate, safety performance, and injuries among construction workers in Spain. As mentioned earlier, the construction industry has a poor OSH record. Construction workers face both physical and psychological demands, and these demands interact with each other. They consider the association of safety attitudes, safety climate, and safety performance. They also review the role of positive factors and work experiences. They then describe a field study of psychosocial risks among construction workers. Interestingly, construction workers reported high levels of job demands as well as high levels of job and personal resources. They conclude with an intensive case study of a high-performing Spanish construction company. They offer a methodology for assessing both work experiences and safety climate dimensions in this industry, a potentially practical application of their research program.

The last part, Part V, explores Innovative Organizational Approaches to viewing occupational health and safety, and returning injured or ill employees back to work. Karlene Roberts and Peter Martelli propose a new approach to organizational safety indicating why a new approach was needed. One reason for this was a dramatic increase in the magnitude of accidents, creating catastrophes in some cases. As organizations become larger, more complex, and interconnected with worldwide impact, larger accidents have taken place. As a result, concerns with reducing risk and increasing reliability have increased. Improving reliability is now as important as productivity in some organizations. Organizations are anticipating an increase in these man-made disasters. Both the design of equipment and of organizations now play a role. Early attempts to manage risk had their roots in mathematical models. This was followed by an emphasis on engineering approaches. More recent work has focused on management, organizational, and systems perspectives. Some catastrophic accidents are bound to happen and are therefore unavoidable. They review disasters such as Three Mile Island and Bhopal in their analysis. Roberts was a founder of high reliability organization (HRO) research in the early 1990s. She considers studies of HROs in a variety of settings (for example, health care, school systems, aviation, and manufacturing). Roberts and Martelli conclude with examples of the application of HRO theory to reduce risk of catastrophic accidents in organizations

Mental health issues in the workplace are a major factor in the growing problem of employee absence. Louise St-Arnaud, Mariève Pelletier, Catherine Briand, Marie-José

Durand, Marc Corbière, and Evelyn Kedl describe their process for assisting and supporting the rehabilitation and return to work of employees following mental health problems. Employees likely exhibit early signs and symptoms such as fatigue, insomnia, anxiety, depression, and irritability. The employee has difficulty being or remaining productive. Employees rarely seek help for fear of appearing weak. It is difficult to withdraw from work because of mental health issues. Stressful workplace and personal life events can contribute to mental health issues at work. Interventions targeting the psychosocial work environment are central to successful return to work and job retention outcomes. The psychosocial work environment includes both the job content and social relations at work; thus the role of one's managers or supervisor in this process is pivotal. Managerial support and commitment are key factors in these interventions. Various stakeholders (for example, management, unions, HR personnel, medical staff, and insurance companies) need to collaborate. A return-to-work coordinator can bring the collaboration about. The authors lay out the necessary steps in providing support throughout sick leave: reassurance, the role of the direct supervisor, identifying obstacles to rehabilitation and return to work, summarizing the concerns and identifying targets for action, working with the supervisor in drafting a return to work plan, and ultimately return to work and job retention. A successful workplace intervention is likely to have benefits to other employees as well.

Conclusions

The statistics on the extent of occupational injuries, illnesses, and death, not only of employees of organizations, but of customers, consumers, and clients of organizations, and community members living near particular organizations, are attention-getting and worrisome. Millions of workers die on the job each year and hundreds of millions of workers are injured. These deaths and injuries have widespread influence on families, organizations, communities, and society as a whole. Much more needs to be done to support medical care of injured workers (Dembe, Fox and Himmelstein, 2002). We have come to a much better understanding of the factors that contribute to these injuries, illnesses, and deaths. While it is unrealistic to expect these to be reduced to zero, considerable room for improvement exists. These will involve changes in individuals, work units, organizations, and society as represented by their governments (Messenger, 2006). While some progress has been seen in some quarters, the challenges that remain are basically worldwide in their importance and magnitude (Kelloway and Day, 2005a; 2005b). We also need to design and implement interventions to increase the wellness of those providing treatment and support to the injured and their families. Our hope is that this collection will not only place, and keep, the importance of worker and citizen health and safety on the forefront, but also offer practical suggestions and approaches to improving both.

References

Almond, D., Edlund, L., and Palme, M. (2009) Chernobyl's subclinical legacy: prenatal exposure to radioactive fallout and school outcomes in Sweden, *The Quarterly Journal of Economics*; 124(4), 1729–1772.

Alvero, A.M., Rost, K., and Austin, J. (2008) The safety observer effect: the effects of conducting safety observations, *Journal of Safety Research*; 39(4), 365–373.

Antonsen, S. (2009) The relationship between culture and safety on offshore supply vessels. *Safety Science*; 47(8), 1118–1128.

Avolio, B.J. (1999) *Full Leadership Development: Building the Vital Forces in Organizations*. Newbury Park, CA: Sage Publications.

Bapuji, H. and Beamish, P.W. (2008) Avoid hazardous design flaws, *Harvard Business Review*; March, 23–24.

Baram, M. (2009) Globalization and workplace hazards in developing countries, *Safety Science*; 47(6), 756–766.

Barling, J., Kelloway, E.K., and Frone, M.R. (2005) *Handbook of Work Stress*. Thousand Oaks, CA: Sage Publications.

Barling, J., Kelloway, E.K., and Iverson, R.D. (2003) High-quality work, job satisfaction, and occupational injuries, *Journal of Applied Psychology*; 88(2), 276–283.

Barling, J., Loughlin, C., and Kelloway, E.K. (2002) Development and test of a model linking safety-specific transformational leadership and occupational safety, *Journal of Applied Psychology*; 87(3), 488–496.

Barnes, C.M. and Hollenbeck, J.R. (2009) Sleep deprivation and teams: burning the midnight oil or playing with fire?, *Academy of Management Review*; 34(1), 56–66.

Barnes, C.M. and Wagner, D.T. (2009) Changing to daylight saving time cuts into sleep and increases workplace injuries, *Journal of Applied Psychology*; 94(5), 1305–1317.

Bergstrom, G., Bodin, L., Hagberg, J., Aronsson, G., and Josephson, M. (2009) Sickness presenteeism today, sickness absenteeism tomorrow? A prospective study of sickness presenteeism and future sickness absenteeism, *Journal of Occupational and Environmental Medicine*; 51(6), 629–638.

Bogner, M.S. (1994) Human Errors in Medicine. Boca Raton, FL: CRC Press.

Bogner, M.S. (2010) *Human Errors in Medicine* (2nd edition). Boca Raton, FL: CRC Press.

Borofsky, G.L. and Smith, M. (1993) Reduction in turnover, accidents and absenteeism: the contribution of a pre-employment screening inventory, *Journal of Clinical Psychology*; 49(1), 109–116.

Brown, K.A., Willis, P.G., and Prussia, G.E (2000) Predicting safe employee behavior in the steel industry: development and test of a socio-technical model, *Journal of Operations Management*; 18(4), 445–465.

Burke, R.J. (2010) Tragic duty. In R. J. Burke and C. L. Cooper (eds) *Risky Business: Psychological, Physical and Financial Costs of High Risk Behavior in Organizations*. Farnham, UK: Gower Publishing, 287–321.

Burke, M.J., Chan-Serafin, S., Salvador, E., Smith, A. and Sarpy, S. (2008) The role of national culture and organizational climate in safety training effectiveness, *European Journal of Work and Organizational Psychology*; 117, 133–152.

Burke, M.J., Holman, D., and Birdi, K. (2006) A walk on the safe side: the implications of learning theory for developing effective safety and health training. In G.P. Hodgkinson and J.K. Ford (eds) *International Review of Industrial and Organizational Psychology*, Chichester, UK: Wiley, 1–44.

Burke, M.J., Sarpy, S.A., Tesluk, P.E., and Smith-Crowe, K. (2002) General safety performance: a test of a grounded theoretical model, *Personnel Psychology*; 55, 429–457

Burke, R.J. (2006) *Research Companion to Working Time and Work Addiction*. Cheltenham, UK: Edward Elgar.

Burke, R.J. and Cooper, C.L. (2008) *The Long Work Hours Culture: Causes, Consequences and Choices*. Bingley, UK: Emerald Publishing.

Burke, R.J. and Cooper, C.L. (2010) *Risky Business*. Farnham, UK: Gower Publishing.

Cellar, D.F., Nelson, Z.C., Yorke, C.M., and Bauer, C. (2001) The five-factor model and safety in the workplace: investigating the relationships between personality and accident involvement, *Journal of Prevention and Intervention in the Community*; 22, 43–52.

Chapman, L.J., Newenhouse, A.C., Pereira, K.M., Karsh, B-T., Meyer, R.M., Brunette, C.M., and Elders, J.J. (2008) Evaluation of a four year intervention to reduce musculoskeletal hazards among berry growers, *Journal of Safety Research*; 39(2), 215–224.

Christian, M.S., Bradley, J.C., Wallace, J.C., and Burke, M.J. (2009) Workplace safety: a meta-analysis of the roles of person and situation factors, *Journal of Applied Psychology*; 94(5), 1103–1127.

Clarke, S. (2006a) The relationship between safety climate and safety performance: a meta-analytic review, *Journal of Occupational Health Psychology*; 11(4), 315–327.

Clarke, S. (2006b) Safety climate in an automobile manufacturing plant: the effects of work environment, job communication, and safety attitudes on accidents and unsafe behavior, *Personnel Review*; 35(4), 413–430.

Clarke, S. (2010) Managing the risk of workplace accidents. In R.J. Burke and C.L. Cooper (eds) *Risky Business*. Farnham, UK: Gower Publishing.

Clarke, S. and Flitcroft, C. (2008) Effects of transformational leadership on perceived safety climate: a longitudinal study, *Journal of Occupational Health and Safety—Australia and New Zealand*; 25, 237–248.

Clarke, S. and Robertson, I.T. (2005) A meta-analytic review of the big five personality factors and accident involvement in occupational and non-occupational settings, *Journal of Occupational and Organizational Psychology*; 78(3), 355–376.

Clarke, S. and Ward, K. (2006) The role of leader influence tactics and safety climate in engaging employee's safety participation, *Risk Analysis*; 26, 1175–1185.

Collins, J.W., Wolf, L., Bell, J.,and Evanoff, B. (2004) An evaluation of a "best practices": musculoskeletal injury prevention program in nursing homes, *Injury Prevention*; 10(4), 206–211.

Committee on Health Care in America (2000) *To Err is Human: Building a Safer Health Care System*. Washington, DC: National Academies Press.

Cooper, M.D., and Phillips, R.A. (2004) Exploratory analysis of the safety climate and safety behavior relationship, *Journal of Safety Research*; 35(5), 497–512.

Cooper, M.D, Phillips, R.A., Sutherland, V.J., and Makin, P.J. (1994) Reducing accidents using goal setting and feedback: a field study, *Journal of Occupational and Organizational Psychology*; 67(2), 219–240.

Cortina, L.M. and Magley, V.J. (2009) Patterns and profiles of responses to incivility in the workplace, *Journal of Occupational Health Psychology*; 14(3), 272–288.

Cullen, J.C. and Hammer, L.B. (2007) Developing and testing a theoretical model linking work-family conflict to employee safety, *Journal of Occupational Health Psychology*; 12(3), 266–278.

Czeisler, C.A. (2006) Sleep deficit: the performance killer, *Harvard Business Review*; 94, 53–59.

Davids, A. and Mahoney, J.T (1957) Personality dynamics and accident proneness in an industrial setting, *Journal of Applied Psychology*; 41, 303–309.

DeJoy, D.M., Schaffer, B.S., Wilson, M.B., Vandenberg, R.J., and Butts, M.M. (2004) Creating safer workplaces; assessing the determinants and role of safety climate, *Journal of Safety Research*; 35(1), 81–90.

Dembe, E. (2009) Ethical issues relating to the health effects of long working hours, *Journal of Business Ethics*; 84(2), 195–204.

Dembe, A.E. (1996) *Occupation and Disease: How Social Factors Affect the Conception of Work-related Disorders*. New Haven, CT: Yale University Press.

Dembe, A.E. (2005) The impact of occupational injuries and illnesses on families and children. In S. Bianchi, L. Casper and R. Berkowitz-King (eds) *Work, Family, Health, and Well-being*. Mahwah, NJ: Lawrence Erlbaum, 397–411.

Dembe, A.E., Erickson, B., and Delbos, R. (2008) The effect of occupation and industry on injury risks from demanding work schedules, *Journal of Occupational and Environmental Medicine*; 50(10), 1185–1194.

Dembe, A.E., Erickson, B., Delbos, R.,and Banks, S. (2005)The impact of overtime and long work hours on occupational injuries and illnesses, *New Evidence from the United States Occupational and Environmental Medicine*; 62 (9), 588–597.

Dembe, A.E., Erickson, B., Delbos, R., and Banks, S. (2006) Nonstandard shift work and the risk of job-related injuries: a National Study from the United States, *Scandinavian Journal of Work, Environment and Health*; 32(3), 232–240.

Dembe, A.E., Erickson, B., Delbos, R., and Banks, S. (2007) Associations between work schedules and the vocational consequences of workplace injuries, *Journal of Occupational Rehabilitation*; 17(4), 641–651.

Dembe, A.E., Fox, S.E., and Himmelstein, J.S. (2002) *Improving Workers Compensation Medical Care: A National Challenge*. Beverly Farms, MA: OEM Press.

DeMont, J. (2009) *Coal Black Heart: The Story of Coal and the Lives it Ruled*. Toronto, Canada: Doubleday.

Drews, F.A., Yazdani, H., Godfrey, C.N., Cooper, J.M., and Strayer, D.L. (2009) Text messaging during simulated driving, *Human Factors*; 51(1), 1–9.

Eklof, M. (2002) Perception and control of occupational injury risks in fishermen—a pilot study, *Work and Stress*; 16(1), 58–69.

Eklof, M. and Turner, M. (2005) Participatory analysis of accidents and incidents as a tool for increasing safety behavior in fishermen—a pilot intervention study, *Work and Stress*; 19, 360–369.

Engkvist, L.L. (2004) The accident process preceding back injuries among Australian nurses, *Safety Science*; 42(3), 221–235.

Ettner, S.L. and Grzywacz, J.G. (2001) Worker's perceptions of how jobs affect health: a social ecological perspective, *Journal of Occupational Health Psychology*; 6(2), 101–113.

Fallon, J.D., Avis, J.M, Kudisch, J.D., Gornet, T.P. and Frost, A. (2000) Conscientiousness as a predictor of productive and counterproductive behaviors, *Journal of Business and Psychology*; 15(2), 339–349.

Fellner, D.J. and Sulzer-Azaroff, B. (1984) Increasing industrial safety practices and conditions through posted feedback, *Journal of Safety Research*; 15(1), 7–21.

Fullerton, C. and Stokes, M. (2007) The utility of a workplace instrument in prediction of workplace injury, *Accident Analysis and Prevention*; 39, 28–37.

Gimeno, D., Elovainio, M., Jokela, M., De Vogli, R., Marmot, M.G., and Kivimaki, M. (2009) Association between passive jobs and low levels of leisure-time physical activity: the Whitehall II cohort study, *Occupational and Environmental Medicine*; 66(11), 772–776.

Glendon, I (2006) Safety culture. In W. Karwoski (ed.) *International Encyclopedia of Ergonomics and Human Factors* (2nd edition). London: CRC Press, 2293–2300.

Glendon, I. (2008a) Safety culture and safety climate: how far have we come and where could we be heading, *Journal of Occupational Health and Safety—Australia and New Zealand*; 25, 249–264.

Glendon, I. (2008b) Safety culture: snapshot of a developing concept, *Journal of Occupational Health and Safety—Australia and New Zealand*; 24(3), 179–189.

Grant, A.M., and Wade-Benzoni, K.A. (2009) The hot and cool of death awareness at work: mortality cues, agency, and self-protective and pro-social motivations, *Academy of Management Review*; 34, 600–622.

Green, F. (2008) Work effort and worker well-being in the age of affluence. In R. J. Burke and C.L. Cooper (eds.) *The Long Work Hours Culture: Causes, Consequences and Choices*. Bingley, UK: Emerald Publishing, 115–136.

Griffin, M.A., and Neal, A. (2000) Perceptions of safety at work: a framework for linking safety climate to safety performance, knowledge, and motivation, *Journal of Occupational Health Psychology*; 5(3), 347–358.

Hämäläinen, P. (2009) The effect of globalization on occupational accidents, *Safety Science*; 47(6), 733–742.

Hämäläinen, P., Saarela, K.L. and Takala, J. (2009) Global trend according to estimated number of occupational accidents and fatal work-related diseases at region and country level, *Journal of Safety Research*; 40(2), 125–139.

Hämäläinen, P., Takala, J., and Saarela, K.L. (2006) Global estimates of occupational accidents, *Safety Science*; 44(2), 137–156.

Harvard Business Review (2006) Pandemic planning checklist for businesses, *Harvard Business Review*; May, 25–26.

Hoffmann, D.A., Jacobs, R., and Landy, F. (1996) High reliability process industries: individual, micro, and macro organizational influences on safety performance, *Journal of Safety Research*; 26(3), 131–149.

Hoffman, D. and Marks, B. (2006) An investigation of the relationship between safety climate and medication errors as well as other nurse and patient outcomes, *Personnel Psychology*; 59(4), 847–869.

Im, H-J., Kwon, Y-J., Kim, S-G., Kim, Y-K., Ju, Y-S., and Lee, H.P. (2009) The characteristics of fatal occupational injuries in Korea's construction industry, 1997–2004, *Safety Science*; 47(8), 1159–1162.

Iverson, R.D, and Erwin, P.J. (1997) Predicting occupational injury: the role of affectivity, *Journal of Occupational and Organizational Psychology*; 70(2), 113–128.

Johnson, S.E. (2007) The predictive validity of safety climate, *Journal of Safety Research*; 38(5), 511–521.

Kelloway, E.K. and Day, A.L. (2005a) Building healthy workplaces: what do we know so far, *Canadian Journal of Behavioral Sciences*; 37(4), 223–235.

Kelloway, E.K., and Day, A.L. (2005b) Building healthy workplaces: where do we need to be, *Canadian Journal of Behavioral Science*; 37, 309–311.

Knutson, K.L., Van Cauter, F., Rathouz, P.J., et al.(2009) Association between sleep and blood pressure in mid-life, *Archives of Internal Medicine*; 169(11), 1055–1061.

Kovalchik, P.G., Matetic, R.J., Smith, A.K. and Bealko, S.B. (2008) Application of prevention through design for hearing loss in the mining industry, *Journal of Safety Research*; 39(2), 251–254.

Krause, T.R., Seymour, K.J. and Sloat, K.C.M. (1999) Long-term evaluation of a behavior-based method for improving safety performance: a meta-analysis of 73 interrupted time-series replications, *Safety Science*; 32(1), 1–18.

Lajunen, T. (2001) Personality and accident liability: are extraversion, neuroticism and psychoticism related to traffic and occupational fatalities?, *Personality and Individual Differences*; 31(8), 1365–1373.

Leigh, J.P., Marcin, J.P. and Miller, T.R. (2004) An estimate of the US Government's undercount of nonfatal occupational injuries, *Journal of Occupational and Environmental Medicine*; 46(1), 10–18.

Luria, G. and Rafaeli, A. (2008) Testing safety commitment in organizations through interpretations of safety artifacts, *Journal of Safety Research*; 39(5), 519–528.

MacKay, J.M., Osmond, M.O., and MacPherson, A. K. (2009) School injuries among Ottawa-area children: A population-based study. *Journal of School Health*; 29, 45–50.

Martin, P.J., Harvey, J.T., Culvenor, J.F., and Payne, W.R. (2009) Effect of a nurse back injury prevention intervention on the risk of injury compensation claims, *Journal of Safety Research*; 40, 33–39.

Mazan, M.R., Svatek, J., Maranda, L., Christian, D., Ghio, A., Nadeau, J. and Hoffman, A.M. (2009) Questionnaire assessment of airway disease symptoms in equine barn personnel, *Occupational Medicine*; 59, 220–225.

McDonald, M.A., Lipscomb, H.J., Bondy, J., and Glazner, J. (2009) "Safety is everyone's job": the key to safety on a large university construction site, *Journal of Safety Research*; 40(1), 53–61.

McPhaul, K.M., London, M., Murrett, K., Flannery, K., Rosen, J., and Lipscomb, J. (2008) Environmental evaluation for workplace violence in healthcare and social services, *Journal of Safety Research*; 39(2), 237–250.

Mearns, K. and Yule, S. (2009) The role of national culture in determining safety performance: challenges for the global oil and gas industry, *Safety Science*; 47(6), 777–785.

Messenger, J.C. (2006) "Decent working time": balancing the needs of workers and employers. In R.J. Burke (ed.) *Research Companion to Working Time and Work Addiction*. Cheltenham, UK: Edward Elgar, 221–241.

Mullen, J. (2005) Testing a model of employee willingness to raise safety issues, *Canadian Journal of Behavioral Science*; 37(4), 272–282.

Neal, A. and Griffin, M.A. (2006).A study of the lagged relationships among safety climate, safety motivation, safety behavior, and accidents at the individual and group level, *Journal of Applied Psychology*; 91(4), 946–953.

Neal, A., Griffin, M.A., and Hart, P.M. (2000) The impact of organizational climate on safety climate and individual behavior, *Safety Science*; 34(1–3), 99–109.

Olsen, O.E., and Lindee, P.H. (2009) Risk on the ramble: the international transfer of risk and vulnerability, *Safety Science*; 47, 743–755.

Peters, G.A., and Peters, B.J. (2007) *Medical Error and Patient Safety: Human Factors in Medicine*. Boca Raton, FL: CRC Press.

Probst, T.M. (2002) Layoffs and tradeoffs: production, quality, and safety demands under the threat of job loss, *Journal of Occupational Health Psychology*; 7(3), 211–220.

Probst, T.M., and Brubaker, T. L. (2001) The effects of job insecurity on employee safety outcomes: cross-sectional and longitudinal explanations, *Journal of Occupational Health Psychology*; 6(2), 139–159.

Probst, T.M., Brubaker, T.L., and Barsotti, A. (2008) Organizational under-reporting of injury rates: an examination of the moderating effect of organizational safety climate, *Journal of Applied Psychology*; 93(5), 1147–1154.

Quick, B.L., Stephenson, M.T., Witte, K., Vaught, C., Booth-Butterfield, S. and Patel, D. (2008) An examination of antecedents to coal miners' hearing protection behaviors: a test of the theory of planned behavior, *Journal of Safety Research*; 39(3), 329–338.

Roberts, K., Desai, V., and Kuo, Y (2008) Decision making in high reliability organizations. In W. Starbuck and G. Hodgkinson (eds) *Handbook of Organizational Decision Making*. London: Oxford, 194–217.

Roscigno, V.J., Lopez, S.H., and Hodson, R. (2009) Supervisory bullying, status inequalities and organizational context, *Social Forces*; 87(3), 1561–1589.

Sasson, J. R. and Austin, J. (2005) The effects of information, feedback, and conducting behavioral safety observations on office ergonomic behavior, *Journal of Organizational Behavior Management*; 24(4), 1–30.

Sax, H.C., Browne, P., Mayewski, R.J., Panzer, R.J., Hittner, K.C., Burke, R.L., and Coletta, S. (2009) Can aviation-based team training elicit sustainable behavioral change?, *Archives of Surgery*; 144(12), 1133–1137.

Schabracq, M.J., Winnubst, J.A.M., and Cooper, C.L. (2003) *The Handbook of Work and Health Psychology*. New York, NY: John Wiley.

Schaufeli, W.B., Taris, T.W., and Bakker, A.B. (2008) It takes two to tango: workaholism is working excessively and working compulsively. In R.J. Burke and C.L. Cooper (eds) *The Long Work Hours Culture: Causes, Consequences and Choices*, Bingley, UK, Emerald Publishing, 203–226.

Schulte, P.A., Rinehart, R., Okun, A., Geraci, C.L., and Heidel, D.S. (2008) National prevention through design (PtD) initiative, *Journal of Safety Research*; 39(2), 115–121.

Shannon, H.S., Mayr, J., and Haines, T. (1997) Overview of the relationship between organizational and workplace factors and injury rates, *Safety Science*; 26(3), 201–217.

Shi, X. (2009) Have government regulations improved workplace safety? A test of the asynchronous regulatory effects in China's coal industry, 1995–2006, *Journal of Safety Research*; 40(3), 207–213.

Spielholz, P., Cullen, J., Smith, C., Howard, N., Silverstein, B., and Bonauto, D. (2008) Assessments of perceived injury risks and priorities among truck drivers and trucking companies in Washington State, *Journal of Safety Research*; 39, 569–576.

Stephenson, M.T., Witte, K., Vaught, C., Quick, B.L., Booth-Butterfield, S., Patel, D., and Zuckerman, C. (2005) Using persuasive message to encourage voluntary hearing protection among coal miners, *Journal of Safety Research*; 36(1), 9–17.

Susser, P. (2006) Limiting exposure of the legal kind. *Harvard Business Review*; May, 34–36.

Teagarden, M.B. (2009) Learning from toys: reflections on the 2007 recall crisis, *Thunderbird International Business Review*; 51(1), 5–15.

Tompa, E., Culyer, A.J., and Dolinsch, R. (2008) *Economic Evaluation of Interventions for Occupational Health and Safety: Developing Good Practice*. Oxford, UK: Oxford University Press.

Tompa, E., Dolinsch, R., and Laing, A. (2009) An economic evaluation of a participatory ergonomics process in an auto parts manufacturer, *Journal of Safety Research*; 43, 41–47.

van Ginneken, J. and Hale, A. (2009) From hanger on-to trendsetter: decision making on a major safety initiative in a steel company maintenance department, *Safety Science*; 47(6), 884–889.

Vila, B. (1996) Tired cops: probable connections between fatigue and the performance, health and safety of patrol officers, *American Journal of Police*; 15(2), 51–92.

Wachter, R.M (2004) The end of the beginning: patient safety five years after "To err is human", *Health Affairs*; 23, 534–545.

Wachter, R.M. (2010) Patient safety at ten: unmistakable progress, troubling gaps, *Health Affairs*; 29, 1–9.

Wallace, J.E., Lemaire, J.B., and Ghali., W.A. (2009) Physician wellness: a missing quality indicator, *The Lancet*; 374(9702), 1714–1721.

Wassell, J.T. (2009) Workplace violence intervention effectiveness: a systematic literature review, *Safety Science*; 47(8), 1049–1055.

Wells, R., Norman, R., Frazer, M., and Laing, A. (2001) University of Waterloo Ergonomics Program Implementation Blueprint. http://www.ergonomics.uwaterloo.ca/bprint.html.

Wright, T. (2004) The political economy of coal mine disasters in China: "Your rice bowl or your life," *The China Quarterly*; 179, 629–646.

Zohar, D. (2000) A group-level model of safety climate: testing the effect of group climate on micro-accidents in manufacturing jobs, *Journal of Applied Psychology*; 85(4), 587–596.

Zohar, D. (2002a) The effects of leadership dimensions, safety climate, and assigned priorites on minor injuries in work groups, *Journal of Organizational Behavior*; 23, 75–86.

Zohar, D. (2002b) Modifying supervisory practices to improve subunit safety: a leadership-based intervention model, *Journal of Applied Psychology*; 87(1), 156–163.

CHAPTER

2 The Business Case for Occupational Safety, Health, Environment and Beyond*

ELYCE ANNE BIDDLE, VILMA G. CARANDE-KULIS, DEE WOODHULL, STEVE NEWELL, AND REEPA SHROFF

In a volatile economy, firms are constantly facing increased global competition, rapidly changing technology, and decreased access to scarce resources. Under these conditions, occupational safety and health (OSH) efforts to insure a safe and healthful work environment must compete with other organizational needs. Without compelling information about the value of OSH efforts to the organization, management may view these programs and activities as a lower priority than projects that have established a clearer connection to their bottom line.

In addition to informing investment decisions, demonstrating the value of OSH efforts can also position OSH professionals as essential contributors to business' bottom line. Demonstrating the value can also strengthen the moral argument for "doing the right thing" in protecting the health and safety of workers.

This chapter will provide a conceptual basis for deriving the value of OSH actions within the context of business operations. It will also provide information on the practical application of established methods for estimating the value contribution of OSH actions, including details for calculating financial measures commonly used by business. Finally, the chapter will present the value proposition method that can be viewed as the next generation of the business case for OSH.

How is Value Defined?

The challenge for OSH professionals is to describe the value of OSH efforts in terms that are understood and accepted within the business community. However, value is a relative term, with meanings grounded in multiple disciplines. For purposes of simplicity and

* The findings and conclusions in this report are those of the author(s) and do not necessarily represent the views of the National Institute for Occupational Safety and Health.

clarity, the definition of value used in this chapter will be based on concepts found in economics, accounting, and general business.

In traditional economics, Adam Smith stated in his *The Wealth of Nations* Book 1, chapters IV and V that the concept of value has two distinctive meanings. The first meaning is called value in use and it is defined as the inherent usefulness of an object. Value in use is not an intrinsic quality of a commodity, but its capacity to satisfy, directly or indirectly, needs or desires. The second meaning is known as value in exchange and is defined as the value associated with the power of purchasing other goods. Value in exchange is the worth of a commodity in terms of its capacity to be exchanged for another commodity, which is usually money. The concept is referred to as market value. The existence of use value has been understood as a prerequisite for commodities to have value in exchange.

In accounting, value has been defined as the monetary worth of services provided, a specific asset, group of assets, or the business as a whole (Barron's, 2005). The framework for measuring value in the United States can be found in General Accepted Accounting Principles (GAAP), which are established by the Financial Accounting Standards Board (FASB). GAAP includes the standards, conventions, and rules that accountants follow when recording and summarizing transactions and when preparing financial information. Also included in the GAAP is a series of principles to help guide the recording and reporting functions to best insure the transparency, comparability, reality, and acceptability of financial results.

In business management, value is often an informal term that includes all forms of value that determine the health and well-being of the firm. Business value expands beyond economic or financial value to include other types of value, such as employee value, customer value, supplier value, channel partner value, alliance partner value, managerial value, and societal value. Many of these values are not directly calculated in monetary terms nor are they all pertinent to this discussion of how to demonstrate value in a practical fashion.

When defining the significance of OSH efforts, customer value is one of the more important criteria. The value can be expressed in terms of utility, quality, benefits, or customer satisfaction. Customer values are received by the end-customer as a result of an OSH action or practice implemented to control the risk of disease or injury. The end-customer may include external clients or customers as well as individuals within the organization who are an integral part of the business process.

The organization can also be viewed as a network of internal and external relationships. Value in this context is described as value networks or value chains. Each point in the network has an interest in the business process, such as a stakeholder group, a resource, end-consumers, interest groups, regulators, or the environment itself. To create value for the organization, there is a collaborative, creative, and synergistic process among the groups. If the organization is viewed as a network of value-creating entities (in this case, the OSH practitioner), the question becomes how each point in the network contributes to overall firm performance. While it would be beneficial if this value could be monetized into a single measure, it may not be feasible.

As a final note, Warren Buffett provides a most insightful definition in his commonly stated phrase: "Price is what you pay. Value is what you get." Whether value is measured in accounting, economic, or business terms, the value of OSH practices and programs is determined by the *impact* or the *effect* they have on the organization.

How is Value Measured?

Although there are a number of ways to measure, estimate, or demonstrate value, one of the more widely adopted methods in the business community is accomplished through developing a business case. A quick search of the Internet reveals a variety of definitions for the term business case. The following list presents verbatim those definitions that are grounded in the fields of project management, decision science, or financial management.

- A business case captures the reasoning for initiating a project or task. Wikipedia at http://en.wikipedia.org/wiki/Business_case.
- An explanation of how a new project, product, and so on is going to be successful and why people should invest money in it. Longman Business English Dictionary at http://lexicon.ft.com/term.asp?t=business-case.
- A type of decision-making tool used to determine the effects a particular decision will have on profitability. A business case should show how the decision will alter cash flows over a period of time, and how costs and revenue will change. Specific attention is paid to internal rate of return (IRR), cash flow, and payback period. Analyzing the financial outcomes stemming from choosing a different vendor to sell a company's product is an example of a business case. Business Dictionary at http://www.businessdictionary.com/definition/business-case.html.
- Information necessary to assess benefits of a project against costs and resources to assess whether the proposal should go ahead. The Department for Business and Innovation Skills in the UK at http://www.berr.gov.uk/aboutus/corporate/projectcentre/glossary/page10895.html.
- Structured proposal that justifies a project for decision makers. Includes an analysis of business process performance and requirements, assumptions, and issues. Also presents the risk analysis by explaining strengths, weaknesses, opportunities, and threats. US Department of Interior, Bureau of Land Management at http://www.blm.gov/wo/st/en/prog/more/bea/Glossary.html.
- The business case provides justification for undertaking a project, in terms of evaluating the benefit, cost, and risk of alternative options and rationale for the preferred solution. Its purpose is to obtain management commitment and approval for investment in the project. Association for Project Management in the UK at http://www.apm.org.uk/Definitions.asp.
- A form that provides detailed information about a proposed standard's business implications and its impact on processes and resources. Ontario Health Care Information Exchange at https://www.ehealthontario.ca/portal/server.pt.
- A collection of descriptive and analytic information about an investment in resource(s) and/or capabilities. International Enterprise Architecture Institute at http://www.internationaleainstitute.org/ea-terms-definitions/.

Each of these definitions have similarities and merit, but the following definition has been adopted by the Centers for Disease Control and Prevention: *Investing in Health and Safety: A Business Case Resource Guide* will be used as the basis for the remaining discussion.

> *The business case assesses the quantitative and qualitative performance of an intervention from a business perspective. Ideally, a business case is an ex ante or a priori structured proposal that assists executives, medical and financial officers in decisions to invest in health protection interventions. The business case can also take the form of an ex post proposal in cases where the success or failure of a current intervention needs to be examined or a rationale is needed for securing funds to revamp, revise, continue or expand an existing program.*
>
> (Carande-Kulis, Biddle and Sotnikov, 2009)

What Tools are Available to Develop the Business Case?

There are a number of general guidelines for developing the business case, but few that address the OSH field. Furthermore, the number of systems or full models—those that include a model, data collection instruments, and instructional documentation—to capture the benefits and costs to the business of implementing OSH interventions are also limited.

In 2004, the US National Institute for Occupational Safety and Health and the World Health Organization (WHO) co-organized the conference "Economic Evaluation of Occupational Health and Safety Interventions at the Company Level" to explore the current status of the use of tools to demonstrate the economic gains from OSH actions. Six key economic or financial evaluation tools that evaluated the impacts of OSH interventions from an individual company perspective were presented at this conference (Eijkemans and Fingerhut, 2005). These tools ranged from individualized approaches suitable for small businesses to complex computerized systems designed for the corporate client. The following examples are three of the most widely used models or methods to develop a business case for OSH issues that were presented during that conference.

Productivity Assessment Tool

One of the earliest cost-benefit analysis tools for OSH, the Productivity Assessment Tool, was developed and published in *Increasing Productivity and Profit through Health & Safety* by Oxenburgh in 1991. This tool was developed for the service and manufacturing sectors and was designed to show that productivity and profit for an enterprise are compatible with safe and healthful working conditions for its employees (Oxenburgh and Marlow, 2005). This computerized tool or program evaluates the potential costs and benefits of specific changes in working conditions by exploring the changes in the employee productivity.

The Productivity Assessment Tool consists of four parts—data on employees, the workplace, the intervention, and a report. Table 2.1 is presented to demonstrate the concept of the Tool.

This model measures productivity changes against what is termed the "ideal state." Simply put, this is the production level if all resources were operating at full capacity. The model captures the annual hours paid by the employer minus the hours that the employee is not actively producing. Losses of productive time include absences from injury, illness, training, vacation and holidays, or other absences such as maternity or military service leave. The hours of productive time are multiplied by the wage of the worker.

Table 2.1 The Productivity Assessment Tool

	Initial case enter data on:	Test case(s) enter expected changes for:
Data concerning the employees	• productive hours • wage costs • overtime • reduced productivity	• productive hours • wage costs • overtime • reduced productivity
Data concerning the workplace	• recruitment • insurance • reduction in waste • energy use • other overheads	• recruitment • insurance • reduction in waste • energy use • other overheads
The intervention	Costs, or estimated costs, for the intervention	
The reports	Cost-benefit analysis calculations and reports of the workplace and the employees	

Source: Oxenburg, Marlow and Oxenburgh, 2004, Figure 4.1.

This is not an individual wage for each employee, but rather an average for an employee category or occupation. The most robust of the available programs will allow up to five employee categories to be considered. Any additional wages, such as overtime, should be added to finalize the annual productive value.

The program collects data concerning the employee using a series of screens with sections for the initial and test cases. The first of the series asks for data on the number of employees, hours per week, and the absences associated with the individual employee or employee group. Employer costs, administrative, managerial, and supervisory costs, are captured in the next screen. The final screens in the series for capturing employee data request a percentage of reduced productivity. This information is also used to identify the need for intervening or modifying the working conditions for the group of employees being examined. Oxenburgh provided Table 2.2 as an overview to the *Reduced Productivity* data screen

Table 2.2 Oxenburgh's overview to the Reduced Productivity data screen

Reason for reduced productivity	Typical interventions that would lead from these factors
Low skill	Improve or increase training
Hand tools	Replace or improve hand tools with a design better suited to the work tasks
Capital	Improve maintenance, replace machinery
Other	Factors not covered above
Reduced productivity (%) and cost per year for the year for the employee group based on employee costs	

Source: Oxenburg, Marlow and Oxenburgh, 2004, Figure 4.4.

Capturing data concerning the workplace is completed through two screens. The first screen collects information on allocated costs, which includes overhead costs that should be proportioned to the employee group being analyzed. A second screen captures recruitment costs, which are the costs associated with employment of new employees and the skill loss when employees leave. Intervention costs are entered in the allocated costs screens under the test case column and include capital costs, management, and consultant time and costs. The effects of the intervention are entered on the remaining screens as appropriate.

In summary, this model presents estimated productivity changes and health effects of a proposed action and produces savings per year and payback periods for use in creating other financial metrics. By far, ergonomic interventions have constituted the largest share of the analyses using The Productivity Assessment Tool.

CERSSO

The Regional Center for Occupational Safety and Health (CERSSO) developed the Tool Kit for use in Central American garment factories (Amador-Redezno, 2005). This computer-based cost-benefit tool was deemed an "instrument designed for you to test it within the confidentiality of your business and which through a simple manner can help show you how much money you are losing by not investing in the Safety and Health of your employees" (Biddle et al., 2005). This six-step model begins with defining the magnitude of the problem and ends with an analysis of the costs and benefits of an OSH investment—integrating epidemiology, risk assessment, industrial engineering, and accounting discipline.

Table 2.3 presents a summary of the steps to complete the CERSSO model entitled "Self Evaluation of the Cost-Benefit on the Investments in Occupational Safety and Health in the Textile Factory."

Table 2.3 A summary of the steps to complete the CERSSO model

Parts	Measures
Step 1 Definition of the magnitude of the problem according to causes and effects	1.1.a. Description of operations
	1.1.b. Prioritizing the causes (risks and demands)
	1.2. Description of the male and female employees in their operations
	1.3. Description of the CAUSES (risks and demands) by their operations.
	1.4. Description of EFFECTS and their relationship with the causes
Step 2 Risk appraisal	2.1. Appraisal of the probability of the effect
	2.2. Appraisal of the severity of the effect
	2.3. Appraisal of the risk
Step 3 Definition of the preventive measures to be undertaken	3.1. Definition of the preventive measures to be undertaken

Table 2.3 A summary of the steps to complete the CERSSO model *concluded*

Parts	Measures
Step 4 Graphing the relationship between the preventive measures and their positive impact	4.1. Graphing the relationship between the preventive measures and their positive impact
Step 5 Evaluating the cost of prevention and its effects	5.1 Identifying the costs of the preventive measures made at the source, individuals and preventive medical actions
	5.2. Identifying the direct costs caused by the potential effects
	5.3. Identifying the indirect costs caused by the potential effects
	5.4. Totaling the costs
Step 6 Analysis of the costs-benefits	6.1. Compare and contrast the costs of the measures taken and the costs of the potential effects

ROHSEI

Fifteen member companies of the ORC Occupational Safety and Health Group—ALCOA, AlliedSignal, ARCO, Bayer, Bristol-Myers Squibb, Colgate-Palmolive, Dow, Duke Power, Eli Lilly, IBM, Johnson & Johnson, Monsanto, M&M Mars, Rhone-Poulenc Rorer, Schering-Plough—formed a task force to work with ORC Worldwide and Arthur Andersen to tailor traditional financial investment analysis approaches and apply them to achieve a better understanding of the business impacts of health, safety, and environmental investments (Linhard, 2005).

The "Return on Health, Safety and Environmental Investments" (ROHSEI) process and tools were developed through interviews with financial, health and safety, and operational professionals, data collection from more than a dozen companies, focus group sessions, and field testing. Since 1997, ROHSEI has demonstrated that analytical tools currently used and accepted by the financial community can be applied to health and safety investments when appropriate data elements underpin the analysis. The process allows users to evaluate health and safety investments on a cost/performance basis. For each alternative, the ROHSEI process facilitates consideration of direct benefits and costs as well as hidden impacts, such as worker productivity. Building the business case employs the following four steps:

1. Understand the opportunity or challenge.
2. Identify and explore alternative solutions.
3. Gather data and conduct analysis.
4. Make a recommendation.

Figure 2.1 highlights the relationship among these four steps and the business case development. It also introduces the four tools that support the analysis: a Business Case Summary, a Causal Loop Diagram, a Direct Impact module, and a Decision Matrix.

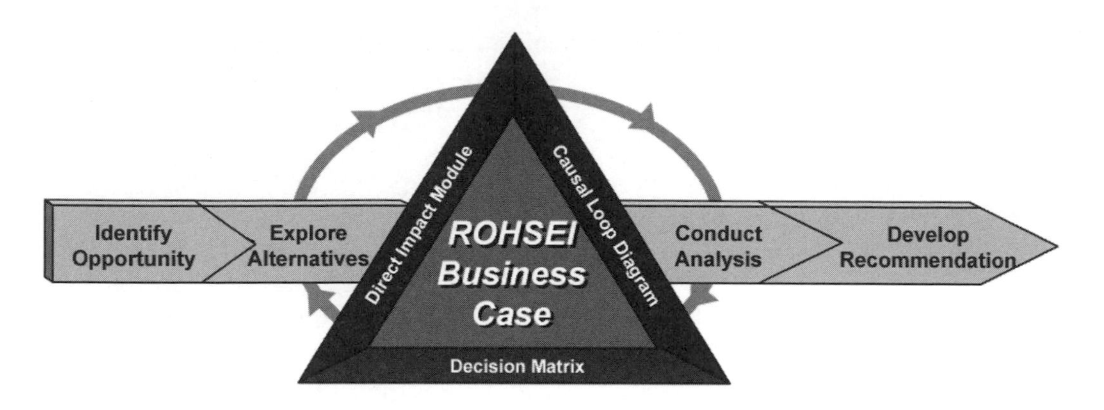

Figure 2.1 Overview of the ORC Worldwide ROHSEI method

Table 2.4 demonstrates how the tools are aligned with the process steps. For example, the Causal Loop Diagram is a tool designed to brainstorm alternative solutions, explore relationships, and identify other impacts of the project. It helps develop a comprehensive view of how each of the alternative investments impacts business performance, considering both direct and hidden benefits and costs.

Table 2.4 How the tools are aligned with the process steps

ROHSEI Process	ROHSEI Tools			
Understand the opportunity or challenge				Business case summary
Identify alternative solutions	Causal loop diagram			Business case summary
Gather data and conduct analysis	Causal loop diagram	Direct impact module	Decision matrix	Business case summary
Recommend a solution based on the analysis				Business case summary

Centers for Disease Control and Prevention (CDC) Business Case Guide

Also in 2004, the Centers for Disease Control and Prevention (CDC) Office of Public and Private Partnership in the National Center for Health Marketing held a brown bag lunch to begin discussions on "Building The Business Case for Prevention: public health policy research agenda." The fourteenth year class of the Public Health Leadership Institute consisting of four of the top management officials within CDC (Ileana Arias PhD, Director of the National Center for Injury Prevention and Control; Hamid Jafari PhD, National Center for Immunization and Respiratory Diseases; Verla Neslund JD, CDC Foundation; Tanja Popvic MD PhD, Chief Science Officer for CDC) embraced the need for CDC to develop a definition and template for creation of a business case. It was understood that the mission of CDC is to improve the quality of life and reduce disease, disability, and injuries.

CDC addresses this mission through a broad array of activities including establishing business partnerships. Businesses are important channels of safety and health protection and promotion for CDC. As a result, the *Investing in Health and Safety: A Business Case Resource Guide* was developed with the intent to provide guidance which would allow consistency, flexibility, and transparency, and have a broad utility to CDC, businesses, academics, and health and safety practitioners (Carande-Kulis, Biddle and Sotnikov, 2009).

The guidance provides a methodological approach for conducting business cases for health and safety actions, and includes those actions implemented by businesses, on the premises of business, or under the direction of business. It describes the techniques and procedures used to develop business cases from the business perspective. The document identifies the following seven steps, shown in Table 2.5, to develop the business case for investing in safety and health.

Table 2.5 Seven steps to develop the business case for investing in safety and health

Steps	Components
Step 1. Describe the current situation	Describe current interventions
	Identify the health protection problem
Step 2 Consider business and national health and safety goals	Consider business goals
	Consider national goals
Step 3 Identify intervention options	Develop a long list of options
	Select a short list of options
Step 4 Define the analytic framework	Define the audience
	Define the perspective
	Define the time frame and analytic horizon
	Consider study design
Step 5 Assess outcomes, costs, and benefits	Measure health and non-health outcomes
	Measure or estimate costs
	Assess and value benefits
Step 6 Identify preferred option(s)	Calculate financial metrics
	Conduct sensitivity analyses
	Rank and prioritize options
Step 7 Finalize the business case	Business case template
	Report the business case
	Consider factors influencing approval
	Final thoughts

The Next Generation of the Business Case: The Value Proposition

The previous section illustrates tools or methods that have been used to develop OSH business cases since the late 1900s. Despite the light that the results have shed on the value of OSH efforts and the assistance in OSH decision-making efforts, the next generation of the business case should be expanded to include the impact on non-financial measures to a much greater extent. The new business case methods must demonstrate that mitigating potential safety and health hazards with effective and efficient solutions creates a competitive advantage for the firm. The new business case methods need to demonstrate that OSH professionals are important partners with business executives in managing enterprise risks—which includes the risk of adverse safety and health incidents. The next generation of the business case must include measures to demonstrate the contribution of OSH to corporate social responsibility, sustainability, and product stewardship.

An effort to provide such a methodology began in 2003 with American Industrial Hygiene Association and the American Board of Industrial Hygiene sponsoring the Value of the Profession Study. The goal of the multi-year study was to determine which mechanisms allow the industrial hygienist to demonstrate business impact of industrial hygiene programs and interventions and to create a strategy to provide the basis for efficient and effective illustration of the value of occupational health actions.

By June 2008, the Value of the Profession Strategy was finalized by an ORC Worldwide-led team (Elyce Biddle, Steve Newell, Reepa Shroff, and Dee Woodhull). The Strategy included the eight steps shown in Figure 2.2.

The formulative phase of the strategy is reflected in the first two steps. These steps provide the background for determining the value of industrial hygiene activities in current and future time frames. Identifying the OSH hazards—one of the primary functions of an industrial hygienist—is captured in the first step of this phase. This phase also includes gathering those business objectives which might be influenced by the work of the industrial hygienist. Because a number of value studies could be undertaken, the second step prioritizes those potential value studies with the goal of insuring that the best opportunity to demonstrate the value of the industrial hygiene program or intervention is seized.

Collectively, the next five steps describe the necessary methods to develop the value proposition. The first step of this phase is a familiar and routine task for industrial hygienists and other occupation health and safety practitioners, conducting risk assessments of those jobs or tasks associated with processes or services that have been selected for evaluation. Ideally, risk assessments would be conducted prior to implementing any programs or activities to mitigate risks, and again following the implementation as a measure of improvement in risk management. At this point, the Strategy provides an opportunity to select the methods of assessing the value—either a quantitative approach, a qualitative approach, or a combination of both. Which method is selected depends on a number of factors including the needs of the organization, the time available for analysis, and the availability of tangible data.

Both the quantitative and qualitative methods determine the effects of implementing programs or activities on employee health (injury or illness), risk management, and the business process. The quantitative approach determines the monetary impact by capturing detailed cost data and generating customary financial business metrics, such as net present value (NPV), return on investment (ROI), and discounted payback period (DPP), which are meaningful to business management.

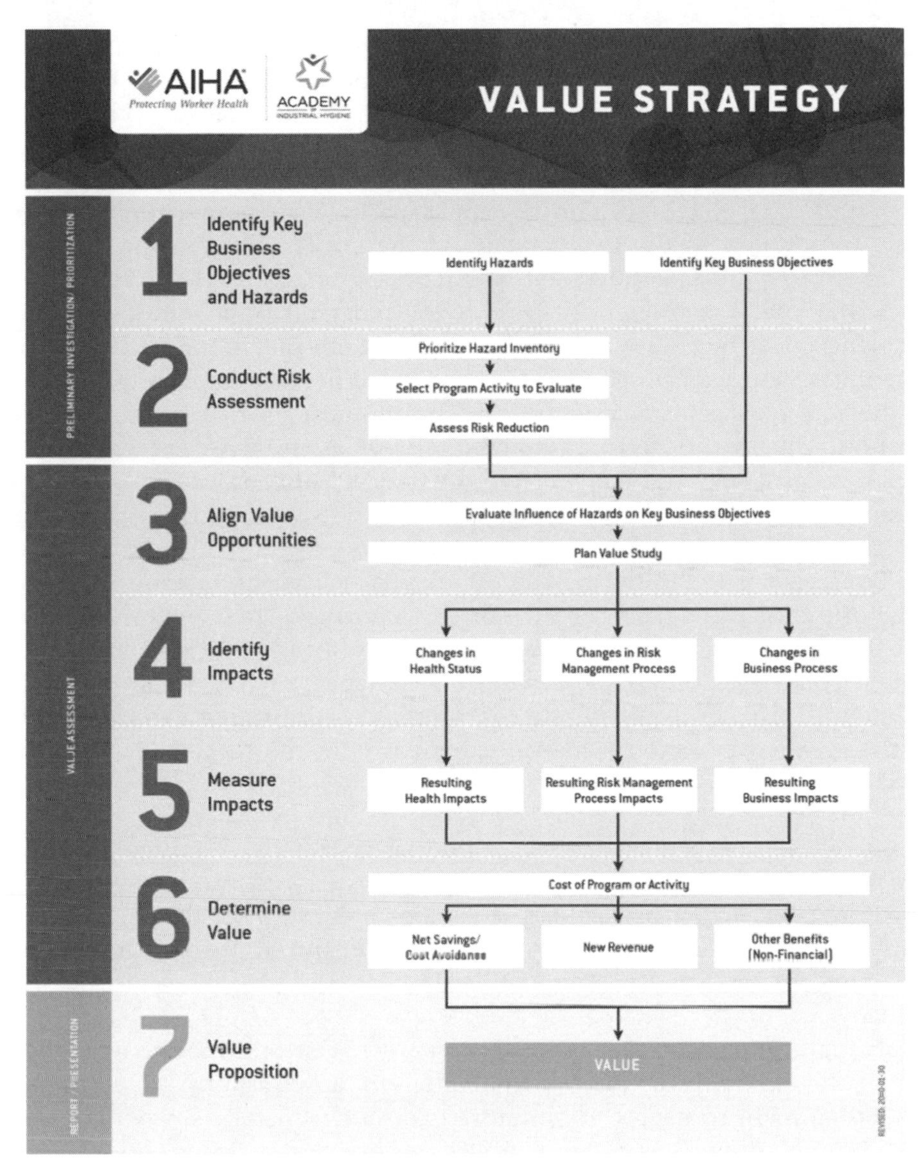

Figure 2.2 Value of the Profession Strategy

Used with permission of AIHA® 2010

The qualitative method captures the value of the contribution of the occupational health program or intervention by tracking its impact on health, the risk management process, and the business process but also through an *evidentiary cause and effect analysis* patterned after legal methodology. The qualitative method isolates and extracts other factors that could have produced the same effects. The results are generally expressed in narrative explanations or non-monetary numerical values, such as the percent change in output.

In general, a quantitative analysis using generally accepted financial business metrics is preferable to a qualitative approach. However, the Strategy architecture can tie the quantitative and qualitative approaches together and provide common framework for capturing and presenting benefits. Regardless of the approach, there must be adequate time allocated to explore the changes in employee health outcomes, changes in the requirements for conducting the industrial hygiene functions, and changes in any downstream business processes of the organization. These changes can be converted into value—whether monetized savings, increased capacity, or a reduction in resource requirements.

The eighth and final step is to develop a package for presentation to the target audience. In addition to the requirements of the target audience, the organizational culture determines the exact presentation content, form, and style. In the quantitative approach, the effects of implementation of the programs or activities on health, risk management, or the business process are the sources of value in the analysis. Benefits of implementation are determined by calculating the difference in costs related to health status, the risk management process, and the business process before and after the intervention. The benefits derived through cost savings and new revenue are expressed in terms of financial metrics, such as NPV, ROI and DPP, that are meaningful to business management. Contributions to business objectives are summarized and presented in specific terms.

The Strategy was tested by the ORC Worldwide-led research team by determining the value of industrial hygiene activities at 15 companies. These tests were designed to evaluate the ability to implement the strategy. However, in addition to demonstrating that the strategy could be employed by an industrial hygienist, a series of unexpected findings unfolded. Most importantly, significant contributions to the business and operations were found in a wide range of interventions implemented by industrial hygienists. Industrial hygienists have worked to:

- eliminate lead from a raw material stream that saved tens of thousands of dollars in operating costs and kept a facility from closing;
- substitute a less toxic material for a chromate primer that saved an aircraft company nearly a half-million dollars in processing costs and added capacity to build an additional aircraft each year. This increased the revenue stream several million dollars annually;
- install engineering controls at a small company to control exposure to nanoparticles that resulted in a ten-fold increase in production capacity; and
- use containment strategies to minimize exposure to potent active pharmaceutical powders that resulted in employee health improvement, reduced personal protective equipment usage, and reduced industrial hygiene sampling expense. This action also assured regulatory compliance, reduced the need for cleaning, and increased employee productivity.

Each case study explored in the research study illustrated essential contributions to business value that are rarely associated with industrial hygiene. One site visit identified a key industrial process that generates billions in revenue annually that would not exist without the active involvement of the industrial hygienist. A challenge to the profession is to identify and document such critical contributions.

The study also identified the relationship between the hierarchy of controls and the value of increasing investments to improve workplace exposures and, subsequently, generate significant financial returns on those investments. In some of the case studies and site visits, the research team observed that as one selects hazard control measures higher in the industrial hygiene hierarchy of controls, business value increased. In a few cases, recovery of initial investments, the greatest cost savings, and other benefits were found to result from eliminating hazards through engineering controls and through the use of personal protective equipment by workers. Other case study results show that with little capital investment, material substitution and containment projects also can have very large pay offs while reducing the potential for worker exposures to hazardous materials. In short, increased investments in industrial hygiene programs or interventions, when using the hierarchy of controls for guidance, have shown to not only have positive impacts for protection of worker health, but often produce a substantial positive business return.

Financial Metrics

As illustrated in the previous examples, the steps and elements required to develop a business case can vary substantially by system design or by the program or intervention being analyzed. The methods can vary depending on the number of employees being affected, the length of time required to implement the program or intervention, or the length of time until the effects of the change are felt. The methods can also vary by the business type and size or the requirements set by the management of the business. However, one element that can be found in all business case analysis is the calculation of financial metrics. For that reason, a thorough understanding of how to derive and interpret the basic financial metrics is important.

Financial metrics describe the effect that an investment has on profit and the financial condition of the company. While accounting standards are published and interpreted in the United States through the Financial Accounting Standards Board (FASB), the same is not true for more general financial metrics. Definitions may vary somewhat by source and may diverge from GAAP. The following are common financial measures used to evaluate business investments within a corporate or commercial enterprise, including short- and long-term investments. Within this context, OSH activities or programs are the investments being evaluated, whether they affect capital investment or working capital management

CASH FLOW (CF)

Cash Flow (CF) is the basis for deriving the majority of financial metrics for the business case. The CF statement provides a list of the actual or undiscounted investment outflows (costs and expenses) that will be required to implement the intervention, the actual or undiscounted inflows (monetized benefits) that the intervention is expected to produce, and the time those inflows will occur during the analytical period. Each benefit or cost identified leads to either an expected CF result, or a value which is monetized in CF terms. CF entries should include non-cash charges such as depreciation and can reflect after-tax values.

Cash flows can be entered daily, monthly, or annually. Tables 2.6 and 2.7 provide examples of CF statements associated with the "status quo" (also known as a base case) and another one for a proposed intervention or program. These examples provide the net CF for each year under consideration, since they generally serve as the starting point for budgeting and business planning activities. A number of external factors, such as inflation, changes in tax rate, and the overall economic environment may influence the CF in future years. For example, costs in the third or fourth year of an OSH program may be substantially higher because of inflation in the costs of materials and labor required to implement the program.

Table 2.6 Cash flow for a status quo intervention or program

Benefits or Gains (Cash Inflows in $)	Year 1	Year 2	Year 3	Year 4	Year 5	Total
Benefit 1	45	66	165	228	279	783
Benefit 2	428	588	641	699	777	3,133
Benefit 3	781	677	620	755	819	3,652
Total Cash Inflows	1,254	1,331	1,426	1,682	1,875	7,568
Costs and Expenses (Cash Outflows)						
Cost 1	(90)	(87)	(87)	(95)	(110)	(469)
Cost 2	(165)	(165)	(255)	(280)	(320)	(1,185)
Cost 3	(975)	(777)	(645)	(700)	(710)	(3,807)
Total Cash Outflows	(1,230)	(1,029)	(987)	(1,075)	(1,140)	(5,461)
Cash Flow Summary						
Total Cash Inflows	1,254	1,331	1,426	1,682	1,875	7,568
Total Cast Outflows	(1,230)	(1,029)	(987)	(1,075)	(1,140)	(5,461)
Net Cash Flow	24	302	439	607	735	2,107

Table 2.7 Cash flow chart for a proposed intervention or program

Benefits or Gains (Cash Inflows in $)	Year 1	Year 2	Year 3	Year 4	Year 5	Total
Benefit 1	120	170	150	275	300	1,015
Benefit 2	500	615	704	755	812	3,386
Benefit 3	866	876	812	900	1,010	4,464
Total Cash Inflows	1,486	1,661	1,666	1,930	2,122	8,865
Costs and Expenses (Cash Outflows)						
Cost 1	(90)	(95)	(88)	(85)	(89)	(447)
Cost 2	(400)	(350)	(387)	(320)	(300)	(1,757)
Cost 3	(1,010)	(849)	(597)	(650)	(650)	(3,756)
Total Cash Outflows	(1,500)	(1,294)	(1,072)	(1,055)	(1,039)	(5,960)
Cash Flow Summary						
Total Cash Inflows	1,486	1,661	1,666	1,930	2,122	8,965
Total Cast Outflows	(1,500)	(1,294)	(1,072)	(1,055)	(1,039)	(5,960)
Net Cash Flow	(14)	367	594	875	1,083	2,905

Incremental cash flow shows the difference between the status quo CF and the CF associated with implementing a new program or intervention. Simple CF does not consider uncertainty and the value of time.

These examples do not present the Discounted Cash Flow (DCF), which accommodates for the uncertainty and value of time in the real world by discounting the CF stream. Discounting adjusts the value of future CF by giving more "value" or weight to the near term CF and less "value" to those in the more distant future. It is important to know when you should include a discounted cash flow in your business case presentation. If the intervention or programs being considered cover long periods of time or if the magnitude of the inflows and outflows are different within each time period, a DCF should be presented. A DCF should also be presented if the timing of the CF from each intervention or program differs substantially within the analysis period.

Table 2.8 Incremental cash flow

Benefits or Gains (Cash Inflows)	Year 1	Year 2	Year 3	Year 4	Year 5	Total
Benefit 1	75	104	(15)	47	21	232
Benefit 2	72	27	63	56	35	253
Benefit 3	85	199	192	145	191	812
Total Cash Inflows	232	330	240	248	247	1297
Costs and Expenses (Cash Outflows)						
Cost 1	0	(8)	(1)	10	21	22
Cost 2	(235)	(185)	(132)	(40)	20	(572)
Cost 3	(35)	(72)	48	50	60	51
Total Cash Outflows	(270)	(265)	(85)	20	101	(499)
Cash Flow Summary						
Total Cash Inflows	232	330	240	248	247	1297
Total Cast Outflows	(270)	(265)	(85)	20	101	(499)
Net Cash Flow	(38)	65	155	268	348	798

NET PRESENT VALUE (NPV)

The Net Present Value (NPV) is the sum of the discounted values of a CF stream of net benefits (benefits – costs) over time. Mathematically, NPV is represented as:

$$\text{NPV}= \sum_{t=0}^{n} A_t(1+i)^{-t}$$

where, A_t represents the series of annual net CF of the intervention, i represents the designated discount rate, t is each expected year of implementation and n is the total expected years in the analytic horizon. NPV is a direct measure of the size of the benefits, net of costs, at the end of the analytic horizon, which the business would have gained by undertaking the program or implementing the intervention, accounting for the value of money. The discount rate for NPV and other measures calculated from the business perspective is usually the opportunity cost of capital for the business that is affected. The opportunity cost, also known as the minimum attractive rate of return (MARR) or hurdle rate, encompasses the market interest rate for lending and borrowing and the risks associated with the investment opportunities. Sensitivity analysis may be used to look at the impact of the MARR on the NPV since the MARR is a difficult rate to measure or obtain.

The NPV is a preferred financial metric because it is not affected by the analytic horizon as long as the analytic horizon is greater than or equal to the useful life of the intervention. Table 2.9 demonstrates the NPV calculation associated with a proposal for a hypothetical intervention where the discount rate is assumed to be 8 percent in each time period.

Table 2.9 Net Present Value calculation

Year	Annual net cash flows	Discount factor for 8% interest	Annual discounted value
0	(317.2)	1.0000	(317.200)
1	295.5	0.9259	273.603
2	248.2	0.8573	212.782
3	245.0	0.7938	194.481
4	475.2	0.7350	349.272
5	591.3	0.6806	402.439
			NPV = 1115.377

PAYBACK PERIOD

The *payback period* is the length of time needed for the business to recover an investment through the CF (described above) and is generally expressed in years. In other words, how long does it take for the intervention or program to pay for itself? The simple payback period is the smallest positive integer p such that:

$$\text{Payback period} = \sum_{t=0}^{p} A_{t,x} \geq 0$$

where $A_{t,x}$ represents the annual net CF of intervention x.

Using data found in Table 2.9, the annual net CF presented are shown in the bottom row of Table 2.10. Here, the payback period occurs in period 2 because the sum of annual net CF for the project is <0 until year 2. Alternatively, the payback period can be calculated to reflect portions of a year. Using the following example, the cumulative net CF are negative until sometime during year 2. Therefore the payback period = 1.0 + (21.7 / 248.2) = 1.09, approximately at the beginning of the second month of year 2.

The payback period metric is generally both simple to calculate and easy to understand. As a result, this metric is routinely used by companies and is sometimes used as a crude measure of risk. The option with the shorter payback period is considered less risky. Despite these attributes, the payback period remains a rough estimate and even if all the assumptions and data are precise, the exact payback day is rarely known. If the net CF is never positive throughout the time horizon, then the payback cannot be calculated.

Table 2.10 Payback period calculation

For the year ending December 31, $ in 1,000s							
	Year 0	Year 1	Year 2	Year 3	Year 4	Year 5	
	2002	2003	2004	2005	2006	2007	Total
Net Cash Flow (CF)	(317.2)	295.5	248.2	245	475.2	591.3	1,538.0
Cumulative Net CF	(317.2)	(21.7)	226.5	471.5	946.7	1,538.0	

Any changes in CF (negative or positive) beyond the payback date are not accounted for. Finally, in the simple payback period, the CF entries are not discounted and therefore this metric does not incorporate the value of time. The analyst, however, may choose to discount the CF entries making the metric adjusted for the value of time. In this case, the measure is called discounted payback period.

RETURN ON INVESTMENT (ROI)

Return on Investment is a widely used term with multiple definitions in the field of accounting. Examples of the various types of returns on investments include Return on Invested Capital, Return on Capital Employed, Return on Total Assets, and Return on Net Worth. Therefore, it is important that the methods for calculating this metric are clearly explained in the business case report.

For the purposes of this paper, the Simple ROI is less of an accounting term than a generalized term for the expected value of an investment in terms of added revenue or profits, or averted expenses.

Simple ROI = $(P_b - P_c)/P_c$

Where P_b represents the gains or benefits from the intervention and P_c represents the cost of that intervention. ROI can be presented as a ratio or as a percentage, that is, the simple ROI times 100 percent. As a ratio, the ROI measures the effectiveness of the investment by calculating how many times the net benefits (benefits from investment minus initial and ongoing costs) recover one dollar invested. As a percentage, the ROI measures the net benefits per hundred dollars invested.

For example, an equipment redesign intervention to decrease the risk of injury in the assembly line is undertaken, at a cost of $1.25 million. It is expected to be in place for at least ten years. During that time it is expected to generate a discounted savings of $1 million in averted medical costs and lost productivity. Additional discounted revenue streams from commercializing the technology are expected to produce $3 million. The Simple ROI is ($4 million-$1.25 million)/$1.25 million = 2.2, which is generally expressed as a ratio, 2.2:1 or percentage, 220 percent. Consequently the investment produces a return of 2.2 dollars per dollar invested or 220 dollars per 100 dollars invested.

INTERNAL RATE OF RETURN (IRR)

This financial metric determines the discount rate at which the NPV is zero. The IRR can be seen as the reverse of NPV, in that IRR computes the break-even rate of return showing the discount rate below which an investment produces a positive NPV. Like the NPV, IRR takes into account the time value of money by considering the CF over the lifetime of a program or intervention. However, unlike the NPV, the IRR is an indirect method for measuring the value of an intervention, but nonetheless is a useful metric if a unique value exists. Mathematically, the IRR is represented as:

$$IRR = \sum_{t=0}^{n} \frac{A_t}{(1+i)^t} = 0$$

where A represents the annual net discounted CF of the intervention at time t, i represents the interest rate, and n is the expected intervention's length. Notice that the IRR formula is merely the NPV formula set equal to zero, with CF known. Although the measure is conceptually simple, solving for the IRR can be more complex. Three basic methods are used to solve for the unknown interest value: trial and error, graphic representation, and a financial calculation or computational solution.

Programs or interventions that have large cash outflows during or at the end of its time horizon (as opposed to the normal case of one or more cash outflows followed by a series of cash inflows) can pose difficulties when employing the IRR as a financial metric. These types of analysis can have no solution, multiple solutions, or the solution can lead to an improper decision. To illustrate the latter assume two interventions with the following CF (see Table 2.11).

Table 2.11 Financial metric comparison

Intervention	Expected net cash flow		Financial metric	
	Year 0	End of Year 1	IRR	NPV (i=10%)
A	($100,000)	$120,000	20%	$9,091
B	$83,333	($100,000)	20%	($7,576)

Using the IRR as the financial metric and assuming a minimum attractive rate of return of 10 percent, both interventions would be desirable. However, the NPV suggests that intervention B may not be an acceptable funding opportunity.

Comparison of Financial Metrics

Each financial metric has value and presents different information for consideration by the decision maker. The following case example should clarify the differences in these financial metrics. In this example, the analyst assesses two proposed mutually exclusive interventions both lasting four years. Development of CF and calculation of financial metrics can become more difficult when interventions are not mutually exclusive or have different timelines. A full discussion of more complex computational situations or conditions is beyond the scope of this paper, but can be readily found in financial management, project evaluation, or managerial accounting texts (Brigham, 1982; Au and Au, 1992; Sullivan and White, 1995).

Each proposed intervention in this example has a cost of $10,000, and the MARR for both is 12 percent. Table 2.12 presents the net CF for each intervention. Table 2.13 presents the cumulative CF for each intervention, which are necessary to calculate the payback periods. And, finally, Table 2.14 presents the calculation of all financial metrics for both interventions. In this example, all financial metrics indicated that intervention A is better than intervention B.

Table 2.12 Net cash flow calculations for competing interventions

Year	Net cash flow ($)	
	Intervention A	Intervention B
0	(10,000)	(10,000)
1	6,500	3,500
2	3,000	3,500
3	3,000	3,500
4	1,000	3,500

Table 2.13 Cumulative cash flow calculations for competing interventions

Year	Cumulative cash flow ($)	
	Intervention A	Intervention B
0	(10,000)	(10,000)
1	(3,500)	(6,500)
2	(500)	(3,000)
3	2,500	500
4	3,500	4,000

Table 2.14 Calculation of payback period, NPV, IRR, and ROI for interventions A and B

Metric	Calculation	Results
$Payback_A$	2 + $500/$3000	2.17 years
$Payback_B$	2 + $3000/$3500	2.86 years
NPV_A	$-\$10,000 + \$6,500/(1.12)^1 + \$3,000/(1.12)^2 + \$3,000/(1.12)^3 + \$1,000/(1.12)^4$	$966.01
NPV_B	$-\$10,000 + \$3,500/(1.12)^1 + \$3,500/(1.12)^2 + \$3,500/(1.12)^3 + \$3,500/(1.12)^4$	$630.72
IRR_A	$-\$10,000 + \$6,500/(r)^1 + \$3,000/(r)^2 + \$3,000/(r)^3 + \$1,000/(r)^4$	18%
IRR_B	$-\$10,000 + \$3,500/(r)^1 + \$3,500/(r)^2 + \$3,500/(r)^3 + \$3,500/(r)^4$	15%
ROI_A	$966.01/$10,000	9.7%
ROI_B	$630.72/$10,000	6.3%

The "best" financial metric to be used when conducting a business case will depend on a number of factors. For example, the analyst could calculate and present all measures or only the customary measures used by the organization or industry in the analysis.

Alternatively, Brigham states that the accuracy of these metrics depends on the timing and magnitude of the CF. Regardless, for the metric to lead to consistently accurate decisions, it must exhibit the following three properties:

- the method must consider all CF throughout the entire life of an intervention;
- the method must consider the time value of money; that is, it must reflect the fact that dollars that come in sooner are more valuable than distant dollars;
- when the method is used to select from a set of mutually exclusive interventions, it must choose the intervention that maximizes the firm's financial performance.

As mentioned earlier, changes in CF beyond the payback date are not included in the calculations and, therefore, violate the first property. Undiscounted payback period violates the second property. However, it should be noted that many firms use payback period when the initial investment is small. The NPV, IRR, and ROI methods all satisfy the first and second properties. All three financial measures lead to identical and correct accept/reject decisions for independent interventions. However, only the NPV method satisfies the third property under all conditions. If two interventions are independent, NPV and IRR measures lead to the same conclusion. However, if both are mutually exclusive and not independent, the resulting measures may not lead to the same conclusions. Exclusive interventions are those when intervention *A* happens, then intervention *B* cannot, or vice-versa. Independent interventions are those when the outcome of intervention *A* has no effect on the outcome of intervention *B*. So, if intervention *A* and *B* are mutually exclusive, they *cannot* be independent. If events *A* and *B* are independent, they *cannot* be mutually exclusive (Brigham, 1982).

Selection of the financial measure or measures for inclusion in the business case is guided by the audience for that business case. Individual businesses routinely have preferences of measures. Some businesses prefer seeing the NPV while others prefer the IRR. The analyst should explore these preferences when the audience is a single business. If the audience is an industry or group of businesses, then the selection of the financial measure(s) to include may require additional exploration to determine the preferences of that group. However, with the completion of CF analysis, calculating the remaining financial measures may be prudent.

IDENTIFY PREFERRED PROGRAMS, ACTIVITIES, OR INTERVENTIONS

Financial metrics aid in identifying the preferred programs, activities, or interventions through the use of decision rules. Generally, decision rules are determined by the specific organization in accordance with the financial strategies and their market position. However, there are general rules of thumb that are useful in the absence of company-specific rules. Despite whether the author of the business case is the final decision maker, it is important to understand these general rules if for no other reason than to eliminate any programs, activities, or interventions from your business case presentation that are clearly not feasible. When evaluating a single action, the rules are as shown in Table 2.15.

When comparing multiple interventions, Table 2.16 provides appropriate decision rules.

Table 2.15 Decision rules for a single program or intervention

Metric	Decision rule
NPV	Accept if NPV ≥ 0; otherwise reject
Payback	Generally acceptable if within short-term time frame; 1–2 years
IRR	Accept if IRR ≥ MARR; otherwise reject
ROI	Accept if ROI ≥ 0

Table 2.16 Decision rules for multiple interventions

Metric	Decision rule
NPV	Select highest NPV value
Payback	Accept proposal with the shortest payback period
IRR	Select highest IRR
ROI	Accept if the largest positive ROI

Conclusions

The business case is not a new tool or method in the business community, but it is relatively new to the OSH world. As was demonstrated through the application of the AIHA Value Strategy, reducing the risk to the worker can have a positive value to the business enterprise. As reported by Goetzel et al. it has been demonstrated through the use of developing the business cases that worksite health promotion and disease prevention programs save health care expenditures and produce a positive ROI for individual firms—Johnson & Johnson in 2002, Citibank in 1999–2000, Procter and Gamble in 1998, Chevron in 1998, California Public Retirement System in 1994, Bank of America in 1993, and Dupont in 1990.

As businesses continue to be under increasing pressure to be cost effective and more efficient, it becomes imperative that OSH professionals understand how to prepare and present the business case to successful compete for scarce resources. OSH professionals must bridge the information gap by providing business decision makers evidence in the terms they understand—and have used since the early 1900s.

It is perhaps even more important for OSH professionals to understand the relative value of the interventions—programs or activities—they recommend for mitigating risks. The business case skills they develop can provide them with a new perspective regarding which solutions are best. For example, some OSH activities may not generate a positive NPV, but the results demonstrated by the business case will indicate that they are the best option to meeting regulatory requirements. Additionally, case studies have shown that commonly-held beliefs with respect to the cost-effectiveness of respiratory protection versus engineering controls may be overturned when business case analysis is applied. Engineering controls are often the more cost-effective solution, as well as the more protective. Adding business case analysis to the set of tools OSH professionals have at their disposal can provide benefits on two levels—increasing the degree of protection for employees, and justifying the cost of OSH investments to management.

References

Amador-Redezno R. (2005) An overview to CERSSO's self evaluation of the cost-benefit on the investment in occupational safety and health in the textile factories: a step by step methodology, *Journal of Safety Research;* 36(3), 215–229.

American Industrial Hygiene Association (2009) *Strategy to Demonstrate the Value of Industrial Hygiene.* http://www.ihvalue.org.

Au, T. and Au, T. (1992). *Engineering Economics for Capital Investment Analysis* (2nd edition). Englewood Cliffs, NJ: Prentice Hall.

Shim, J.K. and Siegel, J.G. (2005) *Dictionary of Accounting Terms.* Hauppauge, NY: Barron's Educational Series, Inc.

Biddle, E., Ray, T., Owusu-Edusei, K., and Camm, T. (2005) Synthesis and recommendations of the economic evaluation of OHS interventions at the company level conference, *Journal of Safety Research;* 36(3), 261–267.

Brigham, E.F. (1982) *Financial Management Theory and Practice.* New York, NY: The Dryden Press.

Carande-Kulis, V. and Biddle, E. (2009) *Making Investments in Health and Safety: A Business Case Resource Guide.* Washington, DC: US Government Printing Office.

Eijkemans, G. and Fingerhut, M. (2005) Forward, *Journal of Safety Research;* 36(3), 207–308.

Financial Accounting Standards Board (2009) *Financial Accounting Standards Board.* http://www.fasb.org.

Financial Accounting Standards Board (2009) *Generally Accepted Accounting Principles.* http://www.fasab.gov/accepted.html.

Goetzel, R.Z., Ozminkowski, R.J., Bruno, J.A., Rutter, K.R., Isaac, F., and Wang, S. (2002) The long term impact of Johnson & Johnson's Heath & Wellness Program on employee health risks, *Journal of Occupational and Environmental Medicine;* 44(5), 417–424.

Linhard J. (2005) Understanding the return on health safety and environmental investments, *Journal of Safety Research;* 36(3), 257–260.

Oxenburgh M. (1991) *Increasing Productivity and Profit through Health & Safety.* North Ryde, NSW: CCH International.

Oxenburgh M. and Marlow, P. (2005) The Productivity Assessment Tool: computer-based cost benefit analysis model for the economic assessment of occupational health and safety interventions in the workplace, *Journal of Safety Research;* 36(3), 209–214.

Oxenburgh, M., Marlow, P. and Oxenburgh, A. (2004) *Increasing Productivity and Profit through Health and Safety: The Financial Returns from a Safe Working Environment* (2nd edition). Boca Raton, FL: CRC Press.

Smith, A. (1937) *The Wealth of Nations* (Book 1, Chapter IV and V). New York, NY: Modern Library, Inc. (Original work published in 1776).

Sullivan, W. and White, J. (1995) *Capital Investment Analysis for Engineering and Management* (2nd edition). Englewood Cliffs, NJ: Prentice Hall.

CHAPTER **3**

Reporting and Investigating Accidents: Recognizing the Tip of the Iceberg

TAHIRA M. PROBST AND MAJA GRASO

Each year, workers around the globe experience approximately 260 million occupational injuries and 350,000 fatalities due to injuries sustained at work (Hämäläinen, Takala and Saarela, 2006). Other estimates suggest fatalities may run as high as 2 million per year when deaths due to illness are included (ILO, 2009). Nonetheless, even relying upon conservative estimates, this translates into a rate of 700,000 injured workers and 970 deaths per day. In the US alone, 4 million work-related injuries and illnesses were reported in 2007 (Bureau of Labor Statistics, 2008), representing a rate of 4.2 cases for every 100 full-time equivalent workers. In the European Union (EU), nearly 6,000 people die each year as a consequence of work-related accidents and 500 million working days were lost as a result of workplace accidents and work-related health problems (Eurostat, 2008). It is estimated that every 3.5 minutes somebody in the EU dies from work-related causes and every 4.5 seconds an EU worker is involved in an accident that forces them to stay at home for at least three working days (European Agency for Safety and Health at Work, 2008).

Despite these staggering numbers, a growing body of research suggests that these figures may severely underestimate the true number of non-fatal occupational injuries (for example, Hämäläinen, Takala and Saarela, 2006; Leigh, Marcin and Miller, 2004; Lowery et al., 1998; Probst, Brubaker and Barsotti, 2008; Probst and Estrada, 2010; Rosenman et al., 2006). While the factors contributing to this are numerous and varied, such underestimation can occur when organizations fail to report employee injuries and illnesses to the appropriate regulatory authority (*organizational-level under-reporting*) or when employees fail to report injuries and illnesses occurring at work to their employer (*individual-level under-reporting*).

Thus, as Figure 3.1 illustrates, the oft-cited statistics drawn from national and international surveillance methods only represent the tip of the proverbial iceberg. The accuracy of such injury surveillance systems can be compromised at either the employee- and/or organization-levels (Weddle, 1996). For any surveillance system to be accurate, employees must first notify their employers when they are injured at work. If this does not occur, employers are not able to accurately record this injury.

Figure 3.1 The accident reporting iceberg

Second, organizations must accurately report documented injuries and illnesses experienced (and reported) by their workers to the appropriate regulatory authority. Failure at either stage will result in flawed surveillance data.

The purpose of this chapter is to provide a selected review of commonly used processes that organizations and countries have in place for reporting, investigating, and tracking employee injuries and illnesses. Next, we define the concept of accident under-reporting and review research on the prevalence of and individual and organizational correlates of under-reporting. Following this, we develop a theoretical framework for understanding and predicting accident reporting behaviors derived from the Health Beliefs Model (HBM; Becker, 1974) and Behavioral Reasoning Theory (BRT; Westaby, 2005). Finally, we propose a number of possible interventions that organizations can utilize to improve the accuracy of accident reporting and suggest directions for future research in this area.

Before proceeding, it is important to note that we primarily concentrate on psychosocial and organizational factors related to workplace accidents and under-reporting. Such a focus is not meant to devalue the important contributions to be made by focusing on, for example, a comprehensive approach to ergonomics, engineering process modifications, and/or government policy interventions. Rather, it is meant to conform to the stated focus of this book on behavioral and psychological factors and to acknowledge the limited scope of what can be realistically covered in a single chapter.

Investigating and Reporting Accidents in the Workplace

Accidents can range in severity from a seemingly innocuous near miss incident to something that results in the death of an employee. Regardless of their severity, most organizations and many countries require the reporting and investigation of workplace accidents. The purpose of such investigations is to determine the individual, organizational, and/or job-related factors that were involved in causing the accident in the hopes that similar events can be prevented (or minimized) in the future. The section below first describes the typical reporting process used by organizations and then discusses the process of reporting workplace accidents up the chain to the appropriate governmental regulatory authority.

INVESTIGATING AND REPORTING ACCIDENTS TO EMPLOYERS

Although conducted in reaction to a specific event, accident investigations should be proactive in that organizations establish the guidelines and procedures for such investigations well before they are ever needed. Thus, organizations need to have an established protocol for the composition of an accident investigation team that can appropriately examine the accident from different perspectives. Such a team should typically include the immediate supervisor of the injured worker, any witnesses, the designated safety officer of the company, and an employee representative chosen by the employees to represent them (Washington State Department of Labor and Industries, 2009). In other words, the accident investigation team should be comprised of a deliberately diverse team of individuals that maximizes the thoroughness and objectivity of the investigation procedure.

When an employee is injured, the very first step involves obtaining medical attention. Once the injured employee is attended to, the preliminary stage of an investigation can begin. This phase is akin to a *fact-finding mission* (Geller, 2001). Thus, the accident scene should be secured and photographed and witnesses should be interviewed in order to answer questions such as the following (Washington State Department of Labor and Industries, 2009):

- Where and when did the accident occur?
- Who was present?
- What was the employee doing before and at the time of the accident?
- What happened during the accident?

Once the accident scene has been secured and data collected, the second phase of an accident investigation involves *establishing the chain of events leading to the accident and identification of the root causes of the accident.* As noted above, causal factors could include individual, job, and/or organizational variables (see Christian et al., 2009 for a recent meta-analytic review). For example, individual factors contributing to an accident could consist of a lack of appropriate knowledge, skills, and/or training on the part of the employee. Low levels of safety motivation, certain personality characteristics, and/or distorted risk perceptions could also play a role in an accident. Job-related factors might include aspects of the tasks themselves (for example, some jobs require inherently more risky behaviors), the workload, ergonomic factors, and other environmental characteristics. Finally, organizational factors such as a lack of safety leadership, a poor organizational safety climate, few resources, and/or poor communication can all contribute to the occurrence of accidents. Often, there is no single identifiable cause of an accident, but rather a confluence of factors is to blame (Christian et al., 2009; Geller, 2001). Without an investigation into these causal factors, potential problems cannot be fixed and preventative action cannot be taken.

It is also important to recognize that there are both proximal and distal causes of any accident (Christian et al., 2009). For example, the precipitating event that caused the injury might have been a failure to properly follow lockout/tagout procedures. The proximal causes leading to this failure might be a lack of employee safety motivation and/or a lack of safety knowledge. The distal causes of this lack of motivation and/or knowledge could then be traced to any number of factors such as a poor organizational safety climate, a failure to provide adequate training to employees, and/or a general propensity to engage in risk-taking behavior on the part of the employee. Numerous other scenarios are also possible.

Once the proximal and distal causes of the accident are indentified, the third and final phase of the accident investigation involves the *development and implementation of recommendations to prevent or minimize such events in the future*. Depending on the results of the investigation, such recommendations may necessitate changes on the part of the employee (for example, attendance at safety training), the nature of the job tasks (for example, installation of automatic shut-off switches), and/or the organization itself (for example, long-term efforts to improve the safety climate). Finally, although not technically part of an accident investigation, there should be some formal attempt to gather follow-up data regarding the effectiveness of the implemented recommendations at improving the individual, job, and/or organizational risk factors identified during the investigation.

A similar process should be used in regards to investigating and reporting near miss incidents as well. The rationale behind near miss reporting systems is based on the injury triangle model. First proposed by Heinrich (1931), this model assumes two things. First, for every one serious accident or death, there are approximately 30 accidents with lost days, and 300 accidents without injuries (that is, near misses). There is some debate on the exact ratio of near misses to incurred accidents. For example, Bird and Germain (1996) later refined this to estimate for every one death or catastrophic property loss, there were 30 minor injuries and/or property damage incidents, and 600 near misses. Nonetheless, the underlying principles and assumptions are similar (Ritwik, 2002; Nielsen, Carstensen and Rasmussen, 2006) and collectively, these models can be thought of as "iceberg" models. While severe safety incidents are the most visible and salient, numerous minor and potential incidents lurk beneath the surface.

A second assumption of such models is that near misses and severe injuries share the same underlying causal processes. It is argued that near misses and accidents are only differentiated by the slightly different circumstances that surrounded each event. As a result, it is crucial to pay as much attention to the reporting and investigation of near misses as it is actual accidents. Further, since the number of near misses occurring relative to the number of accidents is far greater, near misses provide numerous low-cost, no injury opportunities to learn from the circumstances from which they arose and to implement necessary precautions before these circumstances result in a full-blown lost-time injury or worse (Barach and Small, 2000; Nielsen, Carstensen and Rasmussen, 2006;

Ritwik, 2002). Unfortunately, despite the potential usefulness of near miss reporting and investigation, near misses often do not command the same sense of urgency as an actual injury, leading employees to frequently bypass near-miss reporting processes. An extended discussion of reasons associated with a failure to report accidents or near misses is presented later in this chapter.

REPORTING ACCIDENTS TO REGULATORY AUTHORITIES: A SELECTED REVIEW OF NATIONAL SURVEILLANCE PROGRAMS

Just as employees are expected to report accidents and injuries to their employer, so too are organizations typically required to report workplace injuries and illnesses to the appropriate governmental regulatory authorities. The compilation of such reports across organizations form the basis for national surveillance programs and are additionally used for purposes including inspection targeting, performance measurement, safety standards development, resource allocation, and the identification of high-risk and low-hazard industry sectors (OSHA, 2005).

The United States

In the US, the Occupational Safety and Health Act of 1970 created the Occupational Safety and Health Administration (OSHA) within the Department of Labor. One of OSHA's missions is to maintain a reporting and recordkeeping system to monitor job-related injuries and illnesses. In order to facilitate this nationwide surveillance system, OSHA requires businesses with more than ten employees to complete annual logs of workplace injuries and illnesses. A summary of these logs must be posted for employees to see and records of the logs must be maintained for five years for inspection upon request by OSHA and/or any state regulators. The OSHA log data are used to compute injury rates by industry, employer size, and other various classifications. These rates are also often used during the bidding process to identify and hire "safe" contractors. Thus, it is advantageous for contractors to have low injury rates (Leigh, Marcin and Miller, 2004).

The European Union

The European Agency for Safety and Health at Work is the main bureaucratic body responsible for providing guidelines and suggestions for occupational injury surveillance. In an effort to standardize injury rate statistics, the Framework Directive on Health and Safety in the Workplace covers all workers in the EU and requires that all accidents leading to an absence of more than three calendar days be included in the European Statistics on Accidents at Work (ESAW) database (Eurostat, 2001).

Nonetheless, each member country of the EU has its own specific reporting requirements and processes. For example, in Slovenia, the Safety and Health at Work Act requires that employers report to the Labour Inspectorate all incidents resulting in the death of an employee, or any accident that results in time off work for at least three consecutive days. In addition, employers are required to report any collective accidents, dangerous situations, and officially established occupational diseases. Individuals covered under this act include all employers and employees, which also includes self-employed individuals and voluntary apprentices, organized working actions operations, and rescue operations.

Developing countries

Unfortunately, many developing nations do not have clear, established, or consistently enforced processes for occupational injury monitoring (Hämäläinen, Takala and Saarela, 2006). Many developing countries often cite a lack of monetary resources as the primary reason preventing them from implementing those procedures (Hämäläinen, Takala and Saarela, 2006). Due to the absence and/or unreliability of the available data, it is difficult to obtain with great confidence any accurate estimates of the global rates of occupational accidents.

Definition and Prevalence of Accident Under-reporting

Despite pervasive reporting requirements both within organizations and nationally, a growing body of research suggests that a significant proportion of work-related injuries and illnesses are not captured by organizations and/or the national surveillance systems. In other words, substantial numbers of workplace injuries are under-reported. Before discussing the prevalence and potential causes of under-reporting, it is important to clearly define commonly used terms that are used when discussing accident reporting.

KEY TERMS RELATED TO ACCIDENT REPORTING

While specific reporting requirements may differ from country to country, in the US a *reportable event* (that is, one that must be recorded in the log of workplace illnesses and injuries and reported to OSHA) is any work-related injury or illness that results in: death, loss of consciousness, days away from work, restricted job duty or transfer, or medical treatment beyond first aid (Bureau of Labor Statistics, 2005). Such events that are reported to OSHA (or the appropriate regulatory authority) are referred to as *recordable events*. An organization's *recordable rate* is then calculated using the following equation: (N/EH) x 200,000, where N = the number of illnesses and injuries recorded in the company's OSHA log, EH = total hours worked by all employees during the calendar year and 200,000 = base number of hours for 100 equivalent full-time workers (that is, 40 hr/wk, 50 wk/yr). This results in a standardized incidence rate (number of annual injuries per 100 workers) that can be used to compare injury rates across companies and industries regardless of number of employees or hours worked (Bureau of Labor Statistics, 2008).

Of course, definitions regarding what constitutes a recordable event vary from country to country. For example, in the UK, organizations must report recordable events to the Health and Safety Executive under the guidelines of the Reporting of Injuries, Diseases and Dangerous Occurrences Regulations (RIDDOR; HSE, 2008). Events are recordable if they result in: death, major injury, loss of consciousness, or three days away from work. However, "dangerous occurrences" (also sometimes referred to as *near misses*) are also required to be reported. Thus, any unplanned and uncontrolled event that could have resulted in injury but did not needs to be reported.

Unfortunately, we know that not all events that meet the definition of a recordable event are actually reported. These types of events are called *unreported events*. *Organizational under-reporting* occurs when there are discrepancies between the number of events that meet the definition of a recordable event and the number of events that are actually reported to the appropriate regulatory authority. Thus, accident under-reporting is defined as a function of both (1) the number of reportable events reported to the regulatory authority (that is, recordables) and (2) the number of reportable events that are not logged into the appropriate log of workplace injuries and illnesses (that is, unreported events). As the discrepancy between the number of reported and unreported events increases, under-reporting can be said to increase. Thus, we argue that under-reporting is not adequately captured simply by the total number of unreported events. Rather, to understand the depth of the problem, one needs to ascertain both the number of unreported events as well as the number of reported events.[1]

To illustrate this point, consider in Figure 3.2 two organizations who have both failed to accurately report three accidents, but Company One properly reported four other accidents, whereas Company Two reported zero other accidents. Although they both engage in under-reporting of their accident rates, Company Two demonstrates less accurate reporting behavior (that is, failed to report 100 percent of reportable accidents). On the other hand, whereas Company One is more accurate about reporting (that is, reported 57 percent of all accidents), it also experienced more accidents overall. In an ideal situation, of course, all accidents would be reported (or better yet, there would be zero reportable events) and there would be zero unreported accidents.

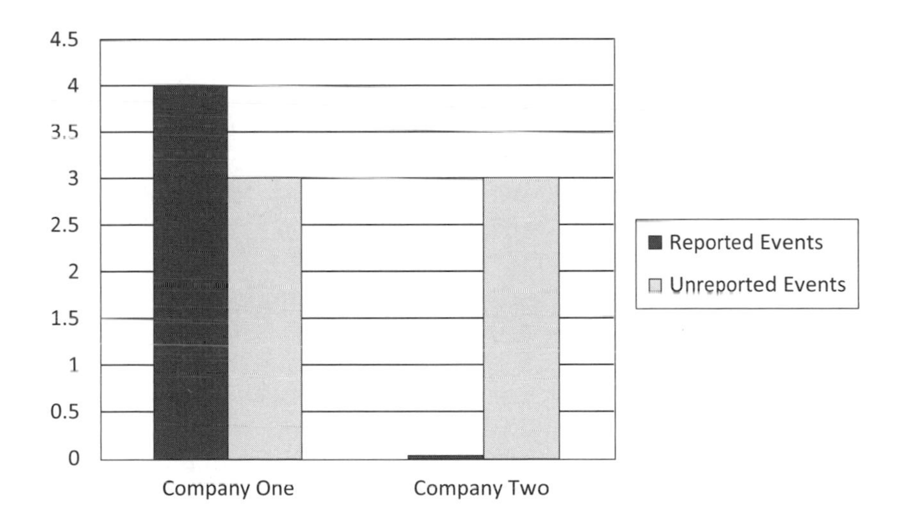

Figure 3.2 Illustration of two possible organizational under-reporting scenarios

1 One might argue for an alternative conceptualization of under-reporting as simply a function of unreported accidents and total experienced accidents. However, this becomes problematic statistically-speaking since the latter number is dependent on the former, whereas reported and unreported accidents are independently distributed.

PREVALENCE OF ORGANIZATIONAL UNDER-REPORTING

While specific estimates of the extent of organizational under-reporting vary, numerous studies have documented its prevalence. In a study of 433 construction companies contracted to build the Denver International Airport (DIA), Glazner et al. (1998) found that injury rates based on workers' compensation claims with payment and/or lost-work-time at the DIA site were more than twice the published national rates for that industry and location. Other studies have compared counts of work-related injuries and illnesses from non-employer sources such as medical records or workers' compensation claims with national data from the Bureau of Labor Statistics (BLS) Survey of Occupational Injuries and Illnesses and have consistently found similar levels of under-reporting (for example, Leigh, Marcin and Miller, 2004; Pransky et al., 1999).

These earlier studies were limited, however, in that they compare the incidence rate of companies to the BLS estimates for companies of the same size and in the same industry sector. However, the individuals and companies in those earlier studies were not actually matched with data that the organizations had provided to the BLS. Thus, to a certain extent, those studies were comparing apples to oranges. To rectify this shortcoming, Rosenman and colleagues (2006) compared data from all companies and individuals in Michigan that were sampled in three years of the annual BLS survey with the illness and injury data from those exact same companies and individuals that were reported to other databases within Michigan (for example, workers' compensation). In comparing the OSHA recordable rates provided by the organizations (that is, their reported illness/injury rate) with the actual illness/injury data drawn from the workers' compensation databases (that is, their real experienced injury rate), the authors were able to more accurately determine that the current national surveillance system misses up to 68 percent of workplace illnesses and injuries. Similarly, in a study of 38 construction contractors, Probst, Brubaker and Barsotti (2008) found that nearly 78 percent of all incidents meeting the definition of a recordable event went unreported.

Thus, even if we use the most conservative of estimates, half of all reportable events are never passed on to the appropriate regulatory authority. Based on the results from the other reviewed studies, that number is likely much higher.

INDIVIDUAL UNDER-REPORTING

Inidividual-level under-reporting is defined similarly as organizational under-reporting in that it involves a comparison between the number of *experienced workplace injuries and illnesses that are reported* to the company and the number of *experienced injuries and illnesses that are not appropriately reported* to the employer. Thus, as with organizational under-reporting, as the discrepancy between the number of unreported and reported accidents increases, under-reporting increases.

Despite their similar definitions, measuring under-reporting at the individual-level is somewhat more difficult than at the organizational-level. At the organizational-level, there are precise data regarding the number of events actually reported to the regulatory authorities (for example, the OSHA logs or RIDDOR data). These data can be compared to workers compensation data and/or to medical records data (obtained, for example, via an Owner-Controlled Insurance Program). On the other hand, it is much more difficult to accurately capture the number of events that employees should have reported to their organization. First, the criteria for what constitutes a reportable event varies from company to company. In some companies, there is a "report everything" policy which includes close calls, near misses, and unsafe conditions and/or behaviors. Others require only that actual injuries be reported. Thus, there is no standardized measure of what constitutes a reportable event as there is at the national level.

More problematic, even if one defines a reportable event using the same criteria as the OSHA recordable events, there is no objective measure of what actually gets reported to the employer (that is, reported events). As we discussed in the previous section, at least half of all reportable events that employees report to their employer do not make it into the official log of workplace illnesses and injuries. Thus, relying on the OSHA or RIDDOR logs would severely underestimate the number of events that employees had reported to their organization. As a result, researchers typically rely upon self-report data from employees to estimate the number of reported and unreported events. For example, Probst and Estrada (2010) used a measure derived from Smecko and Hayes (1999) which asked employees to indicate how many safety incidents they *experienced and reported* and how many they *experienced but did not report* to their supervisor over the past 12 months. A safety incident could include any unplanned event that led to injury, property damage, and/or other loss to the company.

Of course, reliance on self-report safety data can raise methodological concerns. First, self-report data can be inaccurate simply due to an inability to correctly recall safety incidents. For example, the literature suggests that many minor accidents might be forgotten due to extended recall periods. Specifically, research suggests that the accurate recall of workplace accidents may only extend back four weeks (Landen and Hendricks, 1995). However, in many studies—due to the low base rate at which injuries occur—researchers ask employees to consider events over the prior 12 months.

In addition to the problem of inaccurate recall, self-report measures may also be misleading due to impression management goals of the employee. Thus, there might be incentives for employees to respond to survey questions about reporting in a specific way. However, it is important to note that previous studies do indicate that self-report measures of accidents and unsafe behaviors are related to independent observations of these variables (Lusk, Ronis and Baer, 1995). Further, if anything, social desirability responding would act to suppress the variance on these measures as employees would probably tend to underestimate rather than overestimate these events (Hofmann and Stetzer, 1996).

One potential method of dealing with the issue of accurate recall would be to utilize new technologies allowing mobile data collection via the use of handheld devices such as a Palm Pilot, whereby longitudinal data on safety incidents and reporting behavior would be collected at set intervals (for example, once a week) for the duration of the timeframe of interest. This would not address the impression management concerns. However, overt or covert observational methods might be used to complement such data. These methods, of course, require a great deal of time and effort to collect and code the data.

Given the methodological challenges associated with collecting data on individual under-reporting, it is difficult to develop precise estimates of the extent to which employees under-report their injuries to their employers. However, in a multi-organization survey study of 425 employees from five industry sectors, Probst and Estrada (2010) found that employees failed to report 71 percent of all work-related injuries to their company. Similarly, Probst (2006) found that unreported accidents occurred at nearly double the rate of reported accidents, that is, for every reported accident nearly two went unreported. Finally, in a survey study of copper miners, Probst and Graso (2010) found that more than four safety incidents went unreported for every single incident reported to the organization, representing a failure to report over 80 percent of experienced events.

Individual and Organizational Correlates of Reporting Behavior

Although there may be difficulty establishing exactly how pervasive under-reporting is, there is generally consensus that under-reporting does exist and is a serious problem both at the individual- and organizational-levels. Thus, it is important to determine the causes of such under-reporting and possible outcomes.

Clearly, there are significant consequences of under-reporting at both levels. Organizations with high levels of accident under-reporting do not have fewer accidents; they just have fewer reports of accidents. Thus, while the appearance of fewer accidents may have short-term benefits (for example, a lower workers' compensation loss rate), these organizations are likely to pay a heavy price when it comes to the long-term health and safety of their employees and the costs associated with the failure to rectify the root causes of the injuries or accidents (Pransky et al., 1999). This is in addition to any government-imposed penalties and fines that may accrue if such organizational under-reporting is documented and found to be egregious in nature.

Similarly, research has shown that there are detrimental effects for the employee associated with not reporting an accident at work. Not only does the employee take on the financial responsibility of any medical claims that may result (since they cannot take advantage of workers' compensation if they do not report the accident), but also untreated injuries can worsen and over time cause even greater problems for the employee and potentially their co-workers (Gallagher and Myers, 1996). Additionally, employees who work with an untreated injury contribute to the problems of presenteeism, that is, health-related productivity loss experienced by organizations that is associated with employees showing up for work while ill or injured (Loeppke et al., 2003).

Given the prevalence of under-reporting and the serious nature of its consequences, it is important to determine factors that predict and contribute to individual- and organizational-level under-reporting. Table 3.1 summarizes variables that researchers have theorized and/or empirically-demonstrated to be predictive of under-reporting.

PREDICTORS OF INDIVIDUAL-LEVEL UNDER-REPORTING

As can be concluded from the contents of Table 3.1, the majority of under-reporting research has focused on determining why employees may fail to report on-the-job injuries and accidents to their employers. Far less research has focused on antecedents of organizational-level under-reporting. Additionally, with few exceptions, it is important to note that many of the studies of correlates of individual under-reporting do not actually measure under-reporting as defined in this chapter. Rather, most researchers assume (correctly!) that employees often fail to report all experienced accidents and injuries and simply gather descriptive data by asking employees to provide the reasons for such behavior. Thus, there is little empirical analysis of the extent to which these variables are actually predictive of discrepancies between reported and unreported events.

Table 3.1 Antecedents of individual and organizational under-reporting

Predictors of individual-level under-reporting	Predictors of organizational-level under-reporting
• Individual variables • Psychological safety climate • Job insecurity/fear of job loss • Improper diagnosis or causal attributions • Fear of reprisals • Consideration of future safety consequences • Age • Organizational tenure • Organizational and work-group variables • Organizational safety climate • Supervisor enforcement • Lack of training • Misguided safety incentive programs • Work group norms/peer pressure • Production pressure • Onerous and/or lack of reporting systems • Organizational justice perceptions • Punitive vs. non-punitive reporting consequences	• Organizational variables • Organizational safety climate • Collective bargaining agreements • Organizational size • Industry sector • Regulatory and other external variables • Government penalties and fines • Insurance premiums/Experience Modification Rates • Fear of litigation • Fear of negative publicity exposure

Nonetheless, surveys of employees have generated many possible explanations for individual-level under-reporting including: demographic characteristics such as age and organizational tenure (Weddle, 1996); perceived lack of management responsiveness (Clarke, 1998); fear of reprisals or loss of workplace perks and pay incentives (Webb et al., 1989; Pransky et al., 1999; Sinclair and Tetrick, 2004); and an acceptance that injuries are a fact of life in certain lines of work (Pransky et al., 1999). Additionally, there may be an identification problem in which the individual involved does not realize that their incident meets the definition of an accident; this may point to a lack of adequate safety training or improper diagnosis or causal attributions regarding the event (Pransky et al., 1999). Finally, overly onerous (Glendon, 1991) or punitive reporting systems can cause employees to think twice before they choose to report an incident. For example, using an organizational justice framework, Weiner, Hobgood and Lewis (2008) propose that if employees do not feel they will receive fair (that is, just) treatment when they report an incident, they are less likely to do so.

Misguided safety incentive systems have also been implicated in the under-reporting phenomenon. Although well-intended, many serve to reward outcomes (that is, being accident free; see Figure 3.3) rather than behavior (that is, complying with safety policies and procedures). As a result, employees may actually be encouraged to under-report their accidents in order to preserve their ability to receive safety rewards provided by their company (Pransky et al., 1999). Such incentive systems exemplify what Kerr (1975) referred to as *"the folly of rewarding A while hoping for B."* Compounding this, work group norms

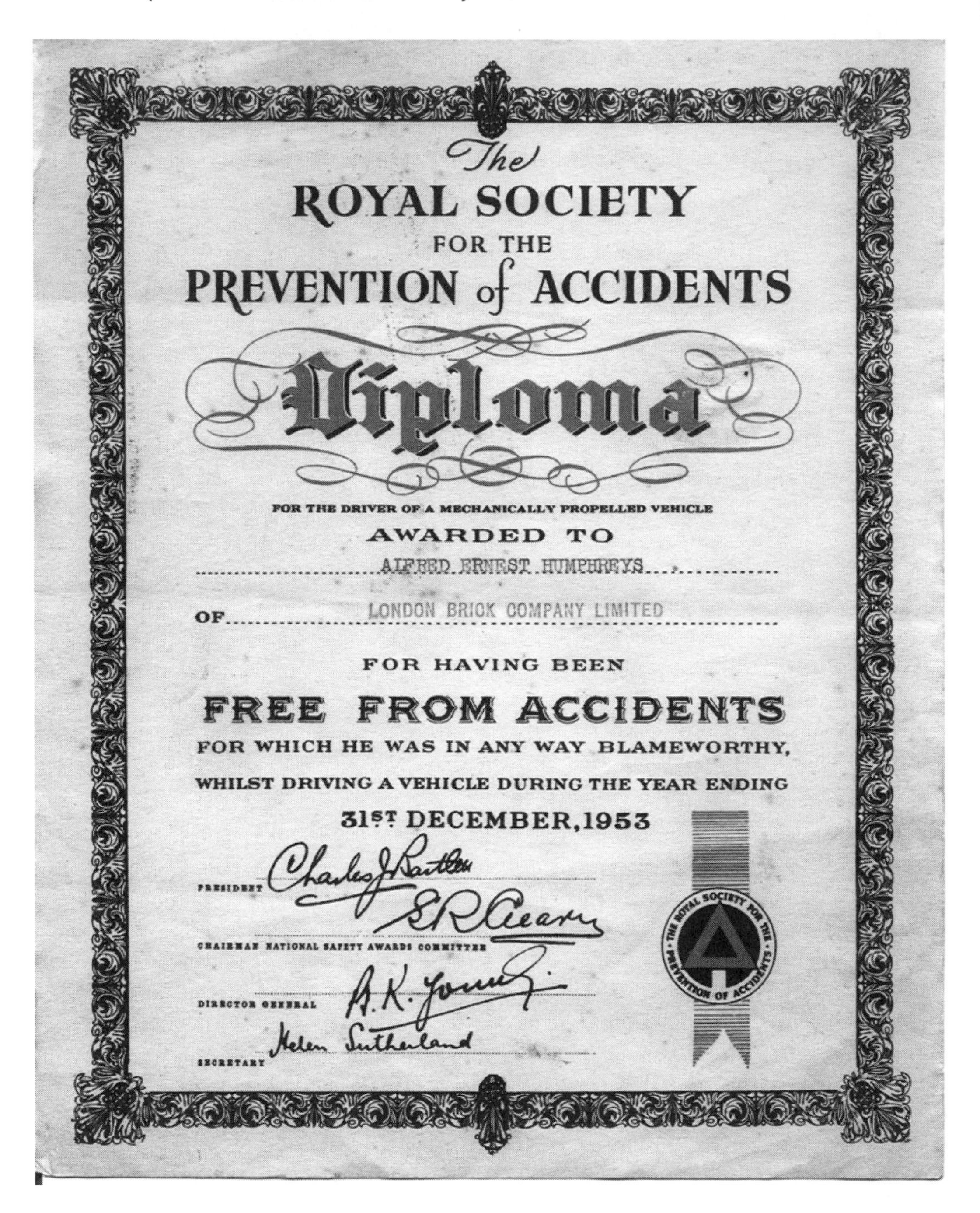

The
ROYAL SOCIETY
FOR THE
PREVENTION of ACCIDENTS
Diploma
FOR THE DRIVER OF A MECHANICALLY PROPELLED VEHICLE
AWARDED TO
ALFRED ERNEST HUMPHREYS
OF LONDON BRICK COMPANY LIMITED
FOR HAVING BEEN
FREE FROM ACCIDENTS
FOR WHICH HE WAS IN ANY WAY BLAMEWORTHY,
WHILST DRIVING A VEHICLE DURING THE YEAR ENDING
31ST DECEMBER, 1953

PRESIDENT

CHAIRMAN NATIONAL SAFETY AWARDS COMMITTEE

DIRECTOR GENERAL

SECRETARY

THE ROYAL SOCIETY FOR THE PREVENTION OF ACCIDENTS

Figure 3.3 An early example of accident-free incentives

Note: This certificate reads, "The Royal Society for the Prevention of Accidents Diploma for the driver of a mechanically propelled vehicle awarded to Alfred Ernest Humphreys of London Brick Company Ltd. for having been free from accidents for which he was in any way blameworthy whilst driving a vehicle during the year ending 31st December 1953."

and accompanying social pressure may serve as additional disincentives for individual employees to report their accidents to supervisors (Sinclair and Tetrick, 2004).

A growing body of research has attempted to empirically identify variables that explain a significant portion of the variability in intra-individual differences between reported and unreported events. Thus, these studies do not overtly ask employees why they chose not to report accidents, but rather use measures of purported antecedents to predict within-subject levels of under-reporting behaviors. For example, Probst (2006) found that job insecurity (that is, fear of job loss) was a significant predictor of accident under-reporting. Not only did job insecurity contribute to employees taking risks at work and being injured, but it also doubled the likelihood that employees would choose not to report such accidents. As job insecurity increased, employees under-reported more accidents.

Probst and Estrada (2010) found that the extent of individual under-reporting could be predicted both by individual perceptions of the organizational safety climate (also referred to as psychological safety climate; Clarke, 2009) and the degree to which supervisors enforce safety policies. When employees perceived their organizational safety climate to be positive, they engaged in far less under-reporting (ratio of unreported to reported accidents was 1.5:1). Even more dramatically, when employees reported having supervisors who enforced safety policies, they not only experienced far fewer accidents, but they also fully reported all of those accidents. On the other hand, among employees who perceived a poor safety climate and/or lax enforcement, the ratio of unreported to reported accidents was greater than 3:1.

Probst, Graso, Estrada and Greer (under review) conducted a two-part study investigating the role of a personality characteristic called consideration of future safety consequences (CFSC) in predicting accident reporting behaviors. Hypotheses were based on the notion that compliance with safety regulations often requires short-term immediate investments in time and effort, yet yields long-term benefits to an employee. For example, by complying with certain rules in regards to safety equipment or following a strict protocol for performing a particular task, employees might enhance their long-term safety, have fewer work-related injuries, and contribute toward establishing an overall healthy safety atmosphere. At the same time however, workers may find themselves burdened by the sometimes exhaustive demands that those safety regulations put on them. In their study, CFSC was found not only to be related to fewer experienced accidents, but it was also related to more accurate reporting of such accidents to one's employer.

Finally, research has shown that a strong organizational emphasis on production can have a detrimental impact on employee health and safety (for example, Landsbergis, Cahill and Schnall, 1999; McLain and Jarrell, 2007). Probst and Graso (2010) examined the extent to which such pressure is also related to employee attitudes and behaviors regarding accident reporting. As might be expected, employees who perceived higher levels of production pressure were less likely to have positive attitudes regarding the reporting of accidents. Furthermore, as perceptions of production pressure increased, so too did employee rates of accident under-reporting.

In addition to knowing why employees choose not to report accidents and injuries, it might also be instructive to consider the perceived negative consequences of reporting such events. An understanding of negative outcomes associated with reporting may provide insights into reasons for accident under-reporting. In their study of pulp and paper mill employees, Probst and Estrada (2010) found that 64 percent of all respondents indicated they had experienced at least one negative consequence as a result of reporting an accident. These consequences ranged from poor interpersonal treatment (for example, being blamed for the incident or gossiped about) to adverse job performance outcomes (for example, loss of scorecard points, disciplinary action; poor performance review) and reassignment to less favorable tasks. Similarly, Probst and Graso (2010) found that prior experience with negative consequences of reporting accidents was predictive of higher levels of under-reporting. In other words, employees who felt they had been "burned" by the system in the past were reluctant to fully report experienced events.

PREDICTORS OF ORGANIZATIONAL-LEVEL UNDER-REPORTING

Although most research has focused on determining individual-level reasons for failing to report occupational injuries, it is equally important to determine why organizations may also under-report their rate of workplace injuries to regulatory authorities. However, while there has been a great deal of research documenting the prevalence of under-reporting, there has been far less attempt to empirically evaluate predictors of such under-reporting. Nonetheless, researchers suggests that government penalties for safety violations, higher insurance premiums, and collective bargaining agreements may all serve to increase incentives for organizations to under-report the actual numbers of accidents and injuries experienced by employees (Collison, 1999; Conway and Svenson, 1998; Zacharatos and Barling, 2004). Barach and Small (2000) add a fear of litigation and possible negative publicity stemming from high injury rates to this list.

In a similar vein, Zahlis and Hansen (2005) argue that there is a disconnect between what organizations measure (OSHA recordables) and the results that really matter (workers' compensation costs and expenses). According to them, organizations have become overly focused on poor measures (that is, OSHA recordables) for a number of good reasons: 1) state and federal regulators require them; 2) the occupational safety and health industries track them; 3) large contracts are granted (or not) based on them; 4) rating bureaus use them; 5) executives believe them; 6) managers are rewarded based on them; and 7) administrators can manipulate them. Given the high stakes of an organization's OSHA injury rate, Zahlis and Hansen (2005) argue that it is not surprising that organizational under-reporting occurs.

Using medical records data provided by an Owner-Controlled Insurance Program, Probst, Brubaker and Barsotti (2008) were able to compare the official OSHA recordable rates of 38 construction contracting firms with their actual rates of experienced injuries that met the definition of an OSHA recordable. They found that there were significant differences between the rate of reported injuries ($M = 3.11$ per 100 employees) and the rate of unreported injuries ($M = 10.90$). In other words, for every three injuries that were properly recorded an additional 11 went unrecorded in the log. More interestingly, the researchers were able to demonstrate that the rate of under-reporting was significantly predicted by the organizational safety climate. Specifically, organizations with a poor safety climate had a significantly higher rate of unreported injuries (nearly 17 per 100 workers) than organizations with a positive safety climate (approximately three per 100 workers). However, there was no significant difference in the injury rates reported to OSHA (3.98 vs. 3.64). Thus, according to the data reported to OSHA (and used to bid on future contracts), poor and positive safety climate organizations appeared to have comparable injury rates. However, their analyses revealed that this was due to substantially higher rates of under-reporting by the poor safety climate organizations.

While Probst, Brubaker and Barsotti (2008) acknowledged such discrepancies could be due to a deliberate manipulation of the numbers, they also proposed that organizations with poor safety climates may simply not devote the resources needed to accurately track recordables; safety personnel may not be adequately trained to correctly identify recordable injuries; and, incentive systems may reward managers and administrators for coding injuries as something other than a recordable. Regardless of the mediating mechanism, organizational safety climate appears to be a significant predictor of organizational-level under-reporting.

Developing a Theoretical Model to Predict Accident Reporting Behaviors

Although there has clearly been a great deal of research aimed at determining why accident under-reporting occurs, there has been little attempt to explain this behavior within established theoretical frameworks. In this section, we propose two alternative theoretical frameworks for the prediction of accident under-reporting both at the individual- and organizational-levels: the Health Beliefs Model (HBM) and Behavioral Reasoning Theory (BRT).

THE HEALTH BELIEFS MODEL: AN EVALUATION OF THREATS, BENEFITS, AND CUES TO ACTION

The HBM is a cognitive behavioral theory of health behavior that consists of three key assumptions (National Cancer Institute, 2005): 1) behavior is influenced by cognitions (that is, what individuals know affects how they act); 2) knowledge is necessary (but not sufficient) for prompting behavior change; and 3) individual perceptions, skills, and social context will influence behavior. Thus, the HBM is a psychological model that attempts to explain and predict health-related behaviors by focusing on the attitudes and beliefs of individuals (Janz and Becker, 1984). Although developed to predict health-related behaviors specifically, such a model could apply to the reporting of accidents, since such reporting can have a direct impact on the health and well-being of affected employees (see Figure 3.4).

According to the HBM, the development of healthy behaviors is a function of multiple variables (Rosenstock, Strecher and Becker, 1994). First, individuals must be aware of the "perceived threat" (that is, the risks and seriousness of the consequences associated with failure to report an accident). Second, individuals must be aware of the "perceived benefits" of the strategies designed to improve reporting behaviors. Third, interventions to increase accurate accident reporting are expected to be more effective if "cues to action" are offered that provide specific suggestions for improving accurate reporting. Finally, increased self-efficacy (the belief that one has the ability to take corrective action) is thought to increase as a result of providing training and guidance in developing appropriate reporting behaviors and attitudes. Therefore, the HBM can best effect change if interventions are grounded in an understanding of how affected the target population

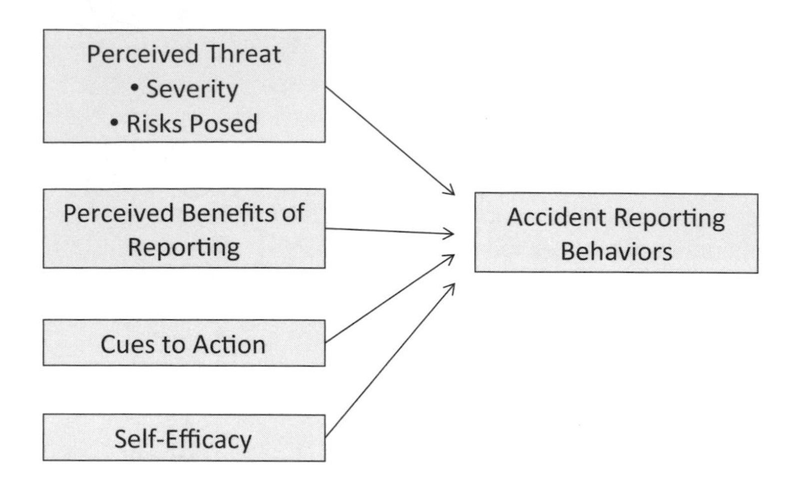

Figure 3.4 Using the Health Beliefs Model to predict accident reporting behaviors

feels by accident under-reporting, whether they believe it is serious, and whether they believe action can reduce under-reporting at an acceptable cost.

In an effort to predict compliance with hospital reporting requirements concerning needlestick injuries, Tabak, Shiaabana and ShaSha (2006) found support for the validity of the HBM. Specifically, individuals who complied with reporting requirements perceived a greater severity of the risks posed by needlestick injuries (for example, severity of potentially contractable diseases) than non-compliers. They perceived greater benefits and fewer disadvantages associated with reporting injuries compared to non-compliers. Finally, compliers had a stronger overall health motivation than non-compliers. Together, these data suggest the potential usefulness of the HBM in predicting and perhaps improving reporting behaviors. Using this model as a theoretical foundation for effecting change at the individual-level, organizations might focus on educating employees about: the causes and consequences of under-reporting, how to recognize manifestations of under-reporting, how to develop a personal action plan to engage in accurate reporting, and how to prevent the occurrence or reoccurrence of under-reporting in the future.

Similarly, at the organizational-level, there are few rewards associated with accurate reporting of workplace illnesses and injuries and plenty of disincentives. Therefore, organizations need to be convinced of the seriousness and risks associated with having flawed national surveillance data. They must believe that there are benefits associated with accurate reporting (rather than benefits associated with having a low recordable rate). Any interventions to increase accurate accident reporting must be accompanied by specific methods to assist organizations in providing accurate reports. The revisions that OSHA made to the log of workplace illnesses and injuries are a good example of a concerted attempt to clarify what kinds of injuries and illnesses meet the definition of a recordable event. As a result, employers hopefully face less ambiguity and have greater self-efficacy regarding their ability to correctly identify and log qualifying events into this required document.

BEHAVIORAL REASONING THEORY: USING REASONS, MOTIVES, AND INTENTIONS TO PREDICT ACCIDENT REPORTING

A second theory that might be usefully applied in order to develop predictions about accident reporting behaviors is called BRT (Westaby, 2005; see Figure 3.5). BRT is rooted in behavioral intention theories (for example, theory of planned behavior; Ajzen, 1999), which predict behavior based upon individual attitudes toward the behavior, subjective norms (that is, social pressure), and perceived control over (that is, the ease/difficulty of enacting) the behavior. BRT expands upon such theories by incorporating context-specific reasons for and against specific behaviors into the model. Westaby (2005) defined reasons as "the specific subjective factors people use to explain their anticipated behavior" (p. 100). According to the theory, reasons are expected to be influential drivers of human behavior, because they help people satisfy their needs to justify, defend, and understand their behavioral decisions (Westaby, Probst and Lee, 2010). Although BRT has been successfully applied in a wide a variety of contexts (for example, intention to work following terminal illness diagnosis, Westaby, Versenyi and Hausmann, 2005; leader decisions to employ youth workers, Westaby, Probst and Lee, 2010; voter intentions, Graso et al., 2010), it has not yet been applied to the context of accident reporting. Nonetheless, one can derive predictions about such behavior at both the individual and organizational levels.

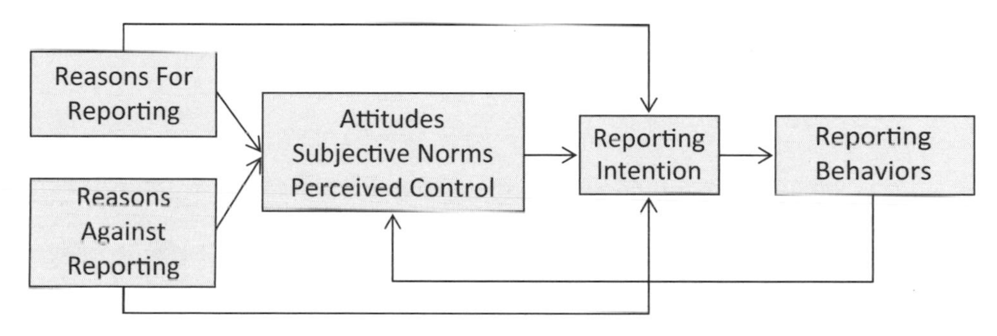

Figure 3.5 Using Behavioral Reasoning Theory to predict accident reporting behaviors

At the individual-level, employees may have a variety of reasons for reporting an accident (for example, enabling correction of problem, receipt of workers compensation), as well as reasons against reporting (for example, being blamed or ostracized, losing benefits, or accepting injuries as a fact of life; Pransky et al., 1999; Sinclair and Tetrick, 2004). These reasons are not only hypothesized to directly influence intentions to report accidents, but are also expected to influence one's perceptions regarding subjective norms, perceived control, and attitudes toward the behavior. For example, if reasons against reporting greatly outweigh reasons for reporting an accident, then it is predicted employees would have more negative attitudes toward reporting. On the other hand, the more reasons employees have for reporting accidents, the more likely they should (a) have positive attitudes toward reporting accidents, (b) feel that other people think that they should report accidents—presumably because other people would also recognize these positive reasons, and (c) perceive enhanced control over reporting accidents (Westaby, Probst and Lee, 2010; Westaby, 2005).

In turn, if an employee has positive attitudes toward reporting an injury, feel that there are social expectations to report an injury, and believe that reporting would be easy for them to do, then they will have greater intentions to actually do so. However, if upon reporting an accident, employees experience negative consequences (for example, demotion or transfer to less desirable tasks), then this may influence the number and availability of reasons against reporting an accident the next time a similar situation presents itself.

This model can be applied in a similar fashion to the prediction of organizational-level reporting. In this case, the focus is on the behaviors of organizational leaders and supervisors. For example, if organizational leaders view reporting of injuries as a positive act, the organizational norms favor a strong safety climate, and the leadership believes that they have control over reporting workplace injuries, they would be predicted to express stronger intentions to report experienced workplace injuries. However, organizations may also have numerous reasons for and against complete injury reporting (for example, accurate estimates of injury-related losses in worker health, productivity and/or increased costs vs. fear a report will trigger an OSHA accident investigation or cause difficulties when bidding for new contracts). Such reasons would be expected to influence perceptions about norms, attitudes, and perceived control, as well as behavioral intentions toward reporting the event.

Future Research Opportunities

Many of the variables presented in Table 3.1 can be placed within the theoretical frameworks described above. Future research in this area would do well to utilize these frameworks to move beyond a piecemeal approach to documenting and identifying individual factors (often in isolation from other contextual variables) related to under-reporting. Rather, these frameworks can be used to develop comprehensive multi-level models of accident reporting behavior that could then be subject to empirical test. Such models should include variables operating at the individual-, workgroup-, organizational-, and national-levels that contribute to the problem of under-reporting.

Workplace interventions to improve the accuracy of accident reporting could also be developed in conjunction with these theoretical models and would allow for a competitive test of the alternative propositions derived from the models. Many researchers have developed recommendations for improving safety incentive systems and reporting systems. Yet, the effectiveness of such interventions are rarely empirically tested. For example, Reason (1997) argues that there are five preconditions necessary for organizations to report accurately: (1) indemnity against disciplinary action; (2) confidentiality of reporting; (3) separating the agency who collects and analyzes the data from the regulatory authority; (4) quick and useful availability of feedback; and (5) ease of using the reporting system. Based on the literature review summarized in Table 3.1, many of these same recommendations would apply at the individual-level: (1) no-fault reporting where accident investigations are seen as fact-finding as opposed to fault-finding; (2) confidential and/or anonymous reporting; (3) visible and positive organizational response to reports of hazardous situations and/or injuries; and (4) a simple straightforward reporting system. Such recommendations would appear to fit within the theoretical frameworks of the HBM and BRT, but again these have largely not been empirically evaluated in this context.

Future research should also concentrate not just on predicting under-reporting, but better understanding what types of injuries and illnesses go unreported. The inclusion of actual loss data in future studies (that is, workers' compensation claims rates and costs) would allow for a more in-depth analysis of the kinds of injuries that are being unreported in workplace injury and illness logs. Similarly, in self-report surveys, researchers should determine if employees fail to report certain types of accidents more often than others. For example, in their study of copper miners, Probst and Graso (2010) used open-ended questions to ask employees how many total accidents they had experienced and reported and how many they had experienced but not reported. They then asked workers to indicate how many of the accidents within each category had resulted in lost-time, first-aid, no injury, and property/equipment damage.

Using this metric, they found that nearly 52 percent of all accidents went unreported. However, the highest rates of under-reporting occurred with events requiring only first aid (89 percent unreported) or "no injury" (61 percent unreported). On the other hand, only one-third of all lost-time injuries and 24 percent of all damage to property or equipment went unreported. This would seem to indicate that employees are more willing to report more severe injuries (particularly those requiring time off from work) and those resulting in property damage, perhaps due to the higher visibility of such events. On the other hand, smaller, less noticeable events that apparently cause "little or no" harm tend not to get reported. This comports with a study conducted by Nielsen, Carstensen and Rasmussen (2006) which asked metal workers to indicate their willingness to report several types of hypothetical events. In that study, employees indicated they would be most willing to report lost-time incidents followed by minor injuries and then near misses.

Conclusions

In closing, while any review of national and international injury, illness, and fatality statistics is sobering, a large and growing body of research suggests these data may only represent the tip of the iceberg. Just as injury triangles have been developed to represent the exponential relationship between near misses, minor accidents, and major injuries/deaths, this chapter has attempted to argue that a similar relationship holds true between accident under-reporting by employees, under-reporting by organizations, and ultimately national surveillance system data. Using the most conservative of estimates, it appears that for every one injury captured in the national surveillance system data, at least two were reported to organizations, and at least four were actually experienced by employees. This would imply, for example, that there were 16 million (as opposed to the 4 million officially reported) work-related illnesses and injuries in the US in 2007.

Given the prevalence and seriousness of the under-reporting phenomenon, we described commonly used processes that organizations and countries have in place for reporting, investigating, and tracking employee injuries and illnesses. More importantly, we reviewed research on empirically-established individual and organizational correlates of under-reporting and proposed two possible theoretical models to use as a framework for future research on understanding and predicting accident reporting behaviors.

Finally, based on these models, we proposed several interventions that organizations can utilize to improve the accuracy of accident reporting and suggested directions for future research in this area.

References

Ajzen, I. (1991) The theory of planned behavior, *Organizational Behavior and Human Decision Processes;* 50(2), 179–211.

Barach, P. and Small, S.D. (2000) Reporting and preventing medical mishaps: Lessons from non-medical near miss reporting systems, *British Medical Journal;* 320(7237), 759–763.

Becker, M.H. (1974) The Health Belief Model and personal health behavior, *Health Education Monographs;* 2(4), 324–473.

Bird, Jr., F.E. and Germain, G.L. (1996) *Practical Loss Control Leadership*. Loganville, GA: International Loss Control Institute.

Bureau of Labor Statistics (2005) *Occupational Safety and Health Definitions*. http://www.bls.gov/iif/oshdef.htm.

Bureau of Labor Statistics (2008) *Workplace Injuries and Illnesses in 2007*. http://www.bls.gov/news.release/osh.nr0.htm.

Christian, M.S., Bradley, J.C., Wallace, J.C., and Burke, M.J. (2009) Workplace safety: A meta-analysis of the roles of person and situation factors, *Journal of Applied Psychology;* 94(5), 1103–1127.

Clarke, S. (1998) Organizational factors affecting the incident reporting of train drivers, *Work & Stress;* 12(1), 6–16.

Clarke, S. (2009) Accidents and safety in the workplace. In S. Cartwright and C.L. Cooper (eds) *The Oxford Handbook of Organizational Well-being,* Oxford, UK: Oxford University Press, 31–54.

Collison, D.L. (1999) "Surviving the rigs": Safety and surveillance on North Sea oil installations, *Organization Studies*; 20(4), 579–600.

Conway, H. and Svenson, J. (1998) Occupational injury and illness rates, 1992–1996: Why they fell, *Monthly Labor Review;* 121(11), 34–8.

European Agency for Safety and Health at Work (2008) *European Week Aims at Cutting Workplace Accidents and Diseases*. http://osha.europa.eu/en/press/press-releases/eu-health-and-safety-week-launched-to-reduce-workplace-accidents-and-diseases.

Eurostat (2001) *European Statistics on Accidents at Work (ESAW), Methodology—2001 edition*. Luxembourg: Office for Official Publications of the European Communities.

Eurostat (2008) *The Social Situation in the European Union 2008: New Insights into Social Inclusion*. Luxembourg: Office for Official Publications of the European Communities.

Gallagher, R.M. and Myers, P. (1996) Referral delay in back pain patients on worker's compensation: Cost and policy implications, *Psychosomatics: Journal of Consultation Liaison Psychiatry;* 37, 270–284.

Geller, E.S. (2001) *Working Safe: How to Help People Actively Care for Health and Safety*. Boca Raton, FL: CRC Press.

Glazner J.E., Borgerding J., Lowery J.T., Bondy J., Mueller K.L., and Kreiss, K. (1998) Construction injury rates may exceed national estimates: Evidence from the construction of Denver International Airport, *American Journal of Industrial Medicine;* 34(2), 105–112.

Glendon, A.I. (1991) Accident data analysis, *Journal of Health and Safety;* 7, 5–24.

Graso, M., Probst, T.P., Westaby, J.D., Gruys, M. (2010) Selecting Leaders: Race, Gender, and Age and the 2008 Election. Poster submitted to the Society for Industrial and Organizational Psychology, Atlanta, GA.

Hämäläinen, P., Takala, J., and Saarela, K.L. (2006) Global estimates of occupational accidents, *Safety Science;* 44(2), 137–156.

Health and Safety Executive (2008) *A Guide to the Reporting of Injuries, Diseases and Dangerous Occurrences Regulations 1995*. http://www.hse.gov.uk/pubns/priced/l73.pdf.

Heinrich, H.W. (1931) *Industrial Accident Prevention*. New York, NY: McGraw-Hill.

Hofmann, D.A. and Stetzer, A. (1996) A cross-level investigation of factors influencing unsafe behaviors and accidents, *Personnel Psychology;* 49(2), 307–339.

International Labor Organization (2009) *World Day for Safety and Health at Work 2009: Facts on Safety and Health at Work*. http://www.ilo.org/wcmsp5/groups/public/---dgreports/---dcomm/documents/publication/wcms_105146.pdf.

Janz, N.K. and Becker, M.H. (1984) The health belief model: A decade later, *Health Education Quarterly;* 11(1), 1–47.

Kerr, S. (1975) On the folly of rewarding A, while hoping for B, *Academy of Management Journal;* 18, 769–783.

Landen, D.D. and Hendricks, S. (1995) Effect of recall on reporting of at-home injuries, *Public Health Reports;* 110(3), 350–355.

Landsbergis, P.A., Cahill, J., and Schnall, P. (1999) The impact of lean production and related new systems of work organization on worker health, *Journal of Occupational Health Psychology;* 4(2), 108–130.

Leigh, J.P., Marcin, J.P., and Miller, T.R. (2004) An estimate of the U.S. government's undercount of nonfatal occupational injuries, *Journal of Occupational and Environmental Medicine;* 46(1), 10–18.

Loeppke, R., Hymel., P.A., Loafland, J.H., Pizzi, L.T., Konicki, D.L., Anstadt, G.W., Baase, C., Fortuna, J., and Scharf, T. (2003) Health-related workplace productivity measurement: General and migrane-specific recommendations from the ACOEM expert panel, *Journal of Occupational and Environmental Medicine,* 45(4), 349–359.

Lowery, J.T., Borgerding, J.A., Zehn, B., Glazner, J.E., Bondy, J., and Kreiss, K. (1998) Risk factors for injury among construction worker at Denver International Airport, *American Journal of Industrial Medicine;* 34(2), 105–112.

Lusk, S.L., Ronis, D.L., and Baer, L.M. (1995) A comparison of multiple indicators: Observations, supervisor report, and self-report as measures of workers' hearing protection use, *Evaluation & the Health Professions;* 18(1), 51–63.

McLain, D.L. and Jarrell, K.A. (2007) The perceived compatibility of safety and production expectations in hazardous occupations, *Journal of Safety Research;* 38(3), 299–309.

National Cancer Institute (2005) *Theory at a Glance: A Guide for Health Promotion Practice* (2nd edition). Washington, DC: US Department of Health and Human Services.

Nielsen, K.J., Carstensen, O., and Rasmussen, K. (2006) The prevention of occupational injuries in two industrial plants using an incident reporting scheme, *Journal of Safety Research;* 37(5), 479–486.

OR-OSHA (2007) Conducting an Accident Investigation. http://www.orosha.org/pdf/workshops/102w.pdf.

OSHA (2005) OSHA Recordkeeping Handbook: The Regulation and Related Interpretations for Recording and Reporting Occupational Injuries and Illnesses. http://www.osha.gov/recordkeeping/handbook/index.html.

Pransky, G., Snyder, T., Dembe, A., and Himmelstein, J. (1999) Under-reporting of work-related disorders in the workplace: A case study and review of the literature, *Ergonomics;* 42(1), 171–182.

Probst, T.M. (2006) Job Insecurity and Accident Under-reporting. Poster presented to the 2006 Conference of the Society of Industrial and Organizational Psychology, Dallas, TX.

Probst, T.M., Brubaker, T.L., and Barsotti, A. (2008) Organizational under-reporting of injury rates: An examination of the moderating effect of organizational safety climate, *Journal of Applied Psychology;* 93(5), 1147–1154.

Probst, T.M. and Estrada, A.X. (2010) Accident under-reporting among employees: Testing the moderating influence of psychological safety climate and supervisor enforcement of safety practices, *Accident Analysis & Prevention*; 42, 1438–1444.

Probst, T.M. and Graso, M. (2010) Pressure to produce = Pressure to reduce accident reporting? Poster submitted to the Society for Industrial and Organizational Psychology, Atlanta, GA.

Probst, T.M., Graso, M., Estrada, A.X., and Greer, S. (under review) Extending the consideration of future consequences to safety outcomes, *Safety Science*.

Reason, J.T. (1997) *Managing the Risks of Organizational Accidents*. Aldershot, UK: Ashgate.

Ritwik, U. (2002) Risk-based approach to near miss, *Hydrocarbon Processing;* October, 93–96.

Rosenman, K.D., Kalush, A., Reilly, M.J., Gardiner, J.C., Reeves. M., and Luo, Z. (2006) How much work-related injury and illness is missed by the current national surveillance system, *Journal of Occupational and Environmental Medicine;* 48(4), 357–365.

Rosenstock, I.M., Strecher, V.J., and Becker, M.H. (1994) The Health Belief Model and HIV risk behavior change. In J. Peterson and R. DiClemente (eds), *Preventing AIDS: Theory and Practice of Behavioral Interventions,* Plenum Press: New York, NY, 5–24.

Sinclair, R.R. and Tetrick, L.E. (2004) Pay and benefits: The role of compensation systems in workplace safety. In J. Barling and M. Frone (eds) *Psychology of Workplace Safety*, Washington, DC: American Psychological Association, 181–201.

Smecko, T. and Hayes, B. (1999) Measuring Compliance with Safety Behaviors at Work. Paper presented at the 14th annual conference of the Society for Industrial and Organizational Psychology. Atlanta, Georgia, April.

Tabak, N., Shiaabana, A.M., and ShaSha, S. (2006) The health beliefs of hospital staff and the reporting of needlestick injury, *Journal of Clinical Nursing;* 15(10), 1228–1239.

Washington State Department of Labor and Industries (2009) Accident Reporting and Investigating Summary. http://www.lni.wa.gov/wisha/rules/corerules/PDFs/296-800-320.pdf.

Webb, G.R., Redman, S., Wilkinson, C. and Sanson-Fisher, R.W. (1989) Filtering effects in reporting work injuries, *Accident Analysis and Prevention;* 21(2), 115–123.

Weddle, M.G. (1996) Reporting occupational injuries: The first step, *Journal of Safety Research;* 27(4), 217–223.

Weiner, B.J., Hobgood, C., and Lewis, M.A. (2008) The meaning of justice in safety incident reporting, *Social Science and Medicine;* 66(2), 403–413.

Westaby, J.D. (2005) Behavioral Reasoning Theory: Identifying new linkages underlying intentions and behavior, *Organizational Behavior and Human Decision Processes;* 98(2), 97–120.

Westaby, J.D., Probst, T.M., and Lee, B.C. (2010) Leadership decision-making: A behavioral reasoning theory analysis, *The Leadership Quarterly*; 21, 481–495.

Westaby, J.D., Versenyi, A., and Hausmann, R.C. (2005) Intentions to work during terminal illness: An exploratory study of antecedent conditions, *Journal of Applied Psychology;* 90(6), 1297–1305.

Zacharatos, A. and Barling, J. (2004) High performance work systems and occupational safety. In J. Barling and M. Frone (eds) *Psychology of Workplace Safety*, Washington, DC: American Psychological Association, 203–222.
Zahlis, D.F. and Hansen, L.L. (2005) Beware the disconnect, *Professional Safety;* 50(11), 18–24.

PART 

Individual Factors

CHAPTER

4 Accident Proneness: Back in Vogue?

SHARON CLARKE

Introduction

Accident proneness is a long-lived and much-debated concept, with discussion and research of this topic spanning 90 years. Investigation of "accident proneness" originated in early studies of accident data, which found that the distribution of accidents across individuals is not that which would be expected by chance; furthermore, the data consistently revealed that a very few people were involved in a disproportionately high number of accidents (Greenwood and Woods, 1919; Greenwood and Yule, 1920; Newbold, 1926). Whilst, this small sub-group of accident repeaters might have been dismissed as statistical outliers, studies were also able to demonstrate stability in individuals' accident records by correlating accident involvement over two successive time periods. This meant that accident repeaters were not just "unlucky," but were consistently more likely to be accident-involved over time compared to non-accident repeaters. Such findings led to speculation that increased accident liability was due to a stable set of personal characteristics, or "accident proneness" (Farmer and Chambers, 1926; Marbe, 1926). Much of the research in this area has adopted either a statistical or a psychological approach (Shaw and Sichel, 1971), with a few references in medical and psychiatric journals to accident proneness as a personality disorder. However, as discussed by Burnham (2008), accident proneness never gained the status of a recognized psychiatric syndrome. This chapter will overview the history of accident proneness research, leading to a review of psychological factors associated with those who demonstrate differential accident involvement and, finally, concluding with implications for organizational policy and practice in relation to accident reduction.

Accident Proneness—The Statistical Approach

Much of the debate and controversy surrounding accident proneness has arisen as the result of the statistical approach, which focused on fitting accident data to theoretical distributions in order to test hypotheses based on the accident proneness concept (McKenna, 1983; Shaw and Sichel, 1971). If all individuals have an equal liability to accidents (that is, accidents are randomly distributed and occur by chance), the Poisson distribution will be a good fit to accident data (Hypothesis 1).[1] However, if an unequal initial liability to accident involvement is assumed, such that some individuals have a greater accident liability than others, the negative binomial distribution will be a good fit (Hypothesis 2). Evidence supporting Hypothesis 2 has been reported consistently across a number of studies (for example, Hakkinen, 1958; Newbold, 1926), which have found that the negative binomial distribution is a better fit to accident data compared to the Poisson distribution. Researchers have taken these findings as evidence that accidents are not random events, but that individuals have differential liability to accidents due to enduring personal characteristics (that is, supporting the existence of "accident proneness").

This stance has generated fierce debate, as critics argued that a negative binomial fit could equally be explained by a failure to control, or inadequate control, for risk exposure (Smeed, 1960). Thus, individuals' unequal liability to accident involvement is a function of their exposure to risk (that is, situational factors, such as type of occupation), rather than personal characteristics, such as personality or intelligence. Furthermore, researchers (for example, Arbous and Kerrich, 1951) argued that negative binomial fit is not dependent on the assumption of initial unequal liability, if one cedes that involvement in an accident may alter the probability of involvement in subsequent accidents.

This latter possibility leads to two further possibilities, that: individuals have equal initial liability, but the probability of subsequent accidents is altered after the first accident (Hypothesis 3); individuals have unequal initial liability and the probability of subsequent accidents is altered after the first accident (Hypothesis 4). In considering the effect of an accident on subsequent accidents, Blasco, Prieto and Cornejo (2003) found that the time-lags between accidents for bus drivers were not distributed as expected by chance; rather, once a bus driver had experienced an accident, subsequent accidents tended to occur at shorter time intervals than expected by chance, following which the time-lags increased and the probability of having a further accident reduced. Furthermore, this tendency was found in all sub-groups of drivers (whether their accident frequency was classed as high, average, or low), although it was more difficult to detect in the low accident sub-group, due to the low density of accidents.

These findings demonstrate evidence that not only may individuals differ in their accident liability in terms of accident frequency, but also in terms of their tendency to experience accident clusters. Cresswell and Froggatt (1963) investigated the possibility that individual vulnerability to accidents varies over time, but as temporary "spells," rather than as an enduring personal characteristic. They argued that individuals experience temporary "spells" of lowered efficiency, which increase their accident liability for a limited period (Hypothesis 5). Taking a statistical approach, Cresswell and Froggatt argued that two models, the short distribution ("spells" plus chance accidents) and the long distribution ("spells" plus no other accidents), would be a good fit to their accident data. This, however, was not the case, and their analyses could be equally interpreted as supporting accident proneness (Hypothesis 2), rather than the existence of temporary spells (Irwin, 1964).

A recent meta-analysis (Visser et al., 2007), based on studies of injuries (requiring medical attention) in the general population published 1966–2005, found that the distribution of accidents failed to match the pattern expected if they were distributed

1 If a random event has a mean number of occurrences in a given time period, then these occurrences will follow a Poisson distribution. For example, the number of cars passing a fixed point over a given time interval.

randomly (that is, the Poisson distribution); instead some individuals were found to suffer injuries more often than would be expected by chance alone (overall odds ratio for observed versus expected repeater: OR = 1.42, 95% CI = 1.05-1.92, $p < 0.05$). Given the consistent finding that accidents are not random events that are evenly distributed across individuals, one can conclude that there is sufficient evidence to reject Hypothesis 1. However, given the review of the "accident proneness" literature, there remains insufficient evidence to accept any of the alternative hypotheses (Hypotheses 2–5).

As highlighted by McKenna (1983), supporters of accident proneness have argued that stability in accident records over time (as demonstrated by high correlations between accidents in two successive time periods) is evidence that accident proneness reflects a stable set of personal characteristics; on the other hand, detractors have focused on those studies that have failed to demonstrate high correlations. As with the negative binomial distribution, the correlation coefficient is not a rigorous test, given that alternative explanations cannot be ruled out: for example, a high correlation may equally result where stability is due to unequal risk exposure (McKenna, 1983). More recently, af Wåhlberg and Dorn (2009) argued that low correlations between time periods have arisen in previous studies due to the use of samples with low numbers of accidents over relatively short time periods; therefore, restricting the amount of variance and limiting the possible size of the correlation coefficient. Using five samples of UK bus drivers, af Wåhlberg and Dorn demonstrated that the size of correlation between time periods was significantly associated with the mean number of accidents ($r = .79$); with larger samples of high-accident bus drivers over longer time periods, it was possible to show considerable stability in accident records. Although the authors called for a revival of the concept of accident proneness, it must be noted (as in previous studies) it was not possible to rule out alternative explanations for stability in accident records over time, such as unequal risk exposure.

Accident Proneness—The Psychological Approach

Despite clear evidence that accidents are not random events (Visser et al., 2007), there remains little understanding of the psychological mechanisms that link personal characteristics and individual difference factors to accident involvement. The statistical approach to accident research, and the conceptual confusion surrounding the concept of "accident proneness," have hampered efforts to develop the psychological approach in this area (McKenna, 1983). In their meta-analysis, Visser et al. (2007) found a high degree of variability in the definition and operationalization of accident proneness; they also noted the tendency for psychologically-based research to use terms related to differential accident or injury liability, rather than the value-laden term of "accident proneness." Accident research has tended to emphasize the influence of situational factors, rather than personal factors, as predictors of accident involvement.

Furthermore, it is rare to find empirical research that measures both situational and personal factors within the same study; where personal factors (such as personality, age, and gender) are measured, they are often only considered as control variables to isolate the effects of situational factors. This may be partly due to the spectre of "accident proneness" that hangs over the study of personal factors and partly to avoid blame for accidents falling to the individual (and so de-emphasize the importance of organizational and societal responsibility for accident prevention). A further barrier to the psychological approach is the argument that the reliability of accident proneness (that is, the size of the correlation between accidents over a number of years) sets the ceiling for the impact of any psychological factors, as accident proneness is assumed to be stable over time (McKenna, 1983).

For example, if the correlation for accidents in two successive time periods is 0.30, this restricts the variance that might be accounted for by any psychological factor to < 9 percent. However, as noted previously by af Wåhlberg and Dorn (2009), such correlations may have been underestimated, due to the use of short time periods and low-accident samples in previous studies. Indeed, the authors found a mean correlation of 0.28 for five samples of bus drivers across two consecutive years, but with increased time periods and numbers of accidents, mean correlations across samples of 0.44 and 0.48 were reported. Furthermore, the argument assumes that psychological factors must be stable, and so excludes the influence of temporary factors. Nevertheless, there is evidence to support a significant effect of stress, caused by life events, on accident involvement (for example, Legree et al., 2003).

Despite the dominance of the statistical approach, a number of studies have taken a psychological approach and have been able to demonstrate that accident involvement has a significant association with a wide range of personal characteristics, including attention and motor function (Hakkinen, 1958), decision-making style (French et al., 1993) and Type A behavior pattern (TABP; Nabi et al., 2005). Taking a psychological, rather than a statistical approach, to accident research, should enable us to develop a deeper understanding of the individual factors, and the underlying psychological mechanisms, linked to accidents.

Investigation into the proximal causes of accidents has highlighted the dominant role played by human error and other psychological factors, particularly cognitive ability and information-processing (for example, Arthur Barrett, and Alexander, 1991; Avolio, Kroeck and Panek, 1985; Groeneweg, 1992; Wagenaar and Groeneweg, 1987). A study of unsafe acts committed by drivers (Reason et al., 1990) distinguished between two distinct categories: errors and violations. Reason (1990) classified errors as slips and lapses (execution failures where actions fail to occur as intended) and mistakes (planning failures, where planned actions fail to achieve the desired outcome).

Reason et al. (1990) argued that different underlying psychological mechanisms account for the occurrence of errors and violations: whilst errors result from faulty information-processing at an individual level, violations are deliberate deviations from safe practice that "can only be described with regard to a social context in which behaviour is governed by operating procedures, codes of practice, rules, norms and the like" (p. 1316). They reported that errors remained stable across age groups, but that violations were found to decrease significantly in older age groups; men also reported significantly more violations than women. Whilst research indicates that young men in particular commit the highest levels of driving violations (Chang and Yeh, 2007), it has been argued that overtly risky behavior only accounts for a small proportion of young people's accidents (McKnight and McKnight, 2003).

Such accidents occur largely as the result of errors and so the higher crash rates seen in younger drivers tend to disappear rapidly with increasing experience. Whilst younger drivers are involved in the highest proportion of accidents, as people get older (particularly over 75) their accident liability begins to increase. Older drivers experience an increased risk of accidental injury of 30–45 percent (Li, Braver and Chen, 2003), even taking into account their increased frailty and susceptibility to injury. However, one must also consider a range of exogenous factors affecting the relationship between age and accident involvement. For example, if driving distance is taken into account, the higher accident liability of older drivers disappears (Langford, Methorst and Hakamies-Blomqvist, 2006). The propensity for errors and violations is likely to contribute substantially to an individual's susceptibility to accidents, which cannot be simply accounted for in terms of demographics. This chapter will now review the literature linking individual difference variables to accident involvement.

Individual Differences in Cognitive Abilities

Accident research has demonstrated a consistently strong relationship between individual cognitive factors, errors, and accident involvement. For example, Brown (1990) found that attentional errors accounted for 40 percent of road accidents, whilst perceptual errors and judgmental errors accounted for a further 25 percent and 10–15 percent, respectively. Furthermore, Edkins and Pollock (1997) found that inattention was responsible for 70 percent of train driver errors. Attentional errors occur more frequently when the behavior is routine and has become automated; for example, lack of attention due to distraction off-task (Reason, 1990). Individuals with low perceptual load are more likely to be distracted by irrelevant stimuli (Forster and Lavie, 2008), with greater distraction increasing the likelihood of accidents (for example, drivers weaving in and out of heavy traffic are less likely to be distracted by billboards than those on an deserted motorway).

Thus, cognitive abilities related to attention and information-processing are likely to be important underlying factors in an individual's vulnerability to accident involvement. Supporting evidence for the role of both attention and information-processing factors has been consistently demonstrated. Arthur, Barrett and Alexander (1991) conducted a meta-analytic review of information-processing and cognitive ability variables; they found small-moderate effects for auditory selective attention ($\rho = .26$) and perceptual style ($\rho = .15$). Avolio, Kroeck and Panek (1985) found significant correlations between six measures of information-processing and accidents ($.13 < r < .43$). Porter (1988) reported that poor visual attention (and also experience of major life events) was most consistently related to accidents, whilst Arthur, Strong and Williamson (1994) found significant correlations between three versions of a computer-based visual attention test and self-reported accidents ($.26 < r < .38$).

Cognitive interpretation of information may also play a significant role, as demonstrated by Langham et al. (2002), who examined reasons for collisions with highly conspicuous police vehicles parked on the hard shoulder of the motorway. They found that collisions occurred due to vigilance failure and false hypotheses about road conditions (drivers would assume that the vehicle was moving, not stationary), rather than sensory failure (drivers did not see the vehicle).

The emphasis on information-processing and cognitive ability in accidents has led researchers to examine the role of intelligence in accident involvement. Gottfredson (2004) has argued that superior information-processing skills are required to avoid accidents, including learning and recalling relevant information, identifying problem situations quickly, and reacting swiftly to unexpected situations. However, there is little evidence that individuals with high intelligence are more able to avoid accidents than low-intelligence individuals (Hakkinen, 1958; McKenna, Duncan and Brown, 1986; Smith and Kirkham, 1982).

Most studies have found little or no correlation between intelligence and accidents; although Smith and Kirkham (1982) found a small but significant association (r = -.17). Rather than having a direct effect on accident involvement, intelligence may act as a buffer against the negative effects of other dispositional factors, such as personality. Perkins and Corr (2006) report a significant interactive effect of neuroticism and cognitive ability on job performance, such that a high cognitive ability buffers the negative effects of neuroticism on job performance. Extending the findings of this research to safety performance, cognitive ability may similarly buffer the negative effects of neuroticism (and possibly other personality traits) on accident involvement.

Research has demonstrated that accidents often occur due to: a lack of attention; memory lapses and slips of action—collectively, cognitive failures. Broadbent et al. (1982) developed the "Cognitive Failures Questionnaire (CFQ)" which is a self-report measure of failures in perception, memory, and motor function. It is not a measure of intelligence (being largely unrelated to performance on IQ tests) but instead reflects success at appropriately distributing attention, particularly under stress and across multiple tasks (Larson et al., 1997). The CFQ is a widely used instrument that has demonstrated excellent reliability and validity (Broadbent et al., 1982; Merckelbach et al. 1996; Vom Hofe, Mainemarre and Vannier, 1998). Broadbent et al. (1982) suggested that the CFQ has a single factor structure, which reflects a general cognitive failure factor. However, although later research has supported various two, three, or four factor models, more recently Rast et al. (2009) found support for a three factor model—Distractibility, Forgetfulness, and False Triggering—which demonstrated factor invariance across age groups (with participants aged between 24 and 83). Forgetfulness increased with age; distractibility was relatively stable (across ages 24–63), but showed a significant drop after the early sixties (perhaps as people retired from work). False Triggering (interrupted processing of sequences of cognitive and motor actions) remained stable across age groups and was highly correlated with distractibility (r = .77). Thus, although Forgetfulness may increase with age, the remaining two factors, Distractibility and False Triggering, which are both related to attention and motor functioning, seem to be quite stable over time. This evidence supports a relatively enduring tendency for cognitive failures that may reflect an individual's propensity to become accident-involved. High CFQ scorers tend to be involved in a higher number of accidents and to require hospitalization more frequently (Larson and Merritt, 1991; Larson et al., 1997). Based on a large-scale UK survey of 7,980 people, of those who reported cognitive failures, 18 percent also reported minor injuries and 7 percent also reported accidents at work (Simpson et al., 2005). Wallace and Vodanovich (2003a) investigated the relationship between work injuries and scores on the CFQ in a sample of electrical workers; they found that high scores on CFQ (in particular on items related to physical blunders, such as accidentally bumping into someone) were significantly predictive of both work injuries and vehicle crashes.

Reported risk factors associated with cognitive failures include: depression, anxiety, risk taking, general life stress, work stress, difficulty sleeping, general health, and neuroticism (Simpson et al., 2005). That there is an association between individual proneness to cognitive failures (or error-proneness) and increased vulnerability to stress is widely accepted (Broadbent, Broadbent and Jones, 1986; Reason, 1988). However, Reason (1990) argued that it is not so much that stress induces a high cognitive failure rate, but rather that certain cognitive styles can lead to both absent-mindedness (or lack of attention) and inappropriate matching of coping strategies to stressful situations. Reason and Mycielska (1982) consider that this is related to the amount of attentional capacity that people have available to deal with stress after other matters have been dealt with. Such arguments would support an individual difference explanation: rather than cognitive failures being just a product of temporary increases in general life or work-related stress, they reflect stable and enduring individual differences in the extent to which responses to stress influence accident involvement.

There is evidence to suggest that such individual differences may originate in dispositional factors, such as personality traits. Reason and Mycielska (1982) reported studies indicating a link between error-proneness and the obsessionality personality trait (as measured by a version of the Middlesex Hospital Questionnaire, an instrument developed for primary use in clinical settings to measure various personality traits): the more obsessive an individual, the lower is their propensity to make errors. Wallace and Vodanovich (2003b) investigated the link between cognitive failures and conscientiousness. They reported that conscientiousness moderated the relationship between cognitive failures and injuries at work, such that the relationship between cognitive failures and injuries was stronger for low scorers on conscientiousness. These findings may suggest that personality influences both the tendency for cognitive failures, and also the extent to which failures can be recovered before they result in accidents or injuries.

Individual Differences in Personality Traits

A number of reviews have been conducted that support links between various personality traits and accident involvement. An early literature review by Keehn (1961) concluded that extraversion and neuroticism were associated with higher injury liability. Later, Hansen (1988) identified six personality characteristics, where there was good empirical support for an association with greater accidental injuries: external locus of control (LOC), extraversion, aggression, social maladjustment, neuroticism, and impulsivity. More recently, Clarke and Robertson (2005) conducted a comprehensive meta-analysis of the relationship between personality traits and accidents (categorizing a wide range of personality characteristics into the "Big Five" personality framework). They reported a moderate effect size for both (low) conscientiousness ($\rho = .27$) and (low) agreeableness ($\rho = .26$) with higher accident involvement (including both work and traffic accidents). In addition, a significant association was found for neuroticism with work accidents ($\rho = .28$) and for extraversion with traffic accidents ($\rho = .24$).

Conscientiousness includes a number of different aspects: competence, order, dutifulness, achievement striving, self-discipline, and deliberation. It has been found to correlate well with criterion measures of job performance across various occupational settings (Barrick and Mount, 1991; Salgado, 1997; 1998; Tett, Jackson and Rothstein, 1991). Low scorers on conscientiousness exhibit behaviors that are characterized by a focus on satisfying immediate needs, regardless of future consequences for oneself or others (West, Elander and French, 1993); they tend to demonstrate little forward planning and have a tendency to ignore rules and regulations (Arthur and Doverspike, 2001). Miller, Lynam and Jones (2008) found that individuals who are low scorers on conscientiousness are characterized by a lack of impulse control, which is related to higher levels of antisocial and risky behavior.

In a work context, Salgado (2002) found that low conscientiousness was the most significant predictor of deviant work behaviors (including rule breaking). Furthermore, individuals who are low on conscientiousness often fail to reflect upon on-task processes such that cognitive failures are more likely to result in workplace accidents (Wallace and Vodanovich, 2003b). Wallace and Chen (2006) argued that conscientiousness will influence safe work behavior through motivational processes, such as self-regulation (Higgins, 1997).

The achievement striving aspects of conscientiousness will lead to a promotion regulatory focus (that is, concern for accomplishing a greater quantity of work more quickly); however, the dependability aspects of conscientiousness will relate to a prevention regulatory focus (that is, concern for adhering to work-related rules, responsibilities, and regulations). It was found that the effect of conscientiousness on safe work behavior was fully mediated by self-regulatory processes, through both of these processes, but that the negative effect of a promotion focus was not sufficient to negate the positive effect of a prevention focus. Thus, high scorers on conscientiousness are likely to avoid accidents through their maintenance of a prevention regulatory focus, with an emphasis on compliance with rules and procedures. However, as noted by Wallace and Chen (2006), compliance is only one element of safe behavior and does not equate to overall safe work performance.

Agreeableness includes elements of trust, compliance, and altruism. People who are high on agreeableness are pleasant, tolerant, tactful, helpful, not defensive, and generally easy to get along with (Hough, 1992). Different aspects of agreeableness, including trust and altruism, have been associated with lower accident rates in the workplace (Davids and Mahoney, 1957). However, the opposite pole of agreeableness (including belligerence, hostility, and aggression) has been more extensively studied in relation to accidents.

Low agreeableness is associated with high emotional arousal and inadequate interpersonal strategies, such that individuals are less able to cooperate with others effectively and more liable to respond aggressively to situations. Such characteristics have been associated with increased likelihood of antisocial and risky behavior (Miller, Lynam and Jones, 2008). Mesken, Lajunen and Summala (2002) suggest that interpersonal violations on the road (that is, aggressive behaviors toward another road user) are associated with higher negative affect and emotional arousal, which in turn influence perception and information processing (Deffenbacher, Oetting and Lynch, 1994), increasing accident risk. High aggression has been associated with greater accident involvement in railway workers (Sah, 1989), pilots (Conger et al., 1959) and bus drivers (Roy and Choudhary, 1985).

Emotional stability has been consistently associated with higher job proficiency across occupations (Salgado 1997; 1998), whilst neuroticism (characterized by anxiety, hostility, depression, self-consciousness, and impulsiveness) has been identified as a significant predictor of workplace accidents (Clarke and Robertson, 2005). The higher accident liability of neurotics may be related to their distractibility, as they tend to be preoccupied with their own anxieties and worries, and therefore more easily distracted from the task at hand (Hansen, 1989; Iverson and Erwin, 1997). Neuroticism is associated with lower behavioral control, so that individuals high in neuroticism tend to demonstrate approach behavior in relation to threatening stimuli and a decreased latency in disengaging from such stimuli (Derryberry, Reed and Pilkenton-Taylor, 2003). Such behavior would mean that neurotics tend to find themselves in more dangerous situations. Furthermore, neurotics tend to respond more negatively to threatening situations and use less proactive coping strategies (Bosma, Stansfeld and Marmot, 1998). This is consistent with Kaplan et al.'s (2009) meta-analysis, which found that negative affectivity (NA) was significantly associated with occupational injury (ρ = .20); where NA is a tendency to experience negative emotions, which has been strongly associated with neuroticism. Neurotic individuals are more likely to experience emotions associated with anger and aggression; however, in combination with high agreeableness, it is likely that these individuals will be able to self-regulate their aggressive or angry responses to a situation. This would suggest that a combination of high neuroticism (N) and low agreeableness (Ag) increases the likelihood of an aggressive response (Ode, Robinson and Wilkowski, 2008). Such individuals would be less able to control their negative emotional reactions to situations, increasing their accident liability.

Acute reactions to stressors, including anxiety and fatigue, can have the effect of decreasing cognitive and performance capacities, such as reaction times and judgment, increasing the probability of errors (Steffy et al., 1986). As neurotics are less likely to seek active control of the environment (Judge, 1993), this may affect their likelihood of taking adequate precautions to prevent injury (for example, wearing protective equipment, such as gloves, masks, and safety goggles). Neurotics may be more vulnerable to accidents due to their tendency to respond negatively to threatening situations and use less proactive coping strategies. In contrast, those high in extraversion and conscientiousness are more likely to view potential stressors as a challenge and to adopt problem-solving coping (Watson and Hubbard, 1996). Grant and Langan-Fox (2006) showed that the effect of high N in combination with high conscientiousness (Cs) leads to higher stress exposure. However, the combination of high N/low Cs is likely to lead to higher accident liability, as this combination is most associated with the use of maladaptive coping strategies (Grant and Langan-Fox, 2006). The failure to cope with stressors will lead to higher levels of strain, which can result in more procedural violations (that is, non-compliance with safe work practices) and higher error propensity (Fogarty and McKeon, 2006).

Extraverts tend to be socially out-going, confident, and experience more positive emotions. Iverson and Erwin (1997) argued that these socially adjusted aspects of extraversion, as reflected in the construct of positive affectivity (PA), will reduce extraverts' vulnerability to accident involvement, as high PA is associated with greater self-efficacy (George and Brief, 1992; Judge, 1993), which in turn is reflected in task engagement and more accurate and systematic decision-making skills (Staw and Barsade, 1993). This should lead extraverts to engage in more thoughtful and careful appraisal of situations, reducing their accident risk. In combination with low N and high Cs, high scorers on extraversion experience low strain (Grant and Langan-Fox, 2006), which reduces error-proneness and accident liability.

Context was found to play a significant role in the relative influence of extraversion on accident involvement, with extraversion having a significant effect on traffic accidents, but not work accidents (Clarke and Robertson, 2005). This finding may reflect the role of the positive aspects of extraversion operating in the workplace, whereas driving allows the expression of a greater range of volitional behavior, such as sensation-seeking. In addition to social adjustment, extraversion is also characterized by the tendency to seek changes in self-stimulation to a far greater extent than introverts. This tendency results in significantly poorer performance on vigilance tasks, in particular, under monotonous conditions (Koelega, 1992). It has been argued that extraversion moderates the relationship between fatigue and driving errors, such that extraverts are particularly prone to driving errors when fatigued (Verwey and Zaidel, 2000). High sensation seekers have a greater tendency to take risks when driving, due to their increased need for novelty and thrills, and therefore have greater accident liability (Jonah, 1997). In addition, Thiffault and Bergeron (2003) found that high sensation seekers may be more sensitive to road monotony and thus more prone to fatigue-related driving errors.

Openness is one of the least studied dimensions of the "Big Five" personality taxonomy. High scorers on openness are imaginative, unconventional, curious, broadminded, and cultured. Although there is little evidence that openness is consistently associated with accident involvement (Arthur and Graziano, 1996; Clarke and Robertson, 2005), studies of risk taking have found that openness is significantly related to "risk propensity" (that is, a preference for higher levels of risk in activities).

Studies of risk taking have found an association with openness, in addition to low conscientiousness and low agreeableness (Kowert and Hermann, 1997; Nicholson et al. 2005). Nicholson et al. (2005) found that these personality dimensions played a significant role in risk-taking behavior across domains (recreation, health, career, finance, safety, and social). Soane and Chmiel (2005) showed that only a small proportion of their sample was consistently risk taking across domains (less than 3 percent), but that these people were significantly less agreeable and less conscientious than those who were consistently risk-averse. In particular, low conscientiousness was associated with risk taking across domains (Soane and Chmiel, 2005). These findings are consistent with the characteristics of low scorers on conscientiousness: a focus on satisfying immediate needs (West, Elander and French, 1993), a tendency to ignore rules and regulations (Arthur and Doverspike, 2001), and a lack of impulse control (Miller, Lynam and Jones, 2008). Furthermore, low scorers on agreeableness tend to experience higher negative affect and emotional arousal also leading them to taking greater risks (Miller, Lynam and Jones, 2008).

There is consistent evidence that individual differences in personality traits are associated with increased accident liability; therefore, possessing certain personality traits increases one's likelihood to become involved in accidents across domains. There is also evidence that these personality traits act indirectly through psychological mechanisms to affect accident liability: primarily, cognitive failures/error-proneness, violations/non-compliance, risk taking, and increased reactivity to stress. However, relatively little research has focused on how personality traits may interact to increase or decrease vulnerability to accidents. Nevertheless, some combinations of personality traits, such as low Ag/high N and high N/low Cs, may be particularly associated with accident liability. It is also important to consider the circumstances under which general tendencies of dispositional factors may not apply; for example, conscientiousness can lead to "blind compliance" where following the rules is prioritized over risk assessment of the situation, which indicates that breaking the rules and improvising would be a safer course of action; agreeableness can lead to adherence to group norms of unsafe behavior in order to get along with people. Further research on combinations of personality traits may highlight how these tendencies might be mitigated. Other personality dimensions, which do not lend themselves readily to inclusion in the "Big Five" personality taxonomy, have been studied in relation to accidents, notably LOC (Hansen, 1988; Arthur, Barrett and

Alexander, 1991). The role of LOC in accident liability will be considered in the next section, within the context of the broader construct of core self-evaluations.

Individual Differences in Core Self-evaluation

Core-self evaluation (CSE) reflects an individual's overall perception of self-worth; it comprises self-esteem, generalized self-efficacy, LOC, and neuroticism (Judge, Locke and Durham, 1997). These characteristics reflect individuals' evaluation of their own self-worth, their ability to cope with a range of situations, their belief in their ability to influence the environment successfully, and their ability to remain calm and secure and to demonstrate low reactivity in everyday situations. The traits that comprise CSE are: evaluative (that is, traits that are evaluative rather than descriptive and can directly affect other attitudes and affective evaluations); fundamental (that is, relating fundamentally to one's self-concept); and, wide in scope (that is, broad rather than narrow traits) (Johnson, Rosen and Levy, 2008). Johnson, Rosen and Levy (2008) argue that CSE traits relate to individuals' beliefs about their own self-regulatory and behavioral capacities.

CSE has been found to have a significant effect on job satisfaction and job performance (Judge et al., 2003), but has not, as an overall construct, been examined in relation to work-related or other types of accidents. Nevertheless, CSE is likely to have a significant effect on individuals' accident involvement as it reflects their beliefs in the controllability of the environment and their perceived ability to successfully effect change in that environment. Johnson, Rosen and Levy (2008) have argued that neuroticism is the most fundamental element, given its strong emotional rather than cognitive nature, which in some sense acts as an antecedent to self-esteem, general self-efficacy, and LOC (Judge, Van Vianen and De Pater, 2004). Thus, one needs a level of emotional stability in order to have positive self-esteem/self-efficacy and an internal LOC.

Neuroticism has been examined extensively as a risk factor for accident involvement: neurotics tend to be more error-prone as they are easily distracted from the task at hand (Hansen, 1989; Iverson and Erwin, 1997); they tend to find themselves in more dangerous situations as they demonstrate approach behavior in relation to threatening stimuli and a decreased latency in disengaging from such stimuli (Derryberry, Reed and Pilkenton-Taylor, 2003); and, they are less likely to take adequate safety precautions as they fail to seek active control of the environment (Judge, 1993).

From an empirical perspective, it has been argued that self-esteem and generalized self-efficacy are interchangeable (given meta-analytic estimates of ρ = .86; Judge et al., 1998). Self-esteem is the individual's appraisal of self-worth; whereas self-efficacy is an estimate of the individual's ability to perform and cope successfully with situations. Given that generalized self-efficacy is measured across situations it reflects a person-level concept, bringing it close in meaning to self-esteem. Individuals with low self-esteem tend to perform at lower levels and tend to react strongly to situations, but to cope with them passively. Such tendencies may lead individuals with low self-esteem to be more accident-involved; indeed, Smith and Heckert (1998) found a significant negative correlation between self-esteem and accidents (r = -.25).

Generalized self-efficacy reflects individuals' assessment of their capability to perform certain tasks and enhances feelings of control. A significant relationship between self-efficacy and accidents has also been reported (Cellar et al., 2004). This may relate to the potential role of perceived control in relation to occupational safety. Perceived control over safety (that is, the individual's belief that he or she is knowledgeable about safety and is capable of controlling his or her safety behavior) was found to correlate significantly with self-reported occupational injuries (Huang et al., 2004; Huang et al., 2006) and to fully mediate the effects of perceived safety climate on injuries (Huang et al., 2006). However, other studies have failed to demonstrate any correlation between perceived control over hazards and occupational injuries (Leiter, Zanaletti and Argentero, 2009).

Although relatively little research has examined the effects of self-esteem and self-efficacy on accidents, more studies have looked at the impact of LOC. Ng, Sorensen and Eby (2006) argue that an internal LOC is associated with the belief that outcomes can be controlled, and so, internals should possess a greater need for self-determination and competence than externals do. Thus, LOC is related to one's intrinsic motivation to dedicate effort to activities, with higher levels of motivation leading to better task performance (Judge and Bono, 2001). Internals are more likely to adopt a proactive approach to managing safety issues in the workplace and have a reduced vulnerability to accident involvement. In contrast, individuals with an external LOC are likely to believe that accidents are random events over which they have little control and, therefore, take a more laissez-faire attitude to safety. Furthermore, externals are less likely to prevent the development of stressful conditions and to be less proactive in the face of negative situations, making them more vulnerable to the negative effects of stress.

Externals take more risks in the workplace (Salminen and Klen, 1994), engage in higher levels of unsafe work behavior (Kuo and Tsaur, 2004) and are more accident-involved (Janicak, 1996; Jones and Wuebker, 1993). Generally, stronger relationships have been reported in relation to work accidents, rather than traffic accidents. A meta-analysis of traffic accidents (Arthur, Barrett and Alexander, 1991) found that LOC had a small-moderate effect on accident liability, suggesting that those with a more external LOC were more accident-involved. In a meta-analysis of nine occupational studies, although they did not look at the effect on occupational accidents or injuries, Christian et al. (2009) found that LOC had a moderate effect ($\rho = .35$) with safety performance at work; this effect was stronger with safety participation ($\rho = .43$) than with safety compliance ($\rho = .25$). Therefore, internals have a tendency to participate in safety-related activities and also to follow safety rules and regulations. Safety participation includes: engaging in safety activities, making safety suggestions, helping co-workers, monitoring others' behavior, and catching mistakes. It reflects a more proactive approach to safety than just following safety rules and requires the belief that engaging in such activities will affect the level of safety in the workplace.

Given that an internal LOC is related to enhanced motivation and task performance (Ng, Sorenson and Eby, 2006), this would be consistent with the behavior of internals and also research that has linked LOC with citizenship behavior, such as initiative performance (Blau, 1993). In relation to safety behavior, Neal and Griffin (2006) found that motivation leads to increased safety participation, which in turn further increases motivation, thus acting as a positive spiral. Self-efficacy may also be associated with safety participation, given that it has a significant association with proactive behavior (that is, showing initiative in developing new ideas and solving problems; Parker, Williams and Turner, 2006) and making improvement suggestions (Axtell et al., 2000). Ng, Sorenson and Eby (2006) argue that LOC is related to attitudinal and behavioral outcomes at work via three main cognitive processes: self-evaluation of well-being, internal motivation, and a cognitive orientation of maintaining active behavioral control. Positive self-evaluations are likely to be reflected in general well-being and affective reactions (such as job satisfaction). Judge, Heller and Mount (2002) found in their meta-analysis that emotional stability was related to job satisfaction at 0.29; Ng,Sorenson and Eby (2006) found that LOC was related to job satisfaction at 0.33. Meta-analytic correlations between job satisfaction and safety behavior (ρ = .29) and occupational accidents (ρ = .16) have been reported; whilst, using structural equation modeling, safety behavior was found to mediate the relationship between job satisfaction and occupational accidents (Clarke, 2010). In addition, general well-being acted as a direct predictor of occupational accidents (ρ = .13). Therefore, CSE may act as a protective factor in relation to accident involvement as it leads to better general well-being and job satisfaction, more internal motivation and tendency to take active control of the environment, including safety participation.

Overall, CSE may potentially play an important role in occupational safety. In particular, CSE may be related to individuals' willingness to engage in safety activities, as well as acting as a protective factor in relation to accident involvement. This conclusion may relate most specifically to the more conscious aspects of CSE (self-esteem, self-efficacy, and LOC), rather than emotional stability. There is consistent evidence that neuroticism increases accident liability through increased vulnerability to stress and error-proneness. This may relate to the emotional aspects of neuroticism, that is, the fundamental tendency to experience negative emotions, such as anxiety and worry.

Accident Proneness—An Individual Difference Variable?

The concept of "accident proneness" suggests that relatively stable and enduring individual differences account for accident liability, rather than temporary or situational factors. In evaluating the evidence to support an individual difference explanation for differential accident liability, empirical studies which include both situational (or organizational) factors and personal/dispositional factors are useful; however, they are also comparatively rare.

Within occupational settings, a limited number of studies have compared the relative influence of situational and personal factors on occupational injuries or accidents (for example. Glasscock et al., 2006; Iverson and Erwin, 1997; Paul and Maiti, 2008). Iverson and Erwin (1997) examined quality of work life and dispositional variables (positive affectivity and negative affectivity) in relation to occupational injuries in a manufacturing plant. Three of the work variables were significant predictors of occupational injuries (routinization, $r = -.42$, supervisory support, $r = -.27$, and co-worker support, $r = -.27$) and both affectivity variables, PA ($r = -.32$) and NA ($r = .21$). Paul and Maiti (2008) developed a structural equation model based on sociotechnical and personal factors for miners. Regression coefficients demonstrated a significant effect for job stress (-.09) and "negative personality" (-.25) (which comprised impulsivity, negative affectivity, depression, and risk taking) on safe work behavior, which in turn was related to work injuries (-.14). Safety environment (.29), work hazards (-.09) and social support (.40) were all found to have significant effects on work injuries via safe work behavior. Glasscock et al. (2006) examined environmental stressors (psychological work demands: defined as demands on attention and task difficulty); safety LOC; Type A behavior pattern; perceived farm stressors (including time pressure and role conflict, but also farming-specific stressors, such as weather, problems with machinery, and economic concerns); stress symptoms; and, safety behavior.

Significant accident risk factors emerged as: perceived economic problems (OR = 2.14, 95% CI = 1.09-4.20, $p < .05$), farmer considers safety when purchasing equipment (OR = 2.34, 95% CI = 1.12-4.89, $p < .05$); and the interaction, safety checks by stress symptoms (OR = 7.01, 95% CI = 1.12-43.91, $p < .05$). The latter effect indicated that safety-related behavior (no regular safety checks) combined with high stress symptoms led to much greater accident risk. Personality factors did not emerge as significant risk factors for farming injuries. Overall, these studies indicate that stable and enduring personality factors tend to have moderate effects on occupational injuries (Iverson and Erwin, 1997; Paul and Maiti, 2008), although the study conducted by Glasscock et al. (2006) showed no significant effect for personality factors. However, in comparison, some situational factors were reported with moderate-large effect sizes. Similarly, Wallace and Chen (2006) measured both safety climate and conscientiousness in relation to safety compliance; conscientiousness was correlated ($r = .13$, $p <.05$), but safety climate had the stronger relationship ($r = .45$, $p < .01$).

The role of occupational stress has also been examined in relation to accident involvement. As noted by Glasscock et al. (2006), although personality factors did not emerge as significant risk factors, accident risk was most strongly predicted by stress-related factors. Hemingway and Smith (1999) demonstrated that occupational stressors were significantly predictive of reported injuries in a hospital setting; with organizational climate contributing no additional variance after controlling for occupational stressors. Fogarty and McKeon (2006) examined the role of organizational climate (including: demands, clarity, leadership, and goal congruence), individual morale, and personal distress in relation to medication errors by nurses in Australian hospitals. They found that all effects were mediated via procedural violations; organizational climate had a distal effect, with personal distress and morale directly affecting violations. Whilst it is possible to gain some appreciation of the relative importance of situational and dispositional factors, the lack of research examining possible interactive effects means that there remains limited understanding of the underlying psychological mechanisms.

The importance of stress as a risk factor in accidents has been long-recognized, although the mechanisms underlying this relationship are not well-understood (Clarke and Cooper, 2004). For example, Legree et al. (2003) found that the strongest correlations with driver at-fault accidents were: emotional state (stressed vs. calm) and heightened stress due to life events ($r = -.22$ and $-.23$ respectively, both $p < .01$). Opponents of the accident-proneness concept argued that accidents occur due to transient factors (such as life stress) rather than stable and enduring traits (for example, Cresswell and Froggatt, 1963). If this were the case, as argued by McKenna (1983), psychological tests could have a stronger association with accidents than accidents themselves:

> *The importance of this finding is that it would question the long and generally held belief that it is impossible for a psychological test to correlate higher with accidents than accidents correlate with themselves. It has been assumed that if accident involvement is not a stable phenomenon then it cannot be studied. This is not necessarily true. In other words, it would still be possible to study differential accident involvement even if those who were involved in accidents at one point in time were not involved at another.*
>
> (McKenna, 1983, p. 69).

However, considering stress to be just a transient influence underestimates the influence of personality factors in the stress process, including exposure, reactivity, choice, and effectiveness (Bolger and Zuckerman, 1995). Personality traits can influence the likelihood of encountering stressors (exposure); the extent to which stressors result in strain (reactivity); selection of strategies for coping with stressors (choice); and, the extent to which coping is successful (effectiveness). Thus, whilst periods of acute stress (due to either work or life events) can have a temporary detrimental effect on cognitive and emotional functioning, dispositional factors, such as personality traits, will have an enduring effect on the stress process—and accident liability—over time.

It would seem possible to have both a set of stable influences on accident liability (such as personality and cognitive ability) as well as transient factors (such as stressors, emotional states, and psychological strain). Differential accident involvement might be described as both a stable and a transient phenomenon, where we need to understand both sets of factors (and the interaction between them) in order to understand accident liability. Furthermore, we need to have an understanding of the time-based mechanisms of the impact of stressors (cf. Griffin and Clarke, 2011) in order to appreciate the impact of stressors on accident involvement. For example, Frese and Zapf (1988) identified a number of potential models to describe the stress process over time—such as the dynamic accumulation model, where strain continues to increase, even after the stressors which caused the initial response have been removed. This model would suggest that one is not simply more vulnerable to accidents specifically when "under stress."

Furthermore, as noted earlier, stable and transient factors cannot be considered as independent, certain personality traits (such as neuroticism) predispose one to react more negatively to stressors, adopt maladaptive coping strategies, and place oneself in more stressful situations. Furthermore, research has shown that best predictor of behavior may be the interaction between state and trait (Rusting, 1998), prompting the need for research that includes mood states as well as dispositional factors to investigate how these factors influence cognitive and emotional functioning (and so the implications for accident involvement). For example, there is evidence that when moods and traits are consistent (for example, an extravert in a positive mood state, or a neurotic in a negative mood state) that this can aid information-processing and so task performance (Tamir, Robinson, and Clore, 2002; Tamir and Robinson, 2004).

Practical Implications for Organizations

There is consistent evidence that accidents are not random events that are evenly distributed across individuals. However, it is clear that simply analyzing accident records to identify accident repeaters and remove them from the workplace, or place them in situations of low risk, is unlikely to be a successful strategy. From a psychological perspective, the literature shows that the propensity for errors and violations will contribute substantially to an individual's susceptibility to accidents, but that this cannot be simply accounted for in terms of demographics (for example, young men are particularly prone to accidents due to immaturity and rash behavior) or "accident proneness" (defined as a stable and enduring personality trait). Experience is an important factor in relation to accidents—thus, there remains a need to support inexperienced workers with adequate task-related and safety training.

Nevertheless, an overview of individual difference variables associated with increased accident liability has emphasized that possessing certain personality traits does indeed increase one's likelihood of becoming involved in accidents across domains. In relation to workplace accidents, some personality traits—particularly neuroticism, (low) conscientiousness and (low) agreeableness—increase the likelihood of work accidents. There is also evidence that these personality traits act indirectly through psychological mechanisms to affect accident liability: primarily, cognitive failures/error-proneness, violations/non-compliance, risk taking, and increased reactivity to stress. However, relatively little research has focused on how personality traits may interact to increase or decrease vulnerability to accidents. Although some combinations of personality traits, such as low Ag/high N and high N/low Cs, may be particularly associated with accident liability, there is currently insufficient research to design a battery of personality tests to detect "accident proneness" as part of selection procedures.

Personality traits can influence the likelihood of encountering stressors (exposure); the extent to which stressors result in strain (reactivity); selection of strategies for coping with stressors (choice); and, the extent to which coping is successful (effectiveness). Thus, whilst periods of acute stress (due to either work or life events) can have a temporary detrimental effect on cognitive and emotional functioning, dispositional factors, such as personality traits, will have an enduring effect on the stress process—and accident liability—over time. Richardson and Rothstein (2008) found that interventions that aimed to help participants to build personal resources and improve stress management skills can be highly effective.

Such interventions should be considered as part of wider initiatives to improve both health and safety, rather than as a targeted stress reduction program in isolation. In addition, training passive employees to become more proactive (using more active coping strategies and building individuals' ability to manage demands confidently) can help those individuals cope more effectively with stress and so reduce their accident liability. Strategies could also seek to increase employees' perceived control so that they can cope more effectively (Spector, 1998).

In addition to personality traits captured within the "Big Five" taxonomy, CSE may potentially play an important role in occupational safety. In particular, CSE is related to individuals' safety participation, as well as acting as a protective factor in relation to accident involvement. This conclusion relates most specifically to the more conscious aspects of CSE (self-esteem, self-efficacy, and LOC), rather than emotional stability. For low scorers on CSE, improvements may be achieved through enhancing individuals' perceptions of control; for example cultivating interpersonal relationships (using mentoring or group cohesion) can enable employees with an external LOC (and low self-esteem/self-efficacy) to trust colleagues to help them maintain control at work (Ng, Sorenson and Eby, 2006).

Training can also be useful in building employees' perceptions of their own capability, in terms of self-efficacy (Parker, Williams and Turner, 2006) and their control beliefs (Meier et al., 2008). The purpose of such interventions is to enable individuals to increase their perceptions of control in the workplace and so encourage them to engage in more safety-related activities. Whilst safety compliance is linked to reduced organizational accident rates, safety participation has the stronger effect in terms of accident reduction (Clarke, 2006). Thus, whilst enforcing safety rules is important, safety improvement should not be reliant upon safety compliance, but should aim to foster a safety culture which encourages safety participation as well as compliance.

Situational factors still account for a greater proportion of the variance in accidents than personality factors; however, current estimates are likely to underestimate the effect of personality factors, given that interactions between personality and situational factors have not been considered to date, and the pervasive influence of personality traits in the stress process. This would imply that global safety interventions, based on the assumption that all employees will respond to the intervention in the same way, are likely to encounter problems based on the influence of individual differences. A more successful strategy might involve discretionary variations by local managers who can implement more individualized measures based on their understanding of the workforce. Such understanding is likely built on trust between managers and their employees within a positive safety climate.

References

af Wåhlberg, A. and Dorn, L. (2009) Bus driver accident record: The return of accident proneness, *Theoretical Issues in Ergonomics Science*; *10*(1), 77–91.

Arbous, A.G. and Kerrich, J.E. (1951) Accident statistics and the concept of accident proneness, *Biometrics*; *7*(4), 340–432.

Arthur, W., Barrett, G.V., and Alexander, R.A. (1991) Prediction of vehicular accident involvement: A meta-analysis, *Human Performance*; *4*(2), 89–105.

Arthur, W. and Doverspike, D. (2001) Predicting motor vehicle crash involvement from a personality measure and a driving knowledge test, *Journal of Prevention and Intervention in the Community*; *22*(1), 35–42.

Arthur, W. and Graziano, W.G. (1996) The five-factor model, conscientiousness, and driving accident involvement, *Journal of Personality*; *64*(3), 593–618.

Arthur, W., Strong, M.H., and Williamson, J. (1994) Validation of a visual attention test as a predictor of driving accident involvement, *Journal of Occupational and Organisational Psychology*; *67*(2), 173–182.

Avolio, B.J., Kroeck, K.G., and Panek, P.E. (1985) Individual differences in information processing ability as a predictor of motor vehicle accidents, *Human Factors*; *27*(5), 577–587.

Axtell, C.M., Holman, D.J., Unsworth, K.L., Wall, T.D., Waterson, P.E., and Harrington, E. (2000) Shop floor innovation: Facilitating the suggestion and implementation of ideas, *Journal of Occupational and Organizational Psychology*; *73*(3), 265–285.

Barrick, M.R. and Mount, M.K. (1991) The big five personality dimensions and job performance: A meta-analysis, *Personnel Psychology*; *44*(1), 1–26.

Blasco, R.D., Prieto, J.M., and Cornejo, J.M. (2003) Accident probability after accident occurrence, *Safety Science*; *41*(6), 481–501.

Blau, G. (1993) Testing the relationship of locus of control to different performance dimensions, *Journal of Occupational and Organizational Psychology*; *66*(2), 125–138.

Bolger, N. and Zuckerman, A. (1995) A framework for studying personality in the stress process, *Journal of Personality and Social Psychology*; *69*(5), 890–902.

Bosma, H., Stansfeld, S.A., and Marmot, M.G. (1998) Job control, personal characteristics, and heart disease, *Journal of Occupational Health Psychology*; *3*(4), 402–409.

Broadbent, D.E., Broadbent, M.H.P., and Jones. J.L. (1986) Performance correlates of self-reported cognitive failure and of obsessionality, *British Journal of Clinical Psychology*; *25*(4), 285–299.

Broadbent, D.E., Cooper, P.F., FitzGerald, P., and Parkes, K.R. (1982) The Cognitive Failures Questionnaire (CFQ) and its correlates, *British Journal of Clinical Psychology*; *21*(1), 1–16.

Brown, I.D. (1990) Drivers' margins of safety considered as a focus for research on error, *Ergonomics*; *33*(10–11), 1307–1314.

Burnham, J.C. (2008) The syndrome of accident proneness (Unfallneigung): Why psychiatrists did not adopt and medicalize it, *History of Psychiatry*; *19*(3), 251–274.

Cellar, D.F., Yorke, C.M., Nelson, Z.C., and Carroll, K.A. (2004) Relationships between five factor personality variables, workplace accidents, and self-efficacy, *Psychological Reports*; *94*(3), 1437–1441.

Chang, H-L. and Yeh, T-H. (2007) Motorcyclist accident involvement by age, gender, and risky behaviors in Taipei, Taiwan, *Transportation Research Part F: Traffic Psychology and Behaviour*; *10*(2), 109–122.

Christian, M.S., Bradley, J.C., Wallace, J.C., and Burke, M.J. (2009) Workplace safety: A meta-analysis of the roles of person and situation factors, *Journal of Applied Psychology*; *94*(5), 1103–1127.

Clarke, S. (2006) The relationship between safety climate and safety performance: A meta-analytic review, *Journal of Occupational Health Psychology*; *11*(4), 315–327.

Clarke, S. (2010) An integrative model of safety climate: Linking psychological climate and work attitudes to individual safety outcomes using meta-analysis. *Journal of Occupational and Organizational Psychology*; 83(3), 553–578.

Clarke, S. and Cooper, C.L. (2004) *Managing the Risk of Workplace Stress: Health and Safety Hazards*. London, UK: Routledge.

Clarke, S. and Robertson, I.T. (2005) A meta-analytic review of the big five personality factors and accident involvement in occupational and non-occupational settings, *Journal of Occupational and Organisational Psychology*; *78*(3), 355–376.

Conger, J.J., Gaskill, H.S., Glad, D.D., Hassell, L., Rainey, R.V., and Sawrey, W.L. (1959) Psychological and psychophysical factors in motor vehicle accidents, *Journal of the American Medical Association*; *169*(14), 1581–1587.

Cresswell, W.L. and Froggatt, P. (1963) *The Causation of Bus Driver Accidents: An Epidemiological study*. London, UK: Oxford University Press.

Davids, A. and Mahoney, J.T. (1957) Personality dynamics and accident proneness in an industrial setting, *Journal of Applied Psychology*; *41*(5), 303–309.

Deffenbacher, J.L., Oetting, E.R., and Lynch, R.S. (1994) Development of a driving anger scale, *Psychological Reports*; *74*(1), 83–91.

Derryberry, D., Reed, M.A., and Pilkenton-Taylor, C. (2003) Temperament and coping: Advantages of an individual differences perspective, *Development and Psychopathology; 15*(4), 1049–1066.

Edkins, G.D. and Pollock, C.M. (1997) The influence of sustained attention on railway accidents, *Accident Analysis and Prevention*; *29*(4), 533–539.

Farmer, E. and Chambers, E.G. (1926) *A Psychological Study of Individual Differences in Accident Liability*. Industrial Fatigue Research Board Report no. 38, London, UK: HMSO.

Fogarty, G.J. and McKeon, C.M. (2006) Patient safety during medication administration: The influence of organizational and individual variables on unsafe work practices and medication errors, *Ergonomics*; *49*(5–6), 444–456.

Forster, S. and Lavie, N. (2008) Failures to ignore entirely irrelevant distractors: The role of load, *Journal of Experimental Psychology: Applied*; *14*(1), 73–83.

French, D.J., West, R.J., Elander, J., and Wilding, J.M. (1993) Decision-making style, driving style, and self-reported involvement in road traffic accidents, *Ergonomics*; *36*(6), 627–644.

Frese, M. and Zapf, D. (1988) Methodological issues in the study of work stress: Objective vs. subjective measurement of work stress and the question of longitudinal studies. In C.L. Cooper and R. Payne (eds) *Causes, Coping, and Consequences of Stress at Work*, Chichester, UK: Wiley, 375–411.

George, J.M., and Brief, A.P. (1992) Feeling good-doing good: A conceptual analysis of the mood at work-organizational spontaneity relationship, *Psychological Bulletin*; *112*(2), 310–329.

Glasscock, D.J., Rasmussen, K., Carstensen, O., and Hansen, O.N. (2006) Psychosocial factors and safety behaviour as predictors of accidental work injuries in farming, *Work and Stress*; *20*(2), 173–189.

Gottfredson, L.S. (2004) Life, death, and intelligence, *Journal of Cognitive Education and Psychology*; *4*(1), 23–46.

Grant, S. and Langan-Fox, J. (2006) Occupational stress, coping and strain: The combined/interactive effect of the Big Five traits, *Personality and Individual Differences*; *41*(4), 719–732.

Greenwood, M. and Woods, H.M. (1919) *The Incidence of Industrial Accidents upon Individuals with Special Reference to Multiple Accidents*. Report no. 4. London, UK: Industrial Fatigue Research Board.

Greenwood, M. and Yule, G.U. (1920) An enquiry into the nature of the frequency distributions representative of multiple happenings, with particular reference to the occurrence of multiple attacks of disease or repeated accidents, *Journal of the Royal Statistical Society*; *83*(2), 255–279.

Griffin, M.A. & Clarke, S. (2011) Stress and well-being at work. In: S. Zedeck (ed) *APA Handbook of Industrial & Organizational Psychology*. Volume 3: Maintaining, Expanding and Contracting the Organization'. Washington DC: American Psychological Association, 359–397.

Groeneweg, J. (1992) *Controlling the Controllable: The Management of Safety*. Leiden, Netherlands: DSWO Press.

Hakkinen, S. (1958) *Traffic Accidents and Driver Characteristics: A Statistical and Psychological Study*. Finland's Institute of Technology, Scientific Researches, No. 13, Helsinki.

Hansen, C.P. (1988) Personality characteristics of the accident involved employee, *Journal of Business and Psychology*, *2*(4), 346–65.

Hansen, C.P. (1989) A causal model of the relationship among accidents, biodata, personality and cognitive factors, *Journal of Applied Psychology*; *74*(1), 81–90.

Hemingway, M.A. and Smith, C.S. (1999) Organisational climate and occupational stressors as predictors of withdrawal behaviours and injuries in nurses, *Journal of Occupational and Organisational Psychology; 72*(3), 285–299.

Higgins, E.T. (1997) Beyond pleasure and pain, *American Psychologist*; *52*(12), 1280–1300.

Hough, L.M. (1992) The 'Big Five' personality variables—construct confusion: Description versus prediction, *Human Performance*; *5*(1–2), 139–155.

Huang, Y-H., Chen, P.Y., Krauss, A.D., and Rogers, D.A. (2004) Quality of the execution of corporate safety policies and employee safety outcomes: Assessing the moderating role of supervisor safety support and the mediating role of employee safety control, *Journal of Business and Psychology*; *18*(4), 483–506.

Huang, Y-H., Ho, M., Smith, G.S., and Chen, P.Y. (2006) Safety climate and self-reported injury: Assessing the mediating role of employee safety control, *Accident Analysis and Prevention*; *38*(3), 425–433.

Irwin, J.O. (1964) The personal factor in accidents: A review article, *Journal of the Royal Statistical Society*; *127*(3), 438–451.

Iverson, R.D. and Erwin, P.J. (1997) Predicting occupational injury: The role of affectivity, *Journal of Occupational and Organisational Psychology*; 70(2), 113–128.

Janicak, C.A. (1996) Predicting accidents at work with measures of locus of control and job hazards, *Psychological Reports*; *78*(1), 115–121.

Johnson, R.E., Rosen, C.C., and Levy, P.E. (2008) Getting to the core of self-evaluation: A review and recommendations, *Journal of Organizational Behavior*; *29*(3), 391–413.

Jonah, B.A. (1997) Sensation seeking and risky driving. In T. Rothengatter and E. Carbonell Vaya (eds.) *Traffic and transport psychology: Theory and application*, Oxford, UK: Pergamon, 259–267.

Jones, J.W. and Wuebker, L.J. (1993) Safety locus of control and employees' accidents, *Journal of Business and Psychology*; *7*(4), 449–457.

Judge, T.A. (1993) Does affective disposition moderate the relationship between job satisfaction and voluntary turnover?, *Journal of Applied Psychology*; *78*(3), 395–401.

Judge, T.A. and Bono, J.E. (2001) Relationship of core self-evaluations traits—self-esteem, generalized self efficacy, locus of control, and emotional stability—with job satisfaction and job performance: A meta-analysis, *Journal of Applied Psychology*; *86*(1), 80–92.

Judge, T.A., Erez, A., Bono, J.E., and Thoresen, C.J. (2003) The core self-evaluations scale: Development of a measure, *Personnel Psychology*; *56*(2), 303–331.

Judge, T.A., Heller, D., and Mount, M.K. (2002) Five-Factor Model of personality and job satisfaction: A meta-analysis, *Journal of Applied Psychology*; *87*(3), 530–541.

Judge, T.A., Locke, E.A., and Durham, C.C. (1997) The dispositional causes of job satisfaction: A core-evaluations approach, *Research in Organizational Behavior*; *19*, 151–188.

Judge, T.A., Locke, E.A., Durham, C.C., and Kluger, A.N. (1998) Dispositional effects on job and life satisfaction: The role of core evaluations, *Journal of Applied Psychology*; *83*, 17–34.

Judge, T.A., Van Vianen, A.E.M., and De Pater, I.E. (2004) Emotional stability, core self-evaluations, and job outcomes: A review of the evidence and an agenda for future research, *Human Performance*; *17*, 325–346.

Kaplan, S., Bradley, J.C., Luchman, J.N., and Haynes, D. (2009) On the role of positive and negative affectivity in job performance: A meta-analytic investigation, *Journal of Applied Psychology*; *94*(1), 162–176.

Keehn, J.D. (1961) Accident tendency, avoidance learning and perceptual defense, *Australian Journal of Psychology*; *13*(2), 157–169.

Koelega, H.S. (1992) Extraversion and vigilance: 30 years of inconsistencies, *Psychological Bulletin*; *112*(2), 239–258.

Kowert, P.A. and Hermann, M.G. (1997) Who takes risks? Daring and caution in foreign policy making, *Journal of Conflict Resolution*; *41*(4), 611–637.

Kuo, C-C. and Tsaur, C-C. (2004) Locus of control, supervisory support and unsafe behaviour: The case of construction industry in Taiwan, *Chinese Journal of Psychology*; *46*(3), 293–305.

Langford, J., Methorst, R. and Hakamies-Blomqvist, L. (2006) Older drivers do not have a high crash risk: A replication of low mileage bias, *Accident Analysis and Prevention*; *38*(3), 574–578.

Langham, M., Hole, G., Edwards, J. and O'Neil, C. (2002) An analysis of 'looked but failed to see' accidents involving parked police cars, *Ergonomics*; *45*(4), 167–185.

Larson, G.E., Alderton, D.L., Neideffer, M. and Underhill, E. (1997) Further evidence on dimensionality and correlates of the Cognitive Failures Questionnaire, *British Journal of Psychology*; *88*(1), 29–38.

Larson, G.E. and Merritt, C.R. (1991) Can accidents be predicted? An empirical test of the Cognitive Failures Questionnaire, *Applied Psychology: An International Review*; *40*(1), 37–45.

Legree, P.J., Heffner, T.S., Psotka, J., Medsker, G.J. and Martin, D.E. (2003) Traffic crash involvement: Experiential driving knowledge and stressful contextual antecedents, *Journal of Applied Psychology*; *88*(1), 15–26.

Leiter, M.P., Zanaletti, W. and Argentero, P. (2009) Occupational risk perception, safety training, and injury prevention: Testing a model in the Italian printing industry, *Journal of Occupational Health Psychology; 14*(1), 1–10.

Li, G., Braver, E. and Chen, L. (2003) Fragility versus excessive crash involvement as determinants of high death rates per vehicle-mile of travel among older drivers, *Accident Analysis and Prevention; 35*(2), *227*–235.

Marbe, K. (1926) *Praktische Psychologie der Unfälle und Betriebsschäden.* Munich, Germany: R. Oldenbourg.

McKenna, F.P. (1983) Accident proneness: A conceptual analysis, *Accident Analysis and Prevention; 15*(1), 65–71.

McKenna, F.P., Duncan, J., and Brown, I.D. (1986) Cognitive abilities and safety on the road: A re-examination of individual differences in dichotic listening and search for embedded figures, *Ergonomics; 29*(5), 649–663.

McKnight, A.J. and McKnight, A.S (2003) Young novice drivers: Careless or clueless?, *Accident Analysis and Prevention; 35*(6), 921–923.

Meier, L.L., Semmer, N.K., Elfering, A., and Jacobshagen, N. (2008) The double meaning of control: Three-way interactions between internal resources, job control, and stressors at work, *Journal of Occupational Health Psychology; 13*(3), 244–258.

Merckelbach, H., Muris, P., Nijman, H., and de Jong, P. J. (1996) Self-reported cognitive failures and neurotic symptomatology, *Personality and Individual Differences; 20*(6), 715–724.

Mesken, J., Lajunen, T., and Summala, H. (2002) Interpersonal violations, speeding violations and their relation to accident involvement in Finland, *Ergonomics; 45*(7), 469–483.

Miller, J.D., Lynam, D.R. and Jones, S. (2008) Externalizing behavior through the lens of the five-factor model: A focus on agreeableness and conscientiousness, *Journal of Personality Assessment; 90*(2), 158–164.

Nabi, H., Consoli, S.M., Chastang, J-F., Chiron, M., Lafont, S., and Lagarde, E. (2005) Type A behavior pattern, risky driving behaviors, and serious road traffic accidents: A prospective study of the GAZEL cohort, *American Journal of Epidemiology; 161*(9), 864–870.

Neal, A. and Griffin, M.A. (2006) A study of the lagged relationships among safety climate, safety motivation, safety behaviour, and accidents at the individual and group levels, *Journal of Applied Psychology; 91*(4), 946–953.

Newbold, E.M. (1926) A contribution to the study of the human factor in the causation of accidents. Industrial Health Research Board, London, no. 34. Reproduced in W. Haddon. E.A. Suchman and D. Klein, (eds) *Accident Research.* New York, NY: Harper & Row, 397–410.

Ng, T.W.H., Sorensen, K.L. and Eby, L.T. (2006) Locus of control at work: a meta-analysis, *Journal of Organizational Behavior; 27*(8), 1057–1087.

Nicholson, N., Soane, E., Fenton-O'Creevy, M., and Willman, P. (2005) Domain specific risk taking and personality, *Journal of Risk Research; 8*(2), 157–176.

Ode, S., Robinson, M.D. and Wilkowski, B.M. (2008) Can one's temper be cooled? A role for agreeableness in moderating Neuroticism's influence on anger and aggression, *Journal of Research in Personality; 42*(2), 295–311.

Parker, S.K., Williams, H.M., and Turner, N. (2006) Modeling the antecedents of proactive behavior at work, *Journal of Applied Psychology; 91*(3), 636–652.

Paul, P.S. and Maiti, J. (2008) The synergic role of sociotechnical and personal characteristics on work injuries in mines, *Ergonomics; 51*(5), 737–767.

Perkins, A.M. and Corr, P.J. (2006) Cognitive ability as a buffer to neuroticism: Churchill's secret weapon?, *Personality and Individual Differences; 40*(1), 39–51.

Porter, C.S. (1988) Accident proneness: A review of the concept. In D.J. Oborne (ed.) *International Reviews of Ergonomics: Current Trends in Human Factors Research and Practice (Volume 2),* London, UK: Taylor & Francis, 177–206.

Rast, P., Zimprich, D., Van Boxtel, M. and Jolles, J. (2009) Factor structure and measurement invariance of the cognitive failures questionnaire across the adult life span, *Assessment; 16*(2), 145–158.

Reason, J. (1988) Stress and cognitive failure. In S. Fisher and J. Reason (eds) *Handbook of Life Stress, Cognition and Health.* New York, NY: John Wiley.

Reason, J.T. (1990) *Human Error.* Cambridge, UK: Cambridge University Press.

Reason, J.T., Manstead, A.S.R., Stradling, S.G., Baxter, J., and Campbell, K. (1990) Errors and violations on the road: A real distinction?, *Ergonomics; 33*(10–11), 1315–1332.

Reason, J.T. and Mycielska, K. (1982) *Absent-minded? The Psychology of Mental Lapses and Everyday Errors.* Englewood Cliffs, NJ: Prentice-Hall.

Richardson, K.M. and Rothstein, H.R. (2008) Effects of occupational stress management intervention programs: A meta-analysis, *Journal of Occupational Health Psychology; 13*(1), 69-93.

Roy, G.S. and Choudhary, R.K. (1985) Driver control as a factor in road safety. *Asian Journal of Psychology and Education; 16*(3), 33–37.

Rusting, C.L. (1998) Personality, mood, and cognitive processing of emotional information: Three conceptual frameworks, *Psychological Bulletin; 124*(2), 165–196.

Sah, A.P. (1989) Personality characteristics of accident free and accident involved Indian railway drivers, *Journal of Personality & Clinical Studies; 5*(2), 203–206.

Salgado, J.F. (1997) The five factor model of personality and job performance in the European community, *Journal of Applied Psychology; 82*(1), 30–43.

Salgado, J.F. (1998) Big Five personality dimensions and job performance in army and civil occupations: A European perspective, *Human Performance; 11*(2–3), 271–288.

Salgado, J.F. (2002) The Big Five personality dimensions and counterproductive behaviours, *International Journal of Selection and Assessment; 10*(1–2), 117–125.

Salminen, S. and Klen, T. (1994) Accident locus of control and risk taking among forestry and construction workers, *Perceptual and Motor Skills; 78*(3), 852–854.

Shaw, L. and Sichel, H.S. (1971) *Accident Proneness.* Oxford, UK: Pergamon.

Simpson, S.A., Wadsworth, E.J.K., Moss, S.C. and Smith, A.P. (2005) Minor injuries, cognitive failures and accidents at work: Incidence and associated features, *Occupational Medicine; 55*, 99–108.

Smeed, R.J. (1960) Proneness of drivers to road accidents, *Nature*; 186, 273–275.

Smith, D.I. and Kirkham, R.W. (1981) Relationship between some personality characteristics and driving record. *British Journal of Social Psychology; 20*(4), 229–231.

Smith, D.L. and Heckert, T.M. (1998) Personality characteristics and traffic accidents of college students, *Journal of Safety Research; 29*(3), 163–169.

Soane, E. and Chmiel, N. (2005) Are risk preferences consistent? The influence of decision domain and personality, *Personality and Individual Differences; 38*(8), 1781–1791.

Spector, P.E. (1998) A control theory of the job stress process. In C.L. Cooper (ed.), *Theories of organizational stress.* Oxford, UK: Oxford University Press, 153–169.

Staw, B. M. and Barsade, S.G. (1993) Affect and managerial performance: A test of the sadder-but wiser vs. happier and smarter hypotheses, *Administrative Science Quarterly; 38*(2), 304–331.

Steffy, B.D., Jones, J.W., Murphy, L.R., and Kunz, L. (1986) A demonstration of the impact of stress abatement programs on reducing employees' accidents and their costs, *American Journal of Health Promotion; 1*(2), 25–32.

Tamir, M. and Robinson, M.D. (2004) Knowing good from bad: The paradox of neuroticism, negative affect, and evaluative processing, *Journal of Personality and Social Psychology*; *87*(6), 913–925.

Tamir, M., Robinson, M.D., and Clore, G. L. (2002) The epistemic benefits of trait-consistent mood states: An analysis of extraversion and mood, *Journal of Personality and Social Psychology; 83*(3), 663–677.

Tett, R.P., Jackson, D.N., and Rothstein, M. (1991) Personality measures as predictors of job performance: A meta-analytic review, *Personnel Psychology*; *44*(4), 703–742.

Thiffault, P. and Bergeron, J. (2003) Fatigue and individual differences in monotonous simulated driving, *Personality and Individual Differences*; *34*(1), 159–176.

Verwey, W.B., and Zaidel, D.M. (2000) Predicting drowsiness accidents from personal attributes, eye blinks and ongoing driving behaviour, *Personality and Individual Differences*; *28*(1), 123–142.

Visser, E., Pijl, Y.J., Stolk, R.P., Neeleman, J., and Rosmalen, J.G.M. (2007) Accident proneness, does it exist? A review and meta-analysis, *Accident Analysis and Prevention*; *39*(3), 556–564.

Vom Hofe, A., Mainemarre, G., and Vannier, L. (1998) Sensitivity to everyday failures and cognitive inhibition: Are they related?, *European Review of Applied Psychology; 48*(1), 49–55.

Wagenaar, W.A. and Groeneweg, J. (1987) Accidents at sea: Multiple causes and impossible consequences, *International Journal of Man-Machine Studies*; *27*(5–6), 587–598.

Wallace, C. and Chen, G. (2006) A multilevel integration of personality, climate, self-regulation, and performance, *Personnel Psychology*; *59*(3), 529–557.

Wallace, J.C. and Vodanovich, S.J. (2003a) Can accidents and industrial mishaps be predicted? Further investigation into the relationship between cognitive failure and reports of accidents, *Journal of Business and Psychology*; *17*(4), 503–514.

Wallace, J.C. and Vodanovich, S.J. (2003b) Workplace safety performance: Conscientiousness, cognitive failure, and their interaction, *Journal of Occupational Health Psychology; 8*(4), 316–327.

Watson, D. and Hubbard, B. (1996) Adaptational style and dispositional structure: Coping in the context of the five-factor model, *Journal of Personality*; *64*(4), 737–774.

West, R.J., Elander, J. and French, D. (1993) Mild social deviance, Type A behaviour pattern and decision-making style as predictors of self-reported driving style and traffic accident risk, *British Journal of Psychology*; *84*(2), 207–219.

CHAPTER 5 *Injury Proneness*

NEARKASEN CHAU

Every year, 120 million work-related injuries, 210,000 of them fatal, occur worldwide (International Labour Office, 1998). They have severe human and socioeconomic consequences (Caisse Nationale de l'Assurance Maladie des Travailleurs Salariés, 2005; Dembe, 2001) that may increase social inequalities in health (Khlat et al., 2008).

Occupational injuries are determined by working conditions and the ability of workers to deal with them. Working conditions include a wide range of job demands related to the particular tasks carried out, the workplace environment, issues regarding posture, the materials and tools used, organizational factors, and pressure from management to achieve production targets by working quickly (Chau et al., 2008b; Kunar, Bhattacherjee and Chau, 2008). Relevant characteristics of workers include job knowledge and experience, the physical and mental capability to do the work, the degree to which an individual observes and assesses occupational hazards, personality, and propensity toward risky behavior (Chau et al., 1995a; 2002; 2004c; 2007; 2008b; 2010; Gauchard et al., 2003; Khlat et al., 2008; Kunar, Bhattacherjee and Chau, 2008). Young age (<25–30 years) and older age (>40–50 years), health status, obesity, presence of diseases, disabilities, and also lifestyle factors such as smoking, alcohol abuse, psychotropic drug use, lack of sports and physical activities (leisure pursuits, and domestic activity including do-it-yourself and gardening) are well known to increase the injury risk among various populations (Chau et al., 2005b; 2009c; 2010; Gauchard et al., 2003).

Older age is associated with reduced physical strength and more disability (Chau et al., 2005b; Mathiowetz et al., 1985), leading to higher risk of injury, particularly among people carrying out the most demanding occupational activities or those that require greater strength or skill (Chau et al., 2009c; Khlat et al., 2008). The impact of older age on injury is a public health problem because of the lengthening of working life driven by the rise in life expectancy (Institut National de la Statistique et des Etudes Economiques, 2001), which results in more people working at an older age. Most disabilities arise during the working years, and progressively impact on a worker's capacity to do his or her job, leading to recurrent absenteeism and, in extreme cases, to dismissal and exclusion from the labor market. Within the context of the European Year of People with Disabilities 2003 (European Foundation for the Improvement of Living and Working Conditions, 2003), there has been a growing interest in supporting the participation of people with illnesses and disabilities in working life, in order to both promote social inclusion and meet the demand for labor (European Foundation for the Improvement of Living and Working Conditions, 2004).

Every year, young people start work lacking job knowledge and experience, and research has revealed them to be subject to a high risk of injury (Breslin et al., 2008; Cellier, Eyrolle and Bertrand, 1995; Chau et al., 2007; 2008b; Salminen, 2004). Many workers are confronted by rapid turnover, which leaves them with a lack of job knowledge and experience. Indeed, this issue affects people in most jobs and of different ages, and thus many older workers may accumulate disabilities and never acquire sufficient job knowledge and experience.

We need to understand and recognize the mechanisms through which these factors contribute to injury in order to identify potential targets for preventive measures and develop injury reduction programs that go beyond conventional methods by considering the various risks to which different occupational groups are subject. The present work reports on the roles of injury risk factors using data from a number of our previous studies that focused on injuries requiring sick leave in various working populations.

Role of Working Conditions

Working conditions are associated with a number of occupational hazards that can lead to job-related injury. One study in railway workers reported that environmental hazards were involved in 25 percent of injuries, technical malfunctions in 16 percent, inadequate organization in 14 percent, lack of know-how/job knowledge in 23 percent, and other human factors in 32 percent (Chau et al., 2007). The population of railway workers was chosen because it encompasses many jobs (mechanic, driver, maintenance worker, construction worker, painter, welder, boilermaker, manual worker, employee, manager, and so on) and covers a wide population for which the annual injury incidence rate is the same as for workers within the French general insurance scheme (Caisse Nationale de l'Assurance Maladie des Travailleurs Salariés, 2005).

A population-based study in France (Chau et al., 2008b) showed that many workers were exposed daily to a number of job demands including high physical workloads, having to use pneumatic tools, other vibrating hand-tools, hammers, machine-tools or vibrating platforms, and carrying out manual handling tasks. They can also be required to work in awkward postures, at a fast pace, at heights, in adverse weather, and in workplaces exposed to noise, cold, or heat. These demands were associated with a two- to five-fold higher risk for occupational injury (Figure 5.1) and concerned not only workmen (the group most at risk) but also people in a number of other jobs such as craftsmen, farmers, foremen, mechanics, and clerks. Principal component analysis showed that the demands were one-dimensional; the first eigenvalue was, at 2.64, markedly higher than the second and the third eigenvalues of 0.61 and 0.36, respectively (Falissard, 1998) and thus validated the use of their number as the measure "cumulative job demands" (CJD). In this study, we found that many workers are exposed to a number of job demands daily: CJD was 1 in 27 percent of subjects, 2–3 in 21 percent, and ≥4 in 12 percent.

We found a strong exposure-response relationship between the CJD score and injury: odds ratios (compared to a CJD of 0) were 1.9 when CJD was 1, 4.4 for a CJD of 2–3, and 9.9 for a CJD ≥4. Note that the odds ratio is an approximation of the relative risk. The ratios remained high when controlling for potential confounders (age, gender, smoking habit, alcohol abuse, presence of diseases, reported fatigue, job category): 1.5 with a CJD of 1; 3.0 with a CJD of 2–3; and 5.4 with a CJD of ≥4.

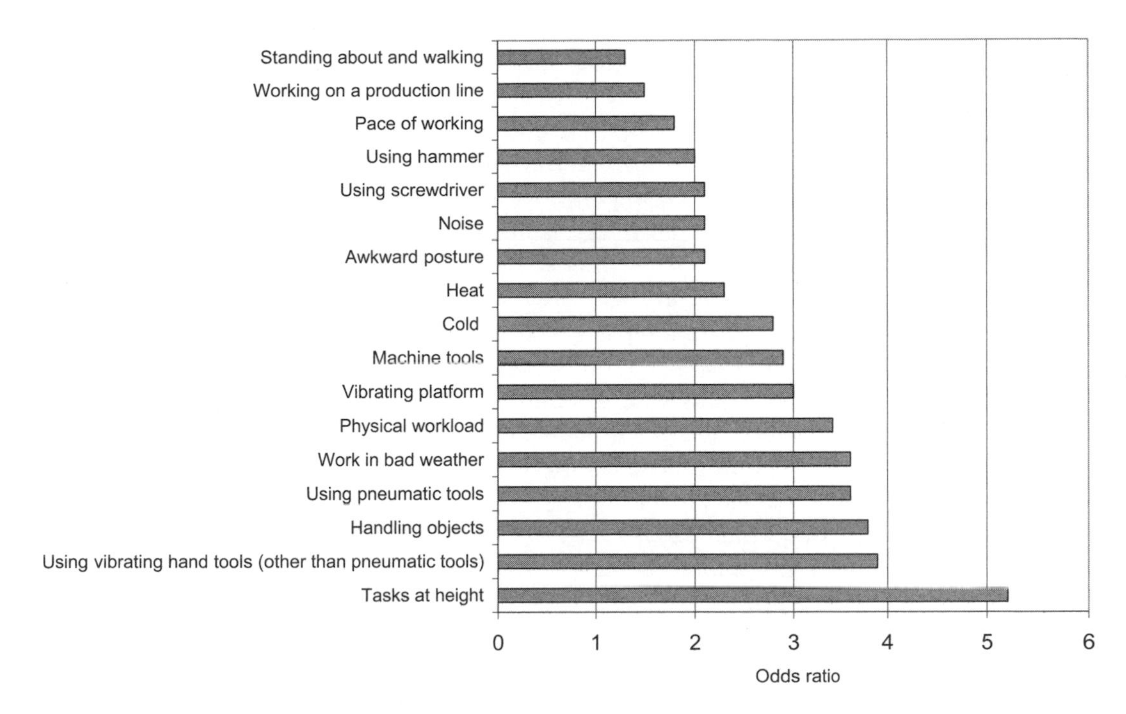

Figure 5.1 Increasing risk of occupational injury associated with high job demands

It should be noted that these job demands strongly related to psychosomatic disorders (Lorhandicap Group, 2004), physical and cognitive functional limitations (Chau, Khlat and the Lorhandicap Group, 2009c), and premature mortality (before 65 or 70 years of age) (Bourgkard et al., 2008). Consequently, they increased social inequality, particularly in health (Chau et al., 2009c; Dahlgren and Whitehead, 2006; Khlat et al., 2008).

Hand tool- and material handling-related hazards affect many workers in various industries. They represented the greatest risk factors among for example Indian coal miners (adjusted odds ratios of about 4) while hazards related to use of machines, environmental/working conditions, and geological/strata control were associated with a two-fold higher risk (Kunar, Bhattacherjee and Chau, 2008).

Role of Lifestyle and Other Individual Characteristics

Research over recent decades has shown that poor health status, poor living conditions, and unhealthy lifestyle, especially smoking, alcohol use, psychotropic drug use, overweight/obesity, fatigue, sleep disorders, musculoskeletal disorders, other diseases, and disabilities, are common and are associated with a higher risk of occupational injury (Chau et al., 2004c; Gauchard et al., 2001; Gauchard et al., 2003; Harma et al., 1998; McCaig, Burt and Stussman, 1998; Simon-Rigaud, 1995; Sprince et al., 2002; Wells and Macdonald, 1999; Zwerling et al., 1997). Indeed, they impair a worker's physical and mental abilities, particularly in task performance and in identifying and assessing occupational hazards. Lower socioeconomic categories are also associated with an increased injury risk, even when controlling for job demands (Chau et al., 2008b) because they are associated with impoverished living conditions, unhealthy lifestyle, and poor health status (Dahlgren and Whitehead, 2006; Galea, Nandi and Vlahov, 2004; Khlat et al., 2008).

Table 5.1 reports the findings of studies in various populations. Nakata and colleagues (2006) reported an increased risk of non-fatal occupational injury among smokers, both active and passive, working for small-medium-scale manufacturing enterprises in Japan.

When investigating the roles of unhealthy lifestyle/behaviors and of poor health and disability, we should keep in mind that they can result from ageing, living conditions seen predominantly in lower socioeconomic groups, and also from adverse working conditions. Initiating smoking, smoking more intensively, and alcohol abuse are associated with high job demands and adverse working conditions (Chau et al., 2009b). The role of adverse working conditions in poor health and disability is well known (Bourgkard et al., 2008; Chau et al., 2005a; 2005b; 2009c; International Labour Office, 1998; Leigh et al., 1999). In addition, many working people smoke and use medications or other legal psychoactive substances in order to cope with work-related difficulties, and such use is more common in manual workers (Chau et al. 2009b; Lapeyre-Mestre et al. 2004; Legleye et al., 2009; Peretti-Watel et al., 2009). It should be noted that smoking and alcohol use continue to result in substantial morbidity worldwide (9.0 percent and 8.4 percent, respectively, of the total burden in the European Union) (Dahlgren and Whitehead, 2006).

Lifestyle factors, other individual characteristics, and job demands are generally so strongly interdependent that the role of some may be concealed by the impact of others, as shown by analysis using a log-linear model of data in a population-based study conducted in north-eastern France (Bhattacherjee et al., 2003). For example, alcohol abuse, measured with the Deta-Cage questionnaire (Beresford et al., 1990), had a significant odds ratio of about 2 but a non-significant odds ratio when adjusted for all study risk factors. Similarly, cognitive disability had a significant odds ratio of 1.4, which became non-significant when adjusted for all covariates. Those investigating numerous risk factors should therefore take account of their inter-correlations.

Some particularities are of interest. We found that overweight (body mass index > 25 kg/m^2) was associated with a higher risk of falls on same level (adjusted odds ratio 2.0) and falls to a lower level (1.7) but played a protective role for handling and carrying objects (0.6) among construction workers (Chau et al., 2004a). Obesity (body mass index ≥ 30 kg/m^2) was not associated with falls overall but was strongly associated with falls requiring sick leave of eight days or more among railway workers (adjusted odds ratio 2.1) (Gauchard et al., 2003). Older age ($\geq$50 years) was also associated with falls requiring sick leave of eight days or more among these workers (adjusted odds ratio 1.8).

Consumption nearly every day of alcohol drink was strongly linked with injury sustained when getting down from a vehicle among railway workers (adjusted odds ratio 6.2) (Gauchard et al., 2003). The risk was greatest for train drivers, a specific feature of whose job is to remain in the same position, seated in the cab, throughout the journey. Descending from a vehicle by stairs or steps is a complex locomotor task that involves highly eccentric muscle action at both the knee and the ankle (McFadyen and Winter, 1988) as well as requiring adequate somatosensory function (Cavanagh, Mulfinger and Owens, 1997). The long period in the same posture may lead to modifications in muscular activation and somatosensory control, generating muscular response disorders that lead to a bad landing on the floor and thus a fall. For these workers, falls were linked with both lack of sports (1.8) and lack of do-it-yourself and gardening activity (1.4).

Table 5.1 Associations of individual factors and occupational injury: odds ratios adjusted for potential covariates

	Working population[1]	Construction workers[2]	Railway workers[3]	Coal miners[4]
Age <30 yr	1.5	1.3	1.5	
Male	1.8			
Five years or less in present job		1.3		
Smoking	1.6	1.3	1.3	
Sleep disorders		2.0	1.3	
Frequent psychotropic drug use	2.0			1.7
Poor health				1.8
Musculoskeletal disorders	1.6			
Physical disability		1.4		
Hearing disorders		1.3		
No sports activity		1.2		
No do-it-yourself and gardening activity			1.2	
Job category				
Executives, intellectual professionals	1.0			
Workmen	3.2			
Farmers, craftsmen, tradesmen	3.0			
Clerks	2.2			
Technicians	2.2			
Foremen	2.9			

1 Working population based study (Bhattacherjee et al., 2003; Chau et al., 2008b).

2 Case-control study on male construction workers (Chau et al., 2002).

3 Case-control study on male railway workers (Chau et al., 2004c).

4 Study on French coal miners (Bhattacherjee et al., 2007).

Among construction workers, no sports activity was associated with injury due to handling and carrying objects (Chau et al., 2004a).

We also found among construction workers that younger age (<30 years) was associated with increased risk of injury due to hand tools (adjusted odds ratio 2.2) and that workers with hearing disorders or sleep disorders were more affected by injuries involving moving objects (2.0) (Chau et al., 2004a). Hearing disorders were highly correlated with prolonged sick leave. They led to a reduction in noise perception, particularly warning messages, and more serious injury because of a lack of avoidance or protective measures.

Falls on the same level or to a lower level related to increasing age and to hearing disability as well as to cognitive disability (concentration, attention, orientation, problem-solving, and memory), even when controlling for sex, age, and job category (Gauchard et al., 2006a). Balance control is a complex sensorimotor function requiring the central processing of afferent information from the visual, vestibular and somatosensory systems in the vestibular nuclei, leading to the organization of motor responses, such as gaze control by ocular reflexes of visual and vestibular origin and posture stabilization by the vestibule-spinal reflex. Damage to any of these systems influences the common output of the postural system, resulting in an increased risk of falls (Gauchard et al., 2003; Vouriot et al., 2004). Certain occupational exposures such as that to anesthetic gases among operating room personnel can lead to impairing information and its central integration, and consequently to inappropriate organization of sensorimotor stabilization strategies and thereby favoring imbalance (Vouriot et al., 2005). Smoking and alcohol use also alter balance control and thus increase the risk of falls (Chau et al., 2008b; Gauchard et al., 2003).

The role of sleep disorders in occupational injury depends on their severity. Many people regularly consume sleeping pills and continue to suffer from insomnia. In one study in construction workers we found that, compared to workers with no sleep disorders (sleep of six hours or more per day and sleeping well and without regular consumption of sleeping pills), those with less than six hours sleep per day and/or not sleeping well but without regular consumption of sleeping pills had an age-adjusted odds ratio of 1.7, while those who regularly consumed sleeping pills, slept for six hours or more per day and slept well had an odds ratio of 2.8, and those with regular consumption of sleeping pills but with less than six hours sleep per day or not sleeping well had an odds ratio of 10.0 (Chau et al., 2002).

Certain self-reported personality traits, risk perception, and risk-taking behavior, particularly due to production pressure, have also been found to be associated with an increased risk of injury (Chau et al., 1995a; 1995b; Ghosh, Bhattacherjee and Chau, 2004; Kunar, Bhattacherjee and Chau, 2008). Work accidents were found to be associated with scores in Benton's Visual Retention test, scores in the Eysenck Personality Questionnaire on neuroticism, and 24-hour general tiredness (Issever et al., 2008).

Some individual factors were also found to be strong contributors to occupational injuries among other specific working populations such as coal miners in India. Indeed, a recent case-control study (Kunar, Bhattacherjee and Chau, 2008) reported that a lack of formal education, smoking, regular consumption of alcohol, and presence of disease were associated with a two- to three-fold higher risk, and risk-taking behavior due to production pressure was associated with a ten-fold higher risk. Having a large family (≥5 dependants) was associated with a five-fold higher risk. The authors stated that discussions with mine management and supervisors revealed that workers with large families were in a less safe mental state at work because they had more commitment as well as responsibility toward their family members.

The role of individual characteristics differs between various types of accidents. The study on construction workers revealed that younger age (<30 years) related to injuries by moving objects, sleep disorders to falls to a lower level, or injuries by moving objects, and lack of sporting activity to injuries due to handling or carrying objects (Chau et al., 2002). The role of individual characteristics may also vary with the severity of injuries. The same study reported that injuries requiring a <15-day sick leave were associated with younger age and smoking (adjusted odds ratios 1.8 and 1.5, respectively) whereas injuries requiring 15+ days sick leave were associated with sleep disorders and five years or less in present job (adjusted odds ratios about 2). The results differed somewhat when considering injuries requiring hospitalization (about one-third of the total). Younger age, smoking, and five years or less in present job related to injuries with no hospitalization (adjusted odds ratios 1.4–1.7), while sleep disorders were more related to injuries with hospitalization than with those without hospitalization (adjusted odds ratios 2.9 vs. 1.7, respectively).

The role of individual factors also differs between jobs categories. The study on construction workers quoted above found that sleep disorders played a role in cases involving plumbers and electricians (adjusted odds ratio 3.8) and civil engineering workers (2.5); young age was relevant among workers carrying out finishing works in buildings (1.9), five years or less in the present job among plumbers and electricians (2.6), and physical disability and no sports activity among masons (1.9) (Chau et al., 2004b).

The risk associated with CJD score was stronger among the workers with frequent drug use for fatigue (adjusted odds ratios 2.3, 6.2, and 12.7 for CJD 1, CJD 2-3 and CJD ≥4 respectively, vs. CJD 0) than among the workers with no such drug use (adjusted odds ratios 1.7, 3.9, and 8.2, respectively) (Chau et al., 2008b).

Finally, there are some disparities in the confounding effects of individual factors in the association between level of job demand and injury. Indeed, controlling for age, sex, smoking, presence of musculoskeletal disorders, frequent drug use for fatigue, and job category decreases the odds ratio between CJD >4 and injury (from 9.9 to 5.4) more than the odds ratio between CJD 2-3 and injury (from 4.4 to 3.0) and that between CJD 1 and injury (from 1.9 to 1.5) (Chau et al., 2008b). These findings highlight the important roles of both job demands and individual characteristics.

Roles of Age and Experience

The roles of age and experience are complex. Every year, young people start work lacking job knowledge and experience (Chau et al., 1995a; 2007; Salminen, 1994; Wong, 1994), and research has revealed them to be subject to a high risk of injury (Cellier et al., 1995; Chau et al., 2002; 2004c; 2007; McCaig, Burt and Stussman, 1998). These studies define young age as <20 or <30 years, which embraces both adolescence and young adulthood.

Some studies have highlighted the role in injury of altered health status, musculoskeletal disorders, and other diseases and disabilities (Chau et al., 2008b; Zwerling et al., 1997) common among workers older than about 40 (Barbotte et al., 2001; Chau et al., 2005b; Gauchard et al., 2006a). Disease and disability affect both working skill and how occupational hazards are assessed and monitored. One study showed a 2.6-fold higher risk for workers aged above 45 compared with those aged below 30 (Ghosh, Bhattacherjee and Chau, 2004). A relationship has been reported between cumulative physical job demands and work injury; the risk in workers aged above 40 was double that in younger individuals (Chau et al., 2008b). Older age is associated with lack of postural control (Poulain and Giraudet, 2008; Sullivan et al., 2009) favoring falls, and the risk of falling to lower level may be higher than that of falling on the same level because it is more difficult to control one's balance on less stable raised platforms or on stairs.

Lower physical strength and increased disability (Chau et al., 2005b; Mathiowetz et al., 1985) mean that older workers are at greater risk of injury when carrying out the most demanding working activities or those that require greater strength or skill (Chau et al., 2009c; Khlat et al., 2008). We found that the CJD score was associated with a higher injury risk for workers aged 45 or over (odds ratio 3.5 for CJD 1, 5.0 for CJD 2–3, and 14.5 for CJD ≥4, vs. CJD 0) than for those aged under 30 (1.4, 4.2 and 9.9, respectively) and 30–44 (1.5, 4.4, and 6.5, respectively). The differences between age groups remained when controlling for all factors studied (Chau et al., 2009a).

The roles of individual characteristics may also differ between age groups. Obesity, smoking, musculoskeletal disorders, and drug use for fatigue related to injury in workers aged 45 or over (adjusted odds ratios 1.8–2.8) whereas smoking related to injury (adjusted odds ratio 1.9) for workers aged under 30 (Chau et al., 2009a).

The role in injury of lack of experience (as measured by length of service) is well known, and some studies have focused on the first five years in a given job (Chau et al., 2004b; 2004c; 2006) because of the relatively small samples used. Many workers have to deal with rapid turnover, which leaves them with a lack of job knowledge and experience. This issue affects most jobs and different ages, and may result in many older workers accumulating disabilities and never gaining sufficient job knowledge and experience. Age and experience can be distinguished as individual factors that change with the course of time, but that could be controlled in an epidemiologic design. Older age is often associated with greater experience, regardless of disease and disability, whereas experience and disability do in fact play opposite roles in injury. Two questions are especially pertinent. First, what length of service reflects a lack of experience? Second, what are the respective roles of younger and older age, length of service and job, when controlling for other factors, and are they related to injury type? We need to understand and recognize the mechanisms, through which these factors contribute to injury, as potential targets for preventive measures and injury reduction programs that go beyond conventional methods by considering the various risks to which different age groups are subjected. It has been difficult to separate the role of age and length of service in most studies because of their collinear nature, especially when they were categorized in two classes only (Blom, Pokorny and Van Leeuwen, 1987). A prospective study on a large population of sufficient subjects in various age brackets and lengths of service in a number of job groups was therefore necessary.

A large prospective cohort study was recently conducted among 164,814 male workers with permanent contracts at the French National Railway Company at some time between January 1, 1998 and December 31, 2000 (three years) to assess the part played in injury of age, length of service with the company, and type of job (Chau et al., 2010). During the three-year follow-up (446,120 person-years) 15,195 injuries necessitating at least one working day lost were observed. This study demonstrated that:

- workers aged under 25 were subject to a higher risk of injury from handling materials/ and machine parts during assembly, collision with moving objects or vehicles and using hand-tools;

- older workers were subject to a higher risk of fall and injury resulting from handling materials and machine parts during assembly, lifting/handling objects or equipment, collision with moving objects or vehicles and using hand-tools;
- age did not influence falls on same level or injury when operating machines/equipment;
- the relative risk decreased steadily with increasing length of service, and this trend was similar for nearly all types of injuries; and
- risks associated with various jobs, when controlling for age and length of service, reflected both occupational activities and the working environment.

This study reveals that the mechanical/diagnostic/electro-technical operators and boilermakers-welders, railway maintenance operators, transport production operators, signposting/telecommunication/energy-electric traction, and specialized mechanical operators had significantly high risks (when adjusted for age and length of service). They featured greater risk of most injury types: handling materials and machine parts during assembly, lifting/handling equipment or objects, collision with/by moving objects or vehicles, operating machines/equipment or using hand-tools. These workers routinely handled large/heavy objects or materials, often in hazardous environments (restricted work space, ground in poor condition and holes in ground, slippery ground, congested ground, sloping ground or railway embankment, reduced visibility at night), and they often stated that they underestimated the risk (Chau et al., 2007). The increasing injury risk during the first four years of service for the subjects aged <25 and the steady decreasing risk according to increasing length of service were observed for most job categories (Chau et al., 2010).

Repeated Occupational Injuries

Some workers have repeated injuries within a short period. Repeated injuries may reflect the magnitude of injury risk associated with various factors and their persistence over time.

Studies on repeated injuries are rare. One case control study (Garchard et al., 2006b) reported that 27 percent of male railway workers had suffered from repeated injuries (two or more) over a two-year period, and that the correlates differed greatly between repeated injuries and occasional injuries (only one). It revealed that the significant risk factors for repeated injuries were: <5 years in present job (adjusted odds ratio 1.8), sleep disorders (2.0), smoking (1.8), no do-it-yourself and no gardening activity (1.7) whereas occasional injuries related to <5 years in present job only (adjusted odds ratio 1.3). Univariate analysis showed that age <30 was associated with both occasional injuries and repeated injuries, and request for a job change with repeated injuries.

Occupational Fractures

Occupational fractures are frequent while epidemiological studies are rare. One study in construction workers in north-eastern France reported that they represented 23 percent of occupational injuries, and they were more common among masons (25 percent) and civil engineering workers (21 percent) than among carpenters, roofers, plumbers, electricians, and people carrying out finishing work in buildings (11–16 percent) (Chau et al., 2002).

One study in railway workers reported that fractures represented 10 percent of occupational injuries, and that they affected more mechanical maintenance operators (27 percent) and railway maintenance operators (14 percent) than people in other jobs (4–12 percent) (Chau et al., 2004c).

More than 80 percent of fractures were due to falls (on the same level or to a lower level), handling tools or objects, and using construction machinery and devices, and fractures concerned mainly the upper limbs (especially the hands), followed by the lower limbs (especially the foot), and trunk.

We found that the individual risk factors differed between the two populations. Among construction workers fractures related to sleep disorders only (adjusted odds ratio 2.4) whereas among railway workers they related to five years or less in present job (adjusted odds ratio 2.5) and no do-it-yourself and no gardening activity (odds ratio 1.8).

Preventive Measures

There is evidence that adverse working conditions are the main contributors to occupational injuries, but individual factors also play a role. The pathways leading from adverse working conditions to occupational injuries may be quite diverse. First, stress and job demands directly elevate the risk of injuries. Second, they generate fatigue, sleep disorders, anxiety, certain diseases (musculoskeletal disorders, cardiovascular disease, for example), physical, sensorial, and intellectual impairments and consequently physical and cognitive functional limitations (Chau et al., 2005a; 2005b; 2008a; 2008b; 2009b; Caisse Nationale de l'Assurance Maladie des Travailleurs Salariés, 2002; the Lorhandicap Group, 2004) that are common injury risk factors. Third, strenuous work is associated with harmful health behaviors (initiating smoking, smoking more intensively, psychotropic medication) and obesity (Chau et al., 2009b; Lalluka et al., 2008; Lapeyre-Mestre et al., 2004; the Lorhandicap Group, 2004; Peretti-Watel et al., 2009), which in the short term may elevate the risk of injuries (Chau et al., 2002; 2004c; 2008b; Gauchard et al., 2003; Khlat et al., 2008), and in the long term are major determinants of chronic diseases and functional limitations that can in turn favor occupational injuries (Chau et al., 2004b). Fourth, job demands may alter health status and consequently living conditions and lifestyle such as a lack during leisure time of sports and physical activity, which play a protective role against occupational injury (Chau et al., 2004b; 2008b; Gauchard et al., 2003; Khlat et al., 2008).

Our findings reveal a number of salient issues, which require implementation of specific preventive measures. There is a need to:

- improve working conditions, particularly the working environment, work organization, and the materials and tools used, reduce the level and number of occupational demands, and limit production pressure;
- provide specific training with regard to appropriate job knowledge, task performance, using tools/machines, handling objects/machines, and occupational hazard

assessment from a worker's first years in a job, especially for younger workers at the beginning of their working life;
- ensure that a worker's skill corresponds to his occupational activity, particularly for older workers (>40 years), and those with reduced physical and mental abilities;
- provide injury prevention for older workers in the context of the lengthening of working life. It should cover falling to a lower level, lifting/handling equipment and objects, as well as other tasks and environments involving excess risk;
- address the availability of sports and physical activities and encourage workers of all ages to take part; these can improve health status and physical and mental skills (especially for falls);
- help workers to gain awareness of risks relating to their physical and mental working abilities; for example limitations due to musculoskeletal disorders, which are common among workers;
- help workers to gain awareness of risks relating to smoking, alcohol use, psychotropic drug use, and overweight or obesity; and
- help workers to gain awareness of risks relating to their job, age, and experience.

The workplace can be a natural setting for a broad discussion on working conditions, disease prevention, and health promotion that, in addition to addressing determinants of health directly related to the working conditions, also considers such issues as smoking, drug use, and health care. Job demand measurements such as the CJD are a simple index that may be useful for health professionals who may need to monitor the subjects most at risk during working life.

Occupational physicians could help workers to find remedial measures. Their interventions may involve risk assessment, health surveillance, management, scientific research, and health education (Porru et al., 2006). They can also work in cooperation with other physicians, employers, workers and their organizations, in particular for workers with an injury or an occupational disease before/when returning to work (Guillaume et al., 1990; Kunar, Bhattacherjee and Chau, 2008; Otero Sierra et al., 1997; Otero Sierra et al., 2000).

Acknowledgements

The author would like to thank Jean-Marie Mur, Philippe Perrin, Ashis Bhattacherjee, Myriam Khlat, Pascal Wild, Eve Bourgkard, Lahoucine Benamghar, Gérome Gauchard, Dominique Deviterne, Alexandre Vouriot, Apurna Kumar Ghosh, Bijay Mihir Kunar, Christian Touron, Domique Dehaene, Christian Siegfried, Jean-Louis Dangelzer, Martine Français, René Jacquin, and Alain Sourdot for their valuable cooperation in the design and conduct of various studies.

He is also indebted to the Lorhandicap Group that includes Nearkasen Chau, Francis Guillemin, Jean-François Ravaud, Jésus Sanchez, Sylvie Guillaume, Jean-Pierre Michaely, Carmen Otero Sierra, Bernard Legras, Alice Dazord, Marie Choquet, Luc Méjean, Nadia Tubiana-Rufi, Jean-Pierre Meyer, Yvon Schléret, and Jean-Marie Mur, for conducting the Lorhandicap study on the general population in north-eastern France.

He further thanks Michèle Baumann and William Francis for their help for reading of the manuscript.

References

Barbotte, E., Guillemin, F., Chau, N., and the Lorhandicap Group (2001) Prevalence of impairments, disabilities, handicaps and quality of life in the general population: a review of recent literature, *Bulletin of the World Health Organization;* 79(11), 1047–1055.

Beresford, T.P., Blow, F.C., Hill, E., Singer, K., and Lucey, M.R. (1990) Comparison of CAGE questionnaire and computer-assisted laboratory profiles in screening for covert alcoholism, *Lancet;* 336(8713), 482–485.

Bhattacherjee, A., Bertrand, J.P., Meyer, J.P., Benamghar, L., Otero Sierra, C., Michaely, J.P., Ghosh, A.K., d'Houtaud, A., Mur, J.M., Chau, N., and the Lorhandicap Group (2007) Relationships of physical job tasks and living conditions with occupational injuries in coal miners, *Industrial Health*; 45(2), 352–358.

Bhattacherjee, A., Chau, N., Otero Sierra, C., Legras, B., Benamghar, L., Michaely, J.P., Ghosh, A.K., Guillemin, F., Ravaud, J.F., Mur, J.M., and the Lorhandicap Group (2003) Relationships of job and some individual characteristics with occupational injuries in employed people: A community-based study, *Journal of Occupational Health*; 45(6), 382–391.

Blom, D.H.J., Pokorny, M.L.I., and Van Leeuwen, P. (1987) The role of age and experience in bus drivers' accidents, *International Journal of Epidemiology*; 16(1), 35–43.

Bourgkard, E., Wild, P., Massin, N., Meyer, J.P., Otero Sierra, C., Fontana, J.M., Benamghar, L., Mur, J.M., Ravaud, J.F., Guillemin, F., Chau, N., and Lorhandicap Group. (2008) Association of physical job demands, smoking and alcohol abuse in subsequent premature mortality: A 9-year follow-up population-based study, *Journal of Occupational Health*; 50(1), 31–40.

Breslin, F.C., Tompa, E., Zhao, R., Pole, J.D., Amick Iii, B.C., Smith, P.M., and Hogg-Johnson, S. (2008) The relationship between job tenure and work disability absence among adults: a prospective study, *Accident; Analysis and Prevention*; 40(1), 368–75.

Caisse Nationale de l'assurance Maladie des Travailleurs Salariés [National Compensation System for Diseases of Salaried Workers] (2005) *Statistiques Nationales des Accidents du Travail, des Accidents de Trajet et des Maladies Professionnelles—2003 [National Statistics of Occupational Accidents and Occupational Diseases—2003].* Paris, France: Caisse Nationale de l'Assurance Maladie des Travailleurs Salariés.

Cavanagh, P.R., Mulfinger, L.M., and Owens, D.A. (1997) How do the elderly negotiate stairs?, *Muscle & Nerve Supplement;* Supplement 5, S52–S55.

Cellier, J.M., Eyrolle, H., and Bertrand, A. (1995) Effects of age and level of work experience on occurrence of accidents, *Perceptual and Motor Skills;* 80(3), 931–40.

Chau, N., Baumann, M., Ravaud, J.F., Choquet, M., Falissard, B., and Lorhandicap Group. (2008a) *Association of Cardiovascular Disease with High Physical Job Demands among Working People: A Population-based Study*. The 12th Biennial Congress of the European Society for Health and Medical Sociology—ESHMS, Oslo, August 28–30th.

Chau, N., Benamghar, L., Siegfried, C., Dehaene, D., Dangelzer, J.L., Français, M., Jacquin, R., Sourdot, A., Touron, C., and Mur, J.M. (2006) Determinants of occupational fracture proneness: A case-control study in construction and railway workers, *Journal of Occupational Health*; 48(4), 267–270.

Chau, N., Bhattacherjee, A., Bertrand, J.P., Meyer, J.P., Guillemin, F., Ravaud, J.F., Ghosh, A.K., Mur, J.M., and Lorhandicap Group. (2005a) Associations of occupational hazards and individual characteristics with occupational injuries and disabilities in Lorraine coal miners. In *Advances in Mining Technology and Management*, A. Bhattacherjee, S.K. Das, and U.M.R. Karanam (eds), Kharagpur: Indian Institute of Technology, 543–552.

Chau, N., Bhattacherjee, A., Kunar, B.M., and Lorhandicap Group. (2009a) Relationship between job, lifestyle, age and occupational injuries, *Occupational Medicine;* 59(2), 114–9.

Chau, N., Bourgkard, E., Bhattacherjee, A., Ravaud, J.F., Choquet, M., Mur, J.M., and Lorhandicap Group. (2008b) Associations of job, living conditions and lifestyle with occupational injuries in working population: A population-based study, *International Archives of Occupational and Environmental Health;* 81(4), 379–389.

Chau, N., Choquet, M., Falissard, B., and Lorhandicap Group. (2009b) Relationship of job demands to initiating smoking in working people: A population-based study, *Industrial Health*; 47(3), 319–25.

Chau, N., d'Houtaud, A., Gruber, M., Monhoven, N., Gavillot, C., Pétry, D., Bourgkard, E., Guillaume, S., and André, J.M. (1995a) Personality self-representations of patients with hand injury, and its relationship with work injury, *European Journal of Epidemiology*; 11(4), 373–382.

Chau, N., Gauchard, G., Dehaene, D., Benamghar, L., Touron, C., Perrin, P., and Mur, J.M. (2007) Contributions of occupational hazards and human factors in occupational injuries and their associations with job, age and type of injuries in railway workers, *International Archives of Occupational and Environmental Health*; 80(6), 517–25.

Chau, N., Gauchard, G.C., Siegfried, C., Benamghar, L., Dangelzer, J.L., Français, M., Jacquin, R., Sourdot, A., Perrin, P. and Mur, J.M. (2004a) Relationships of job, age, and life conditions with the causes and severity of occupational injuries in construction workers, *International Archives of Occupational and Environmental Health*; 77(1), 60–66.

Chau, N., Khlat, M., and Lorhandicap Group. (2009c) Strong association of physical job demands with functional limitations among active people: A population-based study in North-eastern France, *International Archives of Occupational and Environmental Health;* 82(7), 857–66.

Chau, N., Mur, J.M., Benamghar, L., Siegfried, C., Dangelzer, J.L., Français, M., Jacquin, R., and Sourdot, A. (2002) Relationships between some individual characteristics and occupational accidents in the construction industry. A case-control study on 880 victims of accidents occurred during a two-year period, *Journal of Occupational Health*; 44(3), 131–139.

Chau, N., Mur, J.M., Benamghar, L., Siegfried, C., Dangelzer, J.L., Français, M., Jacquin, R., and Sourdot, A. (2004b) Relationships between certain individual characteristics and occupational accidents for various jobs in the construction industry: A case-control study, *American Journal of Industrial Medicine*; 45(1), 84–92.

Chau, N., Mur, J.M., Touron, C., Benamghar, L., and Dehaene, D. (2004c) Correlates of Occupational Injuries for Various Jobs in Railway Workers: A Case-control Study, *Journal of Occupational Health*; 46(4), 272–280.

Chau, N., Pétry, D., Gavillot, C., Guillaume, S., Beaucaillou, C., Bourgkard, E., Gruber, M., Monhoven, N., and André, J.M. (1995b) Implications professionnelles des lésions sévères du membre supérieur [Occupational consequences of severe injuries of upper limb], *Archives des Maladies Professionnelles de Médecine du Travail et de Sécurité Sociale;* 56(1), 12–22.

Chau, N., Ravaud, J.F., Otero Sierra, C., Legras, B., Macho, J., Guillemin, F., Sanchez, J., Mur, J.M., and Lorhandicap Group. (2005b) Prevalence of impairments and social inequalities: A community-based study in Lorraine, *Revue d'épidémiologie et de Santé Publique*; 53(6), 614–628.

Chau, N., Wild, P., Dehaene, D., Benamghar, L., Mur, J.M., and Touron, C. (2010) The role of age, years of employment, and job in work-related injuries: A 446, 120 person-years follow up study in railway workers, *Occupational and Environmental Medicine*; 67(3), 147–153.

Dahlgren, G. and Whitehead, M. (2006) *Levelling Up (Part 2): A Discussion Paper on European Strategies for Tackling Social Inequities in Health.* Copenhagen: World Health Organization Regional Office for Europe. Studies on Social and Economic determinants of Population, No. 3.

Dembe, A.E. (2001) The social consequences of occupational injuries and illnesses, *American Journal of Industrial Medicine;* 40(4), 403–17.

European Foundation for the Improvement of Living and Working Conditions (2003) *Illness, Disability and Social Inclusion.* Luxembourg: Office for Official Publications of the European Communities.

European Foundation for the Improvement of Living and Working Conditions (2004) *Illness and Employment. Retaining the Link to work: Summary.* http://www.eurofound.eu.int.

Falissard, B. (1998) *Comprendre et Utiliser les Statistiques dans les Sciences de la Vie* [Understand and Use Statistics in Life Sciences](2nd edition). Paris: Masson.

Galea, S., Nandi, A., and Vlahov, D. (2004) The social epidemiology of substance use, *Epidemiologic Reviews*; 26, 36–52.

Gauchard, G., Chau, N., Mur, J.M., and Perrin, P. (2001) Falls and working individuals: Role of extrinsic and intrinsic factors, *Ergonomics*; 44(14), 1330–1339.

Gauchard, G.C., Chau, N., Touron, C., Benamghar, L., Dehaene, D., Perrin, P., and Mur, J.M. (2003) Individual characteristics in occupational accidents due to imbalance: A case-control study in the employees of a railway company, *Occupational and Environmental Medicine;* 60(5), 330–335.

Gauchard, G.C., Deviterne, D., Guillemin, F., Sanchez, J., Perrin, P., Mur, J.M., Ravaud, J.F., Chau, N., and Lorhandicap Group (2006a) Prevalence of sensorial and cognitive disabilities and falls, and their relationships: A community-based study, *Neuroepidemiology*; 26(2), 108–118.

Gauchard, G.C., Mur, J.M., Touron, C., Benamghar, L., Dehaene, D., Perrin, P., and Chau, N. (2006b) Determinants of accident proneness: A case-control study in railway workers, *Occupational Medicine*; 56(3), 187–190.

Ghosh, A.K., Bhattacherjee, A., and Chau N. (2004) Relationships of working conditions and individual characteristics with occupational injuries: A case-control study in coal miners, *Journal of Occupational Health*; 46(6), 470–480.

Guillaume, S., Pétry, D., Chau, N., André, J.M., Merle, M., and Manciaux, M. (1990) Impact socio-professionnel de l'épicondylalgie [Sociooccupational impact of epicondylalgy], *Archives des Maladies Professionnelles de Médecine du Travail et de Sécurité Sociale* [Archives of Occupational Diseases, Occupational Mediciene and Social Security]; 51(1), 37–45.

Harma, M., Suvanto, S., Popkin, S., Pulli, K., Mulder, M., and Hirvonen, K. (1998) A dose-response study of total sleep time and the ability to maintain wakefulness, *Journal of Sleep Research;* 7(3), 167–174.

Institut National de la Statistique et des Etudes Economiques [National Institute for Statistics and Economic Studies] (2001) *Projections de Population à l'horizon 2050. Un Vieillissement Inéluctable* [Projections of population in 2050. An ineluctable ageing]. Paris, France: Institut National de la Statistique et des Etudes Economiques, No. 762, Mars.

International Labour Office (1998) *Encyclopaedia of Occupational Health and Safety, Vol 3* (4th edition). Geneva: ILO.

Issever, H., Ozdilli, K., Onen, L., Tan, O., Disci, R., and Yardimci, O. (2008) Examination of personal factors in work accidents, *Indoor and Built Environment*; 17(6), 562–566.

Khlat, M., Ravaud, J.F., Brouard, N., Chau, N., and Lorhandicap Group. (2008) Occupational disparities in accidents and roles of lifestyle factors and disabilities. A population-based study in North-eastern France, *Public Health*; 122(8), 771–783.

Kunar, B.M., Bhattacherjee, A., and Chau, N. (2008) Relationships of job hazards, lack of knowledge, alcohol use, health status and production pressure-related risk taking behavior to work injury of coal miners: A case-control study in India, *Journal of Occupational Health*; 50(3), 236–244.

Lalluka, T., Lahelma, E., Rahkonen, O., Roos, E., Laaksonen, E., Martikainen, P., Head, J., Brunner, E., Mosdol, A., Marmot, M., Sekine, M., Nasermoaddeli, A., and Kagamimori, S. (2008) Associations of job strain and working overtime with adverse health behaviors and obesity: Evidence from the Whitehall II study, Helsinki Health Study, and the Japanese Civil Servants Study, *Social Science & Medicine;* 66(8), 1681–1698.

Lapeyre-Mestre, M., Sulem, P., Niezborala, M., Ngoundo-Mbongue, T.B., Briand-Vincens, D., Jansou, P., Bancarel, Y., Chastan, E., and Montastruc, J.L. (2004) Taking drugs in the working environment: A study in a sample of 2106 workers in the Toulouse metropolitan area, *Therapie*; 59(6), 615–623.

Legleye, S., Peretti-Watel, P., Baumann, M., Beck, F., and Chau, N. (2009) *Associations between Demanding Occupational Conditions and Tobacco, Alcohol and Cannabis Use among French Working Men and Women*. 39th World Congress of the International Institute of Sociology. Yerevan, June 11–14.

Leigh, J., Macaskill, P., Kuosma, E., and Mandryk, J. (1999) Global burden of disease and injury due to occupational factors, *Epidemiology*; 10(5), 626–631.

Lorhandicap Group (2004) Relationships of demanding work conditions with fatigue and psychosomatic disorders: A community-based study, *Occupational and Environmental Medicine*; 61(11), e46–46.

Mathiowetz, V., Kashman, N., Volland, G., Weber, K., Dowe, M., and Rogers, S. (1985) Grip and pinch streght: Normative data for adults, *Archives of Physical Medicine and Rehabilitation*; 66(2), 69–74.

McCaig, L.F., Burt, C.W., and Stussman, B.J. (1998) A comparison of work-related injury visits and other injury visits to emergency departments in the United States, 1995–1996, *Journal of Occupational and Environmental Medicine*; 40(10), 870–875.

McFadyen, B.J. and Winter, D.A. (1988) An integrated biomechanical analysis of normal stair ascent and descent, *Journal of Biomechanics;* 21(9), 733–44.

Nakata, A., Ikeda, T., Takahashi, M., Haratani, T., Hojou, M., Fujioka, Y., and Araki, S. (2006) Non-fatal occupational injury among active and passive smokers in small- and medium-scale manufacturing enterprises in Japan, *Social Science & Medicine;* 63(9), 2452–63.

Otero Sierra, C., Varona, W., Chau, N., Macho, J.M., Teculescu, D., Bernal, M., Caillet, G., and Mur, J.M. (1997) Comparaison des systèmes de prise en charge de maladies professionnelles en France et en Espagne [Comparison of compensation systems for occupational diseases in France and Spain], *Archives des Maladies Professionnelles de Médecine du Travail et de Sécurité Sociale*; 58(6), 539–551.

Otero Sierra, C., Chau, N., Varona, W., Macho, J.M., Caillet, G., Vallayer, C., Petiet, G., Touranchet, A., Bernal, M., and Mur, J.M. (2000) Les maladies professionnelles: situation et vécu du salarié et conséquences [Occupational diseases: situation and experience of workers and consequences], *Archives des Maladies Professionnelles de Médecine du Travail et de Sécurité Sociale*; 61(4), 250–260.

Peretti-Watel, P., Legleye, S., Baumannn, M., Choquet, M., Falissard, B., Chau, N., and Lorhandicap Group. (2009) Fatigue, insomnia and nervousness: gender disparities and roles of individual characteristics and lifestyle factors among economically active people, *Social Psychiatry and Psychiatric Epidemiology;* 44(9), 703–709.

Porru, S., Placidi, D., Carta, A., and Alessio, L. (2006) Prevention of injuries at work: the role of the occupational physician, *International Archives of Occupational and Environmental Health*; 79(3), 177–192.

Poulain, I. and Giraudet, G. (2008) Age-related changes of visual contribution in posture control, *Gait & Posture*; 27(1), 1–7.

Salminen, S.T. (1994) Epidemiological analysis of serious occupational accidents in southern Finland, *Scandinavian Journal of Social Medicine;* 22(3), 225–227.

Salminen, S. (2004) Have young workers more injuries than older ones? An international literature review, *Journal of Safety Research*; 35(5), 513–21.

Simon-Rigaud, M.L. (1995) Physical activities and health: results of a national survey of workers. *Bulletin de l'Académie Nationale de Médecine;* 179(7), 1429–1436.

Sprince, N.L., Park, H., Zwerling, C., Lynch, C.F., Whitten, P.A., Thu, K., Gillette, P.P., Burmeister, L.F., and Alavanja, M.C. (2002) Risk factors for machinery-related injury among Iowa farmers: a case-control study nested in the Agricultural Health Study, *International Journal of Occupational and Environmental Health*; 8(4), 332–338.

Sullivan, E.V., Rose, J., Rohlfing, T., and Pfefferbaum, A. (2009) Postural sway reduction in aging men and women: Relation to brain structure, cognitive status, and stabilizing factors, *Neurobiology of Aging*; 30(5), 793–807.

Vouriot, A., Gauchard, G., Chau, N., Benamghar, L., Lepori, M.L., Mur, J.M., and Perrin, P. (2004) Sensorial organisation favouring higher visual contribution is a risk factor of falls in an occupational setting, *Neuroscience Research*; 48(3), 239–247.

Vouriot, A., Gauchard, G., Chau, N., Benamghar, L., Nadif, R., Mur, J.M. and Perrin, P. (2005) Chronic exposure to anesthetic gases affects balance control in operating room personnel, *Neurotoxicology*; 26(2), 193–198.

Wells, S. and Macdonald, S. (1999) The relationship between alcohol consumption patterns and car, work, sports and home accidents for different age groups, *Accident; Analysis and Prevention*; 31(6), 663–665.

Wong, T.W. (1994) Occupational injuries among construction workers in Hong Kong, *Occupational Medicine;* 44(5), 247–252.

Zwerling, C., Whitten, P.S., Davis, C.S., and Sprince, N.L. (1997) Occupational injuries among workers with disabilities: the national health interview survey, 1985–1994, The *Journal of the American Medical Association*; 278(24), 2163–2166.

PART III

Work Environment Factors

CHAPTER

6 Painful Hours? The Potential Costs of Extra Work Hours and Schedule Inflexibility to Workers' Physical Well-being

LONNIE GOLDEN AND BARBARA WIENS-TUERS

Overview

The hours that people work—the number, timing, and control of those hours of work—matter greatly for individuals' well-being. Contemporary economic research has more recently begun to realize the role of work in influencing subjective well-being and satisfaction (Easterlin, 2006; Pouwels, Siegers and Vlasbom, 2008). Longstanding psychological research explicitly includes pain as one of the inverse correlates with subjective well-being and happiness, which has become part of the domain of behavioral economics (Kahneman and Krueger, 2006). A key purpose of the research presented in this chapter is to answer the call for more research on the "health effects on workers who lack the ability to predict and control their work schedules" (Johnson and Lipscomb, 2006).

Research in the occupational health and safety field often finds that having greater discretion or control over the timing of one's work helps workers to alleviate some of the negative effects of long hours on the incidence of work-related injuries and illnesses (Boden, 2005; Costa, Sartori and Akerstedt, 2006; Dembe et al., 2007). However, the evidence is decidedly mixed regarding the ability of work time control to improve mental health, such as diminishing the degree of psychological distress experienced by workers (Hughes and Parkes, 2007). The present research attempts to add to the wealth of attention from studies on the duration of work (for example, Dembe et al., 2007) a focus on the extent to which workers' lack control over the timing of their work hours have notable differences in a range of self-reported pain and injury indicators. Both long and involuntary extra hours of labor expose workers to greater risks of illness and injuries, both acute and cumulative. Individual and social spillover costs, in the form of physical well-being, are all too often neglected in the conventional economic literature. Ultimately, the hope is that such research will steer labor economists in the direction of considering more seriously the specific conditions of work that create physical and mental health risks, and reach beyond the conventional, limited sphere of income, non-work time, the amorphous notion of worker utility and presumption of compensating wage differentials. This study is intended to contribute to the behavioral economics literature that appears to more explicitly recognize that individuals pursuing ever greater income might underestimate the potential deleterious effects this has on their own current and future physical health (Helliwell, 2003).

Two key indicators of control over hours for workers are considered here—working overtime on a mandatory rather than strictly voluntary basis, and an ability to influence the start or end times of one's daily work schedule. The research asks whether or not workers whose overtime work is perceived to be required tend to experience more frequent (back, arm, or neck) pain and risk of injuries than those whose overtime work is not mandatory and those who work no extra hours at all? From the results it may be inferred how a working condition such as lack of control over work schedules poses a threat to individuals' well-being that may offset the potential benefits. Working more hours is considered a positive indicator of productivity or effort, and as such, generally associated with greater (current or future) income associated with paid overtime work or status in salaried jobs (for example, Altman and Golden, 2008). A chief purpose here is to contrast empirically the separate but perhaps reinforcing effects of a longer duration of hours per se and lack of control over the scheduling of a given number of work hours. Another distinction will be to contrast the experience of acute injuries at work from the more cumulative injuries such as pain from repetitive motion.

The first section of the chapter briefly reviews the empirical literature on the physical well-being implications for workers who work overtime hours or have influence over their own daily work schedules. The second section introduces the General Social Survey (GSS) data applied and presents descriptive statistics on selected measures of the association between the relevant work characteristics and outcomes. The third section contains the empirical estimations of the physical health outcomes generated by inflexible work schedules including mandatory overtime work. The chapter concludes by discussing implications of the results for further research and public policy regarding the regulation of work hours to prevent the observed longer run costs not just to employees, but ultimately to employers and society.

Research Evidence on Physical Health Risks and the Nature of Working Hours

Research in the fields of occupational health and safety, occupational health psychology, employment relations, and work organization documents cases of adverse effects of long, extra or irregular work hours on a range of physical health and injury risks (Sparks, Faragher and Cooper, 2001; Landsbergis, 2003; Caruso et al., 2004; Nicol and Botterill, 2004; Dembe et al., 2005; Grosch et al., 2006; Burke and McAteer, 2006; Burke, 2009). Workers with long hours face elevated risks of health complaints (Fenwick and Tausig, 2001). Workplace practices that lead to greater work time doing repetitive tasks may lower worker well-being or raise cumulative trauma disorders (Brenner, Fairris and Ruser, 2004). Overtime work especially creates a greater risk of injuries and accidents on the job via fatigue (Rosa, 1995; Danna and Griffin, 1999; van der Hulst, 2003; Dong, 2005;

Dembe et al., 2005). However, while those working 60 or more hours were found to be more likely to report new injuries and diagnoses, these might reflect prior health, demographic characteristics, and type of compensation (Allen, Slavin and Bunn, 2007). There is an increased likelihood for illness and injury among employees working in long-hour schedules, particularly during unconventional shift work times (for example, night and evening shifts when fatigue-related errors are made by employees working in demanding schedules (Dembe, 2009)). As men's working hours increase, particularly over 50 hours per week, the increase in work hours is found to indirectly contribute to hypertension, reduced sleep time, physical activity time, and job dissatisfaction (Artazcoz et al., 2009; Courtemanche, 2009).

Workers indicating some experience with fatigue in the previous two weeks are almost three times more likely to experience health-related lost production time than those not reporting fatigue (Brogmus, 2007; Ricci et al., 2007). In addition, truck drivers have a high prevalence of back disorders, which have been linked with their often long hours spent driving and little job control (Jensen and Dahl, 2009). Across all types of jobs generally, working 49 or more hours is associated with more job stress, as compared to those working 35 to 39 hours. Working 70 or more hours is associated with worsening job stress, back pain, arm pain, getting hurt at work, poor physical health, and general self-reported health (Grosch et al., 2006). However, the effect is not consistently linear, since working 49 to 69 hours per week is actually associated with less arm pain than those working standard workweeks. This might reflect that healthy, motivated individuals self-select into longer hours (Clauretie, 2007). On the other hand, many, if not most, overtime workers may be non-fatigued, motivated workers with favorable work characteristics (Beckers et al., 2004). Thus, work hours are positively related to both job stress and mental strain, but not necessarily to physical health problems or injuries (Ng and Feldman, 2008; Barnett, 2004).

When it comes to health, injury, and fatigue effects, the rigidity or flexibility of daily work schedules may be a contributing factor that is independent of the length of work hours (Ng and Feldman, 2008; Beckers et al., 2008). Greater levels of flexibility in a workplace tend to be associated with less self-reported stress and strain, and better physical health (Grzywacz, Casey and Jones, 2007; Butler et al., 2009). Managers' and other workers' capacities to withstand intensive and uncertain working conditions are buttressed by greater flexibility in the nature of work (MacEachen, Polzer and Clarke, 2007). While the duration of working hours is associated with greater frequency of musculoskeletal disorders and psychological health complaints (Raediker et al., 2006), associated pain and strain may be attenuated by a greater internal locus of control (LOC) among the workers involved. Associations between work hours and self-reported health are moderated by the reasons given for working overtime and schedule autonomy. Schedule autonomy lessens the frequency of physical health symptoms (but not fatigue) for a given number of hours worked per week (Tucker and Rutherford, 2005). Workers with a more external than internal LOC report higher stress and consequently, poorer well-being and health outcomes (Meier et al., 2008).

A lack of control over either the volume or scheduling of work hours may reinforce, compound, or exacerbate the effects of long hours on workers (Fenwick and Tausig, 2001; Bliese and Halvorsen, 2001; Berg et al., 2004). Greater variation over time in workers' hours tends to reduce their well-being (Askenazy, 2004; Heisz and LaRochelle-Côté, 2006). For employees working longer than a standard 40-hour week, having flexibility might help mitigate the work stress of long work hours. However, a disproportionate share of all employees who control their work schedules, are professional and managerial employees (Gershuny, 2005; Lesnard and de Saint Pol, 2009). In such jobs, there may be additional stressors due to the responsibilities involved and longer daily hours, but also more internal LOC and flexibility over schedule (Golden, 2009).

External pressure to work, without discretion for workers has been especially threatening to well-being (Green, 2004). Among those working more than 50 hours a week and facing some supervisory pressure to work overtime, a dramatically higher proportion of workers report experiencing an injury, illness, and somatic stress levels (Cornell University Institute for Workplace Studies, 1999). People who work more hours or days than they prefer, due to employer expectations, also feel more overworked (Galinsky et al., 2005). Among those who are not permitted at their job to change their own work schedules toward their preferred schedule, a much higher than average, 45 percent, experience symptoms of overwork (Galinsky and Bond, 2001). Nurses who work mandatory overtime and uncertain (for example, on-call) hours experience significantly higher musculoskeletal disorders, particularly shoulder pain, to a lesser extent back pain and neck pain and thus perhaps contributes to their relatively high rate of occupational burnout (Trinkoff et al., 2006; Johnson and Lipscomb, 2006; Aiken et al., 2002).

Well-Being and Overtime Work: Analysis of GSS Data

This section uses the 2002 GSS Quality of Working Life (QWL) module to empirically explore the relationship between various indicators of well-being and the type of overtime and inflexible work. The 2002 GSS module conducted uses full probability sample design and a total sample size of 2,765, 1,796 of whom were employed. The specific QWL survey question for mandatory overtime is: "When you work overtime, is it mandatory (required by your employer)?" Any worker who reported at least one day in a month during the last year [when] they worked beyond their usual schedule, and answered yes to the question that overtime is mandatory, is then separated from workers with extra hours where the overtime is not mandatory, and from workers with no extra hours at all.

Table 6.1 shows that of the 1,796 employed people in the survey, 461 people answered yes, overtime is mandatory (MOT). That means about 26 percent of employed workers in the US regard their overtime work as mandatory when they work it. Of all those employed, over 19 percent report both that they actually worked beyond their usual schedules in the last year and that when they worked overtime it was mandatory. Among full-time workers this rate is over 21 percent. This rate is slightly higher though generally consistent with other recent estimates from other samples of the extent of the employed work force facing MOT work (Cornell University Institute for Workplace Studies, 1999; Friedman and Casner-Lotto, 2003; Berg, et al., 2004). Workers with required extra hours average more than two hours per week and two days more per month than their counterparts without mandatory extra hours.

Table 6.2 shows that working overtime that is mandatory appears to be associated with earning less own or family income than working overtime voluntarily, although the former raises income above that which occurs with no extra hours at all. Working extra hours appears to be a phenomenon associated more with salaried than hourly jobs.

Table 6.1 General Social Survey 2002 basic descriptive information

	Number	Percent working at least one day beyond usual schedule (n=970)	Percent facing mandatory overtime (n=459)	Percent mandatory overtime and worked beyond usual schedule (n=342)	Percent with flexible schedule (often or sometimes) (n=928)	Percent mandatory overtime and no flexible schedule (rarely or never) (n=239)
Full Sample	2,765	-	-	-		
Employed	1,787	61.4%	25.7%	19.1%	53.9%	13.9%
Full-time	1,744	67.2	27.7	21.1	53.1	15.2
Part-time	312	35.3	16.1	9.0	57.6	8.1
Salaried			26.7		64.4	10.6
Hourly			25.6		43.3	17.0

Number of hours worked *last week* (mean)	Mandatory overtime (n=461)	No mandatory overtime (n=1293)	Difference (col. 1-col. 2)	All employed workers (n=1796)
Full-time	47.6	45.3	*+2.3 hours*	45.9
Part-time	23.3	22.7		22.6
Number of days worked extra per month (mean)	8.9**	4.9	*+4 days/mo.*	5.5

Source: 2002 General Social Survey and authors' calculations.

** Difference between mandatory overtime and no mandatory overtime is significant at < 0.05

In addition, the proportion of the sample that often or sometimes is allowed to vary their starting or ending times of work was 53 percent (43 percent of hourly, 64 percent of salaried). The proportion facing both MOT and lack daily schedule flexibility was 15 percent among full-time workers (11 percent of salaried and 17 percent of hourly). Those whose extra work is voluntary are those who tend to have access to daily schedule flexibility, whereas those whose overtime work is mandatory tend to have relatively less flexibility in their work schedule.

Descriptive Results: Associations between Mandatory Overtime and Physical Health Outcomes

Table 6.3 presents the proportions in the range of responses of the key physical health outcomes and tests for statistically significant differences in such proportions. Virtually all the QWL questions involve scaled or multiple option answers, from always/often to rarely never, and from excellent to poor. Workers working extra hours beyond their usual

Table 6.2 Flexibility, job status and income by type of overtime

Characteristics	Extra hours: MOT n=342	Extra hours: not MOT n=733	Extra hours: all n=1075	No extra hours n=677	All employed n=1787
Flexible daily work schedules					
Often/sometimes	46.5††	61.4	56.7**	50.4	53.8
Way paid					
Salaried	38.6	41.9	40.8**	23.6	33.8
Hourly	49.1	47.9	48.3**	63.1	53.3
Other	12.3	10.2	10.9	13.2	11.9
Respondent's income category	$25,000–29,000	$25,000–29,000	$25,000–29,000	$20,000–22,000	$22,500–24,999
Family income category	$35,000–39,000	$40,000–49,000	$40,000–49,000	30,000–34,999	*$35,000–39,000*

Source: 2002 General Social Survey

** Difference between all extra hours and no extra hours is significant at $\rho < 0.05$

†† Difference between extra hours: MOT and extra hours: not MOT is significant at $\rho <$

number at least once a month self-rate their physical health and potential limitations on daily activities associated with it, as poorer than those who report working no overtime at all. When such overtime work is required, their mean number of days in the last 30 days with not good physical health was higher on average than those whose extra work was not mandatory, but not statistically significantly greater. Similarly, daily fatigue (frequency of feeling used up at the end of the day) was considerably greater for workers with overtime work, but the increased frequency of fatigue when overtime is mandatory was not statistically significant.

Because differences between the mandatory and non-mandatory sample segments are present but ultimately too small (or standard errors too large) to yield statistically significant differences, it appears that it is the long hours per se, more than a lack of choice regarding extra work hours, that is associated with the frequency of poor physical health and fatigue. However, both the long hours and the perception that they are required contribute to work stress. Almost four in ten workers with MOT work report being always or often stressed from work. Thus, when extra hours are considered mandatory, it adds to the frequency of experiencing work stress. Within job types, salaried workers appear to experience work stress more often (and less rarely) than hourly paid workers.

Tables 6.4 and 6.5 show that the number of times an employed worker reports being hurt at work in the last 12 months is positively related to extra hours of work. Table 6.4 shows that injury rates are higher (that is, zero times of injury are lower) among workers who work extra hours, regardless of whether extra work is mandatory. However, experiencing back pain sometime in the past 12 months is higher if overtime work is mandatory.

Table 6.3 Selected health outcomes by type of overtime work

	Extra hours: MOT n=342	Extra hours: not MOT n=733	All extra hours n=1075	No extra hours n=677	All employed n=1787
How many days in past 30 did poor mental or physical health keep you from doing usual activities such as self-care, work, or recreation? (HEALTHY DAYS)					
Mean number of days (SD)	1.7 (5.2)	1.3 (4.0)	1.4 (4.4)	1.6 (5.1)	1.5 (4.7)
Zero Days (%)	75.4	77.1	76.6*	80.7	77.4%
In last 30 days, how many days physical health was NOT good?					
Mean number of days (SD)	2.8 (6.4)	2.6 (5.9)	2.7 (6.1)	2.5 (6.1)	2.6 (6.1)
Zero Days (%)	60.4	62.6	61.8**	68.1	64.3
How often during past 30 days felt used up at end of day? (USEDUP)					
Very often/often	47.1	45.3	45.9**	36.4	42.5
Sometimes	35.1	34.7	34.8	32.1	31.0
Rarely/never	17.8	19.7	19.2**	31.1	25.6
How often is work stressful? (STRESS)					
Always/often	38.6†	34.5	35.8**	22.8	26.6
Sometimes	42.4	45.6	44.8**	39.7	39.8
Hardly ever/never	18.7	19.7	19.5**	37.4	33.6

	Salaried	Hourly
Always	8.9	9.2
Often	29.1**	17.1
Sometimes	44.5	41.4
Hardly ever	13.3**	22.1

This is associated with the working condition of MOT, even if no extra days were actually worked in the previous month. The same association occurs regarding pain in the upper extremities. In the case of both back pain and arm (including wrist and hand) pain, it is the mandatory nature, not just the extra duration of hours that matters.

Table 6.4 Frequency of injuries: by type of overtime and injury

Type of overtime	OT is mandatory: worked extra hours (n=342)	OT is mandatory: no extra hours worked (n=113)	Extra hours: not mandatory (n=733)	Extra hours: all (n=1075)	No extra hours (n=677)
In the past 12 months, how many times have you been injured on the job? (HURTATWK)					
Zero injuries (%)	87.1	91.2	87.7	87.5*	90.4
In the past 12 months, have you had back pain every day for a week or more? (BACKPAIN)					
Yes	34.2++	34.5++	25.9	28.2	28.6
In the past 12 months, have you had pain in the hands, wrists, arms or shoulders every day for a week or more? (PAINARMS)					
Yes	33.9++	33.6++	25.1	27.9	29.1

* Difference is statistically significant between extra hours and no extra hours

\+ Difference is statistically significant between mandatory and not mandatory.

Table 6.5 illustrates that the duration of weekly work hours does matter, after some point. The frequency of experiencing a workplace injury, and experiencing back- or arm-related pain, rises after 60 hours per week. Those working fewer than 60 hours are no more prone to having such chronic pain or cumulative injuries than those working standard or even part-time hours. Thus, when overtime is required rather than purely a worker choice, there is a far greater association with experiencing both back pain and arm pain. The bottom of Table 6.5 shows that working both beyond one's usual schedule and overtime hours that are mandatory (MOTEXTRA) occurs more frequently among those who are full-time workers, particularly those reporting weekly hours (HRS1) more than 50 per week. Also, weekly hours are relatively higher among those who did not work beyond their usual schedule, but when they do extra work it is mandatory (MOTNOEXTRA).

Table 6.5 Injuries and pain by hours worked per week

Hours per week, all jobs	<=35 hours n=411	36-40 n=608	41-50 n=395	51-60 n=253	60-89 n=55	All Employed n=1722
In the past 12 months, how many times have you been injured on the job? (HURTATWK)						
Zero injuries (%)	88.6	88.7	88.9	88.1	81.8	87.9
In the past 12 months, have you had back pain every day for a week or more? (BACKPAIN)						
Yes	28.2	27.47	29.87	22.53	34.55	27.70
In the past 12 months, have you had pain in the hands, wrists, arms or shoulders every day for a week or more? (PAINARMS)						
% MOTEXTRA:	9.7	16.3	24.3	30.0	32.7	19.1
% MOTNOEXTRA	26.3	35.3	58.0	52.6	54.5	41.6

Table 6.6 shows that having a daily work schedule whose starting and ending times are flexible is inversely associated with the number of days when health is not good. It also shows that inflexible work schedules are associated with feeling always stressed from work and less likely to never feel fatigued. A combination of both overtime work being mandatory and schedules being inflexible seems to reinforce feelings of poor physical health and frequency of both work stressfulness and fatigue. Table 6.7 shows that more flexible schedules are associated with reduced frequency of injuries, but not significantly so in the case of both back and arm pain. However, having both an inflexible daily work schedule and facing the working condition of MOT (whether actually worked or not) is a toxic combination when it comes to experiencing back and arm pain (although not necessarily for reporting getting hurt at work). Table 6.8 shows that there is little difference by type of overtime work in the degree to which employees perceive their employer to be committed to providing a safe and healthy workplace environment. Table 6.9 shows that heavy lifting and repetitive hand movements are more common in jobs that involve MOT work, but such tasks appear to be evenly distributed across all level of hours per week worked. Table 6.10 shows that, just as with extra work at one's main job, those who hold a multiple number of jobs more frequently experience injury, back pain, and arm pain than those who have one job. Some of this might be due to them working on average more than three hours per week longer than those with a single job.

Table 6.6 Both indicators of inflexible working hours

	Schedule not flexible n=794	Schedule is flexible n=928	Facing mandatory overtime (whether or not actually worked) n=459	Worked OT but NOT mandatory (whether or not worked) n=733	Schedule not flexible AND OT is Mandatory n=239
In last 30 days, how many days physical health was NOT good?					
Zero Days (%)	60.4	66.2*	62.8	63.8	59.9
How often during the past month have you felt used up at the end of the day? (USEDUP)					
Very often/often	41.1	42.6	46.0	40.4	45.8
Sometimes	32.4	34.5	33.8	33.2	34.4
Rarely/Never	26.3*	20.6	20.1	24.9	19.4
How often do you find work stressful? (STRESS)					
Always	10.3*	7.8	11.1	8.2	13.4
Often	20.8	22.5	24.6	20.7	23.9
Sometimes	39.2	44.6	41.6	42.3	38.9
Hardly ever	18.2	18.6	17.0	18.9	16.6
Never	0.7*	6.4	5.5	8.4	6.9

Table 6.7 Inflexible work hours

	Schedule not flexible n=794	Schedule is flexible n=928	Mandatory overtime (whether worked OT or not)	OT NOT mandatory (whether or not worked)	Not flexible AND mandatory OT n=239
In the past 12 months, how many times have you been injured on the job? (HURTATWK)					
Zero injuries (%)	85.1	90.3*	88.2	87.8	86.6
If yes, how many times? Mean (sd)					
	2.89** (2.84)	2.25 (2.20)	2.06 (1.65)	2.80 (2.82)	1.94 (1.54)
In the past 12 months, have you had back pain every day for a week or more? (BACKPAIN)					
Yes	29.3	27.2	34.6**	25.9	39.3**
In the past 12 months, have you had pain in the hands, wrists, arms or shoulders every day for a week or more? (PAINARMS)					
Yes	28.7	27.5	33.8**	26.1	35.6**

Table 6.8 Safety questions by type of overtime

	Extra hours: MOT n=342	Extra hours: not MOT n=733	Extra hours: all n=1075	No extra hours n=677	All employed n=1787
The safety of workers is a high priority with management where I work. (SAFETYWK)					
Strongly agree	44.4	44.9	44.7	40.8	42.9
Agree	43.6	45.3	44.7	48.5	45.6
Disagree	8.2	7.6	7.8	7.1	7.4
Strongly Disagree	2.9	1.5	2.0	2.1	2.1
There are no significant compromises or shortcuts taken when worker safety is at stake (SAFEFRST)					
Strongly agree	41.8	42.6	42.3	39.4	40.9
Agree	43.6	46.4	45.5	47.0	45.5
Disagree	9.9	8.1	8.7	8.9	8.6
Strongly Disagree	3.8	2.3	2.8	2.2	2.6
The safety and health conditions where I work are good (SAFEHLTH)					
Strongly agree	36.8	37.1	37.0	35.5	36.6
Agree	52.9	54.8	54.2	55.7	54.1
Disagree	8.8	6.8	7.4	6.9	7.2
Strongly Disagree	1.5	1.0	1.1	1.3	1.2
Where I work, employees and management work together to ensure the safest working conditions (TEAMSAFE)					
Strongly agree	38.0	36.3	36.8	36.3	36.4
Agree	48.5	52.4	51.2	50.2	50.2
Disagree	10.8	8.3	9.1	9.6	9.2
Strongly Disagree	2.3	1.9	2.1	2.2	2.1

Table 6.9 Physical working conditions and overtime type

Type of Overtime	Extra hours: MOT n=342	Extra hours: not MOT n=733	Extra hours: all n=1075	No extra hours n=677	All employed n=1787
Does your job require you to do repeated lifting, pushing, pulling or bending? (HVYLIFT)					
Yes (%)	54.7**	41.1	45.4	47.1	45.8
Does your job regularly require you to perform repetitive or forceful hand movements or involve awkward postures? (HANDMOVE)					
Yes (%)	57.6**	47.6	50.8	50.8	50.5
By hours per week, all jobs	<=35 hours n=411	36-40 n=608	41-50 n=395	51-60 n=253	60-89 n=55
Does your job require you to do repeated lifting, pushing, pulling or bending? (HVYLIFT)					
Yes (%)	47.2	45.6	46.1	42.7	47.3
Does your job regularly require you to perform repetitive or forceful hand movements or involve awkward postures? (HANDMOVE)					
Yes (%)	49.9	52.3	50.6	45.9	52.7

Difference statistically significant at 10% level(*) or less or 5% level (**) or less.

Table 6.10 Effects of holding more than one job

	One job n=1421	Jobs or work other than main job n=294
Mean hours of work	41.2 (14.3)	44.3 (15.9)
In the past 12 months, how many times have you been injured on the job? (HURTATWK)		
Zero injuries (%)	89.7	84.4**
If yes, how many times? mean(SD)		
	2.2 (2.1)	1.7 (1.5)
In the past 12 months, have you had back pain every day for a week or more? (BACKPAIN)		
Yes (%)	26.7	32.7*
In the past 12 months, have you had pain in the hands, wrists, arms or shoulders every day for a week or more? (PAINARMS)		
Yes (%)	26.7	33.1**

Econometric Analysis

Econometric analysis is useful in isolating the potential effect of inflexibility of work on physical health indicators, holding constant various personal and job characteristics. Because the main outcomes are from scaled or multiple option questions, ordinal variables such as excellent, good, fair, and poor, the estimation technique used is a multinomial logistic regression. In an ordered logistic (or proportional odds) model, relationships are estimated between selected outcomes and a set of independent variables. The dependent variable in our case is the individual's self-reported frequency of experiencing of pain, injury at work, work stress, and fatigue. The model which is estimated for the true frequency of an outcome, given by:

$$O_j = \beta_1 MOT_j + \beta_2 FLEX_j + \beta_3 X_{2j+} \beta_4 Z_{4j} + u_j$$

The models are tested using the 2002 GSS and its supplement, the QWL. The dependent variable Oj is one of the selected outcomes reported as ordered categories. The independent variables are the presence of MOT and flexible schedule (FLEX), and a vector of control variables for job characteristics (Z), such as occupation and industry, task requirements, whether the job is a salaried or hourly or "standard" employment arrangement (as opposed to non-standard job arrangements, such as independent contractors and agency temporaries), and (X) for demographic characteristics, including age (and exponential), gender, race, foreign or native born, and living in a Standard Metropolitan Statistical Area (SMSA). The first model contains the full sample, with the key independent variables of focus being: having extra days worked that are required, are at least one per month = 1 and no extra days per month = 0 and a similar (1,0) dummy variable for whether the respondent reports being able to change their own daily work schedules often or sometimes, or otherwise. It is estimated along with the several control variables, including the number of hours of work, and u_j is also the error term. Controlling for the number of hours will allow us to observe if there is an add-on effect of being required to work overtime or an offsetting effect by having a flexible daily work schedule.

Hypotheses and Limitations of the Data

There are, unfortunately, several limitations and complications associated with applying these particular survey data and interpretations of the results. One is that the indicators are self-rated subjective health reports. What individuals are thinking rather than objective measures may be more prone to errors. Similarly, it is difficult to disentangle whether individual self-reports are responding to the effects of required extra hours or alternatively, being in less desirable jobs generally. In addition, there is a potential "healthy worker" effect that suggests that health is endogenous with working extra hours—the causality may run in both directions if healthier individuals are willing to work and can endure more overtime work. Moreover, there may be some simultaneity if workers that experience more overtime and also work stress share some common, unobserved traits that are outside of this model. There might be some interpretation problems given that GSS QWL survey questions use the reference period for hours as last week while the reference period for physical outcomes was in the last 30 days (Grosch et al., 2006).

A worker working 40 hours this week may have worked 50 or 60 the previous week. Thus an advantage gained by using extra days in the last month is that there is a potentially more direct association captured between the frequency or amount of overtime work and its physical outcomes, which may be lagged or cumulative.

Tables 6.11 and 6.12 contain a summary of the β coefficients and standard errors of the ordered logistic regressions, the direction of their effect, and statistical significance. Controls for occupation and industry are included but not reported in the table. The first estimation, using all employed workers, row two in both tables, illustrates the effect of working MOT. The statistically significant odds ratio suggests that both sustained back pain and arm pain is exacerbated by having required extra or overtime work. Note that this occurs despite controlling for their number of hours of work, as well as whether their jobs tend to entail heavy lifting and frequent or repetitive hand movements, their particular occupation and industry of employment, their salary vs. hourly paid status, and whether they had a second job. Indeed, lacking control over extra work appears to be more important for explaining back pain than the number of hours of work.

However, back pain is associated also with the extra work that stems from a worker having a second job. In the case of arm-related pain, having required extra work also seems to be a source of such pain. In this case, the inflexibility magnifies the strong positive effects on arm pain of working 60 or more hours per week and holding a second job. In the case of injury at work, there appears to be no more frequent injuries traceable to extra work being required. Among the control variables, the perceived safety of the workplace seems to be a key factor in safety outcomes. (Only for getting injured on the job, do the occupation and industry of the worker matter, once all the other control variables are in place.)

In addition, having salary status is associated with a considerably lower frequency of experiencing an on the job injury. Among occupations (unreported results), the incidence of physical health outcomes by occupational classification is quite uneven. The incidence of back pain appears to be exacerbated by overtime work being mandatory in certain occupations–executive, administrative, managerial; technicians and related support; sales; farming, fishing, and forestry; precision production; transportation; machine operators, assemblers, inspectors; and somewhat in administrative support occupations—relative to workers in those occupations who have overtime work that is not mandatory.

Extra hours that are not mandatory are associated with a higher incidence of back pain in a few occupations as well—sales; service; construction trades and laborer occupations. When overtime is mandatory, workers in certain occupations report a higher rate of experiencing arm-related pain than those whose overtime in that occupation are not mandatory–executive, administrative, managerial; professional specialty; administrative support; farming, fishing, and forestry; construction trades; machine operators and transportation. Extra work hours itself is associated with more arm pain, relative to those who have no extra work, only in executive, administrative, and managerial positions.

Work stress seems to be largely connected to the duration of hours. Mandatory extra work and inflexible schedules are dwarfed by the effect of work hours. Workers with fewer than full-time hours report less stress. Workers with greater than 40 hours per week report progressively higher greater stress as the number of hours climbs. Stress is no higher among those holding more than one job. In addition, work stress appears to be more a scourge of salaried jobs but not hourly paid jobs. Fatigue appears to be virtually exclusively a function of working more than a standard 40-hour work week and is not influenced by inflexibility of overtime work or schedules, but is a consequence of demanding physical labor.

Table 6.11 Logistic regression results—direct physical health outcomes

Odds Ratio (SE)	In the past 12 months, have you had back pain every day for a week or more? (backpain)	In the past 12 months, have you had pain in the hands, wrists, arms or shoulders every day for a week or more? (painarms)	In the past 12 months, how many times have you been injured on the job? (hrtatwk)
Work hours			
MOTEXTRA	1.36** (0.19)	1.32* (0.19)	0.96 (0.20)
FLEX	1.01 (0.13)	1.21 (0.15)	1.00 (0.19)
<=35 hours	1.01 (0.17)	0.95 (0.15)	0.88 (0.21)
41–50 hours	1.12 (0.17)	0.99 (0.15)	1.06 (0.23)
51–60 hours	0.73* (0.14)	0.73 (0.14)	0.97 (0.26)
60–89 hours	1.35 (0.44)	2.15** (0.70)	1.68 (0.71)
secondwk	1.32* (.197)	1.30* (0.19)	1.25 (0.25)
Safety at work			
safetywk2	1.06 (0.13)	1.27* (0.16)	1.31 (0.24)
safetywk3	1.51* (0.33)	1.66** (0.36)	2.18** (0.60)
safetywk4	1.97* (0.73)	2.74** (1.04)	4.50** (1.90)
hvylift	1.31* (0.19)	1.23 (0.18)	3.07** (0.66)
handmove	1.90** (0.25)	2.09** (0.28)	1.27 (0.24)
Employment and job characteristic*			
salary	0.97 (0 .14)	0.85 (0.13)	0.63** (0.14)
Demographics			
male	0.76* (0.11)	0.86 (0.12)	1.20 (0.34)
nonwhite	0.83 (0.12)	0.91 (0.14)	0.86 (0.17)
insmsa	0.84 (0.11)	1.03 (0.14)	0.67* (0.15)
foreign	1.22 (0.23)	1.49** (0.29)	0.94 (0.17)
Logistic regression results are reported as odds ratios * $p < .10$ ** $p < .05$	n = 1722 LR $chi^2(60)$ = 131.51 Prob > chi^2 = 0.0000 Log likelihood = -950.4 Pseudo R^2 = 0.0647	n = 1722 LR $chi^2(60)$ = 166.56 Prob > chi^2 = 0.0000 Log likelihood= -933.83 Pseudo R^2 = 0.0819	n = 1722 LR $chi^2(60)$ = 179.81 Prob > chi^2 = 0.0000 Log likelihood = -528.83 Pseudo R^2 = 0.1454

Results are controlled for industry, occupation respondent's income level. For hrs1, 36–40 hours worked last week is the omitted category; For safetywk1, the safety of workers is a high priority with management where I work—strongly agree—is the omitted category.

Table 6.12 Logistic regression results—indirect physical health outcomes

Odds ratio (SE)	Work stress: find work stressful—always or often	Fatigue: often or very often felt used up at the of the day
Work hours		
MOTEXTRA	1.23 (0.17)	1.08 (0.14)
FLEX	0.87 (0.11)	0.94 (0.10)
<=35 hours	0.77** (0.13)	1.07 (0.16)
41–50 hours	1.41** (0 .21)	1.58** (0.22)
51–60 hours	1.65** (0 .29)	2.36** (0.40)
60–89 hours	2.85** (0 .88)	3.62** (1.14)
secondwk	1.11 (0 .17)	0.98 (0.13)
Safety at work		
safetywk2	1.24** (0.15)	1.11 (0 .12)
safetywk3	1.72** (0.37)	1.25 (0.26)
safetywk4	4.56** (1.72)	4.94** (2.11)
hvylift	1.01 (0.14)	1.28* (0.17)
handmove	1.61** (0.21)	1.81** (0.22)
Employment and job characteristics*		
salary	1.30* (0.17)	1.23 (0.16)
Demographics		
male	0.82 (0.10)	0.67** (0.08)
nonwhite	0.78* (0.11)	0.75** (0.10)
insmsa	0.93 (0.12)	0.99 (0.12)
foreign	1.02 (0.20)	0.93 (0.17)
	Number of obs = 1722 LR chi^2(60) = 162.05 Prob > chi^2 = 0.0000 Log likelihood = -977.90 Pseudo R^2 = 0.0765	Number of obs = 1722 LR chi^2(60) = 186.55 Prob > chi^2 = 0.0000 Log likelihood = -1078.434 Pseudo R^2 = 0.0796

Logistic regression results reported as odds ratios. Results are controlled for industry, occupation respondent's income level. hrs1cat2: 36–40 hours worked last week is the omitted category.

Summary of Findings and Their Implications

MOT work is a key factor in determining chronic pain or injuries. However, flexible schedules do not appear to do much to ease these pains. It is likely that the control variables for occupation, number of hours, and salary status have outweighed the effect of flexible work schedules. Access to flexibility comes hand-in-hand with longer work hours, salaried status, and certain occupations (Golden, 2009). Because the duration of hours also matters for all of the self-reported direct and indirect physical health indicators, both this and control over extra work hours beyond normal hours are more salient factors than the timing of the work day, at least in this particular sample.

The findings have implications for understanding the economics of labor supply and well-being, and for public policy intended to improve worker well-being. The nuances of the results suggest that extra hours and the mandatory nature of some overtime work should be treated in research and policy as having separate and distinct effects on workers' well-being. When a worker cannot refuse unwelcome extra hours of work, their well-being is diminished by more than just the accompanying loss of desired leisure hours. They become exposed to risks to bodily pain, particularly cumulative or chronic pain. (Acute pain or accident risks are associated with long work hours, whether they are strictly voluntary or not so.) The long duration of hours and extra days of work generally create their own negative effects on indicators of work stress and some risks for injury at work. The adverse effects of long hours or extra days appear to be often compounded by overtime being mandatory. Because overtime work tends to bring in additional current or expected future income rewards, the net welfare effect of overtime work is, a priori, ambiguous (Golden and Wiens-Tuers, 2005). Pain and physical discomfort is becoming recognized by some (behavioral) economists as an erosion of potential utility (subjective well-being) of workers (for example, Kahneman and Krueger, 2006).

Thus, the results suggest that pain from work is likely to be ameliorated by both more opportunities for voluntarily reduced work weeks and an ability to refuse extra work. Moreover, limitations on hours would likely decrease the frequency of work stress. To the extent that the inability to refuse extra work tends to offset any positive effects of overtime work, such as current and future compensation increases, an ability to do so might allow workers to realize a higher level of overall well-being. Most tests of compensated wage differential theory find little additional monetary reward for the working condition of MOT work (for example, Ehrenberg and Schumann, 1984). Indeed, the burdens of working at less desirable times of the work day, such as evenings and nights, and the risk of occupational injury, have over time become more and more borne by lower-wage workers (Hamermesh, 1999).

For public policy, the results suggest that any regulation of work hours designed to counter the potential adverse physical well-being effects of long or involuntary extra work ought to focus on providing both limits on very long hours beyond 60 hours per week (or by implication, 12 per day), and greater legal rights of refusal and rights of requests regarding adjustments in work hours. This might involve consideration of adopting the International Labor Organization's (ILO) (2005) principle that the loss of wages accompanied by threats of dismissal if workers refuse to do overtime beyond the scope of their employment contract or national laws falls under the ILO's definition of forced labor (e.g., see Belser et al , 2005). A further step would be to apply the US's own

Occupational Safety and Health Act's (OSHA) general duty clause, requiring employers to remove excessive hours as a known workplace hazard (Andersen, 2004).

There is also a case for requiring employers to pay a premium for involuntarily imposed, particularly on short notice, extra hours beyond the current time-and-a-half rate. This could be applied toward hourly paid (typically non-exempt) employees and perhaps even a straight-time pay equivalent for salaried (typically exempt) employees. Also fruitful might be extending the Fair Labor Standards Act (FLSA) in ways that would enhance an employee's legal right to refuse employer-requested overtime, beyond the health care sector employees which about a dozen US states have adopted. It may also involve adopting rights to request proposed in the current Congress (H.R. 1274), which would require employers to consider written requests from employees to shorten their own standard work week or to shift their daily start and end times of work.

An enhanced legal right to refuse employer-requested overtime work hours could be targeted first to workers who are afflicted or affected by it most, such those in the lower income brackets or employed in sectors where inflexible scheduling practices, long hours, and injury risks are most pervasive—such as construction and business and repair services (Dembe, Delbos and Erickson, 2008). However, because national indicators of subjective well-being are positively related to levels of economic freedom (Helliwell, 2003), such regulation must be carefully designed so as to not suppress overtime work that workers seek and work purely voluntarily. Nonetheless, the findings suggest there is a strong case for policies that would induce employers to adopt less inflexible work scheduling practices that would limit the potential spillover costs borne not only by individuals, but ultimately organizations and the entire work force.

References

Aiken, L.H., Clarke S.P., Sloane D.M., Sochalski, J., and Silber, J.H. (2002) Hospital nurse staffing and patient mortality, nurse burnout, and job dissatisfaction, *Journal of American Medical Association; 288*(16), 23/30, 1987–1993.

Allen Jnr., H.M., Slavin, T., and Bunn, W.B. III. (2007). Do long workhours impact health, safety, and productivity at a heavy manufacturer?, *Journal of Occupational & Environmental Medicine*; *49*(2), 148–171.

Altman, M. and Golden, L. (2008) Why do people overwork? Over-supply of hours of labor, labor market forces and adaptive preferences. In R. Burke and C. Cooper (eds) *The Long Work Hours Culture: Causes, Consequences and Choices,* Bingley, UK: Emerald Group Publishing, 61–83.

Anderson, T. (2004) Overwork robs workers' health: interpreting OSHA's general duty clause to prohibit long work hours, *New York City Law Review; 7*(Spring) 85–160.

Artazcoz, L., Cortès, I., Escribà-Agüir, V., Cascant, L., and Villegas, R. (2009) Understanding the relationship of long working hours with health status and health-related behaviours, *Journal of Epidemiological Community Health; 6*(3), 521–527.

Askenazy, P. (2004) Shorter work time, hours flexibility and labor intensification, *Eastern Economic Journal; 30*(4), 603–14.

Barnett, R.C. (2004) Work Hours as a Predictor of Stress Outcomes. Extended Abstracts from Conference: Long Working Hours, Safety, And Health: Toward A National Research Agenda, University of Maryland, Baltimore, Maryland, April 29–30, 2004.

Beckers, D.G.J., van der Linden, D., Smulders, P.G.W., Kompier, M., Taris, T.W., Geurts, S.A.E. (2008) Voluntary or involuntary? Control over overtime and rewards for overtime in relation to fatigue and work satisfaction, *Work and Stress;* 22(1), 33–50.

Beckers, D.G.J., van der Linden, D., Smulders, P.G.W., Kompier, M., van Veldhoven, M.S.P.M., van Yperen, N.W. (2004) Working overtime hours: Relations with fatigue, work motivation, and the quality of work, *Journal of Occupational and Environmental Medicine; 46*(12), 1282–1289.

Belser, P., de Cock M. and Mehran, F. (2005) ILO Minimum Estimate of Forced Labour in the World. Geneva: International Labour Office.

Berg, P., Appelbaum, E., Bailey, T., and Kalleberg, A. (2004) Contesting time: Comparisons of employee control of working time, *Industrial and Labor Relations Review; 57*(3), 531–549.

Bliese P. and Halversen, R. (1996) Individual and non-homothetic models of job stress: An examination of work hours, cohesion and well-being, *Journal of Applied Social Psychology; 26*, 13, 1171–1189.

Boden. L.I. (2005) Running on empty: Families, time, and workplace injuries, *American Journal of Public Health; 95*(11), 1894–1897.

Brenner, M.D., Fairris, D., and Ruser, J. (2004) Flexible work practices and occupational safety and health: Exploring the relationship between cumulative trauma disorders and workplace transformation, *Industrial Relations;* 43(1), 242–266.

Brogmus, G.E. (2007) Day of the week lost time occupational injury trends in the US by gender and industry and their implications for work scheduling, *Ergonomics; 50*(3) 446–474.

Burke, R.J., (2009) Working to live or living to work: Should individuals and organizations care?, *Journal of Business Ethics; 84*(Supplement 2), 167–172.

Burke, R.J. and McAteer, T. (2006) *Work hours and work addiction: The price of all work and no play.* In J. Langan-Fox, C.L. Cooper, R.J. and Klimoski (eds), *Research Companion to the Dysfunctional Workplace*, Cheltenham, UK: Edward Elgar Publishing, 239–273.

Butler, A., Grzywacz, J., Ettner, S., and Liu, B. (2009) Workplace flexibility, self-reported health, and health care utilization, *Work & Stress*; 23(1) 45–59.

Caruso, C.C., Hitchcock, E.M., Dick, R.B., Russo, J.M., and Schmitt, J.M. (2004) *Overtime and Extended Work Shifts: Recent Findings on Illnesses, Injuries and Health Behaviors*. Cincinnati, OH: National Institute for Occupational Safety and Health.

Courtemanche, C. (2009) Longer hours and larger waistlines? The relationship between work hours and obesity, *Forum for Health Economics and Policy;* 12(2), Article 2, http://www.bepress.com/fhep/12/2/2.

Clauretie, T.M. (2007) A note on the relationship between overtime work and age, *Journal of Legal Economics; 14*(1), 23–32.

Cornell University Institute for Workplace Studies (1999) *Overtime and the American Worker.* Ithaca, NY: New York State School of Industrial and Labor Relations.

Costa, G., Sartori, S., and Akerstedt, T. (2006) Influence of flexibility and variability of working hours on health and well-being, *Chronobiology International; 23*(6), 1125–1137.

Danna, K. and Griffin, R.W. (1999). Health and well-being in the workplace: A review and synthesis of literature, *Journal of Management; 25*(3), 357–384.

Dembe, A. (2009) Ethical issues relating to the health effects of long working hours, *Journal of Business Ethics*; *84*(2), 195–208.

Dembe, A.E., Delbos, R., and Erickson, J.B. (2008) The effect of occupation and industry on the injury risks from demanding work schedules. *Journal of Occupational and Environmental Medicine*; *50*(10), 1185–1194.

Dembe, A.E., Delbos, R., Erickson, J.B., and Banks, S.M. (2007) Associations between employees' work schedules and the vocational consequences of workplace injuries, *Journal of Occupational Rehabilitation;* 17(4), 641–651.

Dembe, A.E., Erickson, J.B., Delbos, R.M., Banks, S., and Reville, R. (2005) The impact of overtime and extended work hours on occupational injuries and illnesses: new evidence from the United States, *Occupational and Environmental Medicine; 62*(9), 588–597.

Dong, X. (2005) Long workhours, work scheduling and work-related injuries among construction workers in the United States, *Scandinavian Journal of Work, Environment and Health; 31*(5), 329–335.

Easterlin, R.A. (2006) Life cycle happiness and its sources: Intersections of psychology, economics, and demography, *Journal of Economic Psychology; 27*(4), 463–482.

Ehrenberg, R. and P. Schumann. (1984) Compensating wage differentials for mandatory overtime, Economic Inquiry; *22*(4), 460–478.

Fenwick, R. and M. Tausig. (2001) Scheduling stress: Family and health outcomes of shift work and schedule control, *The American Behavioral Scientist; 44*(7), March, 1179–98.

Friedman, W. and Casner-Lotto, J. (2003) *Time is of the Essence: New Scheduling Options for Unionized Employees.* Berkeley, CA: Work in America Institute and Labor Project for Working Families.

Galinsky, E. and Bond, J.T. (2001) *Feeling Overworked.* New York, NY: Families and Work Institute.

Galinsky, E., Bond, J.T., Kim, S., Backon, L., Brownfield, E., and Sakai, K. (2005) *Overwork in America: When the Way We Work Becomes Too Much.* New York, NY: Families and Work Institute.

Gershuny, J. (2005) Busyness as the badge of honor for the new superordinate working class, *Social Research; 72*(2), 287–314.

Golden, L. (2009) Flexible daily work schedules in US jobs: Formal introductions needed?, *Industrial Relations; 48*(1), 27–54.

Golden, L. and Wiens-Tuers, B. (2005) Mandatory overtime work in the United States: Who, where, and what?, *Labor Studies Journal; 30*(1), 1–26.

Green, F. (2004) Work Intensification, discretion and the decline in well-being at work, *Eastern Economic Journal; 30*(4), 615–625.

Grosch, J.M., Caruso, W.C.C., Rosa, R.R., and Sauter, S.L. (2006) Long hours of work in the US: Conditions and health, *American Journal of Industrial Medicine; 49*(11), 943–952.

Grzywacz, J.G, Casey, P.R., and Jones F.A. (2007). The effects of workplace flexibility on health behaviors: A cross-sectional and longitudinal analysis, *Journal of Occupational and Environmental Medicine; 49*(12), 1302–1309.

Hamermesh D. (1999) Changing inequality in work injuries and work timing, *Monthly Labor Review;* October, 22–31.

Heisz, A. and LaRochelle-Côté, S. (2006) Work hours instability, *Perspectives on Labour and Income*; 7(12), 17–20.

Helliwell J. (2003) How's life? Combining individual and national variables to explain subjective well-being, *Economic Modeling; 20*(2), 331–360.

Hughes, E.L. and Parkes, K.R. (2007) Work hours and well-being: The roles of work-time control and work-family interference, *Work & Stress*; *21*(3), 264–278.

Jensen, A. and Dahl, S. (2009) Truck drivers hours-of-service regulations and occupational health, *Work: A Journal of Prevention, Assessment and Rehabilitation*; *33*(3), 363–368.

Johnson, J.V. and Lipscomb, J. (2006) Preface: Long working hours, occupational health and the changing nature of work organization, *American Journal of Industrial Medicine; 49*(11), 921–929.

Kahneman, D. and Krueger, A.B. (2006) Developments in the measurement of subjective well-being, *Journal of Economic Perspectives; 20*(1), 3–24.

Landsbergis, P.A. (2003) The changing organization of work and the safety and health of working people, *Journal of Occupational and Environmental Medicine*; *45*(1), 61–72.

Lesnard, L. and de Saint Pol, T. (2009) Patterns of workweek schedules in France, *Social Indicators Research*; *93*(1), 171–176.

MacEachen, E., Polzer, J., and Clarke, J. (2007) You are free to set your own hours: Governing worker productivity and health through flexibility and resilience, *Social Science and Medicine*; *66*(5), 1019–1033.

Meier, L.L., Semmer, N.K., Elfering, A., and Jacobshagen, N. (2008) The double meaning of control: Three-way interactions between internal resources, job control, and stressors at work, *Journal of Occupational Health Psychology*; *13*(3), 244–258.

Nicol, A. and Botterill, J. S. (2004) *On-call work and health: a review, Environmental Health: A Global Access Science Source; 3*(1), *15*.

Ng, T. and Feldman, D. (2008) Long work hours: a social identity perspective on meta-analysis data, *Journal of Organizational Behavior*; *29*(7), 853–880.

Pouwels, B., Siegers, J., and Vlasblom, J.D. (2008) Income, working hours, and happiness, *Economics Letters; 99*(1), 72–74.

Raediker, B., Jansen, D., Schomann, C., and Nachreiner, F. (2006) Extended working hours and health, *Chronobiology International; 23*(6), 1305–1316.

Ricci, J.A., Chee, E., Lorandeau, A.L., and Berger, J. (2007) Fatigue in the US workforce: Prevalence and implications for lost productive work time, *Journal of Occupational and Environmental Medicine; 49*(1), 1–10.

Rosa, R. (1995) Extended workshifts and excessive fatigue, *Journal of Sleep Research; 4*(2), 51–56.

Sparks, K., Faragher, B., and Cooper, C. (2001) Well-being and occupational health in the 21st century workplace, *Journal of Occupational and Organizational Psychology; 74*(4), 489–509.

Spurgeon, A. (2003) *Working Time: Its Impact on Safety and Health*. Geneva: International Labour Office.

Trinkoff, A., Le, R., Geiger-Brown, J., Lipscomb, J., and Lang, G. (2006) Longitudinal relationship of work hours, mandatory overtime, and on-call to musculoskeletal problems in nurses, *American Journal of Industrial Medicine; 49*(11), 964–971.

Tucker, P. and Rutherford, C. (2005) Moderators of the relationship between long work hours and health, *Journal of Occupational Health Psychology; 10*(4), 465–476.

Van Der Hulst, M. (2003) Long work hours and health, *Scandanavian Journal of Work Environment Health; 29*(3), 171 –188.

Appendix: All Relevant Variables in 2002 GSS and Table Abbreviations

OVERTIME WORK AND HOURS

MOREDAYS	How many days per month do you work extra hours beyond your usual schedule?
MUSTWORK	When you work extra hours, is it mandatory (required by your employer)?
EXTRADAYS	At least one day per month worked beyond usual schedule.

MOTEXTRA	Worked beyond usual schedule at least one day per month and it was mandatory.
MOTNOEXTRA	Did not work beyond usual schedule but overtime work is mandatory.
HRS1	How many hours did you work last week, at all jobs? (recoded ranges).
SECONDWK	Worked more than one job (n=247) vs. no work on other than main job has (n=1421).
FLEX	Allowed to change starting and quitting time on a daily basis often or sometimes, formed from: CHNGTIME How often are you allowed to change your starting and quitting times on a daily basis?

HEALTH AND WELL-BEING INDICATORS

HEALTHYDAYS	How many days in past 30 did poor mental or physical health keep you from doing usual activities such as self-care, work, or recreation?
STRESS	How often do you find your work stressful?
USEDUP	How often during the past month have you felt used up at the end of the day?

PHYSICAL HEALTH INDICATORS

HURTATWK	In the past 12 months, how many times have you been injured on the job?
BACKPAIN	In the past 12 months, have you had back pain every day for a week or more?
PAINARMS	In the past 12 months, have you had pain in the hands, wrists, arms or shoulders every day for a week or more?

WORKING CONDITIONS

SAFETYWK	The safety of workers is a high priority with management where I work
SAFEFRST	There are no significant compromises or shortcuts taken when worker safety is at stake.
SAFEHLTH	The safety and health conditions where I work are good.
HVYLIFT	Does your job require you to do repeated lifting, pushing, pulling or bending?
HANDMOVE	Does your job regularly require you to perform repetitive or forceful hand movements or involve awkward postures?

DEMOGRAPHIC CHARACTERISTICS (CONTROLS)

age	Age in years (and age-squared)
male	Respondent is male
nonwhite	Respondent is non-white
insmsa	Respondent within an SMSA and a large or medium size central city
foreign	Respondent was born in a foreign country
rincome	Respondent's own income (bracket)

Occupations*

occcat1	Executive, administrative, managerial
occcat2	Professional specialty
occcat3	Technicians and related support
occcat4	Sales
occcat5	Administrative support
occcat6	Service
occcat7	Farming, fishing, forestry
occcat8	Mechanics and repairers
occcat9	Construction trades
occcat10	Extractive
occcat11	Precision production
occcat12	Machine operators, assemblers, inspectors
occcat13	Transportation
occcat14	Laborers

Industries*

indcat1	Agriculture, forestry, fisheries
indcat2	Mining
indcat3	Construction
indcat4	Manufacturing-nondurables
indcat5	Manufacturing-durables
indcat6	Transportation, communications, public utilities
indcat7	Wholesale trade
indcat8	Retail trade
indcat9	FIREA
indcat10	Business and repair services
indcat11	Personal services
indcat12	Entertainment, recreation services
indcat13	Professional services
indcat14	Public administration

* Industry and occupational variables are based on the 1980 Census industrial and occupational classifications.

CHAPTER **7**

Workplace Bullying: A Toxic Part of Organizational Life

STIG BERGE MATTHIESEN AND BRITA BJØRKELO

Introduction

The interplay that leads to workplace bullying is toxic for organizational life. In this chapter we explore workplace bullying in more detail, its basic characteristics, but also some of the conditions that lead to this unwanted type of behavior. Various sub-types of workplace bullying will be presented. We will also outline and elaborate on some strategies to stop this kind of negative social exchange.

Concept clarification

How can workplace bullying or workplace harassment be defined? In his pioneering book *The Harassed Worker*, Brodsky (1976) coined workplace harassment as persistent attempts on the part of one or more persons to annoy, wear down, frustrate, or elicit a reaction in another. The most common definition of workplace bullying, used by most researchers in recent years, was formulated by Einarsen and colleagues (2003, p. 15).

> *Bullying at work means harassing, offending, socially excluding someone or negatively affecting someone's work tasks. In order for the label bullying (or mobbing) to be applied to a particular activity, interaction or process it has to occur repeatedly and regularly (e.g. weekly) and over a period of time (e.g. about six months). Bullying is an escalating process in the course of which the person confronted ends up in an inferior position and becomes the target of systematic negative social acts. A conflict cannot be called bullying if the incident is an isolated event or if two parties of approximately equal "strength" is in conflict.*

In the US, some researchers have applied the term "emotion abuse" to describe workplace bullying (for example, Keashly and Harvey, 2005). A recent review study by Aquino and Thau (2009) uses the term of "workplace victimization." According to Aquino and Thau, workplace victimization occurs when an employee's well-being is harmed by one or more members of the organization and psychological or physiological needs are unmet or thwarted. Examples of unmet needs may materialise as loss of sense of belonging, a feeling that one is an unworthy individual, and a loss in fundamental beliefs in the ability to predict and cognitively control one's environment and interpersonal trust. The process that leads up to these unmet needs develops when an individual is faced with humiliating negative behavior for over a period of time that he or she is unable to stop and where the employee is in a position where they perceive a power imbalance. Thus, bullying develops gradually through an escalating process, the core being the victim's experience of being exposed to systematic, continuous, and partly intentional aggression in a situation (in this case, the workplace) in which such behavior should not occur (Keashly, 1998). The central feature of imbalance of power (Einarsen and Skogstad, 1996) excludes situations where two equal (for example, gender, ethnicity, power, position) persons are in conflict. The core aspect of this feature is that targets of bullying, regardless of their individual characteristics, find it difficult to defend or protect themselves against the unwanted negatively perceived behavior (Zapf and Einarsen, 2005).

A work situation characterized by low control combined with high strain has been found to be particularly stressful (Karasek and Theorell, 1990) and may be one of the reasons why bullying is associated with severe consequences on physical and psychological health (see, for example, Bechtoldt and Schmitt, 2010; Hansen et al., 2006; Matthiesen and Einarsen, 2001; 2004; Mikkelsen and Einarsen, 2002; Nielsen, Matthiesen, and Einarsen, 2008; Tehrani, 1996; Tracy, Lutgen-Sandvik, and Alberts, 2006). Therapautic contact with individuals exposed to bullying at work has shown that they typically perceive the bullying to be intentional and directed against them, that they lack opportunities to evade it, that they lack adequate social support that could act as a "buffer," that they experience the bullying sanctions as unfair or out of place and as over-dimensioned, and that they feel personally or socially vulnerable, and that the actions they have been exposed to makes them feel extremely insulted, humiliated, and ashamed (Einarsen et al., 1994; Matthiesen et al., 2003; Zapf and Gross, 2001). In addition to the potentially severe consequences workplace bullying may have for the individuals involved, it may also lead to considerable costs for the workplace in which it occurs (Salin, 2003). Later in this chapter we will examine the process of events that lead up to workplace bullying as defined here, but we will next indicate the prevalence of workplace bullying.

Prevalence of Workplace Bullying

Most studies conducted since the start of workplace bullying research have used a prospective survey approach (for example, Einarsen and Raknes, 1997; Mikkelsen and Einarsen, 2001; Vartia, 1996; Zapf, Knorz and Kulla, 1996). Bullying has been included as one of several topics in a wide range organizational studies typically assessed by questionnaires. Results have shown that the prevalence varies greatly from 1 per cent to above 50 per cent depending upon the applied measurement strategy, occupation, or sector, as well as country (Martino, Hoel and Cooper, 2003; Nielsen, Matthiesen and Einarsen, 2010). A review which included 14 sub-samples and a total of 7,118 participants demonstrated that 8.6 percent reported being bullied during the last six months (Einarsen, 1996). Specifically, 1.2 per cent were bullied weekly, 3.4 per cent "now and then" and 4 per cent once or twice. A decade later, the prevalence numbers for workplace bullying seem to have been considerably reduced in Norway. A national representative study, with 2,539 respondents participating, revealed that 4.6 per cent employees reported to be exposed to workplace bullying (Einarsen et al., 2007a).

And 0.6 were bullied weekly, 1.3 per cent "now and then," and 2.5 per cent once or twice. In other words, over a period of about 15 years, the occurrence of bullying in Norway may have undergone a nearly 50 per cent reduction.

Theoretically, bullying is a long lasting process consisting of recurring negative acts. Large representative samples in Sweden (Leymann, 1996) and Norway (Einarsen and Skogstad, 1996) have also found the average duration of bullying to be rather long lasting, varying between 15 and 18 months (Zapf et al., 2003). In the Norwegian national representative study, it was found that a considerable number of bullying incidents, four in ten cases, had lasted for more than one year (Einarsen et al., 2007a). A recent meta-analytic study of workplace bullying across countries applied 102 prevalence estimates of bullying from 86 independent samples with a total of 130,000 respondents (Nielsen et al., 2010). On average, these statistically independent samples provided a prevalence rate of workplace bullying of 14.6 percent, when bullying is considered across countries. It should be noted, however, that the prevalence rate for studies when a definition of bullying was not provided to the victims was found to be 18.1 percent. The rate was consistently lower when the respondents (potential victims) in survey studies, be it convenience sample studies or representative sample studies of various workforces, were given an established definition of workplace bullying, such as the Einarsen et al. definition (2003) previously referred to. When a bullying definition was addressed, 11.3 percent of those taking part in the studies exploring workplace bullying were exposed to this kind of negative conduct.

Prevalence rates of bullying therefore seem to be highly influenced by the research strategy applied. Keashly and Jagatic (2003) suggest that the difficulty in determining the exact prevalence of workplace bullying may be due to lack of common terminology and well-developed methodology. Another explanation may be that the interpretation of bullying varies across nations, which then calls for integrated research approaches (Fevre et al., 2010).

The Process of Bullying

Is it useful to distinguish between harassment and workplace bullying? In Norway, the Work Environment Act (Section 4.3) declares that workplace harassment is prohibited at work. The terms bullying or mobbing are not mentioned in this Section of the Act. Does this mean that harassment and workplace bullying should be seen as synonymous concepts? In our opinion, it is beneficial to differentiate between harassment and workplace bullying. One or a few extreme negative incidents can be seen as harassment, according to the Norwegian Work Environment Act.

In the definition of bullying proposed by Einarsen and colleagues (2003), bullying is described as a long lasting phenomenon with repeated negative acts for period of six months or more. Harassment, however, in accordance with the Norwegian Work Environment Act, can take place with only one or a few humiliating incidents. Figure 7.1 presents a model of how harassment may develop into workplace bullying. The model, adapted from our efforts to consider a link between bullying and racial discrimination (Matthiesen, Glasø, and Lewis, 2009), illustrates how workers may be exposed to a negative or offending situation (sequence 1, situation^{1}) that may be experienced as harassment (sequence 2, harass^{1}). The model describes a situation in which an individual may be mocked based on his or her ethnicity and how this may lead to an attribution or interpretation about why the harassment is occurring (sequence 3, attr^{1}).

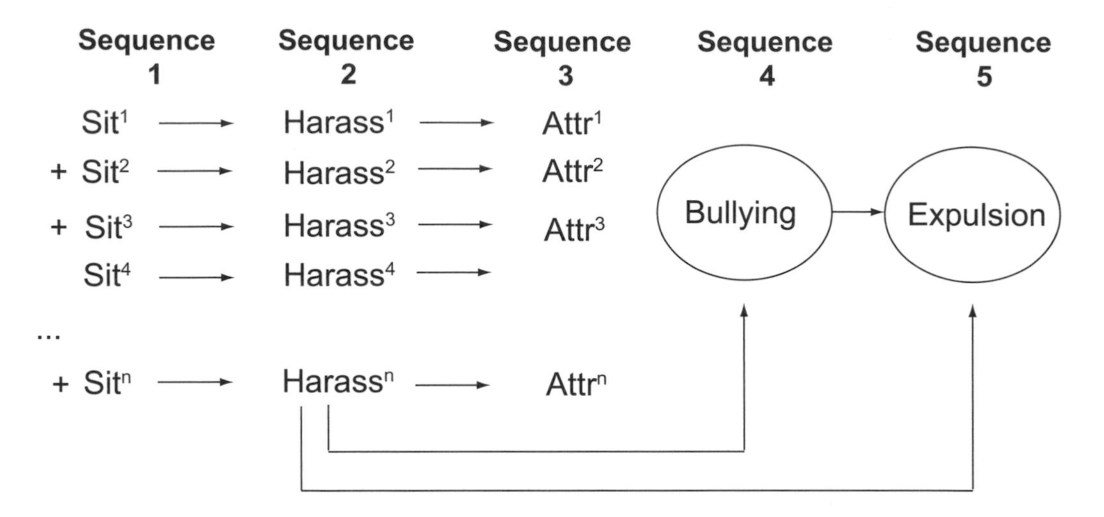

Figure 7.1 A potential development from exposure to a negative situation (sequence 1), to workplace bullying and expulsion (sequence 4 and 5)

Note: A potential development from exposure to a negative situation (sequence 1) to experiencing being harassed or discriminated (sequence 2). Harassment or discrimination may be attributed to ethnical background, and/or other issues (sequence 3). Repeated harassment or discrimination over a given number of situations (situation 1, situation 2, situation n) may lead to an experience of being bullied at work (sequence 4). The harassment or discrimination may also lead to expulsion, resulting in that the individual quits or exits or has to leave the organization or that the individual exits working life in general (sequence 5).

Abbreviations applied in Figure 1: Sit= situation, harass= harassment or discriminating event, attr= attribution or how to explain the occurring events.

As indicated in Figure 7.1, negative situations such as these may be repeated and may accumulate (sit^2, sit^3, sit^4, ... sit^n) with repeated exposure to harassing behaviors ($harass^2$, $harass^3$, $harass^4$, ... $harass^n$). Harassing actions may be ascribed by the individual perceiving it as occurring because of their ethnic characteristics ($attr^2$, $attr^3$, $attr^4$, ... $attr^n$). One example of such an incident may involve an individual being denied permanent employment which may be interpreted by the individual as relating to his or her ethnic background. Another situation may involve the denial of interesting work assignments or tasks, being asked to do routine work well below one's level of competence instead. When harassing or discriminating events continue to occur, a feeling of being harassed or discriminated against may develop and transform itself into a feeling of being bullied at work (sequence 4 in Figure 7.1). If the bullying behaviors concern ethnic content, this may be attributed as the cause and may be described as racist bullying. Finally, sequence 5 in Figure 7.1 deals with employee exit or expulsion which may be the culmination of a bullying process (Leymann, 1996). Due to repeated situations and acts such as these, an employee may decide to leave the organization (cf. arrow from sequence 2 to sequence 5). Exit may also be a consequence of effects associated with long lasting workplace bullying (cf. arrow from sequence 4 to sequence 5). Thus, exit from an organization may be either voluntary and involuntary.

How many harassing or negative acts must occur before an individual experiences it as bullying? Workplace bullying can be understood in terms of the dose-response perspective. According to this, a person must be exposed to a certain number of bullying episodes (dose), before the feeling bullied sets in (response). The dose-response perspective is well known within medicine and epidemiology. For instance, scores of adverse childhood experiences were found to have a strong dose-response graded relationship to the probability of lifetime and recent depressive disorders, with an increased odds ratio probability of about 2.5, as compared to a control group (Chapman et al., 2004). It is also found that some indications of a dose-response link existed between bullying and sick leave (Kivimäki, Elovainio and Vahtera, 2000). However, the dose-response perspective has not been widely applied empirically within the work bullying research field. Little is known about the "dose" of bullying episodes that is a prerequisite for the unique and subjective feeling of being bullied. And the number of bullying episodes that must take place before the onset of the unique feeling of being bullied will most likely vary from one person to another. Distinctive individual features such as former work experience, personal vulnerability, childhood experiences, age, and educational level represent some of the conditions that may determine with how strongly one feels bullied.

A model to illustrate and further inform understanding of bullying has been suggested by Zapf (2004). He draws a number of concentric circles (see Figure 7.2), in which the outer circle consists of various social stressors that take place within an organization. The next inner circle symbolizes a situation in which social conflicts arise and build up over time (for example, when people have to cooperate throughout a period of organizational restructuring, with decisions that have to be improvised, and time pressure to fulfill all the extra work tasks).

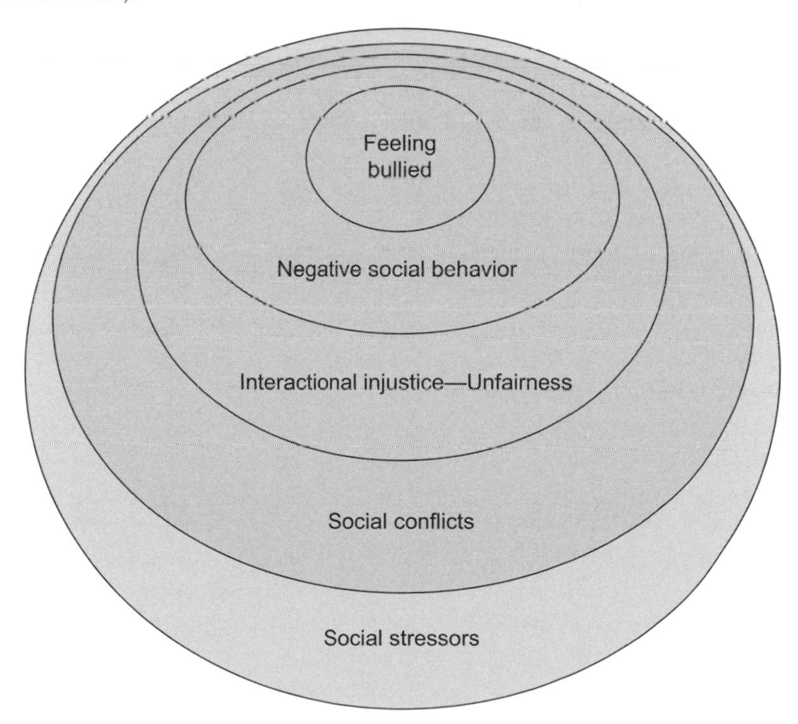

Figure 7.2 An illustrative view of the bullying process (Zapf, 2004)

The next inner circle includes situations in which unfair work practices or interactional injustice occurs (for example, when resources or benefits are perceived by some to be unfairly divided). Zapf's next inner circle includes negative acts or negative social behavior. The Negative Acts Questionnaire (Einarsen, Hoel and Notelaers, 2009) describes a host of such events (for example, repeated "attacks" against a person, social isolation from colleagues, slanders or rumors about an individual being spread). The innermost circle in the Zapf model consists of bullying or mobbing, the subjective and victimized feeling of being the target of bullying. One example may be a company undergoing organizational change with downsizing and layoffs. Here uncertainty and the speed of the transition process may evoke stressing episodes (social stressor circle) and social conflict (for example, between union representatives and top management or between ground floor personnel). The latter may escalate due to competition for the scare resources (social conflicts circle).

In the process of layoffs, controversial and unfair decisions may be made in relation to who gets to stay and who has to go (interactional injustice—unfairness circle). Bullying may be a result when repeated unfair or unjust actions occur over a period of time as decisions made may influence both work content, workplace, and work group interactions (negative social behavior circle). Due to the perceived insensitive and uncaring behavior from superiors some employees or workers may end up feeling bullied (innermost circle). The Zapf model comprises an easy-to-comprehend framework to illustrate the phenomenon of bullying, seen as an escalating social conflict process (Zapf and Gross, 2001).

Types of Bullying

Workplace bullying can also be understood from a situational perspective. Different types of social situations can cause workplace bullying. Einarsen (1999) makes a distinction between work-related actions that make it difficult for victims to carry out their work or involve taking away some or all of their responsibilities and actions that are primarily person-related. Based on empirical and theoretical evidence, this categorization may be broadened to include the following additional bullying types: social isolation (for example, exclusion from daily communication or social events), personal attacks (for example, ridicule and insulting remarks), verbal threats such as criticism and up front humiliation and rumors where one's social reputation is attacked (Zapf, 1999). Actions such as previously mentioned may occur in a range of different situations and settings and with many different kinds of origins and precursors. Matthiesen (2006) has suggested that ten basic sub-types of bullying may in fact exist (see Table 7.1).

One of these ten sub-types of bullying is *predatory bullying* in which the target has done little or nothing provocative that may reasonably justify the behavior of the bully but still finds him or herself in a situation where a predator demonstrates power or exploits an accidental target into compliance (Einarsen, Matthiesen and Mikkelsen, 1999). *Dispute-related bullying* develops from an interpersonal conflict which often involves social control reactions to perceived wrongdoing. Studies have shown that bullying cases typically are triggered by a work-related conflict in which the social climate between the conflicting parties have gone sour and later escalates into a person-focused conflict where the total destruction of the opponent is seen as legitimate actions by the parties (Leymann, 1990;

Table 7.1 Some proposed subtypes of workplace bullying

1. Dispute-related bullying
2. Predatory bullying
3. Scapegoating
4. Sexual harassment
5. Humor-oriented bullying
6. Work-related stalking
7. Extreme media exposure bullying
8. Bullying of workplace newcomers
9. The judicial derelicts (secondary bullying)
10. Retaliation from whistleblowing

Zapf and Gross, 2001). In such highly escalated conflicts, both parties may deny the opponent's human value, thus clearing the way for manipulation, retaliation, elimination, and destruction (van de Vliert, 1998). If one of the parties acquires a disadvantaged position in this struggle, he or she may become a target of bullying (Björkqvist, Österman and Hjelt-Bäck, 1994).

Scapegoating is another type of work harassment which may be described as displaced frustration directed toward an employee or workers that an individual believes "deserves it" (Brodsky, 1976; Thylefors, 1987). Such types of bullying may occur in situations where stress and frustration are caused by a source who is either indefinable, inaccessible, respected, or too powerful to be attacked and the group turns its hostility toward a less powerful person. Although a field of research in itself (for a review, see Pryor and Fitzgerald, 2003), it may also be argued that *sexual harassment* may been seen as a sub-type of work harassment where an employee, for example a powerful and old co-worker or superior, directs repeated and unwanted sexual attention toward a young female employee. The unwanted attention may be combined with threats about future job prospects in order to coerce the target to subjugation, or may in itself act to create a hostile work environment.

Humor-oriented bullying occurs when person-oriented humor is directed toward someone in an out-group position and the jokes and humorous behavior is imbalanced or asymmetrical. Many workplaces have a widespread use of ridiculing, teasing or interpersonal humor. When people-oriented humor plays out between equals, that is, work colleagues within the same in-group, it may increase job satisfaction or work commitment (Matthiesen and Einarsen, 2002). When humor is uni-directional and at the systematic expense of others such humor may function as bullying.

Work-related stalking is a form of bullying that involves systematic and repeated exposure to behaviors that may be inoffensive and harmless in themselves (for example, sending letters or gifts, making telephone calls, or waiting outside a person's home or workplace) (Purcell, Pathe, and Mullen 2004). Stalking can be defined as a course of conduct in which one individual inflicts upon another repeated unwanted intrusions and communications, to such an extent that victims fear for their safety (Pathe and Mullen, 1997). Most episodes of stalking covered by the media seem to consist of rejected ex-partners after separation or divorce, bombarding or terrorizing their former wives or husbands with telephone calls, SMS-messages, or e-mails. Celebrities such as film, music, or sports figures may be stalked in their workplaces; in addition, ordinary workers may also be stalked both inside and outside of their workplaces. In Norway, a tourist bus driver was stalked for years by one of the accompanying female tourists he met in his job. The male driver was terrorized with thousands of letters and telephone calls and stalked day and night. The stalker was finally imprisoned due to the vast number of bullying episodes that she initiated, despite several warnings.

Extreme media exposure bullying is a type of bullying politicians and other high social status members of society may be exposed to, for example, media celebrities, film, and music stars and top leaders, particularly when they transgress (for example, Tiger Woods). If these pillars of their communities are accused of criminal, illegal activities, or in many case simply "stupid" behaviors, and the media compete to have the most provacative headlines, this may develop into extreme media exposure bullying. This is particularly the case if the accusations are incorrect or exaggerated. The person in the spotlight may feel subjected to bullying. Extreme media exposure cannot be countered easily with a legal defense. Some years ago, a former Norwegian cabinet minister committed suicide because of a number of such persistent and harsh incidents.

Workplace newcomer bullying or rite de passage bullying is a form of behavior observed for a long time that is especially relevant in some occupations (for example, within the police or military service) (Brodsky, 1976). In such cases newcomers in the work place are met with intimidating behavior that may be regarded as a cultural tradition with the aim of "testing" the newcomer. When the rites are systematic and long lasting they may develop into bullying. An old sailor once told us a story about a young colleague who on his first voyage was unable to cope with and endure the humiliating and frequent rite de passages he was faced with as a new sailor. The outcome in this case was fatal; he ended up drowning himself.

Judicial or system bullying occurs when an individual feels bullied by "the system" (for example, various bureaucrats and their decisions or the legal system). An individual previously exposed to bullying may attempt to fight for judicial justice or support from the organization or from the authorities which may lead to them ending up at the receiving end of aggression and passive obstruction from a wide range of people or roles thought to be places of rescue. Judicial or system bullying bears resemblance to what has been labeled as secondary bullying which occurs when an individual exposed to bullying feels ignored by others (for example, employer, health and safety authorities, labor union) after he or she reports the bullying (Einarsen, 1999).

The final type of bullying is *retaliatory acts after whistleblowing.* Near and Miceli (1985) define whistleblowing as an act that takes place when an employee witnesses wrongdoing at the work place (for example, unethical conduct, corruption, violence or bullying against others, criminal acts) from a fellow employee or a superior (or a group of employees or superiors). The whistleblower tries to stop the wrongdoing by informing someone who is in the position to stop the wrongdoing. The whistleblowers may voice their concern internally (for example, to a superior within the company), but may also do it externally (for example, informing the rightful authorities, revealing the case in the media informing a local nature conservation association, to give but a few examples). Sometimes whistleblowing leads to a victimization process where the organization or its members "shoots the messenger" (Paul and Townsend, 1996), and the retaliation becomes repeated and systematic and develops into workplace bullying of the individual who attempted to do something about what he or she had witnessed (Bjørkelo et al., 2008).

In a Norwegian survey conducted among a group of some 200 members of a support group for employees previously exposed to bullying at work, whistleblowing turned out to be the second most frequent reason given for workplace bullying when they were asked to rank reasons for why exactly they were targeted for bullying (Nielsen, 2003). One way whistleblowers may be met is by punishing or sanctioning them with informal forms of ostracism (De Maria and Jan, 1997; Williams, 2001) or to strip them of work tasks (Miethe, 1999). Callanan reported on the repeated abuse of individuals in a long-stay ward for chronically ill patients with mental health problems and described his situation in the following way:

> *I used to go over to the canteen at lunch time for a meal, and they wouldn't come and sit with me—not that they disapproved of what I had done, but they didn't want other people to see. They might nod their head, but they wouldn't sit ... none of them would hold a conversation, they would always find an excuse. You felt very much as an outsider*
>
> (Beardshaw, 1981, p. 37).

Whistleblowers may also be terminated from their jobs, or not have their work contracts renewed. They may experience rumors about their "disloyalty" being spread widely, including to other companies, making it difficult to obtain another job when they in fact have performed responsible followership and tried to help a third party (Alford, 2008; Miceli and Near, 2005). Several studies have documented how whistleblowers may suffer from physical and psychological problems when their efforts are followed by retaliation and workplace bullying (Bjørkelo, et al., 2008; Rothschild, 2008; Rothschild and Miethe, 1999; Soeken and Soeken, 1987). Consequences on health have also been found to influence colleagues who may suffer from a variety of stress symptoms such as insomnia and anxiety (McDonald and Ahern, 2002). However, despite formal and informal individual and work task types of retaliation or bullying, and potential physical and mental after effects, most employees exposed to bullying or harassment state that the worst is not being taken seriously or believed and listened to (Bjørkelo et al., 2008; Hoel and Cooper, 2000).

Bullying Interventions

According to Hauge, Skogstad and Einarsen (2009) "bullying will thrive in stressful working environments" (p. 349). How should one therefore approach individual and situational factors in a working environment that may trigger workplace bullying? According to French psychiatrist, psychoanalyst, and family therapist, Marie-France Hirigoyen (2004) the workplace ideally should respond as soon as possible. The individual at the receiving end should collect evidence in the form of dates, and witnesses in order to defend him or herself in the face of word against word situations. According to Hauge, Skogstad and Einarsen (2009), the workplace should also pay attention to the fact that many of the individuals that themselves acknowledge to have bullied others report that they also are exposed to bullying, and that they in general experience high amounts of stress at work.

Empirical studies have shown that many organizations apply anti-bullying measures in accordance with recommendations from the academic literature, particularly when human resources personnel responsible for taking action were young and early in their career (Salin, 2008). Salin also found that large organizations that adopted sophisticated human resoruce management practices (for example, formal systems for appraisal, pay based on performance, training, and employee attitude surveys) were more likley to address workplace bullying issues as part of their general focus on personnel issues. This study also observed that anti-bullying procedures frequently seem to be applied as a reactive more than a proactive action.

One important practical implication would be to embrace a more proactive stance toward workplace bullying. A proactive approach would be characterized by keeping an eye out for potential bullying instances without being ordered or asked to do so, and solving potential bullying problems early, for example by encouraging the reporting of potentially problematic events at work (Bateman and Crant, 1993; Furnham, 1997; Miceli, Near and Dworkin, 2009). Preliminary evidence suggests that positive organizational climates may encourage whistleblowing (Near, Baucus and Miceli, 1993) which may be one way to alert management and others about workplace bullying (Rayner and McIvor, 2006). As individuals exposed to bullying at work also may bully others, interventions should both include a focus on improving the overall work environment, as well as dealing effectively with existing cases of bullying (Hauge, Skogstad and Einarsen, 2009).

To our knowledge, relatively few large-scale intervention programs have been conducted in traditional workplaces that have documented bullying and have also measured the effect of the intervention. However, in the education sector, with its emphasis on reducing school bullying, intervention activity has been undertaken over a number of years (Olweus, 2003). According to Olweus (1994) one needs to work at the general level, at the school level, the class level, and at the individual level to make such interventions effective. For example, a school environment that minimizes student bullying has been found to be characterized by positive interest, warmth, and involvement, firm limits, and non-physical and non-hostile reactions. It is reasonable to translate these key principles into a setting in which most adults spend at least one-third of their waking hours, namely at work. Table 7.2 offers some suggestions for how intervention programs for reducing school bullying may be applied in a workplace setting (see for example, Olweus, 1994, p. 1186 and Olweus 2003, p.72).

Based upon the design of such intervention programs in schools, a total organization approach should include rules and routines that regulate action, and strategies for handling bullying at work in a way that is measurable and that may be evaluated. One of the core components is the need to ensure awareness and top management involvement regarding anti-bullying policies as a general prerequisite. This should then be linked to the legal regulations that refer to bullying and harassment in their jurisdictions. This is consistent with suggestions by Einarsen and Hoel (2008) who argue that in order to prevent and manage bullying at work it is important to build a culture "where bullying and mistreatment of employees are not tolerated" (p. 167).

Core components at the *organizational level* include the application of questionnaire surveys, the arrangement of a bullying awareness day, and the development of routines for detection of bullying actions during social events (for example, lunch hours and at the business Christmas party). According to Einarsen and Hoel (2008), having high work ethic, as well as clear goal, roles, and responsibilities on an organizational level may

Table 7.2 Intervention program strategies in a workplace setting (some suggestions inspired by Dan Olweus' intervention program to stop school bullying)

General prerequisites ++ General awareness and top management involvement regarding anti-bullying policies.
Measures at organizational level ++ Applying questionnaire surveys. ++ Bullying awareness day. ++ Routines for detection of bullying actions during social events (e.g., lunch hours and at the business Christmas party). + Develop a coordination group in charge of the implementation process. + Manager and staff representative meeting and discussion groups.
Measures at the unit level ++ Anti-bullying policies at each unit that contains clear examples of unwanted acts and behaviors. ++ Arrange regular meetings with managers, staff, human resources, and personnel officers about psychosocial factors, including bullying.
Measures at the individual level ++ Serious talks with employees perceived and identified as performing bullying acts and employees that perceive themselves to be at the receiving end of the same acts. These talks should include talking about expected behavior (anti-bullying policies with clear examples), and about the laws that regulate bullying and the psychosocial work environment at work. ++ Serious talks with colleagues and witnesses. These talks should include talking about expected behavior (anti-bullying policies with clear examples), and about the laws that regulate bullying and the psychosocial work environment at work. + Development of individual intervention plans. + Meeting and discussion group with manager and staff representatives that use vignettes and scenarios about bullying and harassment at work

++ Core component; + highly desirable component

prevent and be useful in managing bullying at work. These factors may help to reduce the fact that "the organization itself is the bully" (D'Cruz and Noronha, 2009, p. 44), which may be the case when production demands are excessive and the entire work regime is oppressive (Hoel and Beale, 2006). These general suggestions which set out to create a social climate that is open, that respects diversity, and that deals with conflicts quickly and openly rather than avoiding them, are consistent with recommendations for preventing and managing bullying at work as outlined by Einarsen and Hoel (2008).

At the *unit level,* core components include the creation of anti-bullying policies that contain clear examples of unwanted acts and behaviors in a fitting context (for example, working individually on apparatus of any kind versus in collaborative work in an open office landscape). Regular meetings with managers, employees, and human resource professionals that address psychosocial factors including bullying are also recommended as a core part of such a total organization approach. According to Einarsen and Hoel (2008), leadership styles and practices for management should apply to all employees and include fairness, respect, and sensitivity, and leaders are recommended to educate themselves in conflict management.

At the *individual level,* it is expected that serious talks with employees perceived and identified as performing bullying acts as well as with employees that perceive themselves to be at the receiving end of the same acts are conducted. Talks such as these are important as "most people, even most of those accused of bullying, will generally be opposed to bullying" (Einarsen and Hoel, 2008, p. 167). In detail, these talks should include going through anti-bullying policies and give clear examples, as well as directly address the laws that regulate bullying and the psychosocial work environment at work. Serious talks with the same aims should also be conducted with colleagues and potential witnesses. These talks should strive for impartiality and fairness and may aim at investigating: (1) whether bullying has occurred and discussions regarding how it may be stopped; (2) if it is not bullying how good working conditions can be restored for the involved parties; (3) finding out whether there is need for changing any organizational practices to prevent bullying.

In addition to core elements at these three levels, additional desirable components such as developing a coordination group in charge of the implementation process, and the arrangement of meeting and discussion groups with manager and staff representatives (organizational level), developing individual intervention plans, and arranging meetings and discussion groups that actively apply and discuss vignettes and scenarios about bullying and harassment at work with managers and staff representatives present (individual level) would pay dividends. As a participant in one research study reported: "The HR manager, another manager, and colleagues had a meeting arranged and mediated and in the end both the manager and the employer accepted a share of the responsibility" (Rayner and McIvor, 2008, p. 64). However, at the end of the day, managers, supervisors, and leaders are responsible for "the existence, prevention, and constructive management of bullying at work" (Einarsen and Hoel, 2008, p. 168).

Some describe the exposure to bullying as a lesson in solitude and betrayal, and how such experiences make employees desperate and in despair, leading to a position of social and psychological paralysis (Mikkelsen, Kullberg and Eriksen-Jensen, 2007). According to Mikkelsen, Kullberg and Eriksen-Jensen, one of the most important intervention strategies at an individual level is therefore to treat these employees with empathy and take them and what they describe seriously. Secondly, colleagues are also in a position to make a difference. According to Rayner and McIvor (2008) lack of support from colleagues may exacerbate an already difficult situation and contribute directly "to bullying and harassment and as a spiral of conflict" (p. 41). If another individual, or several colleagues, had spoken up about the bullying of their co-workers "then a truly zero-tolerance culture would be achieved" (p. 59). Thus, the role of colleagues is of great importance as they provide practical and emotional support. However, work colleagues become even more effective if they show that bullying is not "silenced to death" but acted on (Mikkelsen, Kullberg and Eriksen-Jensen, 2007). Colleague support is especially crucial for minority employees as they seem to receive less such support than other employees (Giga, Hoel, and Lewis, 2008).

Conclusions

The International Labour Organization (ILO) has recognized workplace bullying in the broader context of violence at work. In a 2000 monograph, the ILO observed that workplace bullying by itself may be relatively minor but cumulatively it can become a very serious form of violence (Yamada, 2003). Workplace bullying is a complex multi-causal phenomenon with severe negative impact on those affected. Bullying seems to be more widespread in some nations than others (Nielsen, Matthiesen and Einarsen, 2010). Many different antecedent factors may cause workplace bullying, for example role stress (Matthiesen and Einarsen, 2007) and destructive leadership (Einarsen, Aasland and Skogstad, 2007b). Workplace bullying may also impact the organization in various negative ways (Salin, 2009). The negative conduct and experiences that workplace bullying represents is neither the product of chance nor of destiny. Instead, it should be understood as an unwanted form of systematic and repeated interpersonal interactions between individuals in their daily work. Personal factors and situational or contextual factors, taken together, explain the nature and characteristics of the phenomenon. As this chapter has indicated, solid research-based information on the causes and consequences of workplace bullying are now emerging that should serve as the foundation for development of sound interventions and preventive strategies.

References

Alford, C.F. (2008) Whistleblowing as responsible followership. In I. Chaleff, R.E. Riggio and J. Lipman-Blumen (eds) *The Art of Followership: How Great Followers Create Great Leaders and Organizations*. San Francisco, CA: Jossey-Bass, 237–251.

Aquino, K., and Thau, S. (2009) Workplace victimization: Aggression from the target's perspective, *Annual Review of Psychology:* 60, 717–741.

Bateman, T.S. and Crant, J.M. (1993) The proactive component of organizational behavior: A measure and correlates, *Journal of Organizational Behavior;* 14(2), 103–118.

Beardshaw, V. (1981) *Conscientious Objectors at Work*. London: Social Audit Limited.

Bechtoldt, M.N. and Schmitt, K.D. (2010) 'It's not my fault, it's theirs'—explanatory style of bullying targets with unipolar depression and its susceptibility to short term therapeutical modeification, *Journal of Occupational and Organizational Psychology;* 83(2), 395–417.

Bjørkelo, B., Ryberg, W., Matthiesen, S.B., and Einarsen, S. (2008) "When you talk and talk and nobody listens": A mixed method case study of whistleblowing and its consequences, *International Journal of Organisational Behaviour;* 13(2), 18–40.

Björkqvist, K., Österman, K., and Hjelt-Bäck, M. (1994) Aggression among university employees, *Aggressive Behavior;* 20(3), 173–184.

Brodsky, C.M. (1976) *The Harassed Worker*. Toronto, Canada: Lexington Books.

Chapman, D.P., Whitfield, C.L., Felitti, V.J., Dube, S.R., Edwards, V.J., and Anda, R.F. (2004) Adverse childhood experiences and the risk of depressive disorders in adulthood, *Journal of Affective Disorders;* 82, 217–225.

D'Cruz, P. and Noronha, E. (2009) Experiencing depersonalised bullying: A study of Indian call-centre agents, *Work organisation, Labour & Globalisation;* 3(1), 26–46.

De Maria, W. and Jan, C. (1997) Eating its own: the whistleblower`s organization in vendetta mode, *Australian Journal of Social Issues;* 32(1), 37–59.

Einarsen, S. (1996) *Bullying and Harassment at Work: Epidemiological and Psychosocial Aspects*. Unpublished Doctoral dissertation, University of Bergen, Bergen.

Einarsen, S. (1999) The nature and causes of bullying at work, *International Journal of Manpower;* 20(1/2), 16–27.

Einarsen, S., Aasland, M.S., and Skogstad, A. (2007b) Destructive leadership: A definition and a conceptual model, *Leadership Quarterly;* 18, 2007–2216.

Einarsen, S. and Hoel, H. (2008) Bullying and mistreatment at work: How managers may prevent and manage such problems. In A. Kinder, R. Hughes and C.L. Cooper (eds) *Employee Well-being Support: A Workplace Resource*. Chichester, UK: John Wiley & Sons Ltd, 161–173.

Einarsen, S., Hoel, H., and Notelaers, G. (2009) Measuring exposure to bullying and harassment at work: Validity, factor structure and psychometric properties of the Negative Acts Questionnaire-Revised, *Work & Stress;* 23(1), 24–44.

Einarsen, S., Hoel, H., Zapf, D., and Cooper, C.L. (2003) The concept of bullying at work: The European tradition. In S. Einarsen, H. Hoel, D. Zapf and C.L. Cooper (eds) *Bullying and Emotional Abuse in the Workplace*. London, UK: Taylor & Francis, 3–30.

Einarsen, S., Matthiesen, S.B., and Mikkelsen, E.G. (1999) *Tiden Leger Alle Sår? Senvirkninger Av Mobbing i Arbeidslivet [Time is a Great Healer? Health Effects after Bullying at Work]*. Bergen: University of Bergen.

Einarsen, S. and Raknes, B.I. (1997) Harassment in the workplace and the victimization of men, *Violence and Victims;* 12, 247–263.

Einarsen, S., Raknes, B.I., Matthiesen, S.B., and Hellesøy, O.H. (1994). *Mobbing og Harde Personkonflikter. Helsefarlig Samspill på Arbeidsplassen [Bullying and Tough Interpersonal Conflicts. Health Injourious Interaction at the Work place]*. Bergen, Norway: Sigma Forlag.

Einarsen, S. and Skogstad, A. (1996) Bullying at work: Epidemiological findings in public and private organizations, *European Journal of Work and Organizational Psychology;* 5(2), 185–201.

Einarsen, S., Tangedal, M., Skogstad, A., Matthiesen, S.B., Aasland, M.S., Nielsen, M.B., Bjørkelo, B., Glasø,L. and Hauge, L.J. (2007a) *Et Brutalt Arbeidsmiljø? En Undersøkelse av Mobbing, Konflikter og Destruktiv Ledelse i Norsk Arbeidsliv [A Brutal Work Environment. An Exploration of Bullying, Conflicts and Destructive Leadership in Norwegian Working Life]*. Bergen, Norway: Universitetet i Bergen.

Fevre, R., Robinson, A., Jones, T., and Lewis, D. (2010) Researching workplace bullying: The benefits of taking an integrated approach, *International Journal of Social Research Methodology;* 13(1), 71–85.

Furnham, A. (1997) *The Psychology of Behaviour at Work. The Individual in the Organization*. Hove, East Sussex: Psychology Press.

Giga, S.I., Hoel, H., and Lewis, D. (2008) *A review of Black and Minority Ethnic (BME) employee experiences of workplace bullying*: Unite the Union & the Department for Business, Enterprise and Regulatory Reform.

http:/www.unitetheunion.com/resources/equalities/black_and_ethnic_minority_righ.aspx.

Hansen, Å.M., Hogh, A., Persson, R., Karlson, B., Garde, A. H., and Ørbæk, P. (2006) Bullying at work, health outcomes, and physiological stress response, *Journal of Psychosomatic Research;* 60, 63–72.

Hauge, L.J., Skogstad, A., and Einarsen, S. (2009) Individual and situational predictors of workplace bullying: Why do perpetrators engage in the bullying of others?, *Work and Stress,* 23(4), 349–358.

Hirigoyen, M.-F. (2004) *Stalking the Soul*. Canada: Helen Marx Books.

Hoel, H. and Beale, D. (2006) Workplace bullying, psychological perspectives and industrial relations: Towards a contextualized and interdisciplinary approach, *British Journal of Industrial Relations;* 44(2), 239–262.

Hoel, H. and Cooper, C. L. (2000) Working with victims of workplace bullying. In H. Kemshall and J. Pritchard (eds) *Practice in Working with Victims of Violence* (Vol. 8). London, UK: Jessica Kingsley Publishers, 101–118.

Karasek, R. A. and Theorell, T. (1990) *Healthy Work: Stress, Productivity and the Reconstruction of Working Life*. New York, NY: Basic Books.

Keashly, L. (1998) Emotional abuse in the workplace: conceptual and empirical issues, *Journal of Emotional Abuse;* 1(1), 85–117.

Keashly, L. and Harvey, S. (2005). Emotional abuse in the workplace. In S. Fox and P. E. Spector (eds) *Counterproductive Work Behavior*. Washington DC: American Psychological Association, 201–235.

Keashly, L. and Jagatic, K. (2003) By another name: American perspectives on workplace bullying. In S. Einarsen, H. Hoel, D. Zapf and C.L. Cooper (eds) *Bullying and Emotional Abuse in the Workplace*. London, UK: Taylor & Francis, 31–61.

Kivimäki, M., Elovainio, M., and Vahtera, J. (2000) Workplace bullying and sickness absence in hospital staff, *Occupational & Environmental Medicine;* 57(10), 656–660.

Leymann, H. (1990) Mobbing and psychological terror at workplaces, *Violence and Victims;* 5(2), 119–126.

Leymann, H. (1996) The content and development of bullying at work, *European Journal of Work and Organizational Psychology;* 5, 165–184.

Martino, V.D., Hoel, H., and Cooper, C.L. (2003) *Preventing Violence and Harassment in the Workplace*. Dublin: European Federation for the Improvement of Living and Working Conditions.

Matthiesen, S.B. (2006) *Bullying at the Workplace. Antecedents and Outcomes*. Unpublished PhD thesis, University of Bergen, Bergen, Norway.

Matthiesen, S.B., Aasen, E., Holst, G., Wie, K., and Einarsen, S. (2003) The escalation of conflict: a case study of bullying at work, *International Journal of Management and Decision Making;* 4(1), 96–112.

Matthiesen, S.B. and Einarsen, E. (2001) MMPI-2 configurations among victims of bullying at work, *European Journal of Work and organizational Psychology;* 10(4), 467–484.

Matthiesen, S.B. and Einarsen, S. (2002) Arbeidsliv, humor og mobbing—hvor går grensen? [Humor and bullying in working life—where are the boundaries?]. In S. Tyrdal (ed.) *Humor og Helse [Humor and Health]*. Oslo, Norway: Kommuneforlaget, 165–186, 220–222.

Matthiesen, S.B. and Einarsen, S. (2004) Psychiatric distress and symptoms of PTSD among victims of bullying at work, *British Journal of Guidance and Counselling;* 32(3), 335–356.

Matthiesen, S.B. and Einarsen, S. (2007) Perpetrators and targets of bullying at work: Role stress and individual differences, *Violence and Victims;* 22(6), 735–753.

Matthiesen, S.B., Glasø, L., and Lewis, D. (2009) Når jobben blir ugrei: Om diskriminering av innvandrere på arbeidsplassen [When the job is troublesome: About discrimination of immigrants at the workplace]. In G. Sandal (ed.) *Kulturell Mangfold i Arbeidslivet. Utfordringer og Virkemidler [Cultural diversity in working life. Challenges and means for change]*. Bergen, Norway: Fagbokforlaget, 79–98.

McDonald, S. and Ahern, K. (2002) Physical and emotional effects of whistleblowing, *Journal of Psychosocial Nursing & Mental Health Services;* 40(1), 14–27.

Miceli, M.P. and Near, J.P. (2005) Standing up or standing by: what predicts blowing the whistle on organizational wrongdoing? In J.J. Martocchio (ed.) *Research in Personnel and Human Resources Management* (Vol. 24). Oxford, UK: Elsevier Ltd, 95–136.

Miceli, M.P., Near, J.P., and Dworkin, T.M. (2009) A word to the wise: how managers and policy-makers can encourage employees to report wrongdoing, *Journal of Business Ethics;* 86(3), 379–396.

Miethe, T.D. (1999) *Whistleblowing at Work. Tough Choices in Exposing Fraud, Waste, and Abuse on the Job*. Colorado: Westview Press.

Mikkelsen, E.G. and Einarsen, S. (2001) Bullying in Danish work-life: Prevalence and health correlates, *European Journal of Work and Organizational Psychology;* 10(4), 393–413.

Mikkelsen, E.G. and Einarsen, S. (2002) Basic assumptions and post-traumatic stress among victims of workplace bullying, *European Journal of Work and Organizational Psychology;* 11(1), 87–111.

Mikkelsen, E.G., Kullberg, K., and Eriksen-Jensen, I.L. (2007) *Mobning på Arbejdspladsen [Workplace Bullying—Causes and Solutions].* København: FADL's forlag.

Near, J.P., Baucus, M.S., and Miceli, M.P. (1993) The relationship between values and practice. Organizational climates for whistleblowing, *Administration & Society;* 25(2), 204–226.

Near, J. P. and Miceli, M.P. (1985) Organizational dissidence: The case of whistle-blowing, *Journal of Business Ethics;* 4, 1–16.

Nielsen, M.B. (2003) *Når Mobberen er Leder. En Studie av Sammenhengen Mellom Lederstiler og Psykiske Traumereaksjoner hos et Utvalg Mobbeofre [When the Bully is the Boss. A Survey of the Association between Leadership Styles and Crisis Trauma Reactions in Bullied Victims]* (Unpublished student thesis). Trondheim, Norway: University of Trondheim.

Nielsen, M.B., Matthiesen, S.B., and Einarsen, S. (2008) Sense of coherence as a protective mechanism among targets of workplace bullying, *Journal of Occupational Health Psychology;* 13(2), 128–136.

Nielsen, M.B., Matthiesen, S.B., and Einarsen, S. (2010) The impact of methodological moderators on prevalence rates of workplace bullying: A meta analysis, *Journal of Occupational and Organizational Psychology*, 83, 955-979.

Olweus, D. (1994) Annotation: Bullying at school: Basic facts and effects of a school-based intervention program, *Journal of Child Psychology and Psychiatry;* 35(7), 1171–1190.

Olweus, D. (2003) Bully/victim problems in school. Basic facts and an effective intervention programme. In S. Einarsen, H. Hoel, D. Zapf and C. L. Cooper (eds) *Bullying and Emotional Abuse in the Workplace.* London, UK: Taylor & Francis, 62–78.

Pathe, M. and Mullen, P.E. (1997) The impact of stalkers on their victims, *British Journal of Psychiatry;* 170, 12–17.

Paul, R.J. and Townsend, J.B. (1996) Don't kill the messenger! Whistle-blowing in America—A review with recommendations, *Employee Responsibilities and Rights Journal;* 9(2), 149–161.

Pryor, J.B. and Fitzgerald, L.F. (2003) Sexual harassment research in the United States. In S. Einarsen, H. Hoel, D. Zapf and C.L. Cooper (eds) *Bullying and Emotional Abuse in the Workplace.* London, UK: Taylor & Francis, 79–100.

Purcell, R., Pathe, M., and Mullen, P.E. (2004) Stalking: Defining and prosecuting a new category of offending, *International Journal of Law and Psychiatry;* 27, 157–169.

Rayner, C. and McIvor, K.M. (2006) *Put Up or Shut Up? Team Dynamics in Surfacing Bullying,* Book of abstracts. The Fifth International Conference on Bullying and Harassment in the Workplace "The way forward". Trinity College, Dublin, 167–168.

Rayner, C. and McIvor, K. (2008) *Research Report on the Dignity at Work Project.* University of Portsmouth: Unpublished report. www.port.ac.uk/research/workplacebullying/filetodownload,52783,en.pdf.

Rothschild, J. (2008) Freedom of speech denied, dignity assaulted: what the whistleblowers experience in the US, *Current Sociology;* 56(6), 884–903.

Rothschild, J. and Miethe, T. D. (1999) Whistle-blower disclosures and management retaliation. The battle to control information about organization corruption, *Work & Occupations;* 26(1), 107–128.

Salin, D. (2003) Ways of explaining workplace bullying: A review of enabling, motivating and precipating structures and processes in the work environment, *Human Relations;* 56(10), 1213–1232.

Salin, D. (2008) The prevention of workplace bullying as a question of human resource management: measures adopted and underlying organizational factors, *Scandinavian Journal of Management;* s(3), 221–231.

Salin, D. (2009) Organisational responses to workplace harassment: An exploratory study, *Personnel Review;* 38(1), 26–44.

Soeken, K.L., and Soeken, D.R. (1987) A survey of whistleblowers: Their stressors and coping strategies *Whistleblowing Protection Act of 1987* (Vol. 1st sess.). Washington: Supt. of Docs., Congressional sales office, US GPO, 156–166.

Tehrani, N. (1996) The psychology of harassment, *Counselling Psychology Quarterly;* 9(2), 101–117.

Thylefors, I. (1987) *Syndabockar. Om Utstøtning och Mobbning i Arbetslivet [Scape Goats. About Removal and Bullying at the Work place].* Stockholm, Sweden: Natur och Kultur.

Tracy, S.J., Lutgen-Sandvik, P., and Alberts, J.K. (2006) Nightmares, demons, and slaves. Exploring the painful metaphors of workplace bullying, *Management Communication Quarterly;* 20(2), 148–185.

van de Vliert, E. (1998) Conflict and conflict management. In P.J.D. Drenth, H. Thierry and C.J.J. de Wolff (eds) *Handbook of Work and Organizational Psychology (2nd edition), Book 3: Personnel Psychology.* Hove, UK: Psychology Press, 351–376.

Vartia, M. (1996) The sources of bullying—psychological work environment and organizational climate, *European Journal of Work and Organizational Psychology;* 5, 203–205.

Williams, K. (2001) *Ostracism: The Power of Silence.* New York, NY: Guilford Press.

Yamada, D. (2003) Workplace bullying and the law. Toward a transnational consensus? In S. Einarsen, H. Hoel, D. Zapf and C.L. Cooper (eds) *Bullying and Emotional Abuse in the Workplace.* London, UK: Taylor & Francis, 399–411.

Zapf, D. (1999) Organisational, work group related and personal causes of mobbing/bullying at work, *International Journal of Manpower;* 20(1/2), 70–85.

Zapf, D. (2004) *Negative Social Behavior at Work and Workplace Bullying.* Paper presented at the The Fourth International Conference on Bullying and Harassment in the Workplace, University of Bergen, Norway.

Zapf, D. and Einarsen, S. (2005) Mobbing at work: Escalated conflicts in organizations. In S. Fox and P. E. Spector (eds) *Counterproductive Work Behavior.* Washington DC: American Psychological Association, 237–270.

Zapf, D., Einarsen, S., Hoel, H., and Vartia, M. (2003) Empirical findings on bullying in the workplace. In S. Einarsen, H. Hoel, D. Zapf and C.L. Cooper (eds), *Bullying and Emotional Abuse in the Workplace.* London, UK: Taylor & Francis, 103–126.

Zapf, D. and Gross, C. (2001) Conflict escalation and coping with workplace bullying: A replication and extension, *European Journal of Work and Organizational Psychology;* 10(4), 497–522.

Zapf, D., Knorz, C., and Kulla, M. (1996) On the relationship between mobbing factors, and job content, social work environment and health outcomes, *European Journal of Work and Organizational Psychology;* 5(2), 215–23.

CHAPTER 8 Violence in the Workplace

DAVID LESTER

Violence in the workplace takes many forms ranging from harassment (both sexual and non-sexual) such as mobbing, a term to cover situations where people in an office join together to harass an individual, all the way to extreme violence such as murder. Violence in the workplace can come from many sources. Fellow employees, both current workers and those recently fired, occasionally aggress against those who worked with them, a phenomenon known as "horizontal workplace violence" (Thobaben, 2007). From media accounts, there seem to be "fads" in this. For example, in the 1980s, many incidents of postal workers aggressing against fellow workers were reported, while in the 1990s school children aggressing against teachers and classmates seemed to be common. It is not clear whether there was actual suggestion or contagion occurring in these cases or whether the media changed the focus of its attention, thereby giving rise to apparent fads in workplace violence.

Violence in the workplace can come also from customers of the workplace. For example, in July, 1993, Gian Ferri entered the offices of a law firm, Pettit & Martin in San Francisco, where Ferri had been a client earlier, and killed eight and wounded six others before committing suicide. Staff in psychiatric facilities frequently face violent behavior from the patients, as do correctional staff from the inmates (Hatch-Maillette et al., 2007). In some cases, intimate partner violence is the cause of workplace violence—for example, Kimberly Price was shot to death by her estranged husband in June 2005 as she walked into the beauty salon where she worked (Swanberg and Logan, 2007). On occasions the aggressor can seem to pick random targets, as when Timothy McVeigh bombed the federal building in Oklahoma City in April, 1995, killing 168 individuals. Sometimes, the dangerous situations are surprising—for example, Anderson, Westneat and Reed (2005) found that 42 percent of female long-haul truckers reported being victims of workplace violence.

The violence is often witnessed by others, and this can result in psychological distress to these witnesses. Not only may workers witness the murder of others in their workplace, but they may also be witness to suicides in their workplace. Those who witness this violence are often traumatized by the experience. One of the most traumatic instances of this is experienced by the drivers of subway trains who hit and kill suicides jumping in front of their train. The incidence of post-traumatic stress disorder in these drivers has been documented (Williams et al., 1994).

There are some "workplaces" that are especially prone to "workers" being the target and the witness of violence. Wars are the most extreme situations, but workers such as police (Kelloway, Barling and Hurrell, 2006), nurses (Spector et al., 2007), emergency department staff (Peek-Asa et al., 2007), psychiatric unit staff (Peek-Asa et al., 2009), home care staff (Letizia & Casagrande, 2005), and peacekeeping soldiers (Pompili et al., 2009) also experience violence as a regular occurrence in their working life, for some both as the targets of violence and as the agents of violence. For example, police officers are often the victims of assault and murder by those they confront, but they also often assault and kill those that they confront. Being the victim of aggression is obviously a source of great distress, but being the aggressor also can lead to great distress and psychiatric problems for the aggressor.

An Example of Non-Lethal Violence

Mobbing is an example of workplace violence at the less violent end of the spectrum of workplace violence. The term "mobbing" comes from the animal world where, for example, songbirds will fly in a group toward a threat, such as an owl or a hawk, and harass the intruder until it flies away. The term has recently been applied to situations where colleagues gang up on an individual in the workplace, and it has been documented in many situations, both in the business world and in academia (Gravois, 2006). Those exposed to mobbing are stigmatized by colleagues or superiors through rumor, innuendo, intimidation, humiliation, discrediting, and isolation (Pompili et al., 2008), and they often experience depression and anxiety of psychiatric proportions. Mobbing threatens the emotional well-being and professional ability of its victims. In Europe, estimates of the prevalence of mobbing range from 4 percent in Italy to 15 percent in Finland (Paoli & Merillié, 2001)

Mobbing can result in the victims experiencing severe stress, being forced out of their job or quitting. Pompili and his colleagues (2008) studied 102 individuals referred by unions, lawyers, or doctors to a psychiatric unit in Italy for evaluation who were or who had been employed. Those who reported having been mobbed were found to have higher levels of psychiatric disturbance on the Minnesota Multiphasic Personality Inventory (MMPI-2) than those who had not been mobbed, and just over half of those who reported being mobbed were judged to be at some risk of suicide. Mobbing is similar to bullying with the difference that bullying is typically carried out by a single individual while mobbing is carried out by a large group of people (Fogg, 2008).

For a review of follow-up studies on the psychiatric distress experienced by victims of non-fatal workplace violence in general see Hogh and Viitasara (2005).

Murder in the Workplace

The field of workplace violence is, clearly, large, and there are several recent handbooks devoted to the topic (for example, Perline and Goldschmidt, 2004; Kelloway, Barling and Hurrell, 2006). In this chapter, however, the discussion will be limited to workplace violence in which workers are murdered.

In the 1980s, when several postal workers committed mass murder, and in the 1990s when several disgruntled workers in other businesses followed suit, it began to seem as if the workplace could be a very dangerous locale. Homicide was the third leading cause of occupational deaths in 1980–1985 according to the National Institute for Occupational Safety & Health (1992), more so for women than for men. Although most workplace murders do not involve workers killing co-workers (armed robberies are the most common source of workplace murder (Booth et al., 2009), some workplace murders are mass murders by present or former co-workers.

Perline and Goldschmidt (2004) listed 118 incidents of workplace violence in America between 1982 and 2002 with at least one person killed or injured. Those with the most fatalities were the 13 incidents labeled as terrorist/hate crimes (including the September 11, 2001 attack on the World Trade Center and the Pentagon), six transportation incidents (including plane crashes), and one civil disorder incident (a riot). The numbers injured and killed were calculated for this chapter from the data provided by Perline and Golschmidt (Table 8.1).

Table 8.1 The lethality of different types of workplace violence

Type	Number	Killed	Injured
Terrorist[a]	13	231.8	131.8
Civil disorder	1	38.0	1421.0
Transportation	6	26.8	21.7
Corporate & business	28	4.5	3.0
School	21	2.8	7.6
Government facilities	19	2.2	1.1
United States Postal Service	21	2.0	1.6
Interpersonal relations	16	1.9	11

a The number injured was not noted for all of these incidents.

Apart from the terrorist, transportation, and civil disorder incidents, the rest are evenly distributed over the remaining categories, and so the 21 incidents at the United States Postal Service (USPS) is remarkable when compared to all other government and corporate facilities combined. Again excluding the terrorist, transportation, and civil disorder incidents, the remaining types of incidents did not differ significantly in the number of victims killed, but they did differ significantly in the number of victims injured. The number of victims injured was higher for school incidents than for the other types. The larger number of victims at schools and corporate and business facilities suggests less focused attacks at those locations as compared to government, USPS, and interpersonal relations where the lower number of victims seems to indicate more focused anger.

In these incidents, 79 of the assailants were arrested and 32 committed suicide. (Others were classified as "dead" or remained unidentified.) Those arrested killed an average of 4.4 victims and injured 39.8, while those committing suicide killed an average of 4.1 victims and injured 4.7. Omitting the terrorist, transportation, and civil disorder incidents, those arrested killed an average of 4.0 victims and injured 22.4, while those committing suicide killed an average of 4.2 victims and injured 3.8. These differences are not statistically significant.

Seger (1993) noted that the profile for the typical workplace killer was:

- middle-aged white male;
- frustrated employee in a menial job;

- professional with personal frustration, such as rejected suitors;
- bitter and dissatisfied;
- quick to perceive injustice;
- blaming others for his problems;
- enormous pent-up rage;
- few support systems (from friends, family, and neighbors);
- familiarity with firearms; and
- depressed and suicidal who sees no solution for his problems.

Middle-aged white males, if fired, have little opportunity of finding good jobs as compared to the opportunities for younger workers. Having expected to have well-paid and meaningful jobs, they face life at the bottom of the pile instead of being at the peak of their careers. Combined with this, there are often personal sources of stress, such as failed marriages and lonely existences. For those who are lonely, their job is their only source of companionship, and it gives them a sense of stability. Friction at work, let alone being fired, removes these sources of gratification.

Seger (1993) searched newspapers for accounts of workplace murders and located 23 incidents, although he does not specify the time period he chose. Fifteen of these were simple murders, five were murder-suicides in which a worker killed others and then himself, two were attempted murders and one involved threats of murder. Nine of the 23 incidents were at postal offices or workplaces. Seger also surveyed 1,000 companies about violence in the workplace, and 32 responded. Twelve did not report violent incidents, but the other 20 did, with incidents ranging from telephone threats to murder. Of the 60 incidents reported, six were murders or attempted murders.

Going Postal

Savino (2000) noted that postal workers had a very low risk of being killed in the workplace. Whereas taxi drivers had a murder rate of 31.54 per 100,000 per year, and police officers 6.46, postal workers had a rate of only 0.26. Being a postal worker seems to be a safe occupation.

But there were an extraordinary number of mass murders of fellow employees by disgruntled postal workers in the 1980s, so many in fact that those who committed similar mass murders were said to have "gone postal" (see Table 8.2).

Not all of these incidents fulfill the criteria for mass murder (three or more people killed in one incident), but in many of these cases, others were wounded. Baxter and Margavio (1996) noted that many of these men were loners, came from violent, alcoholic families, and had served in the military. Several killed their wives or girlfriends before killing co-workers.

Let us look at one of these. Patrick Sherrill was 44 years old. He was a loner, tended to blame others for his misfortunes, and loved guns. He had been reprimanded for poor job performance on August 18, 1986. Two days later he arrived at the post office at 6:45 am dressed in his uniform and carrying his leather mailbag which was full of weapons and ammunition. Sherrill located his supervisor, the man who had reprimanded him, and shot him. He then opened fire on his co-workers who were busy sorting the mail. He killed 14 and wounded seven more. He then shot himself in the head.

Table 8.2 Workplace murders by postal service employees

Date	Name	Location
Aug 19, 1983	**Perry Smith**	**Johnston, SC**
Smith had resigned as a postal worker after 25 years of service, but he came back three months later and killed the postmaster and wounded two co-workers.		
Dec 2, 1983	**James Brooks**	**Anniston, AL**
After having many disputes with his co-workers, Brooks shot the postmaster and wounded a supervisor.		
Mar 6, 1985	**Steven Brownlee**	**Atlanta, GA**
A 12-year veteran at USPS, Brownlee killed two co-workers and wounded a third.		
May 31, 1985	**Joseph Medina**	**New York, NY**
Medina shot at his supervisor and wounded another co-worker before surrendering to police.		
Aug 20, 1986	**Patrick Sherill**	**Edmond, OK**
Sherrill was facing the possibility of being fired when he killed 14 co-workers and then killed himself.		
Dec 14, 1988	**Warren Murphy**	**New Orleans, LA**
Murphy wounded three people and held his girlfriend hostage for 13 hours before surrendering to police.		
Aug 10, 1989	**John Taylor**	**Orange Glen, CA**
After killing his wife, Taylor went to the post office where he killed two co-workers, wounded another and then committed suicide.		
Oct 10, 1991	**Joseph Harris**	**Ridgewood, NJ**
Recently fired, he killed a former supervisor and her boyfriend in their home, and then killed two workers at the post office, and set off explosives before surrendering to police.		
Nov 14, 1991	**Thomas McIlvane**	**Royal Oak, MI**
Recently fired, he went to the post office and killed three employees and wounded seven. He then shot himself in the head and died later in a hospital.		
May 6, 1993	**Larry Jasion**	**Dearborn, MI**
Jasion had been passed over for a position he wanted, and he killed one co-worker and wounded two others before shooting himself.		
May 6, 1993	**Richard Hilburn**	**Dana Point, CA**
Recently fired, Hilburn killed one co-worker and wounded another.		

Fox and Levin (1994) thought that Sherrill chose to murder his co-workers early in the day before customers were in the post office. He also had checked that none of the co-workers whom he liked were working that morning. Although Sherrill did not have any grievances against most of those whom he killed, they were present when he shot the man he hated, and they represented the "post office," the entity he hated. In a similar way, a man who is angry at his wife may also kill all of their children. Fox and Levin saw mass murderers such as Sherrill as similar to *kamikazes*, murdering others in a suicidal mission.

Why did postal workers go postal? Baxter and Margavio (1996) noted that the USPS came under increased pressure in the 1980s from United States Congress to cut expenses and make a profit. The USPS tried to do this in several ways: increasing the mechanization of the mail process, cutting inessential staff (including personnel responsible for workplace safety, human resource personnel, and postal inspectors), and putting great pressure on postal workers to increase productivity. The workers, themselves, had no input into these changes. Supervisors were caught in a bind. Forced to improve efficiency, they acted like brutal overseers with their staff. As a result, postal workers were objectified, pressured, and intimidated. The USPS began to be run like the military. Supervisors used discipline and intimidation to prevent workers from complaining about work conditions. If a worker reported an on-the-job injury, he was cited for unsafe work practices. If a mail carrier requested an inspection of his route to study its length, he was disciplined for poor work habits. Workers were not allowed bathroom visits unless already on break; workers were dismissed even for whistling at work.

The machines introduced to sort mail were noisy and very fast, and working at the machines was very stressful. Workers using them reported great job dissatisfaction. The USPS was able to reduce the required job skills and, therefore, lower pay for the workers. The USPS also lengthened delivery routes but did not increase the time for mail carrier to deliver their mail. Working for the USPS became hellish, and the USPS was, without question, responsible for creating these intolerable working conditions.

The murderers themselves were also high-risk people. For example, Thomas McIlvane was a volatile man and had continual problems with authority. He was discharged from the Marines for insubordination and, as a letter carrier, he had received many suspensions. Eventually he was dismissed, and he lost an arbitration hearing to get his job back. Shortly after this, he went on his rampage at the Royal Oak post office. But, when the workers in the Royal Oak post office heard that the branch manager, Christopher Carlisle, had been murdered, they broke into applause. Psychologists who interviewed the workers found little anger at McIlvane. His co-workers understood full well his frustration.

It isn't always Postal Workers

Fox and Levin (1994) noted that 44 percent of offenders of workplace murders were customers or clients, 24 percent were strangers, and only a third current or former workers.[1] But perhaps workers and former workers commit more *mass* murders?

Certainly, workers in other kinds of companies beside the USPS commit mass murder. For example, on January 27, 1993, Paul Calden came back to the Fireman's Fund Insurance Company in Tampa, Florida, eight months after being fired, and shot and killed three of his former supervisors, wounded two other employees, and then killed himself. In San Leandro, California, on June 21, 2000, Stuart Alexander killed three meat inspectors who had come to examine his sausage-making factory, tried to gun down the fourth, and then surrendered to police.

1 It is likely that most murders committed during robberies have strangers and customers as the victims.

On December 26, 2000, Michael McDermott, an employee at Edgewater Technology in Wakefield, Massachusetts, came to work with an AK-47 assault rifle and killed seven co-workers, mainly those in the accounting and human resources departments whom he held responsible for garnishing his wages to pay overdue taxes to the IRS. He then sat down and waited to be arrested. On February 5, 2001, William Baker, who had been caught stealing from the Navistar International plant in Melrose Park, Illinois, came to the plant the day before he was due to surrender to prison authorities and killed three workers and wounded four others before shooting himself. Baker had worked at the plant for 39 years before being fired in 1994.

It is not always workers and former workers who commit these massacres. On July 29, 1999, Mark Barton, who had already killed his wife two days earlier and his son and daughter the previous day, went to Momentum Securities, a brokerage in Atlanta where he was a day-trader in stocks and shares, and killed four people. He then went to the All-Tech Investment Group across the street where he killed five more people. He fled but then shot himself when the police cornered him at a gas station in a suburb of Atlanta. Barton had suffered massive losses from day-trading which he could not pay, and he had lost his trading privileges.

Each time one these mass murders happens, there is a focus on that particular industry or occupation. After Barton's massacre, there were articles on the brutal world of day-trading and the enormous stresses it places on people (for example, Kadlec, 1999). Sometimes the job does play a role, as we have seen in the analysis of the massacres at the USPS, but those who carry out these slaughters are also deviant individuals. The problem is that these acts are relatively rare. The rarity of mass murderers in the workplace makes identification of them ahead of time incredibly difficult.

Let us look at one example of a workplace rampage.

Joseph Wesbecker

On September 14, 1989, Joe Wesbecker went to the printing plant where he worked (although he was on disability leave at the time) and, firing his semi-automatic assault weapon, killed eight co-workers and wounded many more. He then shot himself in the head with a pistol and died (Cornwell, 1996).

At the time of the massacre, Wesbecker lived alone and had been on disability for about a year. Occasionally he visited and slept with his second ex-wife, Brenda. He was seeing a psychiatrist, Dr Lee Coleman, who had given Wesbecker lithium for his manic-depressive disorder and Prozac for his depression, but Coleman was beginning to think that Wesbecker had a schizoaffective disorder, a psychosis that is a mix of schizophrenia and depression. Wesbecker had been in and out of treatment several times, attempting suicide in 1984 with an overdose and with car exhaust. Over the years, all kinds of psychotropic medications had been tried, but the current medications did not seem to be helping Wesbecker, and perhaps they were making him agitated. Coleman had tried to persuade Wesbecker to go into the hospital on September 11, but Wesbecker refused.

On September 13, Wesbecker drove his son James to his college classes and picked him up after class. He insisted on buying a textbook James needed for class. He spent that night with Brenda, his ex-wife. On September 14, Wesbecker failed to pick James up. He was already on his way to the Standard Gravure printing plant to get revenge.

Wesbecker was born on April 27, 1942, in Louisville to Martha Wesbecker who had married the previous year at the age of 15. Wesbecker's father fell to his death while mending a church roof the next year, and Wesbecker's grandfather (who had become his surrogate father) died when Wesbecker was almost two. The next few years were filled with moves as Wesbecker's mother moved to different sets of relatives and then back to Louisville. He was even placed in an orphanage for a year when he was ten. Although he was back with his mother the next year, life was still unstable—for example, Martha attempted suicide by drinking rat poison soon after Wesbecker arrived back with her.

As a teenager, Wesbecker was rather wild. He dropped out of high school and was arrested several times for disorderly conduct and fighting. He spent a night in jail for siphoning gas out of someone else's truck. He often carried a starter gun which he fired just to scare people.

At the age of 18, Wesbecker went to work as a printer and married Sue White. For the next 12 years, Wesbecker seemed to settle down. He worked hard and moved to Standard Gravure in 1971, bought better and better houses for his family, and had two sons, Kevin who developed curvature of the spine and James who later became a compulsive exhibitionist, causing Wesbecker a great deal of stress.

Wesbecker had some strange traits. He was a perfectionist and seemed to have an excessive desire to be clean. He quarreled with his neighbors. His mother lived with him for a time, and the problems with the two boys began to get worse when they became teenagers. The stress in the marriage grew, and it ended for good in 1980.

Meanwhile the stress at Standard Gravure had become overwhelming. The printing plant had once belonged to the local newspaper, the *Courier-Journal*, but the paper was sold to Gannett (who published *USA Today*). The plant was then sold to Brian Shea who ran it independently. Faced with rising costs and a demand for increased productivity, the plant installed high-speed machines, and the men were forced to work 16-hour shifts. The noise was tremendous, and the fumes from the toluene used in the ink made the men pass out. The men were made to work night and weekend shifts, and there were pay cuts and erosion of job security as men were laid off. Strangely, rather than banding together against the foremen, the men took out their frustration on one another, such as pouring water on the printing paper and fouling up the machines that others were trying to run. In the mid-1980s, the men began to bring guns to work.

Wesbecker attended Parents without Partners and met Brenda Beasley who had two teenage girls. They married in 1981. Wesbecker wanted Kevin to have surgery for his spinal problem, but Kevin refused and the relationship between the two grew distant. James continued to expose himself, and Brenda's ex-husband was concerned about the safety of his daughter, eventually getting custody of his daughters. Wesbecker paid for residential psychiatric care for James, but James continued his exhibitionism. Wesbecker and his ex-wife continued to fight, and Wesbecker won a lawsuit against Sue for slander and had her placed on two years' probation for threatening him.

Wesbecker thought that the foremen at Standard Gravure were deliberately assigning him the most stressful jobs, and he talked to the plant's social worker about this. (Eventually, his psychiatrists wrote to the plant to insist that Wesbecker get less stressful tasks.) It was at this time that Wesbecker attempted suicide and was committed to a psychiatric hospital (on April 16, 1984) where he was diagnosed with a Major Affective Illness, Depressed, Recurrent Type. The hospital's psychologist thought that Wesbecker also had a borderline personality disorder. After his discharge, Wesbecker was put on an antidepressant (one of the many medications that he tried), but Brenda moved out and divorced him in 1984. Despite this separation, they remained good friends and lovers.

Wesbecker continued to press for easier working conditions, even going to the Human Relations Commission in Louisville in May 1987. But his case-worker there made little progress in his negotiations with the plant.

Wesbecker began to buy weapons in 1988 and to read magazines such as *Full Auto Firearms* and *Soldier of Fortune*. He went to shooting ranges with Brenda. His son James was caught exposing himself again and was sentenced to 90 days in jail. Wesbecker was so irritable that, when he had trouble with his lawnmowers, he wrecked them with an axe and drove his car over them. He often talked to his friends and co-workers about bombing the plant or "wiping the whole place out." On September 7, 1988, Dr Coleman got Wesbecker placed on disability leave, but Wesbecker believed that he had been cheated over the amount of his disability pay.

Wesbecker visited a funeral home and arranged and paid for his cremation. He deeded his house to Brenda, and he continued to accumulate an arsenal of guns. As 1989 passed, Wesbecker's son James continued to get into trouble almost every week. In July, Wesbecker discussed suicide with his friend James Lucas.

Wesbecker's grandmother, who had been a second mother to him, died on August 5, 1989, and a few days later Dr Coleman switched Wesbecker to Prozac and began to wean him off the other medications. Wesbecker told his friend Lucas not to go to work because he had a plan to eliminate the place. He had a list of seven people there he wanted to eliminate. Lucas swore (later in court) that he warned the managers at the plant but that they did not take the threat seriously. On September 14, 1989, Wesbecker arrived at the printing plant just after 8:30 am and began his shooting rampage.

Those who were wounded, but who survived the massacre, sued Eli Lilly, the makers of Prozac, arguing that Prozac was responsible for Wesbecker's rampage at the plant. The jury decided that Eli Lilly was not responsible, but the author of the book on the case, John Cornwell (1996), suspected that a deal may have been made "under the table" between Eli Lilly and the plaintiffs.

Murder in Academia

An interesting case of mass murder in the workplace occurred at the University of Iowa on November 1, 1991, when a graduate student from mainland China shot a fellow student, three professors in his department, and a dean before committing suicide. It was a typical disgruntled "employee" mass murder, except for the fact that the perpetrator was an immigrant. Chen (1995) has written about this incident.

Gang Lu was born in 1963 in Beijing, China. His father was a clerk in an automobile supplies shop, and his mother worked in a hospital clinic. He lived with his parents and two older sisters, all of whom who spoiled him. From an early age, Lu showed a rebellious streak. He called Lenin a "bold ass" in kindergarten, and fussed at the requirements that the communists forced upon him, such as visiting Mao's memorial in Tiananmen Square.

Lu excelled academically and easily won admission to Beijing University where he continued to perform outstandingly. In 1985 he graduated and passed the examinations to go to the United States to study. His command of the English language was quite poor, a problem which plagued him in America, but the authorities let him slip through. Lu was accepted at the University of Iowa to join their prestigious space physics program.

However, Lu was already disenchanted with physics. He did not look forward to returning to China with its antiquated laboratories and very low pay for academics. He wanted to participate in the growing capitalism in China. He decided to go to America but to try and change to business studies to prepare himself for becoming a wealthy entrepreneur in China. Interestingly, Lu blamed his parents for the choice of physics as a career, not himself, and this tendency to blame others for his difficulties and poor choices continued in America.

The University of Iowa did not take care of its foreign students well at all. When Lu arrived at Cedar Rapids airport, 25 miles away from the campus, he had to find his own way to the campus, like other foreign students. He managed to get to the campus, find a temporary room, and locate a tiny apartment to live in for the year—a 10-by-15 room with a recess in the wall as a closet—for $150 a month. Many of the foreign students took shabby but cheap rooms partly to save as much money as they could and partly because they spent so many hours on campus and so little time in their rooms.

In his first year, Lu was a teaching assistant, and his students complained that it was difficult to understand him. The university required him to take courses to improve his language skills. The other graduate students found him abrasive. The Reverend Tom Miller on campus helped the foreign students on Saturdays by driving them out to the cheaper suburban stores to shop, after which he tried to convert them to Christianity. In the discussions, Lu challenged everything that Miller said. He argued with roommates over which channel to watch on television, and with everyone about everything.

Lu wanted to find a girlfriend, and he visited a local bar, the Sports Column, by himself, the only Chinese person there, in order to try to find a one. Eventually a few people got to know him and occasionally talked to him, but he mostly drank alone. He also went bowling and played miniature golf. But he rarely joined in the social activities with the other Chinese students on campus and, when he did, he stayed by himself. At the Sports Column and with the other Chinese, Lu was viewed as a benign misfit. He took out personal ads in the local newspapers, but, despite his efforts, he failed to find a girlfriend. He turned to pornography and, on a semester break, he went to Las Vegas and probably went with prostitutes there.

Lu was soon recognized as the best physics student of his year, and he was willing to help out other students with their calculations. But he had not changed his plans, and he went to the foreign student advisor to see about changing to business. She made it clear to him that the visa requirements did not permit this. Lu went to argue with her half a dozen times, but to no avail. The physics department took away his teaching assistantship because of his poor command of the English language and gave him a research assistantship instead, but he felt slighted by the non-renewal of his teaching assistantship.

He continued to do well in his studies, and he worked hard for his new academic advisor, Christopher Goertz, a theoretical space physicist, born in Germany. In the summer, Goertz let Lu accompany him to Paris to attend a conference on space physics, and Lu decided to stay on and tour Europe. Goertz strongly disapproved of this. He wanted Lu to come back to America right away and resume his research.

The third year was difficult for Lu. A new Chinese student, Linhua Shan, arrived, having transferred from Texas A&M University, and Shan proved to be even more brilliant than Lu. Shan roomed with Lu for a while, along with a third roommate, but both soon moved out because they found living with Lu difficult. Lu was a self-centered know-it-all, with no respect for others, cheap, and irascible. He boasted about his friends at the Sports Column and his many sexual liaisons, boasts which were not true. On one occasion, Lu drove two fellow Chinese students to Chicago, but they got into an argument over who should pay for dinner. Lu abandoned his passengers in Chicago and drove back to Iowa alone. Shan, on the other hand, had a fiancé in China and, within a year of arriving at the University of Iowa, was elected President of the Association for Chinese Students. In contrast, Lu gave a Chinese New Year's party in 1991, but no one came.

Christopher Goertz was a brilliant physicist, but a hard task-master. Neither Lu nor Shan cared for him much as person. Goertz felt that Lu was not working hard enough, and he pushed him harder. He also began to view Shan as the better student and to transfer his preference to Shan. Shan's dissertation was going to be brilliant, whereas Lu's was going to be mundane. As Lu's disenchantment with Goertz grew, he complained about him incessantly to the other students and took to staying home more. Goertz responded by pressuring Lu more and, eventually, Lu decided to meet the challenge. He spent more hours in the department, working harder.

Shan was awarded his degree in December, 1990, ahead of Lu, which shattered Lu. Even worse, Shan's grade-point-average was higher than Lu's (4.00 versus 3.84). Lu lost face, and he blamed Goertz for this.

Lu started job hunting in early 1991, and he was so angry at Goertz that he did not plan to ask Goertz for a reference. He went instead to the Chairperson of the Department, Dwight Nicolson. Nicolson, of course, sent him back to Goertz and told Goertz about Lu's visit. Goertz offered to write letters for Lu but carelessly missed the deadline for some of them. Now Lu was furious at both Nicolson and Goertz.

When Lu came to defend his thesis, he was unaware that he had to make a presentation, which is odd since it would have been common knowledge among the graduate students that the defense involved a presentation. He managed to make a brief presentation but, since his English was still poor and he was obviously unprepared, it did not go well. Members of the committee attacked the dissertation because Lu had used computer programs created by others that he had not checked himself. They approved Lu for his degree on condition that he redid his calculations and checked the program. He did this in a week, but again he felt humiliated by the whole process. Because of his poor English, Lu misunderstood the objections and thought that the committee had questioned the scientific principles behind the thesis.

Each year the university awarded a $2,500 prize for the best dissertation, and in 1991 the prize was for the Department of Physical Sciences. Lu found out that the department was going to nominate Shan rather than him, and Shan indeed won the prize. Lu was furious. He appealed again and again, writing letters so that he had documentation of his grievance, moving up the chain of command until he got to the President of the University.

Chen, in his book on this incident, makes it clear that Lu was treated fairly. Lu did not deserve the dissertation award, and jobs for physicists were scarce in America during that period. However, it is also clear that the administrators at the University of Iowa treated Lu as they would any student. They made no allowance for the fact that Lu was a foreign student whose command of English was poor, and none for Lu's cultural background, a background in which "face" was crucial and humiliation devastating. There is, of course, no "administrative" reason why they should have treated Lu differently and with more caring than they did—except for the result. The fact that they did not treat him well, indeed, from the moment of his arrival in the United States, contributed to his mass murder.

During spring and summer, Lu became more and more frustrated by his situation. On May 21, 1991 he went to get a permit for a gun. On May 29 he bought his first gun—a .25 caliber pistol—and he went to several firing ranges to practice. He then traded in the pistol for a .38 caliber Taurus and later added a .22 caliber Jennings.

He stayed home in his apartment renting movies with violence and revenge as the themes, such as *No Way Out* and *Die Hard*. Lu stopped writing home to his family in China, and they became worried at his silence. The awarding of the dissertation prize to Shan was announced on August 28, 1991.

In September, Lu made a trip to Disney World and other attractions in Florida. Because of the Tiananman Square massacre in Beijing, China, in June 1989, the American government had given Chinese students permission to stay in America after their student visas had expired, and Lu did get permission to stay and work. But he was no longer interested. He wanted revenge for the way he had been mistreated.

On October 8, 1991 he drew out $10,000 from his bank account and sent it home to his family. Soon after, a letter came from the Department of Physics requesting donations for the department. Lu sent the department a check for one cent! He then drew out the rest of his money and wrote a letter to send home along with the money.[2] He cleared out his apartment and loaded all of his possessions into his car. In a letter to his sister, he laid out his grievances, and he made it clear that Goertz had been hindering him in getting his dissertation published rather than facilitating it.

On November 1, 1999 Lu had breakfast at a local diner, mailed his letter home from a local store, and walked over to the physics department where the afternoon seminar was held at 3.30 pm. Lu arrived and sat for a few minutes. He left to check whether Nicolson, the Department Chairperson, was in his office. He then went back to the seminar, pulled out his gun and shot Goertz in the back of the head. He shot Shan in the side of his head, and then advanced on Robert Smith, another professor whom Lu blamed for his misfortunes. The rest of the group fled, but Lu blocked Smith's exit from the room and shot him with two bullets. Lu then went and shot Nicolson in his office with two bullets. He went back up to the seminar room and found that Smith was still alive. Lu shot Smith twice in the head, put two more bullets into Goertz and one more into Shan.

Lu left the building and walked over to where Anne Cleary, the Associate Vice President for Academic Affairs, who had ruled negatively on his appeals, had her office. He shot Cleary and a work-study student in the Office of Academic Affairs in the head.[3] As Lu heard the police sirens getting closer, he went into an empty room in the building, took off his jacket and hung it over a chair, and shot himself in the head.

There is, of course, no excuse for murder, let alone mass murder. Graduate students often get mistreated—indeed it is perhaps the norm. Unfeeling task-masters like Goertz are common. Some faculty treat their graduate students as servants and give them little credit for their work. Those faculty are interested only in what they get out of them. They do not care for or care about their students.

2 The letter was intercepted after the incident and read by local authorities.

3 The student survived, although paralyzed from the neck down.

All of this does not excuse Lu's mass murder. But, like the USPS, the climate in the Department of Physical Sciences at the University of Iowa was not supportive for, and perhaps hostile to, some of the students there. This interaction between a potentially violent individual and a hostile or stressful environment can clearly increase the risk of workplace violence.

How to Prevent Workplace Murder

Seger (1993) made several suggestions for preventing workplace murder. First, the design of the environment is important. Reception areas, offices, and desks can be arranged so that violence can be more easily prevented. Such additions as plexiglas partitions, limited access to the workplace, and better lighting can reduce the risk of violence. The use of security guards and security systems, of course, is also useful.

For the employees, pre-employment screening procedures could pick up clues to potentially violence workers. A history of many job changes of short duration, for example, indicates a problem worker. Psychological testing, if conducted by a qualified professional using appropriate psychological tests, can provide important information.

The work atmosphere is critical. Are employees treated with respect? Termination of employees should be done with special care and in a humane manner. The supervisor should not be angry, nor cold and impersonal. Severance benefits, outplacement, and retraining should be available if possible. After termination, the worker should surrender all keys and identification and not be permitted to return to the workplace again at any time.

Employees, and especially supervisors, should be trained both in anger management and in detecting problem workers. Clues include:

- overreaction to new company policies;
- threatening co-workers;
- withdrawing all money from the credit union;
- repeated violations of company rules and policies;
- having an "everyone is against me" attitude;
- talking about past acts of violence;
- referring to a plan that will "solve everything";

and of course

- aggressive and threatening actions;
- intimidating behavior;
- verbal threats;
- paranoid thinking;
- bizarre behavior;
- alcohol and drug abuse;
- emotional mood swings;
- prior assaultive behavior; and
- ownership of weapons.

Seger noted the importance also of helping battered women. Many murders in the workplace are committed against wives and girlfriends by abusive husbands and lovers.

But the rarity of workplace massacres by disgruntled workers makes detection and prevention of potential massacres very difficult, if not impossible.

For employees who are at risk of encountering violent clients, patients, or customers, Beech and Leather (2006) noted the importance training for all staff, labeling such training as the "cornerstone" of managing workplace violence. The training should include theory (understanding violence in the workplace), prevention (assessment techniques and how to take precautions), interaction skills when encountering aggressive individuals, and post-incident action (reporting the incident, reviewing, and investigating the incident, and counseling those emotionally affected by the incident). Beech and Leather urged that training programs should include an evaluation component so that their effectiveness can be assessed and changes made where appropriate.

McPhaul et al. (2008) reviewed tactics which aim to reduce workplace violence in healthcare settings by restructuring the environment. These tactics include: (1) *surveillance* in which the staff can view patients in the ward and can be viewed by other patients and staff; (2) *access control* which limits entry to the facility, wards, sleeping areas, offices, program areas, and medication and other storage facilities; (3) *territoriality* which empowers the legitimate occupants of a space, such as staff offices or parking lots; and (4) *activity support* which aims to make program areas clean, well-lit, and comfortable, with adequate temperature and noise control. McPhaul et al. gave an example of one inpatient addiction treatment facility with no visitor reception area (access control), limited outdoor lighting and surveillance cameras (territoriality), no central area to observe the addicts (surveillance), and a limited and congested dining area (activity support). In addition, this facility was poor in materials used (glass windows rather than tempered glass) and maintenance (leaks and mold were present).

Booth et al. (2009) analyzed 15 cases of workplace violence where the violent individual took hostages. The situations encompassed armed robberies, customers and consumers, employees and former employees, and domestic disputes. The majority of the events were planned and carried out by single white males between the ages of 25 and 40, aggressing against white females with whom the offender had no significant relationship. Booth et al. noted the importance of bringing trained hostage negotiators as quickly as possible to the scene. In all of their 15 cases, the outcome did not involve the death of the hostages or offender, but sometimes these situations do result in murder and suicide.

Bishop et al. (2006) noted the importance of providing critical incident stress counseling for those who are the victims of workplace violence and those who witness the violence. Organizations and institutions should have teams trained to provide this service in place should a violent event occur. For example, after several recent murderous events on university campuses, universities and colleges, which typically have counseling centers available on campus for the students, have set up services to warn students and staff of dangerous events on campus and to provide crisis counseling for those who require it. It is critical to set up, test, and disseminate information about the procedures and service *before* an event occurs.

Although it is impossible to anticipate and prevent all lethal acts of workplace violence, employers and employees can be proactive in reducing the risks of such incidents and changing lethal acts of violence into non-fatal acts, and Miller (2008) has provided a sound set of suggestions and guidelines for this task. However, in a study of 210 workplace homicides in North Carolina from 1994 to 1998, Ta and Loomis (2007) found that the implementation of administrative and environmental measures to prevent workplace violence was extremely poor. For example, the presence of locked entrances was present in only 13 percent of workplaces and video camera surveillance in 9 percent. On the other hand, restricted entrance before and after business hours was present in 86 percent of the workplaces and a barrier between workers and the public in 75 percent of the workplaces. Guidelines for preventing workplace violence are of no use unless they are routinely implemented by employers.

References

Anderson, D.G., Westneat, S., and Reed, D. (2005) Workplace violence against female long-haul truckers, *Security Journal*; 18(2), 31–38.

Baxter, V. and Margavio, A. (1996) Assaultive violence in the US Post Office, *Work & Occupations*; 23(3), 277–296.

Beech, B. and Leather, P. (2006) Workplace violence in the health care sector, *Aggression & Violent Behavior*; 11(1), 27–43.

Bishop, S., McCullough, B., Thompson, C., and Vasi, N. (2006) Resiliency in the aftermath of repetitious violence in the workplace, *Journal of Workplace Behavioral Health*; 21(3–4), 101–188.

Booth, B., Vecchi, G.M., Finney, E.J., van Hasselt, V.B., and Romano, S.J. (2009) Captive-taking incidents in the context of workplace violence, *Victims & Offenders*; 4, 76–92.

Chen, E. (1995) *Deadly Scholarship*. New York, NY: Birch Lane Press.

Cornwell, J. (1996) *The Power to Harm*. New York, NY: Viking.

Fogg, P. (2008) Academic bullies, *Chronicle of Higher Education*; 55(3), B10–B13.

Fox, J.A. and Levin, J. (1994) Firing back, *Annals of the American Academy of Political & Social Science*; 536, 16–30.

Gravois, J. (2006) Mob rule, *Chronicle of Higher Education*; 52(32), A10–A12.

Hatch-Maillette, M.A., Scalora, M.J., Bader, S.M., and Bornstein, B.H. (2007) A gender-based incidence study of workplace violence in psychiatric and forensic settings, *Violence & Victims*; 22(4), 449–462.

Hogh, A. and Viitasara, E. (2005) A systematic review of longitudinal studies of nonfatal workplace violence, *European Journal of Work & Organizational Psychology*; 14(3), 291–313.

Kadlec, D. (1999) Day Trading, *Time*; 154(6), 26.

Kelloway, E.K., Barling, J., and Hurrell, J J. (eds) (2006) *Handbook of Workplace Violence*. Thousand Oaks, CA: Sage.

Letizia, J.M. and Casagrande, K. (2005) Workplace violence: A continued threat to home care employer and employees, *Home Health Care Management & Practice*; 17(4), 327–329.

McPhaul, K.M., London, M., Murrett, K., Flannery, K., Rosen, J., and Lipscomb, J. (2008) Environmental evaluation for workplace violence in healthcare and social services, *Journal of Safety Research*; 39(2), 237–250.

Miller, L. (2008) Workplace violence: Practical policies and strategies for prevention, response, and recovery, *International Journal of Emergency Mental Health*; 9, 259–280.

National Institute of Occupational Safety & Health (1992) *Homicide in US Workplaces*. Washington, DC: NIOSH #92–103.

Paoli, P. and Merillié, D. (2001) Third European survey on working conditions 2000. In *European Foundation for the Improvement of Living and Working Conditions*. Luxembourg: European Community Publications.

Peek-Asa, C., Casteel, C., Allareddy, V., Nocera, M., Goldmacher, S., OHagan, E., Blando, J., Valiante, D., Gillen, M., and Harrison, R. (2007) Workplace violence prevention programs in hospital emergency departments, *Journal of Occupational & Environmental Medicine*; 49(7), 756–763.

Peek-Asa, C., Casteel, C., Allareddy, V., Nocera, M., Goldmacher, S., OHagan, E., Blando, J., Valiante, D., Gillen, M., and Harrison, R. (2009) Workplace violence prevention programs in psychiatric units and facilities, *Archives of Psychiatric Nursing*; 2(2), 166–176.

Perline, I.H. and Goldschmidt, J. (eds) (2004) *The Psychology and Law of Workplace Violence: A Handbook for Mental Health Professional and Employers*. Springfield, IL: Charles C. Thomas.

Pompili, M., Cuomo, I., Dominici, G., Falcone, I., Iacrossi, G., Saglimbene, A., Lester, D., Tatarelli, R., and Ferracuti, S. (2009) Suicidal behaviour in current and former peacekeepers. In L. Sher and A. Vilens (eds) Suicidal Behaviour Among Current and Former Peacekeepers. Hauppauge, NY: Nova Science, 41–55.

Pompili, M., Lester, D., Innamorati, M., De Pisa, E., Iliceto, P., Puccino, M., Nastro, P. F., Tatarelli, R., and Girardi, P. (2008) Suicide risk and exposure to mobbing, *Work*; 31(2), 237–243.

Savino, L. (2000) Risk of post office violence is more myth than reality, *Philadelphia Inquirer*; September 1, A3.

Seger, K.A. (1993) Violence in the workplace, *Security Journal*; 4(3), 139–149.

Spector, P.E., Coulter, M.L., Stockwell, H.G., and Matz, M.W. (2007) Perceived violence climate, *Work & Stress*; 21(2), 117–130.

Swanberg, J. and Logan, T.K. (2007) Intimate partner violence, employment and the workplaces, *Journal of Interpersonal Violence*; 22(3), 263–267.

Ta, M.L., and Loomis, D.P. (2007) Frequency and determinants of recommended workplace violence prevention measures, *Journal of Safety Research*; 38(6), 643–650.

Thobaben, M. (2007) Horizontal workplace violence, *Home Health Care Management & Practice*; 20(1), 82–83.

Williams, C., Miller, J., Watson, G., and Hunt, N. (1994) A strategy for trauma debriefing after railway suicides, *Social Science & Medicine*; 38(3), 483–487.

PART IV Occupational Factors

CHAPTER 9

Psychological and Behavioral Aspects of Occupational Safety and Health in the US Coal Mining Industry

KATHLEEN M. KOWALSKI-TRAKOFLER, CHARLES VAUGHT, LINDA JANSEN McWILLIAMS, AND DORI B. REISSMAN

Overview

In the US mining industry, psychological aspects of safety and health are defined very broadly as psychosocial issues. Psychology is embraced literally as the study of human behavior, and the focus is on studying human behavior as it relates to injuries and fatalities with the goal of mitigating further instances.

This chapter explores the psychological and behavioral dimensions of occupational safety and health (also referred to as OSH) for workers mining coal underground. Mining has a history of disasters that have formed the framework for an array of OSH interventions. Within the mining industry, the severity of the hazardous environment has necessitated a focus on controlling, managing, and changing the physical environment or "engineering out" the hazard. More recently, a growing body of research indicates that specific job/task and organizational-level factors may have a powerful influence on safe work practices and accident deterrence—thus reducing injuries and deaths of coal miners (DeJoy, Gershon and Schaffer, 2004). Although it must be noted that many psychosocial aspects of OSH in mining are relevant to all major mining sectors (that is, coal, metal, non-metal, stone, and sand and gravel) as well as many other hazardous industries (commercial fishing, transportation, agriculture) the human behavior issues addressed here have tended to arise from underground coal mining.

The chapter is organized to first present the reader with an introduction to the underground coal mining environment, followed by lessons learned from mining disasters. The authors present a model to reduce worker exposure. The research in key psychosocial areas is discussed including judgment decision making and leadership in escape, training, and the introduction of refuge chambers into underground mines. Research on the aging mining population, shift work, hazard recognition, job stress, and resiliency is discussed. The authors conclude with a summary and thoughts for the future.

Introduction—Mining Environment

Mining is one of the oldest occupations known to mankind, perhaps second only to agriculture (Hartman and Mutmansky, 2002). Removal of minerals from the earth has often resulted in heavy human losses. Each year, around the world, thousands of miners die as a result of mining accidents.

In 2008, there were 925 underground and 13,982 surface mining operations reporting employment to the US Department of Labor, Mine Safety and Health Administration (MSHA). Most of the underground mines are for coal extraction (n = 665, 72 %), while the majority of surface mines produce sand and gravel (n = 7,132, 51%). The fatality rate and lost time injury rate at underground mining operations has been consistently higher than the rates for surface mines (Figures 9.1 and 9.2).

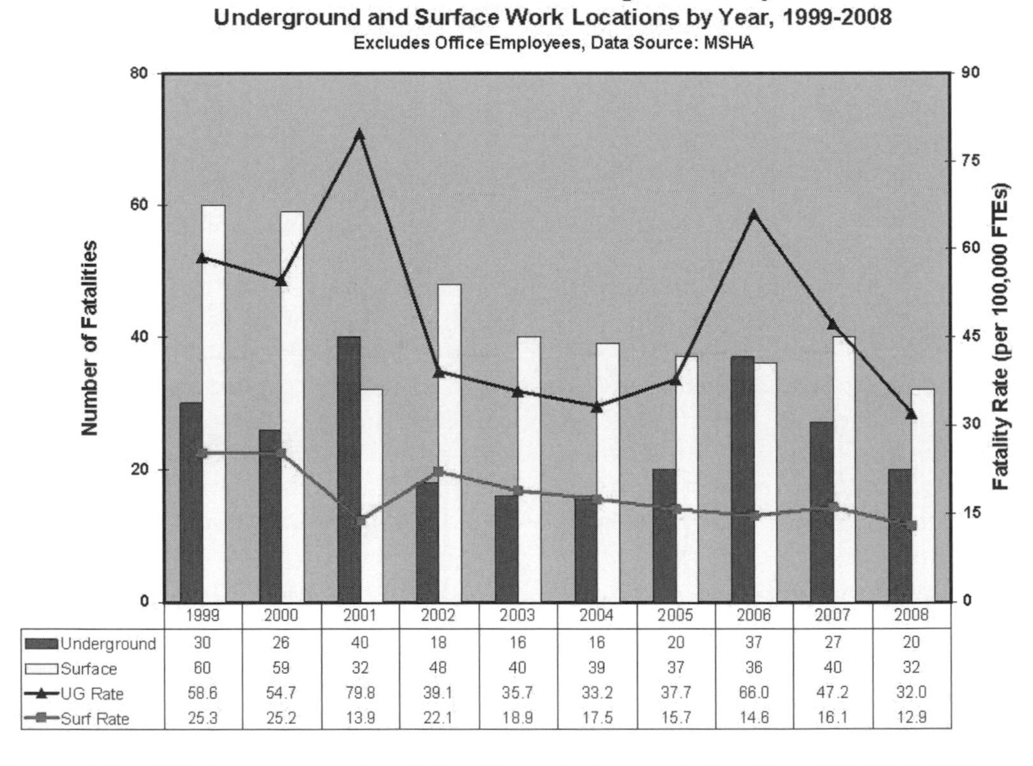

	1999	2000	2001	2002	2003	2004	2005	2006	2007	2008
Underground	30	26	40	18	16	16	20	37	27	20
Surface	60	59	32	48	40	39	37	36	40	32
UG Rate	58.6	54.7	79.8	39.1	35.7	33.2	37.7	66.0	47.2	32.0
Surf Rate	25.3	25.2	13.9	22.1	18.9	17.5	15.7	14.6	16.1	12.9

Figure 9.1 Mining occupational fatality rate by work location (1999–2008)

In addition, coal has the highest number of fatalities of all commodities mined, as illustrated in Figure 9.3.

Many regions of the US are underlain by horizontal coal beds (seams) that cover an enormous area. Sometimes a seam of coal will underlay a significant portion of an entire state.

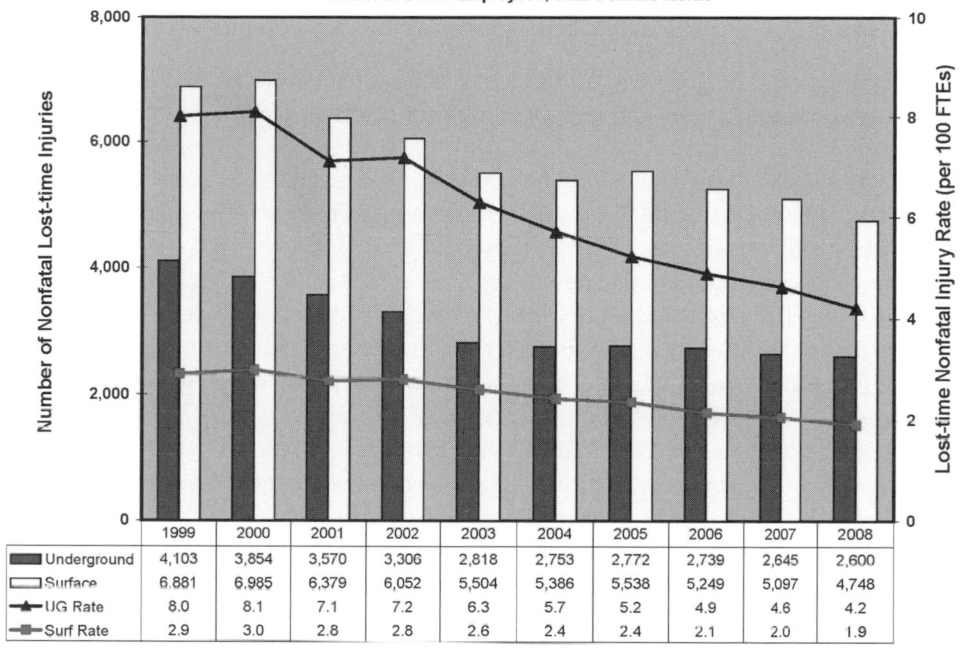

	1999	2000	2001	2002	2003	2004	2005	2006	2007	2008
Underground	4,103	3,854	3,570	3,306	2,818	2,753	2,772	2,739	2,645	2,600
Surface	6,881	6,985	6,379	6,052	5,504	5,386	5,538	5,249	5,097	4,748
UG Rate	8.0	8.1	7.1	7.2	6.3	5.7	5.2	4.9	4.6	4.2
Surf Rate	2.9	3.0	2.8	2.8	2.6	2.4	2.4	2.1	2.0	1.9

Figure 9.2 Mining non-fatal lost time injuries by work location (1999–2008)

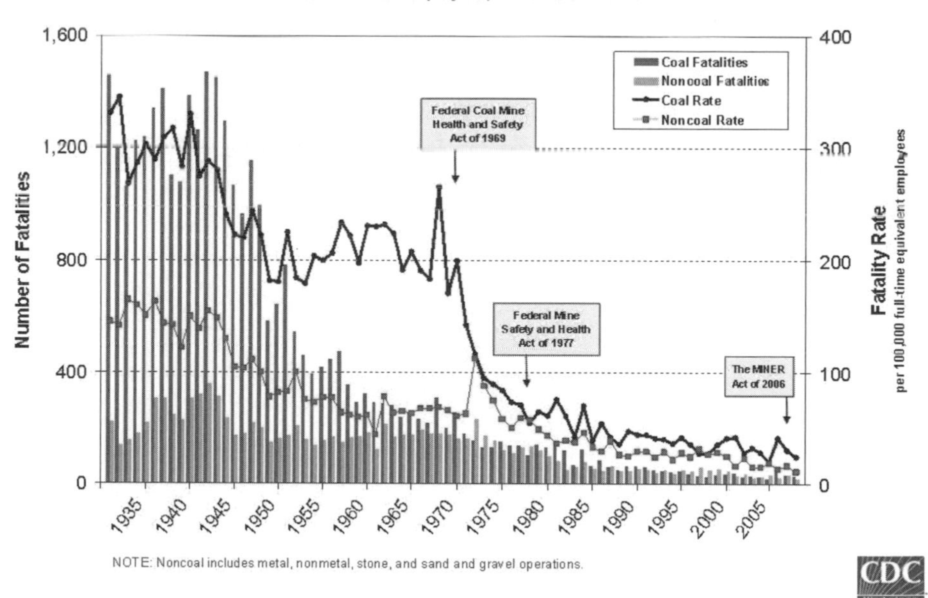

Figure 9.3 Number of mining fatalities and fatality rates by commodity (1931–2008)

These seams may be anywhere from 28 inches to 12 feet or more in thickness. There are two primary underground mining methods used to extract the coal seams—room and pillar, and longwall. With the room and pillar method, the coal seam is "developed" by driving sets of three to eight parallel tunnels, 16 to 20 feet wide, called "entries." These entries, whose centers are 60 to 100 feet apart, may be several thousand feet long. They are connected at right angles by "crosscuts," also 16 to 20 feet wide, at intervals of 60 to 100 feet. The purpose of the crosscuts is to maintain ventilation, and to allow the movement of mobile mining machinery between the entries. Coal is produced as a result of excavating these entries and crosscuts, which constitute a "section" and the points at which coal is actually being extracted are called "working faces." The faces are mined in a cycle. First, a remote-controlled "continuous" mining machine, equipped with a large steel revolving ripping head, takes coal from a face. The mining machine dumps the coal onto "shuttle cars," which haul it to a dumping point ("tailpiece") where it is fed onto conveyor belts and transported out of the mine. After the mining machine reaches a predetermined point at one face, it backs out and goes into the next entry and begins on that face. A "roof bolting" machine is driven into the vacated place and its operators insert steel bolts, some six feet long, vertically into the "roof," or overhead strata. These bolts are installed to prevent the roof from caving in. The pillars of coal created by this system of entries and crosscuts are left to provide additional support.

In a longwall operation the longwall is developed by driving two parallel three-entry sections, approximately 2,000 feet apart, into the coal seam for as much as three miles. The sections, called "longwall setup sections," then turn toward each other and connect. This creates a horizontal block of coal that is then extracted using a "shearer." A shearer is a machine that travels back and forth across the longwall face shearing coal from along its entire width and dumping it directly onto a conveyor belt to be taken outside (see Figure 9.4) As the coal is mined, the longwall retreats toward the point at which the setup began, with the roof caving in behind it as it goes. This process may take months. Once the block of coal is mined, the equipment is moved to another setup and the process begins again.

Figure 9.4 Miner at longwall face

All working faces, including the longwall face, are ventilated with fresh air from the outside. The air is brought into the mine by large fans that pull it down "intake" air shafts. In order to get the air to each face, it is directed through certain designated entries by constructing "stoppings" (concrete block walls) in each crosscut. At the faces, the air is routed by hanging plastic "brattice" curtains. It sweeps across, removing explosive dust and deadly gases and taking them down "return" entries where the exhaust fans pull them outside.

Even under normal conditions, as is widely recognized, an underground coal mine is filled with potential hazards and discomforts. There are limited opportunities for egress in the event of an emergency, workplaces at the face may be confined and noisy, and the only available lighting comes from miners' battery powered cap lamps or powered machines. There are also the usual frustrations of equipment malfunction, mud, water, dust, electrical hazards, and minor injuries such as slips, trips, and falls. Additionally, working in low-height coal is quite challenging to miners' backs and knees, given the need to "duck walk" or crawl in the confined space available.

Workers at the face are not the only ones affected by hazards and emergencies. Dispersed throughout the miles of entryways are a host of support personnel, performing such tasks as laying or repairing track, building stoppings, timbering (installing wooden props in areas needing extra support), cleaning under haulage belts, inspecting hoses, belts and cables, cleaning up roof falls (collapses), pumping water out of low-lying areas, and hauling supplies. Many of these workers work alone or in small crews, sometimes without direct supervision. In most mines today mining activities take place during three shifts, seven days a week.

The potential for injury and emergencies is ever-present. For instance, miners must be aware of oxygen deficiency in locations that may not be adequately ventilated. And, the coal mining process releases dangerous gases, including highly explosive methane gas, that are trapped within the coal seam and their release is part of the mining process. Miners may have to deal with carbon monoxide should there be a fire or explosion underground. In such an event, to give miners a better chance to escape, some of the intake air entries are isolated from others. They may be miles long, but are designed to provide clear air to escaping miners as they make their way out of the mine in the aftermath of a fire or explosion. Sometimes the primary escapeways become compromised in an incident and workers may try to escape through "secondary" escapeways.

As per federal regulation, miners are required to carry oxygen-generating devices for use during an emergency like a fire or an explosion as the mine air becomes unsafe to breathe. These devices are always carried on their belts when inside the mine, and are called "self-contained self-rescuers" (SCSRs) (Figure 9.5). The SCSR is designed to provide one hour of oxygen to the user and comes with goggles (to protect the eyes) and a mouthpiece and nose clip (to isolate the lungs). The units' average weight is 3 to 4 lbs.

A substantial number of miners may face the need to escape from a mine emergency, usually a mine fire, at some point in their career. The basic protocol for escaping from an underground coal mine in an emergency has changed little in the past century. Miners are taught to make every attempt to escape if there is an emergency, following the designated escapeways to safety. If escape is impossible, miners previously were trained to seek temporary safety by erecting a barricade and awaiting rescue. A barricade is erected with available materials such as cement blocks or brattice curtain—used for mine ventilation—

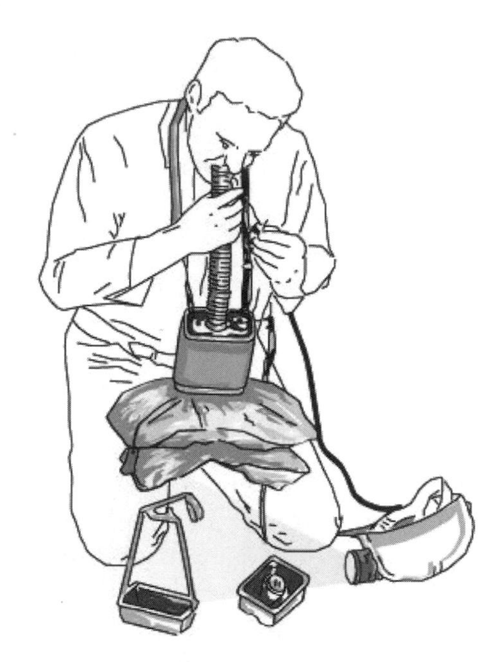

Figure 9.5 Miner donning self-contained self rescuer

with the goal of isolating the miners from toxic air. Since the Sago Mine Disaster in 2006, if escape is impossible, miners are trained to seek shelter in a refuge alternative.

Lessons Learned Through Mining Disasters

Figure 9.6 illustrates mining disaster incidents and fatalities 1900–2008 and Figure 9.7 provides a timeline of major mine disasters and the resulting legislation that they spurred. Each major piece of legislation had an impact on the fatality rates and the direction of research in the industry. Each of the various Congressional acts dealt with more than just responses to disaster. The 1977 Act, for instance, required that miners receive annual refresher training, which is composed of ten courses. Only one of the courses deals directly with escape and emergency evacuation. The rest include such topics as mandatory health and safety standards, first aid, accident prevention, and health.

Within a five-month period in 2006, three separate mining incidents occurred in the US and resulted in the deaths of 19 miners. All three incidents received nationwide attention, particularly the Sago, West Virginia Mine disaster, which occurred on January 2 and resulted in the deaths of 12 miners. The other two incidents, which occurred at the Alma No.1 Mine, also in West Virginia on January 19 and the Kentucky Darby No.1 Mine on May 20, resulted in the deaths of two miners and five miners, respectively. The occurrence of three fatal incidents in five months was a departure from recent trends in underground coal mining safety (refer to Figure 9.6). Before 2006, the frequency of mining disasters had decreased from a high of 20 in 1909 to an average of one every four years during the time period 1985–2005 (Kowalski-Trakofler et al., 2009; McKinney et al. 2002).

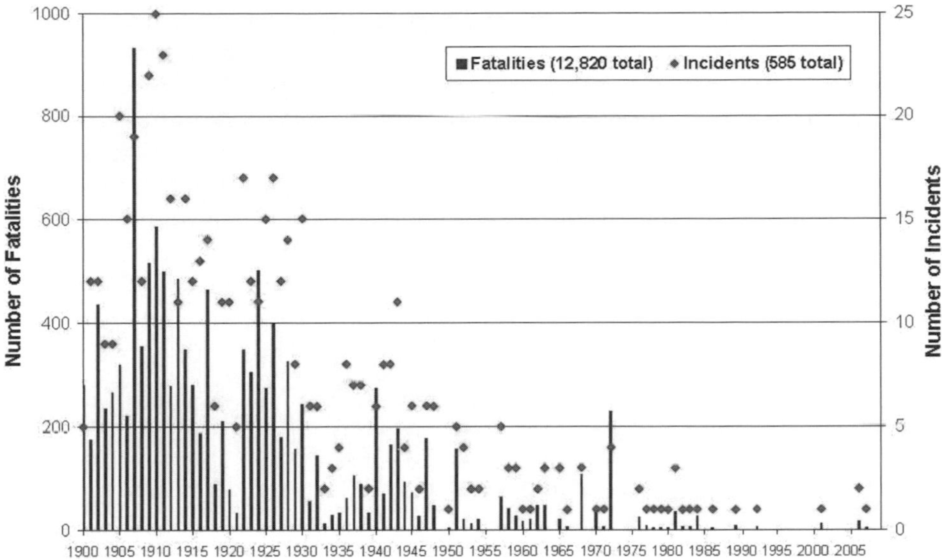

Data source: MSHA

Figure 9.6 Number of fatalities and rates (five-year aggregates) in the mining industry (1911–2008)

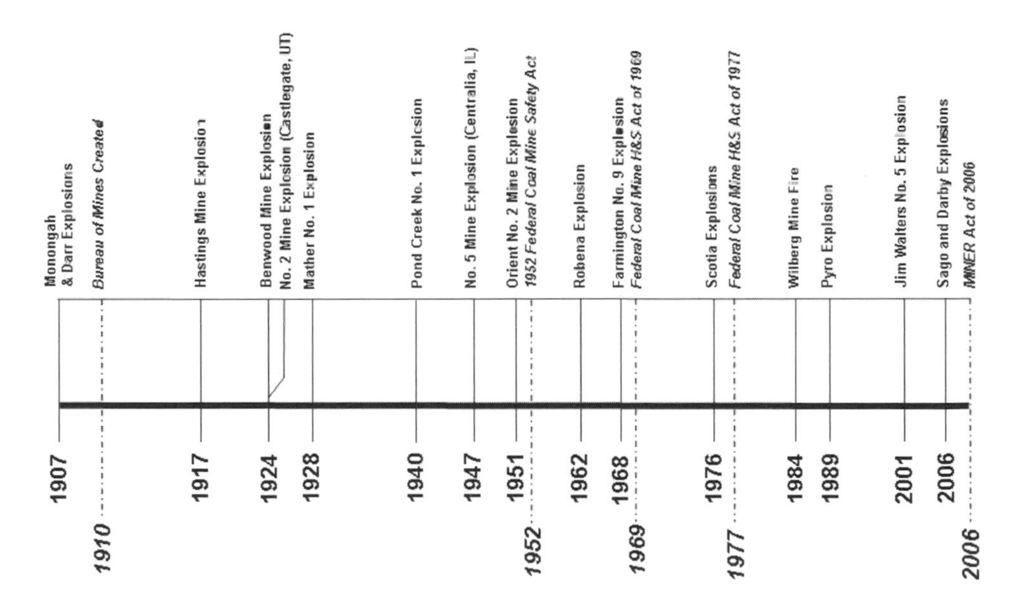

Fgure 9.7 Timeline of mining disasters and resultant legislation

Prior to the Sago incident, mines were only required to provide miners with a single self-contained breathing apparatus (SCSR), which provided one hour of safe air to the user. The sole survivor of the affected Sago mining crew reported that some of his fellow miners thought their SCSR was not working properly. The availability of extra SCSRs might have made a difference in the crew's decision to barricade instead of continuing their escape. These events led to renewed attention to mine safety, health, and training by organized labor, mine operators, lawmakers, and the general public (US). The public outcry resulted in the enactment of the Mine Improvement and New Emergency Response Act (MINER Act, 2006). The MINER Act requires mine operators to develop and maintain better plans for emergency preparedness and response. The legislation requires mine operators to provide caches of SCSRs along escapeways. The protective equipment must be spaced no more than 30 minutes travel time apart along the entire length of each escapeway, thus providing a minimum of two hours of safe air.

The inability of trapped miners to communicate with rescuers during the Sago Mine disaster led to other features in the MINER Act. Mine operators are now required to install wireless two-way communication and mine worker tracking systems between underground and surface workers. Congress subsequently passed an emergency supplemental appropriation to accelerate implementation of (1) emergency oxygen supplies; (2) refuge chambers; and (3) communication and tracking systems.

Occupational Safety and Health Intervention Model to Reduce Worker Exposures

In a hazardous and physically demanding work environment such as underground coal mining, a simple three-tiered model enables researchers and OSH practitioners to systematically design and evaluate interventions to protect workers. These interventions are termed "controls" as they are used to reduce or prevent, albeit control, worker exposure to the health and safety hazards in the work (mine) environment. The first tier of the OSH intervention model is engineering controls, which attempt to remove dangers to workers by optimal process and/or equipment design (technology). Examples of successful engineering solutions include advances in mine roof support technology (prevents roof collapse), noise abatement through equipment design (preserves hearing and enables better signaling), reduction of coal dust dispersion by dust control methods (reduces lung disease and improves visibility), and personal protective equipment technology (such as the SCSR, which generates safe breathing air for the user). Administrative controls represent another line of defense by ensuring appropriate rest and work cycles through shift schedules, safety training, and pre-shift mine safety evaluations. The final OSH intervention model tier is behavioral controls, which focus on whether safe work practices are effectively utilized—including training (knowledge and skills) and proper use of personal protective equipment (for example, SCSRs). This speaks to judgment, decision making and actual work performance (Figure 9.8).

Engineering Controls or interventions are physical manipulations of the sources of the hazard or the manner of exposure to the hazard. Examples include controlling noise, chemical exposure, and heat; erecting barriers; positioning switches for safer use; and redesigning electrical tools and equipment.

Administrative Controls are initiatives by management to modify a work process or exposure (organizational issues). Examples include developing a standard operating procedure and adjusting work practices such as job rotation or better shift schedules. Training is sometimes considered an administrative intervention.

Behavioral Controls focus on influencing workers' and employers' attitudes, knowledge, beliefs, or behaviors concerning work hazards or issues of worker health. Examples include training workers to wear personal protective equipment, using behavior modification techniques such as feedback to promote safer behavior, and encouraging worker health. Training may also be considered a behavioral intervention.

Figure 9.8 Occupational safety and health intervention model to reduce worker exposures

Key Mining Occupational Safety and Health Research Extends Beyond Engineering Controls

Engineering the danger out of the mining environment, the job task, tool, or machinery has represented the vast majority of the safety and health interventions in the US mining industry to date. The importance of training gained recognition in the latter third of the twentieth century, but focused mainly on training workers on the use of technology, tools, machinery, and later, job tasks. Almost 20 years ago, Canter, in discussing issues of escape from structural fire, argued that there is already enough evidence to support the contention that as far as "hardware" solutions are concerned, "such provisions are frequently insufficient and in many cases inappropriate...*human aspects* of the causes and development of fire must be understood if its disastrous effects are to be minimized" (Canter, 1990, p. xii, xiii, 2). Training remains a key component of health and safety in the mining industry, but, while still dealing with "hardware" issues, now pays attention to the human element as well.

Before the 1990s, mining research on behavioral aspects of OSH was conducted mainly through government contracts and reporting mechanisms. Peters (1989) reviewed the earlier research that was focused on organizational and behavioral factors associated with mine safety. Using the context of our OSH interventions model, Peters' review included administrative/organizational issues and individual behavior. The administrative review covered themes such as training, planning, commitment to safety, production pressure, incentive programs, and supervisor-employee relations (DeMichiei et al. in Peters, 1989). Individual behavioral themes gleaned from the review included worker autonomy, absenteeism, role ambiguity, role overload, and role conflict (Goodman et al. in Peters, 1989). These early efforts identified a number of important psychosocial issues in mining, eventually leading to a more structured internal research program by the US Government.

In 1984, the United States Bureau of Mines (now The Office of Mine Safety and Health Research (OMSHR) and the National Institute for Occupational Safety and Health (NIOSH) initiated a program of research to develop performance-based teaching and evaluation methods for assessing critical non-routine health and safety skills (that is, those needed in emergency situations like fires and explosions). This research moved beyond engineering controls and furthered administrative and behavioral control interventions for safety and health in mining through training. Previously, most training had focused on providing miners with routine technical information and experience with machines, tools, job tasks, and personal protective equipment (PPE). Fires and explosions are a major hazard in underground coal mines, yet, from the perspective of most miners, fires and explosions are considered infrequent events. At the time, little was known about the behavior of mine personnel in non-routine circumstances.

A substantial amount of research suggests that worker behavior is a very important contributor to many types of mining accidents. For example, Sanders and Shaw (1988) assessed the extent to which various types of factors contributed to 338 accidents in US underground coal mines. Expert raters assessed the degree to which each of ten types of potential causal factors played a role in each accident. Researchers concluded that "perceptual-cognitive-motor" error of the injured employee was involved to some degree in 93 percent of the cases and when involved, averaged about 33 (of 100) points of causality. The factor was considered a primary causal factor in almost 50 percent of cases and a secondary causal factor in another 24 percent. Management was the second most important causal factor. It was considered a primary factor in 22 percent of the cases and a secondary factor in another 12 percent. A similar study was commissioned by the Queensland Department of Mines and Energy in 2009. Utilizing a Human Factors Analysis and Classification System, researchers reviewed 500 accidents and incidents, and found that human error resulting in unsafe acts was a major contributor, 94 percent of the time.

Mine OSH researchers have begun incorporating principles of adult learning into training and evaluating the efficacy of training using models from the social sciences. Psychological and behavioral OSH research areas in the mining industry now include traumatic incident stress, the effects of the aging mining population on the industry, issues of perception in hazard recognition, the effects of fatigue in shift work, psychological issues related to the introduction of refuge chambers in underground coal mines, potential mental health issues related to the environment, safety culture, the effect of the dynamics of small rural communities in disaster response, and the overall question of how to make the mining workforce more resilient. A few of these areas will be presented in more detail below.

ENHANCING JUDGMENT AND DECISION-MAKING SKILLS

Electrical injuries in mining are not unusual in underground mines. The largest single category of electrical injury is the non-contact electric arc flash. An arc flash is the sudden release of electrical energy through the air when a high-voltage gap exists and there is a breakdown between conductors. An arc flash gives off thermal radiation (heat) and bright, intense light that can cause burns. Temperatures have been recorded as high as 35,000 °F. High-voltage arcs can also produce considerable pressure waves by rapidly heating the air and creating a blast. This pressure burst can hit a worker with great force and send molten metal droplets from melted copper and aluminum electrical components great distances at extremely high velocities. The National Institute for Occupational Safety and Health (NIOSH) examined behavioral control factors using personal interviews with victims and witnesses and an evaluation of the safety climate (Kowalski-Trakofler and Barrett, 2007). A surprise finding in this study was that qualified workers with ten to 16 years of professional experience were making inappropriate behavioral choices that led to the circumstances in which they were injured. Therefore, study recommendations included programs for the seasoned miner that added training in judgment and decision-making skills, while continuing to focus on technical skills and knowledge.

NIOSH evaluated three major mine fires that had forced the evacuation of miners who were working beyond the area of the fire and had to escape through smoke-filled passages in a very hostile environment. Forty-eight of the escaped miners were interviewed about their escape experiences, which provided NIOSH with a rich data base which readily supported a focus beyond engineering and administrative controls to the study of human behavior in escape from mine fires (Vaught et al., 2000). Researchers analyzed the data from the mine fire interviews in a variety of ways over the following decade, including examining individual and group behavior. They discovered that the miners underwent a complex decision-making process as they escaped the smoke-filled mines. Researchers constructed a model of the judgment and decision-making process along with analysis of fire warnings and the uncertainty of information in an emergency environment. The interactive judgment and decision-making model reflects the underlying demand on decision makers in most life and death situations (Figure 9.9).

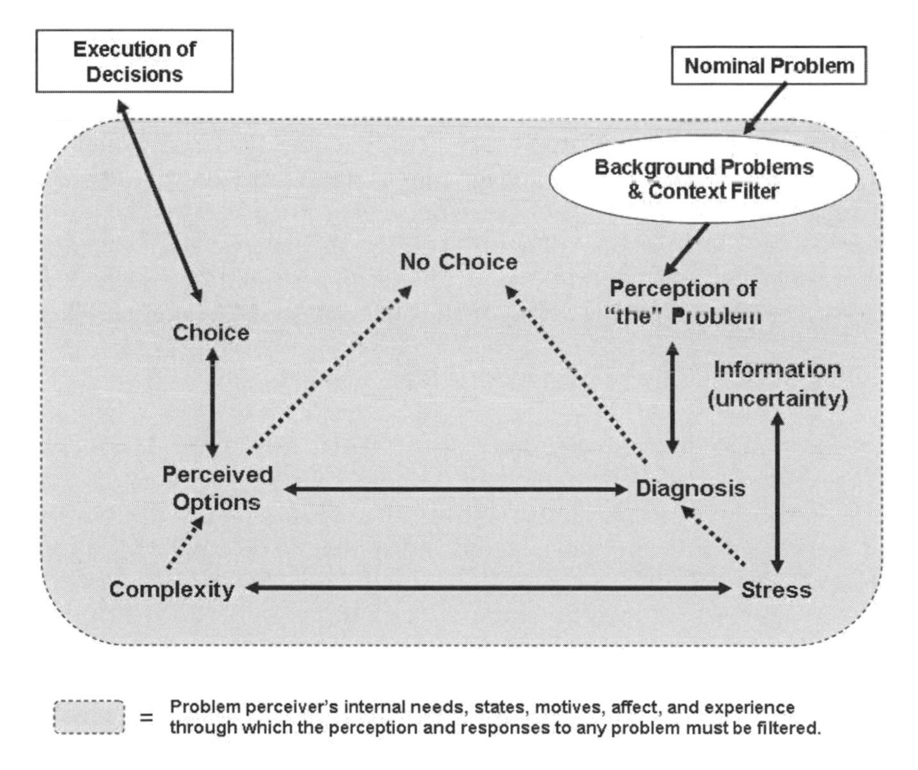

Figure 9.9 Model of judgment and decision making
Source: Vaught et al., 2000.

As miners escape, they go through a multi-step process of judgment and decision making. This process is ongoing and continues from when they first perceive there is a problem until they reach safety. Initially, miners are presented with the nominal problem. In the case of the 48 miners interviewed, this was a mine fire. As miners begin to perceive the problem, background problems and contextual issues factor in. Background problems include information such as knowledge of the fire location or the smell of smoke. Contextual issues include miners initially framing the problem as a routine event, such as smelling smoke from bonds being welded at rail joints, instead of as a non-routine event that could be signaling an emergency situation.

Once the miners perceived the problem, they entered a diagnosis (or analysis) phase. Stress from a variety of sources, including information uncertainty, affected their ability to effectively analyze the situation. After analyzing the situation, miners assessed options available for responding to the circumstances. Then, they selected an option and executed their decision. In some instances, miners made choices and executed decisions only to find that they made the wrong choice. They then re-evaluated the situation, perhaps through further diagnosis, and made new decisions about courses of action. This judgment and decision-making process continued throughout the entire escape.

An emergency makes it necessary to deal with an enormous amount of information in a rather short timeframe, and the information may be faulty. Researchers identified several important points about judgment and decision making in this environment. First, miners often initially placed the warning signs of the problem, such as the smell of smoke, within the context of normal activities, rather than as an emergency situation. This delayed accurate identification of the problem. Second, the diagnosis made by escapees was affected by the nature of the warning message they received, that is, for some the warning came in the form of a phone call while for others the warning was delivered face to face. Those contacted by phone spent time trying to verify the message, whereas those warned face to face tended to act more quickly. Third, miners' perceived options and choices were impacted most by their overall knowledge of the mine and the quality of information available. The researchers determined that "when an individual is warned of danger, that person will act if (1) he or she believes the danger is real and (2) feels that there are viable options. A warning system should be designed to provide the most information possible to comply with these two needs" (Vaught, 2000 p. 114).

EVOLVING LEADERSHIP IN MINE DISASTERS

Information on escapee leadership supports an affiliative model of emergency response, where people help each other rather than a more chaotic depiction of "every-man-for-himself." Although it is common to think that people panic in an emergency, a significant body of social science research has shown that panic is not a valid construct to explain group behavior during crisis situations (Clark, 2002; Quarantelli, 1989). The roles of individuals in a crisis, though not routine, tend to be similar to their normal roles, thus maintaining the social order (Johnson and Johnston, 1988). "The social behavior and cognitive processing of individuals stays remarkably close to what can be seen in ordinary, daily behavior" (Canter, 1990 p. 3). For example, the "Miracle on the Hudson" demonstrated the orderly egress of passengers and maintenance of authority by the flight crew after an emergency aircraft landing in the Hudson River in New York City in 2009 (Prochnau and Parker, 2009). This does not mean individuals are not afraid, and some may exhibit erratic behavior, but the overall tendency in such a situation is to maintain normal behavior and, some research has shown, to help one another (Sime, 1983).

The miner escape interview database allowed researchers to examine group escape and leadership in escape. The majority of miners behaved appropriately and within the accepted social framework and stayed together in escape. An additional analysis of these data was aggregated by escape group and coded for (1) evidence of leadership behavior; (2) evidence showing a lack of leadership; and (3) characteristics of the person leading the group out of the mine safely (Kowalski et al., 1994). The researchers found that some escape groups experienced an apparenont breakdown of leadership during their escape, while new leaders emerged in others. Consensus characteristics showed that successful leaders were aware and knowledgeable; decisive, yet flexible; open to input from others; and a calming influence. They were able to gain the follower's confidence. The leaders were logical decision makers and their leadership role evolved naturally, rather than by an individual seizing power. Effective leadership increased the likelihood of successful evacuation (Kowalski et al., 1994).

In the US mining industry, command leadership in a mine emergency is what may be described as a modified *unified command.* According to the US National Incident Management System (NIMS), unified command allows agencies with different legal, geographic, and functional authorities and responsibilities to work together effectively without affecting individual agency authority, responsibility or accountability (National Incident Management System, 2008). For mining, the unified command is termed a Mine Incident Management Command and may have up to four entities participating; and includes the company representative (mine owner), who is legally responsible for the incident, the state mine authority representative, a federal mine authority representative, and a worker representative (miner union) if the mine has one. MSHA is the agency responsible for determining the cause of the incident and determining fines and penalties. There is not a formal protocol that has been practiced consistently for the interaction of these four groups, as evidenced by the command experiences in the mine disasters of the past decade. The following vignette illustrates the hazards of leadership:

> *A small village in Lassing, Austria—population 2000—became famous after a tragic mining accident in July, 1998. At a depth of 60 meters underground, water and mud broke into a shaft of the mines in Lassing. What is left in memory from this incident ten years later is the huge hole in the earth that swallowed up several houses, the mine workers who survived for ten days, who could not be reached and remain buried in the mine, the rescue leader declaring the death of all mine workers prior to the rescue of the one survivor and the chaos that prevailed for one week. Lassing became a synonym for crisis mismanagement. Initial leadership was lacking and the most crucial after-the-fact finding was that most mistakes were caused by selfish fights over which group would be in the lead agency … [T]he lack of a clear leadership structure in a crisis can be catastrophic.*
>
> (Hersche and Wenker, 2008).

Leadership is a key factor in mine escape and rescue activities, and lack of leadership can be debilitating for missing miners' families, other miners, and the community. In the Sago disaster in West Virginia in 2006, misinformation and poor communication controls led to the release of information stating that all miners were alive followed over an hour later by the report of 12 deaths; this type of communication error can be devastating.

Both command leadership and escapee leadership are important for successful resolution to mine emergencies.

TRAINING TO FACILITATE APPROPRIATE ACTION UNDER DURESS: SETTING EXPECTATIONS

The 2006 incidents at the Sago, Alma, and Darby mines raised a number of issues about mine emergency preparedness and response, particularly as they relate to:

1. miners' donning of and expectations when wearing an SCSR and the need to switch to additional units for escape (refer to Figure 9.5);
2. miners' judgment and decision-making processes under the stress and uncertainty of a mine escape;
3. emergency communications, including equipment, and the transmission of appropriate important information;
4. the layout and marking of emergency escapeways in mines (recently addressed by regulation) and miners' familiarity with escape procedures;
5. way finding and navigation in smoke;
6. the psychosocial aspects of mine emergency escape and response; and
7. evaluation of mine emergency training programs (Gates et al., 2007; Light et al., 2007; Murray et al., 2007).

Many of these issues are not new and have been identified in previous research on self-rescue and escape, including human response issues such as individual and group behavior, judgment and decision-making skills, warnings and communication, way finding (the ability of an individual to move from one point to another through physical space relying on a cognitive map of spatial representations), and leadership in escape (Vaught et al., 1996; 2000). Previous research has also looked at judgment and decision making under stress (Kowalski-Trakofler and Barrett, 2003). It is only within the context of the 2006 mine incidents that these concerns have once again been brought to the surface (Brnich and Kowalski-Trakofler, 2010).

After the Sago disaster, analysis focused on the root cause of the explosion (Gates et al., 2007) without trying to understand the decisions miners made to barricade and to take off and/or share some of the SCSRs. The sole survivor reported that four of the units did not work, yet NIOSH tests indicated the SCSRs had not been used to capacity. This supports the hypothesis that the miners *may* have removed their SCSRs because they thought that the units were faulty.

NIOSH researchers completed one study after Sago to determine what effects or symptoms miners could expect to encounter while donning or wearing a properly-functioning SCSR unit (Kowalski-Trakofler, Vaught and Brnich, 2008). Researchers determined nine key areas representing issues that might influence a miner to remove his/her breathing apparatus. The nine areas included opening and starting problems, coughing when first starting to breathe, taste when breathing, breathing resistance, air being warm and dry, nose clips slipping and uncomfortable, goggles fogging up and the bag not inflating completely. NIOSH provided MSHA recommendations and information focused on cognitive, behavioral, psychological, and physical responses to trauma, which were integrated into training developed for exchanging SCSRs underground.

Additionally, NIOSH developed a new program called "expectations training" that has been implemented by MSHA. Expectations training is "training that provides the trainees with sufficient physical, cognitive, psychological, and behavioral information (beyond the necessary technical information and hands-on experience) to allow them to understand any potential symptoms they might experience while performing a task or action" (Kowalski-Trakofler, Vaught and Brnich, 2008). Thus, miners would be more prepared to deal with the symptoms that can arise from the emergency situation and their life-saving equipment.

USE OF REFUGE CHAMBERS IN MINE ESCAPE AND RESCUE

A substantial number of miners may face the need to escape from a mine emergency, usually a mine fire, at some point in their career. A 1996 study focusing on miners' preparedness to respond to a fire was conducted at seven US underground coal mines. The study revealed that 38 percent of the 180 miners interviewed had evacuated from a mine because of a fire. In addition, 21 percent said they had donned a breathing device because of a fire (Vaught et al., 1996).

The basic protocol for escaping from an underground coal mine in an emergency has changed little in the past century. Miners are taught to make every attempt to escape if there is an emergency, following the designated escapeways to safety. If escape is impossible, miners are now trained to seek temporary safety by going to a refuge alternative. The introduction of refuge chambers provides miners with another option if escape is impossible, but also raises new psychological considerations.

The 2006 MINER Act mandated research be conducted by NIOSH on refuge alternatives. Using this data, MSHA published its proposed rule in 2008 stating mines must install refuge chambers capable of sustaining miners for up to 96 hours in US underground coal mines by 2009 (US Deptartment of Labor, 2008). The final rule on refuge chambers specified that there be annual expectations training on refuge alternatives (CFR 75.1504 (c) (3)), and training on their use should be given quarterly and integrated with mandatory evacuation drills. NIOSH has developed refuge chamber expectations training for miners on the physical and psychological issues they may face (Margolis, Kowalski-Trakofler and Kingsley-Westerman, 2009).

The psychological considerations involved for underground mine workers who choose to remain in refuge chambers include a variety of issues. What are the psychological effects of potentially staying 96 hours in a chamber and what about the group dynamics in a confined space over time in a stressful situation? What supplies are important for maintaining physical and mental health while in the chamber? Under what conditions might miners leave the refuge, given the internal and external situation? Application of research from studies on confined spaces in the military and other industries could benefit the mining industry.

Miners are trained to escape the mine in an emergency. If miners elect to stay in a refuge chamber, they must believe that it is the last alternative and need to have confidence someone will rescue them. Present mine rescue practice in the US has not been changed to accommodate large numbers of trapped miners. In 2002, a drill and escape capsule was used successfully at the Quecreek Mine in Pennsylvania, where nine miners were trapped by an inundation of water after machinery broke through into a sealed-off adjacent mine. Since many US underground coal mines are in hilly or mountainous terrain, and may have less favorable access for this type of rescue than Quecreek, mine rescue teams must be prepared to enter the mine to rescue miners waiting in refuge chambers.

Previously, the US Bureau of Mines contracted for a review of the literature and development of guidelines for designing, constructing, stocking, and maintaining rescue chambers in underground mines (McCoy et al., 1983). Examples of reports reviewed 24 years ago included fallout shelter studies, underwater habitability studies, NASA manned spaceflight human factors research, mine disaster field studies, and laboratory studies on sensory deprivation, confinement, and social isolation.

Predictable psychological reactions to such confinement included anxiety, withdrawal, apathy, aggression, hostility, depression, and irrational and impulsive behavior. Research on the effect of deprivation and isolation on task performance was found to be inconsistent. However, visual illusions and hallucinations were reported in mine disaster field studies where trapped miners were subjected to prolonged periods of darkness (one to two weeks) and uncontrolled hazards (roof falls). Researchers noted a shift in the behavioral dynamics of trapped miners in the two case studies reviewed—with task-oriented behavior emerging in adaptive attempts to escape; followed by more emotion-based behavior as efforts needed to be redirected toward group survival and enhancing social stability. Miners were deemed likely to be confused and disoriented upon entry into the chamber, and consequently very anxious, mainly due to the effect of the disaster. Emergent leadership required different skill sets depending on the behavioral dynamics and duration of the confinement. Managing boredom, restlessness, and fluctuating despair/hope appear to loom larger as confinement persists. Specific stressors noted to cause significant stress included a lack of outside communication, prolonged darkness (sensory deprivation), the presence of severely injured/dying miners (powerlessness to help; guilt; identifying with the suffering), and miners that died (stench, fear of gas poisoning).

Hot, humid, closed, and cramped refuge chamber environments are likely to be uncomfortable and tax coping strategies. Individuals with well-controlled chronic mental illness (for example, depression, generalized anxiety disorder, post traumatic stress disorder (PTSD) or certain chronic physical disorders that can be triggered by stress (for example, asthma, peptic ulcer disease, irritable bowel syndrome, hypertension, coronary artery disease, diabetes) may experience exacerbations in their underlying symptoms if stress overwhelms psychological and social coping strategies.

IMPACT OF THE AGING POPULATION

The approaching departure of "baby boomers" from the workforce is expected to have a profound impact on the US economy and that of other nations around the world. Changes in the workforce will have a greater impact on mining than in many other industries because of past hiring patterns and improved technology. The coal mining boom of the late 1970s led to the employment of many new miners, most of whom were in their twenties. As coal mining became more capital-intensive in the 1980s and 1990s, downsizing and layoffs occurred, and there was a concomitant decline in the hiring of new miners. (Kowalski-Trakofler et al., 2004). According to the US Bureau of Labor Statistics, in 2002 the median age of the coal mine workforce was 45.2 years, while the median age of all workers in the US was 40.1 years (Mallet and Schwerha, 2006). That same year, 57 percent of the coal mining workforce was over 44 years of age. If workers are entering and leaving the industry in a consistent way, comparing ten-year work groups should show similar percentages of workers in each group. Instead, the 45–54 age group is 44 percent of the total, with the 35–44 age group at 23.8 percent and the 25–34 age group at 14.3 percent (Mallett and Schwerha, 2006). Older workers have increased experience and knowledge, which may help them work "smarter." The mining industry today not only faces issues related to an aging population in a physically intense workplace, but the training of new miners to replace the experienced and knowledgeable miners who are ready to retire. The National Mining Association (NMA) estimates a total of 50,000 new employees will be needed in coal mining over the next ten years to meet increasing demand and to replace retiring workers (NMA, 2009). Capturing the institutional knowledge of the older generation of miners to benefit the younger miners is a challenge, along with conducting training for mixed-generation classes.

Coal mine accident statistics from 1978 to 1980, after the last large influx of new miners, suggest that being young and inexperienced leads to higher injury rates among workers. This relationship is consistent across the 15 companies that provided data on the age of their work force, as well as for each of the years 1978, 1979, and 1980: Miners between the ages of 18 and 24 have an injury rate nearly twice that of miners aged 25 to 34, who have a rate about 25 percent higher than miners aged 35 to 44, who in turn have a rate over 40 percent higher than miners who are at least 45 years of age. Hence, a young miner (18–24) is about twice as likely to be injured than is a miner aged 25–44, and about three times more likely to be injured than is a miner 45 years of age or older (National Academy of Science, 1982).

Recently, Mallett and Schwerha (2006) reported that the median age for injured underground coal miners was 43-years-old, based on injury data from MSHA. Data also suggest that these older workers, while injured less often, as the above discussion indicates, sustain more serious injuries with more lost time from the job (Fotta and Bockosh, 2000; Margolis, 2011). In addition, the effects of certain injuries, such as musculoskeletal injuries (MSIs), may be more extreme for older workers. The data show not only that MSIs are a type of injury that tends to happen more frequently to workers over age 30, but that the number of days lost per injury also increases. Over the 11 year period from 1992–2002, over half of all workdays lost were due to musculoskeletal-related injuries. On average, about 40 percent of all injuries that occurred during this period were musculoskeletal in nature (Porter et al., 2008). From an injury prevention perspective, the three-tiered intervention model is useful. Engineering solutions, such as reducing the weight of materials, should be followed by administrative and behavioral interventions. Attention to work organization, informing miners of appropriate PPE, and knowledge of protective behaviors such as correct lifting practices are very useful in reducing the injury rate.

Age-related changes result in diminished physical, sensory, and cognitive capabilities, all of which can affect a miner's safety in the workplace. Mines are challenging environments, and low illumination, noise levels, and difficult terrain are all sources of concern for the aging mining population. Many people, as they age, experience diminished visual acuity and have difficulty seeing in low-lit areas. It is important for miners to wear appropriate safety glasses and be aware of reduced vision in their workplace, using cap lamps to the best advantage. Engineering controls to reduce noise levels of machinery in mines, administrative controls in providing hearing loss information, appropriate PPE, training, and individual behavior can make a significant impact on hearing loss, which is a major health issue in mining. As aging affects balance, slips, trips, and falls become more of an issue, particularly with the uneven nature of mine floors.

SHIFTWORK

Shiftwork, generally defined as working outside normal daylight hours, is a fact of life in the mining industry. Mine workers may work a day, late afternoon, or night shift; they may also work a longer shift (10–12 hours) or overtime. Many mines have rotating shifts, and some may have so many days "on" and then days off. Shiftwork schedules are demanding and likely to produce stress and fatigue (Rosa and Colligan, 1997). Overall research on shiftwork has shown rates of fatigue and number of work accidents are higher in shift workers (Halvani, Zare and Hobobati, 2009).

Although there is limited shiftwork data on the underground coal mining population in particular, a growing body of evidence suggests that long working hours adversely affect both the physical health and mental health of workers. Bise and Breysse (1999) examined the effect of extended shifts on injuries experienced at underground longwall coal mines in the US. They reported finding a trend between the non-fatal days lost incidence rate and shift length. Specifically, for every hour of shift length above eight hours, the non-fatal days lost incidence rate was 1.185 implying that an 18.5 percent increase in the number of non-fatal days lost incidents is predicted when a shift is extended one hour in the range from eight to nine, or nine to ten hours.

Other studies have associated overtime and extended work schedules with an increased risk of hypertension, cardiovascular disease, fatigue, stress, depressions, musculoskeletal disorders, chronic infections, diabetes, general health complaints, and all-cause mortality (Dembe et al., 2005; Caruso et al., 2004). There are relatively few studies comparing long work hours and risk for occupational injuries and illnesses. Some studies have shown evidence of a relationship between long working hours and an increased risk of occupational injury among specific occupations and industries, including mining (Duchon and Smith, 1994). Fatigue has also been shown to result in job dissatisfaction among iron ore miners (Halvani, Zare and Mirmohammadi, 2009).

Shiftwork often results in workers performing their duties out of sync with their circadian rhythms. Circadian rhythms are a major body rhythm, with regular ups and downs in a 24-hour day. People perform best when alertness and internal body activity is high and worst when alertness and activity are low. Alertness affects safety behavior and is a concern for shift workers especially in volatile and constantly changing hazardous environments. There are personal differences in circadian rhythms, but for most people, the high activity portion of their circadian rhythm occurs in late afternoon or early evening. The body's ability to produce energy from food (metabolism) is highest in the afternoon to evening. The least activity usually is in the middle of the night when most people are asleep.

Long working hours, rotating shifts, working out of sync with natural circadian rhythms, and the long commutes often required to reach remote mines can all contribute to limited and/or interrupted sleep. In turn, this leads to fatigue, and fatigue can affect safe performance.

There have been few major studies to date on the effects of shiftwork in the US coal mining industry, although data from shift workers in other types of mining (Duchon and Smith, 1994), and in the medical community, indicate definite safety and health concerns. The effects of shiftwork on occupational health and safety in the US mining industry are an issue worth inquiry.

HAZARD RECOGNITION[1]

In mining, as in most other production-related industries, the safety of the worker is dependent on many interrelated factors, one of which is the workers' ability to recognize hazards in the workplace. The ability to recognize hazards in mining is critical because the work environment is dark, confined, inherently unsafe, and constantly changing during the mining process. The mining process creates exposure to dust, noise, and powerful machinery. Workers must be alert and continuously cognizant of their surroundings. The information necessary to recognize conditions that are precursors of danger is often available in the form of visual cues, which may be difficult to perceive in the low-light environment of an underground mine. MSHA and US Department of Labor descriptive accidents report data have shown that "failure to perceive" a hazard consistently appears as a contributing factor to both fatal and non-fatal injuries.

There had been limited research on training for the recognition of mine hazards and none based on principles of perception until the mid-1990s when researchers applied the military concept of degraded images to training for underground mine workers (Perdue et al 1995; Barrett and Kowalski,1995). At the time, studies suggested that perceptual judgments are susceptible to training and the most extensive base of information came from military studies on target detection (Farnsworth, Malone and Sexton, 1952; Jones, Freitag and Collyer, 1974; Leibowitz, 1967). Laboratory research also suggested that visual degradation of a stimulus hinders its correct identification by slowing both the initial stimulus encoding process and the search for that stimulus in memory. It takes longer to "clean-up" the mental representation and thus, training that cultivates degraded mental representations and creates content for memory identification can shorten the time necessary to identify, and consequently react to hazards. The military research on target detection had found that if the eventual target stimuli are to be searched for and identified under degraded conditions, observers should be trained to recognize them using training stimulus that are similarly degraded (Cockrell, 1979). NIOSH researchers tested the theory that in training miners to recognize hazards and hazardous situations in their highly variable and often visually degraded environment, it would be desirable to give them experience with equally variable representations of these hazards in the training presentations. Previous to this, miners were shown focused, highlighted hazards and told to avoid them. Unfortunately, in an actual mining environment, these hazards are in low light, hazy, and oftentimes competing with other hazards.

NIOSH researchers designed two training programs, one with highlighted hazard visuals and one with degraded visuals. Three separate studies were conducted with underground mines in Pennsylvania, West Virginia, Alabama, and Illinois. Results showed that after the degraded imaging training over a one-year period, incident rates dropped significantly in Alabama (30 percent) and Illinois (27 percent). In each case, however, there was another factor introduced by the company at approximately the same time—management for safety in Alabama, and a flex and stretch program in Illinois. This made it impossible to determine how much of a drop in incident rates was due to training itself. However, in interviews with the trainers, their observations credited the degraded hazard recognition program with a major part in the decrease in injury rates (Kowalski-Trakofler

1 Some text excerpted from Kowalski-Trakofler and Barrett (2003).

and Barrett, 2003). This program has applications for many different hazardous work environments and has been used in the construction and agriculture sectors.

EXPANDED SAFE JOB PERFORMANCE MODEL

NIOSH researchers developed a theoretical Safe Job Performance Model, which expands the basic three-tiered simple model shown in Figure 9.8, in order to define and integrate the various aspects of performing a job safely. This expanded model, shown in Figure 9.10, may be utilized in analyzing specific safety and health problems in mining, in the development of interventions and in the planning and evaluation of training (Kowalski-Trakofler and Barrett, 2003). The core of the model is the safety climate or the work environment of the company or organization. Six components serve as a foundation to support both the organization and the individual to ensure safe job performance. They combine the original three tiers—engineering controls, administrative controls, and behavior controls—with three new components: technical skills, knowledge, and judgment and decision-making ability (Figure 9.10). Technical skills refer to the hands-on skills and abilities needed to get the job done and complete a task successfully. Technical skills explain "how" a worker does the job. Knowledge refers to the basic information needed in order to understand the process of the task. Knowledge is an important underpinning of safe job performance. Workers need to understand the task within the context of the overall job, in addition to having the skills to perform the task. Judgment and decision making refers to the worker's ability to make sound and safe decisions.

NIOSH researchers found that most safety interventions in the mining industry today include technical skills and knowledge, as well as some administrative controls.

Safe Job Performance Model

Engineering Controls
Administrative Controls
Behavioral Controls
Work Environment
Safe Job Performance
Safety Climate
Technical Skills
Knowledge
Judgment and Decision-Making Ability

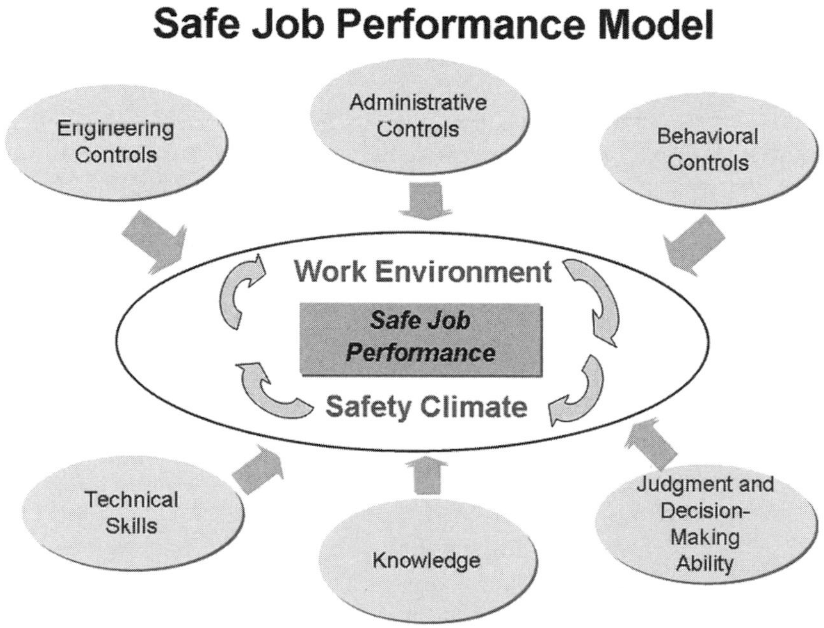

Figure 9.10 Safe Job Performance Model

Source: Kowalski-Trakofler and Barrett (2007).

The addition of further administrative and behavioral controls, plus improved judgment and decision-making ability, can enhance the effectiveness of worker safety programs. This model has application as an evaluation tool for specific safety and health interventions and training programs, as well as overall organizational safety programs.

PERCEIVED JOB STRESS AND HEALTH IMPACT

Five of the ten leading causes of disability worldwide are mental health problems (WHO/ILO, 2000). Even so, the importance of psychological well-being and mental health in the workplace is generally underestimated and seldom included in studies of occupational health. Unfortunately, there are limited psychological studies on the mental health of the US mining population, although issues affecting every workplace population working in a hazardous work environment are most likely relevant.

Althouse and Hurrell (1977) examined how much job stress and psychological strain underground coal miners experience, and how levels of job stress and strain reported by miners who work in mines with high-accident rates compares with the stress and strain reported by miners who work at mines with low-accident rates. Overall, there was surprisingly little difference between the high and low accident mines in terms of reported levels of job stress and psychological strain. The researchers also point out that these findings do not necessarily mean that miners do not experience considerable psychological strain in *both* high-and low-accident mines. The researchers compared the reported stress and strain of coal miners with other nationally sampled blue-collar workers, and found that miners fared better than average on most measures of job stress, and, in fact, were low in subjective job stress experiences. With respect to strain, however, miners were much more irritated than other blue-collar employees. They also experienced greater than average anxiety, depression, and had more physical complaints. However, on average, they expressed higher job satisfaction, lower workload dissatisfaction, and less boredom than other blue-collar workers. Althouse and Hurrell conclude that miners were higher in their affective psychological strain, but lower than the average blue-collar worker on behavioral strain indicators.

DISASTER RESILIENCY OF MINE WORKERS

Based on the extensive studies after the Oklahoma bombing in 1995 and the terrorist events of September 11, 2001 in New York and Washington, DC, the likely outcomes of events such as mining disasters include traumatic incident stress disorders, including acute stress disorder, post-traumatic stress syndrome, and suicides (NIOSH, 2002). At present, only anecdotal evidence supports this idea in mining. Researchers at NIOSH are focused on raising awareness of the issue and developing information for emergency responders (NIOSH, 2002).

Suicides and depression can be the result of inadequate psychological support during and after an emergency response. It has been suggested that the most vulnerable time emotionally is from six months to one year after the event. There is increased anger, self-destructive behavior, and even suicide. "The despair, the helplessness gets so intense … it bursts out" (Lagnado 2002). There were suicides in the aftermath of both the Quecreek and Sago events. Two miners who were at the site of the Sago Mine disaster committed suicide within about six months of the event. Neither man was blamed in the tragedy, nor was it clear why they committed suicide; however, family members claimed that these men were continually bothered by the event. Another suicide victim was the man who successfully pinpointed the location to drill to affect the rescue at Quecreek, but it is not clear how his involvement in the Quecreek emergency may have played a role in his suicide. These cases support the need for specially-trained counselors in disaster mental health. Their services would be beneficial before, during, and after a mine disaster. Currently, interventions after-the-fact and educational programs on the expected human response in crisis may be limited. Individuals who need help are generally referred to the local county mental health office. Unfortunately, local, rural mental health facilities rarely have personnel with specific training in disaster mental health. In some communities, the Red Cross is available to provide qualified emergency mental health support at the time of the crisis, but is not present for follow-up.

Rescue workers, co-workers, and family members are also subject to the psychological after-effects of a traumatic incident. From a psychological perspective, many times the trauma is just beginning when individuals reach safety. Research in this area has shown that interventions may mitigate serious emotional, behavioral, physical, and cognitive consequences to personnel (Everly, Perrin and Everly, 2008). The MINER Act mandates attention to family support. Some mining states are looking into ways to address the needs of mine families, recognizing the needs of family and community during a mine disaster, and the need to base interventions on empirical data. For example, Pennsylvania's Mine Families First legislation mandates that the families of miners involved in an emergency be provided with information, access to counseling and other social services, and other considerations in the event of an emergency.

Humans are efficient survival machines, individually and in groups. Survival is accomplished, not by brute strength or avoidance, but by the ability to cope with a potentially hostile environment by recognizing and solving problems. Today's terminology sometimes refers to this construct as *resilience*—the ability of an individual or organization to both withstand significant adversity and to "bounce back" after a trauma. Resilience has been described as a dynamic process of healthy adaptation in adversity. Resilience is multidimensional and involves personal, organizational, and environmental factors including hardiness, flexibility, optimism, and availability of social resources, sense of connectedness and support, and overall intelligence (Reissman et al., 2010; Reissman, Kowalski-Trakofler and Katz, in press). Resilience is emerging as an umbrella concept for positive behavioral emergency response, with identifiable factors that are applicable to improved escape and rescue strategies. Developing resilient mine workers is a reasonable goal for the industry.

Conclusions

Coal mining disasters have decreased substantially in frequency and number of fatalities in the past 100 years. Engineering hazards out of the environment has been the primary method of reducing these incidents. Engineering improvements that have impacted the health and safety of the mineworker include developing newer, safer mining methods; creating better, safer tools and machinery; understanding and controlling mine gases; more sophisticated roof control and ventilation plans; and overall better ways to remove coal safely from the earth. The health and safety focus today remains in the engineering arena. Yet, since 1988, increasing amounts of research have been completed in the area of human behavior in mining. During the past 20 years, there has been a steady increase in research on miner behavior in mine escape, hazard recognition, communications, expectations training, and, most recently, attention to the human interface with mandated refuge chambers. Training has been developed from this research based on the empirical data. Program evaluation is a key issue. During the past 40 years, knowledge of the causes of work-related disease and disability has grown dramatically; however, ways to evaluate occupational health and safety interventions remain limited. In addition, the industry is continuing to adapt management principles and models identified through social science research. Further benefits are likely to accrue by applying social sciences research and knowledge learned within other hazardous industries.

Acknowledgments

The authors wish to acknowledge colleagues at NIOSH: Michael J. Brnich, Jr., Mining Engineer; Robert Peters, MS Supervisory Research Psychologist; Launa G. Mallett, PhD, Sociologist; Patricia Lenart, BS, IT Specialist; William Reid, Editor, Coal Age.

References

Althouse, R., and Hurrell, J. (1977) An Analysis of Job Stress in Coal Mining. NIOSH (DHEW) 77-217, 1977, 145 pp.; NTIS PB 274-796.

Bise, C.J. and Breysse, P.N. (1999) The effect of shiftwork schedule practices and panel dimensions on injury experience in underground longwall coal mines, *Mineral Resources Engineering*; *8*(4), 349–360.

Brnich, M.J. and Kowalski-Trakofler, K.M. (2010) *Underground Coal Mine Disasters 1900–2010: Events, Responses, and a Look to the Future*. In J. Brune (ed.) Extracting The Science: A Century of Mining Research Celebrating the 100th Anniversary of Original Research with the Formation of the US Bureau of Mines in 1910. Denver, CO: Society for Mining, Metallurgy, and Exploration, 363–372.

Canter, D.V. (1990) Fires and human behavior, *Fire Technology; 20*(2), 1–14.

Caruso, C.C., Hitchcock, E.M., Dick, R.B., Russo, J.M., and Schmit, J.M. (2004) Overtime and Extended Work Shifts: Recent Findings on Illnesses, Injuries, and Health Behaviors. DHHS (NIOSH) Publication No. 2004-143

Clark, L. (2002) Panic: Myth or reality, *Contexts*; *1*(4), 21–16.

Cockrell, J.T. (1979) Effective Training for Target Identification under Degraded Conditions. US Army Research Institute for the Behavioral and Social Sciences, Technical Paper, vol 358.

DeJoy, D.M., Gershon, R.M., and Schaffer, B. (2004) Safety climate: Assessing management and organizational influences on safety, *Professional Safety; 49*(7), 50–57.

DeMarchi, J. (1997) *Historical Mining Disasters*. Beckley, WV: US Department of Labor, Mine Safety and Health Administration, National Mine Health and Safety Academy.

Dembe, A.E., Erickson, J.B., Delbos, R.G., and Banks, S.M. (2005) The impact of overtime and long work hours on occupational injuries and illnesses: new evidence from the United States, *Journal of Occupational and Environmental Medicine*; *62*(9), 588–597.

Duchon, J.C. and Smith, T.J. (1994) *Extended Workdays in Mining and Other Industries: A Review of the Literature*. US Dept of Interior, Bureau of Mines, IC9378

Everly, G., Perrin, P., and Everly, G. (2008) Psychological Issues in Escape, Rescue, and Survival in the Wake of Disaster. CDC contract no. 254-2008-M-24817 for the National Institute for Occupational Safety and Health, Pittsburgh Research Laboratory.

Farnsworth, D., Malone, R., and Sexton, M. (1952) Relative detect ability of hues in air-sea rescue, *Journal of the Optical Society of American*; 42, 289.

Federal Coal Mine Health and Safety Act of 1969 (1969) Pub. L. 91-173, (S 2917), (December 30, 1969).

Federal Mine Safety & Health Act of 1977 (1977) Pub. L. No. 91-173, as amended by Public Law 95-164.

Fotta, B. and Bockosh, G.R. (2000) The aging workforce: An emerging issue in the mining industry. In G.R. Bockosh, N. Karmis, J. Langton, M.K. McCarter, B. Rowe (eds) Proceedings of the 31st Annual Institute of Mining Health, Safety and Research. Blacksburg, VA: Virginia Polytechnic Institute and State University, Department of Mining and Minerals Engineering, 33–45.

Gates, R., Phillips, R., Urosek, J., Stephan, C., Stoltz, R., Swentosky, D., Harris, G.W., O'Donnell, J.R., and Dresch, R.A. (2007) *Report of Investigation; Fatal Underground Coal Mine Explosion, Jan 2, 2006*. US Department of Labor. No. 46-08791.

Halvani, G.H., Zare, M., and Hobobati, H. (2009) The fatigue in workers of Iran Central Iron Ore Company in Yazd, *International Journal of Occupational Medicine and Environment Health;* 22(1), 19–26.

Halvani, G.H., Zare, M., and Mirmohammadi, S.J. (2009) National Institute of Occupational Safety and Health, Kawasaki, Japan, *Industrial Health*; *47*, 134–138.

Hartman, H.L. and Mutmansky, J.M. (2002) *Introductory Mining Engineering*. Hoboken, NJ: John Wiley & Son, Inc.

Hersche, R. and Wenker, O. (2000) Case Report: Lassing mining accident, The Internet Journal of Rescue and Disaster Medicine; ISSN: 1531-2992 Internet Scientific publications, LLC, 1996 to 2008.

Humphrey, H.B. (1998) Historical Summary of Mine Disasters in the United States, Volume II—Coal Mines—1810–1958. *Sec. 4, I.* US Department of Labor Mine Safety and Health Administration National Mine Health and Safety Academy.

Johnson, D.M.J. and Johnson, N.R. (1988) Role extension in disaster: Employee behavior at the Beverly Hills Supper Club fire, *Sociological Focus; 22*, 39–51.

Jones, D.B., Freitag, M., and Collyer, S.C. (1974) Air-to-Ground Target Acquisition Source Book: A Review of the Literature. Prepared for the Office of Naval Research, NTIS AD-A015 079.

Kowalski-Trakofler, K.M. and Barrett, E.A. (2003) The concept of degraded images applied to hazard recognition training in mining for reduction of lost-time injuries, *Journal of Safety Research; 34*(5), 515–525.

Kowalski-Trakofler, K.M. and Barrett, E. (2007) Reducing non-contact electric arc injuries: An investigation of behavioral and organizational issues, *Journal of Safety Research; 38*(5), 597–608.

Kowalski-Trakofler, K.M., Dandrick, A., Brnich, M.J., McWilliams, L.J., and Reissman, D.B. (2009) Underground Coal Mining Disasters and Fatalities: United States, 1900–2006 *MMWR 51/52*(57), 1379–1383.

Kowalski K.M., Mallett, L.G., and Brnich, M.J. (1994) *Emergence of Leadership in a Crisis: a Study of Group Escapes from Fire in Underground Coal Mines*. http://www.cdc.gov/niosh/mining/pubs/pdfs/lcief.pdf.

Kowalski-Trakofler, K.M., Vaught, C., Mallett, L.G., Brnich, M.J., Reinke, D.C., Steiner, L.J., Wiehagen, W.J., and Rethi, L.L. (2004) *Safety and Health Training for an Evolving Workforce: An Overview from the Mining Industry*, (Vol. DHHS (NIOSH) 2004-155). http://www.cdc.gov/niosh/mining/pubs/pubreference/outputid95.htm.

Kowalski-Trakofler, K.M., Vaught, C., and Brnich, M.J. (2008) Expectations training for miners using self-contained self rescuers in escapes from underground coal mines, *Journal of Occupational and Environmental Hygiene*; *5*(10), 671–677.

Kowalski-Trakofler K., Vaught C., and Scharf, T. (2003) Judgment and decision making under stress: An overview for emergency managers, *International Journal of Emergency Management; 1*(3), 278–289.

Lagnado, L. (2002) FDNY tries to rescue its own. Wall Street Journal; March 2, 2002, D1 p. 67.

Leibowitz, J.W. (1967) The Human Visual System and Image Interpretation. Institute for Defense Analyses Research Paper, p. P-319.

Light, T., Herndon, R., Guley, A., Cook, G., Odum, M. and Bates, R. (2007) *Report of Investigation, Fatal Underground Coal Mine Explosion, May 20, 2006* (No. 15-18185). (MSHA) Arlington, VA.

Maiti, J., Shatteerjee, S. and Bangdicala, S.I. (2004) Determinants of work injures in mines—an application of structural equation modeling, *Injury, Control and Safety Promotion;* 11(1), 29–37.

Mallett, L.J. and Schwerha, D.J. (2006) *What Difference Does Age Make? Part 2: Coal Mining Injuries*. Holmes Saf Assn Bull 2006 Jan/Feb. Falls Church, VA: US Department of Labor, Mine Safety and Health Administration, 10–18.

Margolis, K.A., Kowalski-Trakofler, K.M., and Kingsley-Westerman, C. (2009) Refuge Chamber Expectations Training. DHHS (NIOSH) Publication No. 2010-100.

Margolis, K., Kingsley-Westerman, C., and Kowalski Trakofler, K. (2011) Underground Mine Refuge Chamber Expectations Training: Program Development and Evaluation Manuscript Number: SAFETY-D-10-00072R2, Safety Science.

Margolis, K.A. (2010) Underground coal mining injury: A look at how age and experience relate to days lost from work following an injury, Safety Science.

McCabe, K. (2005) *Guide for Performing Arc Flash 990 Calculations*. IEEE P1584 Vol. P1584. New York.

McCoy, J.F., Berry, D.R., Mitchell, D.W. (1983) Development of Guidelines for Rescue Chambers, Volume II. US Bureau of Mines Contract No. JO387210, October 2003, Waltham, MA: Foster-Miller, Inc.

McKinney, R., Crocco, W., Stricklin, K.G., Murray, K.A., Blankenship, S.T., Davidson, R.D., Urosek, J.F., Stephan, C.R., and Beiter, D.A. (2002) *Report of Investigation Fatal Underground Coal Mine Explosions, September 23, 2001, No. 5 Mine*, Jim Walter Resources, Inc., Brookwood, Tuscaloosa County, Alabama I.D. No. 01-01322. Arlington, VA: US Department of Labor, Mine Safety and Health Administration.

Mine Improvement and New Emergency Response Act of 2006 (2006) (MINER Act), Pub. L. No. 108-236 (S 2803) (June 15, 2006).

Murray, K., Pogue, C., Stahlhut, R., Finnie, M., Webb, A., and Burke, A. (2007) *Report of Investigation: Fatal Underground Coal Mine Fire, January 19, 2006* (No. 46-08801). (MSHA) Arlington, VA. http://www.msha.gov/Fatals/2006/Sago/sagoreport.asp.

National Academy of Sciences-National Research Council (1982) *Toward Safer Underground Coal Mines*. NAS.

National Incident Management System (2008) US Department of Homeland Security. http://www.fema.gov/pdf/nims/NIOMS_core.pdf.

National Mining Association (2009) Fast Facts About Minerals. http://www.nma.org/statistics/fast_facts.asp.

National Institute for Occupational Safety and Health (2002) Traumatic Incident Stress: Information for Emergency Response Workers. DHHS (NIOSH) Publication number 2002-107.

Perdue, C.W., Kowalski, K.M., and Barrett, E.A. (1995) Hazard Recognition in Mining: A Psychological Perspective. Information Circular 9422. Bureau of Mines. US Dept. of the Interior.

Peters, R.H., (1989) Review of Recent Research on Organizational and Behavioral Factors Associated with Mine Safety. US Depart of Interior, Bureau of Mines, IC 9232.

Porter, W.L., Mallett, L.G., Schwerha, D.J., Gallagher, S., Torma-Krajewski, J., and Steiner, L.J. (2008) Age Awareness Training for Miners. Information Circular 9505. Dept of HHS, CDC, NIOSH, PRL June.

Prochnau, W. and Parker, L. (2009) *Miracle on the Hudson: The Survivors of Flight 1549 Tell their Extraordinary Stories of Courage, Faith, and Determination*. New York, NY: Ballintine Books. Quarantelli, E.L. (1989) How Individuals and Groups React During Disasters: Planning and Managing Implications for EMS Delivery. Sociology of Panic.

Reissman, D.B., Kowalski-Trakofler, K.M., and Katz, C.L. (in press) Public health practice and disaster resilience: A framework integrating resilience as a worker protection strategy. In S. Southwick, D. Charney, M. Friedman, and B. Litz (eds) *Resilience: Responding to Challenges Across the Lifespan*. Cambridge, UK: Cambridge University Press.

Reissman, D.B., Schreiber, M., Shultz, J.M., and Ursano, R.J. (2010) Disaster mental and behavioral Health. In K.L. Koenig and C.L. Schultz (eds) *Disaster Medicine*. New York, NY: Cambridge University Press.

Rosa, R. and Colligan, M.J. (1997) *Plain Language About Shiftwork*, Vol. DHHS (NIOSH) 97-145, Cincinnati, OH. http://www.cdc.gov/niosh/pdfs/97-145.pdf.

Sanders, M.S. and Shaw, B.E. (1988) Research to Determine the Contribution of System Factors in the Occurrence of Underground Injury Accidents, Project 1545-002. US Deptartment of Interior, Bureau of Mines.

Sime, J.D. (1983) Affiliative behavior during escape to building exits, *Journal of Environmental Psychology; 3*(1), 21–41.

Thrush, P.W. and Staff (eds) (1968) *A Dictionary of Mining, Mineral and Related Terms*. Washington DC: Bureau of Mines, pp.1269.

US Department of Labor Mine Safety and Health Administration (2008) 30 Code of Federal Regulations Part 75. Refuge Alternatives for Underground Coal Mines; Final Rule.

Vaught, C., Brnich, M.J., Mallett, L.G., Cole, H.P., Wiehagen, W.J., Conti, R.S., Kowalski, K.M., and Litton, C.D. (2000) *Behavioral and Organizational Dimensions of Underground Mine Fires*. Pittsburgh, PA: US Department of Health and Human Services, Centers for Disease Control and Prevention, National Institute for Occupational Safety and Health, DHHS (NIOSH) Publication No. 2000-126, IC 9450.

Vaught, C., Fotta, B., Wiehagen, W.J., Conti, R.S., and Fowkes, R.S. (1996) A Profile of Workers' Experience and Preparedness in Responding to Underground Mine Fires. Pittsburgh, PA: US Department of the Interior, Bureau of Mines, RI 9584. NTIS stock number: PB96-147848.

World Health Organization, International Labour Organization (2000) WHO Mental Health Gap Action Programme. http://www.who.int/mental_health/mhgap/en/index.html.

CHAPTER **10**

Psychosocial and Organizational Factors in Offshore Safety

KATHRYN MEARNS

Introduction

Oil is the lifeblood of our modern-day society. Our economies are fuelled by it and our health and well-being is dependent upon it. Oil is not only used to generate power, run our cars, freight our goods and fuel the planes that carry us to the sun; it is also used in plastics, medicines, fertilizers and a host of other ubiquitous products—products we take for granted and would struggle to live without. Economies stand or fall on the price of oil—witness the oil crash of the 1970s (after the Organization of the Petroleum Exporting Companies (OPEC) implemented oil embargoes in response to the Yom Kippur War) and the 2008 economic downturn, which was attributed to failing banks but may have also been partly influenced by the price of oil rising to 147 US$/barrel thus undermining the economic growth that had been dependent on plentiful supplies of cheap oil. The history of oil is fascinating and the interested reader is invited to consult one of the many books on the subject (for example Yergin, 1991). The glamour and wealth generated by the oil industry is testimony to its central role in modern-day society. Terms such as "wild-cats," "roughnecks," and "offshore tigers" have been used to describe the "wells" and "rigs" and the people working on them and the massive business empires of Standard Oil, Halliburton, and The Gulf States were built on the proceeds of oil. However, finding, extracting, and processing oil is a hazardous business and history is full of events that show how dangerous this activity is. Extracting hydrocarbons (oil and gas) at high temperature and pressure is inherently hazardous. The ease with which reserves can be developed and exploited is dependent on many different factors, for example the location and characteristics of the reservoir, the presence of "sour gas" (H_2S) and the type of oil in situ, for example, tar sands, heavy crude, or light, sweet oil. There are only a limited number of places in the world where oil can be found and since most of the easily available resources have already been exploited, the energy companies are being forced into more remote, environmentally sensitive, and challenging areas to extract hydrocarbons, for example Alaska, the northwest Atlantic, and the Barents Sea. These locations present their own particular health and safety hazards for the people working in the industry and their development could also have major environmental implications.

Health and Safety in the Oil and Gas Industry

Over the past 100 years substantial health and safety improvements have been made on the technological, legislative, management, and human factors aspects of oil and gas extraction, transport, and processing. Often these advances have been made in response to accidents and incidents that have affected the industry. The early exploitation of oil probably involved people collecting seepages from sources just below the ground surface but at the turn of the twentieth century the first oil wells were sunk in Texas, closely followed by developments in Baku on the Caspian Sea. The blowouts and fires that occurred at this stage claimed many lives and the technological developments of the time were probably driven as much by loss of revenue than by any other factors. It was not until the industry came under closer scrutiny from government agencies that more focus was put on the costs to human life rather than the costs to the oilfield developer. Reliance on oil as the fuel of choice escalated following the Second World war, with the USA, Middle East, and Russia leading the way in producing and selling this new form of "black gold." In the early 1960s, oil was found on the UK Continental Shelf (UKCS), closely followed by finds on the Norwegian Continental Shelf (NCS). In the UK, Aberdeen became the center of the oil industry just as the traditional industries of granite quarrying and fishing were declining. This was a lifeline to the city and it continues to promote itself as the Oil Capital of Europe. In the Netherlands, the huge Groningen gas field continues to produce and in Norway, the oil and gas industry is a major employer and an important source of income for the government (witness Norway's Petroleum Fund, which was estimated to be worth $US395 billion in June 2009 according to Wikipedia). Although many provinces are now in decline, the Gulf States are still major oil producers and new oilfields are being opened up in Russia and the former Soviet states, for example, Kazakhstan and Uzbekistan. Mexico's oil reserves are in decline but Brazil is currently one of the world's major producers and reserves are still being discovered and exploited in Australia, Canada, and areas of the Far East. However, oil comes at a price and the current chapter will examine that price in relation to the health and safety of people working in the sector, particularly in relation to the offshore oil and gas industry in the UK.

Oil Industry Disasters

The Sea Gem was the first oil industry-related disaster on the UKCS. The rig was a converted steel barge raised on ten legs 15 metres above the water, which supported a helipad, accommodation for 34 people, and a drilling tower plus associated structures. It sank on the 27 December, 1965 killing 13 of the crew and as a result of this accident, the industry started to make use of stand-by vessels to help rescue crews in the event of future accidents. During the 1960s and 1970s there were a number of oil industry accidents leading to the deaths of individual workers, however the next major disaster struck on the 27 March, 1980 when the Alexander Kielland semi-submersible sunk on the Norwegian Ekofisk field following structural failure. A total of 123 people died in this accident, due to a combination of stormy weather conditions, strong currents, and freezing water. This disaster further reinforced the extreme conditions faced by personnel employed in the industry in the North Sea but it was to be superseded by an even greater disaster in 1989, when the Piper Alpha platform, operated by Occidental Petroleum, suffered an explosion and fire claiming the lives of 165 of the 266 men onboard plus two crewmen of a rescue vessel. The events leading up to the disaster are well-documented and can be accessed in full from a number of sources, including Lord Cullen's Public Inquiry into the disaster (Cullen, 1990). In summary, a number of events contributed to the disaster. The design of the platform was partly to blame. Although initially designed as an oil production platform with hazardous operations distant from personnel areas, when gas began to be produced from the field, the accommodation block and other sensitive areas were brought close together. The proximity of the gas compression block to the control room played a major role in the accident. The impact of the loss of the control room where staff with critical functions were deployed when disaster struck, contributed to the unfolding of the disaster. Another contributory factor was the continued flow of oil to the stricken platform from its sister platforms Claymore and Tartan. Even although the operators on Tartan and Claymore could see Piper Alpha burning, they did not believe they had the authority to shutdown production.

This tragic event proved to be a watershed for safety developments in the North Sea with a raft of technological fixes, for example seabed risers and legislative requirements being implemented in the wake of the disaster. Occidental were found guilty of having inadequate maintenance and safety regimes, but they never faced criminal charges for these failures. In total, 106 recommendations emerged from the Inquiry; most of which were implemented by the industry, although somewhat surprisingly "Permit to Work" systems, one of the factors identified as contributing to the disaster has not yet been adequately addressed. One of the most significant recommendations was that the responsibility for regulating safety was moved from the Department of Energy to the Health and Safety Executive (HSE) and a new HSE Offshore Division was created. Furthermore, operating companies were required to produce Safety Cases, demonstrating to the regulator (HSE) that all major hazards had been assessed and measures put in place to mitigate or control them. In addition to major disasters such as Piper Alpha and the Alexander Kielland, helicopter accidents have taken their toll on human life. Since 1976, there have been six fatal accidents in the North Sea alone, involving the loss of 79 lives. The worst disaster was in 1986, when 45 people died in a Chinook helicopter crash. Thus the major hazards faced by personnel working in the industry include "loss of containment," for example, blow-outs, gas leaks, fire and helicopter crashes. In addition to this offshore workers also face the usual litany of occupational accidents such as slips, trips, falls, crushing, cuts, and electrocution and are also exposed to a number of health hazards—noxious fumes, hydrocarbons, chemicals, psychosocial hazards, for example stress and fatigue.

Piper Alpha brought the industry's focus on to the human and organizational factors that contributed to the disaster, with Lord Cullen specifically criticizing Occidental Petroleum, and the oil and gas industry in general, for having a poor safety culture. In many ways, the concept of safety culture becomes a "catch-all" for human and organizational factors. This reference to a poor "safety culture" followed from similar criticisms of the nuclear industry in the aftermath of Chernobyl (IAEA, 1991); ferry transport in the case of the Herald of Free Enterprise (Sheen, 1987) and the rail industry in the King's Cross Fire (Fennell, 1988). More recently, the BP Texas City Refinery disaster in 2005, where 17 people were killed and 150 injured, has also been identified as being due to a deficient safety culture (Baker, 2007). One of the principal findings was that BP management had failed to distinguish between occupational safety measures, for example, slips, trips, and falls and process safety issues such as maintenance of equipment and reporting process upsets. BP's focus on measuring and managing occupational safety meant it had confused declining occupational safety statistics for general improvement in all aspects of safety performance. This was a trap that many oil and gas organizations had fallen into. For example, occupational safety and process safety incidents for the UK oil and gas industry from 2000–2006 indicate a declining trend in occupational safety statistics but a worrying increase in process safety problems. This could partly be due to the ageing offshore platforms many of which have been extended beyond their initial design period, however it could also be due to senior management in the industry making a public commitment in 1997 through its "Step-Change in Safety Initiative" to reduce injuries by 50 percent. This meant that the focus was on reducing injuries to personnel rather than high potential incidents, such as gas or oil leaks arising from the infrastructure of the aging offshore platforms. Following the findings of the Baker panel, the UK oil and gas industry has now made "process safety" one of its key priorities.

In response to its findings, the Baker investigation panel developed a "process safety" survey that was administered to all five of BP's refineries in North America. Two refineries (Toledo and Texas City) had the poorest process safety culture, but the Cherry Point refinery had the best safety culture and as a result, the director of Cherry Point was promoted to oversee better implementation of process safety in BP. This was an interesting development since it was an explicit reward of a senior manager based on his safety performance at a very public level. Safety culture and the associated construct of safety climate continue to be a focus for the offshore oil and gas industry today, particularly among companies and regulators in Europe, for example, Shell's "Hearts & Minds" program (Hudson, 2007; Lawrie, Parker and Hudson, 2006; Parker, Lawrie and Hudson, 2006), studies sponsored by the UK oil and gas industry and the HSE (Mearns et al., 1998; 2001; Mearns, Whitaker and Flin, 2001; 2003) and safety climate auditing approaches supported by the Norwegian Petroleum Safety Authority (Hoivik et al., 2009; Tharaldsen, Olsen and Rundmo, 2008).

The current chapter will explore the research conducted to date on psychosocial and organizational factors in relation to safety in the oil and gas industry, with a specific emphasis on research conducted on the UKCS. The concept of safety culture provides a useful framework to consider the psychosocial and organizational factors in relation to safety performance, however issues relating to health and the working environment are also considered. The chapter will conclude with suggestions as to where the industry should be headed in the future and some of the issues that need to be addressed to enable the future sustainability of the oil and gas sector in terms of health and safety.

Safety Culture, Safety Climate and Safety Outcomes

According to the Advisory Committee for Safety on Nuclear Installations (ACSNI, 1993, p. 23), "The safety culture of an organisation is the product of individual and group values, attitudes, competencies and patterns of behaviour that determine commitment to, and the style and proficiency of, an organisation's health and safety management." This is the mostly widely cited definition of safety culture, however, it is not the easiest of definitions to operationalize thus making it difficult to measure. The associated concept of safety climate has been clearly defined by Zohar (2002) as the perceived value or priority of acting safely as assessed by employees using the daily actions of their leaders (supervisors or managers) as the main cues. According to Zohar (2002) safety climate measurement involves determining the extent to which safety is prioritized in relation to other organizational or work unit goals, most usually safety versus production. This climate can refer to a perceived state of the work unit in relation to the expectations and rewards set by supervisors or it can refer to the organization, where senior management can set the goals, aspirations, expectations, and rewards. Safety climate is determined by individual perceptions aggregated at the group or the organizational level and the strength of the climate is determined by measurement of dispersion, for example, standard deviations (Schneider, Salvaggio and Subarits, 2002) or intraclass correlations (ICCs; Mearns et al., 2009; Wallace, Popp and Modere, 2006). Studies of safety climate have indicated that perceptions of management or supervisor commitment to safety are amongst the best predictors of safety performance as measured by accidents, injuries, safety compliance, and safety citizenship and participation (Clarke, 2006). However, not all studies consider safety climate to be exclusively determined by workforce perceptions of supervisor or management commitment to safety as determined by the priority of safety over other organizational goals (see for example Cheyne et al., 1998; Mearns et al., 1998; 2001; Tharaldsen, Mearns and Knudson (2009). Following from the multi-faceted approach to organizational climate (James et al., 2008) other factors emerge as being of some importance, for example communication, team work, involvement/empowerment, attitudes to reporting incidents, and so on. Nevertheless, the importance of management and supervisor commitment to safety is widely recognized and some studies have started to focus on the role of management and leadership in setting the context for the appropriate safety climate and motivations, expectations, and behavior arising from it (Reid et al., 2008). Findings from this research will be presented in more detail in the final section of the chapter.

In the context of the offshore oil and gas industry, most studies have considered safety climate or culture as multi-faceted. For example, based on interviews and focus groups with offshore workers, Mearns et al. (1997) developed a number of items to be incorporated into a "safety attitudes" scale. A questionnaire containing these items plus measures of safety compliance, safety satisfaction, work pressure, risk perception, job communication, and work clarity was received from 722 employees from 11 offshore installations. Five main "safety attitude" factors were identified through principal components analysis. These factors included "speaking up about safety," "attitudes to violations," "supervisor commitment to safety," "attitudes to rules and regulations," and "Offshore Installation Manager (OIM) commitment to safety." All factors had a Cronbach's Alpha of above 0.70. Multivariate analysis of the data revealed significant differences between installations and between occupational groups regarding how they responded to the factors derived from the Offshore Safety Questionnaire (OSQ). Using self-reported accident/near-miss data over the previous year as the dependent (outcome) variable, the scale measuring "speaking up about safety" predicted 9.1 percent of the variance, whereas scales measuring self-reported safety compliance and satisfaction with safety measures explained 13.6 percent of the variance.

Cox and Cheyne (2000) also developed a safety culture assessment methodology for the UK offshore industry based on questionnaires, behavioral observations, focus groups, in-depth interviews, document analysis, and situational audits. Nine factors were identified from a sample of over 600 employees from five organizations. These factors largely mirrored those found in the research outlined above and included organizational factors such as management commitment, communication, priority of safety, safety rules and procedures; factors reflecting the social environment, that is supportive environment and involvement; individual appreciation such as personal priorities and need for safety and personal appreciation of risk and perceptions of the physical work environment.

In perhaps the most comprehensive study of human and organizational factors on the UKCS, Mearns, Whitaker and Flin (2001; 2003) conducted a benchmarking study using the OSQ to compare safety climate across 13 installations between 1998 and 1999. In 1998, 682 questionnaires were available for analysis whereas in the 1999 survey, the sample was 806 questionnaires. Although 13 installations were surveyed in both 1998 and 1999, only nine of them were common to both years. The results indicated that in the 1998 survey the OSQ consisted of four factors covering attitudes to safety: perceived management commitment to safety; propensity to report accidents and incidents; perceived supervisor competence; and rules and safety implementation. Two factors emerged that covered aspects of safety compliance: general safety compliance and safety compliance under incentives/social pressure. Additional scales addressed involvement in health and safety; communication about health and safety; satisfaction with safety activities; and health and safety policy awareness. As in previous studies, analysis of variance showed significant differences between the installations in their scores on the safety climate scales and Stepwise Discriminant Function Analysis indicated that certain scales "predicted" self-reported accidents for respondents in all job roles, and for a subset of workers closer to frontline activities, for example deck crew and construction personnel. These scales were perceived management commitment to safety, willingness to report accidents, and perceived supervisor competence, with more favorable scores being associated with less likelihood of having experienced an accident. In addition, individuals who had experienced an accident displayed significantly less favorable scores on all OSQ scales except perceived supervisor competence.

The 1999 data showed a similar pattern of results with a comparable factor structure and significant differences between installations on their scale scores. The nine installations common to both years (with a pooled sample size of 521 in 1998 and 624 in 1999) were used to gauge changes across the one-year period. The two samples were closely matched with regard to proportion of supervisors, self-reported accident rate, and tenure. Comparisons could therefore be made on measurements of satisfaction with safety activities; perceived management commitment to safety; perceived supervisor competence; willingness to report accidents; general safety compliance; and safety compliance under incentives/social pressure. In general, performance on all these scales improved from 1998 to 1999 with certain installations showing statistically significant improvements across the period. Those installations that had performed relatively poorly in 1998 performed much better in 1999, however those that were performing well in 1998 experienced a "ceiling effect" and therefore did not show any improvement in performance. Nonetheless, only one installation showed a reduction in its safety climate performance. "Best in class" installations showed higher levels of workforce involvement and communication, higher levels of perceived management commitment to safety, and higher levels of safety compliance.

A further objective of this study was to understand the reasons behind the differences in performance, which is the ultimate objective of the benchmarking approach. For this purpose a Safety Management Questionnaire (SMQ) was designed to measure what was actually being done in terms of health and safety management on the installation at the time of the study. Safety performance indicators used in other health and safety benchmarking programs were developed to cover six main areas: 1) Health and safety policy; 2) Organizing for health and safety; 3) Management Commitment; 4) Workforce Involvement; 5) Health surveillance and promotion; and 6) Health and safety auditing. The health and safety manager responsible for the installation involved in the study recorded the activities relating to these general topics in the SMQ. The participating installations were also required to provide details of accident and incident statistics according to the Reporting of Injuries, Diseases, and Dangerous Occurrences (RIDDOR) scheme (HSE, 1995) and also report near misses and visits to the rig medic. All information related to the period June 31, 1997 to June 31, 1998 (for the 1998 benchmarking survey) and June 31, 1998 to June 31, 1999 (for the 1999 benchmarking survey).

Analysis of data from both the 1998 and 1999 SMQ took the form of rank correlations between four outcome measures (Lost Time Injury or LTI>three days, Near misses; Dangerous Occurrences; total RIDDOR data) and the six sections of the SMQ. A pattern of negative correlations was found with favorable scores on the SMQ associated with lower accident and incident rates. All significant negative correlations involving sub-scale scores were confined to two areas of health and safety management strategy: health promotion and surveillance and health and safety auditing. In particular, high scores on auditing were related to low rates of dangerous occurrences whereas high scores on health promotion and surveillance were associated with low lost-time injury rates. Many other studies have demonstrated the importance of internal, external, and regular auditing activities as a key requirement of any effective health and safety management system but the relationship between worker health/well-being and safety performance have not been so well documented. It is proposed that the benefits of health promotion and occupational health programs could be realized through various processes, for example company investment in these areas may foster perceptions of company commitment and build worker loyalty in areas such as safety compliance. On the other hand, health monitoring and health promotion activities could improve worker health directly and help "immunize" against work-related injury. As an example of this, a chronic bad back can move from the category "occupational illness" to "lost time injury" after a heavy lift. Another possibility is that organizations that have "health" on their agenda are the most mature in their health and safety management policy and actions. "Health" is often the poor relation in the HSE equation and organizations that are focusing on health could well have more sophisticated risk assessment processes (Hope and Mearns, 2007). The importance of a positive work environment in health and safety performance is explored in more detail in the next section.

Work Environment, Health, and Safety in the Petroleum Sector

Major accidents and the impact these have on people's lives and the community around them cannot be underestimated and the industry must continue to focus on the process safety upsets that can escalate into this type of event. But this is not the only type of adverse event that can blight people's lives. According to the UK HSE Health and Safety Statistics, there were 229 deaths and 299,000 reportable injuries in 2007/2008 (HSE, 2009) and a total of 34 million days lost; 28 million due to work-related ill-health and 6 million due to injury.

In the HSE statistics, the oil and gas industry is included under the heading "extractive and utility supply industries", where there were nine fatalities, 390 major injuries, and 1,289 reported "over three-day" injuries in 2006/2007. Incidence rates of work-related ill-health in extractive and utility supply are substantially above the average for all industries, mainly due to the high rate of respiratory disease and vibration-related conditions arising from coal mining and utility supply (asbestosis). At the time of writing there were no statistics available for 2007/2008 but in 2006/07 (based on a two-and-a-half year average), the rate of occupational ill-health in extractive industries was 5,709 per 100,000 people employed (5.7 percent), compared to the average across all industries (that is, 1,688 per 100,000 employed—1.7 percent). The relevant statistics for the global oil and gas industry can be found at http://www2.worksafebc.com/Portals/Petroleum/Statistics.asp. Whereas injuries receive a lot of focus due to their immediate and noticeable impact and their reflection in safety statistics, health effects can remain hidden for longer time periods before being realized and the cause-effect relationships of exposure to health hazards are therefore more difficult to disentangle. Nevertheless, as Parkes (1998) points out, a safe and efficient workforce will also be a healthy workforce and it is perhaps worthwhile to consider the "health" issues first despite the fact that health is often the "poor relation" of health and safety.

Quite apart from the inherently hazardous nature of the job, petroleum plants are not designed and built with human operators in mind, making them ergonomically unsuitable for safe work. Staircases, doors, and gangways tend to be small and narrow, parts of the plant can be difficult to access, for example valves can be hidden behind bulwarks and floors can be slippery or pose a tripping and falling hazard due to ongoing construction and maintenance activities. In addition, the offshore work environment is extremely inhospitable. The platforms tend to be far from land and require helicopter transport to reach them. Weather conditions in the North Sea and on the northwest Atlantic frontier can be atrocious with high winds, heavy rainfall, and intense cold. Furthermore, workers live and work in confined conditions, often with very different types of people, whom they have to get along with for periods for up to six weeks (although the usual rotation pattern is two weeks offshore; two weeks onshore in the UK, and two weeks offshore; three weeks onshore in Norway). Apart from the constant sources of risk arising from the hydrocarbon inventory, offshore workers are exposed to other psychosocial stressors such as noise, vibration, cold, heat, shift patterns (12-hour shifts are commonplace), dull monotonous works sometimes interspersed with periods of intense activity, and little opportunity for developing new skills (Parkes, 1992). Clearly this lifestyle has implications for the physical and mental well-being of employees. Research on the psychosocial aspects of health and safety in the North Sea has a long tradition, stretching back over 25 years. The nature of work in the offshore oil and gas industry and the challenges faced by the people living and working on the remote oil fields in the North Sea was captured by Odd H. Hellesøy, in his book *Work Environment, Statfjord Field: Work Environment, Health and Safety on a North Sea Oil Platform*. Hellesøy (1985) found that 47 percent of sickbay visits were due to somatic complaints with accidents and injuries accounting for 16 percent of visits and personal and work-related concerns responsible for 15 percent of visits. There were significant differences between occupational groups, with drilling and catering personnel more likely to visit the sickbay with injuries arising from accidents. More recently, Parkes and Swash (2005) examined data on 1,944 sickbay consultations on the UKCS made between August 1993 and July 1998. They found that illness accounted for

78 percent of consultations, respiratory problems 28.5 percent; musculoskeletal disorders 23 percent, and accidents 15.3 percent of consultations. Construction personnel were most likely to need treatment for accidents whereas maintenance personnel were most likely to seek consultation for illness. Gastric problems were particularly predominant in production jobs, and musculoskeletal problems in administrative jobs. There were also effects associated with shiftwork with day/night shift workers more likely to experience gastric problems and attend the sickbay more than those who were only involved in day work. Parkes and Swash (2005) also had access to self-reported health data collected from 342 individual workers in 1995–1996 and investigated the relationship between these data and the sickbay visits. Although there was a significant correlation between mean number of consultations and health scores, only the diagnostic category "musculoskeletal disorders" showed a highly significant effect and this type of problem was also associated with symptoms of psychological distress although it is not possible to disentangle cause and effect in these circumstances.

Mearns and Hope (2005) and Mearns, Hope and Reader (2006) studied the general health and well-being of UK offshore workers after earlier research had indicated a significant relationship between proactive management of health (that is, high levels of promotion and surveillance activities) and lower lost time injury rates (Mearns, Whitaker and Flin, 2001; 2003). In order to address the possible reasons for this relationship, the following research questions were posed—Do healthy employees cope better with the offshore environment? Does investment in employee health foster perceptions of company commitment to employees and build loyalty and a desire to perform well in all areas of work life, including safety? Are positive health management practices simply a product of good risk assessments and this effect then extends into all aspects of health and safety management?

A questionnaire comprising eight sections was developed and after piloting it was distributed to 41 installations on the UKCS. A total of 2,199 completed questionnaires were returned of which 1,928 from 31 installations were deemed suitable for analysis. The questionnaire collected data on:

1. perception of factors in the offshore environment that impact on worker health;
2. experience of and satisfaction with the management of occupational health risks;
3. personal health management and goals;
4. perceived colleague and organizational support;
5. health promotion activities in the workplace;
6. perception of health climate and safety climate;
7. safety compliance/risk taking at work; and
8. commitment to the installation.

A second questionnaire was developed targeting the offshore medics who are responsible for maintaining the health and welfare of personnel when they are actually on the installation. This questionnaire asked the medics for general information about their role, experience, and main occupational and general health risks faced by employees. This was followed by a section requesting information on illness and injuries experienced by the personnel that had required a visit to the sickbay over the past 12 months. A "Health Surveillance" section determined how employees were informed about the risks of their work to their health, for example, organized education/information meetings, information leaflets/posters in the workplace, by their supervisor, and so on. The medics were also asked to supply details of health checks and necessary health surveillance activities conducted on the installation (for example, according to Control of Substances Hazardous to Heralth (COSHH) regulations). Section 4 determined whether organized personal health promotion programs or initiatives had taken place on the installation in the previous 12 months and Section 5 focused on whether existing initiatives and health management strategies were being evaluated for their impact. The data from the medics' questionnaire was then used as a measure of "health investment" for the purposes of the study.

In terms of the workforce feedback, respondents identified heavy smoking while offshore, fatigue due to shift work, and stress about work as the factors most affecting their health at work. More than half the sample (54 percent) indicated they experienced feeling under stress or pressure "a few times during each trip" but the majority of respondents believed they coped well with the stress they experienced. Less than a quarter of respondents indicated that they had received support to help them cope with stress. Satisfaction with the management with occupational health risks was generally high, however closer examination of the data revealed that only 8 percent of regular users of hand-held power tools had been checked for vibration white finger and associated conditions. In addition, 64 percent of respondents indicated regular exposure to chemicals but only 29 percent of this sample reported receiving a health check in relation to this exposure. Although levels of training for manual handling, noise exposure, safe use of tools, and correct use of Personal Protective Equipment (PPE) were high across the sample, a quarter of respondents indicated they had not received training in areas they believed would be useful given the health risks they faced in their work.

The majority of respondents believed themselves to be in good health although based on self-report height and weight data, 52 percent returned a BMI score in the overweight category with a further 12 percent falling into the obese category. In relation to this, 49 percent indicated that they find it difficult to eat a healthy diet offshore, although a high proportion indicated good knowledge of the need to eat healthily and take regular exercise. Facilities to exercise varied as a function of what the installation had to offer with some installations having excellent facilities and others having no facility at all. Alcohol consumption while onshore (alcohol is forbidden offshore) also tended to be high with 28 percent of respondents estimating their intake to be between one to ten units and 38 percent indicated an intake of 11–21 units. However, 27 percent indicated a level of consumption between 22–50 units and 7 percent of the sample indicated an average weekly consumption in excess of 51 units. Overall, 17 percent indicated that they felt their current level of alcohol consumption was harmful to their health. Of participants consuming 22–50 units weekly, 67 percent felt this level of consumption was not harmful to their health, while of those consuming in excess of 51 units, 54 percent did not believe their consumption was harmful to their health. This corresponds to the "binge-drinking" patterns observed for Scottish males in the 1998 Scottish Health Survey (Shaw, McMunn and Field, 2000), which reported that 33 percent of adult males (aged 16–74 years) exceeded the maximum consumption levels of 21 units of alcohol per week, while in the current sample, 34 percent of respondents reported an onshore consumption at this level. With regard to smoking behavior, 32 percent of the sample smoked, 27 percent were previous smokers, while 41 percent had never smoked, however, a high proportion of smokers were attempting to quit the habit and stop smoking campaigns were the most prevalent health promotion campaign offshore. Again the levels of smoking reflect those found by Shaw, McMunn and Field (2000).

In accordance with other offshore studies, 36 percent of the sample reported recurring muscular pain (mostly in the lower back), with 67 percent indicating that their work exacerbated this pain. Only 38 percent of those experiencing problems acknowledged that they have received support/advice to help reduce or manage this pain. Nonetheless, 28 percent of the sample had asked the offshore medic for advice regarding their general health or fitness and 45 percent reported receiving unsolicited advice from the medic with regard to the management of their personal health or fitness. On a more worrying note, approximately 20 percent of respondents indicated that they have felt ill while offshore but chose not to report to the medic in order to avoid an onshore referral. The implications of this for worker health and safety have not been investigated but there can be little doubt that, quite apart from being hazardous to one's own health, not reporting that you feel ill could have implications for safety due to reduced performance capabilities. While a majority of respondents felt that the company valued and was concerned about the health of the workforce, there was evidence of uncertainty that management was committed to improving employee health, with scores on the "Organization Health Orientation" scale varying considerably between installations. Similarly scores on health climate and safety climate measures varied considerably between installations, reflecting more and less positive climates onboard. Although, safety climate tended to be positive and levels of safety compliance were high, levels of health climate were comparatively low, no doubt because there has been generally less focus on health than safety in the industry. Finally, the commitment of the workforce to their workplace varied between installations but, overall, there was evidence of strong commitment by the workforce with a high degree of willingness to work hard to ensure the success of the installation they work on. The study did not investigate the role of occupational stress, specifically because a great deal of research had already been conducted on occupational stress offshore. This work is summarized in the following sections.

The Role of Occupational Stress

Occupational stress and its impact on the well-being and performance of offshore workers merits a section on its own. Given the material reviewed above, it is not surprising that researchers would investigate the work stress-employee well-being relationship. One of the earliest studies investigating the relationship between occupational stress, mental health, and accidents was reported by Valerie Sutherland and Cary Cooper (1986, 1991) in their book *Man and Accidents Offshore*. The study was conducted with two samples—190 personnel in 1986 and 310 in 1991. The 1991 sample included 146 staff working for the operating companies and 164 who were contractors. A questionnaire for "stress auditing" was developed from interviews with offshore personnel, asking about aspects of their job, lifestyle, and accident involvement. Job satisfaction, psychological health, and social support were also measured. Most of the participants were British and were well qualified and experienced, having worked offshore for a number of years. An exploratory factor analysis of the "stressor" questionnaire indicated 12 factors: career prospects and reward; safety and insecurity at work; home/work interface; under stimulation, that is, low demand; physical conditions—working and living; unpredictability of work pattern;

living conditions; physical climate and work; organization structure and climate; physical well-being; work overload and transportation (for example, flying in a helicopter). The top three causes of stress concerned pay and conditions, that is, rate of pay, lack of paid holidays, and pay differentials between operating and contracting staff but relationships at home and at work were also of significance and these measures were correlated with job satisfaction and mental health. Accident victims reported less job satisfaction and poorer mental health but again it is difficult to ascertain cause and effect here.

Individuals suffering from stress are known to show a range of physical, emotional, cognitive, and behavioral reactions. Physical effects include increased blood pressure, headaches, and digestive problems. Heart disease is also believed to be linked to long-term stress. The effects on mental health include anxiety and depression, although the causal nature of this relationship is difficult to establish, that is, people who are feeling anxious or depressed may find it harder to cope with their working environment or conversely people who are finding it hard to cope may suffer from anxiety and depression. In a comparison of the mental health of 88 onshore and 84 offshore control room operators Parkes (1992) found no significant differences between the groups on physical symptoms or social dysfunction scores, however there was a significant difference regarding anxiety, with the onshore group showing lower scores. From these earlier studies, it is difficult to determine whether the general mental health of offshore workers differs significantly from norm data. It could be argued that the current offshore workforce is a survivor population and those who could not cope with the rigors of offshore life were selected out long ago. For example, a study of medical evacuations from offshore installations showed that of 1,509 evacuations over a two-year period, only 2 percent were due to psychiatric disorders (Gauld, 1993, cited in Flin and Slaven, 1996). In relation to the subject matter of the current chapter, the key issue is whether stress leads to accidents? The possibility was raised by Sutherland and Cooper (1986; 1991) and also Rundmo (1992) suggested that stress may have an indirect role to play in accident causation amongst Norwegian workers.

In the study by Mearns and Hope (2005), respondents were asked to rate on a five-point scale, the extent to which they felt they were able to cope with any pressures experienced at work. The overall mean rating for the sample of 1928 workers from 31 installations was 1.91 (1 = Generally I cope very well), suggesting that the majority felt they coped well with work stress and pressure. There did not seem to be a significant relationship between self-reported levels of stress and accident involvement. Overall, 21 percent of respondents indicated that they had received support (in the form of advice, information, guidance, and so on) to help them cope with stress experienced in the workplace. When the effectiveness of this support was rated there was considerable variation between installations but the mean overall score was 3.12, suggesting that current forms of support offered were only moderately useful. This is somewhat surprising given that 50 percent of the 24 offshore medics in the sample who responded to the questionnaire reported that they were trained in stress management. Furthermore, 37 percent of the installations offered training courses on stress management for their workforce. The findings of this study were generally positive with many of the installations surveyed involved in a range of health promotion and occupational health surveillance activities. Healthy eating, stop smoking, and exercise campaigns were among the most common health promotion activities whereas manual handling, noise monitoring, safe use of tools, and correct use of PPE were among the most regular occupational health management training programs offered to the workforce.

Conclusions

The preceding sections have identified a series of relationships between psychosocial and organizational aspects of offshore safety, with particular reference to the UK oil and gas industry. Similar patterns of relationships have been identified for the NCS, with studies comparing the two shelves revealing common factors as being of importance (Mearns et al., 2004; Tharaldsen, Mearns and Knudson, 2009). The results of numerous accident investigations, particularly after major incidents such as Piper Alpha and Texas City, have revealed a pattern of failings that usually start with failure at the top of the organization. This has led to the development of research to understand the characteristics of senior managers who are successful safety leaders. Initially, much of the research was focused at the supervisor level, for example see Fleming (1999). Successful supervisors in terms of safety behavior and safety performance were found to show genuine concern for the people under their supervision; they were willing to put in extra effort to protect the team from external pressures and were supportive toward team members. Later the focus moved to the study of site managers, for example see O'Dea and Flin (2001). In this study, 200 OIMs were surveyed about a range of issues including their leadership style and the factors they believed contributed to accidents. Based on the framework of Tannenbaum and Schmidt (1958) which proposes a Telling/Selling/Consulting/Joining approach, 57 percent of the sample preferred a telling/selling approach where the leader has all the control, information and power and uses this authoritarian style to make decisions and issue instructions, which the subordinate simply has to follow. Persuasion may be adopted in order to achieve the subordinate's willing compliance rather than coercing compliance. However, interestingly when OIMs were asked about the most effective ways of improving the organization's safety performance, the majority suggested consulting/joining activities such as "participation in the work activity, building open and trusting relationships with employees, empowering employees by involving them in decision making, communicating with employees, listening to them and acting on their suggestions" (O'Dea and Flin, 2001, p. 52). Yet only 43 percent of OIMs actually preferred this style suggesting a mismatch between known best practice and actual behavior.

Latterly, top management and senior executives have come under increasing scrutiny in terms of how they influence the safety-orientated behavior of their employees and the organization's safety performance. Initially studies considered the role of Transactional and Transformational Leadership in promoting positive safety performance (Barling, Loughlin and Kelloway, 2002; O'Dea and Flin, 2003). The basic style of many managers irrespective of the level in the organization they operate at have been found to be Transactional in nature, with the Transformational style adding a small amount of variance in performance. In studies investigating the role of Authentic Leadership in safety (see Reid et al., 2008), there seems to be more emphasis on "walking the talk"—showing integrity and consistency between words and actions. Taken together with the results of studies on safety culture/climate and health and working environment, it would appear that a strong element of moral responsibility or corporate social responsibility based on care and concern for the workforce and protection against adverse events and conditions is the way the industry should move in the future. It would appear that the "rough, tough" style of the early pioneers where risks had to be taken to secure the prize of "black" gold has evolved over time to become a more participative, sharing, caring approach. In conclusion, Simard and Marchand (1994) propose that given the knowledge and skills to do the job properly are present (due to selection and training), whether a person works safely will be dependent on their level of motivation. Managers at all levels of the organization can play an important role in developing and establishing the type of environment where employees are encouraged to work in a safer way. Safety motivation and safety initiative are more proactive than simply being careful and complying with safety rules, since they have the potential to affect the whole organization and not just one individual. This leads to the development of a positive safety culture where safety is considered to be "the number one priority" when there is a conflict with other organizational goals. The results of many research studies from a range of industries and the findings of major accident inquiries continue to identify the role of management (at all levels of the organization) in promoting and reinforcing safety. The question is when will managers at all levels appreciate that it is their responsibility to ensure that safety management philosophy becomes manifest and the preaching and the practicing converge?

References

Advisory Committee for Safety in Nuclear Installations (1993) ACSNI Human Factors Study Group. Third Report: Organising for Safety, Advisory Committee on the Safety of Nuclear Installations, Health and Safety Commission.

Baker, J.A. III., Bowman, F.L., Erwin, G., Gorton, S., Hendershot, D.C., Leveson, N.G., Priest, S., Rosenthal, I., Tebo, P.V., Wiegmann, D.A., and Wilson, L.D. (2007) The Report of the BP US Refineries Independent Review Panel,Washington, DC.

Barling, J., Loughlin, C., and Kelloway K. (2002) Development and test of a model linking safety-specific transformational leadership and occupational safety, *Journal of Applied Psychology; 87*(3), 488–496.

Cheyne, A., Cox, S., Oliver, A., and Tomas, J.M. (1998) Modelling safety climate in the prediction of levels of safety activity, *Work and Stress; 12*(3), 255–271.

Clarke, S. (2006) The relationship between safety climate and safety performance: A meta-analytic review, *Journal of Occupational Health Psychology; 11*(4), 315–327.

Cox, S.J. and Cheyne, A.J.T. (2000) Assessing safety culture in offshore environments, *Safety Science; 34*(1–3), 111–129.

Cullen, H.L. (1990) *The Public Inquiry into the Piper Alpha Disaster* (Report to the Parliament by the Secretary of State for Energy by Command of Her Majesty Vols. 1 and 2). London: HMSO.

Fennell, D. (1988) Investigation into the King's Cross Underground Fire. London: Department of Transport, HMSO.

Fleming, M. (1999) Effective Supervisory Safety Leadership Behaviours in the Offshore Oil and Gas Industry. Suffolk: HSE Books.

Gauld, S. (1993) *Illness and injury in the offshore workforce*. Unpublished M.Phil thesis, The Robert Gordon University, Aberdeen. In R. Flin and G. Slaven (eds) *Managing the Offshore Installation Workforce*. Tulsa, OK: PennWell Books.

Health and Saftety Executive RIDDOR (1995) The Reporting of Injuries, Diseases and Dangerous Occurrences Regulations. Suffolk: HSE Books.

Health and Safety Executive (2009) The Health and Safety Executive Statistics 2008/2009. Sudbury: HSE Books.

Hellesøy, O.H. (ed.) (1985) Work Environment Statfjord Field: Work Environment, Health and Safety on a North Sea Oil Platform. Oslo, Norway: Universitetsforlaget.

Hope, L. and Mearns, K. (2007) Managing health risks in the offshore workplace: Impact on health climate, safety climate and risk identification, *International Journal of Risk Assessment and Management*; *7*, 152–164.

Hudson, P. (2007) Implementing a safety culture in a major multi-national, *Safety Science; 45*(6), 697–722.

Høivik, D., Tharaldsen, J.E., Baste, V., and Moen, B.E. (2009) What is most important for safety climate: The company belonging or the local working environment? *Safety Science; 47*(10), 1324–1331.

IAEA (1991) Safety Culture. Safety Series 75-INSAG-1. Vienna: International Atomic Energy Agency.

James, L.R., Choi, C.C., Ko, C.E., McNeil, P.K., Minton, M.K., Wright, M.A., and Kim, K. (2008) Organizational and psychological climate: A review of theory and research. In A. D'Amato and M.J. Burke (eds) Psychological and organizational climate research: Contrasting perspectives and research traditions. *A Special Issue of the European Journal of Work and Organizational Psychology.*

Lawrie, M., Parker, D. and Hudson, P. (2006) Investigating employee perceptions of a framework of safety culture maturity, *Safety Science; 44*(3), 259–276.

Mearns, K., Flin, R., Gordon, G., and Fleming, M. (1997) *Organisational and Human Factors in Offshore Safety*. OTH 543 Report, Suffolk: HSE Books.

Mearns, K., Flin, R., Gordon, G., and Fleming, M. (1998) Measuring safety culture in the offshore oil industry, *Work and Stress; 12*(3), 238–254 (Special Issue: Safety Culture).

Mearns, K., Flin, R., Gordon, R., and Fleming, M. (2001) Human and organizational factors in offshore safety, *Work & Stress; 15*(2), 144–160.

Mearns, K., Flin, R., Gordon, R., O'Connor, P., and Whitaker, S. (2003) Factoring the Human into Safety Translating Research into Practice. Volume 1: Benchmarking Human and Organisational Factors in Offshore Safety. HSE Research Report 059. Volume 2: The Development and Evaluation of a Human Factors Accident and Near Miss Reporting Form for the Offshore Industry. HSE Research Report 060. Volume 3: Crew Resource Management Training for Offshore Operations. HSE Research Report 061.

Mearns, K. and Hope, L. (2005) Health and Well-being in the Offshore Environment: The Management of Personal Health. HSE Research Report 305.

Mearns, K., Hope, L., Ford, M., and Tetrick, L. (2009) Investment in workforce health: Exploring the implications for workforce safety climate and commitment, *Accident Analysis and Prevention; 42*(5), 1445–1454.

Mearns, K., Hope, L., and Reader, T. (2006) Health and Well-being in the Offshore Environment: The Role of Organisational Support. HSE Research Report 376.

Mearns, K., Rundmo, T., Flin, R., Fleming, M., and Gordon, R. (2004) Evaluation of social and organisational factors affecting offshore safety—A comparative study, *Journal of Risk Research; 7*(5), 545–561.

Mearns, K., Whitaker, S., and Flin, R. (2001) Benchmarking safety climate in hazardous environments: A longitudinal, inter-organisational approach, *Risk Analysis; 21*(4), 771–786.

Mearns, K., Whitaker, S., and Flin, R. (2003) Safety climate, safety management practice and safety performance in offshore environments, *Safety Science; 41*(8), 641–680.

O'Dea, A. and Flin, R. (2001) Site managers and safety leadership in the oil and gas industry, Safety Science; *37*(1), 39–57.

O'Dea, A. and Flin, R. (2003) The Role of Managerial Leadership in Determining Workplace Safety Outcomes. Health and Safety Executive Research Report RR044.

Parker, D., Lawrie, M., and Hudson, P. (2006) A framework for understanding the development of organizational safety culture, *Safety Science; 44*(6), 551–562.

Parkes, K.R. (1992) Mental health in the oil industry: A comparative study of onshore and offshore employees, *Psychological Medicine; 22*(4), 997–1009.

Parkes, K.R. (1998) Psychosocial aspects of stress, health and safety on North Sea installations, *Scandinavian Journal of Work, Environment and Health; 24*(5), 321–333.

Parkes, K.R. and Swash, S. (2005) Offshore Sickbay Consultations in Relation to Age, Job Factors and Self-reported Health, Health and Safety Executive Research Report, RR364.

Reid, H., Flin, R., Mearns, K., and Bryden, R. (2008) Influence from the Top: Senior Managers and Safety Leadership. Paper SPE 11762 presented at the *Society of Petroleum Engineers International Conference on Health, Safety, and Environment in Oil and Gas Exploration and Production, Nice, France, 15–17 April, 2008.*

Rundmo, T. (1992) Risk perception and safety on offshore petroleum platforms—Part II: Perceived risk, job stress and accidents, *Safety Science; 15*(1), 53–68.

Rundmo, T. (1994) Associations between organizational factors and safety and contingency measures on offshore petroleum platforms, *Scandinavian Journal of Work, Environment & Health; 20*(2), 122–127.

Rundmo, T. (1995) Perceived risk, safety status and job stress among injured and non-injured employees on offshore petroleum installations, *Journal of Safety Research; 26*(2), 87–97.

Schneider, B., Salvaggio, A.M., and Subarits, M. (2002) Climate strength: A new direction for climate research, *Journal of Applied Psychology; 87(2)*, 220–229.

Shaw, A., McMunn, A., and Field, J. (eds) (2000) *The Scottish Health Survey 1998: Volume 1: Findings & Volume 2.* Technical Report, Edinburgh: The Stationery Office.

Sheen, M J. (1987) *M.V. Herald of Free Enterprise*. London: HMSO: Department of Transport.

Simard, M. and Marchand, A. (1994) The behaviour of first line supervisors in accident prevention and effectiveness in occupational safety, *Safety Science; 17*(3), 169–185.

Sutherland, V.J. and Cooper, C.L. (1986) Man and Accidents Offshore: The Costs of Stress among Workers on Oil and Gas Rigs. London: Lloyd's List/Dietsmann.

Sutherland, V.J. and Cooper, C.L. (1991) *Stress and Accidents Offshore*. Houston: Gulf Publishing Co.

Tannenbaum, R. and Schmidt, W.H. (1958) How to choose a leadership pattern, *Harvard Business Review; 36*(2), 95–101, cited in O'Dea & Flin (2001).

Tharaldsen, J-E., Olsen, E., and Rundmo, T. (2008) A longitudinal study of safety climate on the Norwegian continental shelf, *Safety Science; 46*(3), 427–439.

Tharaldsen, J-E., Mearns, K., and Knudson, K. (2009) Perspectives on safety: The impact of group membership, work factors and trust on safety performance in UK and Norwegian drilling company employees, *Safety Science*; *48*(8), 1062–1072.

Wallace, J.C., Popp, E., and Mondore, S. (2006) Safety climate as a mediator between foundation climates and occupational accidents: A group-level investigation, *Journal of Applied Psychology; 91*(3), 681–688.

Yergin, D. (1991) *The Prize: The Epic Quest for Oil, Money, and Power.* New York: Free Press.

Zohar, D. (2002) The effects of leadership dimensions, safety climate, and assigned priorities on minor injuries in work groups, *Journal of Organizational Behavior; 23*, 75–92.

CHAPTER 11 *Safety and Risk in Transportation*

A. IAN GLENDON

Introduction

This chapter considers safety aspects of four common transport modes—air, sea, rail, and road. These operate in many different ways, for example all involve commercial (passenger and freight) and private travel (albeit a minute proportion of rail traffic). Managing the safe operation of each of these modes, involving numerous complex interactions, requires many specialist functions. Table 11.1 summarizes major categories within each travel mode, including commercial, commuting, leisure, and other forms.

Transport is a ubiquitous feature of all our lives with most people undertaking some form of daily travel, while transport brings food and meets other survival needs. As a relatively recent evolutionary development, humans have adapted quickly to the myriad forms of transportation now available, including coping with the inherent complexity of many forms of travel. For example, driving a vehicle involves the most complicated series of tasks that most of us ever engage in, exceeding the complexity of most jobs between daily commutes. Public transport may involve protracted check-in and security processes (Williams, 2007), while interfaces between transport modes may create additional challenges.

Choosing Between Transport Modes

All forms of transport involve some risk. Because they involve trade-offs, risks associated with transport are exclusively speculative. The potential downside (for example, serious injury) is traded against the upside—including arriving safety at your destination or pleasure associated with some travel experiences. Travelers speculate that the benefits of a prospective journey will outweigh the potential harm that might befall them (that is, the risk) during that journey. Most of these decisions are not consciously made, but are arrived at through habit or circumstances.

However, some travel decisions are made consciously—for example, where a genuine choice between travel modes exists or where a journey may/not be necessary. Decision making could then involve deliberate choices about whether to travel and/or by what mode. The risk may be managed by trading off desired benefits (for example, speed, comfort, safety) and the perceived potential for harm. Comparing costs and benefits

Table 11.1 Four transport modes and illustrative uses

Use Mode	Commercial	Commuting	Leisure	Other
Air	Cargo; crop spraying	Relatively small volume (e.g., weekly or to remote locations)	Mostly travel to tourist destinations; also extensive private use and leisure flights (e.g., in "classic" planes)	Military; air show displays; aerial water bombing; weather monitoring; research; surveillance; migration, medical etc
Marine	Fishing; container carriage; oil tanker; harbor master; tugs	Local ferries—e.g., in coastal, inter-island, inland waterways	Ocean cruises; yachting; inland waterways (e.g., barges, liners, powered vessels on rivers, lakes, canals)	Military; powerboat and ocean yacht racing; research (e.g., fish stocks, environmental), coastguard; river police; migration; refugees and asylum seekers
Rail	Freight; onsite (e.g., mining, agriculture)	High density, particularly in urban environments	Travel either to tourist destinations or as a self-contained leisure activity (e.g., steam trains on private tracks)	Track inspection, maintenance and repair vehicles
Road	Freight; bus; taxi; drive in the course of one's work (between destinations, etc)	Very high density, particularly in urban environments	Travel either to tourist destinations or as a self-contained leisure activity (e.g., coach tours, classic car rallies, street car races)	Military; police and emergency response vehicles; etc

of different transport modes can be problematic because of their different externalities and spheres of operation (Rothengatter, 2010). Table 11.2 summarizes some costs and benefits associated with the four travel modes. Because individuals cannot have all the information required to make rational decisions about transport, they use heuristics to simplify decision making. Thus we might select on the basis of perceived control over transport mode (for example, drive own vehicle) rather than on the likelihood of arriving safely at our destination. Identifying key individual factors determining people's choice of transport mode, Moen (2007) found that worry was the prime predictor of safety priorities, followed by negative attitudes toward rules. A summary of how risks might be perceived by individual travelers and the range and sphere of exposure across four transport modes is shown in Table 11.3.

Table 11.2 Qualitative assessment of overall relative cost and benefit levels of four transport modes

Main costs (externalities)	Air	Marine	Rail	Road
Collision deaths/injuries/damage	Generally low frequency, but often salient when they occur	Generally low frequency, but occasionally salient when they occur	Generally low frequency, but occasionally salient when they occur	High and generally only locally visible
Environmental pollution (CO_2, noise, carriage of invasive species, fuel/oil spillage, etc)*	High/moderate	Generally moderate, but individual incidents may be extremely high	Moderate	High
Congestion	Generally moderate; high in some locations (e.g., US)	Generally low	Generally low	Often high
Lifecycle—production/disposal	Generally low (e.g., attributable to closed loop lifetime safety cycle (Akdeniz, 2001))	Generally moderate	Generally moderate	Generally high
Main benefits (to user)	**Air**	**Marine**	**Rail**	**Road**
Reliability	Generally high	Generally moderate	Generally high	Generally moderate
Convenience (time, access, etc)	Moderate	Low	Moderate	Variable
Safety	Generally high	Wide variability—high to low	Generally high	Generally moderate
Cost	High to moderate; often local variability	Generally moderate; may be local variability	Wide variability	Generally moderate; local variability

* Rothengatter (2010) detailed emission rates of different transport modes and quantified potential strategies for alleviating resultant environmental costs.

On the relative risks of travelling by airplane or road vehicle Dijkstra (2006) cited data to claim that in the US it is 22 times safer travelling in a commercial jet than by car. Sivak and Flannagan (2003) calculated that, for any distance where flying is an option, even on the safest roads in the US, driving is approximately 65 times as risky as flying.

Table 11.3 Perceived risk, risk exposure and sphere of risk in four transportation sectors

Risk feature mode	Users' (customers') perceived risk	Risk exposure (from operations)	Risk sphere
Air	Transferred to operators—organizational and individual (e.g., airline pilots)	Trauma risk mainly limited to users and operators—global (diffused) pollution from emissions	Global and local
Marine	Transferred to operators—organizational and individual (e.g., ships' captains)	Trauma risk mainly limited to users and operators—pollution from spillages potentially widespread	Global and local
Rail	Transferred to operators—organizational and individual (e.g., train drivers)	Trauma risk to users and operators; third parties (e.g., suicides, trespassers) often involved	Mainly local
Road	Either transferred to operators—organizational and individual (e.g., truck/bus drivers) or accepted as being under individual's personal control	Multiple third parties potentially at risk as well as users and operators—global (diffused) pollution from emissions	Mainly local

However, these authors noted the different sources of risk in each case, such that driving risk is most closely associated with distance travelled (that is, total exposure), while flying risk is primarily influenced by the number of take-offs and landings—during which 95 percent of global airline fatalities occur—making direct comparisons between these travel modes problematic, further confounded by the fact that many flights begin and end with car journeys.

Evans, Frick and Schwing (1990) also found comparing road and air fatalities to be problematic. For example, while flying risk is approximately equivalent for all passengers, individual (for example, driver age) and vehicle (for example, size) differences as well as environmental circumstances (for example, road type) mean that risk for different driving situations varies widely. Evans et al. calculated that compared with an airline passenger, a "low-risk" driver (40 years of age, alcohol-free, wearing a seat belt, driving a larger-than-average car on rural interstate roads) has a lower fatality rate on trips of less than 969 kilometers by driving rather than flying. In contrast the notional "high-risk" driver's risk of death in less than two kilometers of driving exceeds the likelihood of death on a single flight. These calculations excluded non-fatal injuries, which in the case of road vehicles exceed fatalities by a factor of around 70, and also injuries to third parties—also considerably higher in the case of road vehicles.

While Sivak, Weintraub and Flannagan (1991) confirmed that for "average" or "high-risk" drivers it was always safer to fly than to drive, they determined that even for "low-risk" drivers, non-stop flying was safer for trips of more than 488 kilometers. To aid decision making for individual travelers, these authors generated a fatality probability calculator for high-risk, average, and low-risk drivers selecting either non-stop, 2-, 3-, or 4-segment flights. Barnett (1991) challenged Sivak, Weintraub and Flannagan's calculations as not taking due account of airplane type and driver fatigue, which would reduce the equal-risk level for fatal injury only across the two modes to 209 kilometers. Extending the debate, Evans, Frick and Schwing (1991) drew attention to airlines' differential safety records and other possible confounds. Table 11.4 shows mean safety records of various types of flying. An interesting aspect of the debate on the relative safety of these two modes of travel was that some underlying, but unspecified, assumptions were made, including that rational choice using actuarial data would primarily govern individual travelers' behaviors, that increased use of one mode (say airlines) would mean that relative risks remained essentially unchanged, and that genuine choice existed for all comparable journeys.

Table 11.4 Varying risk levels within aviation (after Amalberti, 2006)

Aviation mode	Mean accident rate
Commercial fixed wing commercial	0.71×10^{-6} per million departures
Chartered flights and non-scheduled operations	5.81×10^{-6}
Helicopters; business flights; general aviation average	8.2×10^{-5} per flight hours
Micro-light; aerial applications—Western countries	10^{-3}
Gyroplane	10^{-2}

Trade-offs also involve exchanging one set of risks for another, so that actions designed to minimize one form of risk might result in a heightened alternative risk. For example, high-profile terrorist attacks such as 9/11 influence people's choice of travel mode (Srinivasan, Bhat and Holguin-Veras, 2006). While an individual's travel choice selection is likely to be driven primarily by their personal risk perception, the total risk for the travelling population might be affected by a range of factors. For example, according to the "dread hypothesis" Gigerenzer (2004, 2006) estimated that in the 12 months after September 11, 2001 ("9/11") six times more Americans were killed on the road by avoiding flying than the total number of people killed on the four fatal flights. A parallel finding by Ayton, Murray and Hampton (2009) revealed an increased rate of cycling injuries—including fatalities—following the July 7, 2005 ("7/7") terrorist attacks on London's public transport system. The authors attributed this increase both to lower dread risk (of low probability, high consequence events) associated with cycling compared with underground train journeys and to the less safe option of cycling compared with train travel. Challenging the dread hypothesis, Ayton, Murray and Hampton considered that public aversion to time delays resulting from increased security measures at airports could have contributed to the decline in post 9/11 air travel.

Also proffering an alternative explanation for Gigerenzer's (2004, 2006) findings, Su et al. (2009) confirmed that while flying decreased, kilometers driven across the US did not increase immediately post 9/11, and that fatal traffic injuries only increased in the north-eastern part of the US. Su et al. considered that the proximity of traumatic events such as 9/11 increased stress levels in this region of the US, thereby impairing local drivers' driving ability to the extent of impacting fatal injury rates, further mediated by alcohol or other drug-related citations.

However, travel choices are also influenced by local and wider cultural factors, for example alternative transport mode availability and preponderance of general use (for example, as in US "car culture"). For example, investigating the possible impact on travel mode choice and safety after the March 11, 2004 ("11/3") Madrid train bomb attacks, López-Rousseau (2005) detected a reduction in both train travel and road vehicle use—fairly small in the latter case—with no subsequent increase in traffic injuries. Citing evidence that dying as a train passenger is 20 times less likely than as a car passenger, López-Rousseau maintained that prior experience with terrorist bomb attacks—resulting in lower dread risk perception, the relatively lower impact of 11/3 compared with 9/11 as well as possible behavior changes (for example, car pooling) partly accounted for Spaniards not confronting the additional risk of traffic injury after 11/3, although considered that this did not necessarily result from deliberate choices.

These studies, along with the incomplete nature of the data, speculative analysis, and interpretation of results, confirm that transportation safety is a highly complex issue, involving individuals' emotional reactions (for example, fear, worry) to situations at least as much as deliberate decision making and cognitive assessment of relative risks of different transport modes in making travel choices. Individual effects will impact public policy and risk management in respect of education and other interventions. For example, as urged by Ayton, Murray and Hampton (2009), interventions may be required to counter increased stress associated with certain forms of travel, as well as educating travelers about the relative risks of different transport modes, for example to counter dread risk perceptions that result from recent or otherwise highly salient adverse events, such as terrorist attacks (Gigerenzer, 2004).

Managing Transport Risks

Transport risk may be managed simultaneously at one or more levels:

1. Personal.
2. Team/group.
3. Organizational—for example, vehicle fleets, airline/shipping/rail companies.
4. Country—for example, legislation and enforcement.
5. National agency—for example, Civil Aviation Safety Authority (Australia) (CASA), National Transport Commission (Australia) (NTC), Australian Maritime Safety Authority (AMSA).
6. International agency—for example, International Maritime Organization (IMO), World Health Organization (WHO), International Civil Aviation Organization (ICAO).

A range of strategies exists for managing transport risks. Traditional strategies for managing risk in each of the four transport modes are summarized in Table 11.5, which also gives a general assessment of the effectiveness of strategies within each sector.

Table 11.5 Traditional strategies for managing transport safety and risk

Strategy mode	Regulation	Enforcement	Education and training
Air	High effectiveness—via international (e.g., ICAO) and national (e.g., Federal Aviation Administration (US) (FAA), Joint Aviation Authorities (JAA)) agencies	Generally high effectiveness—via international—e.g., European Aviation Safety Agency (EASA) and national (e.g., Civil Aviation Authority (UK) (CAA), CASA) agencies	High effectiveness—extensive and continuous for safety critical staff—e.g., Advanced Qualifications Program (of FAA) (AQP), Behavior-oriented observation method (for air traffic control—ATC) (BOOM), Crew resource management (CRM)—Helmreich et al. (1999), Macleod (2005); Line operations safety audit (LOSA)—Thomas (2004), Non-Technical Skills Project (JAA), (NOTECHS)—Flin, O'Connor and Crichton (2008: 302–306), Team resource management (for ATC) (TRM)
Marine	High effectiveness—via international (e.g., IMO) and national (e.g., AMSA) agencies	Variable effectiveness—by national and international—e.g., European Maritime Safety Agency (EMSA) agencies	Highly variable across sector organizations
Rail	Variable effectiveness—by jurisdiction	Generally high effectiveness—via specialist agencies—e.g., Office of Rail Regulation (UK) (ORR) in advanced economies	Continuous for most safety critical roles in advanced economies—e.g., Rail resource management (RRM)—Dédale Asia Pacific (2007)
Road	Highly variable effectiveness—by national/state (etc) jurisdiction	Highly variable effectiveness—by national/state (etc) jurisdiction, usually police or specialist traffic agencies	Highly variable effectiveness—reasonably consistent in advanced economies

While the very different characteristics of each transport mode require distinct risk management methods, generic strategies exist, for example at a systems level within each mode. Some generic risk factors that operate across all four sectors are:

- workload;
- fatigue;
- stress;
- system complexity;
- terrorism (for example, piracy); and
- rate of environmental change.

Some common factors relate to operator capacity (for example, fatigue, workload, stress), while others are associated with external environments (for example, complexity, terrorism, change). However, while risk management strategies in the four sectors might be comparable at a generic level, the way in which each is implemented differs between modes. Table 11.6 outlines four more recently developed generic strategies, all incorporating technology, which complement the traditional strategies described in Table 11.5. The strategies outlined in Table 11.6 have been developed more recently than the traditional strategies, and it could be expected that, while traditional strategies will always be required, there will be considerable scope for further development of newer strategies.

Tables 11.5 and 11.6 refer to a number of bodies or agencies involved in various ways in managing transport safety and risk. Space limitations preclude considering any of these in detail and the number of agencies involved in transport safety is much larger than indicated here—for example, most countries, and often jurisdictions within countries, have specialist agencies for managing various aspects of transport safety.

A third type of strategy involves actions that augment efforts to improve safety in the various transport modes, including gathering data on collisions, crashes, accidents, incidents and disasters—involving loss of life, other injury (traumatic or pathogenic), as well as damage to plant, equipment or the environment (including wildlife) and sometimes also "near incidents" and errors that could have led to more serious outcomes. Where such data are gathered, to be useful they should be competently analyzed and relevant findings transferred to agencies that can implement changes based upon an appropriate mix of strategies outlined in Tables 11.5 and 11.6. Some transport reporting agencies have highly sophisticated databases and analytic techniques. Research may be undertaken to establish specific associations between variables comprising incident etiology.

A third strategy type involves measures designed to mitigate the worst results of incidents should they occur. While these strategies, outlined in Table 11.7, might be considered reactive as opposed to the more proactive, or interventionist, strategies outlined in Tables 11.5 and 11.6, the key to effectively managing safety in any transport mode is appropriately combining strategies from the complete range of those available to address the risks within each sector.

Table 11.6 More recent strategies for managing transport safety and risk

Strategy Mode	Organizational safety (risk management, culture, etc)	Reliability (e.g., achieving mindfulness)	Human factors (HF)	Resilience engineering
Air	Good in most major airlines and jurisdictions—e.g., Air Flow Traffic Management (AFTM)—Turner and Agogino (2007), Central Flow Management Unit (EU air traffic) (CFMU) and among pilots (Evans, Glendon and Creed, 2007)	Some airlines already have or are approaching HRO status	Extensive adoption (e.g., to counter fatigue and distraction)	Mostly resilient during normal operations; some inherent "forgiveness" but system degradation (e.g., multiple cancellations, terrorist attack) can lead to loss of resilience
Marine	Variable across sector organizations—e.g., Marine Accident Risk Calculation System (Norway) (MARCS); the IMO formulates formal safety assessment (FSA) directives	A few organizations approach HRO status	Moderate adoption (e.g., to counter fatigue and distraction)	Mixed resilience due to ever-changing operating environment, which is mostly benign with local perturbations resulting from occasional disasters (e.g., overloaded ferry capsize, pirate attack)
Rail	Variable across sector organizations; some international initiatives—e.g., via European Railway Agency (ERA), European Rail Traffic Management System (ERTMS), European Train Control System (ETCS), International Union of Railways (UIC)	Potential for some large rail sector organizations to achieve HRO status	Moderate adoption in large organizations in advanced economies	Mixed resilience—e.g., under abnormal conditions, safety may be achieved by sacrificing punctuality and traffic volume; or may be resilient in terms of passenger safety but not track maintenance worker safety or for trespassers and suicides (Hale and Heijer, 2006b)
Road	Driving culture variable across jurisdictions; some international initiatives—e.g., European Road Safety Charter (ERSC)	Some fleet/freight carriers and public sector organizations could approach HRO status	Variable adoption	Road environments in most advanced economies very resilient with some degree of "error forgiveness"—many opportunities to improve those in developing economies

Table 11.7 Complementary strategies for managing transport safety and risk

Strategy mode	Research/incident reporting/ data analysis	Accident/incident investigation	Mitigation and collateral damage limitation
Air	Considerable research; generally high reporting/analysis—e.g., Airport Cooperative Research Program (US) (ACRP), Aviation Safety Reporting System (US) (ASRS), British Airways Safety Information System (BASIS); Confidential Human Factors Incident Reporting System (UK) (CHIRP); data sharing—e.g., Flight Safety Foundation (US) (FSF), Global Aviation Information Network (GAIN) (O'Leary, 2002)	Involves international—e.g., International Air Transport Association (IATA), ICAO (annex 13) and national—e.g., Air Accidents Investigation Branch (UK) (AAIB), Australian Transport Safety Bureau (ATSB), Bureau d'Enquêtes et d'Analyses pour la Sécurité de l'Aviation Civile (France) (Bureau of Investigation and Analysis for the Safety of Civil Aviation) (BEA), Safety Trend Evaluation, Analysis and Data Exchange System (IATA-STEADES), National Transport Safety Bureau (US) (NTSB), Transportation Safety Board (Canada) (TSB) organizations	Considerable effort devoted to this
Marine	Some research—e.g., Marine Accident Investigators' International Forum (MAIIF); moderate reporting and analysis	Involves mainly national organizations—e.g., Marine Accident Investigation Branch (MAIB)	Reasonable effort devoted to this
Rail	Moderate research; high reporting—e.g., Confidential Incident reporting and Analysis System (UK) (CIRAS); Rail Safety and Standards Board (UK) (RSSB); some analysis in developed economies (e.g., RSSB 2003a, b; 2004a, b, c; 2005a, b; 2006a, b, c, d, e)	Mostly national organizations involved—e.g., ATSB, NTC, NTSB	Reasonable effort devoted to this
Road	Extensive research—e.g., Framework Program (Europe) (FP7), In-Depth Investigation of Motorcycle Accidents (Europe) (MAIDS), Transport Research Laboratory (UK) (TRL); good reporting and analysis in developed economies—e.g., Observatoire National Interministériel de Sécurité Routière (France) (Inter-Departmental Observatory on Road safety) (ONISR), Programme de Recherche et d'Innovation dans les Transports Terrestres (France) (Program of Research, Experimentation and Innovation in Land Transport) (PREDIT)	Some international (e.g., WHO) and many national organizations involved—e.g., Fatal Accident Reporting System or Fatality Analysis Reporting System (US) (FARS)	Some effort devoted to this

Theoretical Contributions to Transportation Safety

HIGH RELIABILITY THEORY (HRT) AND NORMAL ACCIDENT THEORY (NAT)

These models describe the way in which on the one hand organizations seek to avoid disturbances to normal operations, and on the other how systems are prone to accidents and disasters as part of their normal operations, irrespective of any safety precautions that may be taken. While these have been considered as competing "theories" (for example, Perrow, 2009; Rijpma, 2003; Shrivastava, Sonpar and Pazzaglia, 2009a, b) as its name indicates HRT is primarily about reliability as applied to organizations, while NAT is concerned with system-level safety (Vaughan, 1999). NAT has been criticized on grounds of its ambiguity, limited applicability, and scope for policy or applications (Hopkins, 1999) and for being unable to account for the role of humans in systems (Shrivastava, Sonpar and Pazzaglia, 2009a, b). However, Perrow (2009) maintained that the fact that accidents do still occur demonstrates that even systems that might be considered "safe" can fail, and that NAT is complementary to other approaches, such as where the "drift to deviance" is salient (Vaughan, 1999, 2005). Complex transport systems can be prone to decaying system components over time, variously expressed as disaster incubation theory (DIT, Turner and Pidgeon, 1997) or the "normalization of deviance" (Vaughan, 2005).

Marais, Dulac and Leveson (2004) and Leveson et al. (2009) attempted a synthesis of NAT and HRT within a systems approach to safety from an engineering design perspective. These authors pointed out that both of Perrow's dimensions are scaled rather than categorical states, and that it may be ambiguous as to which quadrant some industries or organizations are located. For example, while air traffic control (ATC) is located in Perrow's quadrant 2 (tightly coupled complex systems), Marais, Dulac and Leveson and Leveson et al. pointed out that safety is designed in as a key part of the mission or rationale for ATC. Marais, Dulac and Leveson identified NAT as a top-down approach to understanding major accidents, while HRT offered a bottom-up reliability perspective.

Perrow's (1984, 1999) original notion was that systems, including but not restricted to transport, that were both tightly (as opposed to loosely) coupled and characterized by complex (as opposed to linear) interactions were particularly prone to "normal accidents"—rare but potentially serious incidents. While aircraft were included in Perrow's "quadrant 2", airways, rail, and marine transport were identified as tightly coupled but with linear interactions (quadrant 1; Perrow, 1984, pp. 97 and 327). Motor vehicles appeared in Perrow's quadrant 3, being loosely coupled and with linear interactions.

Both NAT and HRT maintain that decentralization, in the case of NAT at a system level and for HRT at organization level, assist responses to complex interactions that threaten safety by empowering those adjacent to operations to respond appropriately. Indeed La Porte and Rochlin (1994) characterized HRT as either complementary to, or an extension of NAT. Vaughan (1999) considered that routine nonconformity, mistakes, misconduct, and disasters would be produced by interactions between organizations and their environments, confounded by cognition and choice.

Originating in the US in the 1980s, the high reliability organization (HRO) concept initially focused upon the US ATC system, an electricity generating (nuclear) and distribution company, and US Navy nuclear aircraft carrier operations. Descriptions, definitions and case examples of HROs can be found in Bierly and Spender (1995), Hayes (2006), Hopkins, (2005, 2006), LaPorte (1996), LaPorte and Consolini (1991),

Leveson et al. (2009), Reason (2000), Rosa (2005), Weick and Roberts (1993), Weick and Sutcliffe (2001), and Weick, Sutcliffe and Obsfeldt (1999).

Examples of HROs demonstrating characteristics of Reason's "informed culture" include naval aircraft carriers, nuclear submarines, and ATC. Their just culture involves error management systems that focus upon identifying system failures rather than blaming individuals. Their flexibility means that normal hierarchical operations can be reprogrammed to respond to local circumstances by devolving control to experts "on the ground." Their learning focus involves all workers being trained to recognize and manage errors, a willingness to learn from mistakes, and a collective ability to discover and correct errors before they escalate into crises. This feature has been described as cultures having the "requisite imagination" (Westrum, 1991)—also "collective mindfulness," "organizational mindfulness," or simply "risk awareness," which may represent ways of describing safety culture. Organizational culture has been identified as the source of high reliability in HROs (Weick, 1987).

Mindful organizing involves preoccupation with failure. For example, long periods without incident, rather than breeding complacency generate a search for errors, lapses, and possible routes to major failures. HROs have well-developed near-hit reporting systems—that is, sophisticated reporting cultures (Reason, 1997). They are reluctant to simplify potentially complex issues, as all information could be important. Their workforces are socialized to notice more, explore complexity, and to check on everything.

However, Hopkins (2007) noted that reliability is not necessarily commensurate with safety, while Leveson et al. (2009) stressed that safety and reliability are orthogonal properties, and Shrivastava, Sonpar and Pazzaglia (2009a) pointed out that highly safe organizations were not the same as HROs and that system redundancies (for example, duplications) designed to counter threats might increase costs and opportunities for failure (Perrow, 1994). Van der Schaaf and Wright (2005) provided an example of an HRO criterion applied to safety. An important aspect of their taxonomy is the notion of recovery, which can be either planned (designed-in barriers or defenses against serious errors or faults) or ad hoc. Unplanned (ad hoc) recovery factors involve actions by "sharp end" workers who can detect and understand developing symptoms, and correct untoward events by timely and effective countermeasures.

RESILIENCE ENGINEERING

This recently developed concept considers safety and risk as non-linear. A generic approach that can take varying forms (Amalberti, 2006), it focuses on helping organizations to cope with complexity under pressure and to succeed (Hollnagel, Woods and Leveson, 2006). Organizational resilience may reflect "slack resources" and an ability to respond quickly to problems and to rebound from crises. Low resilience is comparable with low reliability, although as Hale and Heijer (2006a) pointed out, "Organizations can be safe without being resilient" (p. 38). Hale and Heijer (2006b, pp. 136–137) compiled these factors as they applied to railway systems:

- defenses erode under pressure;
- past good performance is taken as a reason for future confidence (complacency) about risk control;

- fragmented problem-solving clouds the big picture—mindfulness is not based on a shared risk picture;
- failure to revise risk assessments appropriately as new evidence accumulates;
- breakdown at boundaries impedes communication and coordination, which do not have sufficient richness and redundancy;
- the organization cannot respond flexibly to (rapidly) changing demands and is not able to cope with unexpected situations;
- not a high enough "devotion" to safety above or alongside other system goals; and
- safety is not built as inherently as possible into the system and the way it operates.

Reflecting previously established components of safety management systems, Wreathall (2006) considered that seven themes of resilient organizations were: top-level commitment, just culture, learning culture, awareness, preparedness, flexibility, and opacity. Such defining features identify resilience as an incremental progression from related concepts previously applied to organizations, including safety culture, normal accidents, and high reliability. Reason's (2008) analysis of a series of historical cases led him to consider that the three critical elements of recovery from crisis—or potential crisis, were: identifying and assessing an expected hazard (classic risk assessment), prior development and testing of appropriate countermeasures, and effectively deploying them—based upon situation awareness. The latter involves correct perception of the situation and understanding its significance in terms of a projected future state. Reason (2008) and Flin, O'Connor and Crichton (2008) deemed situational awareness to be the most important of these components.

Resilience links HRT and NAT insofar as incidents (for example, "disasters") comprise concurrences that border on the ordinary (as in NAT), while resilience engineering seeks to restore safety through system stability—as in becoming an HRO (Hollnagel, 2006) and to engage in mindfulness to predict future potential harm. It adopts comprehensive system-level models—for example, Systems-Theoretic Accident Modelling and Process (STAMP, Leveson et al., 2006) to engineer resilience into safety-critical systems, for example transportation. In a four-category resilience typology, Amalberti (2006) characterized public transportation as an example of a high-risk complex, yet ultra-safe system, where because of the high likelihood of large numbers of casualties, a large accident anywhere could have serious consequences for the organization concerned, and also for the entire sector. The sector was also described as being prone to complacency, yet scrutinized by national, international, and government agencies.

OTHER MODELS OF ACCIDENT/INCIDENT ETIOLOGY

The literature is replete with models (theories, and so on) and their derivatives claiming to represent accident or disaster processes. Following NAT and DIT came Reason's "Swiss cheese" model (Reason, 1997), which has been extensively applied in the investigation of transportation accidents (Young, Shorrock and Faulkner, 2005). Rasmussen (1997) provided a multi-level systems approach to safety and risk management. To an extent all models reflect the era and culture in which they were developed. For example, the notion of individual accident proneness, originally formulated in the 1920s and continuing as a credible explanatory model through to the 1960s, was developed during an era in which blame was typically attributed to individual agents, irrespective of their system role and the environmental constraints or influences operating upon them. As the power of the fundamental attribution error gained credence (Harvey, Town and Yarkin, 1981), drawing attention to the inherent bias in ascribing errors to individuals while ignoring their circumstances, reports increasingly pointed the finger at managerial and wider system influences upon major disasters. Despite continuing attention being drawn to the high "human error" component of accidents, we then entered the era of system (latent) failures and safety culture.

From the 1950s, ergonomics and human factors rapidly gained explanatory power over the next half-century so that in the post-2000 world there have been claims that a rebalancing is required, such that operational factors at the human-mechanized system interface need to be accommodated on an equivalent footing with system-level features (Flin, O'Connor and Crichton, 2008; Reason, 1997; Young, Shorrock and Faulkner, 2005). Young, Shorrock and Faulkner noted that increasing ascription of human error at all levels effectively meant that human error could be regarded as a contributory factor in 100 percent of accidents. One effect would be to render human error effectively useless as a category at a gross level as there would be zero variability and therefore no predictive capacity in any model incorporating human error without a finer grained coding framework. In seeking explanations for major disasters, they argued that investigators should balance system-level failings, managerial shortcomings, and operational ("sharp end") effects at the classic human-machine-system interface.

Managing Transport Safety Risks

MANAGING SAFETY ACROSS ALL MODES

In documenting many of the agencies that manage safety in the main transport modes considered in this chapter, Légé (2008) distinguished between accidental and deliberate (for example, extreme violations, sabotage, terrorist actions) interventions that result in incidents, injuries, and disasters. While Légé's review was limited to 130 sources, the author reported that the number of safety and security transportation references is vast (over 100,000 records), and presumably growing at a rapid rate.

In most, if not all, forms of commercial transportation it is useful to distinguish between "normal" and "crisis" operation modes. A critical feature for the driver, pilot, or operator is to know when each mode applies. This is because attributions to normal mode when the appropriate mode is crisis is very likely to lead to incorrect decision making and actions as a result of misperceiving and/or misunderstanding the system state. This is particularly likely in complex systems (for example, air, rail, marine) and available information is incomplete or ambiguous. Crises may unfold slowly or incrementally over a long period of time or may develop extremely rapidly, for example in the case of sudden structural failure of a critical system component.

Key hazards/high risk aspects for each mode—from Légé (2008) and elsewhere—are outlined in Table 11.8. Key aspects of managing risk across the four transportation sectors, including operator training, error proneness, and risk management implications, are outlined in Table 11.9.

The terrorist threat exists across all modes, being of low likelihood but potentially very high consequences. Murray-Tuite (2008) considered the vulnerability of transport

Table 11.8 Key hazards/high risk aspects for four transport modes

Mode	Key hazards
Air	Crew errors (e.g., speed, inclination, ground proximity), poor visibility (e.g., frost, cloud, darkness), turbulence, microbursts, extreme weather (e.g., high winds, wind shear, lightening, ice, snow, hail, rain), bird strike, runway collision.
Marine	Geography, coastal hazards, extreme weather conditions (e.g., high winds, ice, snow, hail, rain), traffic volume, collisions with other vessels and in port/harbor (Chauvin and Lardjane, 2008; Wellens et al., 2005), lack of local knowledge, crew errors, hazardous cargoes (Arslan and Er, 2008a), piracy (Bruyneel, 2005). Ferry safety is a particular problem for jurisdictions straddling multiple islands (e.g., Philippines, Indonesia) (Bateman, 2006). The fishing industry is particularly high risk (Chauvain and Le Bouar, 2007; Loughran et al., 2002). The International Labor Organization (ILO) publishes information on port and harbor safety (ILO, 2005)—see also Safer Ports (2005).
Rail	Human factors, impaired driver vigilance (e.g., signal siting), shiftwork, fatigue, stress, sudden illness (e.g., heart attack), on-track incursions (e.g., suicides, trespassers) (Lobb, 2006), trackside working (Itoh, Andersen and Seki, 2004), conflicts with road vehicles (e.g., at level crossings) (Mok and Savage, 2005; Health & Safety Executive, 2005), hazardous materials (Glickman and Erkut, 2007), assaults on staff—for example, in pursuit of theft.
Road	Motor vehicle collisions (MVCs), fatigue, stress, alcohol and other drugs, risk-taking (especially young drivers), behavioral adaptation (to environmental risk reduction measures), two-wheeled vehicles, pedestrians, ageing population (various effects on transport use), commercial transport, hazardous materials (Gilbert et al., 2009). It has been estimated that in the region of 1.2m people are killed and around 50 million are injured annually in road accidents (see also WHO, 2004). This figure dwarfs the numbers of deaths and injuries from all other transport modes combined.

Table 11.9 Managing risk in four transportation sectors: operator training, error proneness, and risk management implications

Risk feature mode	Operator training	Error-proneness	Coupling and complexity (Perrow)	Risk management (RM) implications
Air	Highly trained; international medical and fitness requirements; mandatory reassessment at intervals	Error-avoiding	Complex and tightly coupled (quadrant 2—subject to "normal accidents")	Organizational (e.g., passenger, freight) responsibility for RM; individual responsibility (e.g., leisure sector); international legislation/enforcement
Marine	Variable—some highly trained; others not; limited reassessment requirements	Error-inducing	Linear and tightly coupled (quadrant 1)	Organizational (e.g., passenger, freight) responsibility for RM; individual responsibility (e.g., leisure sector); inter/national legislation/enforcement
Rail	Highly trained; medical and fitness requirements and mandatory reassessment at intervals in most jurisdictions	Error-avoiding	Linear and tightly coupled (quadrant 1)	Organizational responsibility for RM; mainly national legislation/ enforcement of sector organizations
Road	Very variable—some highly trained—others not; reassessment required only in a few instances (e.g., some categories of professional drivers)	Error-inducing	Linear and loosely coupled (quadrant 3)	Organizational responsibility for RM (e.g., transport companies in some jurisdictions); national/state legislation/ enforcement of organizations and private vehicle use

networks to terrorist attack. Greenberg et al. (2006) assessed terrorist threats, consequences, and liabilities and the risks for cruise ships, ferries, and containers—see also Chalk (2008). Large-scale terrorist attacks on transport systems tend to receive extensive media coverage (for example, New York, 2001; Madrid, 2004; London 2005) and are therefore subject to risk amplification (Pidgeon, Kasperson and Slovic, 2003).

Referring to maritime and air transportation and the extant legislation governing these domains, Zekos (2000) reported that trans-European networks and environmental protection went hand-in-hand with safety in EU transport policy. Perrow (1994) and Rijpma (2003) characterized marine transport as an "error-inducing" industry, being profit-oriented, poorly organized, and weakly unionized. In contrast, by incorporating numerous safety features, for example as a result of previous accident investigations, aviation was described as an "error-avoiding" industry. While these authors do not specifically mention it, rail might also be considered to be error-avoiding for much the same reasons, while road transport would be error-inducing. One outcome of this distinction is that risk management in each pair of sectors is likely to be quite different.

For example, in the rail and civil aviation sectors, safety advances tend to occur incrementally as major accident and disaster inquiries report on causes and make recommendations to improve system safety and ensure that operational safety knowledge can be shared throughout these sectors. For example the FAA drove a policy to exclude non-standard parts for aircraft maintenance and improved methods for detecting these in the late 1980s and early 1990s following a major air crash. To a lesser extent this process also occurs in the maritime sector. However, as a much more heterogeneous sector, road safety advances much more slowly and less efficiently, and where it occurs at all, action tends to be localized.

In Australia the inter-governmental agency National Transport Commission (NTC, 2009b) is charged with improving productivity as well as safety and environmental performance in its road, rail, and international transport systems. Whether these criteria are mutually compatible or indeed might potentially conflict is a moot point.

CIVIL AVIATION

From the perspective of the lifetime safety cycle (LSC), a philosophy that includes external agency monitoring to ensure that lessons learned from incidents are fed back into the design process, Applegate and Graeber (2005) revealed that successive generations of airplanes demonstrated better safety as a result of improved systems design and implementation. While Applegate and Graeber's prime focus was upon airplane design, including human factors, and system improvements to enhance future safety, implications of maintaining ageing airplanes beyond their designed service date were considered by Akdeniz (2001). By 2015 annual global departures are predicted to reach 30 million and the number of airplanes in service is predicted to reach 23,000. If the accident rate had remained constant since 2000, the expected number of serious accidents could reach one every ten days by 2015. Applegate and Graeber maintained that safety gains would primarily result from reducing the number of accidents associated with human error (contrast Amalberti, 2001).

Noting the 95 percent improvement in accident rate since the dawn of commercial jet aviation, Muir, Thomas and Wilson (2005) considered the multiple passenger safety improvement features that have been integral to this achievement and those that will be required in future generations of aircraft. Foyle and Hooey (2008) provided an overview of various (NASA) models of human performance in the aviation sector. Human factors (also known as HF) continues to feature prominently in the aviation research literature, not only in its traditional guise of information displays (for example, Lim and Khoo, 2005) and the effects of automation (Carver, 2005), but also in baggage screening (Gale, 2005), air traffic management (for example, Kirwan, Rodgers and Schaefer, 2005), aircraft maintenance (for example, Krulak, 2004) and cultural differences (for example, Li et al., 2009; Merritt, 2000).

Dambier and Hinkelbein (2006) and Li and Harris (2006) described analyses of large samples of aircraft accidents. The US-based Aviation Safety Reporting System (ARAS) confidentially collects large numbers of incident reports volunteered by flight crews and de-identifies these reports prior to entering them into the database. Claimed as the largest global repository of voluntary, confidential safety information from frontline aviation personnel, incident narratives are used to support policy, HF research, and training. Established in 1988, by June 2006 over 700,000 reports had been submitted (http://asrs.arc.nasa.gov/). Extrapolating this figure would suggest that by 2010 well over 800,000 incidents would have been recorded.

Reviewing European Civil Aviation Conference (ECAC) and ICAO legislation on air safety, Zekos (2000) considered the single aviation market, ATC (for example, capacity problems), technical requirements, procurement, investigating air accidents, and carrier's liability. Lewinsohn (2005) provided an extensive review of significant US air safety legislation, while van der Geest et al. (2003) considered a model of aviation safety management from a Swiss perspective and the Dutch team of Ale et al. (2006) also modeled air transport safety. Appelbaum and Fewster (2004) addressed global airline safety from the perspective of best practice, while from an interpretive perspective Macrae (2007) considered airline safety as a sensemaking issue.

Reason (2008) noted that controlled flight into terrain (CFIT) resulted in about 74 percent of global commercial aviation accidents, citing a study showing that these accidents had some common features, including certain types of landing approach, lack of ground proximity warning systems (GPWS), and inadequate charts. Reason noted that universals in aviation accidents included unplanned contact with weather and terrain as well as gravity. Moving beyond the well-worn truism that a high percentage of accidents result from human error, Flin, O'Connor and Crichton (2008) cited studies showing that a major contributory factor in a large proportion of aviation accidents, particularly involving CFIT, was poor situation awareness.

Fatigue continues to be the subject of numerous studies within an aviation context (for example, Caldwell et al., 2009; Corbett, 2009; Chaumet et al., 2009; Folkard and Åkerstedt, 2004; Gregory, Xie and Mengel, 2004; Johnson et al., 2004; Killgore et al., 2009; Raslear and Coplen, 2004). Flin, O'Connor and Crichton (2008) cited evidence showing that fatigue had been estimated to be involved in between 4 and 7 percent of civil aviation accidents (and a higher percentage of military aviation accidents). Dijkstra (2006) noted the inherent imbalance under in-flight emergency conditions, during which pilots may have only a very short time to make life or death decisions, while investigation boards can take months and be informed by knowledge of the outcome.

Dekker (2005) contrasted traditional static structuralist safety models with the interpretive approach required to understand the dynamics of accidents that result from a "drift into failure" described as the "incremental movement of systems operations toward the edge of their safety envelope" (p. 181), describing one such aviation accident in detail. Dekker's perspective aligns with Perrow's (1984) view of accidents resulting from normal operations rather than evident failures or errors. Dekker noted the difficulty of contrasting the immediate benefits of early arrival with the problematic amount that was "borrowed from safety" in order to achieve the tangible arrival goal. Dekker argued for control models, which incorporate process as well as structure, describing organizational resilience as a capacity to recognize safe operational boundaries, to recoil from them in a controlled manner, and recovery from any loss of control.

MARINE

Zekos (2000) reviewed European Union (EU) and IMO legislation governing the safety of sea-going vessels, carriage of dangerous goods, marine pollution, port state control, inspections, passenger ferry safety, oil tankers, navigation and marine equipment, transfer of ships, and seafarer training. Atkins (2003) provided an example of the IMO's influence in bringing forward the date of phasing out of single hull oil tankers from 2026 to 2015. She also gave examples of initiatives by EU agencies in the air, rail, and road sectors.

In Rasmussen's (1997) analysis of the Herald of Free Enterprise capsize near Zeebrugge, it was clear that parties who made decisions about ferry design, harbor layout, cargo and passenger management, traffic scheduling, and vessel operation, were unaware of the potential mutual impact of their decisions and actions. Rasmussen also mapped conflicts between parties in the marine sector. He identified governments' and regulators' strategies for legislation as being inadequate during rapid technological change in this sector. Market forces, particularly competition, lack of communication between many parties, inadequate ship designs based upon established practice rather than contemporary needs, and inadequate guidance to operators, are among the forces contributing to conflicts between sector corporations and associations, company managements, and operational and technical staff.

Citing a Marine Incident Investigation Unit (MIIU) study, Reason (2008) noted recurring features of marine accidents, of which around 60 percent were either groundings or collisions. Collisions between large trading vessels and small craft accounted for 83 percent of this accident type, while common contributing factors included failure to keep a lookout and lack of knowledge of the International Collision Regulations by those operating the smaller vessels. Particular locations, pilot-assistance, and time of day (midnight to 04.00 hr) featured prominently in grounding incidents. Reason noted that universals in marine accidents included unplanned contact with rocks, shallows, currents, tides, and other vessels in the vicinity. Allen et al. (2005) described a case study of seafarer fatigue, while McNamara et al. (2005) considered legislative and management approaches to deal with this issue, and Arslan and Er (2007, 2008b) proposed a strategic approach to the problem.

Using a fatigue score index, Raby and Lee (2001) estimated that fatigue was a contributory factor in 16 percent of vessel accidents, 33 percent of personal injury accidents, and 23 percent of combined critical vessel and personal injury accidents in the maritime sector, which peak between 05:00 and 08:00 hrs. The most important contributory factor to the fatigue index was the number of hours worked in the previous 72 hours.

Summarizing findings from marine accident investigations, Raby and Lee (2001) noted that human factors, typically involving action or inactions, contributed to 81 percent of collisions, 69 percent of allisions (striking an object or structure), and 56 percent of groundings. They determined that human factors were less likely to be involved in founderings, sinkings, fires, and floodings, where equipment failure or poor maintenance were more likely to be factors.

Advancing from the era of safety and risk assessment (Fowler and Sørgård, 2000; Guedes Soares and Teixeira, 2001; Lois et al., 2004) researchers from different countries increasingly endorsed safety management and system approaches to maritime safety (Bailey, 2006; Celik, Er and Topcu, 2009; Jalonen and Salmi, 2009; Lindøe, 2007; Trucco et al., 2008), while maritime safety culture was a continuing theme (Darbra et al., 2007; Håvold, 2000; Lappalainen, 2008; Thébault, 2004). Human factors, including stress and human error, also figured prominently in the marine safety literature (Celik and Cebi, 2009; Celik and Er, 2007; Harrald et al., 1998; Hetherington, Flin and Mearns, 2006; Macrae, 2009; Nuutinen and Norros, 2009; Oldenburg et al., 2009; Sherwood Jones and Moore, 2005), while accident data analysis was also addressed (Hansen, Nielsen and Frydenberg, 2002; Toffoli et al., 2005). Others focused upon maritime regulatory, training, and policy frameworks (González-Laxe et al., 2005; Klein, 2007; Oyarce, 2008; Piniella, Rasero and Aragonés, 2005; Psaraftis, 2002, 2006; Tiribelli, 2006; Yercan, Fricke and Stone, 2005).

RAIL

Rochlin (1993) argued that no rail sector organization could be an HRO on the grounds that the technology is "reasonably simple and straightforward"—implying that HROs are exclusively located in Perrow's quadrant 2 (tightly coupled and complex). However, Kauppi et al. (2005) indicated what some aspects of a high reliability rail system might look like, including maintaining situation awareness, and keeping the human in-the-loop at all levels of automation.

While human error has been addressed within a rail sector context (Kim, Baek and Yoon, 2010) a much-studied human factors aspect of rail safety is signals passed at danger (SPADs) (Nikandros and Tombs, 2007). From a UK study, Reason (2008) provided evidence of a highly skewed distribution of SPADS, such that while 93 percent of all signals were SPAD-free, 1 percent attracted 30 percent of SPADs and 0.3 percent attracted 15 percent of SPADs. Features that predispose certain signals to be associated with SPADs "include: location, mounting, visibility, number of aspects and arrest rates" (p. 114).

A number of researchers have considered organizational safety culture and safety climate as significant features of rail sector organizations (Chikudate, 2009; Foulkes et al., 2005; Glendon and Evans, 2007; International Union of Railways, 2004; Jeffcott et al., 2006). Human factors approaches have, inter alia, considered control room design (Bainbridge, Davis and Roberts, 2005), railway signaling (Groeger, Clegg and O'Shea, 2005), and alarm handling (Stanton and Baber, 2008), while fatigue has also been addressed (Dickinson, 2005; Dorrian et al., 2006; Jones et al., 2005; National Transport Commission, 2007; US Department of Transportation, 2006). Other frameworks that have provided a basis for research in this sector include risk taking (Evans, 2005; Sanne, 2008), safety rules (Hale, Heijer and Koornneef, 2003; Lawton, 1998), systems analysis as an aid to understanding the Ladbroke Grove rail crash (Cullen, 2000; Lawton and Ward,

2005), best practice in regulation (Gunningham, 2004; National Transport Commission, 2009a), and citizen engagement (Horlick-Jones, 2008).

Efforts to address some of the more significant issues associated with rail transport include a recent UK initiative to reduce the approximately 200 annual rail suicides, which involve not only pain and suffering but also considerable amounts in financial compensation between rail sector organizations (www.iosh.co.uk)—see also Rådbo, Svedung and Andersson (2008).

ROAD

Funding under EU's FP6 included Traffic Accident Causation in Europe (TRACE). In addition to safety, funding under the seventh European Framework Program (FP7) in transportation focuses upon sustainability and technological advances to improve competitiveness in all transport modes (http://cordis.europa.eu/fp7/transport/home_en.html).

While for the most part, traffic systems are loosely coupled and linear in Perrow's terminology, Rasmussen (1997) documented a case of a road traffic accident that resulted in oil spillage to a drinking water supply—implying that complexity and some degree of coupling may be present in rare circumstances involving motor vehicle collisions (MVCs). The case involved parties at six levels: national government, budgeting and policy; regulatory bodies and associations; local government, planning and budgeting; company planning; physical processes and actor activities; as well as equipment and environment. This type of multi-level analysis implies that risk management must also operate at different levels, and that checks will be constantly required to ensure that risks that are managed at one level are consistent with, and do not conflict or interfere with, the management of risks at other levels. This implies a hierarchical approach to risk management in multi-level systems.

As with other transport modes, human factors aspects of driving have been addressed (Hancock, 2009) for example in terms of cognitive workload (Salmon et al., 2005). Flin, O'Conner and Crichton (2008) cited evidence for fatigue being the major contributing factor in 100,000 crashes and 1,500 fatalities in the US every year, while studies in Australia, the UK, and elsewhere have independently identified fatigue as a major contributory factor in road crashes, particularly of heavy goods vehicles (HGVs) with a significantly raised incidence at night. However, it has been suggested that commercial vehicle drivers are less likely than private vehicle drivers to be involved in fatal and severe injury crashes (Bloomfield, 2005), while Glendon (2007) found that commercial vehicle drivers were less likely than private vehicle drivers to exceed a range of speed limits and to violate other road rules. A growing literature also addresses driver distraction (Regan, Lee and Young, 2008), for example by cellular (mobile) phone use and its effect on crash risk (for example, Hunton and Rose, 2005).

Are motor vehicle collisions an epidemic?

On the basis of numbers of people killed and either temporarily or permanently incapacitated, MVCs have been deemed to constitute a global epidemic (RoadPeace, 2008; World Health Organization, 2009). As with most disease epidemics, the poor—particularly in developing countries—are most severely affected. Nevertheless, is this an appropriate comparison? While characterizing MVCs as an epidemic in terms of numbers killed or incapacitated may be apt, the respective etiologies are quite different, making the analogy inappropriate for at least these reasons:

1. Disease epidemics are examples of pure risk—that is, there is only a downside—that is, victims' suffering and associated effects. While benefits might subsequently flow, for example medical and other scientific advances such as greater understanding of disease pathology and etiology, developing vaccines, or discovering ways of forestalling or mitigating the spread of potential future disease vectors, epidemics are not started deliberately for the purpose of making such advances.
2. Each epidemic arrives as a novel strain—a revised version of a previous genetic form. However, MVC etiology remains essentially unchanged, and unlike many disease vectors, is highly visible—it is all of us. The relentless toll of death and injury reflects the same list of contributing factors: fatigue, alcohol, inattention, distraction, stress, driving violations, bad habits, superstition, and ignorance—supplemented by a lack of situation awareness and empathy for other road users.
3. Sivak and Flannagan (2003) calculated the probability of fatality per kilometer of US interstate highway driving as 4.4×10^{-9}—or about one in a billion per kilometer. Hale and Heijer (2006a) calculated that road traffic exposure revealed an extremely low risk of harm per traffic encounter on Dutch roads—which are likely to be similar to those in other advanced economies. They concluded that, while absolute numbers of people killed and injured gives the impression of the road being a very unsafe environment, it could be regarded as being exceptionally resilient on the basis of encounters that could lead to all injury accidents, which they estimated at 1.5×10^{-5}—well below the probability of human error even in simple tasks. This suggests that road users usually manage these complex interactions very effectively. However, as the vast majority of traffic fatalities and other injuries occur in developing countries, the figures between locations are likely to differ widely.
4. Other ways in which MVCs are unlike disease epidemics include their pattern and distribution, in which the global trend continues upwards, even if reductions occasionally occur in some developed economies. However, downward trends typically reach a plateau from which it is very difficult to achieve further reductions. Furthermore, no deliberate attempt is made to eliminate or reduce the prime vector—exposure to motorized vehicles.

A real challenge for managing risk in this transport mode is finding ways of either making people care sufficiently for enough of the time to ensure the safety of other road users or to create such a forgiving environment that even the most reckless behaviors result in minimal harm to either vehicle operator or third parties. Either of these represents a massive challenge. It is also possible that, because of behavioral adaptation effects (Wilde, 1994) at least some steps toward the second option might preclude serious attempts to instill additional elements of the first. Death and injury on the road can only be addressed by simultaneously acknowledging that the inherent risks of MVCs are a corollary of the widespread benefits of motorized travel. The speculative risk incurred while driving is that you might lose your life (an obvious downside) but you are much more likely to arrive safely (the usual upside). This is the essence of the problem.

DRIVING DILEMMAS

Freedom versus safety. The US Department of Transportation has estimated that 6,000 people were killed and 500,000 injured in 2008 as a result of "driver distraction" from cell phones (www.nhtsa.gov), while Redelmeier and Tibshirani (1997) estimated that during the time when a call is being made, the likelihood of a collision is four times as great as at other times. The "freedom" to use cell phones and other driving distractions contrasts with the seriously compromised level of safety resulting. Legislation and enforcement lags scientific knowledge in this, and other aspects of driving.

The impact of technology. Technology has the potential both to help and hinder driving safety (Horrey, 2009). For example, use of global positioning system (GPS) satellite technology can assist in way finding but also be a serious driving distraction. Researchers continue to explore various aspects of "drive-by-wire" technology (Hayama et al., 2010; Stanton, Young and McCaulder, 1997).

Younger drivers. It is well established that younger drivers are the highest risk driver group, and on many occasions calls have been made to delay licensing drivers until age 21 or 22 years—when drivers begin to resist peer pressure. However, there are at least three problems with this strategy. First, age is confounded with experience, so that implementing such a strategy might shift the risk profile to a higher age group, albeit in slightly attenuated fashion. Second, there is no guarantee that risky behaviors currently "absorbed" by young persons getting behind the wheel of a car would simply disappear—they might be represented in other ways. For example, deprived of a motor vehicle young people could be even more vulnerable as cyclists or pedestrians, particularly after consuming alcohol. Third, because of relatively dramatic development in the adolescent and emerging adult brain, this period is ideal for mastering new and complex skills such as those required for driving (Glendon, 2011a). Delaying the development of these skills would not guarantee a driver's greater lifetime safety—or that of others. The irony of the period of greatest risk taking coinciding with a high capacity for learning adult survival skills, such as driving, needs to be addressed as a composite set of features—for example by early intervention, extended training, and graduated licensing schemes that have been trialed and evaluated as successful in a growing number of jurisdictions (for example, Hallmark et al., 2008; Hedlund, 2007; Neyens, Donmez and Boyle, 2008).

Older drivers. The growing benefits of extensive driving experience may eventually be compromised by physical and cognitive decline. However, if older drivers become older pedestrians they may be at even greater risk. Again the composite of driving risks and benefits (in this case, extended spatial and temporal mobility) need to be addressed concurrently.

Behavioral adaptation. Previously referred to as risk homeostasis theory or risk compensation (Wilde, 1994), this phenomenon has the potential to at least partially revoke some safety improvements made either to driving environments (for example, road widening and straightening; reducing foliage and other visual obstructions; separating motorized from non-motorized traffic) or in-vehicle (for example, anti-lock braking systems; air bags; passenger restraints; roll bars and other vehicle reinforcing features). Under certain conditions, drivers may adjust their driving behaviors to match such higher levels of environmental safety, for example by driving faster, braking later, or reducing attention to the driving task. Possible driver behavioral adaptation needs to be taken account of by those responsible for developing in-vehicle and road environmental safety advances.

The illusion of control. For the most part passengers in some transport modes (for example, train, plane, bus, ferry) willingly allocate control of their safety to a presumed highly trained operating team (including those in control and support functions). Compared with being a passenger in most other transport modes, as an autonomous road user (whether driver, rider, cyclist, or pedestrian) the individual is likely to believe that they are in total control of their own safety, which has been characterized as driver optimism (Moen, 2007). The reality check includes accepting that you are also in part responsible for others' safety and that you are also at the mercy of every other road user with whom you come into contact—with all their misconceptions, violating behaviors, and poor driving practices.

Enforcement activity. While enforcement activity can be effective in the short term, a key issue is whether the desired behavior (for example, reduced rates of breaching signed speed limits, smaller proportions of drivers exceeding designated blood-alcohol concentration limits) will persist in the longer term without enforcement interventions. If driving habits revert to the pre-enforcement state then resources that have been deployed will have had no measurable long-term impact. Evaluation research is required to determine the extent to which various combinations of strategies to improve road safety, particularly interventions, work in the long term (Haworth, 2009; Lees and Lee, 2009). Such research—at least in refereed journals—is very thin on the ground (Glendon, 2011b), rendering determining optimum strategies for improving road safety problematic.

Driving culture. This term, introduced by Zaidel (1992), might be a useful generic description of driving in a jurisdiction, which inevitably comprises a highly variegated mixture of drivers of all ages, both sexes (except in some Islamic states), commercial, public sector, and private vehicles of all shapes and sizes. What are the common dimensions of a driving culture? How can it best be represented? What messages concerning improving road safety can be gleaned from this approach?

Organizational aspects of road safety. Managing fleet safety is a different task than generic road safety—because of the influence of organizational factors. It has been estimated that around half of all occupational fatalities occur on the road (Légé, 2008).

Generic Aspects of Transport Safety

HUMAN FACTORS

Workplace transport is a major factor in occupational accidents (Harley and Cheyne, 2005). In their review of workplace transport operations literature, Harley and Cheyne identified research on individual differences, stress/fatigue, training/competencies and selection, and safety culture/management. Harley and Cheyne identified intelligent transport systems (ITS) (Zhu and Roy, 2003) as an emerging field within workplace transport operations. In-vehicle ITS examples include seatbelt sensors, speed limiting systems, load sensors, fatigue sensors, collision detection sensors, alcohol interlock systems ("alcolocks"), GPS, and intelligent speed adaptation/assistance (ISA) (Carsten and Tate, 2005).

While the "ironies of automation" is not a new phenomenon (Bainbridge, 1987), Amalberti (2001) pointed to the paradox that increasing the degree of automation to reduce human error, for example on aircraft flight decks, can have the unintended effect of reducing overall safety because of crews' incomplete understanding of their operational impact. In this context it is pertinent that only a small proportion of human errors, in combination with systemic failures, ever result in accidents. Reviewing the history of some human error models, Amalberti (2001) and others (for example, Glendon, Clarke and McKenna, 2006) have pointed to the importance of human error as a basic learning device, for example in generating improved safety.

FATIGUE

Åkerstedt (2000) identified fatigue as the most identifiable and preventable cause of transportation accidents, surpassing even alcohol-related incidents. Caldwell, Caldwell and Schmidt (2008) described a range of detection and alertness-management strategies to mitigate fatigue, including work/rest scheduling and education.

Safety improvements follow from adapting work schedules to operators' circadian capacities. Van Dongen et al. (2003) found that chronic restriction of sleep periods to either four or six hours of sleep over 14 consecutive days resulted in significant cumulative reduced cognitive performance on a range of tasks. Such chronic sleep loss might be typical of transport system operators on certain shift patters. Van Dongen et al. (2007) reported some early results of a forecasting model to address reduced cognitive performance in operational settings.

Summarizing findings from a number of studies on the causes of fatigue and its extensive effects on cognitive, motor, communication, and social skills, Flin, O'Connor and Crichton (2008) identified excessive working hours, lack of sleep, stress, temperature extremes, noise, physical work, vibration, and task boredom. Other than the obvious requirement for more sleep, Flin, O'Connor and Crichton identified fatigue countermeasures as including education, sleep hygiene, rest breaks, napping, diet, medication, bright light, and planning—for example using a fatigue management tool for shiftwork and rostering.

DEREGULATION

In a meta-analysis of the effects of transport sector deregulation on safety, Elvik (2006) found that airline deregulation did not appear to influence the safety of air travel, although the only evaluation studies were from the US (11 studies). Road transport deregulation in four countries (13 studies) revealed no adverse effects upon safety. Rail deregulation, which had only been evaluated in the UK and the US (three studies), was associated with improved rail safety, although Elvik noted that no causal relationship could be inferred. While Evans (2007) found an increased number of train crash fatalities following privatization of the UK rail network, he concluded that there was "... no evidence that privatization caused railway safety to deteriorate" (p. 510). There were no marine sector studies of deregulation.

PERSONAL IMPACTS OF TRANSPORTATION DISASTERS

Hagström (1995) detailed the acute psychological impact upon train crash survivors, while Turner, Thompson and Rosser (1995) considered psychological reactions of survivors from the Kings Cross underground fire (Fennell, 1988). Reviewing several studies that detailed the psychological impact upon survivors, the bereaved, and rescue and support personnel of high-profile train, maritime, and air disasters, Lundin (1995) reported on a number of immediate and long-term effects. He noted that "a high and persisting level of psychiatric morbidity was found, mainly involving neurotic and psychosomatic symptoms among survivors" (p. 381). The two main stressors for survivors of train crashes were personal bereavement and somatic injuries. From studies of those affected by maritime disasters, cognitive impairment—particularly when processing threat-related stimuli—and post-traumatic nightmares were frequent symptoms. Feelings of guilt among survivors were common, which were associated with higher levels of psychological distress. Self-reported increased substance use was also a noted feature. Child survivors experienced a range of adverse symptoms ranging from sleep disturbances to heightened alertness to dangers. In the case of some disasters, highly distressing experiences could be exacerbated by intense media coverage. In the case of the residents of Lockerbie after the downing of Pan Am flight 103 in December 1998, Lundin reported that "perceived abuses included invasion of privacy, physical abuse, and insensitive, rude and ghoulish behavior" (p. 387).

ALLOWING INCIDENTS TO OCCUR TO MAINTAIN LEARNING CAPACITY

Amalberti (2001) noted that many transport safety strategies were linear, with managers seeking to eliminate errors and introducing procedures without taking account of the collateral effects of these "overstretched measures", so that, "an incident-free system becomes mute, and its safety can no longer be tuned" (p. 120). Amalberti described the "trap of over regulation," which "is characterized by reduced margins to incidents and accidents ... and numerous violations and deviance" (p. 121). Noting that all (transport) systems will eventually be replaced, Amalberti observed that the real challenge for safety practitioners is managing the transition from old to newer technologies. His safety priorities for ultra-safe transport systems were:

1. Allow systems to age ultra-safely rather than try to eliminate all errors and incidents; however, make genuine efforts to protect the system against catastrophic incidents.
2. Aggregate defense strategies but don't over-optimize systems as this will freeze human and technical adaptive capabilities, while masking minor failures.
3. Allow routine errors as their analysis has little bearing on system safety; however, errors arising from misunderstandings should be subjected to root cause analysis to determine remedies; violations—which paradoxically may be more numerous in ultra-safe systems because system rigidity requires more adaptive processes to manage work constraints—should be made visible and controlled rather than eliminated.

Conclusions

Arising from very different environments and conditions within which each operates, comparing different travel modes from an outcome perspective, such as deaths per distance travelled, is highly problematic. In any case, actuarial data minimally influence people's typical travel choices, these being heavily circumscribed by their other life choices and immediate situations.

Transport operators at the sharp end of transportation, whether road vehicle drivers/riders, airline pilots, ships' captains, or train drivers, make numerous routine decisions. Occasionally they must make decisions under stress, in novel situations, and in very short time periods. Based on their training, experience, and professionalism, they usually make correct decisions under such abnormal circumstances. However, occasionally they make errors, which under normal conditions would be "forgiven" by the environment, but under abnormal circumstances might result in disaster. These "errors" can frequently be traced to system elements that are removed from the sharp end. It behoves transport organization and system managers to identify these system (latent) conditions and to manage the risks associated with them appropriately.

Sociotechnical system change is ubiquitous and may be highly problematic for transportation sector organizations to manage. For example, pressure to automate and to reduce operating costs creates new challenges and risks for all transport modes. Legal factors (for example, increasing propensity to sue) and heightened media scrutiny, are among forces that can amplify these risks. While not a new concept, given that human skills will continue to be required in complex systems (Reason, 2008), appropriately allocating functions between people and machines remains a key aspect of managing transportation safety and risk.

Building in resilience to counter disaster-style events includes genuinely empowering personnel at all levels to challenge what they perceive to be unsafe situations without fear of retribution. National whistleblowing legislation may be required, reinforced by organizational commitment to adhere to the spirit as well as to the letter of such legislation.

Notwithstanding continuing multiple efforts to improve transportation safety, vast disparities exist between jurisdictions, particularly in road fatalities and severe injuries (National Institute for Occupational Safety and Health, 2009; WHO, 2004, 2009). With virtually no research available on transport safety in "third world" countries, it is almost impossible to appreciate what cultural and local factors might operate that differ significantly from those in "advanced economies." While the knowledge gap is massive, the means for its alleviation remain obscure. A sad irony is that because the overwhelming preponderance of transportation casualties occurs in third world countries, the greatest scope for making transportation safety improvements is in these regions. However, the resources required to address these problems, as with other health and safety issues, reside predominantly in advanced economies. Not until this gross imbalance is addressed will transportation safety begin to make significant in-roads into the current global toll of death, serious injury, and other negative impacts.

References

Akdeniz, A. (2001) The impact of mandated aging airplane programs on jet transport airplane scheduled structural inspection programs, *Aircraft Engineering and Aerospace Technology; 73*(1), 4–15.

Åkerstedt, T. (2000) Consensus statement: Fatigue and accidents in transportation operations, *Journal of Sleep Research; 9*(4) 395–395.

Ale, B.J.M., Bellamy, L.J., Cooke, R.M., Goossens, L.H.J., Hale, A.R., Roelen, A.L.C., and Smith, E. (2006) Towards a causal model for air transport safety—An ongoing research project, *Safety Science; 44*(8), 657–673.

Allen, P., Wellens, B., McNamara, R., and Smith, A. (2005) It's not all plain sailing. Port turn-arounds and seafarers' fatigue: A case study. In P.D. Bust and P.T. McCabe (eds), *Contemporary Ergonomics 2005*. London, UK: Taylor & Francis, 563–567.

Amalberti, R. (2001) The paradoxes of almost totally safe transportation systems, *Safety Science; 37*(2–3), 109–126.

Amalberti, R. (2006) Optimum system safety and optimum system resilience: Agonistic or antagonistic concepts? In E. Hollnagel, D.D. Woods, and N. Leveson (eds), *Resilience Engineering: Concepts and Precepts*. Aldershot, UK: Ashgate, 253–271.

Appelbaum, S.H. and Fewster, B.M. (2004) Safety and customer service: Contemporary practices in diversity, organizational development and training and development in the global civil aviation industry, *Management Research News; 27*(10), 1–26.

Applegate, J.D. and Graeber, R.C. (2005) Integrated safety systems design and human factors considerations for jet transport aeroplanes. In D. Harris and H.C. Muir (eds), *Contemporary Issues in Human Factors and Aviation Safety*. Aldershot, UK: Ashgate, 3–23.

Arslan, O. and Er, I.D. (2007) *Effects of Fatigue on Navigation Officers and SWOT Analyze for Reducing Fatigue Related Human Factors on Board*. Istanbul: Technical University.

Arslan, O. and Er, I.D. (2008a) SWOT analysis for safer carriage of bulk liquid chemicals in tankers, *Journal of Hazardous Materials; 154*(1–3), 901–913.

Arslan, O. and Er, I.D. (2008b) A SWOT analysis for successful bridge team organization and safer marine operations, *Process Safety Progress; 27*(1), 21–28.

Atkins, C. (2003) EU transport safety policy—Time to decide, *Health and Safety at Work; 25*(9), 12–12.

Ayton, P., Murray, S., and Hampton, J. (2009). *Terrorism, Dread Risk and Bicycle Accidents*. Paper presented at the BPS Cognitive Psychology Section Annual Conference, University of Hertfordshire, 1–3 September.

Bailey, N. (2006) Risk perception and safety management systems in the global maritime industry, *Policy and Practice in Health and Safety; 4*(2), 59–75.

Bainbridge, J., Davis, G., and Roberts, G. (2005) Control room design: New thinking. In P.D. Bust and P.T. McCabe (eds), *Contemporary Ergonomics 2005*. London, UK: Taylor & Francis, 393–396.

Bainbridge, L. (1987) The ironies of automation. In J. Rasmussen, K.D. Duncan, and J. Leplat (eds) *New Technology and Human Error*. London: Wiley, 271–283.

Barnett, A. (1991) It's safer to fly, *Risk Analysis; 11*(1), 13–13.

Bateman, S. (2006) *Ferry Safety: A Neglected Aspect of Maritime Security? Institute of Defence and Strategic Studies Commentaries, 3 May. www.idss.edu.sg.*

Bierly, P.E. and Spender, J.C. (1995) Culture and high reliability organizations: The case of the nuclear submarine, *Journal of Management; 21*(4), 639–656.

Bloomfield, J.R. (2005) Driving behaviour *in extremis*. In P.D. Bust and P.T. McCabe (eds) *Contemporary Ergonomics 2005*. London, UK: Taylor & Francis, 543–547.

Bruyneel, M. (2005, July) *Piracy Reports in 2005*. Author.

Caldwell, J.A., Caldwell, J.L., and Schmidt, R.M. (2008) Alertness management strategies for operational contexts, *Sleep Medicine Reviews; 12*(4), 257–273.

Caldwell, J.A., Mallis, M.M., Caldwell, J.L., Paulk, M.A., Miller, J.C., and Neri, D.F. (2009) Fatigue countermeasures in aviation, *Aviation, Space, and Environmental Medicine; 80*(1), 29–59.

Carsten, O.M.J. and Tate, F.N. (2005) Intelligent speed adaptation: Accident savings and cost—benefit analysis, *Accident Analysis and Prevention; 37*(3), 407–416.

Carver, E. (2005) Impacts of automation revisited. In P.D. Bust and P.T. McCabe (eds) *Contemporary Ergonomics 2005*. London, UK: Taylor & Francis, 110–114.

Celik, M. and Cebi, S. (2009) Analytical HFACS for investigating human errors in shipping accidents, *Accident Analysis and Prevention; 41*(1), 66–75.

Celik, M. and Er, I.D. (2007) *Identifying the Potential Roles of Design-based Failures on Human Errors in Shipboard Operations. Proceedings of the 7th Navigational Symposium on Marine Navigation and Safety of Sea Transportation* (617–621), 20–22 June, Gydina, Poland.

Celik, M., Er, I.D., and Topcu, Y.I. (2009) Computer-based systematic execution model on human resources management in maritime transportation industry: The case of master selection for embarking on board merchant ships, *Expert Systems with Applications; 36*(2), 1048–1060.

Chalk, P. (2008) *The Maritime Dimension of International Security: Terrorism, Piracy, and Challenges for the United States*. Santa Monica, CA: RAND Corporation.

Chaumet, G., Taillard, J., Sagaspe, P., Pagani, M., Dinges, D.F., Pavy-Le-Traon, A., Bareille, M-P., Rascol, O., and Philip, P. (2009) Confinement and sleep deprivation effects on propensity to take risks, *Aviation, Space, and Environmental Medicine; 80*(2), 73–80.

Chauvin, C. and Lardjane, S. (2008) Decision making and strategies in an interaction situation: Collision avoidance at sea, *Transportation Research Part F: Traffic Psychology and Behaviour; 11*(4), 259–269.

Chauvin, C. and Le Bouar, G. (2007) Occupational injury in the French sea fishing industry: A comparative study between the 1980s and today, *Accident Analysis and Prevention; 39*(1), 79–85.

Chikudate, N. (2009) If human errors are assumed as crimes in a safety culture: A lifeworld analysis of a rail crash, *Human Relations; 62*(9), 1267–1287.

Corbett, M.A. (2009) A drowsiness detection system for pilots: Optalert®, *Aviation, Space, and Environmental Medicine; 80*(2), 149–149.

Cullen, Lord. (2000) *The Ladbroke Grove Rail Inquiry*. Norwich, UK: HSE Books.

Dambier, M. and Hinkelbein, J. (2006) Analysis of 2004 German general aviation aircraft accidents according to the HFACS model, *Air Medical Journal; 25*(6), 265–269.

Darbra, R.M., Crawford, J.F.E., Haley, C.W., and Morrison, R.J. (2007) Safety culture and hazard risk perception of Australian and New Zealand maritime pilots, *Marine Policy; 31*(6), 736–745.

Dédale Asia Pacific (2007) *Guidelines for Rail Resource Management*. Albert Park, VIC: Dédale Asia Pacific.

Dekker, S.W.A. (2005) Why we need new accident models. In D. Harris and H.C. Muir (eds) *Contemporary Issues in Human Factors and Aviation Safety*. Aldershot, UK: Ashgate, 181–198.

Dickinson, C. (2005) Managing fatigue risks. In P.D. Bust and P.T. McCabe (eds) *Contemporary Ergonomics 2005*. London, UK: Taylor & Francis, 537–542.

Dijkstra, A. (2006) Safety management in airlines. In E. Hollnagel, D.D. Woods, and N. Leveson (eds) *Resilience Engineering: Concepts and precepts*. Aldershot, UK: Ashgate, 183–203.

Dorrian, J., Roach, G.D., Fletcher, A., and Dawson, D. (2006) The effects of fatigue on train handling during speed restrictions, *Transportation Research Part F: Traffic Psychology and Behaviour; 9*(4), 243–257.

Elvik, R. (2006) Economic deregulation and transport safety: A synthesis of evidence from evaluation studies, *Accident Analysis and Prevention; 38*(4), 678–686.

Evans, A.W. (2005) *Railways Risks, Safety Values and Safety Costs. Proceedings of the Institution of Civil Engineers: Transport; 158* (pp. 3–9). London: Institution of Civil Engineers.

Evans, A.W. (2007) Rail safety and rail privatisation in Britain, *Accident Analysis and Prevention; 39*(3), 510–523.

Evans, B., Glendon, A.I., and Creed, P.A. (2007) Development and initial validation of an aviation safety climate scale, *Journal of Safety Research; 38*(6), 675–682.

Evans, L., Frick, M.C., and Schwing, R.C. (1990) Is it safer to fly or drive? *Risk Analysis; 10*(3), 239–246.

Evans, L., Frick, M.C., and Schwing, R.C. (1991) Response to Barnett, *Risk Analysis; 11*(1), 17–17.

Fennell, D. (1988) *Report of the Official Inquiry into the Kings Cross Fire*. London, UK: HMSO.

Flin, R., O'Connor, P., and Crichton, M. (2008) *Safety at the Sharp End: A Guide to Non-technical Skills*. Aldershot, UK: Ashgate.

Folkard, S. and Åkerstedt, T. (2004) Trends in the risk of accidents and injuries and their implications for models of fatigue and performance, *Aviation, Space, and Environmental Medicine; 75*(Suppl. I), A161–A167.

Foulkes, J., Stapley, N., Laroya, S., Bowling, K., and Dickinson, C. (2005). Development and validation of the HMRI safety culture inspection model and toolkit. In P.D. Bust and P.T. McCabe (eds), *Contemporary Ergonomics 2005*. London, UK: Taylor & Francis, 603–607.

Fowler, T.G. and Sørgård, E. (2000) Modeling ship transportation risk, *Risk Analysis; 20*(2), 225–244.

Foyle, D.C. and Hooey, B.L. (eds) (2008) *Human Performance Modeling in Aviation*. Boca Raton, FL: CRC Press.

Gale, A. (2005) Human factors in airport baggage screening. In P.D. Bust and P.T. McCabe (eds) *Contemporary Ergonomics 2005*. London, UK: Taylor & Francis, 101–104.

Gigerenzer, G. (2004) Dread risk, September 11, and fatal traffic accidents, *Psychological Science; 15*(4), 286–287.

Gigerenzer, G. (2006) Out of the frying pan into the fire: Behavioral reactions to terrorism attacks, *Risk Analysis; 26*(2), 347–351.

Gilbert, Y., Kumpulainen, A., Lunabba, J., and Raivio, T. (2009) Transport of dangerous goods hubs as part of safe society—Land use planning and risk management, *Risk Management: Research on Risk Management, Assessment and Prevention; 46*(1), 5–6.

Glendon, A.I. (2007) Driving violations observed: An Australian study, *Ergonomics;* 50(8), 1159–1182.

Glendon, A.I. (2011a) Neuroscience and young drivers. In B. Porter (ed.), *Handbook of Traffic Psychology*. Amsterdam: Elsevier.

Glendon, A.I. (2011b) Traffic psychology: A state-of-the-art review. In P. Martin, F. Cheung, M. Kyrios, L. Littlefield, M. Knowles, B. Overmier, and J.M. Prieto (eds), *The IAAP Handbook of Applied Psychology*. Oxford: Wiley-Blackwell, 545–558.

Glendon, A.I., Clarke, S.G., and McKenna, E.F. (2006) *Human Safety and Risk Management* (2nd edition). Boca Raton, FL: CRC Press/Taylor & Francis.

Glendon, A.I., and Evans, B. (2007) Safety climate in Australian railways. In J.R. Wilson, B. Norris, T. Clarke, and A. Mills (eds) *People and Rail Systems: Human Factors at the Heart of the Railway*. Aldershot, UK: Ashgate, 409–417.

Glickman, T.S. and Erkut, E. (2007) Assessment of hazardous material risks for rail year safety, *Safety Science; 45*(7), 813–822.

González-Laxe, F., Prado-Dominguex, J., Martín-Palmero, F.G., and Dopico-Castro, J.A. (2005) How have European Union regulation tools on maritime safety developed after the *Prestige* catastrophe? A special reference to Spain, *Economic Analysis Working Papers, 4*(10), 1–17.

Greenberg, M.D., Chalk, P., Willis, H.H., Khilko, I., and Ortiz, D.S. (2006) *Maritime Terrorism: Risk and Liability*. Santa Monica, CA: RAND Corporation.

Gregory, J.M., Xie, X., and Mengel, S.A. (2004) SLEEP (Sleep Loss Effects on Everyday Performance) model, *Aviation, Space, and Environmental Medicine; 75*(Suppl. I), A125–A133.

Groeger, J.A., Clegg, B.A., and O'Shea, G. (2005) Conjunction in simulated railway signals: A cautionary note, *Applied Cognitive Psychology; 19*(8), 973–984.

Guedes Soares, C. and Teixeira, A.P. (2001) Risk assessment in maritime transportation, *Reliability Engineering and System Safety; 74*(3), 299–309.

Gunningham, N. (2004) *Best Practice Rail Safety Regulation*. Working Paper 31. Australian National University: National Research Centre for OHS Regulation.

Hagström, R. (1995) The acute psychological impact on survivors following a train accident, *Journal of Traumatic Stress; 8*(3), 391–402.

Hale, A.R. and Heijer, T. (2006a) Defining resilience. In E. Hollnagel, D.D. Woods, and N. Leveson (eds) *Resilience Engineering: Concepts and Precepts*. Aldershot, UK: Ashgate, 35–40.

Hale, A.R. and Heijer, T. (2006b) Is resilience really necessary: The case of railways. In E. Hollnagel, D.D. Woods, and N. Leveson (eds) *Resilience Engineering: Concepts and Precepts*. Aldershot, UK: Ashgate, 125–147.

Hale, A.R., Heijer, T., and Koornneef, F. (2003) Management of safety rules: The case of railways, *Safety Science Monitor*; Issue 1, Article III-2.

Hallmark, S.L., Veneziano, D.A., Falb, S., Pawlovich, M., and Witt, D. (2008) Evaluation of Iowa's graduated driver's licensing program, *Accident Analysis and Prevention; 40*(5), 1401–1405.

Hancock, P.A. (2009) On not getting hit: The science of avoiding collisions and the failures involved in that endeavour. In C. Castro (ed.) *Human Factors of Visual and Cognitive Performance in Driving*. Boca Raton, FL: CRC Press, 223–252.

Hansen, H.L., Nielsen, D., and Frydenberg, M. (2002) Occupational accidents aboard merchant ships, *Occupational and Environmental Medicine; 59*(2), 85–91.

Harley, R. and Cheyne, A.J.T. (2005) *Review of Human Factors Involved in Workplace Transport Accidents*. Research Report 398. Norwich, UK: Health & Safety Executive.

Harrald, J.R., Mazzuchi, T.A., Spahn, J., Van Dorp, R., Merrick, J., Shrestha, S., and Grabowski, M. (1998) Using system simulation to model the impact of human error in a maritime system, *Safety Science; 30*(1/2), 235–247.

Harvey, J.H., Town, J.P., and Yarkin, K.L. (1981) How fundamental is "the fundamental attribution error"? *Journal of Personality and Social Psychology; 40*(2), 346–349.

Håvold, J.I. (2000) Culture in maritime safety, *Maritime Policy and Management; 27*(1), 79–88.

Haworth, N. (2009) Interventions to reduce road trauma. In C. Castro (ed.) *Human Factors of Visual and Cognitive Performance in Driving*. Boca Raton, FL: CRC Press, 201–221.

Hayama, R., Higashi, M., Kawahara, S., Nakano, S., and Kumamoto, H. (2010) Fault-tolerant automobile steering based on diversity of steer-by-wire, braking and acceleration, *Reliability Engineering and System Safety; 95*(1), 10–17.

Hayes, J. (2006) *Safety Decision Making in High Hazard Organisations at the Production/Maintenance Interface—A Literature Review*. Working Paper 47. Australian National University: National Research Centre for OHS Regulation.

Health & Safety Executive (2005) *Level Crossings: Summary of Findings and Key Human Factors Issues*. Research Report 359. Norwich, UK: HSE Books.

Hedlund, J. (2007) Novice teen driving: GDL and beyond, *Journal of Safety Research; 38*(2), 259–266.

Helmreich, R.L., Merritt, A.C., and Wilhelm, J.A. (1999) The evolution of crew resource management training in commercial aviation, *International Journal of Aviation Psychology; 9*(1), 19–32.

Hetherington, C., Flin, R., and Mearns, K. (2006) Safety in shipping: The human element, *Journal of Safety Research; 37*(4), 401–411.

Hollnagel, E (2006) Resilience—The challenge of the unstable. In E. Hollnagel, D.D. Woods, and N. Leveson (eds) *Resilience Engineering: Concepts and Precepts*. Aldershot, UK: Ashgate, 10–17.

Hollnagel, E., Woods, D.D., and Leveson, N. (eds) (2006) *Resilience Engineering: Concepts and Precepts*. Aldershot, UK: Ashgate.

Hopkins, A. (1999) The limits of normal accident theory, *Safety Science; 32*(2/3), 93–102.

Hopkins, A. (2005) *Safety, Culture and Risk*. Sydney, Australia: CCH.

Hopkins, A. (2006) *Studying Organisational Cultures and their Effects on Safety*. Working Paper 44. The Australian National University, Canberra, Australia: National Research Centre for OHS Regulation.

Hopkins, A. (2007) *The Problem of Defining High Reliability Organisations*. Working Paper 51. The Australian National University, Canberra, Australia: National Research Centre for OHS Regulation.

Horlick-Jones, T. (2008) Reasoning about safety management policy in everyday terms: A pilot study in citizen engagement for the UK railway industry, *Journal of Risk Research; 11*(6), 697–718.

Horrey, W.J. (2009) On allocating the eyes: Visual attention and in-vehicle technologies. In C. Castro (ed.) *Human Factors of Visual and Cognitive Performance in Driving*. Boca Raton, FL: CRC Press, 151–166.

Hunton, J.H. and Rose, J.M. (2005) Cellular telephones and driving performance: The effects of attentional demands on motor vehicle crash risk, *Risk Analysis; 25*(4), 855–866.

International Labor Organization (2005) *Port Safety and Health Audit Manual*. Geneva: ILO.

International Union of Railways (2004) *"SafeCulture": A Method for Assessing Organisational Safety at Interfaces*. Paris, France: UIC.

Itoh, K., Andersen, H.B., and Seki, M. (2004) Track maintenance train operators' attitudes to job, organisation and management, and their correlation with accident/incident rate, *Cognition, Technology and Work; 6*(2), 63–78.

Jalonen, R. and Salmi, K. (2009) *Safety Performance Indicators for Maritime Safety Management*. Report TKK-AM-9. Helsinki University of Technology: Department of Applied Mechanics.

Jeffcott, S., Pidgeon, N., Weyman, A., and Walls, J. (2006) Risk, trust, and safety culture in UK train operating companies, *Risk Analysis; 26*(5), 1105–1121.

Johnson, M.L., Belenky, G., Redmond, D.P., Thorne, D.R., Williams, J.D., Hursh, S.R., and Balkin, T.J. (2004) Modulating the homeostatic process to predict performance during chronic sleep restriction, *Aviation, Space, and Environmental Medicine; 75*(Suppl. I), A141–A146.

Jones, C.B., Dorrian, J., Rajaratnam, S.M.W., and Dawson, D. (2005) Working hours regulations and fatigue in transportation: A comparative analysis, *Safety Science; 43*(4), 225–252.

Kauppi, A., Wikström, J., Hellström, P., Sandblad, B., and Andersson, A.W. (2005) Future train traffic control: Control by re-planning. In J.R. Wilson, B. Norris, T. Clarke, and A. Mills (eds), *Rail Human Factors: Supporting the Integrated Railway*. Aldershot, UK: Ashgate, 296–305.

Killgore, W.D.S., Grugle, N.L., Reichardt, R.M., Killgore, D.B., and Balkin, T.J. (2009) Executive functions and the ability to sustain vigilance during sleep loss, *Aviation, Space, and Environmental Medicine; 80*(2), 81–87.

Kim, D.S., Baek, D.H., and Yoon, W.C. (2010) Development and evaluation of a computer-aided system for analysing human error in railway operations, *Reliability Engineering and System Safety; 95*(2), 87–98.

Kirwan, B., Rodgers, M., and Schaefer, D. (2005) Human factors in air traffic management: Making a difference. In P.D. Bust and P.T. McCabe (eds) *Contemporary Ergonomics 2005*. London: Taylor & Francis, 59–63.

Klein, N. (2007) The Right of Visit and the 2005 Protocol on the Suppression of Unlawful Acts Against the Safety Of Maritime Navigation, *Denver Journal of International Law & Policy; 35*(2), 287–332.

Krulak, D.C. (2004) Human factors in maintenance: Impact on aircraft mishap frequency and severity, *Aviation, Space, and Environmental Medicine; 75*(5), 429–432.

LaPorte, T.R. (1996) High reliability organizations: Unlikely, demanding and at risk, *Journal of Contingencies and Crisis Management*; *4*(2), 60–71.

LaPorte, T.R. and Consolini, P.M. (1991) Working in practice but not in theory: Theoretical challenges of 'high-reliability organizations', *Journal of Public Administration Research and Theory; 1*(1), 19–47.

LaPorte, T.R. and Rochlin, G. (1994) A rejoinder to Perrow, *Journal of Contingencies and Crisis Management; 2*(4), 221–227.

Lappalainen, J. (2008) *Transforming Maritime Safety Culture: Evaluation of the Impacts of the ISM Code on Maritime Safety Culture in Finland*. Centre for Maritime Studies, University of Turku, Finland.

Lawton, R. (1998) Not working to rule: Understanding procedural violations at work, *Safety Science; 28*(2), 77–95.

Lawton, R. and Ward, N.J. (2005) A systems analysis of the Ladbroke Grove rail crash, *Accident Analysis and Prevention; 37*(2), 235–244.

Lees, M.N. and Lee, J. D. (2009) Enhancing safety by augmenting information in the driving environment. In C. Castro (ed.) *Human Factors of Visual and Cognitive Performance in Driving*. Boca Raton, FL: CRC Press, 167–185.

Légé, P. (2008) *Transport Safety and Security: A Methodological State of the Art*. Bron Cedex, France: Institut National de Recherche sur les Transports et leur Sécurité (INRETS).

Leveson, N., Dulac, N., Marais, K., and Carroll, J. (2009) Moving beyond normal accidents and high reliability organizations: A systems approach to safety in complex systems, *Organization Studies; 30*(2/3), 227–249.

Leveson, N., Dulac, N., Zipkin, D., Cutcher-Gershenfeld, J., Carroll, J., and Barrett, B. (2006) Engineering resilience into safety-critical systems. In E. Hollnagel, D.D. Woods, and N. Leveson (eds) *Resilience Engineering: Concepts and Precepts*. Aldershot, UK: Ashgate, 96–123.

Lewinsohn, J. (2005) Bailing out Congress: An assessment and defense of the Air Transportation Safety and System Stabilization Act of 2001, *The Yale Law Journal; 115*(2), 438–490.

Li, W-C. and Harris, D. (2006) Pilot error and its relationship with higher organizational levels: HFACS analysis of 523 accidents, *Aviation, Space, and Environmental Medicine; 77*(10), 1056–1061.

Li, W-C., Harris, D., Li, L-W., and Wang, T. (2009) The differences of aviation human factors between individualism and collectivism culture. In J.A. Jacko (ed.) *Human-computer Interaction, Part IV*. Berlin, Germany: Springer, 723–730.

Lim, K.Y. and Khoo, E. (2005) Using an animated simulation to assess the visibility of aerodrome information displays. In P.D. Bust and P.T. McCabe (eds) *Contemporary Ergonomics 2005*. London, UK: Taylor & Francis, 583–587.

Lindøe, P.H. (2007) Safe offshore workers and unsafe fishermen—A system failure? *Policy and Practice in Health and Safety; 5*(2), 25–39.

Lobb, B. (2006) Trespassing on the tracks: A review of railway pedestrian safety research, *Journal of Safety Research; 37*(4), 359–365.

Lois, P., Wang, J., Wall, A., and Ruxton, T. (2004) Formal safety assessment of cruise ships, *Tourism Management; 25*(1), 93–109.

López-Rousseau, A. (2005) Avoiding the death risk of avoiding a dread risk: The aftermath of March 11 in Spain, *Psychological Science; 16*(6), 426–428.

Loughran, C.G., Pillay, A., Wang, J., Wall, A., and Ruxton, T. (2002) A preliminary study of fishing vessel safety, *Journal of Risk Research; 5*(1), 3–21.

Lundin, T. (1995) Transportation disasters—A review, *Journal of Traumatic Stress; 8*(3), 381–389.

Macleod, N. (2005) *Building Safe Systems in Aviation: A CRM Developer's Handbook*. Aldershot, UK: Ashgate.

Macrae, C. (2007) *Interrogating the Unknown: Risk Analysis and Sensemaking in Airline Safety Oversight*. Discussion paper No 43. London School of Economics and Political Science: The Centre for Analysis of Risk and Regulation.

Macrae, C. (2009) Human factors at sea: Common patterns of error in groundings and collisions, *Maritime Policy Management; 36*(1), 21–38.

Marais, K., Dulac, N., and Leveson, N. (2004) *Beyond Normal Accidents and High Reliability Organizations: The Need for an Alternative Approach to Safety in Complex Systems*. Cambridge, MA: Massachusetts Institute of Technology.

McNamara, R., Allen, P., Wellens, B., and Smith, A. (2005) Fatigue at sea: Amendments to working time directives and management guidelines. In P.D. Bust and P.T. McCabe (eds), *Contemporary Ergonomics 2005*. London, UK: Taylor & Francis, 568–572.

Merritt, A. (2000) Culture in the cockpit: Do Hofstede's dimensions replicate? *Journal of Cross-Cultural Psychology; 31*(3), 283–301.

Moen, B-E. (2007) Determinants of safety priorities in transport—The effect of personality, worry, optimism, attitudes and willingness to pay, *Safety Science; 45*(8), 848–863.

Mok, S.C. and Savage, I. (2005) Why has safety improved at rail-highway grade crossings? *Risk Analysis; 25*(4), 867–881.

Muir, H.C., Thomas, L., and Wilson, R. (2005) Passenger safety in future very large transport aircraft. In D. Harris and H.C. Muir (eds) *Contemporary Issues in Human Factors and Aviation Safety*. Aldershot, UK: Ashgate, 101–113.

Murray-Tuite, P.M. (2008) Transportation network risk profile for an origin-destination pair: Security measures, terrorism, and target and attack method substitution, *Transportation Research Record: Journal of the Transportation Research Board; 2041*(1), 19–28.

National Institute for Occupational Safety and Health (2009) *Promoting Global Initiatives for Occupational Road Safety: Review of Occupational Road Safety Worldwide*. Washington, DC: NIOSH.

National Transport Commission (2007) *Fatigue Management for Rail Safety Workers: Draft Guidelines*. Canberra, Australia: NTC.

National Transport Commission (2009a) *National Policy Statement on the Recognition of Industry Developed Standards for Rail Safety: Policy Statement*. Canberra: NTC.

National Transport Commission (2009b) *Annual report 09*. Canberra, Australia: NTC.

Neyens, D.M., Donmez, B., and Boyle, L.N. (2008) The Iowa graduated driver licensing program: Effectiveness in reducing crashes of teenage drivers, *Journal of Safety Research; 39*(4), 383–390.

Nikandros, G. and Tombs, D. (2007) *Measuring Railway Signals Passed at Danger*. Paper presented at the 12th Australian Conference on Safety Critical Systems and Software, Adelaide. http://crpit.com/confpapers/CRPITV86Nikandros.pdf.

Nuutinen, M. and Norros, L. (2009) Core task analysis in accident investigation: Analysis of maritime accidents in piloting situations, *Cognition, Technology and Work; 11*(2), 129–150.

Oldenburg, M., Jensen, H-J., Latza, U., and Baur, X. (2009) Seafaring stressors aboard merchant and passenger ships, *International Journal of Public Health; 54*(2), 96–105.

O'Leary, M. (2002) The British Airways human factors reporting programme, *Reliability Engineering and System Safety; 74*(3), 245–255.

Oyarce, X.H. (2008) Consultations on maritime security and safety, *Environmental Policy and Law; 38*(5), 222–223.

Perrow, C. (1984) *Normal Accidents: Living with High-risk Technologies*. New York, NY: Basic Books.

Perrow, C. (1994) The limits of safety: The enhancement of a theory of accidents, *Journal of Contingencies and Crisis Management; 2*(4), 212–220.

Perrow, C. (1999) *Normal Accidents: Living with High-risk Technologies* (2nd Edition). Princeton, NJ: Princeton University Press.

Perrow, C. (2009) What's needed is application, not reconciliation: A response to Shrivastava, Sonpar and Pazzaglia (2009), *Human Relations; 62*(9), 1391–1393.

Pidgeon, N., Kasperson, R.E., and Slovic, P. (eds) (2003) *The Social Amplification of Risk*. Cambridge, UK: Cambridge University Press.

Piniella, F., Rasero, J.C., and Aragonés, J. (2005) Maritime safety control instruments in the era of globalisation, *Journal of Maritime Research; 2*(2), 19–39.

Psaraftis, H.N. (2002) Maritime safety: To be or not to be proactive, *World Maritime University Maritime Affairs Journal*; October, 1–12.

Psaraftis, H.N. (2006) Maritime safety in the post-*Prestige* era, *Marine Technology; 43*(2), 85–90.

Raby, M. and Lee, J.D. (2001) Fatigue and workload in the maritime industry. In P.A. Hancock and P.A. Desmond (eds) *Stress, Workload, and Fatigue*. Mahwah, NJ: Erlbaum, 566–580.

Rådbo, H., Svedung, I., and Andersson, R. (2008) Suicide prevention in railway systems: Application of a barrier approach, *Safety Science; 46*(5), 729–737.

Rail Safety and Standards Board (2003a) *Measurement of Safety Culture in the Rail Industry*. London, UK: RSSB.

Rail Safety & Standards Board (2003b) *Maximising Benefits from CCTV on the Railways—Executive summary*. London, UK: RSSB.

Rail Safety & Standards Board (2004a) *Risk Management Systems*. London, UK: RSSB.

Rail Safety & Standards Board (2004b) *Safety Critical Communications*. London, UK: RSSB.

Rail Safety & Standards Board (2004c) *A Survey of Current Practices in Safety-related Decision Making*. London, UK: RSSB.

Rail Safety & Standards Board (2005a) *Rail-Specific HRA Technique for Driving Tasks: User Manual*. London, UK: RSSB.

Rail Safety & Standards Board (2005b) *How Safe is Safe Enough? An Overview of How Britain's Railways take Decisions that Affect Safety*. London, UK: RSSB.

Rail Safety & Standards Board (2006a) *T059 Human factors Study of Fatigue and Shift Work. Main Report: Guidelines for the Management and Reduction of Fatigue in Train Drivers*. London, UK: RSSB.

Rail Safety & Standards Board (2006b) *T059 Human Factors Study of Fatigue and shift Work. Appendix 1: Working Patterns of Train Drivers—Implications for Fatigue and Safety*. London, UK: RSSB.

Rail Safety & Standards Board (2006c) *T059 Human Factors study of Fatigue and Shift Work. Appendix 2: Review of Coping Strategies to Mitigate Fatigue of Train Drivers*. London, UK: RSSB.

Rail Safety & Standards Board (2006d) *T059 Human Factors Study of Fatigue and Shift Work. Appendix 3: Rail Rostering Culture—Interview findings*. London, UK: RSSB.

Rail Safety & Standards Board (2006e) *T059 Human Factors Study of Fatigue and Shift Work. Appendix 4: Evaluation of Current Tools and Techniques used for Estimating Risks Associated with Shift Patterns*. London, UK: RSSB.

Raslear, T.G. and Coplen, M. (2004). Fatigue models as practical tools: Diagnostic accuracy and decision thresholds, *Aviation, Space, and Environmental Medicine; 75*(Suppl. I), A168–A172.

Rasmussen, J. (1997) Risk management in a dynamic society: A modelling problem, *Safety Science; 27*(2/3), 183–213.

Reason, J.T. (1997) *Managing the Risks of Organizational Accidents*. Aldershot, UK: Ashgate.

Reason, J.T. (2000) Human error: Models and management, *British Medical Journal; 320*(7237), 768–770.

Reason, J.T. (2008) *The Human Contribution: Unsafe Acts, Accidents and Heroic Recoveries*. Aldershot, UK: Ashgate.

Redelmeier, D.A. and Tibshirani, R.J. (1997) Association between cellular-telephone calls and motor vehicle collisions, *The New England Journal of Medicine; 336*(7), 453–458.

Regan, M.A., Lee, J.D., and Young, K. (eds) (2008) *Driver Distraction: Theory, Effects, and Mitigation*. Boca Raton, FL: CRC Press.

Rijpma, J.A. (2003) From deadlock to dead end: The normal accidents-high reliability debate revisited, *Journal of Contingencies and Crisis Management; 11*(1), 37–45.

RoadPeace (2008) *Global Road Deaths—Latest Estimates*. London, UK: RoadPeace.

Rochlin, G. (1993) Defining "high reliability" organizations in practice: A taxonomic prologue. In K. Roberts (ed.) *New Challenges to Understanding Organisations*. New York, NY: Macmillan, 11–32.

Rosa, E.A. (2005) Celebrating a citation classic—and more, *Organization & Environment; 18*(2), 229–234.

Rothengatter, W. (2010) Climate change and the contribution of transport: Basic facts and the role of aviation, *Transportation Research Part D; 15*(1), 5–13.

Safer Ports (2005) *Safer Ports Initiative Guide to Health and Safety Audits*. http://www.saferports.org.uk/spi_2.

Salmon, P. M., Stephan, K., Lenné, M., and Regan, M. (2005) *Cognitive Work Analysis and Road Safety: Potential applications in Road Transport*. In *Proceedings of the Road Safety Research Policing Education Conference 2005*. Wellington, New Zealand, November 14–16.

Sanne, J.M. (2008) Framing risks in a safety-critical and hazardous job: Risk-taking as responsibility in railway maintenance, *Journal of Risk Research; 11*(5), 645–657.

Sherwood Jones, B. and Moore, W. (2005) Slips, strips and falls in the maritime sector. In P.D. Bust and P.T. McCabe (eds) *Contemporary Ergonomics 2005*. London, UK: Taylor & Francis, 490–490.

Shrivastava, S., Sonpar, K., and Pazzaglia, F. (2009a) Normal accident theory versus high reliability theory: A resolution and call for an open systems view of accidents, *Human Relations; 62*(9), 1357–1390.

Shrivastava, S., Sonpar, K., and Pazzaglia, F. (2009b) Reconciliation can lead to better application: A rejoinder to Perrow (2009), *Human Relations; 62*(9), 1395–1398.

Sivak, M. and Flannagan, M.J. (2003) Flying and driving after the September 11 attacks, *American Scientist; 91*(1), 6–8.

Sivak, M., Weintraub, D.J., and Flannagan, M.J. (1991) Nonstop flying is safer than driving, *Risk Analysis; 11*(2), 145–148.

Srinivasan, S., Bhat, C.R., and Holguin-Veras, J. (2006) Empirical analysis of the impact of security perception on intercity mode choice: A panel rank-ordered mixed logit model, *Transportation Research Record: Journal of the Transportation Research Board; 1942*(1), 9–15.

Stanton, N.A. and Baber, C. (2008) Modelling of human alarm response times: A case study of the Ladbroke Grove rail accident in the UK, *Ergonomics; 51*(4), 423–440.

Stanton, N.A., Young, M., and McCaulder, B. (1997) Drive by wire: The case of driver workload and reclaiming control with adaptive cruise control, *Safety Science; 27*(2/3), 149–159.

Su, J. C., Tran, A.G.T.T., Wirtz, J.G., Langteau, R.A., and Rothman, A.J. (2009) Driving under the influence (of stress): Evidence of a regional increase in impaired driving and traffic fatalities after the September 11 terrorist attacks, *Psychological Science; 20*(1), 59–65.

Thébault, L. (2004) Maritime safety culture in Europe, *Managerial Law; 46*(1), 1–59.

Thomas, M. (2004) Predictors of threat and error management: Identification of core nontechnical skills and implications for training systems design, *International Journal of Aviation Psychology; 14*(2), 207–231.

Tiribelli, C. (2006) Time to update the 1988 Rome Convention For the Suppression of Unlawful Acts Against The Safety of Maritime Navigation, *Oregon Review of International Law; 8*(1), 133–156.

Toffoli, A., Lefèvre, J.M., Bitner-Gregerse, E., and Monbaliu, J. (2005) Towards the identification of warning criteria: Analysis of a ship accident database, *Applied Ocean Research; 27*(6), 281–291.

Trucco, P., Cagno, E., Ruggeri, F., and Grande, O. (2008) A Bayesian belief network modelling of organisational factors in risk analysis: A case study in maritime transportation, *Reliability Engineering and Systems Safety; 93*(6), 823–834.

Turner, K. and Agogino, A. (2007) Distributed Agent-based Air Traffic Flow Management, *Proceedings of the Sixth Joint Conference on Autonomous Agents and Multi-agent Systems*, 330–337.

Turner, B.A. and Pidgeon, N.F. (1997) *Man-made Disasters* (2nd Edition). Oxford, UK: Butterworth-Heinemann.

Turner, S.W., Thompson, J., and Rosser, R.M. (1995) The Kings Cross fire: Psychological reactions, *Journal of Traumatic Stress; 8*(3), 419–427.

US Department of Transportation (2006) *Validation and Calibration of a Fatigue Assessment Tool for Railroad Work Schedules: Summary report.* (DOT/FRA/ORD-06/21). Washington, DC: Federal Railroad Administration.

van der Geest, P J., Piers, M.A., de Jong, H.H., Finger, M., Slater, D.H., van Es, G.W.H., and van der Nat, G.J. (2003) *Aviation Safety Management in Switzerland: Recovering from the Myth of Perfection.* Report NLR-CR-2003-316. Amsterdam: Dutch National Aerospace Laboratory (NLR) and Swiss Federal Department of Environment, Traffic, Energy and Communication (DETEC).

Van der Schaaf, T.W. and Wright, L.B. (2005) The development of PRISMA-Rail: A generic root cause analysis approach for the railway industry. In J.R. Wilson, B. Norris, T. Clarke, and A. Mills (eds) *Rail Human Factors: Supporting the Integrated Railway*. Aldershot, UK: Ashgate, 413–421.

Van Dongen, H.P.A., Maislin, G., Mullington, J.M., and Dinges, D.F. (2003) The cumulative cost of additional wakefulness: Dose-response effects on neurobehavioral functions and sleep physiology from chronic sleep restriction and total sleep deprivation, *SLEEP; 26*(2), 117–126.

Van Dongen, H.P.A., Mott, M.S., Huang, J-K., Mollicone, D.J., McKenzie, F.D., and Dinges, D.F. (2007) Optimization of biomathematical model predictions for cognitive performance impairment in individuals: Accounting for unknown traits and uncertain states in homeostatic and circadian processes, *SLEEP; 30*(9), 1129–1143.

Vaughan, D. (1999) The dark side of organizations: Mistake, misconduct, and disaster, *Annual Review of Sociology; 25*, 271–305.

Vaughan, D. (2005) System effects: On slippery slopes, repeating negative patterns, and learning from mistakes? In W. Starbuck and F. Moshe (eds) *Organizations at the Limit: Lessons from the Columbia Disaster*. Oxford, UK: Blackwell, 41–59.

Weick, K.E. (1987) Organization culture as a source of high reliability, *California Management Review; 29*(2), 112–127.

Weick, K.E. and Roberts, K.H. (1993) Collective mind in organizations: Heedful interrelating on flight decks, *Administrative Science Quarterly; 38*(3), 357–381.

Weick, K.E. and Sutcliffe, K.M. (2001) *Managing the Unexpected: Assuring High Performance in an Age of Complexity*. San Francisco, CA: Jossey-Bass.

Weick, K.E., Sutcliffe, K.M., and Obstfeld, D. (1999) Organizing for high reliability: Processes of collective mindfulness. In R.I. Sutton and B.M. Staw (eds) *Research in Organizational Behavior Vol. 21*. Greenwich, CT: JAI Press, 81–123.

Wellens, B., McNamara, R., Allen, P., and Smith, A. (2005) Collisions and collision risk awareness at sea: Data from a variety of seafarers. In P.D. Bust and P.T. McCabe (eds) *Contemporary Ergonomics 2005*. London, UK: Taylor & Francis, 573–577.

Westrum, R. (1991) Cultures with requisite imagination. In J.A. Wise, V.D. Hopkin, and P. Stager (eds) *Verification and Validation of Complex Systems: Human Factors Issues*. New York, NY: Springer, 401–416.

Wilde, G.J.S. (1994) *Target Risk: Dealing with the Danger of Death, Disease and Damage in Everyday Decisions*. Toronto, Canada: PDE Publications.

Williams, C. (2007) *General Aviation Safety and Security Practices: A Synthesis of Airport Practice.* ACRP synthesis 3. Washington, DC: Transportation Research Board.

World Health Organization (2004) *World Report on Road Traffic Injury Prevention*. Geneva: WHO.

World Health Organization (2009) *Global Status Report on Road Safety: Time for Action*. Geneva: WHO.

Wreathall, J. (2006) Properties of resilient organizations: An initial view. In E. Hollnagel, D.D. Woods, and N. Leveson (eds) *Resilience Engineering: Concepts and Precepts*. Aldershot, UK: Ashgate, pp. 275–285.

Yercan, F., Fricke, D., and Stone, L. (2005) Developing a model on improving maritime English training for maritime transportation safety, *Education Studies; 31*(2), 213–234.

Young, M.S., Shorrock, S.T., and Faulkner, J.P.E. (2005) Taste preferences of transport safety investigators: Who doesn't like Swiss cheese? In P.D. Bust and P.T. McCabe (eds) *Contemporary Ergonomics 2005*. London, UK: Taylor & Francis, 393–396.

Zaidel, D.M. (1992) A modeling perspective on the culture of driving, *Accident Analysis and Prevention; 24*(6), 585–597.

Zekos, G.I. (2000) Safety at sea and air transport under EU law, *Managerial Law; 42*(3), 1–19.

Zhu, J. and Roy, S. (2003). MAC for dedicated short range communications in intelligent transport systems, *IEEE Communications Magazine;* December, 60–67.

CHAPTER **12**

Job Stress and Pesticide Exposure Among Immigrant Latino Farmworkers

JOSEPH G. GRZYWACZ, SARA A. QUANDT, AND THOMAS A. ARCURY

Introduction

Pesticide exposure poses a substantial health threat to farmworkers and their families. The US Environmental Protection Agency (US EPA) estimates 10,000 to 20,000 physician-diagnosed cases of acute pesticide exposure occur every year among the nearly 2 million farmworkers in the US. Acute pesticide exposure with high doses can have severe health consequences, including coma and death, whereas low dose exposure can result in skin irritation and gastrointestinal upset. As is frequently the case, however, official counts of physician diagnosed pesticide poisoning overlook the unknown number of farmworkers chronically exposed to low doses of pesticide. Chronic low dose exposure is particularly pernicious because of the unknown long-term health effects to the worker; asthma (Hoppin et al., 2008), diabetes (Montgomery et al., 2008), cancer (Clapp, Jacobs and Loechler, 2008), Parkinsons disease (Ascherio et al., 2006; Gorell et al., 1998; Kamel et al., 2007), Alzheimer's disease (Miller and O'Callaghan, 2008), sterility (Meeker et al., 2008), and spontaneous abortion (Frazier, 2007) are all believed to be partially caused by pesticide exposure. Moreover, pesticides are frequently and unknowingly carried into the home on farmworkers' bodies and clothes, thereby exposing family members, including young children, to these toxic agents.

Pesticide exposure among farmworkers is an environmental injustice (Arcury and Quandt, 2009). The vast majority of farmworkers in the US are Latino immigrants from Mexico: most recent estimates from the National Agricultural Workers Survey (NAWS) indicate that more than 80 percent of all agricultural crop workers are Latino, and 74 percent of crop workers are from Mexico et al., 2005). The burden of chronic low dose exposure is therefore borne, almost exclusively, by one ethnic group. Further, these workers and their families are frequently powerless: many are undocumented, most do not speak much less read English, and most have limited education. Farmworkers are voiceless and faceless.

Relatively little is known about pesticide exposure among farmworkers, particularly the low dose chronic exposure. Lack of understanding is multifaceted, but one reason is that pesticide exposure has not generally fallen under the purview of social and behavioral science. This oversight is problematic because individual behavior is the lynchpin of any strategy to eliminate pesticide exposure, apart from outright banning of pesticides in the agricultural industry. As with other domains of safety, the efficacy of any intervention fundamentally rests on workers' abilities and willingness to engage in advocated safety practices. Importantly, workers' abilities and willingness are shaped by a myriad of cognitive, psychological, social, and cultural factors.

The goal of this chapter is to enable social and behavioral scientists to engage in pesticide exposure research. This goal will be achieved by accomplishing four primary aims. First, we provide a basic background to understand both the farmworker population, and the inherent complexities of pesticide and pesticide exposure research. This background is not intended to cover the entire terrain of pesticide exposure research; rather, it is intended to lay a foundation. Next, we summarize what is known about pesticide exposure among farmworkers. Then, we will focus on the specific issue of job stress and its potential role in pesticide exposure. Finally, we outline high priority areas of needed research. It is important to note from the very outset that the complexity of pesticide exposure as an outcome requires an interdisciplinary effort: addressing the problems resulting from pesticide exposure requires that social and behavioral science theory and methods be partnered with expertise in environmental assessment along with analytic chemists and toxicologists.

Background

CONTEXTUAL BACKGROUND

Farmworkers

Farmworkers are not farmers: each occupation has distinct requirements as well as unique exposures and opportunities. Whereas successful farmers need to keep abreast of new developments in agriculture and frequently acquire this knowledge through post-secondary education and continuing education through cooperative extension programs, farmworkers learn through short-term on-the-job training. Farmers, regardless of the size of their operation, engage in business planning such as deciding which crops to plant; they monitor markets at the local, regional or national levels; they maintain a variety of records (for example, tax records, service records for equipment); and they may manage several employees. Farmworkers, by contrast, are frequently hired for discrete periods to perform specific tasks (for example, planting and harvesting). In short, whereas farmers can be characterized as "managers" or "business owners," farmworkers are generally laborers: they perform strenuous work under a variety of conditions for the sole purpose of production.

Several definitions of migrant farmworker and seasonal farmworker appear in the literature. These definitions have certain key elements in common related to type of work, period of employment, and changing residence to engage in work. Using the definitions found in federal statutes governing migrant health program funds, a *migrant farmworker* is an individual whose principal employment is in agriculture on a seasonal basis, and who, for purposes of employment, establishes a temporary home. The migration may be from farm to farm within a state, interstate, or international. Some migrant farmworkers receive an H2A visa to perform work in US agriculture for a temporary period lasting up to 12 months. In 2008, the US Department of Labor issued 173,103 H2A visas, the vast majority of which (163,695 or 94.5 percent), were issued to individuals from Mexico (Monger and Barr, 2009). A *seasonal farmworker* is an individual whose principal employment is in agriculture on a seasonal basis and who does not migrate. In both cases the definition extends to employment within the past 24 months. For many purposes, the immediate family members (spouse, children) of a farmworker who reside with the farmworker receive the same benefits as do the farmworker; for example, access to health care at migrant clinics and enrollment in migrant education programs.

Although the number of agricultural workers in the US is large, an accurate count of these workers is difficult to establish. Much depends on the definition of what constitutes an agricultural worker. The US Census of Agriculture (United States Department of Agriculture, 2007) indicates that in 2007, 2,636,509 agricultural workers were employed on 482,186 farms. These included 911,439 workers who worked 150 days or more, and 1,725,070 workers who worked 150 days or less; 98,135 farms reported having only workers who worked at least 150 days, 280,894 farms reported having only workers who worked less than 150 days, and 103,157 farms reported having workers who worked both 150 or more days and less than 150 days. A total of 38,784 farms reported hiring migrant farm labor.

Farmworkers are a medically underserved population at substantially greater risk than the general population for numerous environmental and occupational health problems (Arcury and Quandt, 2009; Villarejo, 2003; Villarejo and Baron, 1999). Elevated rates of health problems in the farmworker community are the result of many factors. Fully 25–60 percent of farmworkers live in poverty, depending on whether they are traveling alone or accompanied by family members (Carroll et al., 2005). Despite the existence of the Health Resources and Services Administration (HRSA)-funded Migrant Health system, most farmworkers (and their families) have difficulty accessing and receiving appropriate health care (Arcury and Quandt, 2007). Farmworkers' work environments frequently lack basic necessities like drinking water and cups or clean toilets (Whalley et al., 2009). Farmworker housing is typically poor quality, over-crowded, and does not meet minimal standards for habitation (Gentry et al., 2007; Vallejos, Quandt and Arcury, 2009). In short, the very individuals who bring food to the American table and market find themselves in a context that regularly threatens their mental and physical health and is devoid of basic human rights. Further, despite substantial advances since the 1960 airing of Edward R. Murrow's *Harvest of Shame* highlighted their plight, farmworkers remain a vulnerable population with few protections under the law (Wiggins, 2009).

Pesticides and pesticide exposure

Pesticides are defined by the US EPA as "any substance or mixture of substances intended for preventing, destroying, repelling, or mitigating any pest." There are two important features about this definition. First, pesticides are not restricted to substances intended for insects. "Pests" include insects as well as mice and other animals, unwanted plants (weeds), fungi, and microorganisms like bacteria and viruses. Common household products like bleach-based cleaners (which destroy bacteria and mildew), insect repellant, and products to rid yards of dandelions all fall under the definition of pesticides. Second, pesticides are designed for multiple purposes: they can be used to prevent or repel pests (for example, citronella candles), they can be used to destroy pests (for example, Roundup®), and they can be used to minimize damage by pests (for example, garden dusts to control blight). Importantly, this indicates that pesticides include a wide variety of discrete substances that are designed to achieve specific ends (for example, repel insects, kill weeds). The US EPA estimates that over 1 billion pounds of pesticides are used in the US annually, and those pesticides include nearly 10,000 chemicals (in various combinations) used in over 1,500 pesticide products (Kiely, Donaldson and Grube, 2004).

The US EPA established the Worker Protection Standard (1992) to help protect agricultural workers from pesticides. The Worker Protection Standard requires that, as of January 1, 1996, agricultural employers ensure that their employees receive basic pesticide safety information within five days of working in a field to which a restricted use pesticide has been applied in the previous 30 days. Content required in "basic" training conveys the idea that pesticides may be on or in plants workers come into contact with, in the soil, carried through irrigation water, or drifting in the air from nearby applications. Content also includes basic safety practices for workers to help prevent pesticides from entering their body, including: (1) following directions or signs about staying out of recently treated areas; (2) washing hands with soap and water before eating, drinking, using chewing gum or tobacco, or using the toilet; (3) wearing clothing such as long-sleeved shirts and pants that protects the body from pesticide residues; (4) bathing or showering with soap and water, shampooing hair, and putting on clean clothes immediately after work; (5) laundering work clothes separately from other clothes before wearing them again; and (6) washing immediately in the nearest clean water if pesticides are spilled or sprayed on the body and, as soon as possible, showering, shampooing, and changing into clean clothes. The employer is required to provide this information to workers in a manner they can understand, through the use of a handout or any combination of materials containing required basic information (for example, video). Employers are also required to be able to verify compliance with the required training.

Pesticide exposure is a deceptively simple concept (Hoppin et al., 2006). Pesticide exposure is simply any contact of the body with a pesticide (for detailed review see Hoppin et al., 2006). Unfortunately, despite the simplicity of definition, the science of exposure assessment is exceedingly complex. To understand exposure, the investigator must, at a minimum, know: (1) the agent that is involved; (2) the concentration of the agent; and (3) the length of contact time with the agent. As Hoppin and colleagues point out: "Therefore, exposure to pesticides requires not only the presence of the pesticide, but also that an individual come in contact with the pesticide at a specific time in a specific place" (p. 929). This information is rarely known when conducting pesticide exposure research with farmworkers. Farmworkers typically have no knowledge of the specific pesticides that have been applied to the fields. California and Florida are the only states in the country with laws requiring formal documentation and coordinated surveillance of the specific pesticides applied to specific tracts of land. Therefore, farmers or growers in states outside of California and Florida often fail to keep detailed written records of the pesticides applied to fields, much less their concentration or the amount of time waited before farmworkers entered the fields to perform their tasks. Thus, there is a virtual "perfect storm" of ambiguity when conducting pesticide exposure research with farmworkers in real-world contexts.

Nevertheless, farmworkers' exposure to pesticides is believed to be widespread. Thompson and colleagues (Thompson et al., 2008) reported that 30 to 90 percent of adults in farmworker families had detectable levels of organophosphate pesticides in their urine. Specifically, in samples collected in 2004, 29.2 percent of adults had detectable levels of one dialkylphosphate urinary pesticide metabolite, dimethylphosphate (DMP), while 92.6 percent and 55.0 percent of adults had detectable levels of dimethylthiophosphate (DMTP) and dimethyldithiophosphate (DMDTP), respectively. In the most comprehensive study of farmworker pesticide exposure to date, Arcury and colleagues (2009a) documented that over three-quarters (78.2 percent) of farmworkers (N=287) had metabolites of one or more of 14 distinct pesticides in their urine during the 2007 agricultural season, suggesting virtually ubiquitous exposure to known neurotoxins. Further analyses of these same data suggest that farmworkers' exposure to pesticides varies across the agricultural season (Figure 12.1). Early in the agricultural season at least one organophosphate (OP) pesticide metabolite was found in the urine of over one-third of farmworkers. By August, two or more OP metabolites were detected in over one-half of urine samples provided by farmworkers. These data suggest that: (1) a large proportion of farmworkers are exposed to OP pesticides; (2) farmworkers are exposed to a variety of OP pesticides; and (3) a sizeable proportion of farmworkers are repeatedly exposed to OP pesticides.

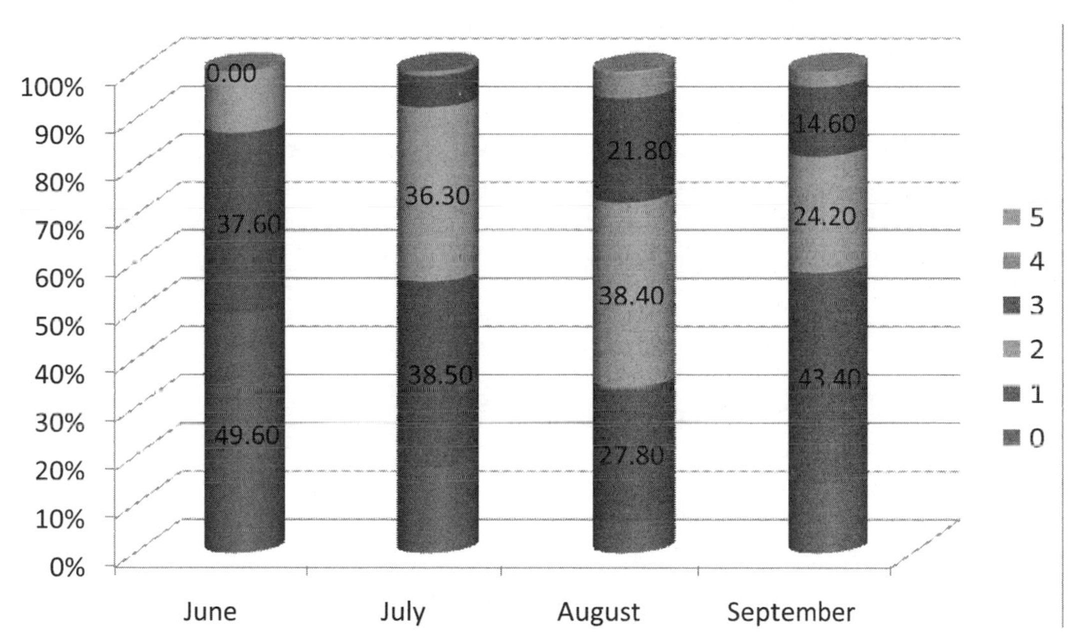

Figure 12.1 Percent of farmworkers in North Carolina with one or more detectable levels of organophosphorus pesticide metabolites across the 2007 agricultural season (Grzywacz et al., 2009, November)

Urinary metabolites provide evidence that farmworkers (or their family members) have come into contact with pesticides; however, there are challenges in interpreting these data. Pesticides currently available are non-persistent, meaning they are metabolized and eliminated from the body within 72 hours: they do not accumulate. This chemical feature raises difficulties for research design because the number and interval of assessments needed to capture "typical" exposure is not obvious. An event-based sampling procedure would be ideal, but this is only possible if researchers know when pesticides are applied. Next, the presence of urinary pesticide metabolites provides no information about the source of the exposure: it is not clear if the individual was exposed, (1) while performing work in the fields; (2) through personal use of various pesticides around the home; (3) via the consumption of unwashed fruits or vegetables obtained through the marketplace; or (4) because pesticides are simply endemic in the environment (for example, accumulation of pesticide residues in homes). Indeed, Arcury and colleagues (Arcury et al., 2009b) finding that greater than 97 percent of farmworkers had the metabolite associated with parathion in their urine throughout the agricultural season suggests that exposure may not be not limited to contact while working in the fields.

Quandt and colleagues (2006) conducted a systematic qualitative review of the literature to construct a comprehensive conceptual framework for understanding farmworkers' exposure to pesticides. Their conceptual framework contrasts proximal and distal determinants of pesticide exposure (Figure 12.2). Those proximal to pesticide exposure—that is, the immediate determinants of exposure—are generally *behaviors* practiced either by farmworkers in the workplace or at home. These include (in the workplace) use of personal protective equipment (PPE) and field sanitation, as well as behaviors performed in the home or place of residence, such as laundry practices. These proximal factors are themselves determined by predictors considered more distal to the exposure. These include *environmental conditions* at work (for example, safety training), at home (for example, number of farmworkers in residence), and in the larger community (for example, total farmland treated with pesticides) which are presumed to affect exposure through individual behavior. The association of environmental conditions with individual behaviors relevant to pesticide exposure is moderated by *psychosocial factors*, including personality attributes, values, beliefs, and knowledge held by farmworkers. Although their comprehensive framework may suggest a rich literature of known "determinants" of pesticide exposure, Quandt and colleagues (2006) concluded that "...the research connecting characteristics of workers' environments and behaviors with actual measures of pesticide exposure [among farmworkers] is meager" (p. 950).

JOB STRESS AND PESTICIDE EXPOSURE

We take a transactional perspective (Lazarus and Folkman, 1984) on job stress wherein job or job-related situations are appraised and interpreted as threatening by the job incumbent, farmworkers in this case. Job or job-related situations may be physical in nature, such as crowded living arrangements, forecasts of consecutive 90 degree temperatures in the fields or, conversely, persistent rain and subsequent inability to work and lost wages. Other job or job-related situations are social or psychological in nature such as the physical separation from family and community for extended periods of time and corresponding feelings of isolation that many farmworkers confront, being the target of discriminatory practices on the job or because one is a "migrant," or living with the ongoing fear of potential deportation if one lacks legal work documents like an H2A visa. Hovey (2000; Hovey and Magaña, 2000; 2002) has delineated the scope of job and job-related stressors inherent in farmworkers daily lives.

The transactional view of job stress fits squarely into the pesticide exposure framework provided by Quandt and colleagues (2006). Although not specifically addressed in the original conceptualization, job stress could be subsumed within the "Work Environment" component of the conceptual framework. Indeed, Quandt and colleagues highlight the potential role of the "organization of work" in creating variation in pesticide exposure, and their narrative references the potential influence of job demands for pesticide exposure. Likewise, personal attributes and characteristics involved in stress appraisal, such as coping style or available supports, were not explicitly addressed in their framework; nevertheless, they could be subsumed under the "Psychosocial Factors" element of Quandt and colleagues' framework.

There are few empirical data directly linking job stress to pesticide exposure. Grzywacz and colleagues (2010) reported results implicating physical job stressors with pesticide exposure. That is, under conditions of low job control, the odds of detecting two of the six dialkylphosphate urinary pesticide metabolites increased with every one unit increase in the level of physical exertion required. These researchers have also reported results suggesting that psychological stressors may also be associated with elevated levels of pesticide exposure (Grzywacz et al., 2009). That is "work intensity," operationalized with four items from the job demands sub-scale of the Job Content Questionnaire (Karasek and Theorell, 1990) but modified to reflect work in the past week (for example, "In the *past week*, including today, how many days did your job require you to work very fast?"), was associated with greater number of detections of organophosphorus (OP) pesticides in the later portion of the agricultural season. A comparable association between work intensity and exposure was not observed in the early portion of the season. Similarly, greater documentation stress, operationalized using items from the Migrant Farmworker Stress Inventory (Hovey and Magaña, 2002a), was associated with greater detection of OP pesticides at the beginning of the agricultural season (June); however, greater documentation stress was associated with fewer detections of OP pesticides at the end of the agricultural season (September). Although they are preliminary, these results suggest that both physical and psychological stressors may contribute to pesticide exposure among farmworkers.

The few studies linking job stress with pesticide exposure are buttressed by a more substantial literature linking job stress to other occupational health outcomes, including unintentional injury and near miss events. Job stress has been associated with greater injury risk within specific industries, such as construction (Goldenhar, Williams and Swanson, 2003), coal mining (Ghosh, Bhattacherjee and Chau, 2004), manufacturing (Kim et al., 2009; Nakata et al., 2006), and health care (Salminen et al., 2003). Evidence from more occupationally heterogeneous cohort studies suggests that job stress poses independent risk for unintentional injuries or accidents while on the job (Swaen et al., 2004). Meta-analysis of data from these and other studies suggest a moderate correlation (r = 0.33 adjusted for attenuation due to measurement, 95 percent confidence interval -0.54 to -0.11) between accidents and injury and job stress assessed at the group level group-level (Christian et al., 2009).

Mechanisms linking job stress with pesticide exposure

While the Quandt model provides a conceptual framework for linking job stress with pesticide exposure, it does not provide a theoretical explanation for an association. Like the broader literature linking stress with occupational injury, there are at least two possible theoretical explanations for associations observed between job stress and pesticide exposure. The first possible explanation, referred to here as the "production hegemony" hypothesis, contends that stressors promote behaviors that place farmworkers at greater risk of being exposed to pesticides. For example, training required by the Worker Protection Standard of the US EPA instructs farmworkers that they can protect themselves from pesticide exposure by wearing long-sleeved shirts and pants while working the fields. This recommendation, however, can be difficult to follow in the context of consecutive 90 degree temperatures with high humidity. In this case, the physical stressor (extreme temperatures) "causes" behavior that places the farmworker at elevated risk of being exposed to pesticides (for example, wearing short sleeves or shirtless). Farmworkers' ability to engage in other behaviors advocated by the Worker Protection Standard such as frequent hand washing can be undermined by psychological production stressors: compressed workweeks following periods of rain may encourage safety shortcuts in order to get "caught up" on the work, or crew leaders without sufficient manpower may push workers to get the work done as fast as possible, thereby allowing little time for workers to wash their hands.

Common across each illustration of the production hegemony hypothesis is the notion that task completion takes priority over personal safety. Although there are no data currently available to test the production hegemony hypothesis linking job stress to pesticide exposure, the plausibility of this explanation is supported by strands of related evidence. Theoretically, Wickens' (1996) notion of "tunneling" suggests that workers focus on the highest priority task, typically production, when under stress and this focus comes at the expense of lower priority tasks such as safety. Turning to empirical strands of evidence, the Cullen report on the Piper Alpha disaster highlighted the dominant culture of poor safety compliance, particularly in the face of elevated production expectations. Thu (1998), studying farm owners and operators, explicitly argued that the narrow temporal window for growing and harvesting and other stressors associated with farming lead farmers to minimize safety standards in favor of production.

Consistent with Thu's (1998) argument and more specific to farmworkers and pesticide exposure, Whalley and colleagues (2009) reported that working in a field where pesticides were recently applied was more common among workers who characterized their boss as being primarily interested in the getting the job done fast and cheap as opposed to workers who reported having a boss that is committed to safety (33.6 percent versus 17.9 percent, respectively). The notion that workers would put themselves at risk for potential pesticide exposure is also consistent with evidence suggesting that workers and growers do not view pesticides as posing substantial personal risk (Arcury et al., 2001; Rao et al., 2004), whereas the importance of productivity and subsequent earning potential hold high salience. Indeed, Elmore and Arcury quote one farmworker from their study who said: "Sometimes I worry about these chemicals affecting me later on. But I have to work" (p. 156). The "need" to work is driven primarily by the fact that the ability to send money to family in their country of origin is among the primary factors pulling immigrant Latinos into farm work (Chavez, 1992).

The second major explanation linking job stress to pesticide exposure is the "distraction" hypothesis. The distraction hypothesis contends that the psychological sequela of job stress leaves workers cognitively unable to protect themselves from pesticide exposure, particularly job stressors appraised as threatening and for which inadequate coping resources are available. For example, the physical separation of farmworkers from family members and community is a persistent stressor for virtually every farmworker who migrates without his/her family (Hovey and Magaña, 2002b). Preoccupation with the stressor or the anxiety that frequently accompanies the stress (Grzywacz et al., 2006; Walter et al., 2002) can result in oversights of advocated safety-related behavior, either on the job (for example, use of appropriate personal protective equipment, frequent hand-washing) or following the workday (for example, taking a shower immediately after work). An important distinction between the production hegemony and distraction hypotheses is that of volition. Under the production hegemony hypothesis workers realize they are not following advocated safety practices, but the behavior is justified in terms of priorities. By contrast, under the distraction hypothesis workers may not be aware of the safety lapse.

As with the production hegemony hypothesis, researchers have not yet published data linking job stressors with pesticide exposure via the distraction hypothesis. However, strands of literature suggest the plausibility of the idea. Arguing from a limited resources perspective, Kanfer and Ackerman (1989) argue the human mind can only process so much information; if a worker is processing emotions such as feelings of loneliness and isolation, he/she has fewer cognitive resources to enable processing other activities such as recognizing safety hazards and taking appropriate precautions. In terms of empirical support, Cullen and Hammer (Cullen and Hammer, 2007) interpreted an observed association between greater worker strain (that is, family-to-work conflict) and poorer compliance with safety behavior in terms of the distraction hypothesis. Beseler and Stallones (2003) interpreted an observed association between elevated depressive symptoms and poorer adherence to safety practices among farmers in terms of the distraction hypothesis. More specific to immigrant workers, researchers have commented that fatigue and distraction are among the mechanisms linking job and job-related stressors confronted by immigrant Latino laborers, including farmworkers, with elevated experiences of accidents and injuries (Salazar et al., 2004; Walter et al., 2002).

Modifiers of the job stress-pesticide exposure relationship

Consistent with the underlying transactional model of stress, there are a substantial number of possible modifiers of job stress-pesticide exposure association. The likelihood of modifiers is also apparent in Quandt and colleagues' (2006) model of pesticide exposure among farmworkers. Some modifiers of the job stress-pesticide exposure association are individual differences. Quandt and colleagues, for example, point to the salience of between-individual differences in knowledge of pesticide risks and advocated safety practices. Although the US EPA's Worker Protection Standard requires that all agricultural workers receive pesticide safety training, evidence indicates that many workers do not receive this training (Arcury et al., 1999; Whalley et al., 2009), and workers frequently do not understand training they receive. Whalley and colleagues (2009), for example, reported that at least 25 percent of workers receiving training understood "none or some" of the training while fewer than 50 percent understood all of the content. Acculturation is another between-person factor that may shape adherence to pesticide safety behavior. Latinos frequently hold a cultural model of illness informed by precepts of humoral medicine, particularly notions that illness arises when "hot" and "cold" elements are combined (Weller, 1983; Rubel, 1960). Showering after work, a behavior advocated in Worker Protection Standard training as a way to minimize pesticide exposure, represents an activity that conflicts with aspects of humoral medicine. That is, the body is metaphorically "hot" following physical labor and water is metaphorically "cold;" precepts of humoral medicine therefore undermine advocated behavior because workers may believe that showering immediately after work poses greater risk for illness than does not showering or delaying showering until the body "cools down" (Quandt et al., 1998). Thus, to the extent that it weakens the strength of humoral medicine-based beliefs, acculturation may modify the link between job stress and pesticide exposure.

The notion of control, broadly conceived, is another between-individual factor that may modify associations between job stress and pesticide exposure among farmworkers (Barling and Kelloway, 1996). Work status or documentation provides a general indicator of control: individuals with an H2A visa allowing them legal entrance into the US may be better equipped to exercise rights to personal safety compared to workers who are undocumented. Recent evidence indicating that farmworkers lacking documentation are less likely to receive basic pesticide safety training (Kandel and Donato, 2009) partially supports the idea that worker status may modify the job stress-pesticide exposure association. More specific aspects of worker control, such as the ability to decide how job-related tasks are implemented and carried out can also affect the job stress-pesticide exposure association. Indeed, Grzywacz and colleagues (2010) reported evidence consistent with such a buffering effect. This possibility recently received limited empirical support when Grzywacz and colleagues found that under conditions of low job control, the odds of detecting two of the six dialkylphosphate urinary pesticide metabolites increased with each unit increase in physical exertion required of the farmworker. By contrast, under conditions of high control there was a null or negative association of physical exertion with pesticide exposure.

Other possible modifiers of the job stress-pesticide exposure association are contextual. A class of potential association modifiers revolves around the adequacy of farmworker housing. If the farm owner or farm labor contractor does not provide housing, farmworkers are faced with acquiring their own housing on the private market in rural agricultural areas with limited available rental housing. In either scenario, the housing quality of farmworkers is poor (Gentry et al., 2007; Vallejos, Quandt and Arcury, 2009), characterized by crowding, poor structural integrity, and the absence of basic showering and laundering facilities, thereby providing a constellation of forces that could modify the link between job stress and exposure. For example, associations between job stress and pesticide exposure due to production hegemony are likely exaggerated in contexts where living conditions do not allow farmworkers to shower immediately after work because there are not enough showers to accommodate the workers. Similarly, associations due to the psychological distraction may be further exaggerated when farmworker housing is located adjacent to fields where pesticides are being applied and housing residents do not close windows or are unable to because of structural defects.

The safety climate of the farm operation provides another salient contextual feature that modifies the putative effects of job stress on pesticide exposure. Rao and colleagues (2004) and others (Quandt et al., 1998) have documented that farm owners, farm operators, labor contractors, and county extension workers believe that farmworkers have limited potential for pesticide exposure. This belief can permeate every aspect of how a farm establishment is run or the types of messages farmworkers receive, including the level of enthusiasm owners/operators put into the Worker Protection Standard training, the provision of requisite materials for field sanitation (for example, provision of soap, water, and paper towels to support frequent hand washing), and encouragement of workers to take necessary precautions to prevent pesticide exposure. The potential of the safety climate as a possible modifier of the association between job stress and pesticide exposure is supported by evidence indicating that individuals who report a climate more conducive to safety also report greater adherence to behaviors advocated by the US EPA's Worker Protection Standards (Whalley et al., 2009).

FUTURE RESEARCH OPPORTUNITIES

The possibilities for future social and behavioral science research focused on pesticide exposure among farmworkers are virtually unlimited. Indeed, the current literature is best described as nascent: virtually any competently conceived and implemented study will contribute to the literature. Nevertheless, in this section we outline high priority areas for job stress and pesticide exposure research. Before doing so, it is important to highlight some of the key challenges of conducting pesticide exposure research.

Research challenges

Difficulties conducting job stress and pesticide exposure research among immigrant farmworkers fall into two general categories. The first category of challenges arises from the unique study population. Arcury and colleagues (2006), however, provide a cogent review of the challenges of conducting research with Latino farmworkers. Farmworkers are an under-researched, vulnerable population (Arcury and Quandt, 2007; Villarejo, 2003), a fact that raises several special ethical considerations including appropriate conventions for insuring participants' full understanding of study procedures, challenges to realizing "informed consent," as well as potential for inadvertent coercion (Cooper et al., 2004). Communication is a challenge. Research instruments and forms can be translated into Spanish, but the extent to which the translations are appropriate may be highly variable. This was recently demonstrated in a study using cognitive interview methods with farmworkers (Grzywacz et al., 2009): the investigators found that farmworkers had substantial difficulty interpreting and responding to Spanish translation of the K-6, a commonly used instrument for assessing psychological distress (Kessler et al., 2002). There are no pre-existing lists of farmworkers that can be used to create a sampling frame for selecting and recruiting potential study participants: researchers need to develop alternative methods for designing study samples representative of the farmworker population. Moreover, many farmworkers prefer to remain inconspicuous and not participate in research because of issues surrounding documentation status. Farmworkers are a highly mobile study population raising difficulties for tracking and retention in research studies.

The second category of research challenges arises from the complexities of capturing and measuring pesticide exposure. The challenges of exposure assessment and biomonitoring of pesticides have been described in detail elsewhere (Barr et al., 2006; Hoppin et al., 2006). Among the fundamental challenges is the limited number of direct measures of pesticide exposure. Measuring pesticide exposure via environmental assessments (for example, surface, handwipe, or air sampling) is valuable because research can identify specific potential sources of specific pesticides, but it is more appropriately described as measures of exposure potential, rather than exposure per se. Similarly, biomonitoring via serum cholinesterase or urine samples is useful for determining whether a study participant has been exposed to pesticides, but the source of exposure or the amount of exposure is not discernable from these measures. Further, in the specific case of biomonitoring, the fact that most pesticides are metabolized with 72 hours of exposure provides a narrow window for measurement. It is therefore exceptionally challenging to characterize farmworkers' typical exposure to pesticides and to link that exposure with specific antecedents like job stress. Readers are encouraged to consult definitive descriptions of the challenges involved in measuring pesticide exposure (for example, Barr et al., 2006; Hoppin et al., 2006) and to work closely with experienced individuals and labs when designing their study.

Research opportunities

The first research priority in building the job stress and pesticide exposure literature is simply to design studies that delineate the job stressors confronted by farmworkers. The classic models of job stress, such as the demand-control model (Karasek and Theorell, 1990) or the effort-reward imbalance model (Siegrist, 1996; Siegrist, Siegrist and Weber, 1986), are not well suited for occupation-specific studies because of restricted range of key job-related attributes (Kristensen, 1995). Further, the extent to which key job-related attributes are relevant in the context of agricultural work remains uncertain. Indeed, in one of the few applications of job stress theory in a farmworker population, Grzywacz, Quandt and Arcury (2008) noted that psychological job demands may be less relevant to farmworker health than physical demands such as ergonomic load, physical exertion, or working in hazardous conditions. A similar observation was made with immigrant Latinos in poultry processing (Grzywacz et al., 2007). Thus, the extent to which instruments frequently used to measure job stress, such as the Job Content Questionnaire (Karasek and Theorell, 1990) capture farmworkers' most poignant job stressors or the stressors with the potential to shape pesticide exposure is questionable.

The Migrant Farmworker Stress Inventory (MFWSI) (Hovey and Seligman, 2006) offers promise for building a farmworker job stress literature. The MFWSI is a 39-item instrument developed based on results of qualitative research undertaken with Latino farmworkers. The instrument has been successfully used with farmworker samples across the US (Hiott et al., 2008; Hovey and Magaña, 2002b; Kim-Godwin and Bechtel, 2004; Magaña and Hovey, 2003), and is consistently associated with indicators of mental health such as depressive symptoms and anxiety. Nevertheless, the MFWSI would benefit from additional refinement, as well as more extensive psychometric evaluation and validation. In particular for this chapter is the need to clearly differentiate job stressors assessed in the MFWSI (for example, availability of drinking water) from those that are job related (for example, crowded housing), and those that are not unique to farmworkers (for example, stressors accompanying migration). Such research is essential for differentiating stressors inherent in farmwork from more ambient stressors confronted by immigrants in general or other marginalized populations. Psychometric studies of the MFWSI based on item response theory and methods would also be valuable for insuring solid measurement of key stressors.

Once job and job-related stressors relevant to farmworkers are identified, the next step in building a critical mass of studies to determine if job stress is associated with pesticide exposure. Because of the complexities involved in measuring pesticide exposure, researchers are encouraged to avoid simple cross-sectional designs where one stress assessment and one measure of pesticide exposure is obtained from each participant at the same time. A more appropriate design would involve collecting measures of recent job stress (for example, in the past week) and then collecting first morning void urine sample the following day and then at 48-hour intervals over the next 10 to 14 days. Collection of urine samples over environmental assessments is advocated because urine samples confirm that pesticides have entered the body. Repeated 48-hour assessments are recommended because of the rapid metabolism of pesticides, and the recommended 10–14 day observation period provides an assessment of pesticide exposure that is proximal to reports of recent stressors. Finally, fielding of this type of study should occur during a period in the agricultural season when pesticides are being used.

Research delineating the role of job and job-related stress with pesticide-specific safety behaviors is also needed. There are several classes of research in the domain that are needed. First, research is needed to identify the most salient job-related stressors relevant to safety behavior. Ideally, this research would study a wide array of plausible stressors and safety behaviors to begin mapping explicit linkages between job stress and safety, as well as to identify those stressors with the strongest effect on safety behavior. Second, research is needed to delineate why job stress affects pesticide safety behavior. That is, does job stress contribute to unsafe behavior because workers are not given the opportunity (that is, the production hegemony hypothesis) or because it contributes to safety errors (that is, the distraction hypothesis)? Although this is probably a false dichotomy, research is needed to understand the mechanisms by which job stress affects behavior. Finally, research is needed to understand what conditions under which job stress contributes to pesticide exposure. In some cases the variability will be due to contextual circumstances, but in other cases variability will be due to individual factors.

Ultimately, research is needed linking all of these pieces of the proposed job stress and pesticide exposure model outlined above. Social and behavioral scientists interested in fielding such a study are encouraged to build an interdisciplinary team of investigators. Occupational Health Psychologists, for example, offer key conceptual insights about the putative linkages between job stress, safety behavior, and subsequent pesticide exposure, and they are well equipped to evaluate measures of several key concepts. However, occupational health psychologists are typically not well-versed in the intricacies of biomonitoring and the factors affecting pesticide metabolism. Expertise in toxicology and analytic chemistry are needed to ensure the extraction of high-quality lab analyses of biological samples and appropriate multivariate modeling when testing associations between indicators of job stress and measures of pesticide exposure. Similarly, expertise in field methods involving hard-to-reach study participants, like farmworkers, is needed, as is expertise in cross-cultural research. In short, although social and behavioral scientists are sorely needed to advance understanding of pesticide exposure among farmworkers and to develop effective intervention strategies, social and behavioral scientists cannot accomplish this work alone.

Conclusions

Pesticide exposure among Latino farmworkers is a pressing occupational health problem that, heretofore, has been largely overlooked by social and behavioral scientists. This chapter was designed to encourage and enable social and behavioral scientists' involvement in this important domain of research. Job stress, broadly defined, likely plays a critical role in understanding pesticide exposure among farmworkers, yet this domain of research remains wide open for empirical study. Social and behavioral scientists need to apply their theoretical understanding of occupational stress and worker safety behavior to pesticide exposure, and they need to apply their expertise in sampling theory, measurement, and psychometrics, and analysis to build the knowledge base essential for developing effective interventions. This chapter provided the background needed for social and behavioral scientists to enlist their expertise in understanding pesticide exposure among Latino farmworkers. All that remains is scientists' willingness to embrace and overcome the complex challenges of pesticide exposure research.

Acknowledgements

This research was supported by a grant from the National Institute for Environmental Health Science (R01- ES008739). The authors appreciate the collaboration of Greene County Health Care, Inc., Snow Hill, NC, Columbus County Community Health Center, Inc., Whiteville, NC, and Student Action with Farmworkers, Durham, NC.

References

Arcury, T.A., Grzywacz, J.G., Chen, H., Vallejos, Q.M., Galvan, L., Whalley, L.E., Isom, S., Barr, D.B., and Quandt, S.A. (2009a) Variation across the agricultural season in organophosphorus pesticide urinary metabolite levels for Latino farmworkers in eastern North Carolina: Project design and descriptive results, *American Journal of Industrial Medicine;* 52(7), 539–550.

Arcury, T.A., Grzywacz, J.G., Isom, S., Whalley, L.E., Vallejos, Q.M., Chen, H., Galvan, L., Barr, D.B., and Quandt, S.A. (2009b) Seasonal variation in the measurement of urinary pesticide metabolites among Latino farmworkers in eastern North Carolina, *International Journal of Occupational and Environmental Health;* 15(4), 339–350.

Arcury, T.A., and Quandt, S.A. (2007) Delivery of health services to migrant and seasonal farmworkers, *Annual Review of Public Health;* 28, 345–363.

Arcury, T.A. and Quandt, S.A. (2009) *Latino Farmworkers in the Eastern United States: Health, Safety, and Justice*. New York, NY: Springer.

Arcury, T.A., Quandt, S.A., Austin, C.K., Preisser, J., and Cabrera, L.F. (1999) Implementation of EPA's Worker Protection Standard training for agricultural laborers: An evaluation using North Carolina data, *Public Health Reports;* 114(5), 459–468.

Arcury, T.A., Quandt, S.A., Barr, D.B., Hoppin, J.A., McCauley, L., Grzywacz, J.G., and Robson, M. G. (2006) Farmworker exposure to pesticides: Methodologic issues for the collection of comparable data, *Environmental Health Perspectives;* 114(6), 923–928.

Arcury, T.A., Quandt, S.A., Cravey, A.J., Elmore, R.C., and Russell, G.B. (2001) Farmworker reports of pesticide safety and sanitation in the work environment, *American Journal of Industrial Medicine;* 39(5), 487–498.

Ascherio, A., Chen, H., Weisskopf, M.G., O'Reilly, E., McCullough, M.L., Calle, E.E., Schwarzschild, M.A., and Thun, M.J. (2006) Pesticide exposure and risk for Parkinson's disease, *Annals of Neurology;* 60(2), 197–203.

Barling, J. and Kelloway, E.K. (1996) Job insecurity and health: The moderating role of workplace control, *Stress Medicine;* 12(4), 253–259.

Barr, D.B., Thomas, K., Curwin, B., Landsittel, D., Raymer, J., Lu, C., Donnelly, K.C., and Acquavella, J. (2006) Biomonitoring of exposure in farmworker studies, *Environmental Health Perspectives;* 114(6), 936–942.

Beseler, C. and Stallones, L. (2003) Safety practices, neurological symptoms, and pesticide poisoning, *Journal of Occupational and Environmental Medicine;* 45(10), 1079–1086.

Carroll, D.J., Samardick, R., Bernard, S., Gabbard, S., and Hernandez, T. (2005) *Findings from the National Agricultural Workers Survey (NAWS) 2001–2002: A Demographic and Employment Profile of United States Farm Workers* (Report 9). Washington, DC: US Department of Labor, Office of the Assistant Secretary for Policy.

Chavez, L.R. (1992) *Shadowed Lives: Undocumented Immigrants in American Society*. Fort Worth, TX: Harcourt Brace College Publishers.

Christian, M.S., Bradley, J.C., Wallace, J.C., and Burke, M.J. (2009) Workplace safety: A meta-analysis of the roles of person and situation factors, *Journal of Applied Psychology;* 94(5), 1103–1127.

Clapp, R.W., Jacobs, M.M., and Loechler, E.L. (2008) Environmental and occupational causes of cancer: New evidence 2005–2007, *Reviews on Environmental Health;* 23(1), 1–37.

Cooper, S.P., Heitman, E., Fox, E.E., Quill, B., Knudson, P., Zahm, S.H., MacNaughton, N., and Ryder, R. (2004) Ethical issues in conducting migrant farmworker studies, *Journal of Immigrant Health;* 6(1), 29–39.

Cullen, J.C. and Hammer, L.B. (2007) Developing and testing a theoretical model linking work-family conflict to employee safety, *Journal of Occupational Health Psychology;* 12(3), 266–278.

Frazier, L.M. (2007) Reproductive disorders associated with pesticide exposure, *Journal of Agromedicine;* 12, 27–37.

Gentry, A.L., Grzywacz, J.G., Quandt, S.A., Davis, S.W., and Arcury, T.A. (2007) Housing quality among North Carolina farmworker families, *Journal of Agricultural Safety and Health;* 13(3), 323–337.

Ghosh, A.K., Bhattacherjee, A., and Chau, N. (2004) Relationships of working conditions and individual characteristics to occupational injuries: A case-control study in coal miners, *Journal of Occupational Health*; 46(4), 470–480.

Goldenhar, L.M., Williams, L J., and Swanson, N.G. (2003) Modelling relationships between job stressors and injury and near-miss outcomes for construction labourers, *Work and Stress;* 17(3), 218–240.

Gorell, J.M., Johnson, C.C., Rybicki, B.A., Peterson, E.L., and Richardson, R.J. (1998) The risk of Parkinson's disease with exposure to pesticides, farming, well water, and rural living, *Neurology;* 50(5), 1346–1350.

Grzywacz, J.G., Alterman, T., Muntaner, C., Gabbard, S., Nakamoto, J., and Carroll, D.J. (2009) Measuring job characteristics and mental health among Latino farmworkers: Results from cognitive testing, *Journal of Immigrant and Minority Health;* 11(2), 131–138.

Grzywacz, J.G., Arcury, T.A., Marin, A., Carrillo, L., Burke, B., Coates, M.L., and Quandt, S.A. (2007) Work-family conflict: Experiences and health implications among immigrant Latinos, *Journal of Applied Psychology;* 92(4), 1119–1130.

Grzywacz, J.G., Quandt, S.A., and Arcury, T.A. (2008) Immigrant farmworkers' health-related quality of life: An application of the job demands-control model, *Journal of Agricultural Safety and Health;* 14(1), 79–92.

Grzywacz, J.G., Quandt, S.A., Early, J., Tapia, J., Graham, C.N., and Arcury, T.A. (2006) Leaving family for work: Ambivalence and mental health among Mexican migrant farmworker men, *Journal of Immigrant Health;* 8(1), 85–97.

Grzywacz, J.G., Quandt, S.A., Vallejos, Q.M., Chen, H., Isom, S., and Arcury, T.A. (2009) *Job-related Stress and Pesticide Exposure among Immigrant Latino Farmworkers.* Paper presentation, Work, Stress, and Health 2009 Conference, sponsored by the American Psychological Association, the National Institute for Occupational Safety and Health, and the Society for Occupational Health Psychology. (November). San Juan, Puerto Rico.

Grzywacz, J.G., Quandt, S.A., Vallejos, Q.M., Whalley, L.E., Chen, H., Isom, S., Barr, D.B., and Arcury, T.A. (2010) Job demands and pesticide exposure among immigrant Latino farmworkers, *Journal of Occupational Health Psychology;*15(3) 252–266.

Hiott, A.E., Grzywacz, J.G., Davis, S.W., Quandt, S A., and Arcury, T.A. (2008) Migrant farmworker stress: Mental health implications, *Journal of Rural Health;* 24(1), 32–39.

Hoppin, J.A., Adgate, J.L., Eberhart, M., Nishioka, M., and Ryan, P.B. (2006) Environmental exposure assessment of pesticides in farmworker homes, *Environmental Health Perspectives;* 114(6), 929–935.

Hoppin, J.A., Umbach, D.M., London, S.J., Henneberger, P.K., Kullman, G.J., Alavanja, M.C., and Sandler, D.P. (2008) Pesticides and atopic and nonatopic asthma among farm women in the Agricultural Health Study, *American Journal of Respiratory andd Critical Care Medicine;* 177(1), 11–18.

Hovey, J.D. (2000) Acculturative stress, depression, and suicidal ideation in Mexican immigrants, *Cultural Diversity and Ethnic Minority Psychology;* 6(2), 134–151.

Hovey, J.D. and Magaña, C.G. (2000) Acculturative stress, anxiety, and depression among Mexican immigrant farmworkers in the midwest United States, *Cultural Diversity and Ethnic Minority Psychology;* 2(3), 119–131.

Hovey, J.D. and Magaña, C.G. (2002a) Exploring the mental health of Mexican migrant farm workers in the midwest: Psychosocial predictors of psychological distress and suggestions for prevention and treatment, *Journal of Psychology;* 136(5), 493–513.

Hovey, J.D. and Magaña, C.G. (2002b) Psychosocial predictors of anxiety among immigrant Mexican migrant farmworkers: Implications for prevention and treatment, *Cultural Diversity and Ethnic Minority Psychology;* 8(3), 274–289.

Hovey, J.D. and Seligman, L. (2006) The mental health of agricultural workers. In J.E. Lessenger (ed) *Agricultural Medicine: A Practical Guide.* New York, NY: Springer-Verlag, 282–289.

Kamel, F., Tanner, C., Umbach, D., Hoppin, J., Alavanja, M., Blair, A., Comyns, K., Goldman, S., Korell, M., Langston, J., Ross, G., and Sandler, D. (2007) Pesticide exposure and self-reported Parkinson's disease in the agricultural health study, *American Journal of Epidemiology;* 165(4), 364–374.

Kandel, W.A. and Donato, K.M. (2009) Does unauthorized status reduce exposure to pesticides?, *Work and Occupations;* 36(4), 367–399.

Kanfer, R. and Ackerman, P.L. (1989) Motivation and cognitive abilities: An integrative/aptitude-treatment interaction approach to skill acquisition, *Journal of Applied Psychology;* 74(4), 657–690.

Karasek, R. and Theorell, T. (1990) *Healthy Work: Stress, Productivity, and the Reconstruction of Working Life.* New York, NY: Basic Books.

Kessler, R.C., Andrews, G., Colpe, L. J., Hiripi, E., Mroczek, D.K., Normand, S.L., Walters, E.E., and Zaslavsky, A.M. (2002) Short screening scales to monitor population prevalences and trends in non-specific psychological distress, *Psychological Medicine;* 32(6), 959–976.

Kiely, T., Donaldson, D., and Grube, A. (2004) *Pesticide Industry Sales and Usage: 2000 and 2001 Market Estimates.* Washington, DC: US Environmental Protection Agency, Biological and Economic Analysis Division of the Office of Pesticide Programs. http://www.epa.gov/oppbead1/pestsales/01pestsales/usage2001.htm.

Kim, H.C., Min, J.Y., Min, K.B., and Park, S.G. (2009) Job strain and the risk for occupational injury in small- to medium-sized manufacturing enterprises: A prospective study of 1,209 Korean employees, *American Journal of Industrial Medicine;* 52, 322–330.

Kim-Godwin, Y.S. and Bechtel, G.A. (2004) Stress among migrant and seasonal farmworkers in rural southeast North Carolina, *Journal of Rural Health;* 20(3), 271–278.

Kristensen, T.S. (1995) The demand-control-support model: Methodological challenges for future research, *Stress Medicine;* 11(1), 17–26.

Lazarus, R.S. and Folkman, S. (1984) *Stress, Appraisal and Coping.* New York, NY: Springer.

Magaña, C.G. and Hovey, J.D. (2003) Psychosocial stressors associated with Mexican migrant farmworkers in the midwest United States, *Journal of Immigrant Health;* 5(2), 75–86.

Meeker, J.D., Ravi, S.R., Barr, D.B., and Hauser, R. (2008) Circulating estradiol in men is inversely related to urinary metabolites of nonpersistent insecticides, *Reproductive Toxicology;* 25(2), 184–191.

Miller, D.B. and O'Callaghan, J.P. (2008) Do early-life insults contribute to the late-life development of Parkinson and Alzheimer diseases?, *Metabolism;* 57(Suppl 2), S44–S49.

Monger, R. and Barr, M. (2009) *Nonimmigrant Admissions to the United States: 2008.* Annual Flow Report. United States Department of Homeland Security, Office of Immigration Statistics: Policy Directorate. http://www.dhs.gov/xlibrary/assets/statistics/publications/ois_ni_fr_2008.pdf.

Montgomery, M.P., Kamel, F., Saldana, T.M., Alavanja, M.C., and Sandler, D.P. (2008) Incident diabetes and pesticide exposure among licensed pesticide applicators: Agricultural Health Study, 1993–2003, *American Journal of Epidemiology;* 167(10), 1235–1246.

Nakata, A., Ikeda, T., Takahashi, M., Haratani, T., Hojou, M., Fujioka, Y., Swanson, N.G., and Araki, S. (2006) Impact of psychosocial job stress on non-fatal occupational injuries in small and medium-sized manufacturing enterprises, *American Journal of Industrial Medicine;* 49(8), 658–669.

Quandt, S.A., Arcury, T.A., Austin, C.K., Saavedra, R.M. (1998) Farmworker and farmer perceptions of farmworker agricultural chemical exposure in North Carolina, *Human Organization;* 57(3), 359–368.

Quandt, S.A., Hernandez-Valero, M.A., Grzywacz, J.G., Hovey, J.D., Gonzales, M., and Arcury, T.A. (2006) Workplace, household, and personal predictors of pesticide exposure for farmworkers, *Environmental Health Perspectives;* 114(6), 943–952.

Rao, P., Arcury, T.A., Quandt, S.A., and Doran, A. (2004) Growers' and extension agents' perceptions of farmworker pesticide exposure, *Human Organization;* 63(2), 151–161.

Rubel, A. J. (1960) Concepts of disease in Mexican-American culture, *American Anthropologist;* 62(5), 795–814.

Salazar, M.K., Napolitano, M., Scherer, J.A., and McCauley, L.A. (2004) Hispanic adolescent farmworkers' perceptions associated with pesticide exposure, *Western Journal of Nursing Research;* 26(2), 146–166; discussion 167–175.

Salminen, S., Kivimaki, M., Elovainio, M., and Vahtera, J. (2003) Stress factors predicting injuries of hospital personnel, *American Journal of Industrial Medicine;* 44(1), 32–36.

Siegrist, J. (1996) Adverse health effects of high-effort/low-reward conditions, *Journal of Occupational Health Psychology;* 1(1), 27–41.

Siegrist, J., Siegrist, K., and Weber, I. (1986) Sociological concepts in the etiology of chronic disease: The case of ischemic heart disease, *Social Science and Medicine;* 22(2), 247–253.

Swaen, G.M., van Amelsvoort, L.P., Bultmann, U., Slangen, J.J., and Kant, I.J. (2004) Psychosocial work characteristics as risk factors for being injured in an occupational accident, *Journal of Occupational and Environmental Medicine;* 46(6), 521–527.

Thompson, B., Coronado, G.D., Vigoren, E.M., Griffith, W.C., Fenske, R.A., Kissel, J.C., Shirai, J.H., and Faustman, E.M. (2008) Para ninos saludables: a community intervention trial to reduce organophosphate pesticide exposure in children of farmworkers, *Environmental Health Perspectives;* 116(5), 687–694.

Thu, K.M. (1998) The health consequences of industrialized agriculture for farmers in the United States, *Human Organization;* 57(3), 335–341.

United States Department of Agriculture (2007) *Census of Agriculture, United States, Summary and State Data, Volume 1: Geographic Area Series, Part 51*. United States Department of Agriculture, National Agricultural Statistics Service. http://www.agcensus.usda.gov/Publications/2007/Full_Report/Volume_1,_Chapter_2_US_State_Level/st99_2_007_007.pdf

United States Environmental Protection Agency (1992) *Pesticide Worker Protection Standard Training 40CFR Part 170*. http://www.epa.gov/oppfead1/safety/workers/PART170.htm.

Vallejos, Q.M., Quandt, S.A., and Arcury, T.A. (2009) The conditions of farmworker housing in the Eastern United States. In T.A. Arcury and S.A. Quandt (eds) *Latino Farmworkers in the Eastern United States: Health, Safety, and Justice*. New York, NY: Springer, 37–7.

Villarejo, D. (2003) The health of US hired farm workers, *Annual Review of Public Health;* 24, 175–193.

Villarejo, D. and Baron, S.L. (1999) The occupational health status of hired farm workers, *Occupational Medicine;* 14(3), 613–635.

Walter, N., Bourgois, P., Margarita Loinaz, H., and Schillinger, D. (2002) Social context of work injury among undocumented day laborers in San Francisco, *Journal of General Internal Medicine;* 17(3), 221–229.

Weller, S.C. (1983) New data on intracultural variability: The hot-cold concept of medicine and illness, *Human Organization;* 42(3), 249–257.

Whalley, L.E., Grzywacz, J.G., Quandt, S.A., Vallejos, Q.M., Walkup, M., Chen, H., Galvan, L., and Arcury, T.A. (2009) Migrant farmworker field and camp safety and sanitation in eastern North Carolina, *Journal of Agromedicine;* 14(4), 421–36.

Wickens, D.D. (1996) Designing for stress. In. J. Driskell and E. Salas (eds) *Stress and Human Performance*. Mahwah, NJ: Erlbaum, 279–295.

Wiggins, M.F. (2009) Farm labor and the struggle for justice in the Eastern United States. In T.A. Arcury and S.A. Quandt (eds) *Latino Farmworkers in the Eastern United States: Health, Safety, and Justice*. New York, NY: Springer, 201–220.

CHAPTER 13

Psychosocial Risks and Positive Factors among Construction Workers

MARISA SALANOVA, EVA CIFRE, SUSANA LLORENS, ISABEL M. MARTÍNEZ, AND LAURA LORENTE

Construction Work from a Psychosocial Point of View: An Overview

Construction is a large, dynamic, and complex industrial sector that plays an important role in the US (Behm, 2008) and in European economies. Construction workers and employers build houses, workplaces, and other buildings, and also maintain the physical infrastructures of cities all over the world. However, job fatalities in the construction industry have long been disproportionate to the number of employees in the business. To date, the European Agency for Safety and Health at Work (2008) shows that the construction industry has one of the worst occupational safety and health records in Europe. New data from the International Work Organization (IWO) in 2007 reveals that 60,000 fatal accidents take place in the construction industry every year. This is the equivalent to one death every ten minutes. Therefore, this sector is one of the most afflicted with occupational accidents.

The most obvious job demands on construction sites are physical (for example, working with heavy equipment, noise, vibrations), chemical exposures (for example, asbestos, lead, epoxy resins), which are frequently the most important causes of absenteeism and disability. More than half the cases of sick leave among construction workers are the result of musculoskeletal complaints and physical disorders, mostly related to the lower back. In this sense, the *Fourth European Working Conditions Survey* (European Foundation for the Improvement of Living and Working Conditions, 2007) indicates that the symptoms most reported by construction workers are backache and musculoskeletal complaints. So it seems clear that construction work is an inherently dangerous occupation. But psychosocial risks also play a key role in this industry as demonstrated by the fact that the aforementioned *Fourth European Working Conditions Survey* (2007) states that musculoskeletal complaints in the construction sector are followed by psychosocial factors such as fatigue and stress (22 percent).

Furthermore, the European Agency for Safety and Health at Work (2008) supports the idea of the importance of psychosocial factors in construction work. It shows that the top ten emerging psychosocial risks relate to the following five main topics:

(1) new forms of employment contracts and job insecurity; (2) an aging workforce; (3) work intensification; (4) high emotional demands at work; and (5) poor work-life balance. Of these emerging psychosocial risks, the first relate more with the construction sector. Research into the influence of irregular forms of employment on worker occupational safety and health reveal that non-permanent workers face higher job insecurity, poorer job conditions, higher job demands, and more occupational accidents. Moreover, stress-related tension and exhaustion appear to be more severe for precariously employed workers than for workers with permanent jobs. Specifically, construction workers have to cope with unpredictable working hours, and casual work enters under this heading since it consists of very short and sometimes unpredictable periods of employment, mixed with periods of unemployment. Furthermore, the pace of work set by colleagues affects over 60 percent of workers in the construction sector.

Empirical research also provides results that stress the role of psychosocial factors in this industry. In this sense, we may state that many construction workers feel stressed to meet certain deadlines and to face periods of unemployment between projects. In addition, there are continuous and rapid changes in the work environment, and colleagues come and go when moving from one project to another. Even in large construction firms, the transition from one work site to another with different site managers can be detrimental to worker morale, especially when there is a lack of communication and/or misunderstanding of company policies (Sobeih et al., 2006).

Moreover in studies conducted among Spanish construction workers, Meliá and Becerril (2007) show that psychosocial risks play a role in this occupational sector, and their findings support, for example, that leadership has direct effects on not only the propensity to quit, but also on the perceived quality of the product. Salanova, Gracia and Lorente (2007) reveal that the most important psychosocial demands for construction workers are quantitative and qualitative (mental) overload, and routine. Moreover, workers report high levels of job disenchantment and medium levels of exhaustion. These results agree with the *Fourth European Working Conditions Survey* (2007) which shows how overload factors, such as quality standards requirement, job performance ratings, and doing complex and routine tasks, are the most specific job demands for the construction sector.

Psychosocial risks are not only important in themselves but, apparently, exposure to additional psychosocial risks is likely to exacerbate the level of danger by workers' increasing risk to injury. In this sense, the *Sixth Spanish National Survey of Work Conditions* (National Institute of Occupational Safety and Health at Work, 2007) indicates that workers perceive psychosocial and/or ergonomic aspects, such as negligence, overconfidence, or lack of attention (45 percent), and tiredness or fatigue (17 percent), as the main psychosocial causes of their work accidents.

In short, both physical and psychosocial risks are a great threat for the construction industry, and are missing in research on this topic. Therefore, this chapter focuses on the specific relationship among the different psychosocial factors and the consequences on health and well-being among construction workers. So far, although there is a lack of research into this topic in this particular occupational sector, we provide different research findings that support the idea that psychosocial risks are also a threat for construction workers in their workplaces.

THE RECIPROCAL INFLUENCE BETWEEN PHYSICAL AND PSYCHOSOCIAL RISKS

So far according to research, physical and psychosocial risks apparently move in different directions. However, some studies have linked them (physical and psychosocial risks) among construction workers. For example, Jansen, Bakker and de Jong (2001) tested and refined the Demand-Control-Support (DCS) Model among 210 construction workers. They hypothesized those mental and physical job demands, low job control, and lack of social support at work have direct and synergistic effects on burnout, and that they mediate the relationships between these potentially physical and psychosocial demanding working conditions on the one hand, and physical health complaints on the other. The results show that lack of social support is the most important determinant of burnout and health complaints among construction workers. In addition, physical demands only relate to burnout when participants have poor job control and report high social support. So, these results show an interaction between both kinds of demands and outcomes. Latza, Pfahlberg and Gefeller (2002) investigated the influence of manual stone and brick handling and psychosocial work factors on the risk of chronic low back pain with a longitudinal study of 488 male construction workers. The results indicate that workers with a low satisfaction with their work achievements more frequently suffer chronic low back pain. Similar risks are observed in the sub-group without chronic low back pain in the baseline survey. A strong effect of time pressure is only present for such workers.

Goldenhar, Williams and Swanson (2003) investigated this link among job stressors and injury or near-miss outcomes in a sample of 408 construction workers. The results show that ten of the 12 work-related stressors directly relate to either injury or near misses, including job demands, low job control, job uncertainty, low training, unsafe climate, skill under-utilization, irresponsibility for the safety of others, safety compliance, exposure hours, and job tenure. Other stressors such as harassment/discrimination, job certainty, lack of social support, skill underutilization, safety irresponsibility, safety compliance, and tenure in construction indirectly relate to either injuries through physical symptoms or to near misses through psychological strain.

In a systematic review based on eight articles published about psychosocial factors and musculoskeletal disorders among construction workers, Sobeih et al. (2006) noted how high job strain is the most commonly investigated factor, followed by job satisfaction, job control, and high quantitative job demands. All the studies report an association between musculoskeletal disorders and at least one psychosocial factor. Many of the reported associations are significant, even after adjusting for demographics and the physical demands of the job.

Finally, in a recent study with 147 active construction workers, Salem et al. (2008) not only revealed how psychosocial factors play a significant role in the construction industry, but also their association with physical factors. The results of a factor analysis indicate a significant association between four work compatibility variables (that is, work environment, physical task, performance, and job satisfaction) and musculoskeletal-stress symptoms among these construction workers.

So far, there is evidence for an association between psychosocial factors and musculoskeletal disorders. Moreover, this information is essential to the construction industry since most intervention programs focus only on construction employees' physical demands.

CONSTRUCTION WORKERS ALSO FEEL POSITIVE EXPERIENCES AT WORK

Although past research has shown that high physical and psychosocial demands related to injuries and strain mainly characterize construction work, workers in this sector also enjoy job and personal resources that contribute to positive experiences.

By considering past and recent research on psychosocial risks among construction workers, the following sections of this chapter present some empirical findings related to the negative psychosocial factors of the work environment and their negative consequences on unwell-being, performance, and accidents in workers, as well as the positive psychosocial factors of this work environment that influence feelings of well-being and psychosocial health at work in this occupational sector. So far, we adopt a holistic perspective of the "Positive Psychology" movement to study the psychosocial factors related to the work environment and construction workers' experiences.

The Positive Psychology movement (Seligman and Csikszentmihalyi, 2000) focuses on human strengths and optimal functioning. Specifically, Seligman, and Csikszentmihalyi (2000, p. 5) state that the purpose of Positive Psychology "...is to begin to catalyze a change in the focus of psychology from pre-occupation only with repairing the worst things in life to also building positive qualities." In a similar vein, Cameron, Dutton and Quinn (2003, p. 4) introduces a new discipline, Positive Organizational Scholarship, which is about "...the study of especially positive outcomes, processes, and attributes of organizations and their members". However, our approach goes one step forward with the emergence of a truly Occupational Health Psychology that includes the entire spectrum of employee health and well-being, ranging from ill-health, unwell-being, and poor functioning to positive health, well-being, and optimal functioning. The objectives are to investigate and to improve employees' health and well-being, and to also promote their optimal functioning in groups and occupational settings.

The following sections are a compendium of empirical- and theoretical-based results among construction workers. The first study goes into safety attitudes, climate, and culture and how they relate to safety performance. There is also a description of theoretical models on climate and attitudes toward safety as well as research results about this topic among construction workers. Secondly, the "Social Cognitive Theory" of Albert Bandura proves useful to explain the negative effects of high levels of self-efficacy (overconfidence) among construction workers. Finally, we present some empirical data to illustrate: (1) the main psychosocial risks and positive factors assessed in the Spanish construction industry with a field study done on several construction companies; and (2) an in-depth case study in a construction company.

Safety Attitudes, Climate/Culture, and its Relationship with Safety Performance

In the last decade, researchers have developed specific theories and methods to investigate the psychosocial aspects of safety performance in organizations, and research on safety performance has taken two forms: (1) at an individual level, considering safety attitudes; and (2) at a group/organizational level through the safety climate and safety culture.

SAFETY ATTITUDES AND PERFORMANCE

Different scholars have provided evidence that when people have positive attitudes, they actually display behaviors that allow them to approach, support, or improve the object of attitude. For example, a worker with positive safety attitudes systematically uses personal protective equipment and adopts safety rules at the workplace. Indeed, the other way round is also true with negative attitudes. Ajzen (1988, p. 117) defines an attitude as "someone's positive or negative evaluation of performing a particular behavior of interest." The current dominant idea indicates that under appropriate conditions, we may expect some relationships between attitudes and behaviors. The dominant theoretical models on these topics are the "Theory of Reasoned Action" (TRA) and its subsequent reformulation in the "Theory of Planned Behavior" (TPB) (for further information, see Ajzen, 2001). Briefly, the TPB claims that attitudes often fail to display strong correlations with behavior because of the large number of factors that potentially prevent the attitude from being converted into behavior, such as intentions, subjective norms caused by others, and the perceived behavioral control, which can be explained as efficacy beliefs (see the next section about self-efficacy).

In organizational contexts, safety attitudes relate to safety performance and relate indirectly to accident rates and self-reported injuries. Specifically, those individuals who have more positive safety attitudes are more likely to remain injury-free. To date, Cheyne et al. (2002) have found that safety attitudes positively and significantly relate to engagement in safety activities. McCabe et al. (2008) also document the positive relationships between manager's attitudes and less accidents and physical symptoms.

Findings about attitudes and their relationship to performance have shown the importance of sociodemographic variables such as age. Relationships among safety attitudes, safety performance, and age have been documented, for example, Siu, Phillips and Leung (2003) analyzed the relationships between these three elements (by considering accident rates and occupational injuries, such as safety performance) among construction workers. They show that older workers had more positive safety attitudes than younger ones. But age has a curvilinear effect on occupational injuries with an inverted U shape in which the frequency of injury increased first with age, and then declines. It seems that older construction workers are more experienced and are, therefore, at less risk at work. Besides, older workers may also be aware that fewer job opportunities are available for them, so they are more committed at work and are willing to comply with safety rules.

SAFETY CLIMATE/CULTURE AND PERFORMANCE

At the group/organizational level, research has focused on the study of safety climate and safety culture and their roles in predicting safety performance (that is, occupational accidents and injuries). Safety climate implies a subjective perception and evaluation of safety issues related to the organization, its members, structures, and processes, based on experience in the organizational environment and social relationships. Different terms have been used to define safety climate, such as the extent to which workers "share" attitudes toward safety which allow them to retain control of and responsibility for injury prevention (Doland and Canter, 1993). With a cognitive approach, Griffin and Neal (2000) argued that the definition of safety climate should be purely in terms of perceptions of the work environment, where the perceptions of the policies, procedures, and practices relate to safety which, at the broadest level, reflect employee perceptions of the value of safety in an organization. On the other hand, safety culture concerns those aspects of the organizational culture which will have an impact on the attitudes and behavior related to increasing or decreasing risks (Guldenmund, 2000).

Safety climate and safety culture have been used interchangeably. Both reflect the attitudes, beliefs, perceptions, and values that employees share in relation to safety. However, safety culture is generally taken to be a more comprehensive construct than safety climate, while the latter is more temporal, subject to commonalities among the individual perceptions of the organization. Cox and Cox (1991) argued that employee attitudes, themselves, are one of the most important indices of safety culture and safety climate. Then, safety climate refers to the perceived state of safety culture at a particular place and a particular time, it is relatively unstable, and is subject to change depending on the features of the current environment or prevailing conditions (Wiegmann et al., 2002).

Some researchers have sought to determine whether different groups of workers within an organization or sector report different safety climates. They suggest that no universal set of safety climate factors exist among industrial sectors or even companies (Arboleda et al., 2003; Cox et al., 1998). In addition, different sub-climates are liable to exist at different levels within an organization. To date, McCabe et al. (2008) found different professional sub-climates to simultaneously co-exist at different levels within an organization (for example, youth, apprentices, and temporary employees) in the construction industry, and they suggest that health and safety programs need to focus specifically on these different safety sub-climates in order to be more effective.

A further step in research is about how safety climate and culture predict safety performance indicators such as perceived risk, accidents, and injuries. For example, the fact that a supervisor never talks about safety might influence his/her subordinates' beliefs that safety is not important at all and, in turn, develop a negative attitude toward safety at the workplace. Alternatively, a stronger safety climate could encourage employees to take greater responsibility in the safety of the organization which influences their engagement in safety behaviors (Hofmann and Stetzer, 1996).

Companies with low accident rates have stimulated the study of safety climate. These companies show a consistently high interest in and commitment to safety performance which relate to the successful implementation of safety intervention programs. This interest shows in the popularity of safety climate and culture surveys within the companies' repertoire of safety measures (for example, national intervention plans, statistical analysis, and publications). Consequently nowadays, there is a growing body of evidence which suggests that safety climate positively influences safety performance, that is, safety practices, safe behavior, and the lack of accidents at work.

In risk environments, such as the construction industry, it is essential to audit safety climate and management practices. However, the special features of the construction industry, as mentioned in above, are such that many workers involved in sub-contracted companies affect the nature and stability of risks, the structure of the companies, the relationships of workers with the main company, and the stability of the social relationships at the workplace. This affects the development of the safety climate over time, which makes longitudinal studies about this topic in the construction industry a difficult task. To date, the cross-cultural research in construction workers from England, Hong Kong, and Spain by Meliá et al. (2008) concludes that under situations such as outsourcing, and lack of social contact of workers with managers and supervisors, it is hard for managers and supervisors to influence the formation and development of safety climate and safety culture among their subordinates. The results of this research show that the worker safety responses in all the samples did not relate to perceived risks. Workers can psychologically protect themselves by perceiving that external factors, and not their own personal safety responses, attribute to risks. We may understand these results as an indicator of the need for appropriate and effective intervention to create positive attitudes among employees and to simultaneously generate climate and safety culture. Companies must provide safety protection and increase safety supervision and enforcement in these special contexts (that is, social support, effective communication, interpersonal relations, enhance training, and so on).

Self-Efficacy and Safety Performance

The previous section highlights the importance of attitudes toward safety performance in the construction industry, as well as the safety climate/culture. But other variables are also important in determining safety performance, such as self-efficacy. This section includes several research findings about the (positive and negative) consequences of self-efficacy in their relationship with safety performance.

SELF-EFFICACY AND POSITIVE OUTCOMES

The framework of Albert Bandura's Social Cognitive Theory (SCT) frames efficacy beliefs into what, at the individual level, defines self-efficacy as "beliefs in one's capabilities to organize and execute courses of action required to produce given attainments" (Bandura, 1997, p. 3). At the group level however, the SCT extends the conception of human agency to collective efficacy beliefs, defined as "group's shared belief in its conjoint capabilities to organize and to execute the courses of action required to produce given levels of attainments" (Bandura, 1997, p. 477). Efficacy beliefs (both self-efficacy and collective efficacy beliefs) play a key role in human functioning because they affect behavior through goals and aspirations, outcome expectations, affective proclivities and perception of impediments, and opportunities in the social environment.

Briefly, efficacy beliefs have effects on people's thinking, acting, and feelings. In this sense, efficacy relates with human behavior and, therefore, with performance. Efficacy beliefs have a strong motivational effect because they influence decisions (selective effects), effort, and persistence (motivational effects) through self-regulatory mechanisms which depend on the environment. Therefore, a person showing high levels of efficacy in an activity feels involved and connected with it, so we may expect positive results. Along these lines, there are many studies that link high levels of self-efficacy with positive outcomes in different settings, areas, or domains. For example, high levels of efficacy beliefs have a strong connection with work engagement and motivation, and psychological well-being at both the individual and organizational levels.

To date, Latham (2005) has found positive relationships among self-efficacy, motivation, commitment, and job performance. Xanthopoulou et al. (2008) discovered that work engagement mediates the relationship between self-efficacy and (in-role and extra-role) performance. These works are examples of decades of empirical research that has generated numerous studies that demonstrate positive relationships between self-efficacy and different motivational and behavioral outcomes, such as work performance, in a variety of work and organizational settings (Stajkovic and Luthans, 1998). As explained before, this is because when efficacy beliefs levels are high and individuals believe they can control their environment effectively, employees are more likely to perceive job demands as challenging, and job and other personal resources as being abundant. Consequently, individuals are more likely to engage in their tasks and perform well (Salanova et al., 2010).

WHEN SELF-EFFICACY HAS NEGATIVE CONSEQUENCES: THE CASE OF OVERCONFIDENCE

Given these positive outcomes being related to self-efficacy research, one may well think that the consequences of high levels of self-efficacy are always desirable. However, research also had shown the "dark" side of self-efficacy. For example, Salomon (1984) found that when people consider a task easy, they invest less effort and learning is lower. Whyte, Saks and Hook (1997) also postulated that self-efficacy could act as a source of inappropriate persistence; that is, in those domains in which an individual displays high self-efficacy and has been successful in the past, he/she may not persist long enough, and even develop overconfidence. Vancouver and colleagues (2001; 2002) conducted several studies about this topic and concluded that high self-efficacy leads to relaxation and reduces future performance over time at the intra-person level, but not at the inter-person level. They also showed that self-efficacy leads to overconfidence and, hence, increases the likelihood of committing logic errors during tasks. Finally, Yeo and Neal (2006) also found similar relationships between self-efficacy and performance in tasks that involve learning. They indicated that the positive relationships between efficacy beliefs and performance are due to an error of analysis in the study. That is, the results are based on cross-sectional studies and only take into account the effects between groups. But longitudinal studies, which reveal intra-changes over time, show that these negative effects of efficacy beliefs are evident.

So far, although research suggests that self-efficacy usually associates with positive outcomes, it may also relate to less desirable outcomes. Even Bandura (1997) affirmed that an optimistic view raises aspirations and maintains motivation, thus allowing people to take greater advantage of their talent, thereby contributing to psychological well-being and personal achievements. This indicates that an optimistic assessment of one's self-efficacy relates to positive results, but not to an overly optimistic assessment since an exaggerated sense of personal efficacy could "blind" a person who faces difficulties or risks.

Moreover, Bandura noted (personal communication, Stanford, October 2005) that efficacy beliefs have a different impact on both: activities that involve risks and those that imply creative/innovative behaviors. In this sense, Salanova, Lorente and Martínez (2009) conducted research to compare three settings: a learning setting, an innovative setting, and a risky one. Their results show that the greater the self-efficacy in the learning and innovative settings, the better academic performance and the more creative behavior, respectively. They also reveal that whereas the greater the self-efficacy in the risky setting, the lower the safety performance.

Experiencing overconfidence can perhaps motivate people to set unrealistic safety goals. In this sense, Salanova, Gracia and Lorente (2007) found that overconfidence is one of the main perceived causes of accidents in the construction industry. Later, Salanova et al. (2009) showed that overconfident people display less safety performance. Moreover, Real (2007) observed that workers with high self-efficacy are less affected by risk perceptions than workers with low safety efficacy. Hence, overconfident people perhaps perceive risks as less dangerous and, consequently, their responses to a given threat are minimum. Given this scenario, we believe that high levels of efficacy beliefs in risky settings, like the construction industry, may relate to poor safety performance which could lead to negligence at work, or even to occupational accidents.

Furthermore, we can conclude that although many studies demonstrate the positive consequences of self-efficacy, other studies also show the negative effects of overconfidence on safety performance, such as the construction industry. The following sections describe the method and theoretical background that we followed to undertake some of the above-mentioned empirical studies.

Empirical Studies on Psychosocial Factors Management

On the next pages, we describe the way in which we adapted our theoretical models (the "Resources-Experiences-Demands Model", RED Model, at the job level; and the "HEalthy and Resilient Organization Model", the HERO Model, at the organization level) to the Spanish construction industry, following two different approaches which both use qualitative and quantitative methodologies. Firstly, we followed the first steps of the so-called "Action-Research" (AR) approach to assess worker psychosocial factors (Study 1); secondly, we conducted a case study to assess a healthy organization (Study 2). But first we explain the theoretical background of both which helped guide our studies.

THEORETICAL BACKGROUND

Due to the applied character of studies about psychosocial factors on construction work, we consider the so-called AR approach as one of the most suitable methodological approaches to explore the psychosocial factors at construction sites. Briefly, one definition of the AR approach is an "emergent inquiry process in which behavioral science knowledge integrates with existing organizational knowledge and applies to solve real organizational problems [...]. It is an evolving change process that is undertaken in a spirit of collaboration and co-inquiry" (Shani and Pasmore, 1985, p. 439). The AR approach refers to the change process based on systematic data collection, and the selection of an action (intervention) based on results when organizational constrains allow it (Robbins, 2005). Therefore, the aim of this approach is to provide a methodology to handle planned changes such as improving worker's well-being at construction sites.

However, we had to ground this applied methodology on theoretical bases. To do so, we used the RED Model (Salanova et al., 2007) (see Figure 13.1) grounded on the positive psychology movement. It extends the "Dual Process Model" (Schaufeli and Bakker, 2004) which, in turn, extends the "Job Demands-Resources Model" (JDR Model) (Demerouti et al., 2001). The JDR Model indicates that the amount of stress experienced at work results from the combination of job demands and low job resources which are available to cope with these demands. *Job demands* (that is, quantitative overload, role conflict) refer to those physical, psychological, social, or organizational aspects of the job that require sustained physical and/or psychological (cognitive and emotional) efforts or skills which, therefore, relate to certain physiological and/or psychological costs. *Job resources* (that is, social support, job control) refer to those physical, psychological, social, or organizational aspects of the job that: (1) are functional in achieving work goals; (2) reduce job demands and the associated physiological and psychological costs; and (3) stimulate personal growth, learning, and development. Hence, resources are not only necessary to deal with job demands, but are also important in their own right.

The JDR Model focuses mainly on negative results, such as employee burnout. Later, as noted above, Schaufeli and Bakker (2004) extended this model with the Dual Process Model by not only including negative outcomes of stress, but also positive ones, such as work engagement. The model assumes two different underlying psychological processes that play a role in the development of psychological well-being outcomes: the energy-draining process (which leads to exhaustion and long-term burnout) and the motivational process (which leads to high work engagement and then to excellent performance) (for a review, see Schaufeli and Bakker, 2004).

However, this model does not pay attention to the special and somewhat "crucial" resources which, from our point of view, make the model completely meaningful, that is, personal resources. These personal resources affect not only the stress process to know how a person appraises the situation, but also both the actual coping process and the recovery from the job stress process. Thus, individuals with more personal resources handle stress more effectively and may recover faster from experienced stress (Salanova, Bakker and Llorens, 2006; Salanova, Peiró and Schaufeli, 2002). In that sense, we may consider self-efficacy a personal resource that plays a key role in coping with stress (Salanova et al., 2001; Salanova, Peiró and Schaufeli, 2002), grounded on the SCT (Bandura, 2002), which we briefly explained in the previous section of this chapter. Following the RED Model, the findings shown in this chapter mainly include personal resources because we followed the RED Model, and we took into account not only job demands and resources, but also personal resources, to face those demands, as well as the experiences (positive and negative) that this (un)balance may produce. Besides, it is important to note that efficacy beliefs (self-efficacy at the individual level, collective efficacy at the group level) play a key and differential role in this RED Model. In this sense, the RED Model considers that efficacy beliefs act as antecedents of demands and resources, as explained earlier (Salanova et al., 2010).

As we show in the Introduction of this chapter, it is important to study not only the things that are going badly in the construction industry, such as injuries, job stress, and psychosocial risks, but also those things that are going well, such as performance, psychosocial positive factors, and work engagement, in order to obtain a more holistic perspective of the reality. In this sense, for example, the study of healthy organizations among construction companies is a challenge in the area of Occupational Health Psychology. From this point of view, we defined healthy organizations as those that "develop systematic, planned, and proactive efforts in improving the employee and the financial health, through good practices related to the enhancement of the tasks (for example, job design and redesign), the social environment (for example, opened communication channels) and the organization (for example, strategies for reconciling work/private life" (Salanova, 2009; Salanova and Schaufeli, 2009). In our positive model of HEalthy and Resilient Organization, that is, the HERO Model (see Figure 13.1), we consider its components, these being balance and continuous interaction, among (1) healthy practices at the level of: tasks (that is, autonomy, feedback, variety), social aspects (that is, social relationships, social support, healthy leadership), and the organization (that is, learning training, safety culture programs, work/life balance); (2) healthy employees, such as the potential of the positive psychological capital (that is, self-efficacy, optimism, hope, resilience, engagement); and (3) healthy organizational outcomes, such as high organizational performance, good relationships with extra-organizational environment, and coorporate social responsibility.

Figure 13.1 The HEalthy and Resilient Organization (HERO) Model (Salanova, 2009)

Some empirical research relates to the positive emotions of construction workers. For example, Salanova, Gracia and Lorente (2007) found that construction workers indicate job (that is, autonomy and positive interpersonal relationships) and personal resources (that is, mental and emotional competences) that buffer the negative consequences of job demands on well-being. As a result of those resources, workers report high levels of vigor (a dimension of work engagement) and good performance.

Furthermore, a recent study focused on some of the components of the previously described healthy organization in terms of transformational leadership and positive psychological capital (that is, positive affect and work engagement) among 122 construction workers (Llorens, Salanova and Losilla, 2009). This work shows that construction workers experience high levels of positive psychological capital, especially vigor, dedication, and pleasure. Moreover, transformational leadership influences work engagement not only directly but also indirectly via positive affects such as comfort, enthusiasm, pleasure, optimism, resilience, and satisfaction. So what this group resource demonstrates is that it enhances workers positive experiences, such as work engagement.

STUDY 1: A FIELD STUDY ON PSYCHOSOCIAL FACTORS ASSESSMENT

Description of the field study

The first aim of this study is to know the main psychosocial risk among construction workers and to adapt the general theoretical RED Model to the specific characteristics of the construction industry. To achieve this aim, we collected information from three sources: (1) previous research; (2) a pilot study; and (3) a *focus* group with experts in this field. In order to carry out the pilot study, the research team formulated a questionnaire, and according to the construction workers' special characteristics (low qualifications and a large number of foreigners, which complicate the verbal comprehension of items), we shortened the original battery by reducing the number of items. To do so, we performed reliability and validity analyses in order to obtain, whenever possible, single-item scales (that which loaded the most in the original scale and that which more highly inter-correlated with the scale). The scales covering the principal risks were common to most occupations. However, we reworded them by taking into account the construction industry's characteristics in order to adapt the questionnaire to this occupational sector (that is, talking about buildings when organizational settings was more appropriate, using "head of work" when referring to leaders, and so on). Besides, we also developed some specific scales (that is, security climate and attitudes, overconfidence). We named this questionnaire: RED-CONS (Resources, Experiences and Demands among CONStruction Industry), which 37 construction workers completed as part of the pilot study (100 percent men) which were working in different buildings in the Spanish Mediterranean area. The mean age was 31 years old, and 82 percent were Spanish (the rest were Moroccan, Colombian, and Rumanian); 63 percent were bricklayers and the rest were electricians, and aluminum and air-conditioning assemblers. Because these workers had few qualifications, we conducted a semi-structured interview during coffee breaks to complete the questionnaire.

We showed the results of this pilot study to the construction industry experts who participated in the focus group (Salanova, Gracia and Lorente, 2007). The aim was to know more about the situation of the construction industry, mainly in terms of psychosocial risks, work accidents, and safety attitudes, and to discuss the results of the pilot study with 15 experts from the sector: five employers, five experts in Occupational Health Psychology, two trade union representatives, one occupational risk prevention officer, one technician in preventing labor risks, and one representative of a medical insurance company. The information obtained through the focus group helped the research team to both close the final questionnaire (interpreting the results of the pilot study, advising about items which are difficult to understand, suggesting new factors not contemplated in the original study), and to implement the final field study.

When finalizing this step, the theoretical model remained as follows (see Figure 13.2), which we explain in detail above. However, we also included some specific factors of the construction sector, that is, physical demands such as job demands, safety climate, and attitudes toward safety such as specific construction resources, overconfidence as a psychosocial distress aspect, and specific measures of job performance (for example, accidents, incidents).

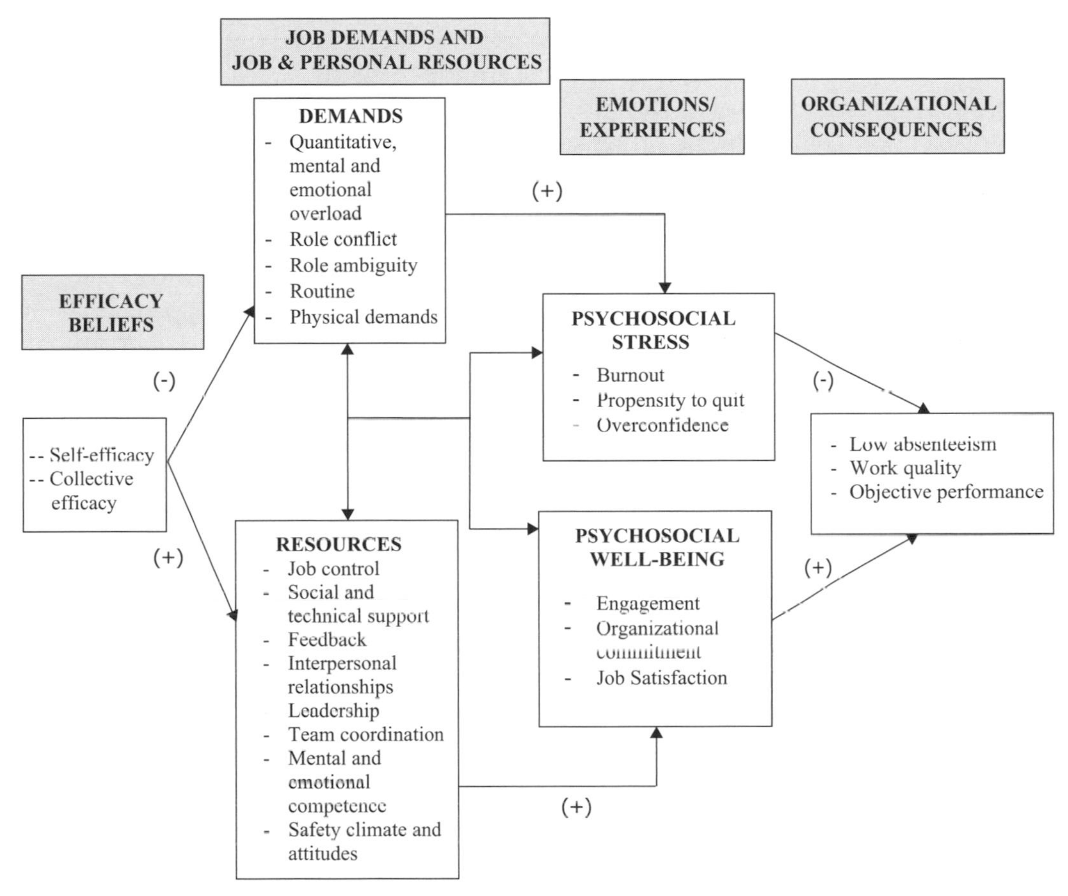

Figure 13.2 The RED Model, adapted to the construction industry

Field study results

Finally, ten of the 16 contacted companies (63 percent) participated in the study. Usually, the Human Resources Manager of each company allowed us to contact the head of each work area whose workers would participate in the study. We handed the questionnaire to each worker during the individual or group face-to-face interview. Finally, 228 employees (100 percent men) from ten different Spanish small- and medium-sized enterprises (SME) in the construction industry participated. Employees' ages ranged from 16 to 64 years (mean = 39.62, s.d. = 11.89), 38 percent of them had a temporary contract, and 18 percent were foreigners. We had to use semi-structured interviews given the study sample's characteristics (that is, low level of education where 34 percent had not completed primary education, and immigrants who might have had problems understanding the specific meaning of the items). We guaranteed confidentiality and anonymity. Workers answered the interview during their breaks either at the beginning or the end of their work shift, and usually in the workplace.

Table 13.1 displays the descriptive analyses and internal consistencies (Cronbach's α) of the scales used in the RED-CONS using SPSS, v. 17.0. The α- values met the criterion of .70 (Nunnally and Bernstein, 1994) with three exceptions: social support, technical support, and feedback. The pattern of correlations shows that variables significantly relate, as expected. Due to the length of the chapter, we have not included the correlations table. However, readers may request it from the first author.

We did Multiple Analyses of Variance (MANOVA) and Analyses of Variance (ANOVA) by comparing the construction industry participants' scores with a heterogeneous general sample of 2,940 Spanish workers. To do so, we took into account the main boxes that compose the *RED Model* whenever possible. Figure 13.3 presents the results. The F values and degree of freedom (df) are available from the first author upon request.

The results show significant differences among all the psychosocial factors assessed, except for one job demand (routine) and one burnout dimension (exhaustion). These analyses reveal that construction workers show lower levels of job demands and higher levels of job and personal resources (except for job control) than the broader heterogeneous sample. Their level of self-efficacy is also lower, which could lead to the higher level of inefficacy (a burnout dimension) shown. Conversely, they show a lower level of cynicism (another burnout dimension) and, remarkably, higher levels for all the indicators of psychosocial well-being analyzed (job satisfaction and the three dimensions of work engagement, that is, vigor, dedication, and absorption).

To complete the field study at approximately one year after the first data collection through questionnaires (Time 1), we returned to the companies to assess objective organizational performance (Time 2). We conducted semi-structured interviews with the Health Prevention Manager or the Human Resources Manager of seven of the ten companies (70 percent) that had participated at Time 1. We assessed objective performance by quality and global performance indicators (that is, Return Of Assets (ROA) as an indicator of how profitable a company is in relation to its total assets; and absenteeism rates). We are currently analyzing this new data.

STUDY 2: A CASE STUDY ON HEALTHY ORGANIZATIONS

We now go on to present the findings of a case study on a construction company. Based on the *HERO Model* described above, we conducted the present study to test the positive psychosocial factors (that is, healthy practices, healthy employees, and healthy organizational outcomes) in the construction industry. Firstly, we present a description of the case study on a construction company and, secondly, we show the main results.

Description of the case study

Following the criterion recommended by George and Bennett (2005) and Gilgun (1994) with a view to conducting a case study in scientific research, we did an empirical case

Table 13.1 Mean (M), standard deviations (SD), and internal consistency (Cronbach's alpha) (n = 228) of the RED Model variables (field study)

	M	SD	α
Job demands			
1. Quantitative overload	2.83	1.89	-
2. Role ambiguity	1.24	1.66	-
3. Role conflict	2.21	2.10	-
4. Routine	3.71	2.05	-
5. Mental overload	3.80	2.06	-
6. Emotional overload	2.95	2.34	-
Job/Personal resources			
7. Autonomy	3.22	2.19	-
8. Social support	2.20	1.58	.40
9. Technical support	3.01	1.71	.36
10. Feedback	3.37	1.54	.39
11. Team coordination	4.60	.97	.77
12. Interpersonal relationships	4.40	1.53	.71
13. Leadership	4.03	1.63	r=.41***
14. Mental competence	4.91	1.29	-
15. Emotional competence	4.49	1.72	-
16. Self-efficacy	4.05	1.67	.82
17. Collective efficacy	4.17	1.30	.90
Psychosocial stress			
18. Burnout: Cynicism	1.51	1.47	.70
19. Burnout: Exhaustion	2.77	1.52	.70
20. Burnout: Inefficacy	1.21	1.47	.82
21. Propensity to quit	1.46	2.05	-
Psychosocial health			
22. Engagement: Vigor	4.79	.95	.73
23. Engagement: Dedication	4.49	1.13	.72
24. Engagement: Absorption	4.47	1.15	.67
25. Satisfaction	5.08	4.89	-
26. Organizational commitment	4.00	1.73	-
Organizational consequences			
27. Work quality	4.23	1.68	-

Note. *** $p < .001$; r = Pearson's correlation; (-) scale composed of 1 item.

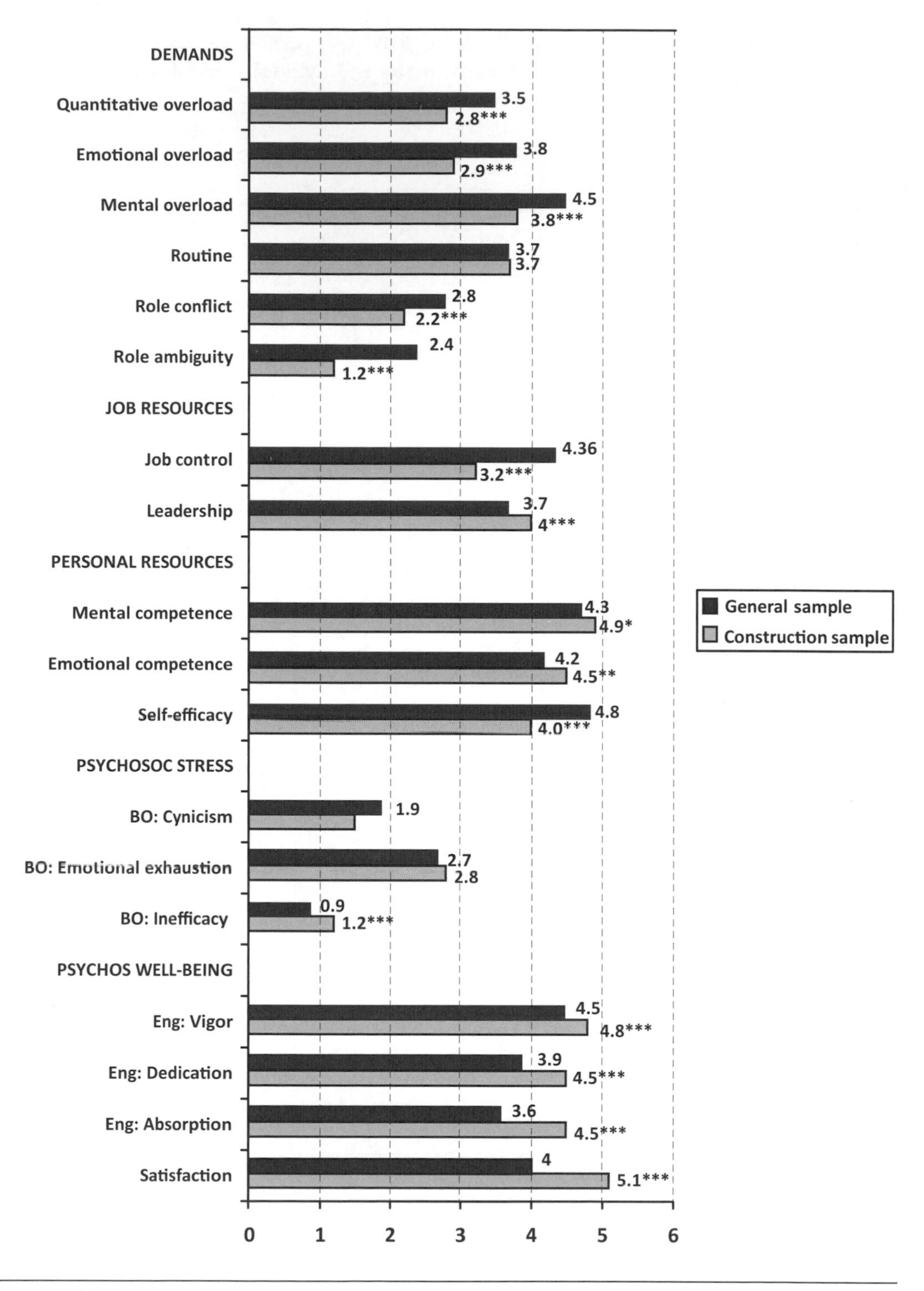

Note: *** $p < .001$; ** $p < .01$; * $p < .05$; BO= Burnout; Eng = Engagement.

Figure 13.3 Descriptive analysis with F differences between the general sample (n=2940) and the construction sample (n=228)

study in December 2008 on a construction company in Spain. The objective of this case study was to test the psychosocial positive factors involved in the evaluation of healthy organizations. We employed a compacted methodology by combining qualitative and quantitative methodology, as well as positive and (traditional) negative (that is, job demands) psychosocial constructs. We also used a new perspective since we were testing not personal but sharing perceptions about the organization. We also elaborated a protocol and a glossary with the main topics.

The *qualitative methodology* consisted in conducting a semi-structured interview with the Human Resources Development (HRD) managers. After the first contact (by telephone), an e-mail was sent to the company which contained the interview guide. The interview lasted two hours and included seven parts: (1) company and interviewed data; (2) company's history; (3) organizational structure; (4) "healthy organization" concept; (5) healthy organizational practices; (6) documental information; and (7) an action plan for the quantitative methodology administration.

We developed two specific instruments for the *quantitative methodology: RED-SME* with two different versions: for workers and for clients, using a seven-point Likert scale of responses (0 "totally disagree/never" to 6 "totally agree/always"). The workers version of the *RED-SME* comprised 133 items which we divided into five parts: (1) sociodemographical data (seven items); (2) job and social demands (24 items); (3) job and social resources (42 items); (4) organizational healthy practices (18 items); and (5) psychosocial health and organizational consequences (42 items). After explaining the objectives of this research, we handed out the questionnaires in the groups which the researchers collected during the work timetable. It is important to note that all the variables, except the sociodemographical ones, referred to the group/company, and that the level of analyses was always collective and not individual.

The sample included 122 employees: 84 percent men; 57 percent had permanent contracts and 55 percent worked part time. Regarding the job, 39 percent worked on buildings, 18 percent in civil work, 16 percent in restoration, 10 percent in production, 8 percent in clerical jobs, 5 percent in the Human Resources Department, and 4 percent did technical office work. Since the company has 145 workers, the sample used in this particular case study (122) goes beyond the minimum of 107 workers required for a representative sample with an error of 0.015 and 90 percent reliability. It is important to note that at the time of the study, and given the economical crisis, the company announced an employment regulation process with the subsequent loss of 22 jobs.

Secondly with the clients' version of the *RED-SME*, we used a seven-point Likert scale of responses (0 "totally disagree" to 6 "totally agree"). Clients should answer by considering the product offered by the company. This questionnaire included 17 items referred to as client's data (five items), service quality (seven items), product satisfaction (one item), loyalty (three items), and complaints about the product (one item). This was actually a telephone survey conducted by two team researchers after receiving the company's prior consent. A representative sample composed of 33 clients (with an error of 0.015 and 90 percent reliability) participated in the study: 100 percent were habitual clients, 40 percent had chosen this company through personal choice, 40 percent had previously obtained a product from this company more than six times, 58 percent of them had made no suggestion for improvement, while 42 percent had established some form of contact with employees while acquiring the product more than four times.

Case study results

The results of the case study on healthy organizations shown are based on the two types of methodology: qualitative (that is, interviews) and quantitative (that is, questionnaires); and on multiple key informants: HDR managers, workers, and clients.

Case study qualitative results The interviews conducted with the HRD managers reveal the following main findings. The results in terms of the company's history show that the company's main successes related to the development of an efficacious and committed human team given the following accomplished goals: (1) the cultural change due to adaptation to society; (2) job and personal sensitivities; (3) constant interest in improving quality, environmental management, and customer satisfaction. The main organizational changes related to two factors: (1) changes in the structural and technical processes; and (2) a new management team oriented to a more structured company and to society. There were remarks about one difficult time when the company had already completed a work (90 percent made) for one promoter which was in a temporary receivership. Consequently the promoter did not pay the company. In order to survive, the company extended its capital, and a collective consciousness spontaneously came about to save the company.

In terms of organizational structure, the company provided the interviewers with the flow schedule to facilitate the distribution of workers in groups and to establish the action plan to hand out questionnaires. In accordance with the healthy organization concept, the interviewees indicated their perception of how healthy the company was according to a degree of six on a scale from "0" (not a healthy organization) to "10" (a very healthy organization). At the same time, the interviewers asked for ways to increase this perception. To do this, the interviewees suggested improving both the communication channels and the job analyses performed in the company. In relation to healthy organizational practices, the company undertook different practices related to Corporate Social Responsibility (CSR), such as annual training and internal promotion planning, work-private life balance programs, work adaptation for handicapped workers, agreements with universities by giving grants to students, agreements with City Councils to subsidize concerts and other activities taking place in the city, investing in sport activities to help improve the careers of young athletes, and the publication of a company magazine to improve internal communication. As an outcome of these healthy organizational practices, the company obtained three different awards: the Quality Management System (ISO 9001), the Environmental Management System (UNE-EN ISO 14001:2004), and more recently, the Occupational Health and Safety Management System (OHSAS 18001: 2007). The company also contributed with documental information such as flow schedules, absenteeism rates, and performance objective data, customer satisfaction survey data, and the CSR objective indicators (for example, number of training hours, number of women who had enjoyed maternity benefits beyond those set out by law, and so on).

Finally, we established the action planning to plan how to hand the questionnaire to workers and clients out. Consequently, we identified 13 "natural" groups of workers. A natural group refers to employees who, irrespectively of their specific job, work in the same department/area, develop social relationships between each other, and share the same leader. Meanwhile, the managers facilitated a list of potential clients.

Case study quantitative results Tables 13.2 and 13.3 display the descriptive analyses and internal consistencies (Cronbach's α) for the scales of both versions of the RED-SME questionnaires using the SPSS software, v.17.0. All the α- values (93 percent for workers and 100 percent for clients) met the criterion of .70 (Nunnally and Bernstein, 1994), with only two exceptions: mental competence and horizontal trust. As expected, the pattern of correlations shows that scales relate significantly (72 percent and 100 percent in workers and in clients, respectively). Because of the length of the chapter, we have not provided the correlations table. However, it is available from the first author upon request.

Compared to the range of the scale, the descriptive analyses show that workers perceive high levels of healthy organizational outcomes (intra-role job performance and organizational commitment), psychosocial health in employees (vigor, dedication, pleasure, and relax), and healthy practices at social (team work and coordination, collective efficacy, mental competences) and organizational levels (vertical trust), but they perceive low levels of job demands (role ambiguity). Moreover the within-group agreements, tested by r_{wg} using the Agree program (Arthur, Bell and Edwards, 2007), show a referent-shift consensus for 87 percent of the variables. Average r_{wg} values range from .47 to .82. This suggests a sharing of employees' perceptions of healthy working conditions in the company with the exception of quantitative overload, routine, emotional overload, emotional dissonance, and support climate (see Table 13.2).

Table 13.3 displays the descriptive analyses for clients. It offers information about the healthy organization outcomes from the clients' point of view. Compared to the range of the scale, clients perceive high levels in all the variables studied. More specifically, the results stress the high levels of service quality, loyalty and, above all, product satisfaction. Furthermore, 97 percent of clients indicate that they had made no complaints about the product. Similarly to workers, the r_{wg} analyses show the referent-shift consensus on 100 percent of the variables. Average r_{wg} values range from .75 to .87. Once more, this suggests the sharing of clients' perceptions about company products and service.

Conclusions

This chapter shows that construction work is an inherently dangerous occupation due to the higher rate of accidents and disabilities in the sector. Furthermore, it also indicates that exposure to additional psychosocial risks is likely to exacerbate the level of danger, thus increasing the workers' risk to injury. However, research into this topic is not abundant. For this reason, this chapter has focused on the specific relationships among constructions workers' different psychosocial factors and health consequences, well-being, and safety performance. The results show that the psychosocial risks at workplaces (that is, task routine, quantitative and qualitative (mental) overload, fast pace of work, unpredictable periods of unemployment, and so on) are threats for construction workers. Finally, but not less importantly, it is also interesting to note that research has systematically revealed how psychosocial factors play a significant role in the construction industry, but how they also relate to physical factors.

However, despite past research showing that high physical and psychosocial demands characterize construction work, which relate to injuries and job strain, the workers in this sector also enjoy job and personal resources that also contribute to positive experiences such as job satisfaction and high work engagement (that is, vigor, dedication, and absorption),

Table 13.2 Mean (M), standard deviations (SD), and internal consistency (Cronbach's alpha) for workers (n = 122) of the HEalthy and Resilient Organization (HERO) Model variables (case study)

Variable	Workers (n = 122)		
	M	*SD*	α
Healthy practices			
Job/Social demands			
1. Quantitative overload	2.52	1.59	.85
2. Role ambiguity	0.99	1.15	.77
3. Role conflict	1.62	1.27	.74
4. Routine	3.35	1.67	.88
5. Mental overload	4.78	1.15	.70
6. Emotional overload	3.15	1.44	.71
7. Mobbing	.86	1.20	.80
8. Emotional dissonance	1.91	1.49	.85
Job/Social resources			
9. Autonomy	4.73	1.33	.76
10. Feedback	4.34	1.28	.67
11. Social support	3.16	1.53	.77
12. Team work	5.16	.91	.77
13. Team coordination	4.93	.89	.66
14. Mental competence	4.93	.90	.56
15. Emotional competence	3.99	1.32	.70
16. Empathy	4.24	1.22	.80
17. Vision	4.43	1.17	r =.42***
18. Inspirational communication	4.22	1.13	.86
19. Intellectual stimulation	3.80	1.21	.78
20. Support	4.08	1.24	.93
21. Recognition	4.22	1.28	.94
22. Collective efficacy	4.96	1.24	.86
Organizational healthy practices			
23. Vertical trust	4.33	1.18	.89
24.Horizontal trust	4.30	.87	.63

Table 13.2 Mean (M), standard deviations (SD), and internal consistency (Cronbach's alpha) for workers (n = 122) of the HEalthy and Resilient Organization (HERO) Model variables (case study) *concluded*

Variable	Workers (n = 122)		
	M	*SD*	α
Healthy practices			
Healthy employees/Psychosocial health			
25. Relax	3.80	1.45	-
26.Enthusiasm	4.13	1.33	-
27. Pleasure	4.74	1.26	-
28. Optimism	4.35	1.39	-
29. Resilience	4.59	1.29	-
30. Satisfaction	4.52	1.27	-
31. Vigor	4.67	.78	.77
32. Dedication	5.26	.85	.85
33. Absorption	4.40	.90	.80
Healthy organizational outcomes			
34. Extra-role performance	4.79	1.08	.72
35. Intra-role performance	4.96	.80	.79
36.Organizational commitment	4.93	.98	.82
37. Service Quality	4.51	.96	.91
38. Healthy results	4.74	1.04	r=.54***

Note: *** p< .001; r = Pearson's correlation; ( ) scale composed of 1 item.

Table 13.3 Mean (M), standard deviations (SD), and internal consistency (Cronbach's alpha) for clients (n = 33)

Variables			
	M	*SD*	α
Service quality	4.05	.87	.88
Product satisfaction	4.70	.68	-
Loyalty	3.39	.52	.95

Note: (-) scale composed of 1 item.

role clarity, and few intentions to quit (Salanova, Gracia and Lorente, 2007). Indeed, research even shows that transformational leadership influences positive states of mind, such as the positive psychological capital like work engagement and construction workers' positive emotions (Llorens, Salanova and Losilla, 2009). However, most research conducted in the construction industry has focused on psychosocial risks, so no positive job characteristics (such as job and organizational resources) and positive outcomes (that is, engagement, positive emotions, job satisfaction) remain unassessed, so little empirical evidence is available. In this sense, it is important to adopt a holistic perspective to study the psychosocial factors (risk and positive factors) related to the work environment and psychological experiences among construction workers in order to take a more integrated viewpoint of the reality by focusing on the new concept of healthy organizations.

Some of the main topics discussed in the chapter include safety attitudes, climate, and culture, and their relationship with safety performance. Employees' attitudes influence their safe or unsafe behavior. In this sense, we note the role played by managers/leaders as they have the key to improve employees' attitudes toward safety at work, which is so important in the construction sector, to not only improve security but to also avoid accidents and work injures. In many cases, attitudes are based on climate and safety culture. In this sense, safety climate and culture relate to safety performance. There is now a growing body of evidence to suggest that safety climate influences safety practices, unsafe behavior, and accidents, and that it is a useful predictive indicator of safety performance. While it seems appropriate to conclude that positive safety climate facilitates safe work behavior, the chapter also presents results about a relationship between safety climate and accidents and injuries. Besides, sociodemographic variables (for example, age) relate to safety performance, although the results are not always conclusive. These results indicate the need for further research into the effect that many variables have on safety performance to be done in specific contexts and at different levels of analysis. Practitioners not only need a general description of the perceived state of safety, they also need precise suggestions for preventive actions based on a separate and clear identification of each major safety issue at each main organizational level. In this sense, it is important to know how to generate and change attitudes, which would be an indicator for training and changing attitudes toward safety behavior.

In relation to safety performance, this chapter also describes its relationship with self-efficacy and its negative consequences when overconfidence develops. According to the *SCT* of Albert Bandura, efficacy beliefs are the basis of personal and collective agency, and influence one's motivation to engage in specific positive behaviors related to performance. However, this chapter reveals that efficacy beliefs do not always relate to specific positive outcomes such as motivation, health, or high performance, but depend on the type of activity being performed. So, it is possible to talk about overconfidence in certain environments (that is, the construction industry). In this sense, we consider it very important to establish the optimum level of self-efficacy in accordance with the setting in which the activity takes place with a view to avoiding the negative consequences of overconfidence, particularly in risky settings.

Finally, this chapter offers empirical data which illustrate: (1) the main psychosocial risks and positive factors assessed in the Spanish construction industry by means of a field study which includes several construction companies; and (2) an in-depth case study in a construction company which also focuses on the evaluation of a healthy organization. Some of the results of the field study agree with those noted in previous studies, for instance, job control. In this sense, and as previously explained, the *European Agency for Safety and Health at Work* (2008) indicates that the pace of work set by colleagues affects over 60 percent of workers. This factor also appears in our study where the level of job control in the construction industry seems significantly lower than in the broader heterogeneous sample. However, this does not happen with other demands, such as routine which, according to the *Fourth European Survey on Life and Working Conditions* (2007), is an overload factor that affects the construction industry. However, our study shows no significant differences for this job demand with the broader heterogeneous sample (that is, they show the same level of routine at work).

At this point, we wish to make a general qualitative interpretation of our results from our theoretical starting point, the *RED Model*. In general, we state that (compared with the heterogeneous sample) construction industry workers show a lower level of job demands, but a higher level of personal and job resources, which results in a medium level of burnout (the same level as exhaustion, a higher level for inefficacy, a lower level for cynicism). Remarkably, however, we note a higher level of job-related well-being (the three dimensions of engagement: vigor, dedication, and absorption; and job satisfaction) than in the general sample. It is important to stress again at this stage the importance of assessing not only negative, but also positive psychosocial factors, that is, a more holistic assessment.

On the other hand, self-efficacy shows significantly lower levels than the heterogeneous sample. According to the *RED Model,* this comparative low level of self-efficacy could affect the low level of job control perceived and, in turn, the inefficacy (burnout) that these construction workers perceive. This is the point at which theory and practice again come together in agreement with Kurt Lewin when he wrote: "*There is nothing more practical than a good theory*" (1952, p. 169).

So our theoretical model uncovers the psychosocial risks of our construction industry study sample: low self-efficacy and low job control. Then, if we intervene in this sample, the practical proposals would emphasize techniques to improve workers' self-efficacy (that is, going to sources of self-efficacy but, at the same time, trying to avoid very high levels of efficacy or overconfidence), and to increase perceived job control. The specific techniques (according to our *AR* approach) would come from the workers themselves through the *feedback-survey* technique. The final aim of this intervention would be to lower the levels of burnout (inefficacy, and even exhaustion) and to maintain the good levels of psychosocial well-being achieved to date over time.

Finally, we took a new step forward while undertaking the case study when we tested the goodness and reliability of the *HERO Model,* specifically in a small- and/or medium-sized construction enterprise (SME). The novelties found are the following: (1) a combined qualitative and quantitative questionnaire battery (*RED-SME*); (2) the traditional and new perspective of Positive Psychology by testing the new concept of healthy organization; (3) three different key informants participate: managers, workers, and clients; (4) the shared perceptions of the working conditions and quality for workers and clients, respectively. The findings of the case study reveal that the methodology is accurate and reliable for testing working conditions in SMEs. Specifically, the analyses of the interview and the questionnaires for workers and for clients stress that we may classify the company under study as a "healthy organization," even in the present situation of a world economical crisis. We expect these findings to possibly contribute to healthy organizations' theoretical knowledge which focuses on improving job resources and healthy practices toward an investment in not only positive psychological capital, but also in healthy and excellent results for society.

References

Ajzen, I. (1988) *Attitudes, Personality and behavior.* Chicago, IL: Dorsey.

Ajzen, I. (2001) Nature and operation of attitudes, *Annual Review of Psychology; 52,* 27–58.

Arboleda, A., Morrow, P.C., Crum, M.R., and Shelley, M.C. (2003) Management practices as antecedents of safety culture within the trucking industry: similarities and differences by hierarchical level, *Journal of Safety Research; 34*(2), 189–197.

Arthur, W., Bell, S.T., and Edwards, B.D. (2007) A longitudinal examination of the comparative criterion-related validity of additive and referent-shift consensus operationalizations of team efficacy, *Organizational Research Methods; 10*(1), 35–58.

Bandura, A. (1997) *Self-efficacy: The Exercise of Control.* (Revised edition 2002). New York, NY: Freeman.

Behm, M. (2008) Construction industry, *Journal of Safety Research; 39,* 175–178.

Cameron, K.S., Dutton, J.E., and Quinn, R.E. (2003. Foundations of Positive Organizational Scholarship. In K.S. Cameron, J.E. Dutton, and R.E. Quinn (eds),*Positive Organizational Scholarship.* San Francisco, CA: Berrett-Koehler, 3–14.

Cheyne, A., Oliver, A., Tomás, J.M., and Cox, S. (2002) The architecture of employee attitudes to safety in the manufacturing sector, *Personnel Review;* 31(*6*), 649–670.

Clarke, S. (2006) Contrasting perceptual, attitudinal and dispositional approaches to accident involvement in the workplace, *Safety Science; 44*(6), 537–550.

Cox, S. and Cox, T. (1991) The structure of employee attitudes to safety: a European example, *Work & Stress;* 5(2), 93–106.

Cox, S.J., Tomás, J.M., Cheyne, A.J.T., and Oliver, A. (1998) Safety culture: The prediction of commitment to safety in the manufacturing industry, *British Journal of Management; 9,* 3–7.

Demerouti, E., Bakker, A.B., Nachreiner, F., and Schaufeli, W.B. (2001) The job demands-resources model of burnout, *Journal of Applied Psychology; 86*(3), 499–512.

Donald, I. and Canter, D. (1993) Attitudes to safety psychological factors and the accident plateau, *Health and Safety Information Bulletin; 215,* 5–12.

European Agency for Safety and Health at Work (2008) *The Construction Sector.* http://osha.europa.eu/en/sector/construction.

European Foundation for the Improvement of Living and Working Conditions (2007) *Fourth European Working Conditions Survey.* http://www.osl.upf.edu/document.htm.

George, A.L. and Bennett, A. (2005) Case Studies and Theory Development in the Social Sciences. Cambridge, MA: MIT Press.

Gilgun, J.F. (1994) A case for case studies in Social Work Research, *Social Work; 39*(4), 371–380.

Goldenhar, L.M., Williams, L.J., and Swanson, N.G. (2003) Modelling relationships between job stressors and injury and near-miss outcomes for construction labourers, *Work & Stress; 17*(3), 218–240.

Griffin, M.A. and Neal, A. (2000) Perceptions of safety at work: a framework for linking safety climate to safety performance, knowledge, and motivation, *Journal of Occupational Health Psychology; 5*(3), 347–358.

Guldenmund F.W. (2000) The nature of safety culture: a review of theory and research, *Safety Science; 34*(1–3), 215–257.

Hofmann, D. and Stetzer, A. (1996) A cross-level investigation of factors influencing unsafe behavior and accidents, *Personnel Psychology; 49*(2), *307*–339.

Instituto Nacional de Seguridad e Higiene en el Trabajo [National Institute of Occupational Safety]and Health at Work] (2007) *VI Encuesta Nacional de Condiciones de Trabajo* [Sixth National Survey of Work Conditions]. http://www.insht.es/Observatorio/Contenidos/InformesPropios/Desarrollados/Ficheros/Informe_VI_ENCT.pdf.

Jansen, P., Bakker, A., and de Jong, J. (2001) A test and refinement of the demand-control-support model in the construction industry. *International Journal of Stress Management; 8*(4), 315–332.

Latham, G. (2005) Work motivation theory and research at the dawn of the twenty-first century, *Annual Review of Psychology*; *56*, 485–516.

Latza, U., Pfahlberg, A., and Gefeller, O. (2002) Impact of repetitive manual materials handling and psychosocial work factors on the future prevalence of chronic low-back pain among construction workers, *Scandinavian Journal of Work, Environment & Health; 28*(5), 314–323.

Lewin, K. (1952) *Field Theory in Social Science: Selected Theoretical Papers by Kurt Lewin*. London, UK: Tavistock.

Llorens, S., Salanova, M., and Losilla, J. (2009) Liderazgo transformacional y capital psicológico positivo: un estudio de caso en una empresa de la construcción [Transformational leadership and positive psychological capital: a case study on a construction firm], *Directivos construcción; 220*(March), 48–55.

McCabe, B., Loughlin, C., Munteanu, R., Tucker, S., and Lam, A. (2008) Individual safety and health outcomes in the construction industry, *Canadian Journal of Civil Engineering; 35*(12), 1455–1467.

Melia, J. L. and Becerril, M. (2007) Psychosocial sources of stress and burnout in the construction industry: A structural equation model, *Psicothema; 19*(4), 679–686.

Melia, J. L., Mears, K., Silva, A., and Lima, L. (2008) Safety climate responses and the perceived risk of accidents in the construction industry, *Safety Science; 46*(6), 949–958.

Nunnaly, J. C. and Bernstein, I.H. (1994) *Psychometric Theory* (3rd edition). New York, NY: McGraw-Hill.

Real, K. (2007) *Information Seeking and Workplace Safety: A Field Application of the Risk Perception Attitude Framework*. Paper presented at annual meeting of the International Communication Association, TBA, San Francisco, CA. http://www.allacademic.com/meta/p170607_index.html.

Robbins, S.P. (2005) *Organizational Behavior.* Upper Saddle River, NJ: Prentice Hall Inc.

Salanova, M. (2009) Organizaciones saludables, organizaciones resilientes [Healthy and resilient organizations], *Gestión Práctica de Riesgos Laborales; 58*(March), 18–23.

Salanova, M., Bakker, A., and Llorens, S. (2006) Flow at work: Evidence for a gain spiral of personal and organizational resources. *Journal of Happiness Studies; 7*, 1–22.

Salanova, M., Cifre, E., Martínez, I.M., and Llorens, S. (2007) *Caso a Caso en la Prevención de Riesgos Psicosociales. Metodología WoNT para una Organización Saludable. [Case to Case in the Psychosocial Risk Prevention: WoNT Methodology for a Healthy Organization]*. Bilbao: Lettera Publicaciones.

Salanova, M., Gracia, E., and Lorente, L. (2007) Riesgos Psicosociales en trabajadores de la construcción [Psychosocial risks among construction workers], *Gestión Práctica de Riesgos Psicosociales; 44*(December), 12–19.

Salanova, M., Grau, R., Llorens, S., and Schaufeli, W. B. (2001) Exposición a las tecnologías de la información, burnout y engagement: el rol modulador de la autoeficacia [Information technology exposure, burnout and engagement: the moderating role of self-efficacy], *Revista de Psicología Social Aplicada; 11*(1), 69–90.

Salanova, M., Lorente, L., and Martínez, I.M. (2009) The dark and bright sides of self-efficacy in predicting learning, innovative and risky performances. Manuscript submitted for publication.

Salanova, M., Peiró, J.M., and Schaufeli, W.B. (2002) Self-efficacy specificity and burnout among information technology employee: an extension of the Job Demands-Control Model, *European Journal on Work and Organizational Psychology; 11*(1), 1–25.

Salanova, M. and Schaufeli, W.B. (2009) *El Engagement de los Empleados. Cuando el Trabajo se Convierte en Pasión* [Work Engagement: When Work becomes a Passion]. Madrid, Spain: Alianza Editorial.

Salanova, M., Schaufeli, W.B., Xanthopoulou, D., and Bakker, A. (2010) The gain spiral of resources and work engagement. In A. Bakker and M. Leiter (eds), *Work Engagement: Recent Developments in Theory and Research*. New York, NY: Psychology Press, 118–131.

Salem, O., Sobeih, T.M., Genaidy, A., Shell, R., Bhattacharya, A., and Succop, P. (2008) Work compatibility and musculoskeletal disorders in the construction industry, *Human Factors and Ergonomics in Manufacturing; 18*(2), 230–252.

Salomon, G. (1984) Television is "easy" and print is "tough": The differential investment of mental effort in learning as a function of perceptions and attributions, *Journal of Educational Psychology; 76*(4), 647–658.

Schaufeli, W.B. and Bakker, A.B. (2004) Job demands, job resources and their relationship with burnout and engagement: A multi-sample study, *Journal of Organizational Behavior; 25*(3), 293–315.

Seligman, M.E.P. and Csikszentmihalyi, M. (2000) Positive psychology: an introduction, *American Psychologist; 55*(1), 5–14.

Shani, A.B. and Pasmore, W.A. (1985) Organization inquiry: Towards a new model of the AR process. In D.D. Warrik (comp.) *Contemporary Organization Development: Current Thinking and Applications*. Glenview, IL: Scott: Foresman, 438–448.

Siu, O., Phillips, D., and Leung, T. (2003) Age differences in safety attitudes and safety performance in Hong Kong construction workers, *Journal of Safety Research; 34*(2), 199–205.

Sobeih, T.M., Salem, O., Daraiseh, N., Genaidy, A., and Shell, R. (2006) Psychosocial factors and musculoskeletal disorders in the construction industry: A systematic review, *Theoretical Issues in Ergonomics Science; 7*(3), 329–344.

Stajkovic, A.D. and Luthans, F. (1998) Self-efficacy and work-related performance: a meta-analysis, *Psychological Bulletin; 124*(2), 240–262.

Vancouver, J.B., Thompson, C.M., Tischner, E.C., and Putka, D.J. (2002) Two studies examining the negative effect of self-efficacy on performance, *Journal of Applied Psychology; 87*(3), 506–516.

Vancouver, J.B., Thomson C.M., and Williams, A.A. (2001) The changing signs in the relationships among self-efficacy, personal goals and performance, *Journal of Applied Psychology; 86*(4), 605–620.

Whyte, G., Saks, A., and Hook, S. (1997) When success breeds failure: the role of self-efficacy in escalating commitment to a losing course of action, *Journal of Organizational Behavior; 18*(5), 415–433.

Wiegmann, D.A., Zhang, H., Thaden, T.L., Sharma, G., and Mitchell, A.A. (2002) *A Synthesis of Safety Culture and Safety Climate Research*. University of Illinois. http://www.humanfactors.uiuc.edu/Reports&PapersPDFs/TechReport/02-03.pdf.

Xanthopoulou, D., Bakker, A. B., Heuven, E., Demerouti, E., and Schaufeli, W.B. (2008) Working in the sky: A dairy study among flight attendants, *Journal of Occupational Health Psychology; 13*(3), 345–356.

Yeo, G. and Neal, A. (2006) An examination of the dynamic relationship between self-efficacy and performance across levels of analyses and levels of specificity, *Journal of Applied Psychology;* 91(5), 1088–1101.

PART V

Innovative Organizational Approaches

CHAPTER 14 A Variegated Approach to Occupational Safety

KARLENE H. ROBERTS AND PETER F. MARTELLI

For too long the occupational health and safety experts solely focused on "slips, trips, and falls." This is an important area since the United States Occupational Safety and Health Administration (OSHA) reports that in 2002 37 percent of occupational injuries occurred from slips, trips, and falls (www.uwsp.edu/safetyloss/). Today many managers and a growing number of occupational safety researchers realize that many important organizational "accidents" happen for other reasons. The purposes of this paper are to:

- set the stage as to reasons it is necessary to take a different approach to organizational safety than we have seen in the past;
- lay out some of the precursors to this newer approach; and
- indicate where the research concerned with this newer research seems to be today.

A Change in Accident Magnitude

Over the last century, organizations and institutions have developed a growing capability to create catastrophic accidents. Someone's error often causes a slip, trip, or fall. Increasingly slips, trips, and falls, and other kinds of errors cause outcomes that are stunning in their destruction of people, organizations, and/or systems of organizations. The first incident of this magnitude studied in the social sciences (Prince, 1920) was The Halifax Explosion in 1917 when Halifax, Nova Scotia, Canada, was devastated by the detonation of a French cargo ship, fully loaded with wartime explosives, that accidentally collided with a Norwegian troop ship in "The Narrows" section of Halifax Harbor. Approximately 2,000 people were killed by the explosion, and it is estimated that over 9,000 people were injured (Armstrong, 2002; Prince, 1920). Prince's thesis only examines the aftermath of the tragedy. This was the largest man-made explosion until the first atomic bomb test explosion in 1945 and is still one of the world's largest man-made, conventional explosions. In fact, the scientists who planned the first atomic bomb attack studied this event.

The general issue of risk mitigation or reliability enhancement in organizations is becoming increasingly important over time because we're building increasingly large,

1 This work was partially supported by National Science Foundation Grant # CMMI 0624296.

complex organizations and systems of organizations with tendrils in many different places in society and in many societies. Error in such complex systems can ramify into disastrous consequences. Take for example, the Society for Worldwide Interbank Financial Telecommunication (SWIFT). SWIFT electronically transfers 97 percent of the financial assets transferred in the world. In 2009 over 3 billion messages were sent among the over 8,300 financial institutions in 208 countries that connect to the SWIFT network (www.swift.com). Transmission errors can have serious negative consequences.

Organizations that are not as technologically sophisticated as SWIFT also have to be concerned with reliability enhancement. The Incident Command System (ICS) is a particular approach used by many public safety professions internationally to assemble and control the temporary systems they employ to manage personnel and equipment at a wide range of emergencies. Although initially developed in response to problems associated with wild land fire fighting, the ICS evolved into an all-risk system supposedly suitable for almost any type of emergency and for emergencies of nearly any size. The ICS is a cornerstone of the US Federal Emergency Management Agency's (FEMA) Integrated Emergency Management System (IEMS), whose objective is to develop and maintain a credible, nationwide emergency management capability involving all levels of government and all types of hazards. ICS systems now operate around the world (Bigley and Roberts, 2002; Flin, 1996). We have seen many situations (for example, Hurricane Katrina) in which natural disasters are compounded by man-made disasters.

In addition to building more organizations that must be reliability enhancing for their own survival and that of a broader public, some organizations that previously dealt with reliability as, perhaps a secondary requirement, are required to turn into organizations in which reliability must rival productivity as the bottom line. For example, water systems and electrical grids must produce clean water and power for everyday consumption. Today they are increasingly forced by external constituencies to consider other forms of reliability. When the punishment for violating rules such as "thou shalt not kill fish," and "thou shalt not ruin the environment" are sufficiently high, organizations must work such prohibitions into their reliability considerations. They are also moving toward the need for enhanced reliability because of the increasing interdependencies within and across them. As Robert Pool states:

> *In a generation or two, the world will likely need thousands of high-reliability organizations running not just nuclear power plants, space flight, and air traffic control, but also chemical plants, electrical grids, computer and telecommunication networks, financial networks, genetic engineering, nuclear-waste storage, and many other complex, hazardous technologies. Our ability to manage a technology, rather than our ability to conceive and build it, may be the limiting factor in many cases.*
>
> (Pool, 1997, p. 276).

It is probable that man-made disasters are impossible without organizations, and thus, an important aspect of organization science is attempting to understand how they occur, how they can be avoided, and how to respond to them when they do occur. As Turner notes, in every case of disaster there is likely to be organizational involvement because "individuals are rarely in a position to create major disasters without official or unofficial access to the energy and other forms of resources controlled by organizations, for organizations have a near-monopoly of control to access to most the sources of energy that could be discharged to produce disasters" (Turner, 1978, p. 160). Disaster production and reliability enhancement strategies are closely associated with risk and risk mitigation. Definitions of risk always include notions about the probability of an event and its consequences. Risk management or reliability enhancement, then, consists of identifying management strategies for predicting and controlling the likelihood of negative events.

Precursors to a Newer Approach to Increasing Organizational Safety

In 1984, a research group called the Center for Catastrophic Risk Management (CCRM) came together at the University of California at Berkeley to study organizations in which errors can have catastrophic consequences. They focused initially on organizations that seemed to behave very reliably, which they called high reliability organizations (HROs). Another group at the University of Michigan began addressing similar issues. While these people represented different disciplines (psychology, political science, physics) they came together with an organizational perspective.

Before discussing where the HRO work stands today it is important to place it in the context of knowledge generation leading up to it. This area of research assumes that problems that increase risk are embedded in both the designs of equipment (done by engineers) and organizations (often done haphazardly by managers—and studied by social scientists), and in their operations (studied by social scientists). Thus, unlike many problems that find their way into social science interest, this problem has its roots in two dissimilar scientific mechanisms for understanding. One is engineering and statistical modeling. The other is the social science approach drawing primarily from sociology and psychology. A third scientific discipline that contributes to this general issue is the human factors approach, a merge of psychology and engineering. Over the years, studies of risk and its mitigation have grown in sophistication as the general fields from which they were drawn became more sophisticated.

Engineering and Modeling Concerns

Concern with risk assessment and management is as old as mankind (Bernstein, 1996). The risks associated with food gathering, animals, health, weather, shelter, and social interactions all had to be recognized and evaluated in one form or another, and then managed.

Mathematical attempts to assess and manage risk have their roots in the 1600s and 1700s with questions about gambling, data analysis, and life. In 1654, a French nobleman, the Chevalier de Méré posed a problem to the famed French mathematician Blaise Pascal. The problem was how to divide the stakes of an unfinished game of chance between two players when one of them is ahead. Pascal consulted a fellow mathematician, Pierre de Fermat, and developed a solution to the problem. The solution was the theory of probability, the mathematical heart of the concept of risk (Bernstein, 1996). Thus, engineering and mathematical approaches to risk have a much longer history than social science approaches.

All of the engineering and mathematical tools we use today in risk assessment and management originated from the developments that took place between 1654 and 1760, with two exceptions. In 1875, Francis Galton discovered regression to the mean. In 1952, Nobel Laureate Harry Markowitz, demonstrated mathematically why diversification is essential in managing risks (Bernstein, 1996).

Prior to the First World War interest in human performance from an engineering perspective began to develop a sub-field called Human Factors (HF). HF is the study of the interaction of humans and their technology. These were efforts to fit men to systems, not to design systems to fit men (and later presumably women). The well-known early 1900s studies by Frederick Taylor and the Gilbreths are also precursors to modern day HF. While engineers did all the early HF work, today it is a behavioral discipline.

The next major developments in engineering were studies of production and time management associated with manufacturing processes (industrial engineering and operations research) and studies intended to improve the efficiency of human operators of machines (ergonomics research). Early in the 1960s, "time studies" in industrial engineering and operations research were seen as the way to improved workforce productivity. Most of the many manufacturing and management processes developed from these studies focused on hardware as a means of reducing accident rates. During the same time period the aerospace and electronics industries faced problems requiring assessment of the reliability of systems made of many components, each with a known failure rate. Based on work in operations research (Von Neumann, 1956), fault tree methods were used by aerospace engineers (Mearns, 1965). The electronics industry used alternative approaches for another decade before adopting fault tree methods that were originally developed in that industry (Bell Telephone Laboratories).

The chemical and process industries also began to use formal risk assessment methods in the 1970s. However, this development took a different path, with much more emphasis on performance based on quantitative and qualitative analytic methods. The chemical and process industries used a wide variety of qualitative and quantitative methods in different plants at different times. Both proactive (before accidents) and reactive (after accidents) methods were developed and applied in these industries.

Expansion of risk assessment and management methods in industrially developed countries came from two directions in the 1970s: (1) the development of nuclear power plants; and (2) the establishment of environmental protection and occupational safety and health governmental agencies (Molak, 1997). The engineering community made its most significant strides in 1975 with the release of the reactor safety study (US Nuclear Regulatory Commission, 1975). This was a probabilistic risk assessment (PRA) process that integrated engineering and environmental considerations into the basic analytical models. A short time later, the offshore engineering community employed similar PRAs to define design and requalification criteria for offshore oil drilling and production platforms (Bea, 1974; Marshall and Bea, 1976).

Process Safety emerged as a separate field from occupational safety in the 1980s. It initially focused on understanding and explaining the nature and causes of major accidents and then on estimating their impacts. An emphasis was placed on plant and equipment design, which lead quantitative risk assessments to focus particularly on equipment failures. A focus on safety auditing systems resulted from the recognition of the importance of humans and was promoted internationally in the 1990s. Many industrial communities employed PRAs with increasing intensity until the early 1990s. Then these communities began to understand the limitations of such processes and to search for improved ways to assess and manage risk. These limitations were centered in the unpredictability and uncontrollability of the multitude of complex factors and interactions that determined the real risks that these systems faced and on the organizational factors.

A major contribution to risk assessment was the development of UK Safety Cases (Spouge, 1999). These Safety Cases were a formalized way to demonstrate the safety of chemical processing plants to their owners and operators. Safety Cases require managers to demonstrate that an adequate Safety Management System (SMS) is in place in each installation, that all major hazards are identified and their risks controlled, and that risks are evaluated and reduced to a level that is as low as reasonably practicable (ALARP). This development was accompanied by a shift away from a prescriptive definition of how safety should be achieved to a goal-setting regime in which the regulator establishes the safety goals, and the owner/operator is responsible for demonstrating capabilities to reach those goals.

Social Science Concerns

Since the social sciences are newer disciplines than are engineering and mathematics, it is not surprising that interest in risk and related issues came much later to these fields. Testing was developed in the First World War to better match people to their work assignments (in today's terminology matching people and jobs through intelligence testing purportedly increases reliability of job performance). The inception of the Second World War brought with it an increase in the development of testing devices. The Army led the field with the development of the Army General Classification Test (AGCT) and other tests. The war also saw an explosion in technology. Because this was total war, involving masses of men and women, it was no longer possible to implement a Taylor-like principle of selecting a few specialized people to do pre existing jobs (Nelson, 1980). The physical characteristics of the equipment now had to be designed to take advantage of human capabilities.

An example of the kind of work that was done is the classic study by Fitts and Jones (1947) of the most effective configuration of control knobs in aircraft cockpits. Two aspects of this study reflect early elements of the HF approach. First it was a study of components, and, second, the researchers were experimental psychologists who had gone into the military and adapted their methodologies to practical problems. While moving away from the study of components, today HF still has a considerable military affiliation.

In the US just after the Second World War, the sociological approach to the study of risk was primarily associated with Quarantelli and his colleagues. In 1951 the National Opinion Research Center (NORC) hired Quarantelli to examine disaster as a possible peacetime prototype of social instability and as a means for preparing for possible future wars. A major part of the NORC project involved a study of the social impact of a tornado that occurred in Arkansas. The project was one of the first to do large-scale tape-recorded interviews and Quarantelli (1954) addressed methodological and administrative issues concerned with using this new technology. The theoretical interest that emerged at the same time was Quarantelli's interest in the concept of panic. At the time panic was conceptualized as an individual difference phenomenon resulting in paralyzing anxiety. Quarantelli's (1954) treatment emphasized the social context in which panic behavior appears, and suggested that panic behavior is extremely rare and almost non-existent in most disasters (as did Clarke, 2006). Later research by this group focused on the emergency period of disasters, giving attention to the way emergency organizations respond to cataclysms in urban communities. The issue of what constitutes a "disaster" was left somewhat flexible. Early on it was decided that organizational theories rooted in classic notions of bureaucratic functioning were inadequate for explaining responses to disaster. The team developed a more dynamic typology that attempted to explain how much pre-impact structure of organizations are maintained and how new structures emerge in emergency situations (Dynes and Quarantelli, 1968).

The wide spread civil disturbances in American cities provided the opportunity for Quarantelli and his colleagues to observe similarities and differences in "natural" disasters and "conflict" disasters. The many consistent themes in the publications of this research group include the myths of disaster behavior, the social nature of disaster, adaptation of community structure in the emergency period, dimensions of emergency planning, and differences among social situations that are conventionally considered as disasters (Dynes, Tierney and Fritz, 1994). The work primarily contributes to the sociological literature on collective behavior and social movement theory, and its focus is on how lacerations in the social fabric caused by a disaster can be repaired.

In his seminal book, *Man-Made Disasters*, the British psychologist, Barry Turner (1978), notes that until 1978 the only interest in disasters was in responses to them. As we saw previously, engineers sometimes examine the precursors to disaster but were primarily interested in technical events. Based on his examinations of three major disasters, Turner discusses two sources of cultural disruption. First, the destructive forces disturb the physical environment and disrupt the everyday conception of the physical world by those affected. The second type of cultural disruption lies in the occurrence of the event itself and its propensity to provoke the question, how could this have happened? Turner identifies six sequences of events associated with the development of disaster. They are:

1. notionally normal starting points: initial accepted beliefs about the world and associated precautionary norms;
2. incubation periods;
3. precipitating event that forces itself to the attention of participants;
4. onset or the immediate consequences of collapse;
5. rescue and salvage – first stage adjustment; and
6. full cultural readjustment.

According to Turner the most important of these stages is incubation—disasters do not happen overnight. He cites limited rationality as one input to disaster. Finally, Turner notes that the distinction between natural and man-made disasters is becoming increasingly blurred as man (and presumably woman) intervenes more in his (her) environment.

In the late 1970s, Ruffell Smith (Smith, 1979) did his now famous study of a full mission simulation of airline flight crew performance. The experiment was originally planned to examine pilot vigilance, workload, and response to stress. The study opened the door to a new realm of human contributions to error and brought to light the importance of aircrews being able to operate as teams. A set of researchers at NASA and other places also began to try to identify what constitutes "pilot error" (in search as they were for the individual difference characteristics that really mattered). These people found that "pilot error" was more likely to have something to do with crew communications and coordination than with "stick-and-rudder" proficiency (Cooper, White and Lauber, 1980).

Something like crew resource management (CRM) was around much before John Lauber first used the phrase in 1977. The development and dissemination of this phrase and similar phrases such as United Airlines' Command, Leadership, and Resource Management (CLR) provided what looked like a tangible program instituted similarly throughout the industry.

A major contributor to this literature is Robert Helmreich. One of his contributions is the "Cockpit Management Attitudes Questionnaire" (CMAQ) (Helmreich, Wilhelm and Gregorich, 1988), a 25-item Likert Scale assessment of attitudes regarding crew coordination, flight deck management, and personal capabilities under conditions of fatigue and stress. Interest in CRM continues and largely takes an individual difference and small group perspective on crew performance. It has largely ignored either internal organizational or larger contextual factors (such as regulation) except for weather.

Relevant work was also taking place in Europe. From an analysis of accident investigations, Elwyn Edwards developed his SHEL model of HF in system design (Nagel and Weiner, 1988). The acronym represents software (documents governing operations), hardware (physical resources), environment, and liveware (the human operators). In elaborating his model through examination of software, Edwards defined a new concept "trans-cockpit authority gradient" (TAG). TAG refers to the fact that the captain must establish a good working relationship with other crewmembers.

From the 1980s until now the other social science interests in reducing errors or risk mitigation took organizational or systems perspectives. In fact, HF work borrowed the "system" concept (becoming Human Factors Ergonomics—HFE) and The Department of Defense paid attention to HFE contributions to the development of weapons systems. *"The essence of the system concept in its most general form is that an entity is composed of sub-entities that, when arranged in a rational organization, are different from the superordinate entity"* (Meister, 1999, p. 89). The most recent development in the HFE area relevant to our concerns is the interest in macro-ergonomics (Hendrick, 1991). Macro-ergonomics draws directly from sociotechnical systems theory (Emery and Trist, 1960). This approach is often referred to as the human-organization-environment-machine interface technology. According to Hendrick, the central focus is on interfacing organizational design with technology to optimize human-system functioning. It is a top-down sociotechnical systems approach to organizational and work system design and the design of related human-machine user and human-environment interfaces. The social science traditions macro-ergonomics draws from (for example, sociology, quality control, social psychology, organizational science, and so on) are much broader than those drawn on in traditional HF research.

In 1984, Charles Perrow published his well-known book, *Normal Accidents* (republished in 1999). He wrote that book as a result of being the only social scientist on the President's Commission to examine the Three Mile Island disaster. He reaches the conclusion that some catastrophic accidents are bound to happen and because they are so catastrophic and unavoidable, as a society we need to close down the activities they support (for example, militaries and commercial nuclear power). He classifies systems in terms of how their components interact (varying from complex to linear) and their degree of coupling (varying from tight to loose). Linear interactions are those of one component with one or more components that precede or follow it. Complex interactions are those in which one component can interact with one or more components outside the normal production sequence. Tightly coupled systems have more time-dependent processes and their sequences are more invariant than loosely coupled systems. When tight coupling is combined with high complexity, Perrow says, the probability of catastrophic outcomes is high.

In 1988, Carol Heimer's *Annual Review of Sociology* chapter established the sociological relevance of psychological work on risk estimation and individual decision making under uncertain conditions (Heimer, 1988). In their 1992 edited volume, the sociologists James Short and Lee Clarke call for a focus on organizational and institutional contexts of risk because hazards and their attendant risks are conceptualized, identified, measured and managed in these entities. The book focuses on risk-related decisions which are "often embedded in organizational and institutional self interest, messy inter- and intraorganizational relationships, economically- and politically-motivated rationalization, personal experience, and 'rule of thumb' considerations that defy the neat, technically sophisticated, and ideologically neutral portrayal of risk analysis as solely a scientific enterprise" (Short and Clarke, 1992, p. 8).

The book's themes revolve around rationality in decision-making, social constructivist approaches, and social policy and power relationships that influence social policy. Institutionalization provides the context in which risk-related decisions are made. Here the fundamental issue is one of resource control and allocation and the means by which their control is achieved. Organizational elites have great power in defining problems, and promoting particular responses to them. Individual preferences do not follow from some logical rational perspective but represent the forces of the contexts in which those individuals are embedded.

In their 1993 *Annual Review of Sociology* chapter these authors (Clarke and Short, 1993) say, "perhaps the most intellectual progress has been made with approaches concerned with how risk identification, evaluation, management, creation, and social meaning are shaped by structural and institutional contexts" (p. 376). Here they focus on risk and social constructionism and on fairness and trust.

More recently Lee Clarke (1999) examined plans. He says:

> *Everyone plans.... Adults who don't plan are considered unstable.... Larger social units plan too.... Planning is not bounded by history or culture.... So planning is a prosaic and ubiquitous, fact of life.... I think there are many interesting things about planning, if we turn our gaze to the symbolic, in addition to functional aspects of it. This book's theme is that* organizations and experts use plans as forms of rhetoric, tools designed to convince audiences that they ought to believe what an organization says. In particular, some plans have so little instrumental utility in them that they warrant the label 'fantasy document'.
>
> (emphasis in original) (pp. 1–2).

Rational planning is possible under conditions of relatively low uncertainty but not under conditions of high uncertainty. Concomitant visions of the future are likely distorted by inadequate and corrupt data. What constitutes effectiveness is unknown. Clarke doesn't feel such plans are produced cynically but more often than not organizations and experts who believe in them produce them. Fantasy plans are morality badges. Clarke draws his cases from evacuation plans for civilian nuclear power plants, nuclear war civil defense, and major oil spills.

In 1987, Paul Shrivastava published his book on Bhopal, the largest industrial accident that has happened to date (Shrivastava, 1987). Shrivastava looked for the root causes of the Bhopal tragedy in somewhat different characteristics than those examined by Perrow (1984). Shrivastava said that human, organizational, and technical failures at Bhopal paved the way for the crisis that ensued (the leakage of toxic gas). Human factors included low employee morale, labor management conflicts, and so on. Organizational factors included the low importance of the Bhopal plant to its parent, Union Carbide, top management discontinuity at the plant, and so on. Technical factors included the tightly coupled nature of the interactive technology.

In Europe, the psychologist, Patrick Lagadec took an approach similar to the sociologists. He attempted to attain in-depth understanding of crisis phenomena. He described (Lagadec, 1993) the essential elements of crisis dynamics, three phases of crisis response (initial phase, thinking and mobilizing phase, and the strategic action phase), and set guidelines for undertaking and developing a learning process.

The Stages are Set

By the early 1990s the engineering and social science stages were fully set for the introduction of HRO research. The earliest work in this arena dealt largely with social psychological or organizational explanations of why catastrophic outcomes do or do not occur in organizations (for example, Rochlin, La Porte and Roberts, 1987; Weick, 1987). Early publications used case study methodology and tended to focus on the culture of reliability enhancement, decision making in HROs, and structuring HROs. These issues are close to those issues thought important by sociologists interested in disaster. Over the years the area has grown more differentiated as more researchers investigated HRO processes or related issues. The number of kinds of organizations investigated has increased and the methodologies are a bit more diverse. For example, Roberts, Rousseau and La Porte (1994) used both quantitative and qualitative assessments of organizational culture in a HRO.

Slowly HRO researchers have inculcated into their work both the issues and methods guiding the earlier engineering and social science work. Mathematical modeling is now as common to the social sciences as it once was to engineering. Some social science researchers incorporated into their thinking concepts of man/machine fit, time studies, fault trees, equipment failures, and so on, all coming from engineering. Simultaneously, some engineers are aware of both the methods and issues of concern to social scientists, such as communication and coordination, limited rationality, collective behavior, incubation, rhetoric about disasters, and so on. Some social scientists and some engineers are fully attuned to the necessity to examine precursors to, onset of, responses to, and cultural realignment after catastrophes.

The first ten years of the twenty-first century were filled with HRO-related activities:

- the theory blossomed;
- the research extended the kinds of organizations examined;
- part of the work now extends HRO concepts into main stream organizational theory; and

- there is a flurry of attempted applications though the success of these attempts is still questionable.

Much of the work appears in organizational behavior journals. Some is in publications addressed to managers. A flurry is published in health care journals. A small amount appears in education, communication, and engineering outlets. A good deal of it is in book chapters rather than refereed journals. One study is book length (Roe and Schulman, 2008).

Theory Development

In 1993 Scott Sagan said:

> *The scholarly literature about complex organizations is large and diverse, but two general competing schools of thought on this specific issue exist. The first is the optimistic view of what I will call 'high reliability theory,' whose proponents argue that extremely safe operations are possible, even with extremely hazardous technologies, if appropriate organizational design and management techniques are followed. The second school, what I will call 'normal accidents theory,' presents a much more pessimistic prediction: serious accidents with complex high technology systems are inevitable.*
>
> (Sagan, 1993, p. 13).

In his book about organizations, accidents, and nuclear weapons, Sagan goes on to compare the two theories and finds HRO theory wanting in predicting misses and near misses. Initially, such a comparison was unwarranted because the two theories overlap in many ways. Unfortunately it continues to be made (for example, Marais, Dulac and Leveson, 2004; Scott, 2003; Rijpma, 2003) taking needed attention away from more productive pursuits.

In addition to further developing concepts inherent in high-reliability theory such as mindfulness (for example, Weick and Putnam, 2006), coordination (for example, Faraj and Xiao, 2006), and latent errors (for example, Ramanujam and Goodman, 2003) the theory itself has been extended. One interesting example is Myers and McPhee's (2006) multi-level investigation of the effect of group interaction and its influence on individual-level membership variables and group assimilation. A model of group socialization was modified to investigate the development and maintenance of highly interdependent workgroups in a high-reliability organization (a municipal fire department). The authors examined individual and crew-level influences on four assimilation outcomes; involvement, trustworthiness, commitment, and acceptance. At the individual level, acculturation predicted all four assimilation outcomes. At the crew level, crew performance affected commitment. Implications are drawn for the influence of group interaction on member assimilation. The study underscores the importance of multi-level research.

The Kinds of Organizations Studied

HRO research began by investigating reliability enhancing processes in US Navy carrier aviation (for example, Rochlin, LaPorte and Roberts, 1987), the Federal Aviation

Administration's air traffic control operations (for example, Schulman, 1993), and commercial nuclear power plants (for example, LaPorte and Lasher, 1988). The early research was criticized because of its reliance on studies of organizations that have command and control over their technical cores and are highly regulated.

In 1999, 2001, and 2004, The Institute of Medicine of the National Academies conducted three studies of the quality of health care in the US (Kohn, Corrigan and Donaldson, 1999; Committee on Quality of Health Care in America, 2001; Page, 2004). These studies unleashed a plethora of publications about health care settings (not highly regulated) as high or low reliability organizations. Most of the articles about reliability enhancement in health care are simply polemics (for example, Carroll and Rudolph, 2006; Clarke, Lerner and Marella, 2007; Welch and Jensen, 2007; Wilson et al., 2005). Among the solid empirical studies in that industry is Gaba et al.'s (2003) comparison of hospital employees' and US Naval aviators' perceptions of safety on a standardized survey (shades of the earlier testing movement. Klein and colleagues (Klein et al., 2006) did a well-crafted qualitative study of "leadership of extreme action teams—teams whose highly skilled members cooperate to perform urgent, unpredictable, interdependent, and highly consequential tasks" (p. 590). Klein and her co-authors find that "dynamic delegation" in such teams enhances their performance. There are a number of other high-quality HRO studies in health care. Xiao and his colleagues at the University of Maryland conduct well-crafted research (for example, Xiao et al., 2002; 2004). They added to high-reliability theory through introducing and assessing the notion of a transactive responsibility system.

Kathleen Sutcliffe and Tim Vogus have paired to do several studies in health care settings. In a well-designed study they found that "the benefits of safety organizing on reported medication errors were amplified when paired with high levels of trust in manager or use of care pathways" (Vogus and Sutcliffe, 2007, p. 1). A longitudinal study of a school reform effort in the UK showed that high-reliability processes could successfully increase student test scores (Reynolds, Stringfield and Schaeffer, 2006). A more recent "longitudinal analysis of outcome data from 12 Welsh secondary schools indicates that four years after the effort was initiated results at all sites were strongly positive. Additional quantitative and qualitative data, gathered four years after the end of the intervention, indicate that the majority of the schools continue using high reliability principles and continued strong progress" (Stringfield, Reynolds and Schaffer, in press). Bea (2000; 2002; 2006) developed an interesting qualitative and quantitative approach to assessing high reliability in the maritime industry.

Possibly the most extensive study of a HRO is Roe and Schulman's (2008) multi-year study of the California Independent System Operator (CAISO), the transmission manager of California's electrical grid. Here we have an organization that does not have command and control over its technical core. These authors put their analyses of issues in high-reliability management into a strategic perspective and discuss the implications of their findings for the high-reliability management of infrastructures in other social and organizational settings.

High-reliability processes have also been examined in other kinds of organizations, including aviation (for example, Burke, Wilson and Salas, 2005); the Columbia space shuttle (for example, Starbuck and Farjoun, 2005); manufacturing (Clarke and Ward, 2006); a military armored brigade (Zohar and Luria, 2008); offshore platforms (for example, Bea, 2002); a police force (Roberts et al., 2008); Scandinavian civil aviation, commercial nuclear power, and oil production (Svenson et al., 2006); submarines (for example, Bierly, Gallagher and Spender, 2008; Roberts and Tadmor, 2002); UK train operations (Jefcott et al., 2006) and wildland and urban fire fighting (for example, Bigley and Roberts, 2002; Christenson et al., 2006).

High Reliability Organization Theory and Mainstream Organizational Theory

Many authors are beginning to link HRO theory to other often well-studied issues in organizational research and other areas. Most frequently these studies link HRO theory to leadership (for example, Bellamy et al., 2005; Clarke and Ward, 2006; Klein et. al., 2006; Vogus and Sutcliffe, 2007); organizational learning (for example, Carroll, Rudolph and Hatakenaka, 2002; Quinn, 2005; Zhao and Olivera, 2006), organizational change or transformation (for example, Burke, Wilson and Salas, 2005; Vogus and Sutcliffe, 2007), innovation (Bierly et. al., 2008) and institutional theory (Burke, Wilson and Salas, 2005). One study links mindfulness in HROs to the vast literature on less mindful behavior (Levinthal and Rerup, 2006). Another investigation relates sensemaking to the growing literature on voice and silence (Blatt et al., 2006), and yet another to bandwagon effects (Fiol and O'Connor, 2003).

Aside from the organizational literature there have been attempts to relate HRO concepts to other concepts. For example, in education HRO has been linked to the fail safe school framework (Bellamy et. al., 2005). There is also an attempt to extend strategic human resource management thinking to theory and research in HROs (Ericksen and Dyer, 2005).

Application

Many attempts at applying HRO theory in real organizations were recently implemented. Most notable are attempts in the health care industry. Leonard, Graham and Bonacom (2004) describe their clinical experience in applying surgical briefings, HRO properties to perinatal care, the value of critical event training and simulation, and the benefits of standardized communication in caring for patients transferred from hospitals to skilled nursing facilities. Madsen, Desai and Roberts (2006) describe an effort to implement HRO processes that ultimately failed in a sub-acute health care facility serving profoundly damaged children. In 2006, Dixon and Schoffer reported an investigation by the Agency for Health Care Research and Quality (AHRQ) that found that most health care workers are not versed on HRO processes. Further, most programs reported they were just at the beginning of the safety journey.

Application of HRO in health care is problematic for several reasons. First, medicine evolved from a mechanical, deterministic model where diagnosis determines treatment and treatment determines outcomes. Second, HRO is a process rather than an implementable structure. Both of these are incompatible with the underlying assumptions of medicine. Third, HRO is a decentralized system trying to operate in a centralized world (Dr Daved Van Stralen, personal communication).

The US Department of Energy (DOE) recently provided requirements and guidance for DOE contractors to insure the development and implementation of effective integrated safety systems that include HRO processes (Unites States Department of Energy, 2006). Both BP and B and W Pantex provide their field personnel with guidelines for incorporating HRO processes in their organizations (BP, 2006, B and W Pantex, 2008). How these have worked is not clear. HRO processes are discussed at NASA, Alaska Airlines, StatOil/Hydro, the Italian Air Force, the Risk Management Association (which provides training for the financial sector), and a number of other organizations. An interesting application to foreign policy-making processes was recently suggested (Meshkati, 2010).

The US Navy submarine and carrier aviation services have long been successful at implementation efforts. Commercial aviation claims the same success—worldwide.

Conclusions

Because human beings are creating more complex organizations and systems of organizations, they have gathered together in limited space resources that can cause tragic catastrophes. Thus, thinking about occupational health and safety in a way that recognizes this is important. HRO research and its application is one way to do that. HRO research has a long and interesting history in engineering and social science research. A flurry of activity relevant to HRO research and application has been undertaken in the last ten years. In the research area, the theory itself is better developed and the research has evolved from solely case study work to quantitative investigations. HRO concepts are now better embedded in the mainstream organizational behavior literature and have spread to other literatures, such as engineering and education. Large numbers of implementation efforts have been tried. Their success or failure rides on the fact that HRO is not "one size fits all." It is a tool box from which discerning managers must pick the tools best suited to their own situations, modify those tools, and be perceptive to the changing nature of their situations and to the tools that will fit those situations. As one of the proponents of HRO in the engineering domain remarked, "It's just one damned thing after another" (Robert Bea, personal communication). Kathleen Sutcliffe mirrored this when she said "this is very hard work" (personal communication).

References

Armstrong, J.G. (2002) *The Halifax Explosion and the Royal Canadian Navy*.Vancouver, BC: UBC Press.

Bea, R.G. (1974) Selection of environmental criteria for offshore platform design, *Journal of Petroleum Technology*; November, 1206–1214.

Bea, R.G. (2000) Performance shaping factors in reliability analysis of design of offshore structures, *Journal of Offshore Mechanics and Arctic Engineering; Transactions of the ASME*; 122(3), 163–172.

Bea, R.G. (2002) Human and organizational factors in reliability assessment and management of offshore structures, *Risk Analysis;* 22(1), 19–35.

Bea, R.G. (2006) Reliability and human factors in geotechnical engineering, *Journal of Geotechnical and Environmental Engineering;* 132 (May), 631–643.

Bellamy, G.T., Crawford, L., Marshall, L.H., and Coulter, G.A. (2005) The fail safe schools challenge: Leadership possibilities for high reliability organizations, *Educational Administration Quarterly*; 41(3), 383–412.

Bernstein, P.L. (1996) *Against the Gods: The Remarkable Story of Risk*. New York, NY: Wiley.

Bierly, P., Gallagher, S., and Spender, J.C. (2008) Innovation and learning in high reliability organizations: A case study of the United States and Russian nuclear attack submarines, *IEEE Transactions in Engineering Management*; 55(3), 393– 408.

Bigley, G.A. and Roberts, K.H. (2002) Structuring temporary systems for high reliability, *Academy of Management Journal*; 44(6), 1281–1300.

Blatt, R., Christianson, M.K., Sutcliffe, K.M., and Rosenthal, M.M. (2006) A sensemaking lens on reliability, *Journal of Organizational Behavior*; 27(7), 897–917.

BP (2006) *Refining and Pipelines Leadership Fieldbook*

Burke, C.S., Wilson, K.A., and Salas, E. (2005) The use of a team based strategy for organizational transformation: Guidance for moving toward a high reliability organization, *Theoretical Issues in Ergonomic Science*, 6(6), 509–530.

B and W Pantex (2008) *High Reliability Operations: A Practical Guide to Avoid the System Accident*. Amarillo, TX: B and W Pantex.

Carroll, J.S. and Rudolph, J. (2006) Design of high reliability organizations in health care, *Quality and Safety in Health Care*; 15(Supplement 1), i4–i9.

Carroll, J.S., Rudolph, J.W., and Hatakenaka, S. (2002) Learning from experience in high hazard organizations. In B. Staw and R. Kramer (eds) *Research in Organizational Behavior*. Amsterdam: Elsevier, 87–137.

Christenson, D.A., DeGrosky, M., Black, A., Fey, B., and Vidal, R. (2006) *High Reliability Organizing Implementation at Sequoia and Kings Canyon National Parks*. Tucson, AZ: Wildland Fires Lessons Learned Center.

Clarke, J.R., Lerner, J.C., and Marella, W. (2007) The role of leaders of health care organizations in patient safety, *American Journal of Medical Quality*; 22(5), 311–318.

Clarke, L. (1999) *Mission Improbable: Using Fantasy Documents to Tame Disaster*. Chicago, IL: University of Chicago Press.

Clarke, L. (2006) *Worst Cases: Terror and Catastrophe in the Popular Imagination*. Chicago, IL: University of Chicago Press.

Clarke, L. and Short, J.F. (1993) Social organization and risk: Some current controversies, *Annual Review of Sociology*; 19, 375–399.

Clarke, S. and Ward, K. (2006) The role of leader influence tactics and safety climate in engaging employee's safety participation, *Risk Analysis*; 26(5), 1175–1185.

Committee on Quality of Health Care in America (2001) *Crossing the Quality Chasm: A New Health System for the 21st Century*. Washington, DC: National Academies Press.

Cooper, G.E., White, M.D., and Lauber, J.K (eds) (1980) *Resource Management on the Flight Deck: Proceedings of a NASA/Industry Workshop*. (NASA CP-2120). Moffett Field, CA: NASA-Ames Research Center.

Dixon, N.M. and Schoffer, M. (2006) Struggling to invent high reliability organizations in health care settings: Insights from the field, *Health Services Research*; 41(4), 1618–1632.

Dynes, R.R., and Quarantelli, E.L. (1968) Redefinition of property norms in community emergencies, *International Journal of Mass Emergencies and Disasters*; 3, 100–112.

Dynes, R.R., Tierney, K.J. and Fritz, C.E. (1994) Forward: The emergence and important of social organization: The contributions of E.L. Quarantelli. In R.R. Dynes and K.J. Tierney, *Disasters, Collective Behavior, and Social Organization*. Newark, DE: University of Delaware Press.

Emery, F.E. and Trist, E.L. (1960) Sociotechnical systems. In C.W. Churchman and M. Verhulst (eds) *Management Science (vol. 2)*. Oxford, UK: Pergamon

Ericksen, J., and Dyer, J. (2005) Toward a strategic human resource management model of high reliability organization performance, *International Journal of Human Resource Management*; 16(6), 907–928.

Faraj, S., and Xiao, Y. (2006) Coordination in fast response organizations, *Management Science*; 52(8), 1155–1169.

Fiol, M. and O'Connor, E.J. (2003) Waking Up: Mindfulness in the face of bandwagons, *Academy of Management Review*; 28(1), 54–70.

Fitts, P.M. and Jones, R.E. (1947) *Analysis of 270 Pilot Errors' Experiences in Reading and Interpreting Aircraft Instruments*. Report TSEAA-694-12A. Wright Patterson Air Force Base, OH: Aeromedical Laboratory.

Flin, R. (1996) *Sitting in the Hot Seat*. New York, NY: John Wiley.

Gaba, D.M., Singer, S.J., Sinaiko, A.D., Bower, J.D., and Ciavarelli, A.P. (2003) Differences in safety culture between hospital personnel and Naval aviators, *Human Factors*; 45(2), 173–185.

Heimer, C.A. (1988) Social structure, psychology, and the estimation of risk, *Annual Review of Sociology*; 14, 491–519.

Helmreich, R.L., Wilhelm, J.A., and Gregorich, S.E. (1988) *Revised Versions of the Cockpit Management Attitudes Questionnaire (CMAQ) and CRM Seminar Evaluation Form*. NASA The University of Texas Technical Report 88-3—revised 1991.

Hendrick, H.W. (1991) Ergonomics in organizational design and management, *Ergonomics*, 34(6), 743–756.

Jeffcott, S., Pidgeon, N., Weyman, A., and Walls, J. (2006) Risk, trust, and safety culture in UK train operating companies, *Risk Analysis*; 26(5), 1105–1121.

Klein, K., Ziegert, J.C., Knight, A.R., and Xiao, Y. (2006) Dynamic delegation: Hierarchical, shared, and deindividualized leadership in extreme action teams, *Administrative Science Quarterly*; 51(4), 590–621.

Kohn, L.T., Corrigan, J.M., and Donaldson, M.S. (1999) *To Err is Human: Building a Safety Health System*. Washington, DC: National Academies Press.

Lagadec, P. (1993) *Preventing Chaos in a Crisis*. London: McGraw-Hill International.

LaPorte, T.R. and Lasher, T (1988) *Cold Turkeys and Task Forces: Pursuing High Reliability in California's Central Valley*. Working paper 88-25, Institute of Governmental Studies, Berkeley CA: University of California.

Leonard, M., Graham. S., and Bonacom, D. (2004) The human factor: The critical importance of effective communication in providing safe care, *Quality and Safety in Health Care*; 13(Supplement 1), i85–i90.

Levinthal, D. and Rerup, C. (2006) Crossing an apparent chasm: Bridging mindful and less-mindful perspectives on organizational learning, *Organization Science*; 17(4), 502–513.

Madsen, P., Desai, V., and Roberts, K.H. (2006) Designing for high reliability: The birth and evolution of a pediatric intensive care unit, *Organization Science*; 17(2), 239–248.

Marais, K., Dulac, N., and Leveson, N. (2004) *Beyond Normal Accidents and High Reliability Organizations: The Need for an Alternative Approach to Safety in Complex Systems*. Paper presented at the Engineering Systems Division Symposium, MIT, Cambridge, March 29–31.

Marshall, P.W. and Bea, R.G. (1976) *Failure Modes of Offshore Platforms*. Proceedings of the International Conference on Behavior of Offshore Structures. National Technical University of Norway, Trondheim, Vol. II. 579–635.

Mearns, A.B. (1965) *Fault tree analysis—The Study of Unlikely Events in Complex Systems*. Proceedings System Safety Symposium. University of Washington and the Boeing Company, Seattle, Washington.

Meister, D. (1999) *The History of Human Factors and Ergonomics*. Mahwah, NJ: Lawrence Erlbaum Associates.

Meshkati, N. (2010) *High Reliability, Resilient Foreign Policy Making*. White Paper, Washington DC: US Department of State.

Molak, V. (ed.) (1997) *Fundamentals of Risk Analysis and Risk Management*. New York, NY: CRC Lewis.

Myers, K.K. and McPhee, R.D. (2006) Influences on member assimilation in work groups in high-reliability organizations: A multilevel analysis, *Human Communication Research*; 32(4), 440–468.

Nagel, D. and Weiner, E. (1988) *Human Factors in Aviation*. London, UK: Academic Press.

Nelson, D. (1980) *Frederick Taylor and the Rise of Scientific Management*. Madison, WI: University of Wisconsin Press.

Page, A (ed.) (2004) *Keeping Patients Safe: Transforming the Work Environment of Nurses*. Washington, DC: National Academies Press.

Perrow, C. (1984, 1999) *Normal Accidents: Living with High Risk Technologies*. New York, NY: Basic Books.

Pool, R. (1997) *Beyond Engineering: How Society Shapes Technology*. New York, NY: Oxford.

Prince S.H. (1920) *Catastrophe and Social Change: Based on a Sociological Study of the Halifax Disaster Columbia Studies in the Social Sciences vol. XCIV*. New York, NY: Columbia University Press.

Quarantelli, E.L. (1954) The nature and conditions of panic, *American Journal of Sociology*; 60(3), 267–275.

Quinn, R.W. (2005) Flow in knowledge work: High performance experience in the design of national security technology, *Administrative Science Quarterly*; 50(4), 610–641.

Ramanujam, R. and Goodman, P.S. (2003) Latent errors and adverse organizational consequences, *Journal of Organizational Behavior*; 24(7), 815–836.

Reynolds, D., Stringfield, S. and Schaffer, E. (2006) The high reliability schools project. Some preliminary results and analyses. In J. Crispeels and A. Harris (eds) *School Improvement: International Perspectives*. London, UK: Routledge, 56–76.

Rijpma, J.A. (2003) Deadlock to dead end: The normal accidents—high reliability controversy, *Journal of Contingencies and Crisis Management*; 11(1), 37–45.

Roberts, K.H., Rousseau, D.N., and La Porte, T.R. (1994) The culture of high reliability: Quantitative and qualitative assessment aboard nuclear powered aircraft carriers, *Journal of High Technology Management Research*, 5(1), 141–161.

Roberts, K.H. and Tadmor, C.T. (2002) Lessons learned from non-medical industries: The tragedy of the USS Greeneville, *Quality and Safety in Health Care*; 11(4), 355–357.

Roberts, K.H., Yu, K.F., Desai, V., and Madsen, P. (2008) Employing adaptive structuring as a cognitive decision aid in high reliability organizations. In G.P. Hodgkinson and W.H. Starbuck (eds) *The Oxford Handbook of Organizational Decision Making*. New York, NY: Oxford, 194–210.

Rochlin, G.I., La Porte, T., and Roberts, K.H. (1987) The self-designing high-reliability organization: Aircraft carrier flight operations at sea, *Naval War College Review*; 40(4), 76–90.

Roe, E. and Schulman, P. (2008) *High Reliability Management: Operating on the Edge*. Stanford, CA: Stanford University Press.

Sagan, S. (1993) The *Limits of Safety: Organizations, Accidents, and Nuclear Weapons*. Princeton, NJ: Princeton University Press.

Schulman, P (1993) The analysis of high reliability organizations: A comparative framework. In K.H. Roberts (ed.) *New Challenges to Understanding Organizations*, New York, NY: Macmillan.

Scott, W.R. (2003) *Organizations: Rational, Natural, and Open Systems*. Upper Saddle River, NJ: Prentice Hall.

Short J.F. and Clarke, L. (eds) (1992) *Organizations, Uncertainties, and Risk*. San Francisco, CA: Westview.

Shrivastava, P. (1987) *Bhopal: Anatomy of a Crisis*. Cambridge, MA: Ballinger.

Smith, R. (1979) *A Simulator Study of the Interaction of Pilot Workload and Error*. Moffett Field, CA: NASA Ames Research Center.

Spouge J. (1999) *A Guide to Quantitative Risk Assessment for Offshore Installations*. CMPT Publication 99/100, London, UK: CMPT.

Starbuck, W.H. and Farjoun, M. (2005) *Organization at the Limit: Lessons from the Columbia Disaster*. Malden, MA: Blackwell.

Stringfield, S., Reynolds, D., and Schaffer, E.C. (in press) Improving secondary students' academic achievement through a focus on reform reliability: Four and nine year findings from the high reliability project, *School Effectiveness and School Improvement*.

Svenson, O., Salo, I., Oedewald, P., Reiman, T., and Skerve, A. (2006) *Nordic Perspective on Safety Management in High Reliability Organizations: Theory and Application*. Roshilde, Denmark: NKS Secretariat.

Turner, B.M. (1978) *Man-Made Disasters*. London, UK: Wykeham.

United States Department of Energy (2006) *Integrated Safety Management Systems Manual*. www.directives.doe.gov.

United States Nuclear Regulatory Commission (1975) *Reactor Safety Study*. USNRC, WASH 1400, Washington, DC: USNRC.

Vogus, T.J. and Sutcliffe, K.M. (2007) The impact of safety organizing, trusted leadership and care pathways on reported medication errors in hospital nursing units, *Medical Care*; 45(10), 997–1002.

Von Neumann, J. (1956) *Probabilistic logics and the synthesis of reliable organisms from unreliable components*. Automata Studies, Annals of Mathematics Studies, No. 34, Princeton University Press, Princeton, NJ.

Weick, K.E. (1987) Organizational culture as a source of high reliability, *California Management Review*; 29(2), 112–127.

Weick, K.E. and Putnam, T. (2006) Organizing for mindfulness: Eastern wisdom and western knowledge, *Journal of Management Inquiry*; 15(3), 275–287.

Welch, S. and Jensen, K. (2007) The concept of reliability in emergency medicine, *American Journal of Medical Quality*; 22(1), 50–58.

Wilson, K.A., Burke, C.S., Priest, H.A., and Salas, E. (2005) Promoting health care safety through training high reliability teams, *Quality and Safety in Health Care*; 14(4), 303–309.

Xiao, Y., Moss, J., Mackenzie, C.F., and Seagull, F.J. (2002) *Transactive Responsibility Systems and High Reliability Teams: A Tentative Formulation*. Proceedings of the Human Factors and Ergonomics Society 46th Meeting, 1428–1439.

Xiao, Y., Plasters, C., Seagull, F., and Moss, J. (2004) Cultural and institutional conditions for high reliability teams, *IEEE International Conference on Systems, Man, and Cybernetics*, 2580–2585.

Zhao, B. and Olivera, F. (2006) Error reporting in organizations, *Academy of Management Review*; 31(4), 1012–1030.

Zohar, D. and Luria, G. (2008) Organizational meta scripts as a source of high reliability: The case of an Army armored brigade, *Journal of Organizational Behavior*; 24, 837–859.

CHAPTER 15

The Best Practices for Managing Return to Work Following Mental Health Problems at Work

LOUISE ST-ARNAUD, CATHERINE BRIAND, MARIE-JOSÉ DURAND, MARC CORBIÈRE, MARIÈVE PELLETIER AND EVELYN KEDL

Mental health problems in the workplace currently represent a major cause of absence from work, and this phenomenon has grown markedly over the last two decades (Gabriel and Liimatainen, 2000; Vézina and Bourbonnais, 2001; Dewa et al., 2002; Henderson, Glozier and Elliott, 2005; Dewa, McDaid and Ettner, 2007; Houtman, 2007). Mental health problems can have particularly incapacitating effects resulting in long periods of disability (Koopsmans, Roelen and Groothoff, 2008), and involve a high risk of relapse (Conti and Burton, 1994; Druss, Schlesinger and Allen, 2001; Gjesdal and Bratberg, 2003; Nieuwenhuijsen et al., 2006; Koopmans, Roelen and Groothoff., 2008).

This increase in absences represents a major economic and public health problem (Henderson, Glozier and Elliott, 2005; Dewa, McDaid and Ettner, 2007). Thus, organizations are starting to feel the need to adopt more comprehensive and integrated approaches to the management of employees' absences in addition to the focus on health and productivity (Watson Wyatt, 2005). The urgency felt in this regard signals a need for good practices in absence management which will foster the return to work and job retention of workers who have been absent for mental health reasons.

Our most recent studies have led to the development of a process to assist and support the rehabilitation and return to work of employees. This process is supported by evidence-based data related to disability management and by the design, implementation, and evaluation of an integrated program of practices supporting return to work following an absence due to a mental health problem.

From the First Signs and Symptoms to Work Cessation: A Difficult Transition

The onset of illness is rarely sudden. The first signs and symptoms often appear when the individual is still working. Feelings of fatigue that can no longer be ignored are often among the first signs. The worker hopes to get over the fatigue during his/her vacation or by taking a few days' rest here and there. However, there comes a time when these periods of respite no longer suffice; fatigue accumulates and an overwhelming feeling of exhaustion sets in. This feeling of exhaustion is often compounded by insomnia, difficulty concentrating, memory loss, irritability and, in some cases, the urge to cry over anything and everything. A decrease in the worker's functional skills, difficulty maintaining the same production rate, irritability toward co-workers or clients, the feeling of losing control and that the situation is going to boil over at any moment, are all symptoms of deteriorating health, and make the worker's situation visible to others in the workplace (co-workers, supervisors, clients, and so on).

Despite these symptoms, many workers hesitate to consult a physician, particularly in the case of men, but also women (St-Arnaud, Saint-Jean and Damasse, 2009). Fear of being seen as weak because of their inability to withstand the pressure at work is among the fears cited in explaining their hesitation to consult a physician and take leave from work. Some workers feel guilty about taking leave, as if their deteriorating health were a sign of weakness and self-neglect, despite real and particularly disabling symptoms (St-Arnaud, Saint-Jean and Rhéaume, 2004; St-Arnaud, Saint-Jean and Damasse, 2009). According to Haslam et al. (2005), mental health problems always generate strong resistance in the workplace because of the prejudice associated with them. The very idea of illness is dismissed and rejected and it is only *in extremis* that it will be accepted.

Work cessation has serious consequences in the workplace. Socially, workers who can no longer perform their role need to have very good reasons. Thus, the illness must be recognized as "serious" enough to justify a withdrawal from work. In this regard, certain types of illness are more easily recognized than others. For example, an individual who has had a heart attack is considered to have a valid reason to take sick leave. However, mental health problems are less obvious, more ambiguous, even dubious in some cases and thus are contested. Individuals often find it difficult to assess their own mental health. They have few points of reference and tend to judge themselves harshly. Some workers wait for approval, in an informal way, from those around them, a word from co-workers or the supervisor, a way to be validated by other people. Knowing this could make it possible to help some workers undertake a consultation process (St-Arnaud, Saint-Jean and Rhéaume, 2004; St-Arnaud, Saint-Jean and Damasse, 2009). The support of co-workers and the supervisor can thus be a crucial determinant in helping the worker consult and undertake treatment.

According to Henderson, Glozier and Elliot (2005), "common" mental health problems such as depression and anxiety contribute more to increasing sickness absences in the workplace than do severe and persistent mental disorders. Adjustment disorders are generally the most common mental health problems among workers (Nieuwenhuijsen et al., 2003). These usually transitory disorders are manifested through various emotional symptoms (anxiety or depression) or behavioral symptoms (irritability, carelessness) in reaction to a stressful event in a worker's personal or work life. Studies suggest that over 50 percent of workers who are on sick leave for a mental health problem have received a diagnosis of adjustment disorder (LISV, 2000, in Nieuwenhuijsen et al., 2003; van der Klink et al., 2003). However, Casey (2001) points out that it is difficult to evaluate the full extent of this disorder since its diagnosis is not considered in most studies on the prevalence of mental disorders. In general, the duration of absence of workers with an adjustment disorder is estimated to be short, with periods ranging from four to six weeks, the time it takes to recover from a stressful event (MSSS, 2009). However, when the stressful situation endures, the symptoms are likely to worsen and lead to a more serious health problem, including major depression (Vézina et al., 1992).

Mood disorders, including major depression, are associated with longer periods of absence (Kessler et al., 2006; Nieuwenhuijsen et al., 2006; Brenninkmeijer, Houtman and Blonk, 2008). The analysis of data from a population survey conducted in France involving a representative sample of workers reveals the prevalence of mood disorders to be 10 percent for men and 14 percent for women (Cohidon, Imbernon and Gorldberg, 2009). This category also includes individuals suffering from bipolar disorder, an illness which generally appears before the age of 35 and is distinguished by the presence of periods of abnormal euphoria and major depression. Kessler et al.'s study (2006) conducted on a representative sample of workers in the US reveals a prevalence rate of 1.1 percent for bipolar disorders and 6.4 percent for depression over a 12-month period. The measurements obtained from these different studies must be interpreted and compared with caution because of the variability in the methodology used to obtain incidence and prevalence rates.

Anxiety disorders cause the longest periods of absence, in particular because individuals find it more difficult to consult. These disorders include panic disorders, phobia, obsessive-compulsive disorder and generalized anxiety disorder. Cohidon, Imbernon and Gorldberg's study (2009) reveals prevalence rates of 17 percent for men and 25 percent for women. The prevalence of anxiety disorders, all diagnoses combined, appears to be higher than that of major depression (Pélissolo et al., 2002; Waghorn and Chant, 2005; or from 20 percent to 25 percent (Kessler et al., 1994; Leon, Portera and Weissman, 1995; Cohidon, Imbernon and Gorldberg, 2009).

In addition to these mental health problems, some workers may have personality dysfunctions. These dysfunctions are not necessarily considered to be an illness although they can create difficulties at the relational or behavioral level. Moreover, a much smaller proportion of workers may have psychotic disorders, including schizophrenia. These health problems are associated to a greater extent with severe mental disorders, and the occupational integration and job retention of workers with these mental health problems remain a major challenge (Corbière et al., 2006a; Corbière and Lecomte, 2009c).

Recognizing the Central Role of Work on Mental Health and Job Retention

Stressful events in an individual's personal life, such as the death of a loved one, caring for a parent or sick child, or conjugal or financial difficulties, can also contribute to weakening the individual's health and lead to an adjustment disorder (St-Arnaud, Saint-Jean and Rhéaume, 2003). However, a great proportion of workers who have been absent from work due to mental health problems stopped working because of difficulties experienced in their work context (St-Arnaud et al., 2007; Cohidon, Imbernon and Gorldberg, 2009). In a study involving 1,850 workers who were on leave due to a mental health problem, as certified by a medical diagnosis, the overwhelming majority of workers referred to difficulties experienced in the context of their work to explain the deterioration in their health and the sick leave (St-Arnaud et al., 2007). In fact, only 9 percent of the subjects

(10 percent of women and 6 percent of men) referred mainly to their personal life in explaining their health problem and sick leave; 32 percent attributed this situation directly to their work (27 percent of women and 43 percent of men), and nearly two-thirds of respondents (63 percent of women and 50 percent of men) attributed it to both their personal life and work. Given the fact that 32 percent of subjects stated that they were absent mainly because of their work and that nearly two-thirds were absent due to both personal and work-related reasons, this means that a total of more than 90 percent of the subjects referred to work-related problems in accounting for the deterioration in their health and the sick leave. The work-related stress identified by the subjects were: work overload (62 percent), non-recognition of effort (48 percent), conflict with the supervisor (31 percent), conflict with co-workers (21 percent), a negative evaluation of their work (19 percent), lack of autonomy in their work (17 percent), and job insecurity (14 percent) (St-Arnaud et al., 2007).

These results are consistent with those in numerous writings, which highlight the fact that in recent years workplaces have undergone a great deal of upheaval which has had an impact on the mental health of workers (Karasek and Theorell, 1990; Dejours 1993; 1995; Niedhammer et al., 1998; van der Doef and Maes, 1999; Stansfeld et al., 1999; Brisson, Larocque and Bourbonnais, 2001; Siegrist and Marmot, 2004; Rugulies et al., 2006; Bourbonnais et al., 2006a; 2006b). Increased competitiveness and competition, accompanied by organizational mergers and staff streamlining have led to new demands in the workplace. These changes cause a complete disruption in the methods of work organization and force some employers to move toward a flexible management of production time and labor force utilization. Moreover, the amount of work demanded from employees increases, while human and financial resources decrease. Work intensification appears to be responsible for a large number of absences related to mental health problems (Vézina et al., 2004; 2008). New management practices such as getting rid of downtime, evaluating individualized performance, and sub-contracting have also been associated with this work intensification. These management practices affect social labor relations, make workers compete with each other, weaken work groups, and undermine the capacity for mutual assistance and generally getting along (Dejours, 2003). The pressure exerted by these changes has an impact on employees' capacity to work and retain their jobs, and also on their mental health. According to Vinet, Bourbonnais and Brisson (2003), the spectacular rise in absences due to mental health problems and the ensuing proportional rise in group insurance premiums attest to the extent and depth of this crisis.

Based on this perspective, returning to work following a mental health problem remains particularly difficult and risky if work-related risk factors are not taken into account. In fact, it is more difficult for individuals who have been absent due to work-related factors to return to work (St-Arnaud et al., 2007). Conversely, an analysis of return-to-work conditions shows a significant association between improved working conditions upon the return to work and resolved mental health problems. Brenninkmeijer, Houtman and Blonk's study (2008) on factors predicting return to work following depression also demonstrates the need to modify the task or the work context in order to foster the recovery of health and the return to work. Taking action on the psychosocial environment at work upon the return to work proves to be a major determinant in restoring health and a successful return to work following a mental health problem.

Challenges of an Intervention Targeting the Psychosocial Environment at Work

In recent years, research in the field of occupational rehabilitation has evolved from a biomedical approach often centered on the individual factors of the illness toward an approach that takes the factors related to the work environment into account (Durand et al., 2003; Franche et al., 2005). According to Franche et al. (2005), making temporary or permanent changes in the work environment remains a crucial component of interventions considered to be effective in the workplace to ensure a successful return to work. In fact, several studies stress the importance of this measure and its effectiveness on the duration of work disability (Hogg-Johnson and Cole, 2003; Amick et al., 2000; Arnetz et al., 2003; Loisel et al., 2001). In terms of mental health at work, this dimension is all the more crucial since the psychosocial environment at work is responsible for a large percentage of work absences (Vézina et al., 2008). In addition, the writings of Brenninkmeijer, Houtman and Blonk (2008) and St-Arnaud et al. (2007) have confirmed the importance of acting on the psychosocial environment at work in order to foster return to work and job retention. Moreover, a systematic review of preventive interventions in the area of mental health has shown the importance of taking action at the individual level, at the workteam level, and at the level of organizational and political structures (Corbière et al., 2009a).

The psychosocial environment at work includes both technical dimensions of work and human dimensions. The technical dimensions relate more specifically to task content. In other words, they condition the "what," "how," and "how much" to do in a given period of time. The human dimensions involve more specifically social relations at work. They refer to the modes of interaction and communication between individuals, either at the vertical level (supervisors and subordinates) or horizontal level (co-workers) (St-Arnaud and Vézina, 1993). These work dimensions directly affect work organization and management practices (Brun, 2009). Thus, the organization's managers and, especially, the employee's direct supervisor are directly involved when dealing with the factors related to the psychosocial environment at work. According to Franche et al. (2005), the latter play a unique role in the organization in terms of making the link between senior management and the worker. They can, among other things, change the work, interpret the organization's policies, and facilitate access to organizational resources. However, the managers and direct supervisors' capacity to act on the factors related to the psychosocial environment at work will depend on the importance attached to this issue by the organization, in particular by senior management. In fact, direct supervisors can often feel caught between the demands of senior management to increase productivity and their responsibilities regarding the health and well-being of employees (Franche et al., 2005).

Support and commitment from senior management remain key factors in the development and implementation of an intervention targeting work organization and management practices. According to Baril and Berthelette (2000), the values of senior executives and the quantity of resources they allocate for the support of an intervention can modulate the capacity for action of the stakeholders involved in changing the work environment. Their values and attitudes have a significant impact on the success of interventions. A positive attitude will be translated into a concern for workers' health and sustained support for interventions in the workplace. Moreover, by favoring a participatory management style in the organization, senior management allows workers and direct supervisors to be stakeholders in the planning and implementation of a return-to-work program (Stock et al., 1999). Relations between management and the unions are also perceived to have a major impact on return-to-work programs (Baril et al., 2003). Instances of confrontational behavior decrease when unions and management share the common goal of ensuring workers' well-being and health upon their return to work. Return-to-work programs are more difficult to implement when the union plays only a marginal role in the program, when the program is imposed by management, or when key elements in collective agreements are not respected. Conversely, unions are more likely to approve the return-to-work measures put forward if the latter are well planned and properly managed. The following factors constitute the conditions that are essential to the success of a return-to-work program: establishing a climate of trust marked by respect, effective communication, and collaboration between the various internal or external stakeholders involved in the return to work (Baril et al., 2003; Stock et al., 1999). On the other hand, legal recourses reduce trust and interfere with the return-to-work process and are considered to be obstacles to the return to work (Baril et al., 2003). Based on this perspective, the value attributed to employees and the importance attached to the work climate influence the worker as a key stakeholder in his/her return to work (Baril and Berthelette, 2000). These factors encourage workers to collaborate in early return-to-work measures if they see that their concerns and suggestions have been taken into account in the various participatory ergonomics projects (Stock et al., 1999). Thus, an organization which is concerned with its employees' health and sustained employment must recognize the central role of work on mental health and job retention. Based on this perspective, identifying factors related to the psychosocial environment at work that are likely to negatively affect the return to work must be an integral part of the protocol used to evaluate workers on sick leave.

The Strategic Role of a Coordinator Responsible for Rehabilitation and Return-To-Work Support Activities

Evidence-based data suggest that, in addition to promoting intervention programs in the workplace, attention should also be focused on a collaborative process between the partners involved in the return-to-work (Durand and Loisel, 2001; Loisel et al., 2001; Durand et al., 2004; Franche et al., 2005). Managers, unions, workers, heads of human resources, medical resources, and insurers must work together and take coherent actions at each step in the return-to-work process (Stock, et al., 1999). Moreover, an increasing number of studies suggest the need to hire an individual to coordinate the activities supporting rehabilitation and return to work (Olsheski, Rosenthal and Hamilton, (2002); Russo and Innes, 2002; Young et al., 2005; Shaw et al., 2008).

The return-to-work coordinator is responsible for assessing the needs related to rehabilitation and return-to-work support, for preparing the return to work, and for facilitating communication between stakeholders in the workplace. According to Shaw et al. (2008), the success of interventions appears to depend more on competency in ergonomics, reassigning modified tasks, communication and conflict resolution, than on competency based on medical training. Moreover, the coordinator needs to act as the interface between several stakeholders who may have different goals and contexts for action (MacEachen et al., 2006). Thus, a major challenge for the coordinator is to win the worker's trust while preserving his/her credibility with regard to managers and other stakeholders. It is essential that the coordinator play a neutral and independent role, free from medical-legal and administrative issues, in performing this task. According to Baril et al. (2003), the functions related to absence control should be distinguished from those related to rehabilitation and return-to-work support. Despite this distinction, the credibility of return-to-work support programs can nevertheless be compromised. In fact, integrating stakeholders with contradictory roles in the same organization can create confusion over the real intentions of the organization.

A Support-based Approach throughout the Sick Leave

The return-to-work coordinator uses best practices to support the worker's rehabilitation and return to work and assists the worker on sick leave throughout his/her return-to-work process. This process involves six major steps:

1) REASSURANCE PRACTICES

Taking leave from work due to a mental health problem is a difficult experience (St-Arnaud, Saint-Jean and Damasse, 2006). Agreeing to take leave from work and, especially, receiving a diagnosis related to a mental disorder, is a difficult experience to accept, in particular for an individual who has always functioned well at work (St-Arnaud, Saint-Jean and Rhéaume, 2003). This first finding helps to understand the vital importance of practices aimed at reassuring and supporting the individual on sick leave. As a first step, the coordinator makes a telephone call to establish contact with the worker. During this call, the worker is informed about activities that could support his/her rehabilitation and return to work, and is invited to participate in these on a voluntary basis.

2) THE CENTRAL ROLE OF THE DIRECT SUPERVISOR

Through their functions, attitudes, and key role with regard to employees, direct supervisors play a significant role in the return-to-work and job retention process (Gates, 1993; McLellan, Pransky and Shaw, 2001; Linton, 1991; Franche et al., 2005, Corbière et al., 2009a). The direct supervisor is the main person responsible for planning the workload, methods of supervision, resource allocation, and evaluation of results. At several levels, he/she can even decide on the organization of work and is authorized to implement a number of measures to make accommodations or adjust the work in order to ensure a worker's return to work and job retention (Gates, 1993; Linton, 1991; Corbière et al., 2006a; Corbière and Shen, 2006b). According to Brun (2009), the management practices implemented by supervisors can be influencing factors for mental health. Studies have also shown that supervisors who adopt supportive behaviors toward a worker returning to work following an absence episode foster greater success in terms of rehabilitation (Corbière and Lecomte, 2007). Direct supervisors thus play a key role in the process, in particular in helping the worker prepare his/her return to work by identifying the factors in the work environment that could be changed in order to facilitate the return to work and ensure job retention. It is important to plan competency development activities aimed at helping supervisors to better grasp the importance of their role and of the factors related to the psychosocial environment at work from the perspective of mental health at work. Indeed, these training activities could contribute to facilitating the shift away from a paradigm of absence control toward a paradigm based on the support of individuals, a shift that is more or less difficult to bring about, depending on the practices and values conveyed in the organization.

3) IDENTIFYING OBSTACLES TO REHABILITATION AND RETURN TO WORK

A few weeks after the sick leave begins, the worker is invited to a first meeting with the return-to-work coordinator to identify, according to how the worker perceives things, the obstacles and facilitators to rehabilitation and a return to work. The clinical, social, and organizational factors are examined during this meeting. The interview starts with a brief review of the worker's employment history up to the last job held before the sick leave. The worker is invited to talk about the personal and organizational factors which contributed to his/her deteriorating health and sick leave, as well as the consultation processes engaged in and his/her current state of health.

An analysis of resources and needs in the area of clinical support and social support is then conducted. Depending on the case, the worker can be referred to more specialized mental health services, or to the organization's employee assistance program (EAP) which offers a referral service to help workers grappling with personal problems (psychologists, guidance counsellors, social workers, and so on). This type of referral is not aimed at reassessing the veracity of the illness as is often seen in the expertise reports requested by some employers. The aim here is to ensure a better treatment plan by providing the worker and his/her attending physician with access to specialized resources. This must be carried out with the agreement of the worker and his/her attending physician, or at the request of the attending physician, who will be informed of the available clinical resources made available by the employer.

Lastly, work-related factors can be addressed during this meeting or discussed subsequently if the worker does not seem to be able to deal with this topic because of his/her health. The idea behind this first meeting is to establish a relationship of trust with the worker and to foster the rebuilding of a positive link with the workplace. Once the worker is able to talk about work, he/she will be questioned about tasks, relations with supervisors and co-workers, and concerns about the idea of returning to work. This process allows the worker to "think" about work and to act on his/her fears about an eventual return to work.

4) SUMMARIZING THE CONCERNS AND TARGETS FOR ACTION

During this discussion about work-related factors, the worker identifies and expresses his/her concerns regarding rehabilitation and the return to work. This exchange is more focused and aims at defining, among all the concerns expressed, those which are more significant and could be discussed with the direct supervisor in order to identify courses of action likely to foster return to work and job retention. In general, this meeting leads the worker to begin thinking about these issues, a thought process which then continues helping the worker clarify any concerns regarding the return to work and his/her subsequent capacity for job retention.

The coordinator works with the individual in order to address the main points, clarify some aspects, and end up with a relatively clear formulation of his/her needs and concerns. By narrating events, but also clarifying their ideas, workers can thus examine their suffering and identify what makes them uncomfortable, what paralyzes them.

This exercise aims to act on the anticipation of return-to-work conditions and strengthen the feeling of self-efficacy by focusing on the worker's power to act. This process of thinking through and summarizing the issues should make it possible to target two or three major concerns related to the psychosocial environment at work which will then be discussed with the direct supervisor. These concerns may relate to workload, the clarification of roles, relational difficulties, and so on.

In addition to the importance of welcoming the worker back to work, providing support at work and developing reassurance practices during the sick leave, the possibility of making changes in the work environment appears to be a major determinant of a successful return to work (Brenninkmeijer, Houtman and Blonk, 2008; St-Arnaud et al., 2007; Caveen, Dewa and Goering, 2006). Difficulties linked to the psychosocial environment at work remain one of the major factors likely to contribute to the deteriorating health and sick leave of workers. Anticipating a return to work in difficult conditions can be a source of anxiety, which can be detrimental to the rehabilitation process (St-Arnaud,Saint-Jean and Damasse, 2006). Conversely, the possibility of acting on the work environment is a major determinant of a successful return to work (St-Arnaud et al., 2007).

5) MEETING THE DIRECT SUPERVISOR AND DRAFTING A RETURN-TO-WORK PLAN

A meeting is later organized with the worker, the direct supervisor, and the return-to-work coordinator in order to define a return-to-work plan which will take account of the factors related to the work environment that can foster the return to work and job retention. First, the return-to-work coordinator reports the worker's concerns. The supervisor is encouraged to adopt an open-minded attitude based on active listening and the search for solutions. Courses of action can be explored while also taking into account constraints related to work organization as expressed by the supervisor. This meeting is led by the return-to-work coordinator who acts as a mediator between the worker and the supervisor in order to assist them in developing a satisfactory action plan. Different levels of action can be considered, that is: temporary adjustment measures to foster a gradual return, permanent adjustments made to the work environment, activities involving conflict resolution or mediation, prospects for reassignment to another workstation or to another work unit, or accommodating measures. Lastly, the return plan must also specify welcoming activities which will support the worker upon his/her return to work. Studies have demonstrated the importance of preparing the return and planning ways to make the worker feel welcome upon his/her return to work.

6) RETURN TO WORK AND JOB RETENTION

The actual return to work is an important step which must be planned well ahead of the day of return (Durand et al., 2003; Baril et al., 2003). It is now known that the return to work does not occur at the end of a complete health recovery, but rather through a continuous process where health is rebuilt gradually through the work activity itself

(St-Arnaud, Saint-Jean and Rhéaume, 2003). The possibility of returning to work gradually, of being welcomed and supported by co-workers and supervisors, and especially, of benefiting from a reorganized psychosocial environment at work is a major determinant of a successful return to work. These are the conditions for a transition from a state of threatened vulnerability to one of reassured vulnerability (St-Arnaud, Saint-Jean and Rhéaume, 2003; St-Arnaud et al. 2007). The first days after returning to work are often marked by a feeling of vulnerability and the fear of relapse. Individuals only gradually regain confidence in their capacity to work and feel able to function effectively in their work (St-Arnaud St-Arnaud, Saint-Jean and Rhéaume, 2004). The welcome and support received from the supervisor and co-workers remains crucial during the return. It should also be possible to adjust the terms and conditions of the return-to-work plan to the real situations encountered by the worker upon his/her return to work. The procedures for a gradual return can easily be ignored in the face of work demands (St-Arnaud, Saint-Jean and Rhéaume, 2004). It is strongly recommended that the employee who has replaced the worker on sick leave be retained so as to ensure the effectiveness of the gradual return to work, not only over time but also in terms of the task (Durand and Loisel, 2001). Lastly, a follow up on the return to work must be conducted with both the worker and the direct supervisor. It is important to check whether interventions in the psychosocial environment at work have been effective over time. Readjustments may be needed, based on the relatively stable progress of the individual's health and the numerous changes that are likely to occur in the way work is organized over time.

The Shift away from an Individual Approach to Rehabilitation toward a Preventive Approach Covering all Workers

Taken individually, each of the interventions addressing the psychosocial environment at work fosters the return to work and job retention of individuals who have been absent from work due to a mental health problem. However, these practices are limited to management on a case-by-case basis. The importance here is to achieve a shift away from a case-by-case approach toward an approach centered on identifying factors in the psychosocial environment at work that are likely to affect other workers. Thus, a cross-sectional analysis of the concerns identified by various workers as well as the targets for action on the psychosocial environment at work put forward under the various action plans will lead to a shift away from an individual approach to rehabilitation toward an organizational approach aimed at all workers. This process involves characterizing the factors related to the psychosocial environment at work identified by workers and direct supervisors when following up on workers on sick leave, and bringing out the factors likely to affect other workers. This characterization process can be conducted using an analytical grid of risk factors related to the psychosocial environment at work (Vézina et al., 2009). Moreover, validating the process with stakeholders in the workplace (human resources direction, union representatives, occupational health officers, and so on) will help to better reflect organizational concerns.

Being able to analyze the risk factors common to several workers will lead to a shift away from an individual approach to rehabilitation toward an organizational approach based on prevention, covering other workers exposed to the same high risk situation. Making this shift from support for rehabilitation toward support for prevention is an essential condition for an effective intervention strategy aimed at fostering the return to work and job retention of workers.

References

Amick, B.C., Habeck R.V., Hunt, A., Fossel, A.H., Chapin, A., Keller, R.B., and Katz, J.N. (2000) Measuring the impact of organizational behaviors on work disability prevention and management, *Journal of Occupational Rehabilitation;* 10(1), 21–38.

Arnetz, B.B., Sjogren, B., Rydehn, B., and Meisel, R. (2003) Early workplace intervention for employees with musculoskeletal-related absenteeism: A prospective controlled intervention study, *Journal of Occupational and Environmental Medicine;* 45(5), 499–506.

Baril, R. and Berthelette, D. (2000) *Les Composantes et les Déterminants Organisationnels des Interventions de Maintien du Lien d'emploi en Entreprise* [*The Organizational Components and Determinants Associated with Maintaining the Employment Link*], Rapport N° R-238. Montréal: Institut de Recherche en Santé et Sécurité du Travail du Québec.

Baril, R., Clarke, J., Friesen, M., Stock, S., Cole, D. and Work-ready group (2003) Management of return-to-work programs for workers with musculoskeletal disorders: a qualitative study in three Canadian provinces, *Social Science and Medicine*; 57(11), 2101–2114.

Bourbonnais, R., Brisson, C., Vinet, A., Vézina, M., Abdous, B., and Gaudet, M. (2006b) Effectiveness of a participative intervention on psychosocial work factors to prevent mental health problems in a hospital setting, *Occupational and Environmental Medicine*; 63(5), 335–342.

Bourbonnais, R., Brisson, C., Vinet, A., Vézina, M., and Lower, A. (2006a) Development and implementation of a participative intervention to improve the psychosocial work environment and mental health in an acute care hospital, *Occupational and Environmental Medicine*; 63(5), 326–334.

Brenninkmeijer, V., Houtman, I., and Blonk, R. (2008) Depressed and absent from work: predicting prolonged depressive symptomatology among employees, *Occupational and Environmental Medicine;* 58(4), 295–301.

Brisson, C., Larocque, B., and Bourbonnais, R. (2001) Les contraintes psychosociales au travail chez les canadiennes et les canadiens, *Revue Canadienne de Santé Publique*; 92(6): 460–467.

Brun, J. (2009) *Management d'équipe: 7 Leviers pour Améliorer le Bien-être et l'efficacité au Travail* [*Team-based Management: 7 Incentives to Enhance Well-being and Efficiency at Work*]. Eyrolles, Paris: Éditions de l'organisation.

Casey, P. (2001) Adult adjustment disorder: A review of its current diagnostic status. *Journal of Psychatric Practice; 7*(1), 32–40.

Caveen, M., Dewa, C.S., and Goering, P. (2006) The influence of organizational factors on return-to-work outcomes, *Canadian Journal of Community Mental Health Problems;* 25(2), 121–414.

Cohidon, C., Imbernon, E., and Gorldberg, M. (2009) Prevalence of common mental disorders and their work consequences in France, according to occupational category, *American Journal of Industrial Medicine*; 52(2), 141–152.

Conti, D.J. and Burton, W.N. (1994) The economic impact of depression in the workplace, *Journal of Occupational and Environmental Medicine;* 36(9), 983–988.

Corbière, M., Lanctôt, N., Sanquirgo, N., and Lecomte, T. (2009b) Evaluation of self-esteem as a worker for people with severe mental disorders, *Journal of Vocational Rehabilitation;* 30(2), 87–98.

Corbière, M. and Lecomte, T. (2009c) Vocational services offered to people with severe mental illness, *Journal of Mental Health*; 18(1), 38–50.

Corbière, M. and Lecomte, T. (2007) *Work Accommodations for Recently Employed People with Mental Illness*. Paper presented at the International Academy of Law and Mental Health, 30th International Congress, Padua, Italy, June.

Corbière, M., Lesage, A.D, Villeneuve, K., and Mercier, C. (2006a) Le maintien en emploi des personnes souffrant d'une maladie mentale [Job retention among people with mental health illnesses]. *Santé Mentale au Québec,* 31(1), 9–36.

Corbière, M. and Shen, J. (2006b) A systematic review of psychological return-to-work interventions for people with mental health problems and/or physical injuries, *Canadian Journal of Community Mental Health at Work,* 25(2), 261–288.

Corbière, M., Shen, J., Rouleau, M., and Dewa, C.A. (2009a) Systematic review of preventive interventions regarding mental health issues in organizations, *WORK, 33*(1), *81–116.*

Dejours, C. (1993). *Travail et Usure Mentale. De la Psychopathologie à la Psychodynamique du Travail* [Work and Mental Wear and Tear. From Psychopathologies to Psychodynamics of Work], (New augmented edition) Paris: Bayard Éditions.

Dejours, C. (1995) Comment formuler une problématique de la santé en ergonomie et en médecine du travail [How to define health questions in ergonomics and occupational medicine], *Le Travail Humain*; 58(1), 1–15.

Dejours C. (2003) *L'Évaluation du Travail à l'épreuve du Réel. Critique des Fondements de l'évaluation* [Evaluating Work through the Test of Reality. A Critique of the Basics of Evaluation]. Paris: Inra Éditions.

Dewa, C.S., Goering, P.R.N., Lin, E., and Paterson, M. (2002) Depression-related short-term disability in an employed population, *Journal of Occupational & Environmental Medicine;* 44(7), 628–633.

Dewa, C.S., McDaid, D., and Ettner, S.L. (2007) An international perspective on worker mental health problems: Who bears the burden and how are costs addressed?, *Canadian Journal of Psychiatry;* 52(6), 346–356.

Druss, B.G., Schlesinger, M., and Allen, H.M. (2001) Depressive symptoms, satisfaction with health care, and 2-year work outcomes in an employed population, *American Journal of Psychiatry*; 158(5), 731–734.

Durand, M.-J. and Loisel, P. (2001) Therapeutic return to work: rehabilitation in the workplace, *Work: A Journal of Prevention, Assessment and Rehabilitation*; 17(1), 57–63.

Durand, M.-J., Loisel, P., Charpentier, N. Labelle, J., and Nha Hong, Q. (2004) *Le Programme de Retour Thérapeutique au Travail (RIT)* [*The Therapeutic Return-to-Work Program*]. Longueuil: Centre de Recherche Clinique en Réadaptation au Travail Prévicap de l'Hôpital Charles LeMoyne.

Durand, M-J., Vachon, B., Loisel, P., and Berthelette, D. (2003) Constructing the program impact theory for an evidence-based work rehabilitation program for workers with low back pain, *Work*; 21(3), 233–242.

Franche, R.L., Baril, R., Shaw, W., Nicholas, M., and Loisel, P. (2005) Workplace based return-to-work interventions: Optimizing the role of stakeholders in implementation and research, *Journal of Occupational Rehabilitation*; 15(4), 525–541.

Gabriel, P. and Liimatainen, M.-R. (2000) *Mental Health in the Workplace*. Genève: Bureau International du Travail.

Gates, L. (1993) The role of the supervisor in successful adjustment to work with a disabling condition: Issues for disability policy and practice, *Journal of Occupational Rehabilitation*; 3(4), 179–190.

Gjesdal S. and Bratberg E (2003) Diagnosis and duration of sickness absence as predictors for disability pension: Results from a three-year, multi-register based and prospective study, *Scandinavian Journal of Public Health*; 31(4), 246–254.

Haslam, C., Atkinson, S., Brown, S.S., and Haslam, R.A. (2005) Anxiety and depression in the workplace: Effects on the individual and organisation (a focus group investigation), *Journal of Affective Disorders*; 88(2), 209–215.

Henderson, M., Glozier, N., and Elliot, K.H. (2005) Long term sickness absence, *British Medicine Journal*; 330(7495), 802–803.

Hogg-Johnson S. and Cole, D. (2003) Early prognostic factors for duration on benefits among workers with compensated occupational soft tissue injuries, *Journal of Occupational and Environmental Medicine*; 60(4), 244–253.

Houtman, I.L.D. (2007) *Work-related Stress*. Dublin, Ireland: European Foundation for the Improvement of Living and Working Conditions. http://www.eurofound.europa.eu/ewco/reports/TN0502TR01/TN0502TR01.pdf.

Karasek, R. and Theorell, T. (1990) *Healthy Work: Stress, Productivity and the Reconstruction of Working Life*. New York, NY: Basic Books.

Kessler R.C., Akiskal H.S., Ames M., Birnbaum H., Greenberg P., Hirschfeld R.M.A., Jin R., Merikangas K.R., Simon G.E., and Wang P.S. (2006) Prevalence and effects of mood disorders on work performance in a nationally representative sample of US workers, *American Journal of Psychiatry*; 163(9), 1561–1568.

Kessler, R.C., McGonagle, K.A., Zhao, S., Nelson, C.B., Hughes, M., Eshleman, S., Wittchen, H.-U., and Kendler, K.S. (1994) Lifetime and 12-month prevalence of DSM III-R psychiatric disorders in the United States: Results from the National Comorbidity Survey, *Archives of General Psychiatry;* 51(1), 8–19.

Koopsmans, P.C., Roelen, C.A.M., and Groothoff, J.W. (2008) Sickness absence due to depressive symptoms, *International Archives of Occupational and Environmental Health*; 81(6), 711–719.

Leon, A.C., Portera, L., and Weissman, M.M. (1995) The social costs of anxiety disorders, *British Journal of Psychiatry*; 166(27), 19–22.

Linton S.J. (1991) A behavioral workshop for training immediate supervisors: The key to neck and back injuries, *Perceptual and Motor Skills*; 73(3), 1159–1170.

Loisel, P., Gosselin, L., Durand, P., Lemaire, J., Poitras, S., and Abenhaim, L. (2001) Implementation of a participatory ergonomics program in the rehabilitation of workers suffering from subacute back pain, *Applied Ergonomics*; 32(1), 53–60.

MacEachen, E., Clarke, J., Franche, R.L., and Irvin, E. (2006) Systematic review of the qualitative literature on return to work after injury, *Scandinavian Journal of Work, Environment & Health; 32*(4), 257–269.

McLellan, R.K., Pransky, G., and Shaw, W. (2001) Disability management training for supervisors: A pilot intervention program, *Journal of Occupational Rehabilitation;* 11(1), 33–41.

Niedhammer, I., Goldberg, M., Leclerc, A., Bugel, I., and David, S. (1998) Psychosocial factors at work and subsequent depressive symptoms in the Gazel cohort, *Scandinavian Journal of Work, Environment & Health*; 24(3), 197–205.

Nieuwenhuijsen, K., Verbeek, J.H.A.M., de Boer, A.G.E.M., Blonk, R.W.B., and Djik J.H. van (2006) Predicting the duration of sickness absence for patients with common mental disorder in occupational health care, *Scandinavian Journal of Work, Environment and Health;* 32(1), 67–74.

Nieuwenhuijsen, K., Verbeek, J.H.A.M., Siemerink, J.C.M.J., and Tummers-Nijsen, D. (2003) Quality of rehabilitation among workers with adjustment disorders according to practice guidelines; A retrospective cohort study, *Journal of occupational and environmental medicine*; 60(Suppl I), i21–i25.

Olsheski, J.A., Rosenthal, D.A., and Hamilton, M. (2002) Disability management and psychosocial rehabilitation: considerations for integration, *Work; 19*(1), 63–70.

Pélissolo, A., André, C., Chignon, J.M., Dutoit, D., Martin, P., Richard-Berthe, C., and Tignol, J. (2002) Anxiety disorders in private practice psychiatric out-patients: prevalence, comorbidity and burden, *Encephale*; 28(6), 510–519.

Rugulies, R., Bultmann, U., Aust, B., and Burr, H. (2006) Psychosocial work environment and incidence of severe depressive symptoms: Prospective findings from a 5-Year follow-up of the Danish work environment cohort study, *American Journal of Epidemiology;* 163(10), 877–887.

Russo, D. and Innes, E. (2002) An organizational case study of the case manager's role in a client's return-to-work programme in Australia, *Occupational Therapy International*; 9(1), 57–75.

Shaw, W., Hong, Q., Pransky, G., and Loisel, P. (2008) A literature review describing the role of return-to-work coordinators in trial program and interventions designed to prevent workplace disability, *Journal of Occupational Rehabilitation*; 18(1), 2–15.

Siegrist, J. and Marmot, M. (2004) Health inequalities and the psychosocial environment—two scientific challenges, *Social Science & Medicine*; 58(8), 1463–1473.

St-Arnaud, L., Bourbonnais, R., Saint-Jean, M., and Rhéaume, J. (2007) Determinants of return-to-Work among employees absent due to mental health problems, *Industrial Relations Journal*; 62(4), 690–713.

St-Arnaud, L., Saint-Jean, M., and Damasse, J. (2006) Towards an enhanced understanding of factors involved in the return-to-work process of employees absent due to mental health problems, *Canadian Journal of Community Mental Health;* 25(2), 303–315.

St-Arnaud, L., Saint-Jean, M., and Damasse, J. (2009) *Rapports sociaux et anticipation des conditions de retour au travail à la suite d'une absence pour des raisons de santé mentale* [*Social relations and anticipation of return-to-work conditions following absence for mental health reasons*]. In M.-F. Maranda and G. Founier (pp. 160–184) (eds) P*sychopathologie du Travail et Maintien Durable en Emploi: Une Question Antinomique?* [*Pathogenic organization of work and maintain sustainable employment: a paradoxical question?*]. Québec: Presses de l'Université Laval.

St-Arnaud, L., Saint-Jean, M., and Rhéaume, J. (2003) De la désinsertion à la réinsertion professionnelle à la suite d'un arrêt de travail pour un problème de santé mentale [From dropping out of work to occupational reintegration following work absence due to a mental health problem], *Santé Mentale au Québec;* 28(1): 193–211.

St-Arnaud, L., Saint-Jean, M., and Rhéaume, J. (2004) Regard de l'autre et dynamique de la reconnaissance: un effet loupe sur les personnes qui ont des troubles mentaux au travail [Other people's view and dynamics of recognition: magnifying effects on people with mental health problems at work], *Revue Travailler*; 12, 99–115.

St-Arnaud, L. and Vézina, M. (1993) *Santé Mentale et Organisation du Travail* [Mental Health and Work Organization], Le médecin du Québec.

Stansfeld, S.A., Fuhrer, R., Shipley, M.J., and Marmot M.G. (1999) Work characteristics predict psychiatric disorder: prospective results from the Whitehall II study, *Occupational and Environmental Medicine;* 56(5), 302–307.

Stock, S., Deguire, S., Baril, R., and Durand, M.J. (1999). Obstacles And Factors Facilitating Return to Work of Workers with Musculoskeletal Disorders. Summary of the Report of the Quebec Qualitative Study in the Electric and Electronic Sector of Workready Phase 1. Montreal Department of Public Health, RRSSS Montréal-Centre, décembre 1999.

http://www.irsst.qc.ca/media/documents/PubIRSST/R-298.PDF

Van der Doef, M. and Maes, S. (1999) The job demand-control (-support) model and psychological well-being: a review of 20 years of empirical research, *Work and Stress*; 13(2), 87–114.

Van der Klink, J.J.L., Blonk, R.W.B., Schene, A.H. and Van der Dijk, F.J.H. (2003) Reducing long term sickness absence by an activating intervention in adjustment disorder: A cluster randomised controlled design, *Occupational Environment Medicine*; 60(6), 429–437.

Vézina, M. and Bourbonnais, R. (2001) *Incapacité de Travail pour des Raisons de Santé Mentale. Portrait Social du Québec* [*Inability to Work for Mental Health Reasons. Social portrait of Quebec*]. Québec: Institut de la Statistique du Québec.

Vézina M., Bourbonnais R., Brisson C., and Trudel L. (2004) Facteurs de risques psychosociaux [Psychosocial risk factors]. In *Manuel d'Hygiène du Travail [Handbook of Occupational Health]*, Montreal: Modulo-Griffon, ch. 19, 362–375.

Vézina, M., Bourbonnais, R., Marchand, A., and Arcand, R. (2008) Stress au Travail et Santé Mentale chez les Adultes Québécois [Stress in the workplace and mental health of adult Quebeckers]. Enquête sur la Santé dans les Collectivités Canadiennes (cycle 1.2). Québec: Institut de la Statistique du Québec.

Vézina, M., Chénard, C., St-Arnaud, L., Gourdeau, P., Lippel, K., Stocks, S., Bourbonnais, R., Brisson, C., Marchand, A., and Bhérer, L. (2009) Grille d'identification des Risques Psychosociaux au Travail [Grid used to identify psychosocial risks at work]. Institut National de Santé Publique. Gouvernement du Québec. http://www.inspq.qc.ca/pdf/publications/744_OutilCaractMilieuTravail.pdf.

Vézina, M., Cousineau, M., Mergler, D., Vinet A. (1992) *Pour donner un Sens au Travail: Bilan et Orientations du Québec en Santé Mentale au Québec* [Giving a Meaning to Work: Quebec's Review and Orientations in Mental Health in Quebec]. Québec: Gaétan Morin édition.

Vinet, A. (2004) *Travail, Organisation et Santé: le Défi de la Productivité dans le Respect des Personnes* [Work, Organization and Health: The Challenge of Achieving Productivity while Showing Respect for People]. Québec: Les Presses de l'Université Laval.

Vinet , A., Bourbonnais, R., and Brisson, C. (2003) Travail et Santé Mentale: une relation qui se détériore. Sous la direction de Michel Audet. Santé mentale et travail [Work and mental health: a deteriorating relationship]. L'urgence de penser autrement l'organisation, Actes du 58e Congrès du Département des Relations Industrielles de l'Université Laval, tenu à Québec en 2003 (pp. 5–37). Sainte-Foy: Les Presses de l'Université Laval.

Waghorn, G.R. and Chant, D.C. (2005) Employment restrictions among persons with ICD-10 anxiety disorders: characteristics from a population survey, *Journal of Anxiety Disorders*; 19(6), 642–657.

Watson Wyatt (2005) *Managing Health Care Costs in a New Era: 10th Annual NBGH*. Washington DC: National Business Group on Health & Watson Wyatt.

Wall, V. et Programme Santé et Sécurité du Travail—Réseau (MSSS) (2009) *Guide de l'employeur Concernant le Traitement des Périodes d'absence pour Invalidité* [*Employers' Guide to Dealing with Periods of Disability Absence*]. Québec: Ministère de la Santé et des Services Sociaux.

Young, A.E., Roessler, R., Wasiak, R., McPherson, K.M., Poppel van, M.N.M. and Anema, J.R. (2005) A developmental conceptualization of return to work, *Journal of Occupational Rehabilitation*; 15(4), 557–567.

Index